VICTORIAN PROSE

John W. Bicknell,

John Clive, David J. DeLaura,

Charles Stephen Dessain, Lawrence Evans,

Howard W. Fulweiler, Wendell V. Harris,

Richard Helmstadter, Thomas Pinney, John M. Robson,

Martin J. Svaglic, G. B. Tennyson,

and Francis G. Townsend

VICTORIAN PROSE

A Guide to Research

Edited by David J. DeLaura

THE MODERN LANGUAGE ASSOCIATION OF AMERICA · NEW YORK

1973

CONTENTS

●

PREFACE

Victorian Prose: A Guide to Research is designed to join two well-received earlier volumes, *Victorian Fiction: A Guide to Research* (1964), edited by Lionel Stevenson, and *The Victorian Poets: A Guide to Research* (2nd ed., 1968), edited by Frederic E. Faverty. Michael Timko made helpful comments on the entire manuscript. The contributors owe a special debt of gratitude to the staffs of the Research and Editorial Offices of the Modern Language Association: Walter S. Achtert, Judy Goulding, William Pell, and Margot Rabiner.

The subheadings in each chapter have been introduced into the Table of Contents in order to make the volume easier to use. Certain topical entries have also been added to the Index. Coverage of important material is complete through 1971; a few items from 1972 have been included. The Index was prepared by Michael Adams.

D.J.D.

TABLE OF ACRONYMS

·

The following acronyms are used in parenthetical references. In addition, such common words as "University," "Studies," "Journal," "Quarterly," and so forth are abbreviated as "Univ.," "Stud.," "J.," "Q.," and so forth.

ABC	*American Book Collector*
AHR	*American Historical Review*
AI	*American Imago*
AL	*American Literature*
AM	*Atlantic Monthly*
AN&Q	*American Notes & Queries*
AQ	*American Quarterly*
AR	*Antioch Review*
ASch	*American Scholar*
BBB	*Bulletin du Bibliophile et du Bibliothécaire*
BC	*Book Collector*
BJA	*British Journal of Aesthetics*
BJRL	*Bulletin of the John Rylands Library*
BLR	*Bodleian Library Record*
BMQ	*British Museum Quarterly*
BNYPL	*Bulletin of the New York Public Library*
BuR	*Bucknell Review*
BUSE	*Boston University Studies in English*
BYUS	*Brigham Young University Studies*
CathW	*Catholic World*
CCC	*College Composition & Communication*

CE	College English
CEA	CEA Critic
CentR	Centennial Review
CHA	Cuadernos Hispanoamericanos
CHR	Catholic Historical Review
CJEPS	Canadian Journal of Economics and Political Science
CL	Comparative Literature
CLAJ	College Language Association Journal
CLQ	Colby Library Quarterly
ConR	Contemporary Review
CQ	Cambridge Quarterly
CQR	Church Quarterly Review
CritQ	Critical Quarterly
DownR	Downside Review
DR	Dalhousie Review
DubR	Dublin Review
DUJ	Durham University Journal
DVLG	Deutsche Vierteljahrsschrift für Literaturwissenschaft und Geistesgeschichte
EA	Etudes Anglaises
E&S	Essays and Studies by Members of the English Association
EC	Etudes Celtiques
EG	Etudes Germaniques
EHR	English Historical Review
EIC	Essays in Criticism (Oxford)
ELH	ELH: Journal of English Literary History
ELN	English Language Notes (Univ. of Colorado)
ELT	English Literature in Transition (1880–1920)
EM	English Miscellany
EML	English Men of Letters
ES	English Studies
ESA	English Studies in Africa (Johannesburg)
ESQ	Emerson Society Quarterly
ETJ	Educational Theatre Journal
EUQ	Emory University Quarterly
Expl	Explicator
FortR	Fortnightly Review
GL&L	German Life & Letters
GRM	Germanisch-romanische Monatsschrifte, Neue Folge
HistJ	Historical Journal
HJ	Hibbert Journal
HLB	Harvard Library Bulletin
HLQ	Huntington Library Quarterly
HMPEC	Historical Magazine of the Protestant Episcopal Church
HR	Hispanic Review
IRSH	International Review of Social History
JAAC	Journal of Aesthetics and Art Criticism
JBS	Journal of British Studies (Trinity Coll., Hartford, Conn.)
JEGP	JEGP: Journal of English and Germanic Philology
JEH ·	Journal of Ecclesiastical History

JHI	*Journal of the History of Ideas*
JP	*Journal of Philosophy*
JRH	*Journal of Religious History*
JRUL	*Journal of the Rutgers University Library*
JSUB	*Jahrbuch der Schlesischen Friedrich-Wilhelm-Universität zu Breslau*
KJ	*Kipling Journal*
KR	*Kenyon Review*
LangQ	*Language Quarterly* (Univ. of South Florida)
LanM	*Les Langues Modernes*
LC	*Library Chronicle* (Univ. of Pennsylvania)
LHR	*Lock Haven Review*
MissQ	*Mississippi Quarterly*
MLN	*Modern Language Notes*
MLQ	*Modern Language Quarterly*
MLR	*Modern Language Review*
MNL	*Mill News Letter*
MP	*Modern Philology*
MTJ	*Mark Twain Journal*
N&Q	*Notes & Queries*
NA	*Nuova Antologia*
NC	*Nineteenth Century*
NCBEL	*New Cambridge Bibliography of English Literature*, ed. George Watson
NCF	*Nineteenth-Century Fiction*
NEQ	*New England Quarterly*
NM	*Neuphilologische Mitteilungen*
NS	*Die Neueren Sprachen*
OL	*Orbis Litterarum*
OS	*Orientalia Suecana* (Uppsala)
P&P	*Past & Present*
PAPS	*Proceedings of the American Philosophical Society*
PBA	*Proceedings of the British Academy*
PBSA	*Papers of the Bibliographical Society of America*
PEGS	*Publications of the English Goethe Society*
PhQ	*Philosophical Quarterly*
PhR	*Philosophical Review*
PLL	*Papers on Language and Literature*
PMLA	*PMLA: Publications of the Modern Language Association of America*
PPR	*Philosophy and Phenomenological Research*
PQ	*Philological Quarterly*
PsyR	*Psychoanalytic Review*
QJS	*Quarterly Journal of Speech*
QQ	*Queen's Quarterly* (Queen's Univ., Kingston, Ont., Canada)
QR	*Quarterly Review*
RAA	*Revue Anglo-Américain*
RDM	*Revue des Deux Mondes*
REL	*Review of English Literature* (Leeds)
Ren	*Renascence*
RES	*Review of English Studies*
RevN	*La Revue Nouvelle* (Paris)

RLC	*Revue de Littérature Comparée*
RMM	*Revue de Métaphysique et de Morale*
RSPT	*Revue des Sciences Philosophiques et Théologiques*
RUS	*Rice University Studies*
SAQ	*South Atlantic Quarterly*
SatR	*Saturday Review*
SB	*Studies in Bibliography*
SEL	*Studies in English Literature, 1500–1900*
SEng	*Studies in English* (Univ. of Texas)
SIR	*Studies in Romanticism* (Boston Univ.)
SLitI	*Studies in the Literary Imagination* (Georgia State Coll.)
SN	*Studia Neophilologica*
SoR	*Southern Review* (Louisiana State Univ.)
SoRA	*Southern Review: An Australian Journal of Literary Studies* (Univ. of Adelaide)
SP	*Studies in Philology*
SR	*Sewanee Review*
SS	*Scandinavian Studies*
SSJ	*Southern Speech Journal*
SSL	*Studies in Scottish Literature* (Univ. of South Carolina)
SUS	*Susquehanna University Studies*
TC	*Twentieth Century*
TCBS	*Transactions of the Cambridge Bibliographical Society*
TLS	*Times Literary Supplement* (London)
TQ	*Texas Quarterly*
TriQ	*Tri-Quarterly*
TSB	*Thoreau Society Bulletin*
TSL	*Tennessee Studies in Literature*
TSLL	*Texas Studies in Literature and Language*
TWA	*Transactions of the Wisconsin Academy of Sciences, Arts, and Letters*
UKCR	*University of Kansas City Review*
UR	*University Review* (Kansas City, Mo.)
UTQ	*University of Toronto Quarterly*
VN	*Victorian Newsletter*
VP	*Victorian Poetry*
VPN	*Victorian Periodicals Newsletter*
VS	*Victorian Studies*
WHR	*Western Humanities Review*
WPQ	*Western Political Quarterly* (Univ. of Utah)
WWR	*Walt Whitman Review*
YFS	*Yale French Studies*
YR	*Yale Review*
YULG	*Yale University Library Gazette*

GENERAL MATERIALS

·

David J. DeLaura

The current lively state of studies in Victorian nonfictional prose cannot be said to be a "revival," since fully competent study in the area is an affair by and large of the past twenty years. In Victorian fiction and poetry, too, sustained study is a recent phenomenon, but the tradition in prose is even more obscure and the issues less fully debated. Much of value to the student of prose will be found in earlier "guides to research" parallel to the present volume: *Victorian Fiction* (1964), edited by Lionel Stevenson, *The Victorian Poets* (2nd ed., 1968), edited by Frederic E. Faverty, and *The English Romantic Poets and Essayists* (rev. ed., 1966), edited by Carolyn W. and Lawrence H. Houtchens.

The kinds of emphasis in the first "patchy" and "tentative" surge of serious Victorian studies in the 1930's can be gathered in Charles F. Harrold's exhaustive "Recent Trends in Victorian Studies: 1932–1939" (*SP*, 1940). His charge, that "The writer on the Victorians sometimes knows too little philosophy, is ignorant of or indifferent to the nature and history of religion, is inadequately grounded in classical and modern languages, and is not yet at home in the general history of ideas," though less pertinent today, is still uncomfortably applicable to much of the admittedly more serious work of recent years. What Harrold's prescription notably lacks, as does his own otherwise outstanding work in Carlyle and New-man, is a sense of the artistry and "form" of the Victorian writers. An altogether new depth of insight and competence was introduced by such works as R. H. Wilenski's *John Ruskin* (1933) and Lionel Trilling's justly celebrated *Matthew Arnold* (1939). But until Walter Houghton's *The Art of Newman's "Apologia"* (1945) and E. K. Brown's *Matthew Arnold: A Study in Conflict* (1948), the more integral study of the art of the Victorian prose writers cannot be said to have begun.

3

A book designed to clarify the progress of Victorian studies, *The Reinterpretation of Victorian Literature* (1950), edited by Joseph E. Baker, is quite anomalous in having only a single chapter on the novel and next to nothing on poetry. But it also fails conspicuously to bring up the artistry and methods of the nonfictional prose writers discussed in almost every chapter. It cannot even be claimed that most of the problems in the history of ideas identified by Norman Foerster in the volume have been very decisively advanced in the interim. These include "the influence of various continental cultures upon England," literature and the fine arts, the divorce of literature and morality, the tradition of aestheticism from Keats to Wilde, literature and science, literature and Christianity, and philosophy and religion. The dearth of serious earlier studies can be judged by the fact that the useful anthology, *Victorian Literature: Modern Essays in Criticism*, edited by Austin Wright in 1961, has a number of essays on the prose writers, but only perhaps three that can still stand as solid contributions. A similar anthology, edited by Robert O. Preyer in 1967, *Victorian Literature: Selected Essays*, has only two selections on the prose writers. Not everything remains to be done, as it did in 1940, but the gaps in our knowledge and our inadequate grasp of the real issues in the area justify the survey they receive in this chapter and in the remainder of this volume.

I. BIBLIOGRAPHY

Much of the work in the area is buried in unread dissertations. The useful *Guide to Doctoral Dissertations in Victorian Literature, 1886–1958* (1960), compiled by Richard D. Altick and William R. Matthews, has been largely superseded by Lawrence F. McNamee's *Dissertations in English and American Literature: Theses Accepted by American, British, and German Universities, 1865–1964* (1968). An alarmingly large supplement, covering the years 1964–68, followed in 1969. The annual Victorian Bibliography, now published in *Victorian Studies*, has been gathered in three volumes through 1964, under the title *Bibliographies of Studies in Victorian Literature*: 1932–44, edited by William D. Templeman (1945; rpt. 1971); 1945–54, edited by Austin Wright (1956; rpt. 1971); and 1955–64, edited by Robert C. Slack (1967). The annual *MLA International Bibliography* and the bibliographies in *The Victorian Newsletter* should also be consulted. *Victorian Poetry* has in recent years included prose writers with the poets in its annual critical review of articles. *Studies in English Literature* publishes an annual critical survey of books on nineteenth-century literature.

Volume III of *The New Cambridge Bibliography of English Literature* (1969), edited by George Watson, is a mine of primary and secondary sources. Particularly valuable for the student of prose are the easily overlooked early sections under General Works. Jerome H. Buckley's *Victorian Poets and Prose Writers* (1966) is a good basic bibliography that pays more than the usual attention to prose. Two excellent bibliographies that appeared in England in 1970 will speed up the assimilation of the enormous body of historical and other "background" studies in the period: Lionel Madden's *How to Find Out about the Victorian Period: A Guide to Sources of Information*, and Josef Lewis Altholz' *Victorian England, 1837–1901*.

III. THE TRADITIONS OF VICTORIAN PROSE · 5

II. ANTHOLOGIES

Students of Victorian prose have not been well served by the anthologists. *English Prose of the Victorian Period* (1938), edited by C. F. Harrold and W. D. Templeman, though long outdated in its bibliographies and illustrative critical texts, remains the most generous collection. But its lengthy introduction, excellent on political and social history, has nothing to say about the art of Victorian prose, and its bibliography under "Literary, Philosophical, and Religious Aspects" is nearly barren of literary materials. The new emphasis in the field is reflected in the introduction to William E. Buckler's shorter but useful *Prose of the Victorian Period* (1958).

A welcome development is the goodly shelf of more specialized anthologies, in addition to the Wright and Preyer volumes noted above, that have recently accumulated. Gordon S. Haight's *The Portable Victorian Reader* (1972) is a rich brew of Victoriana. Gerald Kauvar and Gerald Sorenson present, in *The Victorian Mind* (1969), Victorian selections on a variety of background topics. Richard A. Levine's *Backgrounds to Victorian Literature* (1967) is a good collection of modern interpretative essays. Robert Langbaum's *The Victorian Age: Essays in History and in Social and Literary Criticism* (1967) draws on Victorian and modern sources. Shiv Kumar's woefully uneven collection, *British Victorian Literature: Recent Revaluations* (1969), is to be used with caution. Two easily overlooked sides of the Victorian achievement are nicely caught in Harold Orel's *The World of Victorian Humor* (1961) and in *A Treasury of Scientific Prose: A Nineteenth-Century Anthology* (1963), edited by Howard Mumford Jones and I. Bernard Cohen.

Especially hard to recover is the wealth of Victorian literary criticism by writers other than the major figures covered in this volume. *English Literary Criticism: Romantic and Victorian* (1963), edited by Daniel Hoffman and Samuel Hynes, though its selections are fairly predictable, at least enables the reader to grasp the unity and continuity of nineteenth-century critical interests. Robert L. Peters' *Victorians on Literature and Art* (1961) includes out-of-the-way material and enhances our perception of the complexity of the Victorians' aesthetic concerns. The anthology edited by Walter E. Houghton and G. Robert Stange, *Victorian Poetry and Poetics* (2nd ed., 1968), is admirable in presenting critical prose by the poets and an appendix of major critical statements of the period. Particularly commendable is George Levine's highly original anthology, *The Emergence of Victorian Consciousness: The Spirit of the Age* (1967). All selections date between 1824 and 1837, the "inter-period" least understood by workers in the field.

III. THE TRADITIONS OF VICTORIAN PROSE

No one would dream of asking, What is Victorian poetry, or, What is Victorian fiction? They can be pointed to, in all their abundance, *en série* on library shelves. The situation of Victorian prose is altogether different, since some of the best prose of the period is quite "unliterary" in context and content, and appears in such nonstandard forms as letters, diaries and notebooks, memoirs, books of travel, scientific treatises, histories of various sorts, and social criticism. Students of poetry and fiction are aware of traditions and continuities in their fields; there is much less of that comprehensive and historical grasp on the part of even the better recent students of Victorian prose.

A chief desideratum, then, is an informed and critically alert history of nineteenth-century prose in its diversity and its major lines of development. The best sketch of such a history is Kenneth Allott's introduction to *Victorian Prose, 1830–1880* (1956). He notes, however, that there is no "agreed character and explanation of Victorian prose, in the sense that these exist for Jacobean and Augustan prose," and though he finds Victorian prose diverging from Augustan in diction and imagery, he contents himself largely with cataloging and rejoicing in the individual differences. He is very suggestive on the delayed "Romantic" quality of early Victorian prose, its strengths and weaknesses deriving from "the heavy new demands made on it by emotion." Why the Romantics themselves came to place such demands on prose (including fiction) so late—mostly after 1830—can be grasped in the excellent introductions to two anthologies, Raymond Wright's *Prose of the Romantic Period, 1780–1830* (1956) and Carl R. Woodring's *Prose of the Romantic Period* (1961). Raymond Williams, in the introduction to the second volume of *The Pelican Book of English Prose* (1969), is more interested in fiction than in nonfictional prose. But his acute sense of the "social" dimension of prose, of the implications of the writer-reader relationship, proves how much of the complex tone of Victorian prose is lost in many "contextual" readings. There are provocative if unsystematic remarks on Victorian prose in J. M. Murry's "English Prose in the Nineteenth Century" (in *Discoveries*, 1924) and G. M. Young's "Prose, Old and New" (in *Daylight and Champaign*, 1937).

The important links of the nineteenth century with the seventeenth—especially in religious concerns—include the rise in each period of a "polyphonic" prose. Though studies have been made of the nineteenth century's growing interest in seventeenth-century poetry, such as Joseph Duncan's *The Revival of Metaphysical Poetry* (1959), we lack a parallel study of the implications of the cult of the seventeenth-century prose masters from Coleridge and Lamb to Pater and Gosse. Indeed, a good topic for investigation would be the polemical and other "uses" of the seventeenth century in the nineteenth. Students of Victorian prose have generally showed little concern for the large body of high-quality work done on seventeenth-century prose and its traditions in our century. An excellent collection is Stanley E. Fish's *Seventeenth-Century Prose: Modern Essays in Criticism* (1971), divided into Theories of Seventeenth-Century Style (mostly from the 1920's and 1930's) and Individual Styles (the bulk from the 1960's).

There is little sense currently that Victorian prose has its own natural history, a self-conscious if inchoate body of theoretical and practical assumptions. G. B. Tennyson, in the present volume, offers Carlyle as the inventor of Victorian prose, not only in disparaging poetry and fiction in favor of history and biography, but in creating "the taste for serious works of nonfiction." Ruskin, Arnold, and even Newman are thus "epigones" of Carlyle. This temptingly simplified view of the internal history of Victorian prose will not bear scrutiny. Newman's sermons and controversial works of the twenties and thirties obviously have a quite independent origin; the whole of the Romantic tradition of "personal" prose is not even mentioned; Macaulay and the contemporary historians go for nothing; such key figures in the development of a "symphonic" prose as De Quincey, Landor, and

Christopher North (John Wilson)—all of whom worked well on into the Victorian period—are put out of account.

Apart from Allott's introduction, the best place to begin now is Travis R. Merritt's "Taste, Opinion, and Theory in the Rise of Victorian Prose Stylism" (in *The Art of Victorian Prose*, ed. George Levine and William Madden, 1968). His most original contribution is his history of an "artistic" but "light" style late in the century, in figures like Pater, Saintsbury, and R. L. Stevenson, developed in conscious opposition to the more ornate earlier Victorian styles. He sees this "prose stylism" as flowering and withering very quickly at the end of the century; he fails to note that the real future of stylism was in fiction, from Meredith and James to Conrad, Joyce, Virginia Woolf, and perhaps the American Gothicists. Much more needs to be done for the earlier part of the century, especially in the Romantic essayists and in De Quincey. *Selected Essays on Rhetoric by Thomas De Quincey* (1967) has a long and interesting introduction by Frederick Burwick pointing out links with the Scottish associationists. But De Quincey's theories of style, rhetoric, and eloquence are more clearly set forth in Sigmund K. Proctor's *Thomas De Quincey's Theory of Literature* (1943). David Masson's claims for the new prose, noted in passing by Merritt, are most fully set forth in his remarkable "Theories of Poetry and a New Poet" (*North Brit. Rev.*, 1853). Apart from Pater's "Style" (1888), perhaps the most important Victorian document in the cult of style is Saintsbury's "Modern English Prose" (1876; in *Collected Essays and Papers*, 1923), with its praise of "style" over "meaning" and its prescient admission of Pater to the canon.

Current interest in the Victorian prose writers centers on the major social prophets and literary critics. Earlier interest, culminating in the early twentieth century, is largely focused on the "personal" essay which flourished from Lamb and Hazlitt to Stevenson and eventually foundered in the middle-brow periodicals. Earlier works such as W. C. Brownell's *Victorian Prose Masters* (1902), W. J. Dawson's *The Makers of English Prose* (1906), and Hugh Walker's *The English Essay and Essayists* (1915) have little to offer the modern student. Despite its old-fashioned rhetorical orientation, William Minto's *A Manual of English Prose Literature* (1872) is altogether ahead of its time in its penetrating stylistic comments on De Quincey, Macaulay, and Carlyle. *The Great English Essayists* (1909), by W. J. and C. W. Dawson, has the merit of suggesting some interesting if not always convincing subgenres of the form. Oliver Elton's *A Survey of English Literature, 1780–1880* (4 vols., 1920), intelligently covering a wide range of nineteenth-century prose, perhaps marks the close of the earlier period. A tradition of English prose that cuts across genre boundaries and reveals a unity of viewpoint and technique in some important Victorian prose from Peacock and Thackeray through Arnold and Mallock to Samuel Butler is that of satire. Hugh Walker's *English Satire and Satirists* (1925) opens out a topic that has received far too little special attention.

IV. THE THEMES OF VICTORIAN PROSE

One is hesitant to enforce the critically dangerous separation of "form" and "content" in the treatment of any complex body of literature. It is particularly undesirable in reading Victorian prose since, as John Holloway points out in *The*

Victorian Sage (1953), the *subject* of a good deal of Victorian prose is precisely certain attitudes of mind that are inseparable from highly personal modes of expression. Still, as the following section will show, the key critical problem in Victorian prose is the relationship of a developed body of fact and belief, often strongly asserted, to its highly artful embodiment. Although, as the chapters in the present volume show, our apprehension of the individual careers of the Victorian prose writers has improved markedly of late, very few attempts have been made to grasp the unity and continuity of their collective interests. The sheer bulk of recent work has made the goal more daunting, but it is an all the more imperative need in the field.

The larger background for the study of Victorian prose is provided by important modern work in nineteenth-century English intellectual, social, and political history by such authorities as Asa Briggs, William L. Burn, Kitson Clark, Elie Halévy, David Thomson, G. M. Trevelyan, E. L. Woodward, and G. M. Young. For these, the student is referred to the bibliographies listed above. Here, we can cite only those works that illuminate most directly the literary and cultural context. Some of the better earlier work on the Victorian prophets was itself conceived polemically. A distinctive rationalist line of argument, often structured on the premise of the "warfare" between orthodox religion and a triumphant rationality, was worked out in A. W. Benn's *A History of English Rationalism in the Nineteenth Century* (2 vols., 1906; rpt. 1962), Janet Courtney's *Freethinkers of the Nineteenth Century* (1920), and three works by J. M. Robertson: *Modern Humanists* (1891), *Modern Humanists Reconsidered* (1927), and *A History of Freethought in the Nineteenth Century* (1929). Robert Shafer, a representative of the religious wing of the American New Humanists, developed a telling counterpolemic in *Christianity and Naturalism* (1926).

Basil Willey's two well-known books, *Nineteenth Century Studies* (1949) and *More Nineteenth Century Studies* (1956), gave a new orientation to the field. Willey finds the unity of the prophets to lie in their spiritual struggles, which he treats sympathetically from his own "modernist" religious position. Coleridge for the first time is placed correctly at the head of the file. Several of the key books on the period appeared during these years. Graham Hough's *The Last Romantics* (1947) is a sensitive study of later Victorian culture from Ruskin to Wilde and Yeats. Jerome Hamilton Buckley, in *The Victorian Temper: A Study in Literary Culture* (1951), avoids intellectual and literary history as such, but gives an excellent sense of what might be called "the climate of creativity" during the various phases of Victorian culture. Walter E. Houghton's massive *The Victorian Frame of Mind, 1830–1870* (1957) has been criticized for its encyclopedic character and for its failure to descend to more "popular" sources. But its heavy reliance on literary and "serious" sources provides the literary student with a wide range of fascinating material, perceptively drawn together. Raymond Williams' *Culture and Society, 1780–1950* (1958) provides indispensable insight into a long series of "culture-critics" from Burke and Coleridge to the twentieth century. Stressing "cultural" and social concerns, Williams finds the unity of the tradition in the attempt to preserve inherited "elitist" standards in a democratizing society. A number of the essays in *1859: Entering an Age of Crisis* (1959), edited by P. Appleman and others, deal with intellectual controversies of the age as well as the neglected field of popular culture. J. Hillis Miller's *The Disappearance of God: Five Nineteenth-Century Writers* (1963) is important for its extension to English literature of the methods of Genevan "structuralism." Though controversial in its relative indifference to chronology and to the unity of whole works, the book unquestionably throws the religious issues in the careers of De Quincey and Arnold into a new and striking perspective.

Insight into the unity of Victorian literature, and especially of the prose writers, can be gained in studies of particular themes. B. E. Lippincott's *Victorian Critics of Democracy* (1938) is a balanced if unexciting account of the social and political views of the major prose writers. Gaylord C. LeRoy, in *Perplexed Prophets: Six Nineteenth-Century Authors* (1953), attempts to penetrate to the psychological sources of his authors' social opinions, but his focus is unsteady. Ahead of its time in depth and competence is C. R. Sanders' *Coleridge and the Broad Church Movement* (1942). Alan W. Brown's *The Metaphysical Society: Victorian Minds in Crisis* (1947) conveys a sense of the personal context of intellectual debate in the seventies. Gertrude Himmelfarb's *Victorian Minds* (1967), though not without its own strong prejudices, excellently captures the vigor of Victorian intellectual life. Even more idiosyncratic is Morse Peckham's lively study of "Culture Crisis," *The Victorian Revolutionaries* (1970). There is much of value in J. H. Buckley's *The Triumph of Time* (1966), which sensitively explores the Victorians' pervasive interest in history, process, progress, growth, and decay. (A fully competent, modern discussion of 19th-century English historiography, as a successor to G. P. Gooch's *History and Historians in the Nineteenth Century*, 2nd ed., 1920, is a major unfilled need. One important sector is illuminated in Duncan Forbes's *The Liberal Anglican Idea of History*, 1952.) A welcome study of a central concern of the Victorian prose writers is Herbert L. Sussman's *Victorians and the Machine: The Literary Response to Technology* (1968). An important theme in Carlyle, Ruskin, and Morris is clarified in Alice Chandler's *A Dream of Order: The Medieval Ideal in Nineteenth-Century English Literature* (1970).

Of central importance are literary criticism and theory, since much of the best Victorian prose is some variety of journalism or reviewing, especially in that favorite Victorian form, the biographical-critical essay. Put simply, no one has yet grasped the internal dynamics of the period 1830–1900 with anything like the skill and comprehensiveness with which M. H. Abrams in his now-classic *The Mirror and the Lamp* (1953) synthesized the literary thinking of the Romantics. Some of the books mentioned above, notably Buckley's *The Victorian Temper* and Hough's *The Last Romantics*, are excellent prolegomena to such a history. Volumes III and IV of René Wellek's *A History of Modern Criticism* (1965), which offer judicious and painstaking syntheses of individual critics, have the nearly unique merit of being fully aware of the larger European context. The first chapter of Frank Kermode's *Romantic Image* (1957) throws out dazzling assertions, some highly questionable, about the cult of the image and of the alienated artist in nineteenth-century England. His sweeping hints and guesses cry out for careful confirmation, in context.

Particularly hard to recover is the literary climate of the long period between 1830 and the emergence in the sixties of such authoritative critical voices as those of Arnold, Swinburne, and Pater. The best attempt so far to synthesize early and mid-Victorian aesthetic assumptions appears in the first and last chapters of Alba H. Warren, Jr., *English Poetic Theory, 1825–1865* (1950; rpt. 1966). But the nine figures he chooses (characterizing each on the basis of a single book or essay) are only questionably representative. Perhaps only Carlyle and Ruskin were genuine taste-makers, and neither worked primarily as a literary critic. Some of the following unnamed figures were probably more important in affecting the tastes and judgments of the literate public: Macaulay, the Hallams, Masson, Henry Taylor, the later De Quincey, J. C. Hare, Sterling, G. H. Lewes, Clough, Patmore, Bagehot, Froude, Ludlow, Kingsley. This is not to mention the even lesser-known but frequently recurring names now available in the first two volumes of Walter E. Houghton's *Wellesley Index to Victorian Periodicals, 1824–1900* (1966, 1972)—though even this essential work is obviously not being consulted by all recent users of Victorian periodicals. Lawrence J. Starzyk's "Towards a Reassessment of Early Victorian Aesthetics: The Metaphysical Foundations" (*BJA*, 1971), though not always convincing in generalization, draws on some of this little-used material. Modern studies of Victorian periodicals—many of them mentioned in R. G. Cox's "The Reviews and Magazines" (in *From Dickens to Hardy*, ed. B. Ford, 1958)—are helpful in identifying general editorial policies and reviewing practices. Much of the actual jungle of Victorian "higher" journalism and reviewing remains fairly impenetrable, however, although *Victorian Periodicals Newsletter* is building up a welcome amount of detailed studies of specific journals and topics.

One unfortunate critical result is the frequent failure of students to judge the probable impact of a work on an assumed audience. Too frequently, as A. Dwight Culler and others have seen, the audience is deduced, circularly, from the text. Whereas in fact Carlyle literally created an audience for his message and his special mode of utterance, Newman had little sense of the Dublin audience he wrote for in the fifties, and the acerbities which the modern reader relishes in Arnold may, as Geoffrey Tillotson has claimed, have irritated and lost for him the audience he sought. Such essential critical questions, involving tone and intention, cannot be settled with authority apart from an intimate sense of the literary context. We have nothing for the Victorians comparable to such admirable studies as John Clive's *Scotch Reviewers*: The Edinburgh Review, *1802–1815* (1957) and John O. Hayden's *The Romantic Reviewers, 1802–1824* (1969), but some of the spadework has been done. The development of a "mass reading public" is admirably treated in Richard D. Altick's *The English Common Reader* (1957). More literary in emphasis, but less substantial, is Amy Cruse's *The Victorians and Their Reading* (1935). The assumptions and criteria of the novel-reviewers after mid-century are treated in two valuable works: Richard Stang's *The Theory of the Novel in England, 1850–1870* (1961) and Kenneth Graham's *English Criticism of the Novel, 1865–1900* (1965). For the earlier period, Kathleen Tillotson, in the long first chapter of her well-known *Novels of the Eighteen-Forties* (1954), sheds light on reader assumptions and publishing practices. Some of the unlit Grub Street side of Victorian literary life is revealed in John Gross's entertaining *The Rise and Fall of the Man of Letters* (1967). Particularly welcome would be more studies of persisting traditions and countertraditions in Victorian reviewing, such as those identified in two important articles, R. G. Cox's "Victorian Criticism of Poetry: The Minority Tradition" (*Scrutiny*, 1951) and R. V. Johnson's "Pater and the Victorian Anti-Romantics" (*EIC*, 1954). But little along those lines has been done since.

V. THE ART OF VICTORIAN PROSE

The growth of interest in the artistry of the Victorian prose writers has coincided with a near avalanche of studies in theoretical and practical stylistics that has hardly yet begun to be assimilated, especially by the literary. Obviously, the student cannot be held to a mastery of this complex and questionably useful material before he is allowed to comment on the Victorian prose masters; it would be foolhardy, nevertheless, to attempt serious studies in style without acquiring some sense of the largely unexploited resources of modern stylistics. Unfortunately, the body of earlier European studies in style was a yet-untracked wilderness to most Anglo-American literary scholars when the newer, more technical "stylistic linguistics" began to press its claims upon us. At the risk of disproportioning this chapter, some signposts through the thickets seem in order.

The chapter "Style and Stylistics" in René Wellek and Austin Warren's *Theory of Literature* (1948) first made available to the English-speaking world the names, titles, and procedures of the foremost twentieth-century analysts of style. Another important early survey is Helmut Hatzfeld's "Stylistic Criticism as Art-Minded Philology" (*YFS*, 1949). Much of the major work was done by German-speakers, such as Carl Vossler, Ernst Curtius, Erich Auerbach, and Leo Spitzer; but their subjects were frequently in the Romance literatures. This work was splendidly drawn together in Hatzfeld's *A Critical Bibliography of the New Stylistics, Applied to the Romance Languages, 1900–1952* (1953), and in a second volume (1966) covering the years 1953–65. The sections on general theory of style go well beyond the Romance literatures. Two recent bibliographies, largely confined to works in English, provide good sections on prose: *Style and Stylistics* (1967), by Louis T. Milic, and *English Stylistics* (1968), by Richard W. Bailey and Dolores M. Burton.

Two recent journals, *Style* and *Language and Style*, testify to the lively state of American stylistics, though regrettably little of their content has so far been directly pertinent to Victorian prose. Richard W. Bailey's "Current Trends in the Analysis of Style" (*Style*, 1967) is a good introduction to contemporary linguistics and stylistics. The debate between Bailey and Donald Davie (*Style*, 1967) clarifies some issues. A welcome development is the accelerating production of collections of key modern essays on style, by the following editors: T. A. Sebeok (1960), John Spencer (1964), Roger Fowler (1966), J. V. Cunningham (1966), Seymour Chatman and Samuel Levin (1967), Glen Love and Michael Payne (1969), Howard Babb (1971), and S. Chatman (1971). The claims of many of the new stylisticians are appropriately modest, though the stance of a number of Americans in the field is more aggressive: a familiar line is to admit that linguistics has "not yet" offered much to the critic, but then to disparage all earlier methods of stylistic analysis while in effect following Roman Jakobson's subordination of poetics to linguistics (in Sebeok, *Style and Language*). The reactions of the humanists, insisting on the paramountcy of "meaning" and a "system of values," can be impatient, as in Gordon Messing's review of Sebeok (*Language*, 1961) and F. W. Bateson's "Linguistics and Literary Criticism" (in *The Disciplines of Criticism*, ed. P. Demetz et al., 1968), or firm but conciliatory, as in a number of the essays by René Wellek gathered in *Concepts of Criticism* (1963) and *Discriminations* (1970). The current skirmishing among the ancients and the moderns, the literary critics and the linguisticians, is ultimately part of a larger cultural conflict involving inchoate philosophical positions. Too often it draws strength from the humanist's instinctive and uninstructed recoil in face of the behaviorism and positivism that infect a good deal of contemporary language study. For the moment, much of the work done under the aegis of the new stylistics, whatever its promise, is generally open to the charge of being deficient in historical sense, ignorant of older traditions of rhetorical and generic analysis, and incapable of managing the unity of whole works. The humanist should, however, get a glimpse of the future of "quantification," as opened out in *Statistics and Style*, edited by L. Doležel and R. Bailey (1969), and in Louis Milic's "The Computer Approach to Style" (in *The Art of Victorian Prose*).

Certain works on style that fall outside current controversy deserve attention. Earlier general "literary" approaches to style, such as those by F. L. Lucas, J. M. Murry, and Herbert Read, now regularly dismissed as "impressionistic," can still sensitize the student to language. George Saintsbury's *A History of English Prose Rhythm* (1912; rpt. 1965), despite his generally rejected preoccupation with classical "quantitative" meters, remains valuable as a storehouse of lively characterizations of a wide range of prose writers. Paull Franklin Baum's . . . *the other harmony of prose* . . . (1952) is a good modern introduction to "rhythm" in prose that summarizes earlier views and has a good bibliography. Huntington Brown's short but thoughtful *Prose Styles* (1966) provides a good historical sense of the varieties of prose discourse, including narrative, and of their complex interactions with the practical aspects of life. Josephine Miles's *Style and Proportion: The Language of Prose and Poetry* (1967), filled with provocative (and debatable) perceptions, draws on distinctions first developed in her earlier works. A curiosity is Louis T. Milic's bulky *Stylists on Style* (1969), which invites the student to analyze a large number of historically arranged selections, themselves *on* aspects of style. His long introduction is an ambitious attempt to yoke transformational grammar with traditional rhetoric.

Students of Victorian prose have few models of sustained analysis: two stand out. W. K. Wimsatt, Jr.'s *The Prose Style of Samuel Johnson* (1941) is perhaps the first such modern book-length study in English, and one of the best. His introduction, "Style as Meaning," presents probably the most influential case for the "contextualist" view of the indissolubility of form and content. Jonas Barish's *Ben Jonson and the Language of Prose Comedy* (1960) is important for its close examination of prose and for its intelligent discussion of the prose tradition. Two recent, more theoretical books deserve attention. David Lodge, in *Language of Fiction* (1966), very valuably hints at how the theoretical problems of fiction are analogous to those of nonfictional prose: their referential force toward the outward world of "experience" (in fiction) and "ideas" (in nonfiction) contrasts with the more exclusively inward-turning world of language and symbol (in poetry). Karl Kroeber, in *Styles in Fictional Structure: The Art of Jane Austen, Charlotte Brontë, George Eliot* (1971), stresses the *differences* between fictional and nonfictional style on the ground that "a distinction between narrative and dialogue is usually unimportant in the study of nonfictional prose." One wishes he had taken account of the arguments of Holloway and later critics who stress precisely the variety of "voices" and the dramatization of discussions, the "fictionality," of Victorian prose.

The work of Richard Ohmann deserves special attention because he is interested in nineteenth-century prose and because he is the most literarily sensitive of the recent American theorists of style. His *Shaw: The Style and the Man* (1962) is the boldest full attempt yet made to align grammatical categories with an author's characteristic modes of thought. In a series of essays—for example, "Prolegomena to the Analysis of Prose Style" (in *Styles in Prose Fiction*, ed. Harold Martin, 1959), "Generative Grammars and the Concept of Literary Style" (*Word*, 1964), "Literature as Sentences" (*CE*, 1966)—he has depreciated all other approaches to style and expressed his belief that generative-transformational grammar will clear up stylistic theory. Attacking the "organicism" of a Wimsatt or a Monroe Beardsley, the furthest philosophical extension of his approach is his suggestion that "the elusive intuition we have of *form* and *content* may turn out to be anchored in a distinction between the surface structures and the deep structures" (*CE*, 1966). His "A Linguistic Appraisal of Victorian Style" (in *The Art of Victorian Prose*) interestingly treats Arnold and Carlyle, and ends with the judgment (very much in need of further investigation) that, despite "stylistic tendencies" that divide the Victorians from the Augustans, there is no "Victorian" style, since "the Victorians differ nearly as much from each other as they differ from eighteenth-century writers."

The other chief proponent of this approach is Louis T. Milic, who (in 2 essays in *Contemporary Essays on Style*, ed. Love and Payne) argues even more strongly for a "rhetorical" separation of form and style, and for the rejection of "period styles" in favor of "individual" styles. Close reading in the two schools reveals less divergence than at first appears. But the "organicists" will tend to err on the side of an almost mystical and unanalyzable "nondetachability" of form and content, while the new grammarians, accepting the central transformational distinction between deep and surface structures and the linguists' tendency to define style in terms of "choice" and "deviation" from norms, have reintroduced into criticism a startling reversion to the commonsense and "rhetorical" separation of the two components. This continuing debate is bound to affect studies in Victorian prose.

R. H. Hutton, throughout his various volumes, is virtually the only Victorian before Saintsbury to show a continuing alertness to the art of the Victorian prose writers. Lewis Gates's pioneering *The Studies in Literature* (1899) provided acute remarks on style and rhetorical method that were to flower long after, in studies mentioned above, by Walter E. Houghton and E. K. Brown. But it is scarcely an exaggeration to say that the modern study of the subject commences with John Holloway's *The Victorian Sage* (1953; rpt. 1962). His first chapter, based on jointly aestheticist and positivistic principles, is in effect an important extension of the much-vexed problem of "belief" in literature, especially in discursive prose. The perceptive chapters on individual authors accomplish two critical ends: by adopting from the New Critics an attention to figure and texture, he moved the Victorian prose writers into closer alignment with the central "imaginative" and lyrical norm of modern taste and theory; and by stressing voice and dramatization, he introduced a fictional or "novelistic" norm that has been pursued in later studies.

A series of articles followed in *Victorian Newsletter* that are still worth some attention. A. Dwight Culler ("Method in the Study of Victorian Prose") called critical prose a "mediatorial form" requiring for its understanding a broadly humanistic method, in which formal analysis is not detached from "the deliberate activation of real belief." An exchange between R. C. Schweik and Culler (1956) led the latter to the statement that Holloway worked in "a metaphysical void," his premise being "a thorough-going nominalism." Francis G. Townsend's "Newman and the Problem of Critical Prose" (1957) presents a provocative theory of the relationship of poems to essays ("Every great poem is a concealed essay which has been given external form") and of the different critical tasks required for the two forms. Though the inadequacies of rhetorical analysis are confidently asserted by many contemporary theorists of prose, Martin J. Svaglic's telling examples (1957) suggest how much of the meaning and the inner dynamics of familiar Victorian prose pieces remain unknown in the neglect of such analysis. No one has yet answered his simple question, whether the structure of "Rugby Chapel" is utterly different from that of "The Study of Poetry." A term to this phase of the discussion was made in William E. Buckler's perceptive introduction to his *Prose of the Victorian Period* (1958), summing up and criticizing then recent work and analyzing at length Pater's essay "Style."

George Levine ("Nonfiction as Art," VN, 1966) clarifies and develops some of the problems laid out by Holloway. He sees that Newman convinces us of the reality of his belief only through his "creation" of an imaginative world coextensive with its texture: style, imagery, structure, rhetoric, logic. But he draws back from the problem of the effect on the *reader's* belief, avoiding that more "existential" problem in favor of emphasis on "the quality of Newman's feeling and . . . the ways in which Newman believes." The equally important introduction by Levine and William Madden to their *Art of Victorian Prose* (1968) argues the case even more radically, within the framework of "an expressionist aesthetic in which all language is self-expression." In effect, by an extreme polarization, Victorian prose becomes "art" when it ceases to "mean" in the way it did to its original audience. What had earlier seemed the problem of the high proportion of argumentative "content" in Victorian prose is solved at a stroke, by dismissing an author's "ostensible arguments" and his "assumed outward reality" as somehow irrelevant to his "art." The "poetics" of Victorian prose—in a line stretching from Pater to Holloway to Levine and Madden—has thus achieved one impressively stated, if not unassailable, formulation. A debate is in order to see whether there is a future to Culler's "mediatorial" method (*VN*, 1956), in which the reader's beliefs and the values inherent in the "external" referent are indeed relevant to what actually happens when we read Victorian prose. That debate was begun by Patrick J. McCarthy ("Reading Victorian Prose: Arnold's 'Culture and Its Enemies,'" *UTQ*, 1971), who argues, against Levine and Madden, that the bulk of Victorian prose "is not self-regarding but mediative."

Several of the essays in *The Art of Victorian Prose* suggest new approaches. Walter Cannon's striking view ("Darwin's Vision in *The Origin of Species*") that the "scientific imagination by 1859 . . . had outrun the resources of inherited myth, ritual, drama, and metaphor" matches A. Dwight Culler's conclusion ("The Darwinian Revolution") that "ultimately the Darwinian technique is [not] susceptible of very profound or satisfying literary exploitation." Alan Donagan ("Victorian Philosophical Prose: J. S. Mill and F. H. Bradley") berates Saintsbury for emphasizing the detached power of "style," but he himself urges the questionable view that the critic is interested in thought "only as it has to do with the expression of emotion." John Holloway ("Logic, Feeling, and Structure in Political Oratory: A Primer of Analysis"), adopting a repellent format, ends negatively, stressing the distinction "between the oratorical and the literary imagination." An opposite point is made by Martin Svaglic ("Classical Rhetoric and Victorian Prose"), whose traditional methods of analysis can claim to reveal something of the complex unity of whole works as very few of the other methods in the volume can. G. Robert Stange ("Art Criticism as a Prose Genre") uses Ruskin and Pater to define an original, and neglected, Victorian genre. Though Norman N. Holland's unabashed sexual readings ("Prose and Minds: A Psychoanalytical Approach to Non-Fiction") are open to familiar objections, he outdoes Richard Ohmann by insisting that syntactic choices represent the writer's "own idiosyncratic patterns of defense," and calls for a full-scale correlation of grammar with "the basic psychosocial issues of Victorian culture."

The diversity of the Victorian period (or periods) and the complexity of the age's concerns are much better understood in recent years; one hears fewer pronouncements about "the Victorian mind." But we need to know much more *about* the Victorians, beginning with their lives. For some (Matthew Arnold and Pater), there are no biographies; for many, the standard biographies are much out of date; and certain copious studies (on George Eliot and J. A. Froude) have been judged critically deficient. Far too few studies of the Victorians show a grasp of the European context that informs the best work on the Romantics. Students of the prose sages have showed too little interest in the significance and influence of Spinoza, Kant, Hegel, or Comte. Beyond biography and the cultural and intellectual context, we still know too little about texts and textual history, publishing practices and editorial policies, the periodicals in which the prose writers appeared and in which they were reviewed, and the various "audiences" of the various kinds of publications.

Victorian fiction and poetry exhibit a coherence imposed by recognizable (if evolving) forms and genres. In our ignorance of the traditions in the prose, and in the current antiformalist and neoromantic critical climate, the temptation has been to leap over all intermediate categories and to infer some psychic trait from a particular device or usage. Or an inappropriate form, such as the supposed "realism" of the early George Eliot, is used as a norm for belaboring the prose writers for falling short of a goal they never aspired to. These sophisticated simplicities would be abated by close attention to Northrop Frye's chapter, "Theory of Genres," in *Anatomy of Criticism* (1957). His discussion of the four strands in "fiction"—novel, confession, anatomy, and romance—offers numerous hints for describing the precise intentions and effects of writings demonstrating an interest in ideas. This underexploited approach has recently been clarified by articles in the journal *Genre* and by Paul Hernadi's *Beyond Genre* (1972). This is not to suggest that the current interest in Victorian prose as self-expression is not valuable, only that there are relevant formal and intellectual traditions involved. A good study could be based on Walter Pater's discussion of the essay in the Montaignean tradition as the characteristic vehicle of modern skepticism and relativism. An interesting if undeveloped idea is William R. Brown's (in "William James and the Language of Personal Literature," *Style*, 1971), that "personal literature," in which a structure of ideas is overshadowed by the author's personality, should be considered a genre that includes the meditative poem as well as the essay.

The still inadequately grasped unity of the Victorian sages may lie in a shared, if fragmenting, community of interests, largely "ethical" and "imaginative," derived from the longer tradition of Christian humanism, and treated characteristically by the Victorians as being in a state of severe crisis. The moral and religious elements of the nineteenth-century embodiment of the tradition, with Coleridge at the head, are spelled out by Basil Willey; the social and cultural elements by Raymond Williams. The "humanism" of these sages would be illuminated by studies in the continuity of interest in a view of "mind" that resists fragmentation or simplification: in Coleridge's "balance" of faculties, Carlyle's "region of meditation," De Quincey's "understanding heart," or Arnold's "imaginative reason." An interesting treatment by a professional philosopher of the "ethical" climate of Victorian England can be found in J. B. Schneewind's *Backgrounds of English Victorian Literature* (1970). A good topic for investigation would be how much was known in nineteenth-century England about the Renaissance and, specifically, the Renaissance humanists, and whether this knowledge affected Victorian ideals of mind and imagination.

Edward Alexander observes (*JEGP*, 1969) that, in our welcome present interest in the "art" of Victorian prose, the "higher" ability is still "to recognize the success or failure of a work of art as a function of its author's success or failure in discovering ideas which are large and flexible enough to assimilate the experience of his time." What is still too often lacking is precisely a sense of the forms and strategies that the welter of Victorian ideas-in-conflict took. A good model for such unified study is Paul Fussell's *The Rhetorical World of Augustan Humanism: Ethics and Imagery from Swift to Burke* (1965). That "higher" synthesis has been aided by the appearance in recent years of a number of studies of two or more writers that exhibit simultaneously, though in varying proportions, a concern for cultural debate as well as artistry and modes of argumentation. These would include Alexander's own *Matthew Arnold and John Stuart Mill* (1965), U. C. Knoepflmacher's *Religious Humanism and the Victorian Novel* (1965), George Levine's *The Boundaries of Fiction: Carlyle, Macaulay, Newman* (1968), and David DeLaura's *Hebrew and Hellene in Victorian England: Newman, Arnold, and Pater* (1969). A chief deficiency remains the lack of detailed studies of single masterpieces as competent as Walter Houghton's *The Art of Newman's "Apologia"* and G. B. Tennyson's *"Sartor" Called "Resartus"* (1965).

THOMAS BABINGTON MACAULAY

•

John Clive and Thomas Pinney

I. MANUSCRIPTS AND BIBLIOGRAPHY

The largest collection of MSS is at Trinity College, Cambridge; it contains much unpublished juvenilia, many hundreds of letters, and eleven volumes of Macaulay's journal, 1838–59. This last, of which only a very small part appears in Trevelyan's *Life of Macaulay*, is now being edited for publication by Robert Robson; the project will take some years to complete. The MSS of five *Edinburgh Review* essays are in the British Museum; two others are in the Morgan Library. Not all of the MS of the *History of England* seems to have survived, and what has is now widely dispersed. The portions of the fifth volume now in the Morgan Library and the British Museum appear to be the largest extant fragments. An important collection of the Macaulay family papers is in the Huntington Library. The documents of Macaulay's public career, including many official papers of his writing, are in the Public Record Office, the India Office Library, and the West Bengal Record Office, Calcutta.

There is no single complete bibliography of Macaulay. The British Museum *Catalogue*, the *NCBEL*, Arthur Bryant, *Macaulay* (1932), and Walter Hoyt French and Gerald D. Sanders, *The Reader's Macaulay* (1936) provide the most useful lists; and attention should be drawn to Donald H. Cunningham, "Thomas Babington Macaulay: A Bibliography of Twentieth-Century Periodical Articles and Speeches" (*Bull. of Bibliography and Mag. Notes*, 1971). The *Wellesley Index to Victorian Periodicals* (1966–) gives the only full record of Macaulay's contributions to the *Edinburgh Review*. On the question of Macaulay's earliest contribution to the *Edinburgh*, Jane Millgate's "Father and Son: Macaulay's *Edinburgh* Debut"

(*RES*, 1970) clarifies and confirms the information in the *Wellesley Index*. The problems confronting the bibliographer, should anyone be willing to undertake that role, will be considerable, for Macaulay wrote much and in many forms; moreover, he constantly revised and corrected his texts as they passed through their many editions, a matter almost entirely unstudied as yet.

II. EDITIONS

The *Works* (8 vols., 1866) edited by Macaulay's sister, Lady Trevelyan, is the standard edition, reasonably full but by no means complete; it is most attractively reprinted as the Albany edition (12 vols., 1898). The New Cambridge edition (10 vols., 1900) adds three speeches and some letters from printed sources. The *Works* (9 vols., 1905–07), edited by Thomas Finlayson Henderson, is the only attempt, and not a very satisfactory one, at an annotated edition. *The Reader's Macaulay* (1936) is a good and carefully edited selection, as is *Macaulay: Prose and Poetry* (1952), selected by George M. Young for the Reynard Library. John Clive and Thomas Pinney's *Thomas Babington Macaulay, Selected Writings* (1972) includes some items not ordinarily reprinted, including the Minute on Education, an early essay on the London University, and letters on the Reform Bill crisis. Macaulay's essays, so popular in the nineteenth century that George Otto Trevelyan could say that the demand for them varied "with the demand for coal," have been reprinted in a myriad of forms and combinations since Macaulay's own first selection from them in 1843, but no complete edition has ever been made. The selection in the 1866 *Works* is the basis for most subsequent editions. *Critical and Historical Essays* (3 vols., 1903), edited by Francis Charles Montague, is annotated, but excludes the essays from *Knight's Quarterly Magazine* and the biographies contributed to the *Encyclopaedia Britannica*. The essays are kept in print in three volumes of the Everyman's Library; *Critical and Historical Essays* (1965), edited by Hugh Trevor-Roper, is a selection of nine essays from the *Edinburgh Review*. Macaulay's university prize essay of 1822, "On the Life and Character of William III," was published from the MS by Alan Noel Latimer Munby (*TLS*, 1 May 1969). Macaulay's speeches, though they belong just as much to his art as do his essays, have not attracted editors. George Malcolm Young, *Speeches by Lord Macaulay, with His Minute on English Education* (1935), is a sympathetic presentation of this section of Macaulay's oeuvre, but is out of print, rather scarce, and has had no successors. It followed the very meager selection published by Macaulay (1854 for 1853), representing only a small fraction of the whole. Young was one of the few editors interested in Macaulay's official papers, printing the Education Minute of 1835 both in the *Speeches* and in his selection of 1952; it may also be found in the Clive and Pinney anthology. *Lord Macaulay's Legislative Minutes*, edited by C. D. Dharker (1946), is an extensive though not quite complete reprinting of the minutes that Macaulay wrote in his capacity as fourth member of the Supreme Council of India and is furnished with a long and informative introduction. A volume less easily found, but useful as supplementing Dharker, is Henry Woodrow's edition of *Macaulay's Minutes on Education in India Written in the Years 1835, 1836, and 1837 and Now First Collected from the Records in the Department of Public Instruction* (1862). A very special branch of Macaulay's writing is represented in *Marginal*

Notes by Lord Macaulay, edited by Sir George Otto Trevelyan (1907); the material in that is agreeably augmented by Alan Noel Latimer Munby, *Macaulay's Library* (1966). Like the *Essays*, the *History of England*, as one of the great Victorian best sellers, was produced in a formidable number of editions during the first fifty years following its publication; the pace has much slowed now. Macaulay's final text was the edition of [1857–]1858 in seven volumes over which he labored carefully, and this seems to have been generally used thereafter. The most splendid edition of the *History* is Charles Harding Firth's (6 vols., 1913–15), notable especially for its illustrations. The volumes of the *History* in Henderson's annotated edition of the *Works*, already mentioned, were reprinted in one volume (1907) and in five volumes in the World's Classics (1931). The *History* still appears in Everyman's Library (4 vols.), and an abridgment by Hugh Trevor-Roper was published in 1968.

III. BIOGRAPHY AND LETTERS

The situation here is simple: G. O. Trevelyan's *Life and Letters of Lord Macaulay* (2 vols., 1876) remains first and the rest are nowhere. Trevelyan's *Life*, a charming and artful narrative, is recognized as one of the two or three best literary biographies of the nineteenth century and has served, to compare small things with great, like Boswell's *Johnson*, to keep the memory of its subject alive after the popularity of his work declined. Trevelyan's final text is the edition of 1923, though the text of the 1908 edition is the one regularly reprinted. A limited edition (1959) of the 1908 text is useful for its index. Trevelyan, for all his virtues, needs supplementing now; he was writing too close to his subject to be as frank as strict honesty would require, having to respect the sensibilities of many living people who had known Macaulay. More important, his account reveals hardly anything of the inwardness of Macaulay's experience, being written almost throughout with a certain amused detachment. It is not always like that, but such is the dominant style, with the result that a blandly happy, unproblematic Macaulay is presented. For all that, Trevelyan's *Life* is too good for there to be any question of "replacing" it. An adequate modern biography, besides having to respect Trevelyan, will also have to wait for the information in the letters and journals, whose publication will be a slow affair. After Trevelyan, much the most important biography is Frederick Arnold's *The Public Life of Lord Macaulay* (1862), for the sake of its record of Macaulay's political activity at Leeds and Edinburgh and for the many speeches it includes. Arthur Bryant's *Macaulay* (1932) is a graceful account largely derived from Trevelyan and is an excellent brief introduction; though Bryant was allowed to read Macaulay's journals, there is little evident use of them in his book. Richmond Croom Beatty's *Lord Macaulay: Victorian Liberal* (1938), the most recent biography except for Giles St. Aubyn's brief, popular *Macaulay* (1952), is an unfortunate book. Although Beatty, too, had access to the journals, he was apparently not allowed to make extensive use of them, and his book has little information to add to Trevelyan. In the absence of new information, the hostility of the book's Southern Agrarian view of Macaulay and its insufficient knowledge of the Victorian age are fatal. John Clive's study, *Macaulay: The Shaping of the Historian* (1973), though not strictly a biography, makes use of considerable new biographical information in seeking to describe Macaulay's intellectual development and to interpret his early public career as well as his literary work. It is the fullest and best documented study of Macaulay's early years yet published.

Macaulay's letters have never been collected. About five hundred are printed in Trevelyan, but printed subject to the license of the editorial conventions then prevailing. None appears as Macaulay wrote it, and the extent to which Trevelyan has allowed himself to rearrange, redate, and rewrite the letters is perhaps greater than what Forster allowed himself in editing Dickens or Cross in editing George Eliot. Another extensive publication of Macaulay's letters, more straightforwardly treated, is in *Selection from the Correspondence of the Late Macvey Napier*, edited by Macvey Napier, Jr. (1879), which documents the history of Macaulay's connection with the *Edinburgh Review*. A comprehensive edition of the letters is now being prepared by Thomas Pinney, but even this will exclude the many hundreds of official letters that Macaulay wrote from his various public offices.

Not many new facts or documents have come to light on the subject of Macaulay's public life. An exception is the article by Arthur Stanley Turberville and Frank Beckwith on "Leeds and Parliamentary Reform 1820–1832" (*Pub. of the Thoresby Soc.*, 1943) which includes some lively excerpts from the pamphlet literature produced by that election. Another exception is provided by Gerald and Natalie Robinson Sirkin whose "The Battle of Indian Education: Macaulay's Opening Salvo" (*VS*, 1971) includes a newly discovered letter of Macaulay's supporting the "Anglicist" against the "Orientalist" side in the matter of educational policy for India. But recent treatment of Macaulay's Indian years has generally centered around interpretation rather than new facts or documents. The discussion has been devoted to two principal topics—his Minute on Indian Education and his Penal Code. The question of whether Macaulay has ultimately been proved right in his emphasis on the teaching of English in the education of Indians continues to be debated. The Sirkins support his position in toto. On the other hand, David Kopf in his *British Orientalism and the Bengal Renaissance: The Dynamics of Indian Modernization 1773–1835* (1969) draws attention to those elements of "cultural imperialism" in the Minute that were to give rise to much misunderstanding. What seems clear from Percival Spear's "Bentinck and Education" (*Cambridge Hist. J.*, 1938) is that Macaulay himself has been too much blamed and too much praised. He should not be held solely responsible for making an educational policy upon which Lord William Bentinck, the Governor-General, was in any event determined. Kenneth Ballhatchet, in "The Home Government and Bentinck's Educational Policy" (*Cambridge Hist. J.*, 1951), points to Macaulay's brother-in-law, Charles Trevelyan, as the key figure in persuading Bentinck to adopt the policy. Elmer Cutts, in "The Background of Macaulay's Minute" (*AHR*, 1953), emphasizes Evangelical agitation and pressure for more than half a century before 1835. This, he points out, antedated and was more significant than Utilitarianism in bringing about Macaulay's view of Indian education. But there can be no doubt about the important role played by Utilitarian influence in shaping Macaulay's work as Law Member on the Indian Council, both in the form of his legal minutes and of his Penal Code. In his excellent book, *The English Utilitarians and India* (1959), Eric Stokes defined and examined that influence in detail, finding Macaulay's mind reflective of the assimilation of Utilitarian science to the Whig outlook. An illuminating Indian estimate of the Code and its significance for Indian law today is to be found in Motilal Chimanlal Setalvad, *The Common Law in India* (1960).

IV. CRITICISM

Criticism of Macaulay has not been remarkable either for copiousness or originality in this century, though some of the latest has also been among the best. The main lines of criticism were laid down in the nineteenth century, notably in essays by Bagehot, Gladstone, John Morley, and Taine, and in studies by J. Cotter Morison and John Paget. Matthew Arnold's occasional pained remarks have also had their effect. There is an abundant but less influential American critical literature on Macaulay, which has been fully surveyed to 1940 by Harry Hayden Clark, "The Vogue of Macaulay in America" (*TWA*, 1942). The strategy of the dominant criticism has been to allow to Macaulay vividness, energy, clarity, allusive range, and rhetorical skill on the one hand, and, on the other hand, party prejudice, superficiality, exaggerated statement, mechanical form, and other indications of inadequate imaginative sensitivity. George Malcolm Young, for instance, in his essay on Macaulay in *Daylight and Champaign* (1937), detected "a certain commonness of mind" as perhaps the most deep-seated and insidious defect in the historian's constitution. The only question with a given critic has frequently been which side of the scale to weight more heavily. More often than not, in the very act of condemning Macaulay for his paradoxes, critics have made one of him—the "Philistine on Parnassus," in Lytton Strachey's phrase; or, in William Henry Chamberlin's, "The Magnificent Middlebrow" (*SatR*, 1965). There is no doubt that the establishment of a critical orthodoxy has hindered the fresh and direct study of Macaulay. What is especially needed now—and there are already some contributions of this kind—are studies paying more receptive attention to the complexity and individuality of Macaulay's art and thought.

The appearance of a number of the *Review of English Literature* in 1960 devoted to Macaulay on the centenary of his death conveniently marks an end and a beginning in the discussion of Macaulay's style and of the sensibility underlying it. The end is George Sutherland Fraser's "Macaulay's Style as an Essayist," a sensitive and perceptive restatement of the received (originally Arnoldian) view that Macaulay's style is "mere rhetoric" and that it is emphatically a public style, revealing nothing of the private personality. The beginning is in John Clive's "Macaulay's Historical Imagination," which argues that Macaulay's style—in the widest sense—does in fact reveal the qualities of the man behind it, especially his "strongly developed visual and dramatic imagination and his equally strongly developed fantasy life." Clive sees both the strengths and weaknesses of Macaulay's work as the effects of his histrionic and self-centered imagination, which is at once a source of vividness and an obstacle to sympathetic understanding. In the same issue, Eric Stokes comes at the question of the relation between writer and work from a different angle. After examining the evidence of the great suffering that the marriage of one and the death of the other of his favorite sisters produced in Macaulay, Stokes concludes that the very intensity and vulnerability of his emotional life led Macaulay to avoid, in his writing, the expression of personal feeling: his buried life was one that he feared to know. Hence, Stokes suggests, the artificiality of Macaulay's work comes from his writing under rigid control and against his natural, emotional grain.

The links between Macaulay's personality and his art pointed out by Clive and Stokes were taken up and elaborated in two ambitious studies, both published in

1968: William Madden, "Macaulay's Style," *The Art of Victorian Prose*, edited by Madden and George Levine; and George Levine, "Macaulay: Progress and Retreat," in his *The Boundaries of Fiction*.

Madden provides an anatomy of Macaulay's style in "oratorical," "histrionic," "antithetical," and "judicious" elements, and seeks to relate each of these to the formative influences of Macaulay's life. He agrees with Clive that the main element is the "histrionic," and with Stokes that Macaulay sought to escape from his emotions in literature; but he moves on from these positions to the rather startling conclusion that Macaulay's is, finally, an incoherent style, a chaos of unintegrated tendencies. It is hard to resist the feeling that Madden's essay, fine as it is in detail, has fallen into one of the traps of biographical criticism. It is one thing to show contradictions between what we know of Macaulay's emotional life and the quality of his writings; it is quite another to discover those contradictions within the writings themselves.

Levine's essay, the fullest to appear in many years, is tied to a thesis about the nature of the novel and of the relation of nineteenth-century prose to the novelistic standard. It can, though, be readily separated from that connection without much distortion. The point of departure is the proposition that Macaulay feared his own emotional life and that both his imaginative and his practical lives were devoted to escaping from it. Since his writing was a form of escape, it necessarily exhibits the simplifications inseparable from escapist literature. Taking the *History* as his central text, Levine concludes that it is the means for providing certain childish gratifications to its author. Under all the scholarship there are very simple and elementary interests being served: the delight in strange and wonderful things and the demand for strict poetic justice. Though the *History* resembles fiction, the kind of fiction it resembles is romance; it therefore fails to exhibit that "openness" which Levine particularly seeks but instead provides only the safety and certainty that Macaulay required. Such is the main drift of the essay; but in the course of a very expansive development, based on a wide and intimate knowledge of the subject, it has many excellent things to say about other, less tendentious, topics, such as Macaulay's theory of literature, his idea of the past, and his narrative art. One may note in passing that the novelistic qualities of Macaulay's *History* in which Levine is interested are also discussed by Avrom Fleishman, who, in *The Historical Novel* (1971), takes up the relation between Macaulay's theory and practice of history and Thackeray's *Henry Esmond*, a relation earlier glanced at by Gordon Ray in his *Thackeray, The Age of Wisdom* (1958), but one not yet fully analyzed. Both Madden and Levine have raised questions that will, no doubt, continue to be important in the discussion of Macaulay. At the same time, it seems worth pointing out that the new attention paid to the relation between psychology and creation in the articles of Clive, Stokes, Levine, and Madden, though it has suggested a number of new considerations, has not changed the received judgment as to the kind and quality of Macaulay's writing. It has made such a réchauffé of conventional criticism as Mario Praz's in *The Hero in Eclipse in Victorian Fiction* (1956)—where Macaulay is summarized as a fortunate bourgeois, "serene, energetic, healthy, with a mind free of passion and emotion"—less likely to be repeated. But the opportunity to set forth in adequate detail the distinctive achievements of Macaulay's art is still open to a sympathetic critic.

A start toward this kind of appreciation is made by Jane Millgate, "Macaulay at Work: An Example of His Use of Sources" (*TCBS*, 1970). By close analysis of

Macaulay's various comments on Temple and the Phalaris controversy in relation to their sources, Millgate is able to show in convincing detail that Macaulay, in repeating familiar materials, succeeded in "making them over into something entirely his own." As an illustration of the critical value of source study, Millgate's seems much preferable to the method of Robert D. Horn, "Addison's *Campaign* and Macaulay" (*PMLA*, 1948). After a painstaking examination of the evidence, Horn concludes merely that Macaulay "contented himself with an uncritical fusion of two conflicting accounts" in his treatment of the history of Addison's poem.

Macaulay as a literary theorist, a role he did not at all aspire to, has attracted some attention in recent years. Frederick L. Jones, "Macaulay's Theory of Poetry in *Milton*" (*MLQ*, 1952), proposes that Peacock's *Four Ages of Poetry*, rather than the primitivistic theory of Hazlitt, was the authority behind Macaulay's formula for the opposition between poetry and civilization. No doubt Macaulay had read Peacock, but his idea of the conflict between poetic imagination and critical reason is not to be accounted for by a single source. René Wellek devotes a few pages to Macaulay in the third volume of his *History of Modern Criticism* (1965), though he recognizes that Macaulay very soon ceased to take any interest in literary theory. Wellek provides a fuller context for Macaulay as a theorist than does Jones by relating him to "such 18th-century critics as Wharton, whose double point of view combined primitivism and belief in progress." In "Singer and Seer: Macaulay on the Historian as Poet" (*PLL*, 1967), Ronald Weber works out from the early essays Macaulay's view of the specially privileged position of the historian, whose craft, compounding poetry and philosophy, reconciles the conflict of imagination and reason. But, as Weber observes, the "imagination" of the historian for Macaulay is not a primary power of seeing but an auxiliary power of rendering things vivid. Terry Otten's "Macaulay's Critical Theory of Imagination and Reason" (*JAAC*, 1969) draws on the evidence of a chronological survey of the essays, beginning with the earliest published in *Knight's Quarterly*, to show that Macaulay's theory of the conflict between imagination and reason, though elaborated and qualified over the years, remains consistent. Otten also makes the essential point that Macaulay's idea of the imagination is simply as the image-making power; it has nothing at all of the Germanic or Coleridgean about it. Though it treats the subject only incidentally, the most perceptive discussion of Macaulay's theory of literature—or, more accurately, of his essentially untheoretic "attitudes toward literature"—is George Levine's essay in *The Boundaries of Fiction*.

The ballad theory, on which Macaulay constructed his *Lays of Ancient Rome*, is the subject of two studies: Arnaldo Momigliano, "Perizonius, Niebuhr, and the Character of Early Roman Tradition" (*J. of Roman Stud.*, 1957), comments on the degree to which that theory is nowadays accepted by classical scholars; while the chapter by K. R. Prowse entitled "Livy and Macaulay" (in Thomas Alan Dorey, ed., *Livy*, 1971) examines Macaulay's artistry in his use of material taken from Livy.

Macaulay's two articles on Johnson have generated commentary that may be ranged under three different subjects: Macaulay on Croker, Macaulay on Boswell, and Macaulay on Johnson. Esmond Samuel DeBeer, "Macaulay and Croker" (*RES*, 1959), disposes of the tradition (apparently founded by Gladstone) that Macaulay's attack on Croker's edition of Boswell was in retaliation for the beatings he took from Croker in Parliament. DeBeer's review of the evidence enables him to say plainly that "Macaulay had no personal defeats in debate to avenge." DeBeer also vindicates Macaulay's strictures on Croker's editorial work. He tries, finally, to account for Macaulay's hatred of Croker, but the cause remains something of a mystery. H. A. Morgan's "Boswell and Macaulay" (*ConR*, 1958), though slight and unoriginal, may be noted as representative of the abuse that the renovation of Boswell in this century has drawn down on Macaulay. The admirers of Boswell are now repaying with a vengeance the injustice that Macaulay was certainly guilty of in rendering their hero as a sublime simpleton. Frederick Pottle, *James Boswell: The Earlier Years, 1740–1769* (1966), curtly calls Macaulay "uninformed" about Boswell, which is no doubt true for our post-Malahide era but not true for Macaulay's generation; indeed, Macaulay as well as Croker had talked with men who had known Boswell. An excellent corrective is Francis R. Hart, "Boswell and the Romantics: A Chapter in the History of Biographical Theory" (*ELH*, 1960), an informed and interesting study of the critical history and influence of Boswell's book between its publication and the appearance of Croker's edition. Hart sets Macaulay's paradoxical Boswell in perspective and demonstrates that "only the rhetorical extravagance was original with Macaulay." Lodwick Hartley, in "A Late Augustan Circus: Macaulay on Johnson, Boswell, and Walpole" (*SAQ*, 1968), argues that Macaulay's comments on these writers are not only unoriginal but perversely wrong. The article might have profited greatly from Hart's, but as Oscar Cargill ruefully concluded after working through all the commentary on Henry James's novels, "nobody apparently reads anybody else." David Fong (*UTQ*, 1970) describes some affinities between Johnson and Macaulay in literary theory and method, and points to some significant changes in Macaulay's view of Johnson between 1831 and 1859, very justly concluding that Macaulay was "far from being merely a vulgarizer of the Johnsonian image." It was time that this much should be said in Macaulay's defense.

Other individual essays continue to be criticized in the light of modern scholarship. Thus Penderel Moon, *Warren Hastings and British India* (1947), maintains that Macaulay in his essay on Hastings formed a one-sided view of his character and failed to see the profounder aspects of his achievement as a statesman. Against this one may set the apology, especially interesting as the work of an Indian, presented by R. K. Das Gupta, "Macaulay's Writings on India" (in Cyril Henry Philips, ed., *Historians of India, Pakistan and Ceylon*, 1961). The essays on Hastings and Clive are admitted to be perhaps too severe in their judgments, but they are defended for their honesty, their willingness to assert standards of moral judgment, and their value to other English historians as correctives to "self-flattery in historical writing." Das Gupta sees what hostile critics of Macaulay see in these essays, but he attempts, with less than entire success it may be, to show that what have usually been regarded as defects may really be virtues. Behind the errors of detail and the distortions inherent in any perspective is a definite and defensible idea of Indian history: "the two essays will ever have a value as showing that the task of empire-building . . . cannot be accomplished without a measure of inhumanity and injustice."

The most extensive general critique of Macaulay's historical essays is to be found in Pieter Geyl's "Macaulay in His Essays," *Debates with Historians* (1955). Geyl regarded Macaulay as a man of the eighteenth century whose intellect was more strongly developed than his imagination and whose obsession with "progress" made him incapable of disinterested contact with historic personages, especially with complex and tormented ones. But even Geyl recognized that the essays are "masterpieces through which there speaks to us, directly and insistently, a mind of rare clarity and immense vigor." George Peabody Gooch, in the pages devoted to Macaulay in his *History and Historians in the Nineteenth Century* (1913; new ed., 1952), makes intelligent and relevant critical remarks about the major essays. He insists that the *History* was a far greater achievement than the essays. But Dom David Knowles comes closer to the spirit in which Macaulay wrote his essays when he notes in *Lord Macaulay 1800–1959* (1960) that recent critics "have put up large blocks with all modern conveniences alongside Macaulay's gay wooden bungalows." Nothing, he adds, has replaced the essays taken in bulk as a sketch of the seventeenth and eighteenth centuries, and as a first brilliant overture to the *History*. David Fong, "Macaulay: The Essayist as Historian" (*DR*, 1971), also argues that the essays, particularly the later ones, are worthy preparation for the *History*. Hugh Trevor-Roper, who deals with the influence of Scott on Macaulay in *The Romantic Movement and the Study of History* (1969), had previously made a strong connection between the essays and the *History* in the introduction to his selection from Macaulay's *Essays* (1965). Here he acknowledged the fact that Macaulay's style changed for the better when he turned to serious historical writing, but added that "studied critically, the difference between the *Essays* and the *History* is much less absolute than Acton and others have maintained." And it is, of course, the *History* that has evoked most of the critical comment on Macaulay's work in recent years.

Detailed criticism of Macaulay's *History* began early. The most impressive example from the last century is certainly Paget's "New 'Examen': An Inquiry into the Evidence Relating to Certain Passages in Lord Macaulay's *History*" (1861), which raised sharply argued doubts about Macaulay's treatment of Marlborough, the massacre of Glencoe, the highlands of Scotland, Dundee, and William Penn. It may be found in Paget's *Paradoxes and Puzzles: Historical, Judicial, and Literary* (2nd ed., 1874) and is still worth reading. Sir Winston Churchill, a great admirer of Paget who induced a publisher to reprint the "New Examen" with an introduction by himself in 1934, continued the defense of his illustrious ancestor in the first two volumes of *Marlborough: His Life and Times* (4 vols., 1933–38). In the course of them he questioned Macaulay's use of sources and called him a word-spinner and a liar. He was also skeptical about George Macaulay Trevelyan's thesis, set forth in the section devoted to Macaulay in *Clio, A Muse and Other Essays* (new ed., 1930), which maintained that had Macaulay lived another five years, and thus completed more of the *History*, he would have shown the heroic side of Marlborough "who would now enjoy the full meed of admiration and gratitude still denied to him by his countrymen's little knowledge of what he did." The following index entries from Churchill's second volume indicate the general tenor of his response: "Attitude of Macaulay to Marlborough explained by Professor Trevelyan, 1:144; its treachery insisted on by the present author, 1:144–5." No less an authority on the period than the late Sir Lewis Namier was completely convinced by Churchill that Macaulay's account of Marlborough was wrong, as he indicated in a fascinating letter published in Julia Namier, *Lewis Namier* (1971). But Trevelyan, in a letter to be found in *TLS* (19 Oct. 1933) as well as in the third volume of his *England under Queen Anne* (3 vols., 1931–34), pointed out in reply to Churchill that while Macaulay's treatment of Marlborough was the worst thing in the *History*, Churchill had no right to call him a liar: "A pioneer historian who had to find the straw for his own bricks, and was moreover 'cocksure' by temperament, could make ghastly mistakes without being called a 'liar.' "

Judge Jeffreys would seem more difficult to defend against Macaulay's aspersions than Marlborough. But some twentieth-century scholars have taken a more balanced view of him, among them Seymour Scholfield, *Jeffreys of the Bloody Assize* (1937), George Williams Keeton, *Lord Chancellor Jeffreys and the Stuart Cause* (1965), and, most recently, G. Kitson Clark, in *The Critical Historian* (1967), where he underlines the dangerous effects that could result from Macaulay's letting his imagination play on what he had stored up in his memory. William M. Lamont's "Macaulay, the Archbishop, and the Civil War" (*Hist. Today*, 1964) castigates Macaulay for the "brilliant unfairness" of his treatment of Laud.

In considering these instances of detailed criticism of Macaulay's *History*, it is well to keep in mind this statement by Sir Charles Firth in the preface to his illustrated edition: "The task of illustrating the *History* necessitated a close scrutiny of Macaulay's pages, and while it made some defects and omissions more apparent, it has increased, not diminished, my admiration of what Macaulay succeeded in doing." A detailed expansion of this statement is represented by Firth's own *Commentary on Macaulay's History of England* (ed. Godfrey Davies, 1938). That book first took form as a series of lectures delivered at Oxford in 1914, whose purpose it was not only to criticize Macaulay's statements and his point of view, but also to reveal the extent to which his conclusions had been invalidated or confirmed by later writers or by new documentary materials. Godfrey Davies, the editor, made no general attempt to bring the work up to date, but he did add some bibliographical notes. Firth's book is prescribed reading for anyone seriously interested in Macaulay's historical method. He comments incisively on the conception, structure, style, and arrangement of the *History*, and then goes on to deal with Macaulay's use of authorities, literary and otherwise, the third chapter, his treatment of the army and navy, of Scottish, Irish, and colonial history, foreign affairs, and of James II and William and Mary. He also devotes a chapter to Macaulay's errors, in which he concludes that some of these were due to the fact that Macaulay had the mental habits of the politician rather than the historian.

Those particularly interested in a recent judgment of Macaulay's treatment in the *History* of England's relations with continental Europe should read Mark A. Thomson's *Macaulay* (1959); while those primarily interested in the constitutional aspects of the *History* should consult Godfrey Davies' magisterial article, "The Treatment of Constitutional History in Macaulay's *History of England*" (*HLQ*, 1939). Here Davies concludes that Macaulay missed the essence of the opposition to the early Stuarts, that is, the attempt to establish the supremacy of the law over the prerogative. But he finds him much sounder on the later Stuarts, and praises him for not being content to deal narrowly with constitutional issues, but always eager to explain their general significance. In trying to arrive at any summary judgment of the quality of Macaulay's *History* it is, by the way, well to remember F. W. Maitland's judgment (cited by Trevelyan in his *TLS* letter of 1933) that Macaulay was always right in the points of law he discussed in the *History*; and S. R. Gardiner's assertion in *Cromwell's Place in History* (1902) that Macaulay's judgment of political situations was as superb as his judgment of personal character was weak.

The charge most often brought against Macaulay as a historian—for the most part, though not always, by those who have not carefully read his historical writings —is that Whiggism colored his history, either in the form of obvious political bias or in the form of what Sir Herbert Butterfield has called *The Whig Interpretation of History* (1931), an approach to the past governed primarily by the values, usually

Protestant and progressive, of the present. Can Macaulay justifiably be called a Whig historian? It should be noted, first of all, that his name does not appear in *The Whig Interpretation*, whose author is said to have had Lord Acton, rather than Macaulay, in mind as his principal target. Indeed, it was Sir Herbert himself who in his *George the Third and the Historians* (1957) demonstrated that in his view of the politics of the eighteenth century, as set forth in his essays on Walpole and Chatham, Macaulay made the "Tory" case against the Whigs under George II, and did not for a moment pretend that in 1760 there existed a happy constitutional order which George III wickedly set out to overthrow. As for Macaulay's view of the politics of the late seventeenth century in the *History*, Trevelyan long ago (in *Clio, A Muse*) indicated that Whiggism was not its worst historical fault, characteristically adding: "I wish it had been." Macaulay, after all, had taken a position against Monmouth's Rebellion, against the Whigs's refusal to make peace with Louis, and against Shaftesbury. The extent of his Whiggism, Trevelyan concluded, lay in his belief in religious toleration and in parliamentary government. Andrew Browning's "Lord Macaulay, 1800–1859" (*Hist*J, 1959) supports Trevelyan's judgment, pointing out that Macaulay's opinion of recognized Whig leaders (except Somers) was not high, and that his attacks on Marlborough stemmed from Tory rather than from Whig sources.

If, then, Macaulay's political prejudices in the *History* were not narrowly Whiggish, how else can they be defined? William G. Carleton's "Macaulay and the Trimmers" (*ASch*, 1950) offered an answer to this question in pointing out that the real villains in the *History* tended to be extremists of the left or right; that the work was really a classic defense of the middle of the road, in which "Trimmers" such as William III and Halifax figured as heroes. This persuasive interpretation of Macaulay's historiographic parti pris has been applied to his political stance in general by Vincent E. Starzinger, in his *Middlingness: Juste Milieu Political Theory in France and England, 1815–1848* (1965). Starzinger argues that, unlike Brougham, Macaulay did not alienate himself from the vital center of English politics as it emerged during the events of 1832. One may prefer Henry William Carless Davis' formulation, in *The Age of Grey and Peel* (1929), that even after 1832 Macaulay "moved with the stream and was hardly aware how fast the stream was flowing." But, in any event, some knowledge of his view of politics is essential for an understanding of the *History*; not because that crudely mirrors Whig prejudices, but because in Macaulay's own mind the two spheres of politics and history were inextricably linked. Thus Hugh Trevor-Roper, both in the preface to his abridged edition of the *History* (1968) and in his "Lord Macaulay" (*Listener*, 1965), has argued that part of Macaulay's achievement as a historian was to restore to history the importance of politics by showing (contra Hume) that a society's progress was not distinct from politics, but could be achieved by enlightened, liberal, and rational political action.

In his veritable obsession with progress, Macaulay certainly was a "Whig" historian in the larger sense. George Macaulay Trevelyan's "Macaulay and the Sense of Optimism," *Ideas and Beliefs of the Victorians: An Historic Revaluation of the Victorian Age* (ed. Harman Grisewood, 1949), examined Macaulay's belief in progress within the historical context and perspective of the early Victorian age. This approach has also been followed by Robert L. Schuyler, "Macaulay and His History—A Hundred Years After" (*Pol. Sci. Q.*, 1948), who connects Macaulay's presentism with his desire to diminish social discontent, and by Edwin M. Yoder,

Jr., "Macaulay Revisited" (*SAQ*, 1964), who views the elements of insularity and provincialism to be found in Macaulay's *History* against a Victorian backdrop.

While some recent critics have thus attempted to relate certain aspects of Macaulay's historical writings to his time, others have tried to regard them in the light of his personality. In 1928 Herbert Albert Laurens Fisher, in his lecture on "The Whig Historians" (*PBA*, 1928), traced Macaulay's antimorbid and antimystical feelings to "the overflowing happiness of a wholesome, ardent, hard-headed, limited Scot." If Macaulay, who hated to be reminded of his Scottishness as much as he hated to be reminded of his limitations, has ever turned in his grave it must have been when Fisher pronounced that sentence. Three years later, Lytton Strachey's sketch of Macaulay, in his *Portraits in Miniature and Other Essays*, took a different tack. Having begun by calling the metallic exactness and the "fatal efficiency" of the historian's style one of the most remarkable products of the industrial revolution, Strachey went on to connect that stylistic "barrenness" to the lack of intense physical emotion in Macaulay's life: "The embracing fluidity of love is lacking." A generation later John Harold Plumb resumed this theme in his essay on Macaulay in *Men and Centuries* (1963). It was, he remarked, because Macaulay lacked the roots of life, sexual passion and the sense of tragedy it arouses, that he was unable to penetrate to the heart of human existence.

Criticism of Macaulay as a historian will no doubt continue. After all, as George Richard Potter pointed out in his *Macaulay* (1959), the *History* is "worth every ounce of powder and shot that is fired against it." Let us hope that his defenders can do better than John R. Griffin, with his *The Intellectual Milieu of Lord Macaulay* (1965), a book so well meant and at the same time so full of errors that Macaulay himself might even have relished reviewing it in his best "Montgomery" manner. There are, to be sure, other defenders: those praising his achievements in special fields, for example, J. M. Strawson, "Macaulay as a Military Historian" (*Army Q. & Defense J.*, 1963), and Margaret Wood, "Lord Macaulay, Parliamentary Speaker: His Leading Ideas" (*QJS*, 1958); and, for the comfort of today's general reader, young and old, Jack Valenti, who, in "Macaulay and His Critics," *The Bitter Taste of Glory: Nine Portraits of Power and Conflict* (1971), caps his praise for Macaulay by declaring that reading him is akin to smoking pot, since the carpentry of his sentences gives the reader a kind of floating assurance that he can do it, too. To which the authors of this chapter can only add: but no one has, as yet!

THE CARLYLES

·

G. B. Tennyson

THOMAS CARLYLE*

•

G. B. Tennyson

If genius were cheap, we should do without Carlyle;
but, in the existing population, he cannot be spared.

—EMERSON

After some decades of trying to do without Carlyle, the English-speaking world is again realizing that he cannot be spared. Emerson was writing in 1865 at a time of great American exasperation with Carlyle over his stand on the American Civil War. In a manner that anticipates Carlyle's later detractors and at least rivals in alarm if not effectiveness Carlyle's own obloquies, Emerson preceded his judgment of Carlyle's indispensability with such shrill statements as: "He is as dangerous as a madman. Nobody knows what he will say next or whom he will strike. Prudent people keep out of his way." Such has been not infrequently Carlyle's effect. But he has also had effects of another kind. Matthew Arnold, writing almost twenty years later than Emerson, could recall the rapture of hearing Carlyle's "puissant voice" in the 1840's in the same breath that he recalled the ineffable sweetness of the "religious music" of the voice of John Henry Newman, as though the two had somehow blended into a grand symphony of the early years of Victorian hope and promise. "Happy the man," exclaimed Arnold, "who in that susceptible season of youth hears such voices!" Emerson, of course, is known as one of Carlyle's first champions and Arnold as one of his most distressed critics, and one could indeed find passages to justify both these views. But here we see the roles reversed. For Carlyle affected almost everyone positively *and* negatively at one time or other; the point is that he affected them.

Thomas Carlyle is the test case for the endurance and value of Victorian nonfiction prose. First of all, he helped create Victorianism. Second, he created

---

* In compiling the bibliography of more than 1,200 items consulted for this study the author was immeasurably and capably aided by Mrs. Janet D. Keyes, who is, however, not responsible for the opinions expressed.

Victorian nonfiction prose. In one view, to be sure, Carlyle is the last of the Romantics, having been born in the same year as Keats and having begun his writing career in the early 1820's. But such a view ignores the fact that he outlived Mill, Dickens, Forster, Thackeray, George Eliot, and a host of other Victorians, that he was in any case longer-lived than all the other major Victorians save Newman and Hardy. But more important than life-span, the view of Carlyle as Romantic ignores the fact that, while he forged his thought and style in the 1820's, it did not reach his contemporaries until the thirties and forties. Celebrity came to Carlyle with the publication of *The French Revolution* in 1837, the year of Victoria's accession; it did not leave him, though it changed its character, until 1881, the year of his own death. The intervening years are quintessentially Victorian.

Carlyle taught his contemporaries how to think as he did about many subjects, or at least that they ought to think as he did. He was also accused of having mistaught many of them how to write as he did. But if Carlylese has remained and ought to remain the sole property of its inventor, Carlyle's choice of nonfiction prose as his medium was a choice rightly imitated by many others in the age. Carlyle was the pioneer in nonfiction prose as the vehicle for carrying ideas to a mass audience. All the other Victorian prose writers of consequence followed in his wake—Ruskin with art, Newman with religion, Arnold with culture—but all of them as popular writers of nonfiction were Carlyle epigones. This came about not merely because Carlyle disparaged poetry- and novel-writing in favor of history and biography and forever exhorted his contemporaries to turn to nonfiction; it came about more because Carlyle with his own writing created the taste for serious works of nonfiction. It is hard to believe that the creator of that taste can be disposed of without also disposing of those who followed him.

Beyond creating Victorian nonfiction prose, Carlyle stands in other ways in an especially determinative relationship to other Victorians, for he seems not only to have led the way in reaching a mass audience with intellectual and factual material, but also to have set, or at least exhibited, a career pattern for many of his contemporaries, especially the social critics and moralists. Carlyle began in what can be broadly construed as the area of art and aesthetics. In his case it was specifically literary criticism and an enthusiasm for German Romantic literature. Ruskin with art and painting and his enthusiasm for Turner, Arnold and Morris with the writing of poetry, even Pater at a considerable distance offer parallels. Carlyle moved, inevitably it now appears, to the study of history and historical institutions, partly as a consequence of trying to understand the exceptional man, the poet, the seer, the prophet, the man who later became identified as the Hero, and partly as a consequence of coming to believe that true poetry and literature is history itself. The meaning of history and its men and institutions led—again it now seems so inevitable—to a consideration of present-day institutions and present-day history, which is to say of society, politics, and current events. Finally, Carlyle turned inward and toward the personal and sought to examine something of the meaning of his own experience.

The pattern is only general, not particular, for the chronology shows a continual overlap of interests. *Chartism*, an intensely social document, follows *The French Revolution* but precedes *Past and Present*, the one historical, the other historical and social; *Frederick the Great* appears when Carlyle is in his sixties and after the affectionate and retrospective *Life of Sterling*. Carlyle was not one to abandon an interest once he had taken it up, and in more than one sense Carlyle was more consistent than his contemporaries, for it is all there in *Sartor Resartus*. But the broad outline still shows a moving outward to social and cultural questions from a base in aesthetic ones and a return to the personal and private once the message had been uttered—and had failed to transform the world. The parallel is most striking with Ruskin, Carlyle's acknowledged disciple, who indeed exhibits the pattern more clearly than does Carlyle, even to being totally broken by the frustrations of speaking in vain to a heedless and profligate generation. But, taken broadly, the pattern could be applied to any half-dozen Victorians, from Arnold to Dickens to Tennyson to Browning, and even with some stretching to Mill. Part of it is the human pattern of rise, flowering, and decline; but here it takes the peculiar Victorian-Carlylean form of art-society-self. It has often been noted that Teufelsdröckh was a representative man and that his appeal rested on the affinities he shared with the intellectual and spiritual experiences of many a Victorian reader. It is less often noted that Carlyle was a representative Man of Letters who both pioneered and shared a life experience with a large number of his Victorian fellows.

So, Carlyle's survival as man and writer, as representative Victorian Man of Letters, as the father of Victorian nonfiction prose, in some way affects the survival of all the others. That he survives, however, is increasingly evident—not from the mass of immediate post-death materials, but from the new critical attention of the last two decades. In 1894 a German scholar, Gerhart von Schulze-Gaevernitz, complained of the amount of material written about Carlyle. Since that time the mass has swelled even more. For a generation or more the swell was due largely to the industry of German scholars whose file of dissertations materially helped to make Carlyle even today the most frequently dissertated about of all Victorian nonfiction authors and tied for third among authors of all genres. But during the first four or five decades of this century, the harvests of valuable Carlyle scholarship were lean indeed. Material still came forth from other than the German dissertation mills, but it was at least as often hostile as favorable. As the passions aroused by two wars faded in intensity, Carlyle was again considered as a literary genius and a potent intellectual and social force of the nineteenth century. And as we enter the decade of the centenary of Carlyle's death and to within two and a half decades of the bicentennial of his birth, we can see Carlyle in perspective as neither madman nor inerrant pontiff, but as one of the enduring monuments of our literature who, quite simply, cannot be spared.

I. MANUSCRIPTS AND SOURCE MATERIALS

Carlyle's literary manuscripts survive in far less abundance than would seem probable for a man who collected and retained such a quantity of memorabilia and minutiae as the richly stocked house in Chelsea today attests. The fact that early manuscripts and manuscripts of minor and miscellaneous works survive in far greater measure than those of major works written when Carlyle was famous suggests that some important pieces may yet be in private hands. It is possible that manuscripts of works like *Sartor Resartus* and *The French Revolution* or substantial portions of them may still come to light. Apart from the present study the only effort to list Carlyle manuscripts is Hill Shine's brief notice (*VN*, 1958).

Part of the Carlyle manuscript problem has to do with the confusion that reigned over the estate after Carlyle's death in 1881, and with the sensational "revelations" of the following decades. Since both John Forster and John Carlyle had predeceased Carlyle, the only living executor was James Anthony Froude. The issue of Froude's conduct after Carlyle's death will be discussed below under Biography, but it must be said in regard to the manuscripts that the entire so-called "Froude-Carlyle controversy" so embittered surviving Froudes and Carlyles and others that there would have been an understandable reluctance to release manuscript materials at all. After long legal battles the papers (exclusive of some Jane Welsh material which was finally explicitly bequeathed to Froude) were finally transmitted to Carlyle's niece Mary Aitken Carlyle, and these ultimately found their way to her husband and cousin, Carlyle's nephew Alexander, an industrious Carlyle scholar in his own right. How much of this material Alexander retained is not known, but some is definitely still in private hands. The bulk was put up for auction at Sotheby's in the late 1920's and also after Alexander's death in 1932, with the largest blocks eventually going to Yale University, the foundation of Yale's present impressive holdings. Sotheby's published catalogs of the material under the title *Catalogue of Manuscripts and Documents Pertaining to Thomas Carlyle* in 1928 and again in 1932. Listings also occur throughout the 1930's in the Maggs Brothers catalogs.

The most important surviving single work is *Past and Present* of which the holograph manuscript is in the British Museum and the corrected page proofs are in the Yale Library. Since Carlyle revised his works heavily in proof, it is necessary to consult both holdings for a textual study, as was ably done by Grace Calder in *The Writing of* Past and Present (1949). The British Museum manuscript is briefly described by J. P. Gibson in "Carlyle's *Past and Present*" (*BMQ*, 1927), the Yale manuscript at length by Calder and also earlier by her in "Carlyle's *Past and Present*" (*YULG*, 1931). *Frederick the Great* survives to a large extent but in such far-flung distribution it would require heroic efforts to use it for scholarly work. The manuscript was cut up, even sometimes to mere sections of pages; some of these were used for presentation and gift purposes and the distributed parts and snippets have found their way to many repositories, but no doubt some have been lost forever. The largest segment is at Yale, which also houses the rejectanda of *Frederick* and various drafts and blockings of the book. The whole Yale *Frederick* collection is discussed by Richard Brooks in "Manuscripts Pertaining to Carlyle's *Frederick the Great*" (*YULG*, 1934). Brooks divides the material into eight categories of which the most important is the 380 pages (of the total 2,958) largely comprising Books 17–21. The collection also contains the journal kept by Carlyle in 1858 on his journey to Germany in pursuit of Frederick material and battlefield authenticity. Brooks edited this material in a separate book, *Thomas Carlyle's Journey to Germany, Autumn 1858* (1940). Karl Young's "The Uses of Rare Books and Manuscripts" (*YULG*, 1941) discusses the Carlyle collection at Yale.

The bulk of the *Reminiscences* is in the National Library of Scotland, Edinburgh. This includes also Geraldine Jewsbury's memoir of Jane Welsh Carlyle, Jane's notebook, and Carlyle's manuscripts of the reminiscences of Edward Irving and Lord Jeffrey. Several current projects are under way to re-edit the *Reminiscences*, and these will make use of the National Library of Scotland material. John Clubbe of Duke University is editing a brief unpublished reminiscence by Carlyle of the Scottish painter Alexander Scurving and a commentary by Carlyle on a German biography of him by Friedrich Althaus. Other manuscripts for the *Reminiscences* are presumably still privately held, as Carlyle's notebook journals are known to be.

Of lesser items the National Library of Scotland holds some poems, the rejected portions of "Shooting Niagara," the early "Gropings about Montrose" (see Coleman O. Parsons' "Carlyle's Gropings about Montrose," *Eng. Studien*, 1937), and some unpublished pieces on education and history from the period 1835–50, as well as other miscellaneous short pieces, some unpublished. In addition to *Past and Present*, the British Museum holds the manuscript of Carlyle's "Narrative of a Tour to the Netherlands" of 1842, printed by Alexander Carlyle in *Cornhill* (1922). Carlyle's house, Chelsea, has the manuscript of "Illudo Chartis," printed by Marjorie P. King (*MLR*, 1954), and a fragment of *The French Revolution*. The Pierpont Morgan Library in New York City has the manuscript of Carlyle's unfinished novel *Wotton Reinfred*. Yale holds, besides its *Frederick* collection, Carlyle's unfinished *History of German Literature* from 1830, ably edited by Hill Shine (1951); most of the early poems, edited by G. B. Tennyson in "Carlyle's Poetry to 1840" (*VP*, 1962); "Spiritual Optics," edited by Murray Baumgarten (*VS*, 1968); and a number of miscellaneous prose pieces.

The Forster Collection of the Victoria and Albert Museum holds some interesting Carlyle political pieces and "The Death of Charles Buller," all from the *Examiner* of 1848, some *Frederick* material, and some of *Cromwell*, including the manuscripts of the notorious "Squire Notes" in Carlyle's hand. The *Examiner* material is reprinted (but not from the manuscripts) in Percy Newberry's *Rescued Essays of Carlyle* (1892). The Houghton Library at Harvard University houses in its vaults some 500 of Carlyle's research volumes with copious notes used for *Frederick* and *Cromwell*. This material is listed in William Coolidge Lane's *The Carlyle Collection* (1888). The Houghton also houses some miscellaneous short literary manuscript fragments and a typescript of the *History of German Literature*. The Huntington Library has Carlyle's "Last Words on Trades-Unions, Promoterism, and the Signs of the Times" from 1872 and a short fragment from *Frederick*. Carlyle's two sets of marginalia in John Sterling's *Essays and Tales*, one at Harvard, one at Duke, have both been studied, the former by Anne K. Tuell (*PMLA*, 1939) and the latter by William Blackburn (*SP*, 1947). Carlyle's essay on Lord Chatham, in the New York Public Library, is discussed by Lewis M. Stark and Robert W. Hill in "The Bequest of Mary Stillman Harkness" (*BNYPL*, 1951).

Other research libraries hold scattered literary items and most autograph collections have a line with signature in Carlyle's hand. There is thus still literary material available for scholarly study, but the substantial area of Carlyle manuscript preservation has been the correspondence. Here an entirely different picture prevails from that of the literary manuscripts. To be sure, the manuscripts of the staggering number of letters written by the two Carlyles are scattered throughout the world, but the fact remains that vast numbers of the letters do survive. Charles Richard Sanders of Duke has in the past twenty years located about 9,500 letters from Thomas and Jane Carlyle. The Duke-Edinburgh edition now in progress (discussed below under published correspondence) will make all the extant Carlyle letters available, some 4,500 for the first time. The first volume of the Duke-Edinburgh edition provides a full breakdown of the location of the Carlyle letters. The number of consequential collections exceeds two dozen. The following information is gratefully borrowed from the Duke-Edinburgh findings.

The major repositories of Carlyle letters—those holding more than 100 letters

—in descending order are: The National Library of Scotland, Edinburgh, which holds 4,780 (3,400 by Thomas, 1,380 by Jane); the collection of the Marquess of Northampton of letters to the Ashburtons; the Victoria and Albert Museum; the Alexander Carlyle family in Canada; Trinity College, Cambridge; the collection of Frederick W. Hilles of Yale; Harvard Library; Edinburgh University Library; the Strouse Collection at the University of California, Santa Cruz; the Huntington Library; and Yale Library. There are surely also letters that have hitherto not come to light as well as some that are irrevocably lost.

The abundance of surviving letters and the paucity of surviving literary manuscripts might suggest again the existence of manuscripts in private hands, but it must be remembered that recipients of letters from Carlyle were very likely to retain them as treasures (which accounts for the relative rarity of early Carlyle letters and the frequency of later ones after he became famous). Moreover, there is some reason to believe, from the survival of materials in the Forster Collection, for example, that Carlyle's literary manuscripts often remained with the printer, and in any case he was addicted to substantial revision on proof sheets, which would render some manuscripts less valuable if the sheets were not also preserved. Nevertheless, the Carlyle scholar will continue to yearn for missing manuscripts and perhaps that yearning will one day be satisfied by the emergence of manuscripts still preserved but unknown to scholarship.

II. BIBLIOGRAPHIES

Despite some notable compilations just after Carlyle's death and the work of Alexander Carlyle and David Alec Wilson, Carlyle bibliography really begins with Isaac Watson Dyer's *A Bibliography of Thomas Carlyle's Writings and Ana* (1928). Unfortunately, it almost ends there as well, since there has been no full updating of Dyer and no comparably ambitious undertaking. Still, a few of the later bibliographical gatherings have made valuable contributions.

Before Dyer, the important compilations are Richard H. Shepherd's *Bibliography of Carlyle* (1881), John P. Anderson's bibliography appended to Richard Garnett's *Life of Carlyle* (1887), and Mary Eunice Wead's *A Catalogue of the Dr. Samuel A. Jones Carlyle Collection* (1919), which lists items in the collection at the University of Michigan. Alexander Carlyle's various editions of letters and David Alec Wilson's *Life* (1923–34) also contain extensive lists. Dyer comprehends all of this material.

Dyer's undertaking is far more extensive than anything attempted before or since in Carlyle bibliography, but only 600 copies of it were printed. It lists all of Carlyle's works in all editions then known as well as uncollected periodical pieces and all correspondence then known. It also includes translations of Carlyle into other languages, an area largely ignored in Carlyle studies, and yet one that would repay serious attention, especially in the study of Carlyle's reputation and influence. Beyond all that, Dyer undertakes to list virtually every known book and article about Carlyle to 1928, including even those with only slight and inconsequential mention. Still, he misses some items. Dyer has annotated with a liberal hand, and, while some of the annotation is supererogatory, much is still of use in the study of Carlyle. Dyer's volume also contains a section by James A. S. Barrett, titled "Principal Portraits, Statues, Busts, and Photographs of Thomas Carlyle." This is followed by a commentary on the portraits by James L. Caw. The list of works and editions by Carlyle is still immensely useful, and the portraits section continues to be a valuable research source.

Dyer's work went further than any other toward establishing the Carlyle canon, but the task remains unfinished. Since Dyer's time there have been additions to the canon, and the publication of the complete letters will doubtless add further ones. Some Carlyle contributions and collaborations for *Fraser's Magazine* that Dyer missed are provided in Miriam M. H. Thrall's *Rebellious* Fraser's (1934), including one largely independent review of Cunningham's *Life of Burns* and two possible collaborations with Heraud. At the same time Thrall rejects three articles listed by Dyer on the strength of arguments offered by James A. S. Barrett (*TLS*, 20 Jan. 1927 and 26 April 1928). Hill Shine added external evidence for rejecting two of them (*MLN*, 1936). This makes more doubtful the fourth Barrett ascription, an article on Vitalis in the *Foreign Review* for 1829, also listed in Dyer, but not part of Thrall's concern. Shine would add as a Carlyle piece one reworked by Heraud or Maginn, *Fraser's* "Letter on the Doctrine of St. Simon" (*N&Q*, 1936). Further additions to the Carlyle canon have been provided by G. B. Tennyson in "Unnoted Encyclopaedia Articles by Carlyle" (*MLN*, 1963), which adds to the accepted eighteen contributions Carlyle made to the *Edinburgh Encyclopaedia* the articles "Persia" and "Quakers." Tennyson's "Carlyle's Poetry to 1840: A Checklist and Discussion, A New Attribution and Six Unpublished Poems" (*VP*, 1963) lists all of Carlyle's poetry excluding translations and publishes for the first time six poems from manuscripts at Yale. It also attributes to Carlyle an unsigned poem from *Fraser's*. To date, this is the definitive bibliography of Carlyle's poetry, but it is almost certain that there are other unnoted Carlyle poems, either anonymously published or still in manuscript, that should be added to the known ones. The new letters will probably add items to Carlyle's works. Apart from future additions to the canon there is the problem that nowhere is there a single up-to-date listing with annotation of all Carlyle's works that takes into account the findings since Dyer. The closest approximation to it is the listing in the *NCBEL*. There is also no up-to-date list of translations of Carlyle's works.

Still in the area of specialized bibliographical listings, Edward F. Coffin's "American First Editions of Carlyle" (*ABC*, 1933) lists some items missed even by Dyer. A minor correction to Dyer's listings can be found in Richard C. Johnson and G. Thomas Tanselle, "The Haldeman-Julius 'Little Blue Books' as a Bibliographical Problem" (*PBSA*, 1970). Useful for specialized purposes is the bibliography in Alan C. Taylor's *Carlyle et la pensée latine* (1937), which is rich in translations of Carlyle into Romance tongues, and Lawrence McNamee's *Dissertations in English and American Literature* (1968) and *Supplement* (1969). The annual bibliographies are discussed under General Materials.

Two general compilations—the bibliography in Harrold and Templeman's *English Prose of the Victorian Era* (1938) and the *CBEL*, Volume III (1940) and Supplement (1957)—are now outdated but still of some use. The *CBEL* listing has been largely superseded by the new edition, although the older volumes continue to offer a more workable breakdown into separate categories and not all of the titles were repeated in the new edition. The highly selective listing by Jerome Hamilton Buckley, *Victorian Poets and Prose Writers* (1966) in the Goldentree Bibliography series is suitable for introductory classroom use, but it offers only a beginning and is regrettably not free of error.

The most important bibliography since Dyer is undoubtedly that compiled by Charles Richard Sanders for the *NCBEL* (1969). The listing is especially good on canon, editions (translations are *not* included, alas), and letters and correspondence (both Carlyles are intermixed throughout). All other categories are lumped together in one amorphous listing. In keeping with *CBEL* practice, the criticism section does not pretend to completeness, but it is still quite extensive. Its coverage extends through 1965.

Perhaps the most useful work to date that involves Carlyle bibliography, though it is not confined to that, is Carlisle Moore's review of research and criticism in *The English Romantic Poets and Essayists*, edited by Carolyn Washburn Houtchens and Lawrence Huston Houtchens (1966). It is complete through 1964. Moore proceeds on the pattern established for the MLA Guides to Research, including the present volume, and his comments and appraisals are uniformly just and intelligent. His chapter can easily escape detection because it is tucked away with the Romantics, but Moore and the editors argue persuasively for Carlyle as a transitional figure from the Romantic to the Victorian period, and Moore points out that Carlyle wrote some of his most "original and durable works" before 1832. Moore, nevertheless, treats the whole of Carlyle's work, and he even succeeds in compressing all the criticism of Carlyle into twenty-five pages, a concision that is beyond the capacity of the present author.

Rodger L. Tarr's *Check-list of Twentieth Century English Language Articles on Thomas Carlyle, 1900–1965* (South Carolina Bibliographical Series, 1972) updates Dyer on articles but suffers from its self-imposed limitations. What is clearly needed is a full-scale bibliography to cover the period from Dyer to the present.

III. EDITIONS

There is no definitive scholarly edition of Carlyle's works. The standard edition generally used for scholarly purposes (though there are some omissions) is the Centenary Edition, edited by Henry Duff Traill (1896–99; New York printing carries the dates 1896–1901). It contains more material than the various collected editions published during Carlyle's lifetime, including even the fine People's Edition (1871–74), published under Carlyle's own supervision (rpt. as the Copyright Edition in 1888). Other earlier editions still of some interest are the first collected edition of 1857–58, the excellent Library Edition of 1869–71, and the Ashburton Edition of 1885–88. After the Centenary a few other collected editions appeared, most notably the Edinburgh Edition (1903) and the Centennial (1904?), but none has supplanted the Centenary, and there has been no new full edition in more than half a century.

So it is the Centenary that stands as the edition most suitable for scholarly use, its chief virtue being comprehensiveness. It runs to thirty volumes, with an additional volume edited by Alexander Carlyle as a supplement, *Historical Sketches of Notable Persons and Events in the Reigns of James I and Charles I* (1898). The text of the Centenary is merely satisfactory, the introductions by Traill are unremittingly belletristic, and there is no general index, although each work is individually indexed.

There is a considerable body of Carlyle material not available in any collected edition. Much of this material appeared in separate volumes by divers editors in the first two decades after Carlyle's death. The first to appear was the much-vexed *Reminiscences* (2 vols., 1881) edited by James Anthony Froude, and undertaken again by Charles Eliot Norton (2 vols., 1887; rpt. in one volume in the Everyman series, 1932) in protest against Froude's errors. Norton's, which is generally a more reliable edition than Froude's, was recently reissued with a few additional pages of reminiscence of Sir William Hamilton and with a brief introduction by Ian Campbell (1972). Meantime, Carlyle's comments on a contemporary biography of himself and a reminiscence of the Edinburgh painter Adam Skirving have been edited by John Clubbe for publication in 1973. A full and authoritative edition of all Carlyle's reminiscences would now be in order.

Froude also edited Carlyle's *Reminiscences of My Irish Journey in 1849* (1882) and his *Letters and Memorials of Jane Welsh Carlyle* (3 vols., 1883). Also appearing after Carlyle's death were *Last Words of Thomas Carlyle on Trades-Unions, Promoterism and the Signs of the Times* (1882); *Rescued Essays*, edited by Percy Newberry (1892); *Last Words of Thomas Carlyle* (1892), which includes "Wotton Reinfred"; and two editions of Carlyle's second course of public lectures from 1838 on the history of literature, one edited by J. Reay Greene (1892) and the other by R. P. Karkaria (1892). Both are edited from contemporary notes by Thomas Chisholm Anstey and are closer to being Carlyle's than the sketchy version in Edward Dowden's *Transcripts and Sketches* (1887). There are no comparably full notes for the first and third courses of lectures; the fourth, of course, Carlyle published himself as *On Heroes and Hero-Worship*. Yet other Carlyliana appeared in S. R. Crockett's edition of *Montaigne and Other Essays, Chiefly Biographical* (1897), containing Carlyle's contributions to the *Edinburgh Encyclopaedia*; and in *Collectanea Thomas Carlyle 1821–1855*, edited by Samuel Arthur Jones (1903).

Apart from the *Reminiscences*, perhaps the most important of the material not in any collected edition is Charles Eliot Norton's edition of *Two Note Books of Thomas Carlyle from 23d March 1822 to 16th May 1832* (1898), which elicited James A. S. Barrett's note with corrections (*N&Q*, 1934) and Ian Campbell's note about the whereabouts of the original, "James Barrett and Carlyle's 'Journal'" (*N&Q*, 1970). Later notebook entries are available only from Froude's quotations in his biography of Carlyle, and only one modern author has had access to these later journals—Jacques Cabau, who used them for *Thomas Carlyle ou le Prométhée enchaîné* (1968). Many of these early editions, such as *Two Note Books, Rescued Essays*, and even the *Historical Sketches*, are now very difficult to obtain. Kenneth J. Fielding prepared new introductions for reprints in 1971 of two valuable Carlyle works, the *Last Words* and *Two Note Books*. O. D. Edwards has done the same for Charles Gavan Duffy's *Conversations with Carlyle*, and Fielding has also provided a new introduction for a reprint of the *Catalogue of the Forster Collection* at the Victoria and Albert. All of these are dear in price but at least libraries can now acquire them, even if they remain, as does the recent reprint of the Centenary, beyond the reach of Dr. Johnson's scholar suffering from toil, envy, and want.

Later editions of works not available elsewhere include the various printings and editions of manuscript material by Alexander Carlyle, Coleman Parsons, Richard A. E. Brooks, Hill Shine, Marjorie P. King, G. B. Tennyson, and Murray Baumgarten, all cited above under Manuscripts. It is necessary to specify the volumes cited above and all these subsequent additions to the canon, as well as to remind the reader of the other uncollected periodical pieces cited in Dyer, in order to emphasize again the incompleteness of the Centenary Edition and the need for a truly full and scholarly collected edition. That it would easily add another ten volumes to the Centenary's thirty need not be doubted, nor that it would be warmly received by students of Carlyle.

Only a few anthologies of Carlyle merit consideration in a review of scholarship, the field having been littered with pious chrestomathies and gatherings of sayings of Chairman Thomas. Among more recent collections might be mentioned Arthur Montague D. Hughes's *Selections* (1957), useful mainly for its "Appreciations" by various nineteenth-century figures. Substantial modern collections are confined to Julian Symons' *Carlyle: Selected Works, Reminiscences, and Letters* (1955), stronger on *Reminiscences* and letters than on works; and G. B. Tennyson's *A Carlyle Reader* (1969), the best for balance and overall assessment (and also happily in paperback), but regrettably lacking in annotations. A slender paperback selection, too short to do justice to Carlyle, is available in Herbert Sussman's *Thomas Carlyle*: Sartor Resartus *and Selected Prose* (1970).

Should a new edition of Carlyle be undertaken it would have abundant editions and commentaries for certain individual works to draw upon. These will be discussed individually below under Criticism because they often contain valuable critical material, but the few definitive editions should be noted here: Archibald MacMechan's edition of *Sartor Resartus* (1896; rev. 1905) and Charles Frederick Harrold's edition of the same work (1937); MacMechan's edition of *On Heroes and Hero-Worship* (1901); and A. M. D. Hughes's edition of *Past and Present* (1921). Beyond that it should be pointed out that definitive critical editions are lacking for the essays, *Chartism, Cromwell, The French Revolution, Frederick, German Romance, Latter-Day Pamphlets, Schiller, Life of Sterling, Wilhelm Meister*, and, of course, for virtually all the minor writings.

Finally, a word must be said about the inadequate treatment of Carlyle by the paperback industry. In view of the absurd trivia regularly issued in paperback, it is deplorable that only three major works and one translation by Carlyle should be available n paper—*Sartor* (in Tennyson's *A Carlyle Reader* and in Sussman's anthology), *Heroes*, edited by Carl Niemeyer (1968), *Past and Present*, edited by Richar Altick (1965), and *Wilhelm Meister's Apprenticeship*, edited by Victor Lange (1962). *A Carlyle Reader* also contains several early essays and selections from later works. Julian Symons' anthology has recently been issued in paper covers with an erroneous attribution of editorship on the cover; the contents remain the same as in the hardcover edition. There is a severe abridgment of *Frederick the Great* in paper (1969) and a recent paper edition, by Eugene R. August, of the *Occasional Discourse on the Nigger Question* coupled with John Stuart Mill's rejoinder (1971). Paperback publishers have a clear and present duty to do better by Carlyle.

IV. CORRESPONDENCE

If the absence of a definitive edition of Carlyle's works will continue to frustrate the scholar for a long time to come, he can at least take heart that the situation with regard to the correspondence is much brighter. The cause for cheer is the now-appearing definitive edition of *The Collected Letters of Thomas and Jane Welsh Carlyle*, under the general editorship of Charles Richard Sanders of Duke and the associate editorship of K. J. Fielding of Edinburgh University. Assistant editors are Ian Campbell, John Clubbe, and Janetta Taylor. The edition is known as the Duke-Edinburgh edition and the first four volumes, covering the years through 1828, appeared late in 1970. The full edition will run to about forty volumes.

Although no final assessment of the new edition can be made for many years, it is already clear that the Duke-Edinburgh edition is likely to be the one thing needful in scholarship on Carlyle's correspondence. The editors have wisely resolved to publish every letter, no matter how small, and to publish it complete. They will also republish all previously printed letters for which manuscripts are still lacking. Publication will proceed in sets of four volumes at a time, making available a substantial body of material with each publication. Following each set an index will be issued, and these will all be combined into a master index after the final volume is published. Each volume will contain approximately 300 letters, and the volumes will be issued in proper chronological sequence from the earliest Carlyle letters to the latest. The first volume, for example, contains letters from 1812 to 1821. As the Carlyles age and write more frequently there will be volumes confined to one or two years, for Sanders has found years like the early 1840's in which Carlyle wrote an average of 169 letters per year, while Jane at the same time was averaging 116!

The Duke-Edinburgh edition will be heavily annotated with abundant identifications of persons, places, and allusions, as the first four volumes testify. The final result will be a vivid commentary on a vast span of nineteenth-century life as well as a unique presentation of the life and thought of two of the most arresting figures in the age. Sanders has reported on his project through the years as well as having issued articles on particular aspects of Carlyle's correspondence. Four articles on the editing project are of interest, two early ones issuing progress reports (*VN*, 1954, and *BJRL*, 1955), one more recent and informative on the project as it reached publication stage (in *Editing Nineteenth-Century Texts*, ed. Robson, 1967), and one containing material now in the general introduction, "Carlyle as Editor and Critic of Literary Letters" (*EUQ*, 1964).

In the light of the Duke-Edinburgh letters edition it would almost seem as though no other editions of Carlyle letters will ever be necessary and as though all the numerous previous volumes will be entirely superseded, but it is not so. There will continue to be a need for some of the existing editions, especially those reprinting both sides of a correspondence when Carlyle was engaged with distinguished or especially interesting figures. Moreover, welcome as the Duke-Edinburgh will be, it will still be a long time in reaching completion and students of Carlyle must continue to resort to the many existing collections of the correspondence of the two Carlyles until the full run of the planned edition is complete.

There are several general collections of Carlyle letters in which the most important correspondence can be found, but there is also a truly depressing number of articles and miscellaneous publications that contain letters or portions of them. These cannot all be cited, but the student is advised to make a diligent search in the bibliographies before resting content that he has found all published letters. Likewise, one cannot always rely on Froude's excerpts in the biography, though they are well used for Froude's purposes.

In the meantime, most of the early compilations by C. E. Norton and Alexander Carlyle are still standard. This is no longer true of Norton's edition of Carlyle's

Early Letters, 1814–1826 (2 vols., 1886), but we still must use his *Letters, 1826– 1836* (2 vols., 1888), and Alexander Carlyle's *New Letters of Thomas Carlyle* (1904), and *The Love Letters of Thomas Carlyle and Jane Welsh* (1909), the last issued largely as one of the blasts in the Froude-Carlyle controversy, but now of interest in its own right. The editing in these is not up to the Duke-Edinburgh level. Norton's two-volume edition, with a later supplement, of the *Correspondence of Carlyle and Emerson* (1883, 1886) has now been superseded by the excellent edition by Joseph Slater of *The Correspondence of Emerson and Carlyle* (1964). Norton also edited the *Correspondence between Goethe and Carlyle* (1887). Charles Townsend Copeland edited *Letters of Carlyle to His Youngest Sister* (1899), and Alexander Carlyle published *Letters of Carlyle to John Stuart Mill, John Sterling and Robert Browning* (1923).

More recently John Graham, Jr. has edited *Letters of Carlyle to William Graham* (1950), and Trudy Bliss has provided a volume of Carlyle's *Letters to His Wife* (1953). Edwin W. Marrs, Jr. has edited the most impressive recent collection apart from Slater's and one which contains many hitherto unpublished letters, *The Letters of Carlyle to His Brother Alexander* (1968), which makes available a large number of letters that had long remained in family hands in Canada. These will all be included in the Duke-Edinburgh edition, but it is possible to see through Marrs's edition a kind of miniature (of 800 pages!) of the range of Carlyle's correspondence such as the Duke-Edinburgh will enlarge and enrich.

Among the mass of periodical publications of Carlyle letters or groups of them, only a few bear specific mention: Alexander Carlyle's "Thomas Carlyle and Thomas Spedding" (*Cornhill*, 1921), William A. Speck's "New Letters of Carlyle to Eckermann" (*YR*, 1926), and Grace Calder's "Carlyle and 'Irving's London Circle'" (*PMLA*, 1954). Sanders' many articles on particularly important exchanges between Carlyle and other notable Victorians or on patterns of Carlyle's thought that can be discerned from certain epistolary groupings are well worth looking into. These include articles on the Carlyle-Ruskin correspondence (*BJRL*, 1958), Carlyle and Browning (*JEGP*, 1963), the Carlyle-Leigh Hunt letters (*BJRL*, 1964), and broader studies, "The Victorian Rembrandt" (*BJRL*, 1957), "Carlyle, Poetry, and the Music of Humanity" (*WHR*, 1962), as well as others that are more purely critical but which make use of correspondence. These will be cited under Criticism. W. Forbes Gray's "Carlyle and John Forster" (*QR*, 1937) is based on correspondence. Rodger L. Tarr has provided a contribution to the study of Carlyle's letters in "Carlyle and Henry M'Cormac: Letters on the Condition of Ireland in 1848" (*SSL*, 1968). George Allan Cate is preparing for publication his "The Correspondence of Thomas Carlyle and John Ruskin" (Diss. Duke 1968).

There is, then, good reason to look with satisfaction at the whole area of Carlyle correspondence. A new edition of the Goethe-Carlyle correspondence might well be undertaken, and perhaps other such exchanges where both sides are given would still be in order. But in the main we can take more comfort from the scholarly and critical state of Carlyle correspondence than from any other area of scholarly endeavor concerning Carlyle. After this our journey, like that of Ruskin's alpine pilgrim from the Middle Ages to the Renaissance, will plunge us "with every forward step into more cold and melancholy shade."

V. BIOGRAPHIES

The fact that Carlyle made much of his reputation and indeed his living by writing biography, and the further fact that Carlyle is remembered in some circles solely for his dictum that history is the biography of great men, make his expressed wish that no biography of him be written seem either an affectation or an insult. Biographies of Carlyle have, of course, been written and in goodly number, but that there are few of any really outstanding merit turns an irony back on the ironist. It may just be the intransigence of the material. For Carlyle, though everywhere regarded as an "exciting" writer, did not in fact live a very exciting life. The excitement in a biography of Carlyle must enter through the writing and personality of Carlyle himself rather than his deeds. This may account for some of the biographical excesses of those who have taken up the task of Carlyle biography. After all, fifty years in Cheyne Row can seem a long tedious stretch without a few personality clashes (and there were those) or some hint of Another Woman (there were not any). And when all else fails there are the sexual "revelations." The results are not infrequently like those excoriated by the lady tutor in Dorothy Sayers' *Gaudy Night*, who criticized a former student's popular biography of Carlyle: "She has reproduced all the old gossip without troubling to verify anything. Slipshod, showy, and catchpenny." The tutor then added, "But I believe, poor thing, she is very hard up."

Most Carlyle biographers, however, have not been hard up. Apart from Froude, who was carrying out a commission and reaping the reward of years of devoted attendance on Carlyle, the earliest biographers were simply dutiful Victorian admirers of the Sage. They turned out a large number of biographies in the first two decades after Carlyle's death, most of them of very limited interest today. Those that still bear mention are Moncure D. Conway's *Thomas Carlyle* (1881), William Howie Wylie's *Thomas Carlyle, the Man and His Books* (1881), Thomas A. Fischer's German biography, *Thomas Carlyle* (1882), and, the best of this type, Richard Herne Shepherd's *Memoirs of the Life and Writings of Thomas Carlyle* (2 vols., 1881).

But the work that swept the field, both because of its comprehensiveness and because of the author's known intimacy with Carlyle, was Froude's four-volume biography, the first two volumes titled *Thomas Carlyle: A History of the First Forty Years of His Life, 1795–1835* (1882), and the last two, *Thomas Carlyle: A History of His Life in London, 1834–1881* (1884). When all is said and done Froude's remains the standard biography. But much more needs to be said and done, for Froude's work is not entirely satisfactory as a critical biography and its reputation is slowly sinking again after an earlier fall and rise as a result of what is now known as the Froude-Carlyle controversy. That will be discussed in detail later. First, the work itself.

Froude had available and drew upon, not always accurately or carefully, a vast number of manuscripts, papers, and letters of both Carlyles. He also had his own friendship with Carlyle for the last thirty years or more of Carlyle's life and his own acquaintance with the large Carlyle literary and social circle. There is little doubt that no one was better qualified at the time to write Carlyle's life than Froude. Moreover, what is often forgotten in the light of the Froude-Carlyle conflict is that Froude considered himself a confirmed Carlylean and thought that he was presenting a favorable picture of his subject. And in the main he was; Carlyle emerges as a complex brooding intellectual giant. But Froude did not seek to paint only a complimentary portrait, and he felt especially keenly that Jane Carlyle had been neglected and at times ill treated by Carlyle. This emerges clearly in Froude's biography, but it was also augmented by Froude's publication (thought by many to be too hasty) of Carlyle's own *Reminiscences.* Froude's oversympathetic picture of Jane and his rather cavalier use of the letters and manuscripts form the nucleus of the later controversy. The biography itself contains virtually nothing of the sexual revelations that were to bedevil the issue in after years.

Because Froude's biography shows Carlyle as sometimes irascible and frequently self-centered, it has commended itself to modern readers far more than its contemporary rivals that reverently sought to present only an acceptable public portrait. Further, Froude clearly had more literary skill than any rival biographers in his own day and far more than his later rival David Alec Wilson. Froude's biography, then, is properly still the standard full-length life of Carlyle, but there remains something about it that is not wholly satisfactory. It is not only the excessive dwelling on Jane's alleged sorrows or on Carlyle's acerbity or even the exasperating use of documents; it is rather a certain heaviness, even a gloom (as Froude said of Carlyle, "Gloom clung to him like a shadow") that renders Froude's life somewhat ponderous. It is a rather imposing Victorian funeral monument, and, for all Carlyle's own seriousness of purpose, there is an essential ingredient in his makeup that Froude misses. Perhaps it is that wild and so often humorous demonic element, currently much the rage in Carlyle studies; perhaps it is the Carlyle laugh that was legendary in his own lifetime. Whatever it is, Froude's biography does not adequately reflect it. The work has now come to be indispensable but not quite sufficient. It seems even more a product of its age than the subject it seeks to delineate. What is more, we are no longer certain that it offers a true picture.

The something missing in Froude is, however, not supplied by other biographers, certainly not by the work usually squared off in combat against Froude— David Alec Wilson's *Life of Thomas Carlyle* (6 vols., 1923–34). For, while Wilson explicitly sought to remedy Froude's insufficiencies, his biography is so different as to be almost impossible to compare. Wilson issued his volumes over a decade, the last volume being completed after his death by D. Wilson MacArthur, and each bears a separate subtitle appropriate to the period of Carlyle's life being examined. Wilson sought for accuracy above all, but it cannot be said that he succeeded much better than Froude in that department. Where he clearly surpasses Froude is in the diligence of his pursuit of information, however obscure, about Carlyle's life. Old matriculation slips, provincial newspaper articles, none of these escaped Wilson's sedulous inquiry. But the result is merely a storehouse of curious data, not the intelligent and persuasive ordering of it. Insofar as Wilson has a thesis, it is that Carlyle could do no wrong and no one should be suffered who criticizes him, least of all James Anthony Froude. It is not a thesis that can sustain six vast volumes. Still, Wilson's biography is now the grand compendium of information about Carlyle, and future biographers must look to it for many facts not available elsewhere, even if they must take care to check where they can. Since Wilson sought to answer Froude who was now long in his grave, it is only fair to call attention to W. H. Dunn's pro-Froude assessment, "Wilson's Carlyle" (*SR*, 1932), which compares Wilson's methods to Froude's.

In the battle between Froude's four and Wilson's six volumes it is no longer necessary to declare an unqualified winner. Froude's is clearly the more successful work qua biography and has become an essential part of the study of Carlyle, while Wilson's is an unparalleled repository of data that no scholar can ignore. Yet there remains a need for a thorough and definitive scholarly biography.

Turning from the ambitious multivolume undertakings to the one-volume biographies we find the situation not much improved. Richard Garnett's *Life of Thomas Carlyle* (1887) is still one of the best. He views Carlyle favorably but not slavishly as primarily a literary artist. John Nichols' *Thomas Carlyle* (1892) is derivative of Froude and not as satisfactory as Garnett. R. S. Craig's *The Making of Carlyle* (1908) is anti-Froude, but not very compelling today. Norwood Young's *Carlyle: His Rise and Fall* (1927) takes the prize as the most openly antagonistic book-length study. Young's disapproval of all Carlyle's works and ways makes one yearn for the admiring Victorian obituary biographies or even for the sycophancy of David Alec Wilson. Young need not be regarded seriously in seeking a critical biography of Carlyle.

This leaves only five modern critical biographies, two of them in foreign languages. The earliest is Emery Neff's *Carlyle* (1932). It is probably still the best single-volume critical biography. It is flawed in Neff's incomplete appreciation, one might almost say incomplete understanding, of Carlyle's literary gifts, and for this Garnett is a good corrective, as are the many recent studies of Carlyle's artistry. But Neff endeavors to see Carlyle in the context of his age, and his study is rich in historical and social background and especially strong on economics. He slights the work after *Cromwell* and somewhat exaggerates Carlyle's later "despair." Following Neff there is D. Lammond's insignificant *Carlyle* (1934) and two Continental studies, Victor Basch's *Carlyle, l'homme et l'œuvre* (1938) and Laura Fermi's *Thomas Carlyle* (1939), both of them rare instances of Latin interest in Carlyle but not major undertakings. More important is Julian Symons' *Thomas Carlyle: The Life and Ideas of a Prophet* (1952). It is a commentary on the way Carlyle biography has been so avoided by scholars that there have been only three English-language critical biographies of Carlyle since Wilson.

Symons, by virtue of his work as a professional biographer and his familiarity with Carlyle's writings (he edited a lengthy one-volume anthology), should have produced the definitive critical biography for modern use, but his book, interesting and useful as it is, is not quite that. Symons' strengths lie in crediting Carlyle with many exceptional insights into life and society, and indeed Symons' whole approach to Carlyle as a prophet is one that has become increasingly fruitful in understanding Carlyle's methods and ideas. But Symons also shows himself to be burdened with modern psychological assumptions which make him seek to explain Carlyle by explaining him away. His book too often adopts the tone of condescension that seems to mark any undertaking done with too much reliance on psychology. Further, Symons' whole study falls too readily into the formula for modern treatments of Carlyle, that method whereby the author is enabled to select what he likes of Carlyle and reject what he does not by positing the good as early and the bad as late; between the two occurs a souring and hardening on Carlyle's part that renders him distasteful in old age. Symons makes full use of this questionable method and misses seeing Carlyle whole.

Carlyle studies, then, need a massive scholarly biography that combines the detail and painstakingness of Wilson with the literary grace and sustained thematic coherence of Froude, and a scholarly unbiased one-volume critical biography that combines Neff's social and historical grasp with Garnett's literary appreciation and Symons' deeper-toned understanding of the social and intellectual role of the prophet.

Specialized Biographies. Personal Background and Relations with Others

The needs may be great in general biographies of Carlyle, but they are more than fully met when we look at specialized studies of Carlyle personally or in his relations with others. Froude did not have, but Wilson did, the mass of memoirs, reminiscences, impressions, conversations, and the like that continued to come forth for twenty years after Carlyle's death. Many of these are by distinguished literary associates, and they should be consulted to obtain a full picture of Carlyle in his lifetime. They are also often the sources for some of Carlyle's wittiest and most scathing remarks, a commodity of which no true Carlylean can ever have a surfeit. Beyond that, there have been numerous studies of special aspects of Carlyle's life, from the impact of his Scottish upbringing to his relations with the great and near-great of his day. These too offer an almost frighteningly vast source of material, not only for biographical facts but for a deeper understanding of Carlyle than was possible for Froude or than D. A. Wilson was able to assimilate into his partisan conception of the Master.

Among the earlier personal recollections that still bear mention are those of Henry Larkin (*Brit. Q. Rev.*, 1881), Margaret O. W. Oliphant (*Macmillan's*, 1881), Henry W. Knighton (*Critical Rev.*, 1881), and Stuart J. Reid's *Carlyle* (1881). Also, Henry James (the elder) in *Literary Remains* (1885); David Masson's *Carlyle Personally and in His Writings* (1885), *Edinburgh Sketches and Memories* (1892), and *Memories of London in the 'Forties* (1908); Francis Espinasse's *Literary Recollections and Sketches* (1893); and William Allingham's *A Diary* (1907; reissued with introd. by Geoffrey Grigson, 1967). Countless further references and descriptions of Carlyle by his contemporaries in their own letters and reminiscences are best pursued in the pages of Dyer.

Naturally, this stream of personal reminiscence largely dried up after a generation had gone by, but there have been a few contributions in recent years, largely from hitherto unpublished memoirs and letters: H. Davis' excerpts from the diary of James Shepherd Pike, a New York abolitionist who visited Carlyle several times in the 1860's and likened him to Sam Houston (*AM*, 1939); Arthur Adrian's "Dean Stanley's Report of Conversations with Carlyle" (*VS*, 1957), drawing on unpublished notes; George Hendrick's "William Sloane Kennedy Stalks Carlyle" (*ESQ*, 1961), which uses Kennedy's diary; W. J. Keith's "An Interview with Carlyle" (*N&Q*, 1967), which records an 1868 meeting of Carlyle with John Callander Ross; Edwin Marrs's "Reminiscences of a Visit with Carlyle in 1878 by His Nephew and Namesake" (*Thoth*, 1967), which gives excerpts from a journal kept by Carlyle's nephew Thomas, one of the Canadian branch of the family; and Ian Campbell's "Portrait of Carlyle" (*The Scotsman*, 12 Aug. 1967), which records notes kept by the Scottish painter Robert Herdman in 1875 when he painted Carlyle's portrait.

After the first phase of personal reminiscences had passed, Carlyle studies saw a considerable flow of books and articles about places associated with Carlyle. The parent and certainly the most ambitious of these is still J. M. Sloan's *The Carlyle Country* (1904), although it was but the further extension of John Burroughs' approach in *Fresh Fields* (1885). Sloan pursues the study of biography geographically, tracing the impact on Carlyle of his early residence and associations in Scotland. As biography Sloan's work is of limited usefulness, but the book offers an unrivaled wealth of illustrations of Scottish places known to Carlyle. In the same line are W. Sharp's *Literary Geography* (1904), H. C. Shelley's *Literary By-paths in Old England*, and more narrowly, Rosalie Masson's "Two Edinburgh Literary Homes" (*Chambers*, 1922). There has also been a number of articles on Carlyle's Scottish associations in the *S.M.T. Magazine*: C. Keith on "Where the Carlyles Lived" (1935), W. Jeffrey on Craigenputtock (1938), S. P. B. Mais on "The Scotland of Thomas Carlyle" (1943), A. E. Ballard on "Carlyle's Birthplace" (1945), and, in *Scottish Country Life*, J. Shaw Simpson's "Craigenputtock" (1934).

Along with the Scottish interest there was also early interest in the Carlyle house in Cheyne Row, most fully honored by Reginald Blunt's still charming and definitive *The Carlyles' Chelsea Home* (1895), and by frequent lightweight articles on No. 5 Cheyne Row since Blunt, including H. T. Schorn (*Der Türmer*, 1925), Sydney K. Phelps (*NC*, 1926), F. Young (*Listener*, 1934), and Joanna Richardson (*Listener*, 1960). None is worth pursuing if the reader has Blunt available. The one important later addition to the literature about Cheyne Row is Thea Holme's *The Carlyles at Home* (1965), an engaging and pleasantly illustrated rendering of domestic life in Cheyne Row, including endless servant problems, by the wife of the former curator of Carlyle's house. Other aspects of Cheyne Row life generally appear in studies of the two Carlyles and in connection with Jane Welsh Carlyle.

Antiquarian interest has also centered on Carlyle's relations, especially his Canadian relatives, all of them descendants of his brother Alexander who emigrated to Canada in 1843: James C. Hodgins' "Some Reminiscences of the Carlyle Family" (*Canadian Mag.*, 1921); D. R. Keys's "Bengough and Carlyle" (*UTQ*, 1932), rather more interesting than its title; and Edwin W. Marrs's edition of Carlyle's letters to his brother. Carlyle's niece, Mary Aitken Carlyle, is given her due in Mabel Davidson's "A Lady Who Deserves to Be Remembered" (*SR*, 1923), and his nephew Alexander is memorialized in C. F. Harrold's "Remembering Carlyle: A Visit with His Nephew" (*SAQ*, 1937). Some brief pieces on Carlyle's relations and friends are offered in Rodger Tarr's note on Carlyle's final visit to the Grange (*N&Q*, 1970), and on Mary Aitken Carlyle (*ELN*, 1971), and in Ian Campbell's note on Carlyle and George Cron (*N&Q*, 1971), and on Carlyle and Sir Gideon Dunn (*ELN*, 1972), both having to do with originals of minor Carlyle characters. P. Morgan, in "Carlyle, Jeffrey and the *Edinburgh Review*" (*Neophilologus,* 1970), treats an important early relationship.

More to the point of an intellectual understanding of Carlyle has been Hill Shine's indispensable *Carlyle's Early Reading to 1834* (1953), which records every work and author Carlyle is known to have read in the years before he moved to London. Even though the listing is impressive, with over 3,000 entries, it may be possible to supplement it when the new edition of the letters has been published. Shine's essay on Carlyle's intellectual development is also very valuable. Nothing comparable to Shine's checklist has appeared since, but there have been two articles on Carlyle's reading, C. P. Finlayson's "Thomas Carlyle's Borrowings from the Edinburgh University Library, 1819–1820" (*Biblioteck*, 1961) and Ian Campbell's "Carlyle's Borrowings from the Theological Library of Edinburgh University" (*Biblioteck*, 1969). Campbell and Rodger Tarr have looked at Carlyle's early study of

German (*Ill. Q.*, 1971). There is even a study of Carlyle's contribution to mathematics, one of his early enthusiasms—Peter A. Wursthorn, "The Position of Thomas Carlyle in the History of Mathematics" (*Mathematics Teacher*, 1966)— which praises the originality and "beautiful simplicity" of Carlyle's solution of the real roots of any quadratic equation and reveals that Carlyle's translation of Legendre's *Geometry* "completely supplanted" Euclid in the United States and became the standard text after 1834.

Once we leave Carlyle personally we forthwith come up against the many personal relationships of his long life. Of all his relations with others the most heavily plowed field has been that concerning his relationships with Jane Welsh Carlyle. Since this area constitutes most of the biography of Jane herself, it will be more fully examined in the section on Jane Welsh Carlyle, but here a few central works must be cited. Apart from Froude's picture of the long-suffering wife and Alexander Carlyle's and D. A. Wilson's rejoinders, the following are of note: Elizabeth G. Bell in "A 'Not Unblessed Pilgrimage': The Carlyles' Married Life" (*Cornhill*, 1924) takes Jane's part, while Osbert Burdett in *The Two Carlyles* (1930) strives for greater balance but is still too dependent on Froude. Iris Origo has devoted her attention to the sensitive Ashburton relationship (*Cornhill*, 1950; rpt. in *A Measure of Love*, 1957). The two chief biographies of Jane necessarily concern themselves with the relationship, Townsend Scudder's *Jane Welsh Carlyle* (1939) and Lawrence and Elisabeth Hanson's *Necessary Evil: The Life of Jane Welsh Carlyle* (1952), the latter by far the superior treatment. John Stewart Collis' popular study *The Carlyles* (1971) is not of any scholarly value.

All of the studies of Carlyle and Jane take off from Froude and the issue is always the same: did Carlyle neglect and mistreat Jane? Did he especially offend her in his relationship with Lady Ashburton? Was Jane's life, in short, sacrificed to Carlyle's egoism? The verdict has generally been that much was endured on both sides and that the Carlyles both deserved and somehow enjoyed each other. Lady Ashburton was certainly not the Other Woman, though she occupied much of Carlyle's attention for a time, and Jane was certainly, like Carlyle, "gey ill to live with."

Carlyle's relations with others have been variously investigated. Among his early ardors commentators have sought for the "original" of *Sartor*'s Blumine. The most ambitious pursuit of that elusive lady is Raymond Clare Archibald's *Carlyle's First Love: Margaret Gordon, Lady Bannerman* (1909), but Carlyle's own brief portrait in the *Reminiscences* is still unsurpassed. The claims for Kitty Kirkpatrick had already been advanced by G. Strachey in "Carlyle and the Rose Goddess" (*NC*, 1892), and those for Jane Welsh by Alexander Carlyle in *The Love Letters*. C. R. Sanders also treats Carlyle and Kitty Kirkpatrick as well as Carlyle's relations with other Stracheys in his *The Strachey Family* (1953).

More interesting is Carlyle's relation with the dynamic preacher Edward Irving, examined in Elizabeth Haldane's "Edward Irving" (*QR*, 1934), in Ian Campbell's note (*SSL*, 1971), H. Watt's "Carlyle and Edward Irving: The Story of a Friendship" (*Scots Mag.*, 1934), and, most intelligently, in A. L. Drummond's *Edward Irving and His Circle* (1937) and in Thomas A. Kirby's "Carlyle and Irving" (*ELH*, 1946). A specialized aspect of this relationship is illuminated in Grace J. Calder's "Carlyle and 'Irving's London Circle'" (*PMLA*, 1954). Here again, Carlyle's own assessments in the *Reminiscences* and in the "Death of Edward Irving" are indispensable.

After Irving, Carlyle's closest friend was John Sterling, and Carlyle undertook to write his biography (1851). The association of the two men is explored in Anne K. Tuell's *John Sterling: A Representative Victorian* (1941). Carlyle's relations with the Italian nationalist Giuseppe Mazzini are examined in Harry Rudman's *Italian Nationalism and English Letters* (1940). Grace J. Calder uses unpublished Darwin letters to delineate another Carlyle relationship in "Erasmus Darwin, Friend of Thomas and Jane Carlyle" (*MLQ*, 1959). Beyond these, the truly important Carlyle relationships are at least as much literary as personal—his friendships with Mill, Dickens, Tennyson, Ruskin, and other Victorians. These will be considered below under Criticism.

THE FROUDE CONTROVERSY. It seems more appropriate to denominate the Froude-Carlyle controversy simply the Froude controversy, for Carlyle was dead before the conflict erupted. The main points at issue have already been touched upon in the discussion of Froude's and Wilson's biographies of Carlyle, but the whole brouhaha spawned a literature of its own that is often (although happily not in the *NCBEL*) bibliographically intermixed with other Carlyle studies and can cause confusion to the unwary. For some years now it has been customary to say as little about the Froude controversy as possible in the hope that it would fade quietly away. To some extent it has; the passions generated by the issues no longer excite as once they did, and many have thought that Waldo Hilary Dunn has fully vindicated Froude. But at the same time the issue will not quite die. No biography since Froude's, and certainly none since the bitter turn-of-the-century exchanges between surviving Froudes and Carlyles, can ignore the ramifications of the issue. Even critical studies are affected, especially when they adopt the notion of Carlyle's later despair. Studies of Jane Welsh Carlyle are simply unthinkable without accounting for Froude's views. And the modern mind is even less likely than the Victorian one to pass off so calefactory a charge as impotence.

Carlisle Moore in his succinct treatment of the controversy (in *English Romantic Poets and Essayists*, ed. Houtchens, 1966) rightly sums up the "bones of contention" as three: Froude's use of Carlyle's papers, Carlyle's alleged mistreatment of Jane, and the imputation of sexual impotence to Carlyle. The first charge seems the mustiest of all now, but it does touch upon the scholarship itself, and is actually two-pronged: first, Froude's rights of access to Carlyle's papers and his reluctance to turn them over to Mary Aitken Carlyle and, second, whether in his use of those papers Froude quoted judiciously and accurately. The first aspect of this charge was ultimately settled only after legal maneuvering, but it was finally determined that Froude had a right to use Carlyle's papers for the authorized biography and at the same time that the papers were ultimately the property of Mary. The second aspect involves literary evaluation and is not settled so easily. Waldo Hilary Dunn has made a persuasive case that Froude's quotations and selections were in the main accurate and judicious. We can say at the least that Froude used the papers in a manner not inconsistent with prevailing standards of biographical scholarship.

The second charge, more difficult to assess, has been the burden of many biographical treatments of the Carlyles. In the eyes of Carlyle supporters, Froude's *Life* was the unfunny exemplification of Oscar Wilde's witticism that "every great man has his disciples and it is always Judas who writes the biography." Once again, Froude's champion Dunn effectively made the case for Froude's interpretation.

While it has been held by many that he successfully clears Froude here, the final answer will be given by the definitive biography, and there are grounds to suggest that it will not be unqualifiedly in Froude's favor. That Froude was, however, presenting the case as he saw it is probably beyond dispute.

The third charge is one that will probably never be settled definitively. No amount of research is likely to take us inside the Carlyle bedroom. But on the face of it the charge is improbable. It rests on hearsay evidence from an unreliable witness and what is most startling is that it did not surface until many years after Carlyle's death.

The public aspect of the Froude controversy gathered steam slowly, though the principals were quite fervid from the start. Froude's first two volumes appeared in 1882, one year after Carlyle's death; the final two appeared in 1884. In between he published *Letters and Memorials of Jane Welsh Carlyle* from materials expressly left to him in Carlyle's will. But the first real document in the controversy did not appear until 1898 when David Alec Wilson, the later biographer, published his *Mr. Froude and Carlyle*. To be sure, contemporary reviews of Froude's book had not infrequently taken issue with Froude's portrayal of the Carlyles' married life and some had defended him, but the issue was always the treatment of Jane. Meantime, the controversy over the papers had been going on more or less privately. Mary Aitken Carlyle did feel impelled to take to the pages of the *Times* at one point regarding the Carlyle papers, and Froude's supporter Sir James Fitzjames Stephen published *The Late Mr. Carlyle's Papers* (1886) on the matter. Further, C. E. Norton's 1887 re-editing of the *Reminiscences* was directly occasioned by what he thought to be Froude's errors. But still there was no awareness of the issue of impotence for two decades after Carlyle's death. Froude, affronted by increasingly hostile criticisms of his treatment of Carlyle, privately wrote what was to be later published as *My Relations with Carlyle* (1903). He died in 1894 with the document unpublished.

Wilson's *Mr. Froude and Carlyle*, which took severe issue with Froude on the first two of the three bones of contention (the third not having yet surfaced), was still not enough to elicit a reply. What turned the trick was the publication by Alexander Carlyle of *New Letters and Memorials of Jane Welsh Carlyle* (1903), being those omitted or "mutilated" by Froude in his 1883 edition. The antagonistic tone of the introduction brought forth the Froude children's publication of Froude's *My Relations*. In this slender work Froude defended his interpretation of the marriage and revealed what he claimed to have wanted to suppress, namely that Carlyle was impotent and that Jane Welsh Carlyle had died a virgin. His source for this extraordinary claim was said to be the word of Geraldine Jewsbury, a minor novelist and sometime close associate of Jane's. She had died in 1880 and Carlyle had called her stories of Craigenputtock "mythical." Now the battle was joined. Immediately into the fray leaped Sir James Crichton-Browne, a medical doctor and friend of Alexander Carlyle's, with his "Froude and Carlyle: The Imputation Considered Medically" (*Brit. Medical J.*, 1903). In the same year Crichton-Browne joined forces with Alexander Carlyle, reprinting the medical article and adding other material to produce *The Nemesis of Froude: A Rejoinder to J. A. Froude's "My Relations with Carlyle"* (the title taking off, of course, on Froude's 1848 anti-Tractarian novel, *The Nemesis of Faith*). From these curious documents we learn that Carlyle wore a truss, that he was sexually "normally formed," that no medical examination was ever made at the time of Jane Welsh Carlyle's death that could possibly have determined whether she died *virgo intacta*, and other such immodest details. Crichton-Browne emerges as one of those friends who make it unnecessary to have enemies, but his intentions were noble and after all Froude had raised the issue.

Each side retired for a time, convinced of its own righteousness. Then Frank Harris published "Talks with Carlyle" (*Eng. Rev.*, 1911; rpt. in *Contemporary Portraits*, 1915), in which he claimed that Carlyle had confessed his sexual impotence to him, a virtual stranger. Harris was a notorious liar, and Alexander Carlyle immediately demolished his allegations in his "Frank Harris and His (Imaginary) Talks with Carlyle" (*Eng. Rev.*, 1911). But it stirred up the old issues again. To settle it all D. A. Wilson issued his *The Truth about Carlyle* (1913), with another of those medical forewords by Crichton-Browne. Frank Harris lay strewn about in pieces. The final stroke in this phase of the whole matter was Wilson's six-volume *Life*, which does not neglect to flail out at Froude, at the allegations of impotence, at all who ever thought ill of Carlyle.

By the 1930's it all seemed to have died down. Froude was long since dead, as was Mary Aitken Carlyle (d. 1895). Alexander Carlyle was to die in 1931 and D. A. Wilson in 1933. But nothing had really been settled. How fair Froude's portrait of the domestic relations was continued to be a matter of debate, and since 1903 people had been murmuring about Carlyle's "impotence." Froude had, of course, his own defenders, apart from his family. An early champion was Herbert Paul in *The Life of Froude* (1905), and Waldo Hilary Dunn in *English Biography* (1916) had proclaimed Froude's Carlyle equal to Boswell's Johnson. Dunn became Froude's chief defender and thought to settle the controversy once and for all with *Froude and Carlyle: A Study of the Froude-Carlyle Controversy* (1930), which endeavored to vindicate Froude. With that the controversy entered its modern phase. Dunn was widely regarded as having vindicated Froude as a biographer, but most informed readers recognized that it was impossible on such slender evidence to prove or disprove Froude's imputation about Carlyle's virility. Dunn of course believed he had succeeded on all counts. In this connection see George Saintsbury's "Froude and Carlyle" (*Bookman*, 1930) and Dunn's critique of Wilson cited earlier. Subsequently, others tried to assess Froude's achievement, but they have always stood in Dunn's shadow: L. Iffländer's *J. A. Froudes Lebenswerk* (1940), J. Chartres Molony's "The Fall of an Idol: Effect on Carlyle's Fame of the *Reminiscences* and the Froude Biography" (*Blackwood's*, 1945), and Theressa Wilson Brown's "Froude's *Life of Thomas Carlyle*" in *If by Your Art* (ed. Agnes Starrett, 1948).

Dunn entered the lists again with "Carlyle's Last Letters to Froude" (*TC*, 1956), designed to prove that Carlyle reposed his trust in Froude, which he surely did. Hyder E. Rollins, in "Charles Eliot Norton and Froude" (*JEGP*, 1958), examined Norton's sometimes fierce reaction to Froude, but also showed that passions were aroused on all sides. Then Dunn issued his full-length biography of Froude, *James Anthony Froude* (2 vols., 1961–63), which reiterates the views he had advanced in *Froude and Carlyle*. One of the most recent documents on the matter is Edward Sharples, Jr.'s "Carlyle and His Readers: The Froude Controversy Once Again" (Diss. Rochester 1964), which says that most of the disputed points have been resolved in Froude's favor.

Yet there remain the unconvinced. Gertrude Himmelfarb in *Victorian Minds* (1968) thinks there is something "demonic" in Froude's devotion to Carlyle, a slant that echoes the occasional turning of psychological attention to Froude rather than

Carlyle. Perhaps the mystery will be solved in two current investigations of the controversy. John Clubbe of Duke is reexamining the issue as part of a new abridged edition of Froude's *Life*. K. J. Fielding of Edinburgh is also studying the controversy anew. From these investigations may come the objective assessments that earlier partisanships rendered impossible.

MISCELLANEA. This is the grandma's attic of Carlyle biography. Here are some treasures and many oddities. Among the treasures are the informative studies of Carlyle's central role in the founding of the London Library: *Carlyle and the London Library* (1907) edited by Frederic Harrison; an unsigned article, "Thomas Carlyle and Hagberg Wright" (*TLS*, 3 May 1941); Henry W. Nevison, "Carlyle and the London Library" (*NS*, 1941); Simon Nowell-Smith et al., *English Libraries, 1800–1850* (1958); and Raymond Irwin, *The English Library: Sources and History* (1966). Harrison and Nowell-Smith are the most useful studies on this topic. Also in the miscellaneous category are Herbert L. Stewart's "Carlyle and Canada" (*Canadian Mag.*, 1921) and Frank Yeigh's "Scott, Carlyle, Dickens and Canada" (*QQ*, 1930).

There are several special studies of Carlyle's relationship toward a particular nineteenth-century event or circumstance. The most interesting of these is George H. Ford's "The Governor Eyre Case in England" (*UTQ*, 1948), which is concerned with the involvement of the whole Victorian literary world in that cause célèbre. Ford makes clear that Carlyle's enormous influence helped to enlist on his and Eyre's side such men as Dickens, Ruskin, Tennyson, Tyndall, and later Kingsley, Froude, and indirectly Matthew Arnold. Carlyle also figures in Bernard Semmel's *The Governor Eyre Controversy* (1962), and he is briefly mentioned in regard to the Eyre case in Anthony Preston and John Major's *Send a Gunboat!* (1967). Carlyle's scornful reaction to the Crystal Palace is included in J. E. Lloyd's "Victorian Writers and the Great Exhibition" (*N&Q*, 1951). Carlyle's attitude toward a major Victorian periodical is reflected from letters in W. M. Parker's "Dean Milman and *The Quarterly Review*" (*QR*, 1955). The impact of Carlyle's satire in *Sartor Resartus* on the nineteenth-century phenomenon of dandyism is considered in Ellen Moers's *The Dandy: Brummell to Beerbohm* (1960). Of very special interest in these times is the well-presented article by Gerald M. Straka, "The Spirit of Carlyle in the Old South" (*Historian*, 1957). Straka concentrates on Southern response to Carlyle in the 1850's largely based on the "Nigger Question" and *Latter-Day Pamphlets*. The South tended to interpret Carlyle as suited to its own needs of the moment, which were largely dictated by the mounting threats to slavery, but Straka reprints a most intriguing letter of 1851 from Carlyle to a Virginia gentleman in which, as Straka says, Carlyle "proposes what amounts to emancipation."

E. L. A.'s "Carlyle and the Franklin Tithe-Book" (*More Books*, 1940) and LeRoy E. Kimball's "Thomas Carlyle and Charles Butler of Wall Street" (in *Essays and Studies in Honor of Carleton Brown*, 1940) are isolated studies of a stray Carlyle connection. More difficult to categorize are such curiosities as Frank Miller's *Poems from the Carlyle Country* (1937), chiefly the poems of Miller himself and appreciations on two of Carlyle's associates. There are even a poem on Carlyle, T. C. Wilson's "And to Carlyle" (*Nat. Rev.*, 1934), and miscellaneous queries on Carlylisms (*N&Q*, 1942, 1943, 1944). A Carlyle interest attaches to the monograph in German by Franz Krämer, *Thomas Carlyle of the Scottish Bar, 1803–1855* (1966), which traces the career of a very distant relative of Carlyle's, a powerful

Continental force in the Irvingite (Catholic Apostolic) Church and the author of numerous tracts and religious works, including the 1853 "The Jew Our Lawgiver" for which the famous Carlyle has been unjustly accused of anti-Semitism.

At last we come to the true chamber of horrors in Carlyle studies—the "medical" and psychiatric examinations. The earliest is George M. Gould's *Biographic Clinics: The Origins of the Ill-Health of De Quincey, Carlyle . . .* , etc. (6 vols. [!], 1903). Gould believes that all of Carlyle's medical problems stemmed from eyestrain and an indifference to "enlightened medical science." Anent which Gould concludes: "The more imperative is our duty." This vein was not remined until much later, although Carlyle's constantly upset stomach has always been a component of the biographies. The more fertile ground has been the psychological. Richard Berger's "Carlyles Kampf mit dem Lärm" (*Schalltechnik*, 1936) loses an interesting opportunity to examine Carlyle's extraordinary sensitivity to noise by falling into anecdotalism. Jackson Towne in "Carlyle and Oedipus" (*PsyR*, 1935) adds Freud to Froude to claim that Carlyle had an inordinate attachment to his mother and moreover had the facial expression of a "neurotic type," and that Froude was in love with Jane! W. R. Bett in *The Infirmities of Genius* (1952) was unable to top this, although he did not hesitate to affirm Carlyle's impotence on the basis of his writing style, a conclusion that never seems to strike these writers as at least shaky.

But the prize exhibit in this gallery is James L. Halliday's *Mr. Carlyle, My Patient* (1949). Halliday's method is to use Carlyle's writings indiscriminately as autobiography and thereby make Carlyle out as a patient. He even writes a case history for Carlyle at age twenty-eight. He concludes that the patient should be seen by a psychiatrist and promptly proceeds to serve in that capacity. Carlyle's genius is found to be intimately tied up with his scoptophilia, an intense desire to see nudity, as well as the opposite impulse. He is also sadistic, also anal, also paranoid. One can only conclude with Carlisle Moore that "no more inept work exists in the annals of biography" than Halliday's. Scorn is probably too lofty for it; laughter would suit better.

VI. CRITICISM

General Studies

Since Carlyle's work was subject to criticism as early as 1824 when De Quincey slammed his translation of *Wilhelm Meister* (*London Mag.*, 1824), his output has had a longer time than that of any Victorian to gather about itself a body of critical writing. Thus there is an enormous amount of material. But the general studies tend to emphasize one or another of the four main categories first enunciated by Victorian critics: Carlyle as philosopher, as moralist and teacher, as literary artist, and as powerful social force. There are, of course, many combinations and overlappings of these categories. Nor are they all present in equal measure in any given period: the Victorian period, for example, is stronger on the first two; the modern on the last two. The almost irresistible temptation to travel the byways of Carlyle criticism in the nineteenth century, however, must be resisted in favor of a quick tour down the main road to our own time.

Once Carlyle had established himself and created the taste that he was uniquely qualified to satisfy, he enjoyed generally very high esteem. Early favorable notices by friends and associates like John Stuart Mill and John Sterling (*London and Westminster Rev.*, 1837, 1839) helped, but regard for Carlyle soon became broadly based. Such works as Alexander Hay Japp's *Three Great Teachers of Our Own Time* (1865) or Peter Bayne's *Lessons from My Masters* (1879) express the almost idolatrous view of Carlyle as a moral leader that was shared by the great bulk of Victorian intellectuals during at least one period in their lives. Richard Holt Hutton's *Essays on Some Modern Guides to English Thought in Matters of Faith* (1887) offers a more balanced view that includes valuable literary insights. The numerous parodies, ranging from an early diversion in *Fraser's* (1838) to Trollope's somewhat harsher view in *The Warden* (1855), reflect the Victorian fascination with Carlyle as a stylist. There were, of course, Victorian dissenters, both from the view of Carlyle as a great philosopher and teacher and from the view of him as a master of the language. Thomas McNicoll in *Essays on English Literature* (1861) took severe issue with Carlyle's language and philosophy and after Carlyle's death critical weight leaned ever more toward McNicoll's view. Still, in his lifetime Carlyle exercised tremendous influence based on the generally high esteem his works enjoyed.

Froude's biography no doubt contributed to the critical downfall of Carlyle, but the later Froude controversy contributed more. Beyond that there is always a certain turning away from a literary giant in the period immediately following his death. Since Carlyle had begun to excite Victorian doubts as early as 1850 with the *Latter-Day Pamphets*, there must have been many who by 1881 felt they had waited long enough to have their chance at him. Thus, along with the respectful posthumous assessments came more and more that hedged their acceptance of Carlyle with qualifications or that simply denounced him outright. In this latter category belong such as Edmond Scherer's *Essays on English Literature* (trans. 1891) and J. M. Robertson's *Modern Humanists* (1891). Robertson thought Carlyle a "prophet with a gospel of shreds and patches" and felt him incapable of writing a connected book. More measured but still highly qualified were the judgments of such critics as John Morley, John Burroughs, Edward Caird, Frederic Harrison, and Leslie Stephen. Some, like George Saintsbury in his various critical works of the late nineteenth century, claim a place for Carlyle almost solely on artistic grounds and are willing to do without or substantially moderate his philosophy.

So changed was the critical atmosphere from the days of Japp and Bayne that at the turn of the century W. C. Brownell in *Victorian Prose Masters* (1901) could observe that Carlyle is now neglected but will inevitably come back because of the vitality of his style and vision. He could also assess Carlyle as too idiosyncratic, too egotistical, but still somehow a valuable stimulus to "moral energy." Brownell typically sums up the contradictory assessments of Carlyle in the twenty years after his death and typically fails to make a synthesis of them. We thus enter the twentieth century on a mixed note in Carlyle criticism. The philosopher-teacher with the arresting style has become the eccentric stylist with a questionable philosophy and questionable teachings. Much early twentieth-century criticism never advanced beyond this rather jejune view.

But not all early modern criticism is so spiritless and some central studies should be cited. Gilbert Keith Chesterton's *Twelve Types* (1902) finds much to honor in Carlyle and faults him chiefly for his "mania for spiritual consistency" which led him to extreme positions. Paul Elmer More in the *Shelburne Essays* (1905) holds Carlyle to be the greatest figure in English letters after Dr. Johnson. Hugh Walker in *The Literature of the Victorian Era* (1910) devotes his attention chiefly to the German influence, as does Oliver Elton in *Survey of English Litera-ture, 1780–1830* (1912) as a means of dealing as much as possible only with the early and preferred Carlyle. Louis Cazamian's *Carlyle* (1913; trans. E. K. Brown, 1932) is much concerned to place Carlyle in a social and historical context. Caza-mian's work on the social novel in England would surely seem to fit him to perform this task well, but he perplexingly insists upon calling Carlyle a "supreme utilitar-ian" while also an idealist, and he endeavors to redefine utilitarianism to suit this capricious usage. All of this merely darkens counsel. He also neglects the aesthetic side of Carlyle's genius. He does recognize that Carlyle "fashioned and tempered the soul of an age."

Bliss Perry's *Thomas Carlyle: How to Know Him* (1915) and Augustus Ralli's *Guide to Carlyle* (2 vols., 1920) are both sympathetic general treatments. Almost half of Ralli's book, which Saintsbury thought should have been omitted, is devoted to detailed analysis of individual Carlyle works. Mary Agnes Hamilton's *Thomas Carlyle* (1926) is an attempt to "rescue" Carlyle for the twentieth century by stressing his social teachings and their relation to ideas of the modern labor move-ment. J. M. Robertson in *Modern Humanists Reconsidered* (1927) does not appear to have reconsidered Carlyle very much since his damning judgment of 1895, but he allows that Carlyle has a value as an "awakener" of other people, provided they stop there and do not become awakened to Carlyle's own pernicious ideas. John Macy in "Carlyle: From Ecclefechan to the World" (*Bookman*, 1929) concentrates on Carlyle's style but to very little purpose. He offers the somewhat uncommon modern judgment that *Heroes* is Carlyle's most attractive book. Lytton Strachey in *Portraits in Miniature* (1931) tries to do in short compass for Carlyle what he had done for, or to, his victims in *Eminent Victorians*. The result is a highly readable but quite insubstantial essay. In the same collection Strachey pours his urbane acid to etch a portrait of James Anthony Froude. All good fun in a Bloomsbury way.

There is also in this early material the beginnings of what has proved to be a popular approach to Carlyle's career whatever the position for or against him may be, namely, the view of Carlyle's work as somehow profoundly bifurcated. Early and late is the most neutral way of putting it, but it more often comes out as a division between good and bad, or optimistic and pessimistic, or radical and reac-tionary. Commentators vary as to where exactly to place the shift, but it usually comes out to be somewhere around the time of *Latter-Day Pamphlets* (1850) but can range ten years in either direction. These clear divisions are somewhat muted in the early criticism, but they tend to become ever more prominent as we approach the criticism of our own day.

S. Sagar's *Round by Repentance Tower* (1930) is always described in bibliog-raphies as "a study from the Roman Catholic position." What that means is that Carlyle is examined to see where he went wrong—or rather where he did not go right, that is, to Rome. While that may seem at first less than promising because so doctrinaire, it turns out to produce a study with some genuine merits. The author's special vantage point has made him open to Carlyle's peculiar insight into the agony of a world without God and sensitive to one of Carlyle's central points, his "cry of alarm" at the spiritual peril of the modern world. Sagar also sensibly notes, apropos of the reaction against Carlyle because of Prussian aggression in World War I, that Carlyle "was a great man, but he did not cause the Great War."

Emery Neff's *Carlyle* (1932), discussed previously as a critical biography, deserves mention here as a sound general study with the same cautions as previously expressed regarding his neglect of the later works. The other critical biographies, most notably Symons, should also be consulted as general studies. Louis Cazamian, author of the 1913 study, reprinted two essays from the 1920's on Carlyle in *Essais en deux langues* (1938) in which he expresses the welcome judgment that Carlyle's "intentions morales furent toujours pures." His general view is more balanced than in the earlier study. Herbert J. C. Grierson's "Thomas Carlyle" (*PBA*, 1940; also separately printed) treats Carlyle generally as an Old Testament Prophet, and also adopts the popular modern view of Carlyle as having lost hope after *Past and Present*, but it is a better treatment than Grierson's unfortunate ventures into the area of Carlyle and Nazism (1933). Much more in the Victorian vein is Edward H. Griggs's *Moral Leaders* (1940). He sees Carlyle as the chief avenue for two Continental streams of thought, that of the French Revolution and that of Kantian transcendentalism. Where he obviously differs from the Victorians is in his awareness of Carlyle's present low estate, but he insists that Carlyle will come back in our time. Frank A. Lea in *Carlyle: Prophet of Today* (1943) calls his study a psychography (i.e., psychological biography), and some of it is clearly inspired by wartime fears, but he strives to find Carlyle's virtues. He sees that Carlyle's vision and mission are essentially religious.

The best short introductory essay to Carlyle's work is that by David Gascoyne, *Thomas Carlyle* (1952; British Council Pamphlet). It is a brave assertion of Carlyle's enduring value by a sensitive modern poet. The most recent general study of all of Carlyle's work is Albert J. LaValley's *Carlyle and the Idea of the Modern* (1968), an ambitious and provocative undertaking which frequently illuminates those aspects of Carlyle that have subsequently become hallmarks of the modern sensibility. The study is especially concerned to see the modern dimensions of Carlyle's prophetic literature and to relate him to others, such as Blake and Nietzsche, who moved in similar areas. This study goes far toward showing Carlyle as the pioneering and experimental writer that he was. But the book's modernism is also its weakness and Carlyle is frequently judged by alien and not enduring standards, not to mention being placed too often on the couch. Read with caution, the study will help to open new horizons in Carlyle criticism even as it fails to scan all of the old ones.

LaValley's study reminds us that Carlyle has been frequently treated in works dealing with Victorian literature as a whole and in works that present a general view of Carlyle while concentrating on a particular aspect of his writing or phase of his career. Many of these indeed broke the ground that LaValley has tried to till. Others are less critically venturesome and concerned to give a standard assessment or to relate Carlyle to earlier influences. In this latter category belong such literary histories as Ashley Thorndike's *Literature in a Changing Age* (1920) and Samuel Chew's *The Nineteenth Century and After* (1948; 1967), part of the Baugh *Literary History of England*. Carlyle also of course appears in all standard histories of Victorian literature. Also in a now-standard vein are the general assessments of Carlyle as part of the Romantic movement or as part of the English strain of nineteenth-century idealism. Here one should consult R. H. Murray's *Studies in the English Social and Political Thinkers of the Nineteenth Century* (1929) and Holbrook Jackson's *Dreamers of Dreams* (1948), a graceful if not rigorous study that sees Carlyle as the most influential and original of the group of thinkers that includes Ruskin, Morris, Emerson, and Whitman. In the same vein is Jean Pucelle's *L'Idéalisme en Angleterre* (1955). Other such studies will be examined later.

More directly concerned with Carlyle's relation to Romanticism is Ernest Bernbaum's *Guide through the Romantic Movement* (1949), which quixotically argues that Carlyle ceased to be a Romantic after the 1840's. This theme or a variation of it—Carlyle as not truly or not consistently Romantic—is found again in Morse Peckham's "Towards a Theory of Romanticism" (*PMLA*, 1951), Robert Langbaum's *The Poetry of Experience* (1957), and least effectively in Eugene Goodheart's *The Cult of the Ego* (1968). Such views are attempts to come to grips with the apparent disjunction between the early and the later Carlyle, a real problem in Carlyle studies, both critically and biographically, but one that is too facilely solved by recourse to hypothetical "shifts" and "breaks" and "discontinuities" placed anywhere from 1841 to 1866, or by mysterious lurking unromantic tendencies or unsubduable philistinisms that surface and finally drive out the benign Romantic impulses. Neither Romanticism nor Carlyle is much clarified by such interpretations. At the same time there is clearly a need for greater understanding of what Romanticism becomes as its early exemplars pass away and as it is carried on into the century by such as Carlyle. Anyone pursuing this line should not fail to consult Jacques Barzun's well-thought-out *Classic, Romantic and Modern* (1943; 2nd ed., 1961).

A more enlightened vein of general studies from which the better part of such works as LaValley's descend is represented by the work of Holloway, Buckley, Houghton, and others. Here we find two main lines of interest: Carlyle as an intellectual force and Carlyle as a literary experimenter and proto-modernist. One or the other of these lines has dominated recent studies of Carlyle. Probably too many modern studies have been indebted to Eric Bentley's wayward *A Century of Hero Worship* (1944; 2nd ed. 1957; British title: *The Cult of the Superman*), which must also be considered later in regard to the question of Nazism. Its relevance here lies in Bentley's attempt to link Carlyle and Nietzsche (one of LaValley's pairings also) and to make observations about the idea of heroism in the nineteenth century. Much of Bentley's work is suggestive, much is questionable. More profitable and more influential in recent times has been John Holloway's *The Victorian Sage* (1953), which is not a general study as such, but which isolates and examines with great skill Carlyle's fulfilling of the role of the sage or prophet by means of his rhetoric. Other Victorian sages, such as Newman and Arnold, are included in Holloway's study. Ruskin, who is missing in Holloway, is joined with Carlyle in E. D. Mackerness' "The Voice of Prophecy" in *From Dickens to Hardy* (ed. Boris Ford, 1958).

A combination of the approaches to Carlyle as latter-day Romantic and harbinger of the new occurs in the treatments given him by Morse Peckham, first in *Beyond the Tragic Vision* (1962) and most recently in *Victorian Revolutionaries* (1970). Peckham's attitude toward Carlyle is ambivalent: he praises him for his literary and psychological daring and condemns him for not going farther in the direction that Peckham sees as desirable. *Beyond the Tragic Vision* especially recognizes the modernity and experimentalism of *Sartor Resartus*, which Peckham sees as an attempt to gain some kind of integration of the self in the face of the collapse of traditional values. *Victorian Revolutionaries* is rich on *Frederick the Great* and

Carlyle's "cultured transcendence." While Peckham frequently exasperates, he is concerned with trying to identify the Romantic impulse and the Victorian ethos, which simply cannot be understood without Carlyle, as such commentators as J. H. Buckley and Walter Houghton have seen.

Jerome Hamilton Buckley considers Carlyle at various points throughout *The Victorian Temper* (1951) as "Prophet-Idol-breaker" and as one of those who marked out a common "pattern of conversion" for fellow Victorians. Buckley's book is intelligent and illuminating on Carlyle's role in creating the Victorian ethos. Not so Gaylord C. LeRoy in *Perplexed Prophets* (1953). LeRoy treats Carlyle along with five other nineteenth-century British authors, but he does not treat him very illuminatingly. He bases most of his interpretation on Carlyle's alleged authoritarian character and attributes Carlyle's influence to "authoritarianism being part of the character structure of his age." LeRoy's study is more sophisticated than the grotesque psychiatric studies of the 1930's which it slightly resembles, but it is still not very useful. Quite the opposite is true of Walter E. Houghton's *The Victorian Frame of Mind* (1957), especially in terms of Carlyle's influence on the age. Beatrice Saunders' *Portraits of Genius* (1959) contains a chapter on Carlyle, but it is superficial and has not benefited from recent scholarship. David Daiches' essay *Carlyle and the Victorian Dilemma* (1963; rpt. in *More Literary Essays*, 1968) is in the company of Buckley and Houghton. Daiches says that Carlyle diagnosed the Victorian problem well but did not have a solution. G. B. Tennyson's *Carlyle and the Modern World* (Carlyle Society, 1972) offers a defense of Carlyle against characteristic modern objections, drawing especially on *Latter-Day Pamphlets*.

The Buckley-Houghton view of Carlyle as a potent intellectual force in the age represents an approach that virtually all modern commentators can and must agree upon. Accordingly the large scope of Raymond Williams' *Culture and Society, 1780–1950* (1958) finds considerable place for Carlyle. Williams uses "Signs of the Times" as the essence of Carlyle's views and sees all his thought largely in light of it. He follows the now conventional view of Carlyle as good early and bad late, but he concludes on a note of respect for Carlyle's "essential quality: the word reverence, not for him, but in him." A not dissimilar view of Carlyle is taken by Raymond Chapman in *The Victorian Debate: English Literature and Society, 1832–1901* (1968). Once again we see Carlyle as the epitome of the Victorian confrontation between literature and society and Carlyle as feeling the compulsion to bridge the gap. Carlyle among the self-divided Victorians is also treated rather predictably by Masao Miyoshi in *The Divided Self* (1969) as having sought through *Sartor* to bridge the gap left by Romanticism through "conversion."

There are several more sharply focused studies that nevertheless present general views of Carlyle and treat matters touching his whole literary career. One such is William Savage Johnson's *Thomas Carlyle: A Study of His Literary Apprenticeship, 1814–1831* (1911), which moves through the early years toward *Sartor* as the culmination of the first part of Carlyle's career. Far more valuable but on a somewhat related theme is C. F. Harrold's *Carlyle and German Thought, 1819–1834* (1934), which must also be considered later in regard to Carlyle's relation to German literature. Harrold's is a groundbreaking study that continues to be indispensable for any general understanding of Carlyle's thought. Another specialized work that should be cited here as well as later is G. B. Tennyson's *"Sartor" Called "Resartus"* (1965), which studies not only *Sartor Resartus* but also Carlyle's literary apprenticeship, thereby largely superseding Johnson, and which also studies the literary methods Carlyle was to use throughout his career. Tennyson's treatment of Carlyle is highly sympathetic and has probably influenced the subsequent course of Carlyle study. Jacques Cabau's dense and scholarly *Thomas Carlyle ou le Prométhée enchainé* (1968) endeavors to penetrate to the genesis of Carlyle's work and thus is confined to the early period, 1795–1834. As the subtitle suggests, Cabau sees Carlyle as enormously potent, but nevertheless confined and restrained, largely for psychological reasons. He argues that Carlyle evolved a Romantic rhetoric to turn against Romanticism itself; he sacrificed the freedom of Romanticism in order to engage metaphor in a vocation. Cabau makes many useful observations about the dark side of Carlyle's vision, the demonic element, black humor, thaumaturgy; he points to affinities with surrealism. Thus Carlylean metaphor "affirme les droits de l'imagination, mais aussi ses devoirs—qui sont sa mission." The book contains a very substantial bibliography.

Future general studies must do some of the things that any future critical biography should do, but they must also accommodate the increasing knowledge of Carlyle's impact on his age and his extraordinary literary and psychological enterprise to the older concern for his thought and ideas.

Influence and Literary Relations

Carlyle's influence was protean, for he knew most of the literary men of his day. Even some earlier figures who influenced Carlyle, such as Goethe, were drawn into personal contact whenever possible. A considerable body of criticism has grown up about his influence and his relations with literary men. No full study has ever been made of these matters, or indeed of his influence in a broader sense. So extensive is the number of separate pieces that the clearest way to examine the individual studies is alphabetically by author who influenced or was influenced by Carlyle. At the same time so many of these studies are mere notes that little discussion is called for and many cannot be cited at all, and many of the best treatments are those more properly cited elsewhere under Carlyle's ideas. The remaining mass of separate studies and notes on Carlyle's literary relations are cited here. The value in the following section, it is hoped, will be the bringing together for the first time the many titles in this somewhat chaotic area so that future work can take a more meaningful direction.

ARNOLD. Two valuable studies have been made of this important relationship. Kathleen Tillotson's seminal article (*PBA*, 1956) was preceded by John Kelman's chapter on Carlyle's Hebraism and Arnold's Hellenism in *Prophets of Yesterday* (1924) and Kenji Ishida's article (*Tokyo Stud. in Eng.*, 1933) but followed by David J. DeLaura's yet more substantial study (*PMLA*, 1964). In this superb study DeLaura has shown instance after instance of Arnold's echoing Carlyle's ideas and even phrasings, even at times when Arnold was publicly disenchanted with Carlyle. A similar echoing by Arnold of Carlyle, this time chiefly in regard to aesthetics, is examined by Lawrence J. Starzyk (*Criticism*, 1970). A shrill denunciation of the kind of scholarship that documents Carlyle's influence on Arnold or finds any merit in Carlyle whatsoever rends the air in D. R. M. Wilkinson's "Carlyle, Arnold, and Literary Justice" (*PMLA*, 1971). It serves to illustrate that the anti-Carlyle lobby is by no means dead. Brief notes on aspects of the Carlyle-Arnold relationship are offered by Frederick Page, "Balder Dead (1855)" (*E&S*, 1942), Kathleen Tillotson, "Arnold and Carlyle" (*N&Q*, 1955), Kenneth Allott, "An Arnold-Clough Letter"

(*N&Q*, 1956), and C. J. Rawson on Arnold and Henry Reve (*N&Q*, 1971). Patrick J. McCarthy on Arnold (*UTQ*, 1971) is also instructive on Carlyle. There is now a need for a book-length treatment of the relationship.

BAUDELAIRE. Despite its title, "Carlyle and Some Early English Critics of Baudelaire" by G. T. Clapton (*A Miscellany of Studies in Romance Languages and Literature Presented to Leon E. Kastner*, ed. Mary Williams and James A. de Rothschild, 1932) has little to say about Carlyle and Baudelaire except that Carlyle did not like what he read of Baudelaire in *Fraser's Magazine* or picked up about him from the association with Swinburne. BLAKE. See Harold L. Bruce's "Blake, Carlyle and the French Revolution" (*Gayley Anniversary Papers*, 1922). LaValley's book considers parallels at some length. BONSELS. Alfred Heinrich (*Zeitschrift für französische und englische Unterricht*, 1922) has done the only note, and the subject does not call for more. BOUHOURS. An anonymous note, "Mr. Carlyle and Père Bouhours" (*CathW*, 1871), is the only reference to this slight connection.

BROWNING. There are quite rightly a number of studies of this relationship but unfortunately no full study. The "Memorabilist" has twice noted Carlyle-Browning connections, "Browning as Carlyle's Boswell" and "On *The Ring and the Book*" (*N&Q*, 1943, 1944). More important is the discussion in Richard D. Altick's "Browning's 'Transcendentalism'" (*JEGP*, 1959) on Browning's poem of that name and its relation to Carlyle's ideas. A discussion of Browning's intellectual indebtednesses to Carlyle as well as their personal contacts appears in C. R. Sanders' "Carlyle, Browning, and the Nature of a Poet" (*EUQ*, 1960). The impact of Carlyle's *French Revolution* on a Browning poem is studied in Charlotte Crawford Watkins' "Browning's 'Red Cotton Night-Cap Country' and Carlyle" (*VS*, 1964). And David S. Gadziola's "The Prophet and the Poet: The Relationship of Thomas Carlyle with Robert Browning, Alfred Tennyson, and Arthur Hugh Clough" (Diss. Maryland 1968) studies, in part, the relationship.

BÜCHNER. The German playwright appears to have had affinities and common sources rather than any direct connection with Carlyle, according to R. Majut (*MLR*, 1953). BURNS. The Burns-Carlyle connection is, of course, of some consequence and will appear later in discussion of Carlyle's *Essays*. Here one can note an anonymous early article, "Carlyle and Burns" (*SatR*, 1923). BURROUGHS. Since his literary criticism included Carlyle, there is some connection there. See Joseph M. Garrison, Jr., "John Burroughs as a Literary Critic" (Diss. Duke 1963). BYRON. Carlyle's own Byronism has been sufficiently remarked to provoke a few studies of the relation. See Heinrich Kraeger's chapter in *Der Byronische Heldentypus* (1898); but much more to the point of influence and impact is C. R. Sanders' "The Byron Closed in *Sartor Resartus*" (*SIR*, 1964), which explores far more than its title implies and constitutes the fullest examination of Carlyle's longtime and very serious thought on Byron. A significant part of the literary impact of Byron on Carlyle is treated in Allan C. Christensen's "Heroism in the Age of Reform: Byron, Goethe, and the Novels of Carlyle" (Diss. Princeton 1968).

CHAUCER. Thomas Kirby's brief note (*MLN*, 1946) indicates that Carlyle liked the medieval author. CLOUGH. This important influence is frequently touched on in Paul Veyriras' *Arthur Hugh Clough* (1965). A specific Clough work is seen for its Carlylism in C. Castan's "Clough's 'Epi-strauss-ium' and Carlyle" (*VP*, 1966). COBBETT. A brief comparison of Cobbett and Carlyle as pessimists, with Cobbett emerging as an even darker one than Carlyle, is offered by G. K. Chesterton's "William Cobbett" essay in *RSL, Essays by Divers Hands*, III (1923). A significant influence of Cobbett's thought on Carlyle is argued in Charles H. Kegel's "William Cobbett and Malthusianism" (*JHI*, 1958). COLERIDGE. The extremely important Coleridge-Carlyle relationship deserves a separate study. It is frequently commented upon in general studies of Carlyle, but only a few more specialized studies have treated it at worthwhile length. These include the early study by Nikolaus Schanck, *Die sozialpolitische Anschauungen Coleridges und sein Einfluss auf Carlyle* (1924), and an illuminating chapter in C. R. Sanders' *Coleridge and the Broad Church Movement* (1943). A general piece on Carlyle's reaction to the earlier group that included Coleridge is found in Donald R. Swanson's "Carlyle on the English Romantic Poets" (*LHR*, 1969). CONRAD. See A. L. Hopwood (*RES*, 1972). CONWAY. Carlyle's influence on one of his later biographers is discussed in Mary Elizabeth Burtis' *Moncure Conway, 1832–1907* (1952). DE QUINCEY. More should certainly be done on the Carlyle-De Quincey affinities, but for the moment we have only Walter Y. Durand's "De Quincey and Carlyle in Their Relation to the Germans" (*PMLA*, 1907) and a dissertation, Edward H. Essig's "Thomas De Quincey and Robert Pearse Gillies as Champions of German Literature and Thought" (Northwestern 1952).

DICKENS. Perhaps the most important of all Carlyle's literary relations and influences is that with Dickens. After years of many specialized studies of aspects of the relationship there are now two good book-length works by Michael Goldberg (1972) and William Oddie (1972). Goldberg's is the more literary study, Oddie's the more historical. Between them there is now a full consideration of the literary and personal interaction between these two Victorian giants. One cannot, however, dispense entirely with the many specialized treatments. Of earlier studies that still have merit one should consult Samuel Davey's *Darwin, Carlyle, Dickens* (1876) and Philipp Aronstein's (*Anglia*, 1896), and perhaps the Russian study by T. Shaskolskaya (*Trans. of the Leningrad Pedagogical Inst.*, 1940).

Specific notes on particular works and passages involving Dickens and Carlyle can be cited only briefly: J. A. Falconer on *A Tale of Two Cities* (*MLN*, 1921); W. J. Fisher on Carlyle's influence on Dickens (*Dickensian*, 1927); T. C. D. on Carlyle and *Pickwick* (*N&Q*, 1948); K. J. Fielding on Carlyle, Dickens, and William Maccall (*N&Q*, 1954); Michael Slater on Carlyle's influence on *The Chimes* (*NCF*, 1970; and again in *Dickens 1970*, ed. Michael Slater, 1970) and Rodger Tarr on the same theme (*NCF*, 1972); Blair G. Kenney on Carlyle's influence on *Bleak House* (*Dickensian*, 1970) and Rodger Tarr on the same topic (*Stud. in the Novel*, 1971); Richard J. Dunn on Carlyle's influence on *David Copperfield* (in *Dickens the Craftsman*, ed. Robert Partlow, 1970); and Allan C. Christensen on Carlyle's influence on *Martin Chuzzlewit* (*Stud. in the Novel*, 1971). The last two studies are of particular value in showing how Dickens worked out in his own literary terms ideas derived from Carlyle's *Sartor*.

Extensive thematic studies, apart from the Goldberg and Oddie books, are available in Mildred G. Christian's "Carlyle's Influence upon the Social Theory of Dickens" (*Trollopian*, 1947) and Goldberg's study of Dickens' political development in "From Bentham to Carlyle" (*JHI*, 1972). John Holloway credits Carlyle with great influence on Dickens' symbolism in "Dickens and the Symbol" (in *Dickens 1970*). Carlyle's impact on Dickens' view of American slavery is presented by Arthur A. Adrian (*PMLA*, 1952). The personal as well as the literary associations of the two men are the focus of L. G. Dickens' essay (*Dickensian*, 1957). While there will continue to be future studies of aspects of the Carlyle-Dickens relationship, it is fair to say that this is one area that shows no pressing need for further study.

DISRAELI. James D. Merritt's "The Novelist St. Barbe in Disraeli's *Endymion*: Revenge on Whom?" (*NCF*, 1968) suggests that Carlyle be considered along with the usual candidate Thackeray as the original of Disraeli's character. DOYLE. William D. Jenkins' "Who Might Thomas Carlyle Be?" (*Baker St. J.*, 1966) suggests many interesting influences of Carlyle on Doyle and even the possibility of Doyle's indebtedness to Carlyle for some of the qualities in the character of Sherlock Holmes. See also Stephen F. Crocker's "Watson Doctors the Venerable Bede" (*Baker St. J.*, 1959).

EMERSON. The Emerson-Carlyle association has been perhaps the most extensively examined of all Carlyle's literary relations and only a quick survey can indicate the scope of the material. As early as Emile Montégut's "Littérature américaine" (*RDM*, 1850), the affiliation of the two men had been explored. A few other notable earlier studies, apart from Emerson's own writings, are Peter Wilson's *Leaders in Literature* (1898), Ernst von Wiecki's *Carlyle's 'Helden' und Emerson's 'Repräsentanten'* (1903), J. M. Sloan's (*Living Age*, 1921), and Frank T. Thompson's (*SP*, 1927). More recently, Carlyle has been treated in relationship to Emerson in studies of Emerson and the New England transcendentalists, such as Townsend Scudder's belletristic *The Lonely Wayfaring Man* (1936), Carl F. Strauch's "The Problem of Time and the Romantic Mode in Hawthorne, Melville and Emerson" (*ESQ*, 1964), and William S. Vance's *Carlyle and the American Transcendentalists* (1944). The purely biographical has also continued to dominate much of the criticism of the two, as in E. Seillière's "L'Amitié d'Emerson et de Carlyle" (*J. des Economistes*, 1938), George H. Hartwig's "An Immortal Friendship" (*HJ*, 1939), Robert Pearsall's "Carlyle and Emerson: Horses and Revolutions" (*SAQ*, 1956), and Kenneth W. Cameron's "Emerson's *Nature* and British Swedenborgism" (*ESQ*, 1963) on Carlyle's role in gaining Emerson a British public. There is a Japanese contribution in Akika Tomita's "Lonely Emerson and Whimsical Carlyle" (*Amer. Culture*, 1947).

But the Carlyle-Emerson relationship is really most interesting for the ideas involved. Here there are several useful studies. Helmut Kuhn's "Carlyle, Ally and Critic of Emerson" (*EUQ*, 1948) argues that Carlyle and Emerson balance each other in their response to the crisis of unbelief in the age. More general is Suk-joo Kim's "A Comparative Study of Emerson and Carlyle" (*Eng. Lang. & Lit.*, Korea, 1962). Harold L. Berger's "Emerson and Carlyle—Stylists at Odds" (*ESQ*, 1963) approaches the differences between the two through their respective styles. A further examination of their differences is made by Robert N. Hertz in "Victory and the Consciousness of Battle" (*Personalist*, 1964). But we return to their spiritual similarities in Harold L. Berger's "Emerson and Carlyle: The Dissenting Believers" (*ESQ*, 1965). A useful summary of the Carlyle-Emerson relationship and the Victorian estimate of the two can be found in William J. Sowder's *Emerson's Impact on the British Isles and Canada* (1966). Light on Carlyle's impact on the transcendental movement is offered in Rodger L. Tarr's "Emerson's Transcendentalism in L. M. Child's Letter to Carlyle" (*ESQ*, 1970). Despite all this Carlyle-Emerson scholarship and the valuable edition of and introduction to the correspondence by Slater, the definitive book-length study is still being awaited.

FITZGERALD. A lesser-known Victorian Fitzgerald is the subject of Thomas A. Kirby's "Carlyle, Fitzgerald and Naseby Project" (*MLQ*, 1947). The better-known

Fitzgerald and his response to Carlyle is treated in Clarice Short's "Edward Fitzgerald on Some Fellow Victorians" (*WHR*, 1951).

FORD. Carlyle and Henry Ford are both credited with a belief in social altruism by Leopold Caro in "Od Carlyle a do Fordo" (*Sprawy Obce*, 1932). FORSTER. An unsuspected Carlyle influence on *A Room with a View* is treated in Betty J. M. Belvin's "Expanding Themes in the Novels of E. M. Forster" (Diss. Washington 1958). FULLER. The somewhat ludicrous Margaret Fuller often appears in Carlyle studies because of her well-reported meeting with Carlyle. Ray Cecil Carter's "Margaret Fuller and the Two Sages" (*CLQ*, 1963) reprints Fuller's letter to Emerson on that meeting. GANIVET. Carlyle is claimed as an influence on the Spanish writer Angel Ganivet in D. Montalto Cessi's *Tre studi sulla cultura spagnola* (1967). GEORGE. A surely hitherto unsuspected connection between Carlyle and David Lloyd George is not made very meaningful by the anonymous "On Two Lord Rectors" (*Nation*, 1923). MRS. GASKELL. See Rodger Tarr's "Carlyle's Influence upon the Mid-Victorian Social Novels of Gaskell, Kingsley, and Dickens" (Diss. South Carolina 1969). GIDE. Though at first André Gide appears an unlikely Carlyle epigone, Germaine Brée has shown the considerable impact that Carlyle had on Gide's thought at an important point in Gide's development in her "Rencontre avec Carlyle" (*Revue d'Histoire Littéraire de la France*, 1970).

GOETHE. Not even the Carlyle-Emerson relationship has produced more material than Carlyle's admiration for and correspondence with Goethe. The Goethe material is overall of slightly higher quality. Publication of the correspondence was early undertaken by C. E. Norton (1887); and F. M. Müller (1886) began a long line of critical studies. Other earlier studies include H. H. Boyesen's *Essays on German Literature* (1892), Leon Kellner's (*Die Nation*, 1896), R. Schroeder's "Carlyles Abhandlung über den Goethesche *Faust*" (*Archiv*, 1896), and James Mackinnon's essay in *Leisure Hours in the Study* (1897). In the early part of this century there are Otto Baumgarten (1906), F. M. Stawell (*Int. J. of Ethics*, 1911), and the still essential study by Jean-Marie Carré, *Goethe en Angleterre* (1920). Almost all of the Carlyle-Goethe material then and now is concerned with the young Carlyle's response to Goethe and the influence he freely admitted Goethe had on him.

Still of interest on Goethe's English influence are Karl Holl's "Goethes Vollendung in ihrer Beziehung zu Byron und Carlyle" (*GRM*, 1921) and J. B. Orrick's study (*PEGS*, 1928; rpt. 1966), which is rich on Carlyle and Arnold. B. J. Morse's "Crabb Robinson and Goethe in England" (*ES*, 1932) considers Carlyle's predecessor among English Goethe enthusiasts. Kuno Francke's "Carlyle and Goethe's *Symbolum*" (*PQ*, 1927) is an illuminating study of Carlyle's translation of a Goethe poem. Another interesting study of the same subject is Friedrich Brie's "Carlyle und Goethes *Symbolum*" (*Anglia*, 1943). J. A. S. Barrett (*HJ*, 1931) is chiefly concerned with Carlyle's adaptation of Goethe's ethical thought. Helmut Plagens' *Carlyles Weg zu Goethe* (1938) was followed by another study with precisely the same title by A. Kippenburg (1946). The most concise modern treatment of this theme is William Witte's chapter, "Carlyle's Conversion," in *The Era of Goethe* (1960). The source of Carlyle's well-known phrase "the Open Secret" is ably traced in Joseph Slater's "Goethe, Carlyle and the Open Secret" (*Anglia*, 1958).

HARDY. Benjamin Sankey's "Henchard and Faust" (*ELN*, 1965) argues that Carlyle was the intermediary for Hardy's interpretation of *Faust* in *The Mayor of*

Casterbridge. HERDER. In response to ideas contested between René Wellek and Hill Shine regarding the sources for some of Carlyle's thought, Shine pursued the question of Carlyle's intellectual indebtedness to Herder and developed the topic in admirable depth in "Carlyle's Early Writings and Herder's *Ideen*" (*Booker Memorial Studies*, 1950). HOFFMANN. Although Carlyle translated E. T. A. Hoffmann, no consequential study has examined the literary affinities, but Carlyle is mentioned in Erwin G. Gudde's "E. T. A. Hoffmann's Reception in England" (*PMLA*, 1926). HALLEY. The obscure American dialect writer Marietta Halley borrowed from Carlyle, as is shown by Eston Everett Ericson, "An American Indebtedness to Carlyle" (*N&Q*, 1959). HORN. W. Leopold's (*JEGP*, 1929) is an important article on some of Carlyle's handbook sources for his German literary knowledge in *Sartor*. HUTTON. Because Hutton wrote of Carlyle with some reservations, his relationship has proved interesting to a few. A note by the "Memorabilist," "Richard Holt Hutton and Carlyle" (*N&Q*, 1943), corrects a Hutton misinterpretation. Robert H. Tener's "Sources of Hutton's 'Modern Guides' Essay on Carlyle" (*N&Q*, 1963) lists Hutton's sources for his essay, these being a substantial number of Hutton's own journalistic pieces mainly from the *Spectator*. HUXLEY. That Carlyle had a profound influence on the younger Thomas Henry Huxley is amply demonstrated by Leonard Huxley (*Cornhill*, 1932) and by William Irvine (*Booker Memorial Studies*, 1950).

JEAN PAUL. Quite a substantial literature exists on Carlyle and Jean Paul Friedrich Richter, beginning with H. Breitinger's "Thomas Carlyle: Ein Nachahmer Jean Pauls?" (*Die Gegenwart*, 1885). Important early contributions are by H. Conrad (*Die Gegenwart*, 1891) and Henry Pape, *Jean Paul als Quelle von Thomas Carlyles Anschauung und Stil* (1904). See also Theodor Geissendoerfer (*JEGP*, 1926) and H. Wernekke (*Jean-Paul-Blätter*, 1927). Geissendoerfer again took up the subject (*Hesperus*, 1958) and most recently J. W. Smeed has made excellent contributions in "Carlyles Jean-Paul Übersetzungen" (*DVLG*, 1961) and "Thomas Carlyle and Jean Paul Richter" (*CL*, 1964). There are also many critical studies of *Sartor* that treat Jean Paul. As the wealth of scholarly material shows, there is enough here for a book-length study. Jean Paul's extraordinary style is the central focus, but the relation of style to idea is also important and much light could be cast on both authors by a thorough examination.

JEFFREY. An aspect of the editorial relationship with Francis Jeffrey is treated in Maxwell H. Goldberg's "Carlyle, Pictet, and Jeffrey" (*MLQ*, 1946). JERDAN. See Robert W. Duncan's "William Jerdan and the *Literary Gazette*" (Diss. Cincinnati 1955) and Carlyle's *Reminiscences*. JOWETT. The don who is remembered by the rhyme thought Carlyle powerful but extreme, according to Fanny Price's "Jowett on Carlyle" (*N&Q*, 1943).

KANT. The most valuable study continues to be Harrold's *Carlyle and German Thought*, but there are three other useful works: Margaret Storrs's *The Relation of Carlyle to Kant and Fichte* (1929) and René Wellek's *Immanuel Kant in England* (1931) and his *Confrontations* (1965). KEBLE. Carlyle allegedly called The Great Tractarian "a little ape," and A. M. Coleman in "Keble: A Phrase from Carlyle" (*N&Q*, 1938) wants to know where. Otherwise nothing. KINGSLEY. There are two early studies: W. R. Greg's in *Literary and Social Judgements* (1869) and Maria Meyer's *Carlyles Einfluss auf Kingsley* (1914). A more recent treatment is Robert D. Campbell's "Victorian Pegasus in Harness: A Study of Kingsley's Debt to Thomas Carlyle, and F. D. Maurice" (Diss. Wisconsin 1969). Readers should also consult Cazamian's *Le Roman social en Angleterre* and Tarr's dissertation cited under Mrs. Gaskell. KIPLING. Andrew Rutherford (*KJ*, 1966) points up many affinities, but attempts to cleanse Kipling of any of the bad associations surrounding Carlyle and thus misrepresents Carlyle. W. Keats Sparrow in "The Work Theme in Kipling's Novels" (*KJ*, 1970) points out some Carlyle influence. KÜNZEL. A slight connection through letters is demonstrated in Walther Fischer's *Des Därmstadter Schriftstellers Johann Heinrich Künzel (1810–1873) Beziehungen zu England* (1940). LAGERLÖF. See L. G. Nystrom, "The Influence of Thomas Carlyle on Selma Lagerlöf" (Diss. Southern Methodist 1937). LANGLAND. Curiously, two authors have found similarities between Carlyle and Langland: R. Hittmair in "Die Arbeit bei Langland, Locke, Carlyle" (*GRM*, 1926) and Stanley B. James in "A Mediaeval Carlyle" (*The Month*, 1933).

LAWRENCE. It has been common for critics to point in passing to affinities between Carlyle and D. H. Lawrence, but only Edward Alexander's provocative and provoking article (*UTQ*, 1968) has sought to examine this topic at any length. Alexander studies parallels between the two in terms of the frustrations and excesses of the modern artist who seeks in vain to transform society. He likens the Lawrence-Bertrand Russell relationship to the Carlyle-Mill one and opts for the two spokesmen for reason over Carlyle and Lawrence. While reason and reasonableness need much to be encouraged in these times, it is not clear that Russell really had much more of it than Carlyle or Lawrence and thus the choice posed ends up as a false one. But on the way Alexander makes many telling points and finds many instructive parallels. LOWELL. James Russell Lowell brings us back to Margaret Fuller, for the one article on Lowell and Carlyle is concerned with a source for a Lowell pun in *A Fable for Critics*, H. Ehrlich's "Origin of Lowell's Miss Fooler" (*AL*, 1966).

MACAULAY. A number of studies have been directed to parallels and contrasts between Carlyle and Macaulay. A parallel was noted early in Ludwig Häusser's "Macaulay's Friedrich der Grosse mit einem Nachtrag über Carlyle" (*Hist. Zeitschrift*, 1859), and more extensive comparisons offered by Edmund Gosse (*Littell's Living Age*, 1898) and Otto Krauske (*Hist. Zeitschrift*, 1908). Recent studies have been almost exclusively concerned to use Carlyle and Macaulay as opposites and contrasts. Still essential in this line is Richard C. Beatty's article (*PQ*, 1939) and William H. Rogers' more specialized "A Study in Contrasts: Carlyle and Macaulay as Book Reviewers" (Fla. State Univ. Stud., 1952). Alan John Percivale Taylor in *Englishmen and Others* (1956) devotes a chapter to a stimulating comparison of Carlyle and Macaulay.

MAETERLINCK. There is some possibility that Maeterlinck had read Carlyle and every sign that he might have is examined by Raymond Pouilliart in "Maurice Maeterlinck et Carlyle" (*RLC*, 1964). MARX. No influence is posited, but a similarity in approach is examined in Kenneth Burke's *A Rhetoric of Motives* (1950). MAZZINI. The connection of the Italian nationalist with Carlyle is a very real one and is treated in the biographies. The chief literary treatment is Harry W. Rudman's *Italian Nationalism and English Letters* (1940). See also Michele Saponara's "Una donna tra due poeti" (*NA*, 1958), Charles Dedeyan's "Mazzini, Carlyle et les réfugiés italiens" (*Atti dell' Accademia Lucchese di Scienze, Lettere, ed Arte*, 1953), Francesco Fumora's *Mazzini* (1969), and Paolo Arecchi's short note (*Brocellana*, 1969). MELVILLE. Only recently have Melville's Carlyle affinities been examined. Two short items find Carlyle sources for passages in *Moby-Dick*: Alexander Welsh's "A Melville Debt to Carlyle" (*MLN*, 1958) and Mario L. D'Avanzo's "'The Cassock' and Carlyle's 'Church Clothes'" (*ESQ*, 1968). Two dissertations take on the larger area of literary relations between the two authors: Bruce L. Greenberg's "Thomas Carlyle and Herman Melville" (North Carolina 1964) and Julie Ann Braun's "Melville's Use of Carlyle's *Sartor Resartus*" (California, Los Angeles 1968). MENCKEN. The sages of Chelsea and Baltimore agreed about the preposterousness of democracy, as C. F. Harrold points out in "Two Critics of Democracy" (*SAQ*, 1928).

MEREDITH. More should be done on Carlyle and Meredith than has been so far. Meantime we have John W. Morris' "Thomas Carlyle's Influence on George Meredith's Theory of Literature" (Diss. Tennessee 1954) and the same author's "*Beauchamp's Career*: Meredith's Acknowledgement of His Debt to Carlyle" (*TSL*, 1962). MÉRIMÉE. A. de Suzannet's "Mérimée et Carlyle" (*BBB*, 1933) shows that Mérimée troubled to write to Carlyle to point out errors in *Frederick the Great*. MICKIEWICZ. Carlyle's encounter with the works of the Polish poet Adam Mickiewicz is documented by Wiktor Weintraub's "Carlyle and Mickiewicz" (in *Studi in onore di Etione lo Gatto e Giovanni Maver*, 1962). Though Weintraub makes rather grand claims for this reading, the important aspect of the article is its demonstration of Carlyle's continued broad literary interests in the 1840's.

MILL. From the start the Carlyle-Mill association has generated a high level of criticism. Patrick Proctor Alexander (1866) begins the list and is followed by Edward Jenks (1888), but the definitive study is Emery Neff's (1924; rev. 1926), which uses the two figures as a means of seeing the entire age in perspective in terms of its dominant impulses. Subsequent studies have been more specialized but still of interest. Peter E. Martin's "Carlyle and Mill: The 'Anti-Self-Consciousness' Theory" (*Thoth*, 1965) continues the tradition of seeing them as complements or opposites, as does Anna J. Mill's *Carlyle and Mill: Two Scottish University Rectors* (Carlyle Society, 1965). More sharply focused but still in the comparison-contrast tradition is Henry Ebel's "'The Primaeval Fountain of Human Nature': Mill, Carlyle, and the French Revolution" (*VN*, 1966). See also Murray Baumgarten's "The Ideas of History of Thomas Carlyle and John Stuart Mill" (Diss. California, Berkeley 1966) and Herbert E. Spivey's "Carlyle and Mill on the Individual in Society" (Diss. Duke 1969). Baumgarten published a summary statement of his findings (*MNL*, 1967). Two studies are concerned with very particular incidents. Iva G. Jones's "Trollope, Carlyle, and Mill on the Negro" (*J. of Negro Hist.*, 1967) wags its finger at both Carlyle and Trollope but applauds Mill; and Edward Alexander's "Mill's Marginal Notes on Carlyle's 'Hudson's Statue'" (*ELN*, 1969) adds a footnote to the documentation of the Mill-Carlyle split after the late 1840's.

MILLER. Carlyle's Columbus in *Past and Present* is claimed as the source for a Joaquin Miller poem in Margaret Duckett's "Carlyle, 'Columbus,' and Joaquin Miller" (*PQ*, 1956). NEWMAN. Two contributions to what should be a larger field are Henry Tristram's "Two Leaders" (*Cornhill*, 1928) and J. B. Fletcher's stimulating "Newman and Carlyle" (*AM*, 1905). NIETZSCHE. The Carlyle-Nietzsche link was noticed early in J. H. Wilhelmi's *Thomas Carlyle und Friedrich Nietzsche* (1897) and picked up again after the Nazi perversion of their ideas, as in Walther Spethmann's "Der Begriff des Herrentums bei Nietzsche" (*Neue Deutsche Forschungen*, 1935). By far the most valuable study is Albert Wagner's "Goethe, Carlyle, Nietzsche and the German Middle Class" (*Monatshefte*, 1939), a dense and careful examination of changing cultural notions. Eric Bentley's *Century of Hero-Worship* has done much to stress similarities between Carlyle and Nietzsche; he added further notes in "Modern Hero-Worship: Notes on Carlyle, Nietzsche, and Stefan George" (*SR*, 1944), but the contrasts between the two are cited in Hans Hartmann's "Nietzsche contre Carlyle" (*Etudes Nietzschéennes*, 1949). La-Valley's book also cites parallels, and some parallels with distinctions are pointed out in Tennyson's *"Sartor" Called "Resartus."*

NOVALIS. Despite the thoroughness and excellence of C. F. Harrold's study (*SP*, 1930), this subject needs further exploration. PARRINGTON. See Louis Filler's "Parrington and Carlyle: Cross-Currents in History and Belles-Lettres" (*AR*, 1952). PROCTER. Carlyle knew the minor poet through the Strachey circle and references to this connection are made by Richard W. Armour in "The Life and Works of Bryan Walter Procter ('Barry Cornwall')" (Diss. Harvard 1934). The only other examination, but it is definitive, is in Sanders' *The Strachey Family*. QUINET. That Carlyle even had some impact here can be seen in Henri Tronchon's *Le Jeune Edgard Quinet* (1938). RAMSAY. More of Carlyle's knowledge of Scottish authors is offered in Coleman O. Parsons' "Carlyle on Ramsay and Ferguson" (*MLR*, 1934).

RICHTER. See JEAN PAUL. RIPLEY. An English translator of Kant and a friend of Emerson is the subject of Joseph Slater's "George Ripley and Thomas Carlyle" (*PMLA*, 1952). ROSSETTI. Carlyle wrote a favorable note about the Pre-Raphaelite publication, as reported in H. Jervis' "Carlyle and 'The Germ'" (*TLS*, 20 Aug. 1938). RUSKIN. A book is surely needed on the important Carlyle-Ruskin relationship. Frederick William Roe's valuable *Social Philosophy of Carlyle and Ruskin* (1921) is good on their common social ideas. Otherwise several articles cast some light. Maxwell H. Goldberg's (*TLS*, 16 May 1935) is a specialized correction of some Ruskin-Carlyle correspondence. Sanders' studies of the correspondence and biographies of Carlyle and Ruskin provide much personal information. Van Akin Burd's "Ruskin's Antidote for Carlyle's Purges" (*BUSE*, 1957) is also concerned with correspondence and Ruskin's bowdlerizing of some Carlyle imagery. Charles H. Kegel has studied the details of the personal side of the Carlyle-Ruskin friendship in "An Uncertain Biographical Fact" (*VN*, 1956), arguing for a first meeting between the two between 1846 and 1847, and more broadly in "Carlyle and Ruskin: An Influential Friendship" (*BYUS*, 1964). Donald R. Swanson's "Ruskin and His 'Master'" (*VN*, 1967) is a brief survey of the association of the two. R. Fulford provides an interesting note on Ruskin's later views of Carlyle (*TLS*, 16 April 1971).

SAINT-PIERRE. The tenuous connection between Carlyle and the author of *Paul et Virginie* is examined in Edwin W. Marrs's "Carlyle, Bernardin de Saint-Pierre, and Madame Coffin" (*VN*, 1968). SCHILLER. Since Carlyle's first substantial work was his biography of Schiller, this is an important literary relation, but not much has been done recently. Some early studies are still important: H. Conrad (*Vierteljahrsschrift für Literaturgeschichte*, 1889) is perhaps the earliest to examine it separately. Two other early studies also still bear consideration: Frohwalt Küchler's (*Anglia*, 1903) and A. Hildebrand's (1913). Much slighter is Maria Luisa Astaldi's "Schiller e Carlyle" (*Ulisse*, 1956). A recent and capable study is in William Witte's *Schiller and Burns and Other Essays* (1959). SCOTT. Far too little has been done here, but frequent references occur in general studies of Carlyle and in criticism of his Burns essay and the like. Specifically on the Carlyle-Scott relationship there is only Herbert J. C. Grierson's "Scott and Carlyle" (*E&S*, 1928). SEWELL. The Tractarian priest who wrote an early *Quarterly Review* article on Carlyle apparently never provoked Carlyle's wrath. The connection is treated in Lionel

James's *A Forgotten Genius: Sewell of St. Columba's and Radley* (1945). SHAKE-SPEARE. Apart from criticism on *Heroes*, little has been done with Carlyle's debt to Shakespeare. The matter is treated in Augustus Ralli's *Later Critiques* (1933). SHAW. A necessary but neglected topic. See Julian B. Kaye's *Bernard Shaw and the Nineteenth-Century Tradition* (1958). SMILES. "What Carlyle prophesied," says Asa Briggs, "Samuel Smiles turned to homilies." This highly Victorian influence is studied in Briggs's *Victorian People* (1955).

STERLING. In addition to the criticism on Carlyle's biography there have been studies on the literary and personal relationship. George Gilfillan's "Carlyle and Sterling" in *A Gallery of Literary Portraits* (1845) is the first. Carlyle's book provoked Emile Montégut (*RDM*, 1852). Anne Kimball Tuell in *John Sterling: A Representative Victorian* (1941) gives the best view of the association. STERNE. Endless references to the influence of Sterne and Swift occur in Carlyle studies but there has been little extensive examination of the topic. There is Ronald L. Trowbridge's "Echoes of Swift and Sterne in the Works of Thomas Carlyle" (Diss. Michigan 1968). Jack F. Stewart's "Romantic Theories of Humor Relating to Sterne" (*Personalist*, 1968) includes Carlyle among other Romantics who followed Sterne's ideas on humor. SWEDENBORG. No one yet knows what, if any, the exact influences and responses were on Carlyle's part to Swedenborg and Swedenborgianism, but some ideas may be gleaned from James C. Malin's "Carlyle's Philosophy of Clothes and Swedenborg's" (*SS*, 1961). SWIFT. Sidney M. B. Coulling (*SEL*, 1970) argues that Carlyle's acceptance of Swift's humor and rejection of Swift's satire kept him from becoming "Swift's disciple in any profound sense."

SWINBURNE. There seems to have been more hate than love in Swinburne's mixed reaction to Carlyle, but he still shows evidence of having read and absorbed a good bit of Carlyle. K. L. Knickerbocker's "Sources of Swinburne's 'Les Noyades'" (*PQ*, 1933) finds *The French Revolution* in the background. "C. T." in "Carlyle and Swinburne" (*N&Q*, 1953) looks at Swinburne's anti-Carlyle utterances as having been provoked by some severe Carlyle aspersion on Swinburne. Wendell Stacy Johnson (*ELN*, 1963) reports some of the cutting references the two men made to each other, all having to do with cesspools and refuse, but notes that Swinburne probably borrowed the Tree Igdrasil image in *Hertha* from Carlyle.

TENNYSON. This vital relationship is always referred to in the biographies and has been pursued by Sanders in studies of the correspondence. Among many articles, De Witt T. Starnes has the earliest (*Texas Rev.*, 1921). The indefatigable "Memorabilist" touches on it (*N&Q*, 1943). There are several instances of Tennyson adapting or echoing Carlyle ideas and phrasings. W. D. Templeman pursues an important one in "Tennyson's 'Locksley Hall' and Thomas Carlyle" (*Booker Memorial Studies*, 1950); R. A. Greenberg examines another in "Possible Source of Tennyson's 'Tooth and Claw'" (*MLN*, 1956); and George O. Marshall still another in "An Incident from Carlyle in Tennyson's *Maud*" (*N&Q*, 1959). Clyde de L. Ryals in "The 'Heavenly Friend': The 'New Mythus' of *In Memoriam*" (*Personalist*, 1962) parallels Tennyson's spiritual crisis to Carlyle's in *Sartor*. The best study of the personal relationship is C. R. Sanders' skillful and engaging "Carlyle and Tennyson" (*PMLA*, 1961).

THACKERAY. Little has been done on this subject. Jean-Marie Carré has edited a letter, "Une Lettre inédite de Thackeray sur Carlyle (1846)" (*RLC*, 1949). Of interest too is Russell A. Fraser's "Shooting Niagara in the Novels of Thackeray and Trollope" (*MLQ*, 1958). C. R. Sanders has completed a lengthy study of the

Carlyle-Thackeray relationship that should appear soon. THOREAU. Walter Harding (*TSB*, 1967) and George Monteiro and John C. Wyllie (*Center for Editions of American Authors Newsletter*, 1968, 1969) treat a rather curious word-use in Thoreau's essay on Carlyle from 1847. Thomas Woodson's "The Two Beginnings of *Walden*: A Distinction of Styles" (*ELH*, 1968) includes reference to Carlyle. TROLLOPE. The study cited under Mill on Trollope's racial attitudes as influenced by Carlyle should be considered here as well. Wilson B. Gragg (*NCF*, 1958) profitably approaches the connection through Trollope's parody of Carlyle in *The Warden*. N. John Hall (*NCF*, 1972) shows Trollope, like so many Victorians, echoing Carlyle even while rejecting him. TWAIN. The most extensive consideration of Carlyle's influence on Twain, especially the influence of *The French Revolution* and *Sartor Resartus*, is offered by Howard G. Baetzhold's *Mark Twain and John Bull: The British Connection* (1970). According to D. S. Bertolloti, Jr., the Clothes Philosophy appears in Twain's *A Connecticut Yankee* ("Mark Twain Revisits the Tailor," *MTJ*, 1967).

UHLAND. See T. P. Armstrong, "Carlyle and Uhland: Parallel Passages" (*N&Q*, 1935). UNAMUNO. Several articles detail Carlyle's influence on Unamuno: C. Claveria's (*CHA*, 1949), Anna Krause's (*CL*, 1956), and, most interesting, Peter G. Earle's "Unamuno and the Theme of History" (*HR*, 1964), which considers Unamuno's enthusiasm for Carlyle and other writers of the "emphatic school." VARNHAGEN VON ENSE. See H. G. Fiedler (*MLR*, 1943). WHEELER. Wheeler was an Emerson associate who was zealous in advancing Carlyle's American fortunes, and his activities are chronicled in John O. Eidson's "Charles Stearns Wheeler: Emerson's Good Grecian" (*N&Q*, 1954).

WHITMAN. Quite a considerable amount of material is available on Carlyle's influence on Whitman. Joseph Jay Rubin's "Whitman and Carlyle: 1846" (*MLN*, 1938) identifies Whitman's first mention of Carlyle as 1846 and shows that Whitman enjoyed Carlyle's *Cromwell*. Gregory Paine's "The Literary Relations of Whitman and Carlyle" (*SP*, 1939) explores the whole topic, and Joseph Jay Rubin adds a further note to Paine's findings in "Carlyle on Contemporary Style" (*MLN*, 1942). Fred Manning Smith has two interesting articles on Whitman's intellectual indebtedness to Carlyle, "Whitman's Poet-Prophet and Carlyle's Hero" (*PMLA*, 1940) and "Whitman's Debt to Carlyle's *Sartor Resartus*" (*MLQ*, 1942). Smith argues that Carlyle not Emerson should be thought of as Whitman's master. Alice L. Cooke's "Whitman as a Critic" (*Walt Whitman Newsletter*, 1958) discusses Whitman's disagreements with Carlyle's *Shooting Niagara* and some of his agreements too, as expressed in *Democratic Vistas*. The same topic is pursued in Joseph Jones's "Carlyle, Whitman, and the Democratic Dilemma" (*ESA*, 1960), where Whitman's reaction is described as one of "shock." Finally, W. A. Little's "Walt Whitman and the *Nibelungenlied*" (*PMLA*, 1965) suggests that Carlyle's *Miscellanies* may have been a source for Whitman's knowledge of the German epic. WHITTIER. The widespread abolitionist disillusionment with Carlyle's "Nigger Question" and *Latter-Day Pamphlets* was strongly felt by Whittier, according to Roland Woodwell (*ESQ*, 1968), and provoked replies from the poet. WORDSWORTH. Carlyle's response to the poet is best examined through his own *Reminiscences*. There is also Swanson's article cited under Coleridge. But a fuller study should be undertaken. YEATS. Brian John's "Yeats and Carlyle" (*N&Q*, 1970) points out some suggestive parallels between the two.

Some other studies cover Carlyle's influence on more than one figure. Cazamian in *Le Roman social en Angleterre* claims a powerful social influence for Carlyle on novelists like Mrs. Gaskell and Kingsley. Kathleen Tillotson in *Novels of the Eighteen-Forties* (1954) shows that Carlyle's influence extended deeply to the aesthetics of the novel as well. That Carlyle inspired some Victorian novelists to use official statistics with passion is shown by Sheila M. Smith's "Blue Books and Victorian Novelists" (*RES*, 1970). Yet there are still no full studies of Carlyle's influence on many of the novelists of the age. How the magazines reacted to Carlyle in his own age has been studied only in Jules Paul Seigel's "Thomas Carlyle and the Periodical Press" (Diss. Maryland 1966). Sabura Ota offers "Carlyle's Relation with Modern Japanese Literature" (*Tokyo Stud. in Eng.*, 1967). A number of studies by Yutaka Kikuchi on aspects of Carlyle should be cited here because they are in Japanese and therefore of limited accessibility: "Carlyle's Conception of Sincerity" (*Thought Currents in English Literature*, 1954), "Carlyle's Reverence for Shakespeare," "Carlyle's Poetic Spirit as Referred to by Akutagawa Ryunosuke," "Carlyle's Description of Louis xv in *The French Revolution*" (all in the *J. of Aoyama Gakuin Women's Coll.*, 1960, 1964, and 1969), and "Lafcadio Hearn's Interpretation of Carlyle" (*Gakugei*, 1968).

Such a various gathering as the preceding points on the one hand to the range and variety of Carlyle's own interests and on the other to his interest for and influence upon many others. Probably no single work could fit all this comfortably together, but a broad study of Carlyle's impact on other literary figures could go far toward making the kind of sense and pattern out of his role in nineteenth-century thought that these studies in isolation cannot do.

Carlyle's Thought and Ideas

Religious and Philosophical Ideas

Two main sources of Carlyle's ideas have been generally recognized: Calvinism and German idealist philosophy. The German sources have been more deeply investigated, the most sustained examinations being the work of two eminent Carlyle scholars, C. F. Harrold and Hill Shine. Harrold's study of Carlyle's indebtedness to German philosophic sources, *Carlyle and German Thought, 1819–1834* (1934) remains the definitive study of this subject. Harrold points out where Carlyle misunderstood as well as where he understood, and subsequent criticism has loosely and wrongly taken it as established that Carlyle really did not understand German philosophy at all. Harrold, on the contrary, conclusively demonstrates that Carlyle was deeply indebted to Goethe, Schiller, Novalis and, through them as much as directly, to Kant, Fichte, and Schelling for his view of the world as a symbolic vesture, as in the Clothes Philosophy, and for his conception of the transcendent reality of the divine. Carlyle made fast and loose with the Kantian distinction between Reason and Understanding, which Carlyle interpreted in his own hierarchical way, and perhaps also with the Kantian concept of space and time, although Carlyle is not rigorously consistent on these matters, as Harrold later shows in his thorough introduction to *Sartor Resartus* (1937). What Harrold's study does not do, although it is sometimes supposed to have done so, is to treat Carlyle's response to German literature as such or the literary impact of his German studies. It does, however, supersede the earlier studies by W. Morgan (*QQ*, 1916) and C. E. Vaughan (*E&S*, 1910).

Harrold pursued his study of the nature and sources of Carlyle's thought in several subsequent articles, as well as in the introduction to *Sartor*. "The Mystical Element in Carlyle (1827–1834)" (*MP*, 1932) and "Carlyle and the Mystical Tradition" (*CathW*, 1935) examine the meaning of the Leith Walk experience and relate it to the larger tradition of Christian mysticism, although Harrold is reluctant to equate it fully with the experiences of the more fully developed medieval mystics. C. R. Sanders treats "The Question of Carlyle's Conversion" (*VN*, 1956), but the fullest examination is Carlisle Moore's "*Sartor Resartus* and the Problem of Carlyle's Conversion" (*PMLA*, 1955). Moore argues convincingly that it took Carlyle almost a full decade to move from the "Everlasting No" to the "Everlasting Yea," though the whole experience is compressed in *Sartor*. Harrold also turned his attention to the "Calvinist substructure" of Carlyle's thought in "The Nature of Carlyle's Calvinism" (*SP*, 1936), much superior to Wilhelm Grey's investigation of the same field in *Carlyle und das Puritanertum* (1937). But both see in Carlyle's Calvinistic upbringing the seeds of many of his later ideas. Grey believes that Carlyle's entire work was that of a puritan "Menschheitsprediger," but Harrold sees Carlyle's development as moving from German idealism to a reliance on the underlying Calvinism after the 1830's. Stanford Gwilliam's "Thomas Carlyle, Reluctant Calvinist" (Diss. Columbia 1966) also sees the dominant pattern in Carlyle's thought as that of his childhood Calvinism.

In his *Carlyle's Fusion of Poetry, History, and Religion by 1834* (1937) Hill Shine has incorporated previous articles on this topic (*PMLA*, 1935; *SP*, 1936). Less concerned with sources than Harrold, Shine endeavors to show how Carlyle adapted and amalgamated his ideas into a unique Carlylean blend. Carlyle had struggled with the "German philosophy problem" in 1826–27, then with religion and poetry in an effort to salvage the values in each and to eliminate the conflicts in all. He finally arrived at a fusion. But Shine also sees this fusion as having gradually given way to increasing Calvinism in the later Carlyle. Shine's *Carlyle's Early Reading to 1834* (1953) continues the interest in the development of Carlyle's thought and provides an indispensable resource for any work in this area in the listing of all works Carlyle read up to 1834. Shine's idea of Carlyle's thought as a fusion of his three main intellectual interests parallels some of C. R. Sanders' arguments in *Coleridge and the Broad Church Movement* (1942) where Carlyle is likened to Coleridge in having joined philosophy and religion. And in J. H. Muirhead's *The Platonic Tradition in Anglo-Saxon Philosophy* (1931) we learn that Carlyle's thought was a compound of Puritanism and German idealism. Dwight J. Simpson in "Carlyle and the Natural Law" (*Hist. of Ideas Newsletter*, 1955) takes Carlyle's thought back to even more fundamental philosophic views than Calvinism or German philosophy in that he finds it consonant with the Natural Law of Christian tradition. William H. Marwick in "Carlyle and Quakerism" (*Friends' Q.*, 1968) does not claim Quakerism as a source, but Carlyle's known respect for Quakers prompts him to seek similarities and differences between Carlyle's views and those of the Society of Friends. There are many points of contact, but nothing like identity.

In general, the modern studies combining interest in sources of Carlyle's thought with efforts to clarify and delineate the main lines of that thought are the best guides to Carlyle's religious and philosophical position, but some earlier studies of Carlyle the moral teacher still have value. George M. McCrie's *The Religion of Our Literature* (1875), John Beattie Crozier's *The Religion of the Future* (1880),

John Tulloch's *Movements of Religious Thought in Britain during the Nineteenth Century* (1885), and Joseph Forster's *Four Great Teachers* (1890) all see Carlyle as a powerful religious force even though he does not preach the whole of Christian doctrine. Richard Holt Hutton, however, in *Essays on Some of the Modern Guides of English Thought in Matters of Faith* (1887) sees Carlyle's thought as often destructive and believes that Carlyle was "irreverent" and lacked faith in man. Charles J. Goodwin in "Ethics of Carlyle" (*Int. J. of Ethics*, 1905) also finds Carlyle's metaphysics inadequate because unsystematic, but he praises Carlyle's sincerity, patience, obedience, and silence, a quality Hutton found absent in Carlyle. John R. Wilson examines Carlyle's existentialism (Diss. Kansas 1969).

Some German studies are at variance with one another on Carlyle's religion. Edvard Lehmann in "Die Religion Thomas Carlyles" (*Deutsche Rundschau*, 1910) claims that Carlyle's strength lies in his preaching that Christianity will fade away, while A. Klein in "Die Weltanschauung Carlyles" (*Neue Jahrbücher für das klassische Altertum*, 1916) says that there is no longer any value to Carlyle's teaching because it was really religious. J. Besch in *Sprecher Gottes in unserer Zeit* (1919) thinks Carlyle's message was religious and therefore of value. Herbert Leslie Stewart in "Carlyle's Conception of Religion" (*Amer. J. of Theol.*, 1917) is not even sure Carlyle is a theist. He likens his religious position to Wordsworth's. Both might be surprised to find their theism taken away from them. After disposing of Carlyle's religion, Stewart might be expected to be more severe on Carlyle's philosophy, but his "Carlyle's Place in Philosophy" (*Monist*, 1919) calls him a "brilliant amateur" who saw all the weaknesses of empiricism and utilitarianism and recognized that in grounding morals upon objective reason lay the basis of true metaphysics.

W. H. Dunn's *Lectures on Three Eminent Victorians* (1932) includes one on "Carlyle and the Eternal Verities" which concludes that Carlyle's great virtue was in supplying "moral energy." Dunn's essay is superior to two German studies on similar themes, L. Eckloff's "Thomas Carlyle als Denker-Dichter und Seher" (*Forschungen und Fortschritte*, 1937) and Hans Wittig's "Das innere Gefüge der Gedankenwelt Thomas Carlyles" (*Hist. Zeitschrift*, 1938). Granville Hicks's "Literature and Revolution" (*Eng. J.*, 1935) is unremarkable, as is Desmond Mac-Carthy's "The 'Momentous' View of Life" (*Listener*, 1931).

The best general assessment of Carlyle's intellectual position in nineteenth-century literature is Basil Willey's chapter in *Nineteenth-Century Studies* (1949). With grace and clarity Willey places Carlyle in relation to the religious and philo-sophical currents of his age and also makes telling observations on Carlyle's politi-cal ideas and their proper interpretation. He sees Carlyle's essential position and chief value as religious and considers him in the main a positive force in the age. Here again David Daiches' slighter *Carlyle and the Victorian Dilemma* should be cited for a less sanguine view. Northrop Frye's "The Problem of Spiritual Authority in the Nineteenth Century" (in *Literary Views*, ed. Carroll Camden, 1964; and in *Essays in English Literature from the Renaissance to the Victorian Age Presented to A. S. P. Woodhouse*, ed. M. MacLure and F. W. Watt, 1964) considers how Carlyle sought to provide a de jure authority to set beside de facto temporal authority, the need for spiritual authority being one of the most agonizing problems of the age. See also G. B. Tennyson's *Carlyle and the Modern World*.

While we now have a good grasp of the sources from which Carlyle drew his religious and philosophic ideas and some idea of their impact on the age, there is still no comprehensive study of Carlyle and religion that really unites these emphases. Nor have existing studies done justice to Carlyle's insights into the religious impulse which probably has more to do with his Hero doctrine than politics does. The new-found awareness of Carlyle's feeling for the demonic could also be turned to account in these matters. To take Carlyle seriously is to take his ideas about religion seriously.

Social and Political Ideas

Even though the most penetrating critics have agreed that Carlyle's central thrust is religious and philosophical, it is his social and political teachings that have attracted the main critical attention. This is partly because critics have found his social doctrines more accessible, though not necessarily more commendable, than his religious ones, and partly because our own age has been more obsessed with social than with religious concerns.

It is often hard to dissociate Victorian criticism of Carlyle's social ideas from criticism of his philosophic ones, for both stress his sincerity and moral teaching. Some still notable Victorian assessments mainly of Carlyle's social ideas are William L. Courtney in "Carlyle's Political Doctrines" (*FortR*, 1879); Alfred Francison, *National Lessons from the Life and Works of Thomas Carlyle* (1881); Henry Rose, *The New Political Economy* (1891); H. de B. Gibbins, *English Social Reformers* (1892); Vida D. Scudder, *Social Ideas in English Letters* (1898); and William Roscoe Thayer, *Throne Makers* (1899). In the main these authors are not revolted by Carlyle's opposition to democracy or his support of strong rule, even if they do not always agree with him; rather they stress the moral earnestness of his preaching and the valor of his contest with materialism and empiricism. Thayer, for example, likens him to Dr. Johnson in the eighteenth century and Milton in the seventeenth as the foremost preacher of his age.

Also worth brief mention from the first part of this century are Mary A. Ward's *Prophets of the Nineteenth Century* (1900); Jacques Gazeau's *L'Impérialisme anglais: Son évolution* (1903), a study attributing imperialistic inclinations to Carlyle; John MacCunn's *Six Radical Thinkers* (1907), a sympathetic account; and Louis Cazamian's *L'Angleterre moderne: Son évolution* (1912), which speaks of Carlyle's social ideas as an example of "régression féodale," and otherwise repeats the views expressed in his other studies of Carlyle.

Frederick W. Roe's *The Social Philosophy of Carlyle and Ruskin* (1921) is a good introduction to Carlyle's social ideas by a sympathetic critic. Indeed, some of the better examinations of Carlyle's social position have been those undertaken in comparing Carlyle with another figure, such as Emery Neff's *Carlyle and Mill*. In the case of Roe's book, it is likeness not unlikeness that is stressed. Roe sees in both Carlyle and Ruskin the primacy of the "human factor" and refuses to be drawn into the modern distortions of Carlyle's position. He insists that Carlyle never separated force from morality. Roe considers both Carlyle and Ruskin to be "radical and conservative in mingled strains" and concludes that the two were "heralds of a better order," which he incautiously saw dawning in 1921.

Many general assessments of Carlyle's social thought are concerned to relate him to one or more of the main social thrusts in the age, from Chartism to imperialism. Crane Brinton in *English Political Thought in the Nineteenth Century* (1933) relates him to both, with little or no credit given Carlyle for his contribution to either. The imperialist theme had been struck earlier by Gazeau and was again by

Friedrich Brie. In Brie's *Imperialistische Strömungen in der englischen Literatur* (1928) he held Coleridge and Southey to be imperialists of the school that later included Carlyle. None of the imperialist studies are very convincing and there is really not adequate material to make much of a case for Carlyle's role in late Victorian imperialism, though one can argue for his having contributed to the ideas that nurtured imperialism.

More profitable is the approach to Carlyle through those issues he spoke to so directly in the age: laissez-faire, the condition of England, the role of the modern worker. Bernard N. Schilling in *Human Dignity and the Great Victorians* (1946) reminds us of Carlyle's compassion for the economically depressed and his consistent speaking out for "our common humanity." Humphry House recognizes Carlyle's antipathy to politics which he says stemmed from his anti-eighteenth-century bias in "The Sage Who Despised Politicians" (*Listener*, 1951; rpt. in *All in Due Time*, 1955), but he believes Carlyle lacked any useful practical advice for his contemporaries. M. W. Flinn, however, in his edition of Chadwick's *Report on the Sanitary Condition of the Laboring Population* (1966) notes that Carlyle took an active interest in such matters and once agreed to annotate Chadwick's report even though his main interest was laissez-faire shortcomings rather than sanitation.

A more comprehensive view of Carlyle's social thought is generally to be found in German criticism, which takes Carlyle seriously as a social theorist. Unfortunately, such studies as W. A. Mesek's *Mensch, Geschichte und Staat bei Thomas Carlyle* (1935), C. Puhlmann's *Thomas Carlyle: Eine Studie über seine Welt- und Gesellschaftsanschauung* (1938), Paul Hulsmann's *Der wirtschaftsständische Gedanke in der englischen Literatur* (1939), or Adolf Ballmer's *Carlyles Stellung zu Theorie und Praxis des modernen Kapitalismus* (1940) are scarcely longer than their titles and hardly do justice to their subjects. But there are two substantial German studies in this vein, Friedrich Brie's "Theokratie und Gottesreich bei Thomas Carlyle" (*Hist. Jahrbuch*, 1949) and Jürgen Kedenburg's *Teleologisches Geschichtsbild und theokratische Staatsauffassung im Werke Thomas Carlyles* (1960). Brie's study is one of restrained sympathy for what he sees as Carlyle's advocacy of a theocracy. He argues that Carlyle's irrelevance today may turn out to be far more relevant tomorrow than we had supposed. Kedenburg's even more ambitious study holds that all of Carlyle's ideas—of the state and of history—are permeated by his God-centered view of life. Kedenburg makes perhaps too much of Carlyle's theories of historical periodicity; still, his and Brie's studies mark a healthy resurgence of German Carlyle scholarship after some regrettable excesses during the thirties.

A dominantly nineteenth-century focus, looking either before or after Carlyle for sources and influences of his social ideas, marks a considerable group of studies. Wesley L. Hunner's "Carlyle's Romantic Social Philosophy" (Diss. Wisconsin 1939) relates Carlyle's thought to the Romantic movement, as do William F. Kennedy's *Humanist versus Economist* (1958) and Elizabeth M. Vida's dissertation on German Romanticism and Carlyle (Toronto 1969). Two dissertations see some Carlyle influence on Fabianism, William R. Clark's "The Literary Aspects of Fabian Socialism" (Columbia 1952) and William C. Wilbur's "The Origin and Development of Fabian Socialism to 1890" (Columbia 1953). Carlyle is even credited with having contributed to the Gandhian notion of passive resistance in Harrison Hoblitzelle's "The War against War in the Nineteenth Century" (Diss. Columbia 1959).

Two works try to get at the matter of the medieval sources of Carlyle's thought, a subject frequently encountered in studies of *Past and Present*. Alice K. Chandler in *A Dream of Order: The Medieval Ideal in Nineteenth-Century English Literature* (1970) devotes a chapter to Carlyle, largely to *Past and Present*. She sees Carlyle's medievalism as having stimulated his concern for the poor and she sees Carlyle as transforming Cobbett's agrarian medievalism into a "feudalization of industry," a notion that profoundly influenced late Victorian and modern social legislation. Charles H. Kegel in "Medieval-Modern Contrasts Used for Social Purposes" (Diss. Michigan State 1955) includes Carlyle among other nineteenth-century figures. Kegel later published an article on an aspect of the same topic, "Lord John Manners and the Young England Movement" (*WPQ*, 1961), in which he holds that Manners learned much of his medievalism and his abhorrence of a do-nothing aristocracy from Carlyle's writings.

Carlyle's fondness for certain medieval ideas did not necessarily extend, as it did in Ruskin's case, to a distaste for modern technology. Herbert L. Sussman in *Victorians and the Machine* (1968) maintains that Carlyle was not hostile as such to the machine but that he could never find in the machine "a purpose beyond the purely material." Sussman's slight study is still, however, only a preliminary to a full examination of Carlyle and technology.

Now that it is less a sin to criticize democracy than it was a generation ago, Carlyle's distaste seems a shade less unforgivable than it did then. In *Quack, Quack!* (1935) Leonard Woolf could safely indulge in the quackery of blaming fascism on Carlyle and Carlyle's ideas on sadism and of suggesting that Carlyle was somehow attempting to please the "middle-class inhabitants of Chelsea and Kensington round about 1850." A very silly book. Earlier critics had blamed Carlyle for World War I. Marshall Kelly in *Carlyle and the War* (1915) and Stuart P. Sherman in "Carlyle and Kaiser-Worship" (*Nation*, 1918) are guilty of this foolishness.

Benjamin Evans Lippincott in *Victorian Critics of Democracy* (1938) attains some objectivity in isolating Carlyle's (and Ruskin's) antidemocratic sentiments, but he goes on to mar all by equating them with fascism and asserting that these ideas came to reality with Mussolini and Hitler. C. F. Harrold, predictably, had been wiser in his earlier comparison of Carlyle's and Mencken's criticisms of democracy (*SAQ*, 1927), noting that their criticisms are restatements and developments of Aristotle's. Of some interest here is Warren M. Morgan's "Carlyle's Concept of Democracy" (Diss. Wisconsin 1944), Eric Bentley's uneven *A Century of Hero-Worship* (1944) discussed earlier, and Ernst Cassirer's exemplary *The Myth of the State* (1946) to be discussed below, but William G. Walton's "Carlyle—Forgotten Prophet" (*Amer. Mercury*, 1969) is not an important treatment.

Carlyle's antidemocratic ideas (and the reaction against them) stem in large measure from his doctrine of the Hero, which has itself generated much comment (see below under individual works). But the best treatment of these matters is B. H. Lehman's *Carlyle's Theory of the Hero* (1928) which attempts to account for both the loss and gain to Carlyle's work as a result of his hero theory. Lehman applies Carlyle's criteria to the Sage himself with results that confirm Carlyle's sincerity yet show that his "Hero-Theory lessened his natural fitness" for certain kinds of thought. Friedrich Brie in *Helden und Heldenverehrung bei Thomas Carlyle* (1948) does not add a great deal to Lehman, but he emphasizes that Carlyle always held the Hero to be simultaneously "a commanding and a humble man chosen by God for truth," hardly the fascist caricature of both favorable German and hostile English criticism.

As to the question of Nazism, it can no more be passed over than the Froude controversy. It is still a classroom platitude that Carlyle was a "proto-Nazi," a charge on the same level as that Shakespeare was an anti-Semite. In Carlyle's case the matter has been hobgoblinized since World War I. Then he was held responsible for that conflict and, if truth be told, there is far more evidence, slight as it is, for Carlyle's Prussian sympathies than for his Nazi ones. Some earlier critiques have already been cited. There is also the pseudonymous article "Thomas Carlyle as the Catspaw of the Hohenzollerns" (*Nat. Rev.*, 1923), most charmingly titled but thoroughly asinine. Herbert L. Stewart in "The Alleged Prussianism of Carlyle" (*Int. J. of Ethics*, 1918) sought to counter these criticisms by pointing out that Carlyle's doctrine of Right equaling Might rests on theological grounds and has to do with a very, very long view of history. Stewart acknowledges that the doctrine runs the *risk* of becoming worship of what *is*. But then even more does Pope's.

It is not until the Nazi period that things really wax hot. Here the Nazis are more to blame than overanxious democrats, for the Nazis found in Carlyle a spokesman for some of their dearest convictions. Carlyle praised force, did he not? He liked strong leaders, he advocated obedience, he was a friend of Germany. So speak Wolfgang Keller in "Carlyle und der Führergedanke" (*Zeitschrift für franz-ösische und englischen Unterricht*, 1934), Wilhelm Vollrath in *Thomas Carlyle und H. St. Chamberlain, zwei Freunde Deutschlands* (1935), and H. Borbein in "Thomas Carlyle im Lichte des deutschen Schicksals" (*Neuphilologische Monats-schrift*, 1935). That Carlyle was read—or misread—in Nazi Germany is undeni-able. G. I. Morris in "Divine Hitler" (*NS*, 1935) cites his own experience in a Junker home in 1934 to show that *Heroes* was required reading for the "Abitur." A headmaster had told his students that "Ruskin and Carlyle were the first National Socialists." But the same social experience revealed that Hitler's divinity was dem-onstrated in church by comparison of the Führer to Moses, David, and Isaiah!

But the Nazi fantasies roll on. G. Heinemann in "Vom Führertum, Helden und Heldenverehrung" (*Die Deutsche höhere Schule*, 1935) salutes Carlyle as a forerunner of the *Führer*. P. Aldag in "Thomas Carlyle und die Juden" (*Geist der Zeit*, 1937) lauds Carlyle's anti-Semitism in "The Jew—Our Lawgiver" of 1853, a pamphlet by Thomas Carlyle the Advocate (see Krämer in Miscellanea above) and not by Carlyle at all! H. Dietz in "Thomas Carlyle und die politische Führerauslese des Engländers" (*Zeitschrift für Neusprachlichen Unterricht*, 1938) sees Carlyle as having anticipated Hitler, and Hildegard Gauger in *Die Psychologie des Schweigens in England* (1937) sees the Doctrine of Silence as a distinctly Nordic notion that Carlyle was privileged to advance and thereby become a "Künder des Führer-gedankens," both Carlyle and Hitler being cited as examples of silence! Finally, Theodor Deimel in *Carlyle und der Nationalsozialismus* (1937), the most sustained study, concedes that Carlyle differs from Nazism on two important counts: he has deficient racism (i.e., he does not hate Jews) and he persists in maintaining strong religious elements (i.e., he does not really endorse immoral leaders). All of which makes abundantly plain that Carlyle is a Nazi only by the grossest misread-ing. To leave out Carlyle's religious sentiments is to leave out the essential Carlyle. Deimel recognized this and chose to see Carlyle as simply deficient because of the darkness of the age in which he lived.

That Nazis would find such misreading justifiable is more understandable than that anti-Nazis would, but such is the zeal to place blame. Joseph E. Baker in "Carlyle Rules the Reich" (*SatR*, 1933) admits that Carlyle did not share Hitler's feeling about the Jews but feels he prepared the way for racism anyway. Herbert J.

C. Grierson's *Carlyle and Hitler* (1933) is more equivocal than its title implies. Hitler's name occurs only once in the text; and while Grierson thinks Carlyle led to Nietzsche he declines to speculate on what Carlyle's views would have been on twentieth-century "heroes." Ernest Seillière in *L'Actualité de Carlyle: Un précurseur du national-socialisme* (1939) finds Carlyle and Romanticism jointly responsible. Perhaps emboldened by other criticism and pushed over the brink by the actual outbreak of hostilities, Grierson in "The Hero and the Führer" (*Aberdeen Univ. Rev.*, 1940) confidently asserts, on the kind of absence of evidence he accuses Carlyle of in writing history, that Carlyle's "hero is well on the way to become a Hitler or a Stalin." William McGovern in *From Luther to Hitler* (1941) casts his net wider and hauls up Carlyle and Ruskin among many others as "a prelude to Naziism and Hitler." Irene P. McKeehan in "Carlyle, Hitler, and Emerson" (*Univ. of Colo. Stud.*, 1942) manages by selective misreading to find Carlyle but not Emerson as a forerunner of Hitler. Sympathy for the distress of the laboring poor she identifies as a "democratic sentiment." Carlyle being opposed to democracy could not have had it, and that's that.

Yet there is worse. Cuthbert Wright's "Carlyle and the Present Crisis" (*Commonweal*, 1943) says Carlyle "licked Prussia's bootjacks," if you will, and that his "whole metaphysical, ethical and personal trend was so emblematic of the Nazi soul and the Nazi state" that if he were alive today (1943) the government would throw him in jail and give him a mild taste of martyrdom. J. Salwyn Schapiro in "Thomas Carlyle, Prophet of Fascism" (*J. of Mod. Hist.*, 1945) sounds the ominous but now increasingly familiar note that social philosophers must be revaluated in the light of the present crisis. On such a revaluation Carlyle turns out to be a Nazi. Moreover, he was not a very good writer or thinker, has no followers and no ancestors, contributed to laissez-faire (!), and has importance only in having continued the tradition that led to Nazism. Pierette le Corre-Guiart in "Carlyle et le Neo-Socialisme" (*LanM*, 1953) adds the latest and one could hope final footnote to this curious literature, citing the protofascist character of Carlyle's writing, but noting some discrepancies. The discrepancies are the things we minimize when talking about Carlyle's Nazism.

It is well to remember in this matter that Carlyle died aged and infirm eight years before Adolf Hitler was born and fifty-five years before Hitler through the agency of democracy became Chancellor of Germany. The word Nazism was not in Carlyle's vocabulary nor in anyone else's when he died. Thus what is always being discussed are alleged *affinities* between Carlyle's thought and the doctrines of the Nazi movement. Some of these affinities are, of course, real, just as there are affinities between Carlyle's thought and other forms of socialism, but the merest scholarly restraint should have curbed both English and German commentators from such excesses as the previous studies exhibit, and Carlyle's own tendency toward verbal excess would have proved cautionary to those who were genuinely in search of the truth and not in search merely of a champion or a scapegoat.

Ernst Cassirer in *The Myth of the State* (1946) makes a serious attempt to understand Carlyle's ideas of the hero and of history and in so doing rejects the charge that Carlyle was a fascist or led others to fascism. Cassirer's study delves into the personal background and the influence of Goethe and Fichte. He emphasizes that Carlyle's hero was marked by two criteria, "insight" and "sincerity," and that Carlyle's celebrated "Might is Right" doctrine (which Carlyle repeatedly clarified in his own lifetime) always means "moral right" and "moral might." One cannot help adding that Carlyle's refusal to take the full leap into modernism and the exaltation of the self, which has been deplored by more than one modern critic, is the very reason that Carlyle cannot be called a fascist, for it is the setting of self above the moral law that makes possible fascism and all the other forms of totalitarianism which those same moderns affect to bewail.

Like the Froude controversy, the Carlyle as Nazi theme has died away as far as any direct writings on the topic are concerned, but the ghost continues to haunt the old premises. To point out that scholars are as prone as any other class of humankind to fatuity may not seem entirely satisfactory, though true. The still skeptical should turn to Carlyle himself on the subject of the Hero and ask whether Hitler, Mussolini, or Stalin would readily fall into the company of Odin, Shakespeare, Dante, and Samuel Johnson. To be sure, Carlyle praises "repressive" heroes too—Mahomet, Cromwell, Knox—but it is not clear why these should be taken as solely representative of his view of the Hero. Nor is it clear that Carlyle's praise of them is quite the same thing as the advocacy of gas chambers or slave labor camps. If there is to be any further work on this topic let us hope that it is undertaken by someone who wants to see Carlyle steadily and whole and not by either a whitewasher or a witch-hunter.

Ideas on History

Much of Carlyle's thought on democracy, fascism, and even the Hero emerged from his historical studies. The sources for this thought are treated by Harrold, Shine, and Moore, and are intimately connected with his belief that history is the record of man's contact with the divine. But critics are divided on the histories themselves. Some early studies strike the pros and cons. Lewis G. James (*Westminster Rev.*, 1889) found Carlyle deficient in historical perspective and in understanding of democracy. G. P. Gooch in *History and Historians in the Nineteenth Century* (1913) claimed Carlyle was a master of portrait painting and the "greatest of showmen," but faulty in his blindness to the masses and in his repressive philosophy of later years. Lytton Strachey in *Portraits in Miniature* has already been cited for his frivolous view of Carlyle which extended to Carlyle's histories.

That able Carlyle apologist Herbert L. Stewart (*Pol. Sci. Q.*, 1917) allowed that Carlyle suffered from too much subjectivity in writing history, but claimed for him first place as a historian who recognized the movement of ideas and beliefs in whole societies as opposed to mere political history. George Macaulay Trevelyan in "Carlyle as an Historian" (*NC*, 1899; frequently reprinted) is more measured than Stewart but still claims large areas of Carlyle's histories as valid and valuable. Trevelyan says that men of genius have rarely written history and Carlyle is an exception. His strengths include his feeling for the romance of history and his combination of poetry and realism. *The French Revolution* best fills this description in Trevelyan's view. Carlyle's weaknesses, however, are one-sidedness, excessive hero-worship, and his emotional view of the universe. Karl Bachmann's *Die Geschichtsauffassung Thomas Carlyles* (1938) manages to damn with fulsome praise by claiming that Carlyle's view of history, like Milton's, was that of England as the elect among nations and the sister of Germany. It is not a helpful study.

James W. Thompson and Bernard J. Holm's *A History of Historical Writing* (1942) and F. R. Flournoy's "Thomas Carlyle" (in *Some Modern Historians of Britain*, ed. Herman Ausubel et al., 1951) are slight popular studies that make the customary claims and disclaimers for Carlyle's histories. Only slightly more substantial are the essays by Noel Annan, "Historians Reconsidered" (*Hist. Today*, 1952), and A. J. P. Taylor, "The Art of Writing History" (*Listener*, 1953), the former treating Carlyle as a "romantic historicist" in search of the moral in history, the latter less sympathetic as regards Carlyle's ideas (Hitler surfaces here again) but hospitable as regards his method. Both consider *The French Revolution* Carlyle's masterpiece. Robert E. Kusch in "Carlyle's View of the Eighteenth Century" (Diss. Northwestern 1965) gives chapter and verse for Carlyle's known dislike of the age of negativism.

The most extensive study of Carlyle as historian is that by Louise M. Young in *Thomas Carlyle and the Art of History* (1939), which endeavors to show both the background and theory of Carlyle as historian and to make a claim for Carlyle's blend of philosophy, art, and science in writing history. She devotes her final chapter to Carlyle's position as a historian but it is more a defense of Carlyle's theory and method than an assessment of his position. Of all his works Young claims that it is his histories alone that "are works of art that will endure."

Pieter Geyl's challenging estimate in *Debates with Historians* (1955) is far more critical than Young's. Geyl is especially severe on Carlyle's defenders and he overpraises Eric Bentley's study, but Geyl almost uniquely discerns that the traditional interpretation of Carlyle's shift to reaction about 1850, though he subscribes to it, poses a problem. There is a bifurcation that he recognizes needs to be bridged, even though his essay does not bridge it. Geyl subsequently in *Use and Abuse of History* (1956) numbers Carlyle among the great writers of history, a species now rare because of specialization.

Roger Sharrock's "Carlyle and the Sense of History" (*E&S*, 1966) is a disorganized but scintillating essay that treats as much Carlyle's style as his sense of history. Sharrock maintains that Carlyle, while contributing to the modern deterministic sense of history, himself escaped this fate by virtue of a compassion that sees men "caught in the toils of events" and preserves him from abstract determinism. Also concerned with Carlyle's manner in the writing of history is Carlisle Moore's valuable "Carlyle's *Diamond Necklace* and Poetic History" (*PMLA*, 1943), in which Moore specifically examines the literary consequences of Carlyle's fusion of history, poetry, and religion in the work Moore considers to be an apprentice study for the writing of *The French Revolution*. These consequences are mainly Carlyle's use of fictional techniques in writing nonfiction, a theme that has become popular in recent literary critical approaches to Carlyle.

The aspect of Carlyle's historical thought that has surprisingly generated the greatest amount of comment is the question of progress and periodicity in history and the degree of Carlyle's indebtedness for this latter concept to the Saint-Simonians. Albrecht Ströle's *Thomas Carlyles Anschauung vom Fortschritt in der Geschichte* (1909) is an early venture into this realm, not concerned with Saint-Simonianism, but rather with demonstrating that Carlyle had a genuine concept of progress in history. John W. Stevenson's "Carlyle and the Idea of Progress" (Diss. Vanderbilt 1954) also argues for Carlyle's optimistic belief in an upward spiral of history toward a state of spiritual realization.

But the major thrust of scholarship in this area has been reserved for the question of Saint-Simonianism. More than a half-dozen studies have grappled with the problem with no absolutely final resolution yet reached. David Brooks Confer's *Saint-Simonism in the Radicalism of Thomas Carlyle* (1931) is less concerned, however, than later studies with the question of periodicity and more concerned with aligning Carlyle's social theories with those of the "father of socialism and the institutor of the labor union." Like most subsequent studies, Confer's lays extraordinary stress on Carlyle's correspondence with the Saint-Simonian Gustave d'Eichthal and on Carlyle's lost translation of Saint-Simon's *Nouveau Christianisme*. Confer sees *Past and Present* as the culmination of Carlyle's Saint-Simonianism. In the same vein are Ella M. Murphy's dissertation (Iowa 1933) and her article (*SP*, 1936), Friedrich Hayek's *The Counter-Revolution of Science* (1952), and Richard K. P. Pankhurst's *The Saint-Simonians, Mill and Carlyle* (1957), which clearly attributes Saint-Simonian ideas to both men, as does Dwight N. Lindley's "The Saint-Simonians: Mill and Carlyle" (Diss. Columbia 1958).

The issue of historical periodicity—alternating epochs of belief and unbelief, or organic and critical—has attracted such scholars as Hill Shine and René Wellek. The issue is not so much *whether* Carlyle had such a concept—he clearly did—as just what he meant by it and whether he held it sociologically or romantically, that is, from the rationalist or intuitive point of view. Hill Shine in *Carlyle and the Saint-Simonians: The Concept of Historical Periodicity* (1941) argues that Carlyle, while already moving in the direction of a concept of alternating epochs, acquired a form and focus for such views from his encounter in 1830–31 with Saint-Simonian thought and that his writings after that time—chiefly *Sartor* through *Past and Present*, less so later—reflect precisely this Saint-Simonian formulation of the idea. Shine's scholarship is extremely thorough, yet his conclusions have been tellingly challenged by Wellek and others.

Wellek in "Carlyle and the Philosophy of History" (*PQ*, 1944; rpt. in *Confrontations*, 1965) takes Shine to task for overemphasizing Saint-Simonian influence and also Louise Young for attributing to Carlyle a Hegelian concept of history when Carlyle was really a moralist and Calvinist Christian. Wellek insists that Carlyle has a penetrating awareness of the mystery of history and a healthy avoidance of the schematizing of history so characteristic of sociologists, historicists, and other moderns. Wellek's rejection of sociological interpretations of Carlyle on history was supported by Cassirer in *The Myth of the State*. Although Young had stressed Carlyle's indebtedness to Herder, and C. F. Harrold touched on the matter, Wellek maintained that Herder's concept of palingenesis was more influential for Carlyle's thought than had been acknowledged and that it was from such sources (another is Goethe in the *West-Östlicher Divan*) that Carlyle derived his periodic concepts, not from the Saint-Simonians.

Shine responded to the implied challenge in Wellek and presented a thorough examination of Carlyle and Herder in "Carlyle's Early Writings and Herder's *Ideen*: The Concept of History" (*Booker Memorial Studies*, 1950). While he shows Carlyle's affinities with Herder's concepts of history and nature as revelation, he does not yield in his insistence on Carlyle's Saint-Simonianism in regard to periodicity. It may be that this is a question that admits of no final solution. One must acknowledge that Shine clearly has the edge in the matter of careful examination of Carlyle's writings and scholarship but Wellek's position is in other ways more philosophically sophisticated and more consonant with Carlyle's whole intellectual position and the "feel" of Carlyle's writings. It seems likely that Carlyle, having developed his views in the 1820's, as Shine's own research has amply demonstrated, was still eclectic enough in 1830 to adopt the Saint-Simonian formulation without adopting the Saint-Simonian rationalist assumptions behind it.

Although Saint-Simonianism may benefit from a rest period in Carlyle studies, there is room for more work on Carlyle as a historian. Taking off from Wellek, a future critic might well examine not Carlyle's sources, but his mature philosophy of history, and others could turn to individual historical works, some of which are still poorly served by criticism.

Literary Criticism, Artistry, and Style

Whatever else he is, Carlyle is a literary artist and the most individual stylist in the language. In recent years the literary-critical approach to Carlyle has proved to be the most popular and fruitful approach of all, especially since the earlier preoccupation with Carlyle's philosophy has lost much of its appeal. Of course the better literary-critical studies also treat Carlyle's ideas, but they do so with due regard for his manner of presenting them. Moreover, the literary approach has in our time attracted the most capable minds in Carlyle studies, and one can hope that no future student of Carlyle will ignore his extraordinary literary gifts. The studies considered below range from the most narrowly linguistic to the most broadly critical. They have in common the approach to Carlyle through his art.

Early on, critics recognized that Carlyle's language was a special domain. One of the first responses to its challenge was to catalog kinds and varieties of word use, and the fascination with this approach has never entirely disappeared. M. Krummacher's "Notizen über den Sprachgebrauch Carlyles" (*Eng. Studien*, 1883) is such a catalog; more usefully, Otto Schmeding's *Über Wortbildung bei Carlyle* (1900) was concerned to examine how Carlyle coined words, and Vernon Lee's (Violet Paget's) "Carlyle and the Present Tense" (*ConR*, 1904) is the first study to examine the implications of this essential aspect of Carlyle's style. George Saintsbury repeatedly directed his attention to Carlyle's style and the best of his remarks can be found in his *History of English Prose Rhythm* (1912). One of the best early German considerations of Carlyle's style and also of his writings in a larger sense is Heinrich Kraeger's monograph "Carlyle's Stellung zur deutschen Sprache und Literatur" (*Anglia*, 1899). Kraeger incorporates his earlier piece in *Anglia* on "Wotton Reinfred" and directs intelligent attention to Carlyle's translations and to his word use and German word references.

Later specialized examinations of aspects of Carlyle's diction and style include Carla Weidemann's "Biblische Stilelemente bei Carlyle" (*GRM*, 1927) and Mary B. Deaton's "Thomas Carlyle's Use of Metaphor" (*CE*, 1944), chiefly illustrated from *Sartor*. Harold Wentworth, in "The Allegedly Dead Suffix -dom in Modern English" (*PMLA*, 1941), shows how alive that suffix is in Carlyle's exuberant coinages, since he was by himself responsible for more than half of all such in the nineteenth century. Wentworth's data is further exploited by Robert M. Estrich and Hans Sperber in *Three Keys to Language* (1952). They becloud their interpretation of Carlyle's verbal variety with considerations of a dubiously biographical kind, but what is undeniably clear is that no other nineteenth-century author approaches Carlyle's verbal ingenuity. Earlier catalogs have shown that Carlyle did not rest content with creations in -*dom* but liberally coined with -*ness*, -*hood*, and other suffixes, and also coined by free use of prefixes. The definitive study of these matters is still wanting.

Two German studies carry on the tradition of the word catalog and the detailed sentence study: Wilhelm Döppelheuer's *Untersuchung des Satzbaus in den*

Werken Thomas Carlyles (1961) is especially directed toward German influences, and Hans-Werner Ludwig's *Die Self-Komposita bei Thomas Carlyle, Matthew Arnold, und Gerard Manley Hopkins* (1963) reveals some interesting facts about words compounded with *self-* in the three authors. Not surprisingly, Carlyle uses twice as many such compounds as Arnold and three times as many as Hopkins. One should add, though the author does not, that Carlyle's writings exceed in bulk those of the other two authors by approximately the same measures.

More broadly on the matter of Carlyle's style there have been approaches through painting, symbolism, and rhetoric. One approach has been through Carlyle's visual emphasis. An anonymous piece, "Carlyle the Cinematographer" (*AM*, 1924), makes some telling comparisons, but the most cultivated approach has been through painting. Benjamin B. Chamberlin in "Carlyle as a Portrait Painter" (*SR*, 1928) is one of the first to liken Carlyle to the painter, in this case to postimpressionists. Logan Pearsall Smith in his much reprinted "Carlyle: The Rembrandt of English Prose" (*Reperusals and Recollections*, 1936) makes a great deal of Carlyle's Rembrandtesque chiaroscuro and word painting and too little of everything else in Carlyle. C. R. Sanders has taken up and enriched Pearsall Smith's Rembrandt comparison in his "The Victorian Rembrandt: Carlyle's Portraits of His Contemporaries" (*BJRL*, 1957). Sanders has gathered together many of Carlyle's most brilliant sketches of his contemporaries, but more than that, Sanders argues that Carlyle's incisive portraits are miniature reflections of his whole system of values. As illustration, he assembles Carlyle's comments over a thirty-year period on Queen Victoria. The result is both instructive and enjoyable; one could wish for an entire anthology of such Carlyle pieces.

Francis X. Roellinger's "The Early Development of Carlyle's Style" (*PMLA*, 1957) is still one of the most thorough studies of this topic, even though Roellinger is not convincing in his argument that Carlylese was developed specifically for Teufelsdröckh. James R. Sutherland's *On English Prose* (1957) is of slight value in regard to Carlyle's style which it purports to treat because of its class preoccupation and general lack of sympathy with the subject. Some useful observations appear in the introduction to William E. Buckler's *Prose of the Victorian Period* (1958). The importance of symbols in Carlyle's style has been studied by John M. Lindberg (Diss. Wisconsin 1957), by Robert Louis Peters in "Some Illustrations of Carlyle's Symbolist Imagery" (*VN*, 1959), and by Richard A. Levine in "Carlyle as Poet: The Phoenix Image in 'Organic Filaments'" (*VN*, 1964). A specialized use of an image is noted by G. B. Tennyson, "The True Shekinah Is Man" (*AN&Q*, 1964). Geoffrey Carter's "Carlyle's Use of Metaphor in His Essays" (Diss. Pennsylvania 1969) discerns three main types of metaphor—mechanistic, organicist, and cognitive—in Carlyle's early writings.

Paul West in "Carlyle's Creative Disregard" (*Melbourne Critical Rev.*, 1962) shows some of what can be done in understanding Carlyle through a thoughtful and imaginative response to his style. He calls that style "Cyrenaic," and, while he at times lets his critical imagination run away with him, he nevertheless makes some striking observations about Carlyle's relation to his age through his analysis of style. John Lindberg in "The Decadence of Style: Symbolic Structure in Carlyle's Later Prose" (*SSL*, 1964) tries to cope with the problem of the style of the later acerbic Carlyle, which he sees as having moved from means to ends in Carlyle's career. The essay does not convince, but it treats a valid problem in Carlyle studies. A slightly similar issue is raised in Henry Ebel's "The Contrary Voice: Patterns of Crisis in the Prose of Arnold and Carlyle" (Diss. Columbia 1965).

Carlyle's rhetoric has long been recognized as an inexhaustible world unto itself, difficult of analytical access, but recent studies have had the admirable example of John Holloway to follow in trying to get at it. Holloway's *The Victorian Sage* (1953) treats "philosophy and rhetoric" in the works of six Victorian prose writers, with two chapters devoted to Carlyle. The book is the best indication of the modern direction spoken of earlier whereby matter and manner are jointly investigated as integrally part of one another. Holloway reduces Carlyle's ideas to a few central propositions and shows how his rhetoric is calculated to induce acceptance of those propositions. By skillful use of parallels and juxtaposed passages, Holloway is able to demonstrate that "no part of Carlyle's prose seems quite unrelated to his overriding purpose." Holloway's seminal study has quite rightly exercised an influence on virtually all the good stylistic analysis of Carlyle that has come after him. The studies of symbolism and style cited above reflect some of Holloway's insights.

Among the most important recent studies reflecting Holloway's influence are Tennyson's *"Sartor" Called "Resartus"* and George Levine's challenging "The Uses and Abuses of Carlylese" in *The Art of Victorian Prose* (1968). Levine rightly insists upon considering Carlyle's style part and parcel of his thought and he struggles manfully to salvage what of each he can, but he simply cannot go all the way with the later Carlyle, which is where he concentrates his study in this essay. Nor can Mark Roberts in "Carlyle and the Rhetoric of Unreason" (*EIC*, 1968), but he recognizes some of Carlyle's characteristic methods. The problem is really that of how literally to take Carlyle's more extravagant language, especially in the later period. Levine wants to insist that, however much allowance we make for Carlylean hyperbole and Carlylean transformation of things and even people into symbols, there must still adhere some literal residue, and it is this minimal literal meaning that he so often finds unpalatable. The probable explanation is that we still have not fully mastered the vocabulary to express the necessary kind of reading that a style like Carlyle's requires and finally that in some instances Carlyle *wanted* to be unpalatable.

One recent explicitly rhetorical approach to Carlyle's style making use of the computer, Frederick L. Burwick's "Stylistic Continuity and Change in the Prose of Thomas Carlyle" (in *Statistics and Style*, ed. L. Doležel and R. W. Bailey, 1969), is highly technical and directed toward proving the dubious proposition that Carlyle's rhetoric becomes more and more "exuberantly associational" as he matures. By "associational" the author refers to the rhetorical principles of the Scottish associationist rhetoricians in which he alleges Carlyle would have been trained. It is not at all clear that Carlyle subscribed to associationist principles or desired to illustrate them, although the computer dutifully finds what it is bidden to. Some useful rhetorical principles are illustrated on the way and the rhetorical approach to Carlyle's style probably would yield a good deal more if further pursued. Another quantitative approach to Carlyle's style is offered by Robert L. Oakman (Diss. Indiana 1970).

An excellent means of insight into Carlyle's style, though it does not supply any critical vocabulary, is through parody. Joyce brilliantly parodied Carlyle in the "Oxen of the Sun" chapter in *Ulysses*, and Hugh Kingsmill goes one better in "Some Modern Light Bringers" (*Bookman*, 1932; variously reprinted), wherein he takes on a group of modern writers as though he were Carlyle disposing of their grosser follies and more exasperating inanities. But the whole approach is a highly imaginative form of criticism.

Kingsmill's parodies remind us that Carlyle himself was no mean humorist, but the subject has scarcely been touched by critics. William Samuel Lilly in *Four English Humorists of the Nineteenth Century* (1895) considers Dickens, Thackeray, Eliot, and Carlyle, but he makes only the barest remarks on the actual subject of humor, noting that Carlyle's "playfulness is of the grimmest." Thomas Wentworth Higginson's *Carlyle's Laugh and Other Surprises* (1909) also fails to explore in depth. A. H. Upham in "Rabelaisianism in Carlyle" (*MLN*, 1918) is more specific, citing six features of Carlyle's humor that he finds Rabelaisian.

Two recent studies of Carlyle's humor agree only in part on its effectiveness. Richard J. Dunn in " 'Inverse Sublimity': Carlyle's Theory of Humor" (*UTQ*, 1970) is clear enough on Carlyle's early theory of humor, but he thinks the later Carlyle fell short of his own goal. Ronald L. Trowbridge in "Thomas Carlyle's Masks of Humor" (*Mich. Academician*, 1970), however, makes an effort to redeem Carlyle in general as a humorist. Clarence J. Wolfshohl's "Thomas Carlyle: Comedy and the Comic Vision" (Diss. New Mexico 1969) sees Carlyle's practice in Coleridgean terms. Tennyson's *"Sartor" Called "Resartus"* devotes a section to the philosophic grounds of Carlyle's humor. Max K. Sutton's " 'Inverse Sublimity' in Victorian Humor" (*VS*, 1966) is so far the best examination of Carlyle's kind of humor and its influence on other Victorians. Sutton and Tennyson both trace the philosophic origins of Carlyle's humor to Jean Paul, which is clearly the direction for future criticism.

Carlyle's critical theories have been the subject of some worthwhile study and frequently such studies cast light on Carlyle's own literary practice. Frederick William Roe's *Thomas Carlyle as a Critic of Literature* (1910) is still the best study of this neglected aspect of Carlyle's work. Roe notes that Carlyle excelled in insight and knowledge, but that he was capricious in his sympathies and frequently lacking in detachment. Roe also acknowledges Carlyle's pioneering critical role in the Victorian age. Roe was followed by only two comparable studies, one Elizabeth Nichols, "The Consistency of Carlyle's Literary Criticism" (Diss. Michigan 1931), the other a study chiefly taken up with the origins of Carlyle's critical principles, Alfredo Obertello's *Carlyle's Critical Theories: Their Origin and Practice* (1948). Obertello concludes that Carlyle's true critical service was in bringing German literature to his countrymen and that his own critical principles all rested on moral judgments. And there can be little doubt that Carlyle was an intensely moral critic, and one highly interesting illumination of his moral bent is well traced in Patricia M. Ball's "Sincerity: The Rise and Fall of a Critical Term" (*MLR*, 1964). She shows that it was largely the emotional intensity and spiritual authority of Carlyle that gave to the term *sincerity* its special positive force for Victorians. Koenraad W. Swart in " 'Individualism' in the Mid-Nineteenth Century" (*JHI*, 1962) says even Carlyle did not use the word *individualism* to describe his cultural ideas. The term was in flux in the age.

After Roe the best illustration of Carlyle's critical principles is that set forth by Alba H. Warren, Jr. in *English Poetic Theory, 1825–1865* (1950). Warren is concerned with Carlyle's influence on the poetic theory of the age and not with his total role as a critic, but within his scope he presents much of the essential Carlyle critical position. Warren examines the early essays and sets forth Carlyle's case for the poet as prophet and for poetry as indubitably didactic. He shows that Carlyle's theory of the poet eventually places the poet in the larger context of the Hero. Warren concludes with some praise for Carlyle's large view of the poet as teacher and of literature as more than idle amusement, but he also says that Carlyle is too transcendental and that his type of criticism ultimately blurs distinctions. Warren is certainly right concerning practical criticism in which Carlyle can be an uncertain guide, but Carlyle's case for poetry, or good literature, as more than mere amusement is one that has to be continually remade. Some further light on Carlyle's aesthetics will be found in Lawrence J. Starzyk's article on early Victorian aesthetics (*BJA*, 1971).

Carlyle's critical effort is mainly found in his studies of German literature and a substantial criticism has grown up about this topic. An early attempt to assess his role in bringing German literature to England is Wilhelm Streuli's *Thomas Carlyle als Vermittler deutscher Literatur und deutschen Geistes* (1895). C. E. Vaughn's "Carlyle and His German Masters" (*E&S*, 1910) is a sympathetic account of Carlyle's debt to Goethe and Fichte and has been superseded by later studies such as Wellek's and Harrold's. John Blankenagel in "Carlyle as a Critic of Grillparzer" (*PMLA*, 1927) is much more sharply focused than most other studies and devoted to one of Carlyle's less sterling critical performances, his rejection of Grillparzer along with the more defensible rejections of Klingermann and Müllner, in "German Playwrights" (1829). Blankenagel, a Grillparzer defender, is nevertheless understanding of Carlyle's critical problems in the essay.

V. Stockley in *German Literature as Known in England, 1750–1830* (1929) returns us to the broader view. Carlyle appears frequently as those authors he discussed or translated are cited. Time and again Carlyle was the agent of their English debut. René Wellek's "Carlyle and German Romanticism" (*Zvláštníostikz xenia Pragensia*, 1929; rpt. in *Confrontations*, 1965) remains the best overall treatment of Carlyle's response to Romanticism. Wellek's treatment in the third volume of his *A History of Modern Criticism* (1955) should also be consulted. Karl Lotter's *Carlyle und die deutsche Romantik* (1931) is a lightweight piece of no special distinction. More valuable is Camillo von Klenze's "Carlyle and German Letters" (in *Charles Timothy Brooks*, 1938), which considers also the impact that Carlyle's advocacy had on such subsequent translators as Brooks. Von Klenze sees Carlyle's chief contributions in this area as his reverence for German spiritual depth and intellectual originality. Margarete Lomholt-Thomsen in *Carlyles Forhold til tysk Litteratur* (1941) contributes a Danish slant to this subject but there are no revelations there.

W. Witte has made several good contributions to Carlyle and German studies, and on the general aspects of the topic he offers "Carlyle as a Critic of German Literature" (*Aberdeen Univ. Rev.*, 1942; rpt. in *Schiller and Burns and Other Essays*, 1959), a balanced though not profound study that makes the point that Carlyle was keener as a critic of the first generation of German Romanticism—Goethe, Schiller, Jean Paul—than of the second. Carlyle fell off even more with later German writers if we are to accept the not very objective findings of Solomon Liptzin in *The English Legend of Heinrich Heine* (1954) that Carlyle's failure to respond favorably to Heine has to do with his anti-Semitism. We find more to occupy the mind in Alan Lang Strout's "Writers on German Literature in *Blackwood's Magazine*" (*Library*, 1954), where the first suggestion is made of a possible affinity between Carlyle's treatment of German letters and that of some of the authors of the *Blackwood's* circle, such as John Gibson Lockhart, a suggestion developed at greater length in "*Sartor*" *Called* "*Resartus*," which also devotes a chapter to Carlyle's Germanizing activities. J. W. Smeed in *German Influence on Thomas Carlyle* (Carlyle Society, 1964) maintains his customary high scholarly level. Smeed has also contributed fruitfully to discussion of Carlyle's translations and his relations with Jean Paul.

Part of the study of Carlyle as a critic must consider also what Carlyle did as an editor. Apart from the examples in *Cromwell* and numerous other works (for Carlyle almost always wrote as some sort of editor), there is to hand Carlyle's work in editing the letters and memorials of Jane Welsh Carlyle. Neither C. R. Sanders' "Carlyle as Editor and Critic of Literary Letters" (*EUQ*, 1964) nor Arthur A. Adrian's "Carlyle on Editing Letters" (*VN*, 1967) fully answers the questions that would touch on Carlyle's critical precepts, but they cast light on his practice. Sanders also considers Carlyle's critical principles in his "Carlyle, Poetry, and the Music of Humanity" (*WHR*, 1962), which is concerned with Carlyle's known antipathy to poetry. He carefully catalogs Carlyle's responses to individual poems and poets and is particularly revealing on criteria Carlyle enunciated to Browning. Carlyle, Sanders shows, rejected the mechanical in poetry and sought something transcendent and infinite. Just as Carlyle called poetry away from the mechanical, so he made the same high demands on biography. In *English Biography in the Early Nineteenth Century, 1801–1838* (1966), Joseph W. Reed, Jr. argues that, while Carlyle's theory of biography was both too impractical and too emphatic on the unconscious, he nevertheless served to call nineteenth-century biography to a higher plane and to demand of biographers "artistic responsibility."

Building on Roe, Warren, Wellek, and the studies of Carlyle's German literary criticism and his editorial procedures, a future scholar should be able to write the definitive study of Carlyle as a literary critic, for it is still needed. Louis James is engaged in preparing a very much needed, substantial volume of selections from Carlyle's literary criticism.

Carlyle's artistry in a larger sense is the subject of Arthur Mämpel's *Thomas Carlyle als Künstler* (1935), especially useful for its consideration of Carlyle's early works and its emphasis on the fictional elements in his writing. These have been even more extensively and profitably examined in Carlisle Moore's "Thomas Carlyle and Fiction: 1822–1834" (in *Nineteenth-Century Studies*, ed. Herbert Davis et al., 1940), where Moore examines both the early works of fiction and Carlyle's changing ideas about fiction. Moore argues that it was not so much Carlyle's failures at fiction, though "Cruthers and Johnson" and "Wotton Reinfred" are surely failures, as his preoccupation with transcendental philosophic ideas that turned him away from and eventually, in theory at any rate, against fiction. Moore treated Carlyle's fictional devices again in an article on *The Diamond Necklace* (*PMLA*, 1943).

Just what Carlyle's relationship was to fiction, in theory and practice, is a frequent subject of speculation and can be pursued in critical biographies and studies of particular works, especially those on *Sartor Resartus*, which is the locus classicus for Carlyle's fictional experimentation. Susanne Howe's pioneering *Wilhelm Meister and His English Kinsmen* (1930) considers Carlyle's translation of Goethe's novel and his adaptation of it in Book II of *Sartor* to be definitive for the form and popularity of what she calls "Apprenticeship Novels," which include novels of the Oxford Movement as well as those by authors from Bulwer to Meredith. A recent study by Tennyson, "The *Bildungsroman* in Nineteenth-Century English Literature" (in *Medieval Epic to the "Epic Theater" of Brecht*, ed. John M. Spalek and Rosario P. Armato, 1968), takes as its starting point the German concept of the *Bildungsroman* and endeavors to posit a theory to account for its form in English, citing the novels of the Howe study and others. Carlyle is again held to be the primary avenue through which the form reached England, but unlike Howe, Tennyson sees its English flowering in Dickens.

A stimulating consequence of the contemporary interest in Carlyle's fictional devices is George Levine's *The Boundaries of Fiction: Carlyle, Macaulay, Newman* (1968), which incorporates Levine's earlier "*Sartor Resartus* and the Balance of Fiction" (*VS*, 1964). Levine's examination of fictional devices in Carlyle, especially *Sartor*, brings up to date the Mämpel and Moore investigations of this issue. Levine's study is burdened by fashionable but dubious psychologizing, but it nevertheless contains some excellent analysis of specific fictional techniques found in Carlyle's work. Levine operates on the assumption that some profound deterrent kept Carlyle from working in what he feels was the dominant form of the age, but that assumption may be harder and harder to sustain after the present volume demonstrates the massive role of nonfiction prose in the age, and Carlyle's choice may appear to be less compelled and more elected than it has hitherto.

Two dissertations consider Carlyle's role in the question of the art of Victorian prose: Julia A. Smith's "Narrative Art in Victorian Nonfiction: Theory and Practice in Carlyle, Newman, and Pater" (Texas 1969) and Walter L. Reed's "Meditations on the Hero: Narrative Form in Carlyle, Kierkegaard, and Melville" (Yale 1969). Reed has also published an article on the conversion pattern in *Sartor Resartus*, discussed below under individual works. Elliot L. Gilbert's arresting article on the relation between Carlyle's prophecy and art (*PMLA*, 1972) makes valuable observations on Carlyle's characteristic literary mode. Gordon Cheesewright (Diss. California, Los Angeles 1972) examines the art of Carlyle and others in terms of conversion patterns.

Studies of Carlyle's artistry still have some distance to go. Perhaps the first requisite, now that certain pioneering studies have begun to take the work seriously for its literary brilliance, is for future studies to take equally seriously the author who created the work.

VII. CRITICISM OF INDIVIDUAL WORKS

General biographical and critical studies have naturally had much to say on individual Carlyle works, and no student of Carlyle should pass these by in seeking an understanding of particular works. In some instances these contain the only available criticism. But there has also been an immense number of studies directed toward specific works alone. To be sure, even here attention is not equally distributed. Little or nothing has been done on such works as *German Romance* or *Chartism*, while the *Sartor Resartus* file bulges with studies of all kinds. Thus the mere frequency of studies indicates something about the nature of interest and criticism on Carlyle.

Special studies of individual works are discussed below under the work, listed alphabetically by its best-known title, except for the Essays and Miscellanies which are grouped together under the general title of Essays. If no edition is specially cited it means that a good critical edition is lacking. For contemporary periodical reviews and most other commentary see Dyer and *CBEL*.

CHARTISM (1837). An early routine treatment of this neglected work can be found in Alois Brandl's "Chartisten, Sozialisten, und Carlyle" (*Deutsche Rundschau*,

1912), but it mainly outlines the Chartist position for foreign readers. John Virtue has done the chief work on *Chartism* (Diss. Yale 1935), which provides an annotated edition and a discussion of the work, including a history of the composition. Virtue later printed one of his minor historical findings in "Carlyle's 'Mr. Symmons'" (*Studies in Honor of R. D. O'Leary and S. L. Whitcomb*, 1942), which seeks to identify one Jeliger Symons as the "Mr. Symmons" quoted by Carlyle in *Chartism*.

CROMWELL (1845). Again a neglected work, though frequently touched on in studies of Carlyle as a historian. Wilbur C. Abbott's *Conflicts with Oblivion* (1924) devotes a chapter to *Cromwell* in which he claims that Carlyle's achievement in the work was twofold: he collected a good deal of valuable material in one place, disposing of much chaff and obscurity, and then he "shouted long and hard" until the world came and took a look at it. Bernard Holland in "On a Re-Reading of Carlyle's *Cromwell*" (*Wiseman* [*Dublin*] *Rev.*, 1924) calls it the best work Carlyle ever wrote but too partisan, omitting too many shadows in Cromwell's portrait. D. H. Pennington in "Cromwell and the Historians" (*Hist. Today*, 1958) devotes a section to Carlyle's work, praising him for making Cromwell again exciting as a man and not as a monster and for dispelling the notion that Cromwell was a hypocrite. Two notes with the same title take issue with a particular aspect of *Cromwell*: B. Blackstone's and H. P. Kennedy Skipton's "Carlyle and Little Gidding" (*TLS*, 28 March, 11 April 1936). Both deplore Carlyle's vicious treatment of Nicholas Ferrar and the Little Gidding community, which is in truth deplorably presented by Carlyle; the Skipton note points out the curious disparity between the hostile *Cromwell* portrait of Ferrar and the much juster and kinder presentation in Carlyle's earlier *Historical Sketches*. The shift in viewpoint remains unexplained.

DIAMOND NECKLACE (1837). Carlisle Moore's previously cited essay (*PMLA*, 1943) is the only study, but a fine one, of this truly arresting Carlyle work. Moore draws on Shine and others to show that Carlyle put into practice his ideas of a "divine, poetic history" in his preparatory work for *The French Revolution*. He identifies a number of stylistic devices used by Carlyle to escape from the linearity of conventional history and get at the "three-dimensional solidity" of action. There is as yet no study of the work in relation to the development of detective and mystery fiction.

ESSAYS. The four volumes of Carlyle's *Miscellanies* from 1839 and the many essays after that time have virtually never been studied as a group. Hugh Walker comes closest in *The English Essay and Essayists* (1915), though he also includes longer works. Walker notes that Carlyle's essays from the *Miscellanies* to *Shooting Niagara* touch all of his great interests and that no one else in the age so clearly enunciated and followed his principles as Carlyle and no one did more to establish the intellectual independence of the critic. Walker even goes so far as to say that on all the great points Carlyle was generally right.

The essay "Biography" (1832) is held to be the chief source for Victorian ideas of autobiography by Keith Rinehart in "The Victorian Approach to Autobiography" (*MP*, 1954), for Carlyle enunciates the importance of the poetic joined with the moral. After 1870 the Carlylean concept of biography breaks down in Victorian thought, Rinehart says. Carlyle's essay on Boswell (1832) is touched on in Francis R. Hart's "Boswell and the Romantics" (*ELH*, 1960) as an instance of the Victorian interest in discipleship.

The Walter Scott essay of 1838 has generated some criticism. Leslie Stephen's piece in *Hours in a Library* (1874) is less an assessment of the Carlyle essay than a use of it for a fresh and sympathetic look at Scott. Along the way, however, he has some good things to say of the earlier treatment by "one whose name I would never mention without profound respect, and who has a special claim to be heard in this case." Julia Wedgwood, however, attacked Carlyle's Scott essay (*ConR*, 1878). H. J. C. Grierson in *Essays and Addresses* (1940) includes an article on "Scott and Carlyle" which traces the causes, some of them justified, that contributed to Carlyle's qualified estimate of Scott. Robert C. Gordon in "A Victorian Anticipation of Recent Scott Criticism" (*PQ*, 1957) touches on Carlyle's essay only to snap at it as "Victorian moralism at its worst."

"The State of German Literature" which Carlyle published in 1827 is the actual subject of Werner Leopold's *Die religiöse Wurzel von Carlyles literarischer Wirksamkeit* (1922). Although Leopold seeks to ferret out Carlyle's religious position, the value of his study lies in its close examination of the "State of German Literature" as an example of Carlyle's style and his structuring of a literary piece.

Many individual essays could profitably be studied and a comprehensive study of all Carlyle's essays is in order.

FREDERICK THE GREAT (1858–65). There is no definitive study, no good edition. M. Krummacher's two-part essay, "Sprache und Stil in Carlyles 'Friedrich II'" (*Eng. Studien*, 1888), is actually a word list of colloquialisms and Carlylisms from that work. German critics have naturally been drawn to *Frederick*. Konrad F. Neumann in *Carlyles Friedrich der Grosse* (1932) offers a slight study which finds the work unsatisfactory as history. Neumann has a good section on the contemporary critical reception of *Frederick*. Mämpel's *Carlyle als Künstler*, already cited, bears the subtitle "unter besonderer Berücksichtigung Friedrich des Grossen" and is chiefly directed toward supplying the necessary background to a reading of *Frederick* and an understanding of Carlyle's method. It is strong on Carlyle's dramatic technique and literary artistry and it is still worth consulting for illustrations of Carlyle's symbolic technique. Hermann Knust's "Der bleibende Wert des Heldenbildes Friedrichs des Grossen von Carlyle" (*Neuphilologische Monatsschrift*, 1939) adds nothing to our understanding of the work and is marred by efforts to relate Frederick and Carlyle to Hitler. Richard A. E. Brooks's edition of Carlyle's *Journey to Germany* (1940) should be remembered here because the journal grew out of Carlyle's *Frederick* researches and because Brooks's introduction contains illuminating criticism of Carlyle's historical method, especially in the battle scenes. Brooks argues for the greatness of *Frederick* as a work of history.

L. Ettlinger's "Carlyle on Portraits of Frederick the Great" (*MLR*, 1945) provides an unpublished letter in the State Archives in Berlin from Carlyle on portraits of Frederick, a subject in which Carlyle was intensely interested. Elmer L. Brooks in "B. W. Procter and the Genesis of Carlyle's *Frederick the Great*" (*HLB*, 1953) notes an early suggestion to Carlyle from Bulwer in 1831 that he write on Frederick the Great, but the project was not then carried out. Margot Krohn (*JSUB*, 1965) offers a somewhat disjointed monograph generally about Frederick but containing also much biographical data on Carlyle's composition of the work and his German trip and even the public history of Frederick and miscellaneous jottings about Jane. The whole essay is very long and not very helpful. That Carlyle revised and revised, even at proof-sheet stage, is well known but was documented again in regard to the surviving *Frederick* materials by Alexander F. Clarke in "Belles Lettres" (*Manuscripta*, 1968). Nancy Mitford demonstrates anew that she writes entertainingly in "Tam and Fritz: Carlyle and Frederick the Great" (*Hist. Today*, 1968), but the article and the book that followed, *Frederick the Great* (1971), contribute nothing to our understanding of Carlyle or his work. The paperback abridgment by John Clive (1969) has a short sympathetic introduction but is valueless as an edition because it is so truncated. Most *Frederick* editions are, alas, abridged.

Thus *Frederick* remains inadequately studied as a work of art. It is forbidding in its amplitude and complexity, but it would for that reason all the more repay study.

THE FRENCH REVOLUTION (1837). Again no definitive work, which is all the more surprising for Carlyle's most highly regarded history. The best editions, though not flawless, are by C. R. L. Fletcher (1902) and John Holland Rose (1902). There is also one by C. F. Harrold (1937). Mazzini and Mill wrote essays on the work in the first years after its appearance and these are still worth consulting, as is Frederic Harrison's essay in *The Choice of Books* (1886). Harrison finds the work deficient in "historical science" but enduringly beautiful as a "historical poem." Recent general treatments include two with the same title by Frank A. Lea, "Carlyle and *The French Revolution*" (*Adelphi*, 1941; *Listener*, 1964). Neither is weighty but both are pleasant. Lea praises Carlyle's Romantic method in contrast to Gibbon's classical one and likens his response to the upheaval to Wordsworth's; Carlyle's book, he says, is as true a poem as *The Excursion*. Alfred Cobban (*History*, 1963) believes Carlyle failed to recognize that it was a bourgeois revolution but did uniquely see it was a revolution of *sans-cullotism*. Cobban cites the elements that formed Carlyle's view of the Revolution, such as his Calvinism and his concept of periodicity, and he praises the immediacy and vitality of Carlyle's writing.

Two important recent studies of *The French Revolution* are by Hedva Ben-Israel. In "Carlyle and the French Revolution" (*HistJ*, 1958) Ben-Israel takes away with one hand and gives with the other. His central points are that Carlyle's history is novel in giving history a narrative but that Carlyle's regard for fact is less important than his method of immersing himself in his topic and then letting the story flow forth. He denies that Carlyle had any philosophy of the Revolution or any real understanding of it while still praising the final result as poetic history. The essay is suggestive but inconclusive. Ben-Israel added to this essay and published it in *English Historians on the French Revolution* (1968). Here he is concerned to relate Carlyle to Romantic historiography. But the book version does not clarify the inconsistencies of his earlier appraisal and he alternately argues that Carlyle thought of history as poetry and that he did not. However, the approach is admirably rooted in historical scholarship and the appendix contains a useful bibliography of nine-teenth-century reactions to Carlyle's book.

There have been several studies on the literary and verbal aspects of *The French Revolution*. The following are brief items on specific expressions or passages in the book: Frederick W. Hilles' "'Mother of Dead Dogs'" (*MLN*, 1927), F. Olivero's "The Campaign of 1792 in Carlyle and Goethe" (in *Studi Britannici*, 1931), Jack Lindsay's "A Tale of Two Cities" (*Life and Letters Today*, 1949), and

A. L. A. Mooij's "Carducci, a-t-il paraphrasé Carlyle?" (*Neophilologus*, 1951). A sidelight on Carlyle's use of a metaphor is cast by Robert E. Kusch in "Carlyle and the Milieu of 'Spontaneous Combustion'" (*NM*, 1969); Kusch speculates on possible sources for Carlyle's awareness of the idea. Sara W. G. Graff discusses the artistic unity of *The French Revolution* (Diss. Arkansas 1970).

But the important work on language and method in the book is by C. F. Harrold. His "The Translated Passages in Carlyle's *French Revolution*" (*JEGP*, 1928) shows that Carlyle was faithful to the fact of his translations if not always to the literal text. The same conclusion, more deeply thought out and applied to the meaning of the work, informs Harrold's "Carlyle's General Method in *The French Revolution*" (*PMLA*, 1928), a painstaking comparison of Carlyle's translations and paraphrases of his cited sources. Harrold demonstrates that Carlyle's relentless pursuit of "fact" never meant slavishness to sources, but rather fidelity to the spirit of the event. On the much debated question of Carlyle's sympathies in *The French Revolution*, Harrold concludes that he was partisan of neither side, though he certainly cast doubt on the efficacy of revolution to settle political problems, and that his own view is most notably one of pity and sympathy for all participants. Harrold's studies are still central to an understanding of the book and were not effectively ruled out of account by Ben-Israel's objections. Also valuable in assessing Carlyle's method in *The French Revolution* is H. M. Leicester's "Dialectic of Romantic Historiography" (*VS*, 1971).

Walter Blair in "*The French Revolution* and *Huckleberry Finn*" (*MP*, 1957) finds some parallels between the two books and goes on to argue that Twain developed beyond Carlyle's views. A series of minor notes calling attention to alleged errors in Carlyle's history follows in the tradition of Oscar Browning's "Carlyle as a Historian" (*Athenaeum*, 1888) and *The Flight to Varennes and Other Essays* (1892), which sought to show errors (later disproved) in Carlyle's historical reporting. The later notes of this kind include a series spaced over several months under the title "Errors in Carlyle's *French Revolution*" (*N&Q*, 1921) and Henry Broadbent's "Carlyle's *French Revolution*—A Suggestion" (*TLS*, 21 July 1927). Jules Douady in "Carlyle et l'insurrection des femmes" (*RAA*, 1926) takes issue with Carlyle's treatment in that section and with his treatment overall, claiming that England has yet to produce a historian of the Revolution who writes in the proper spirit. One cannot agree with this estimate but one can say that Carlyle's work itself has not yet found its proper historian.

GERMAN ROMANCE (1827). This work is in contention for the title of Carlyle's most neglected. Studies of Carlyle's German indebtedness of course treat *German Romance* or works or authors included in it, but the only work on this endeavor overall is John Linscheid's *Carlyle's Translation of the German Romances Included in* German Romance (1936), chiefly a study of Carlyle's translating methods and useful primarily for the author's attempt to ascertain which editions Carlyle used in his translation. An instructive note on one of the stories in *German Romance*, Musaeus' "Libussa," is provided by Rodger Tarr (*AN&Q*, 1971).

HEROES AND HERO-WORSHIP (1841). No definitive study exists but the work appears to be in line for serious reconsideration. Archibald MacMechan's and P. C. Parr's early editions (1901, 1910) contain much valuable material and are still the best editions. Most of the rest of scholarly energy in this area has gone into general studies of Carlyle's theory of the Hero. Some early studies compare Carlyle and others: Giuseppi Ravenna's "La teoria dell'eroe in T. Carlyle e F. Nietzsche" (*NA*, 1903), and Ernst von Wiecki's already cited work comparing Carlyle and Emerson. Neither is important. B. H. Lehman's *Carlyle's Theory of the Hero* (1928) is highly relevant here and should be consulted. Paul Wissman's "Carlyles Buch über Helden und Heldenverehrung im Dienste Nationalpolitischer Schulung" (*Zeitschrift für Neusprachlichen Unterricht,* 1935) reveals its bias in its title and need not be trifled with. Frederic E. Faverty has a sympathetic short account in *Your Literary Heritage* (1959), and there has also been a recent paperback edition by Carl Niemeyer (1966). One should overlook the introduction.

DeLaura's "Ishmael as Prophet: *Heroes and Hero-Worship* and the Self-Expressive Basis of Carlyle's Art" (*TSLL*, 1969) and Robert E. Kusch's "Pattern and Paradox in *Heroes and Hero-Worship*" (*SSL*, 1969) constitute the best literary work on *Heroes*. Both are concerned with Carlyle's artistry, but they do not always agree. DeLaura sees the unity of *Heroes* in the "deeply personal character" of Carlyle's effort to define the "character, the message, and the social role of the prophet, especially in the nineteenth century." DeLaura traces Carlyle's developing concern for his own role as prophet and he sees the "ultimate hero" of the book to be Carlyle himself. In the face of such a psychological reading and its attendant temptations DeLaura maintains his literary equilibrium and continues to focus on the work he calls "the most openly 'prophetic' book of the nineteenth century in England and a masterpiece of Romantic art." Kusch, by contrast, takes Carlyle to task for failure to sustain his theme when he comes to the eighteenth century because of "logical and aesthetic difficulties" having to do with Carlyle's view of that age, and he regrets that Carlyle did not choose Goethe as his eighteenth-century hero. He does observe other useful formative patterns in the work—the Tree Igdrasil, for example—but overall he finds it wanting in unity. Kusch and DeLaura are not so far apart as may seem. Kusch is seeking a visible, literary unity; DeLaura one that lies deeper and touches the psychological wellsprings of Carlyle and his age. DeLaura's study is itself the deeper of the two, but a unity that comprehends both points of view might still be discriminated by a future critic.

Three specialized studies of *Heroes* deserve mention. Martin M. Crow in "The Hero as Desperado" (*Texas Lib. Chron.*, 1946) defends Carlyle's Hero doctrine from attacks, most specifically from a long-forgotten attack by a Texas author, Judge Alfred W. Arrington in his 1847 *Duelists and Duelling in the South-West*, who held that Carlyle would have approved of the southwestern desperado. Not so, says Crow, who rejects Arrington's assertion that "Thomas Carlyle is the desperado of literature." The piece is most interesting for unearthing Arrington and his pre-Arnoldian phraseology. W. Montgomery Watt in "Carlyle on Muhammed" (*HJ*, 1955) traces Carlyle's sources for his portrait of Mohammed in *Heroes* and notes that Carlyle was in the forefront of favorable European treatment of the Prophet. Carlyle's conception of Mohammed, says Watt, "is a true one" and still valuable to historians today. Alan Carey Taylor in "Carlyle interprète de Dante" (*EA*, 1959) notes many Carlyle references before *Heroes* but concentrates on Carlyle's estimate in that work. It rests, he says, almost wholly on Carlyle's reading of *The Divine Comedy* and no other Dante work.

ILLUDO CHARTIS (ca. 1826). This work was evidently an exercise in the mode later developed for *Sartor* and was first uncovered and examined in that light by Marjorie

P. King in "*Illudo Chartis*: An Initial Study in Carlyle's Mode of Composition" (*MLR*, 1954), cited earlier, and then by Tennyson. Ronald L. Trowbridge in "Carlyle's *Illudo Chartis* as a Prophetic Exercise in the Manner of Swift and Sterne" (*SSL*, 1968) points out specific parallels and echoes from the two previous authors reminding us of how deeply read in their works Carlyle was.

LATTER-DAY PAMPHLETS (1850). Few indeed are those who have ventured into this tulgey wood; more's the pity, for *Latter-Day Pamphlets* needs its scholar. Evan A. Reiff in "Studies in Carlyle's *Latter-Day Pamphlets*" (*Univ. of Iowa Stud.*, 1937) undertook to defend both the consistency and viability of Carlyle's social views in that work, and he, of course, has never been heard from again. He relates some of Carlyle's utterances to his Irish journey of the previous year but argues that his radicalism was also consonant with previous expressions. One later defender, A. Bryant, provided a brief untitled commentary on the work praising Carlyle as a forerunner of socialism (*Illustrated London News*, 26 June 1948). Judith M. C. Miller's dissertation (Arizona 1970) offers a defense, as does Tennyson's *Carlyle and the Modern World*.

"LECTURES" (1837–39). Because they were never published by Carlyle, the other three lecture series preceding *Heroes* have not truly been available for study. But some comments appear in the later transcriptions of two of the series. See Editions. Ethel M. F. Fulton's "A Study of the Public Lectures Given by Thomas Carlyle" (Diss. Toronto 1969) considers what is known of the lectures and the importance of the series for Carlyle's reputation at the time.

OCCASIONAL DISCOURSE ON THE NIGGER QUESTION (1849). Surprisingly, this has just been issued in paperback in an edition by Eugene R. August titled *Carlyle: The Nigger Question, Mill: The Negro Question* (1971). In his introduction August emphatically deplores Carlyle's views, but he draws so much upon sleazy documents such as Halliday's "psychosomatic biography" to support his interpretation that at times he appears to protest too much. The edition is annotated and contains some interesting illustrative materials.

PAST AND PRESENT (1843). Grace Calder's excellent *The Writing of* Past and Present (1949) considers Carlyle's mode of composition by careful comparison of manuscripts and proofsheets, and concludes that Carlyle's revisions make the final version more "finished and artistic" than the original. She isolates many specific types of revisions, most notably expansions and additions of greater concreteness, but allows that the final result still has an unexplainable magic. Calder's work is an almost unique example in Carlyle studies of literary criticism based on thorough examination of substantial manuscript materials.

The early excellent and still standard edition by Arthur Montagu D. Hughes (1918) and the paperback edition by Richard Altick (1965) have instructive historical material, Hughes's the more complete, Altick's the more up to date. Other studies are less important. Stanley Thomas Williams (*SAQ*, 1922) stresses the positive side of Carlyle's message in the book. Lewis H. Chrisman's study (*Methodist Rev.*, 1927) is an appreciation, while A. L. Rowse in "Books in General" (*ES*, 1943), writing on the centenary of the work, is far less enthusiastic. He finds the style "appalling" but the book still the "most balanced" Carlyle wrote on the

Condition-of-England question. A recent scholarly edition and translation of *The Chronicle of Jocelin of Brakelond* by H. E. Butler (1949) makes no mention of Carlyle, leaving us with only Fritz Schneider's unreliable Past und Present *und der Chronica Jocelini de Brakelonda* (1911) for a source study. Work could be done here. John T. Fain's "Word Echoes in *Past and Present*" (*VN*, 1955) notes some of Carlyle's echoing and intensifications for artistic effect, and Edwin W. Marrs, Jr., in "Dating the Writing of *Past and Present*" (*N&Q*, 1967), argues persuasively that the book was begun by November of 1842 and completed in March 1843, not quite the seven weeks of Froude's assertion.

REMINISCENCES (1866, 1881). No separate study, unfortunately, of one of Carlyle's most beautiful works, but Edward Sharples is said to be readying a new edition. See also above, Biographies, The Froude Controversy.

SARTOR RESARTUS (1833–34). On the basis of the number of separate studies it has generated as well as its inevitable inclusion in all general studies of Carlyle, *Sartor Resartus* is clearly Carlyle's most popular work. It has enjoyed numerous editions, including several of high scholarly quality—those by A. MacMechan (1896), J. A. S. Barrett (1905), P. C. Parr (1913), and C. F. Harrold (1937)—each with valuable introductions, especially Harrold's with its treatment of Carlyle's ideas. It exists in paper in Tennyson's *Carlyle Reader* (1968). It continues to attract the chief attention in the modern revival of interest in Carlyle as a stylist. The many studies can roughly be divided into five categories: *Sartor* overall, genesis, philosophy, artistry, and specialized studies.

G. B. Tennyson's *"Sartor" Called "Resartus"* (1965) is the most comprehensive study of the work and can be said to have incorporated and superseded many of the earlier studies on origin, background, style, and structure. Tennyson devotes the early part of his book to a study of Carlyle's literary apprenticeship and pre-*Sartor* writings, a topic that also chiefly occupied William Savage Johnson in his earlier cited study, *Thomas Carlyle: A Study of His Literary Apprenticeship,* and David L. Maulsby in *The Growth of* Sartor Resartus (1899), but Tennyson places greater stress on Carlyle's German literary studies. Tennyson also traces the complex publication history of *Sartor* through the 1830's. The latter part of his study is given over to an examination of the style, structure, and meaning of *Sartor*. Tennyson claims a dynamic artistic form for Carlyle's book in which matter and manner complement each other and reinforce Carlyle's intellectual bearing, which Tennyson affirms to be ultimately God-centered, radical and experimental though it was. It seems most becoming here to quote Carlisle Moore's estimate of the book as "an invaluable contribution to the study of Carlyle as both artist and thinker."

There are no other comparable separate studies, but readers should be reminded again to consult standard literary histories, general criticism, and critical biographies of Carlyle in considering *Sartor*. An admirable adaptation of Tennyson's approach applied to larger issues in modern literature is found in Russell Kirk's discussion of *Sartor* in *Enemies of the Permanent Things* (1969), in which *Sartor* is seen as an example of "ethical fantasy," a commodity Kirk values as both salutary and rare.

Many commentators have considered the relation of Carlyle's famous Leith Walk experience to *Sartor*. John T. Wells's belletristic *Thomas Carlyle: His Religious Experiences as Reflected in* Sartor Resartus (1899) was followed by Alfred

Carl Lorenz who argues in *Diogenes Teufelsdröckh und Thomas Carlyle* (1913) that all of Book ii is purely autobiographical and not symbolic of anything, an astonishingly narrow view. P. H. Elander in "Thomas Carlyles 'religiöse Krise' und deren Darstellung in Selbst-biographischen Roman" (*SN*, 1942) also traces the Leith Walk experience to purely psychological and biographical factors, but Hermann Plagens in an article with the same title (*Archiv*, 1944) retorts that it was precisely a *religious* experience and cannot be explained away by talk of disappointment in finding a suitable vocation, as Elander tries to do. Plagens is right. The definitive discussion of these matters was provided by Carlisle Moore in "*Sartor Resartus* and the Problem of Carlyle's 'Conversion'" (*PMLA*, 1955), in which Moore argues that the experiences of Teufelsdröckh in Book ii of *Sartor*, while clearly based on Carlyle's own, by no means literally recapitulate in detail or in time sequence what happened to Carlyle himself. Moore maintains that Carlyle really required almost a decade to work out the full consequences of the Leith Walk experience, that is, to move from The Everlasting No to The Everlasting Yea, while in *Sartor* it is all compressed. Moore's explication of the experience has not only the virtue of illuminating *Sartor* but also that of clarifying why it was not until the decade after Leith Walk that Carlyle found his proper voice.

Other studies of the origin of *Sartor* find analogues in works Carlyle knew or may have responded to. The least persuasive is S. B. Liljegren's argument in "The Origin of *Sartor Resartus*" (*Palaestra*, 1925) that Carlyle was responding to novels of fashion, especially Bulwer's *Pelham*. More to the point is Susanne Howe's study *Wilhelm Meister and His English Kinsmen* (1930) which treats both Carlyle's translation of the Goethe novel and *Sartor*, Book ii, in the tradition of the *Bildungsroman* and which sees Carlyle's work as having shaped much subsequent English fiction. Berenice Cooper in "A Comparison of *Quintus Fixlein* and *Sartor Resartus*" (*TWA*, 1958) explicitly affirms *Sartor*'s independence as a work of art and seeks only to note some arresting parallels with the Jean Paul story. Her essay is more authoritative than Henri Plard's very general "Le *Sartor Resartus* de Carlyle et Jean Paul" (*EG*, 1963), but Plard does add some notes on Kierkegaard and the stimulating assertion that the important Jean Paul book for *Sartor* is *Hesperus*. Lore Metzger in "*Sartor Resartus*: A Victorian *Faust*" (*CL*, 1961) argues that *Sartor* is based on the pattern of *Faust*, a work he claims stood "at the fixed center of the spiral of Carlyle's philosophy" for Teufelsdröckh he claims is a compound of Faust and Mephistopheles. Metzger, like so many critics, tends to view *Sartor Resartus* as almost exclusively composed of Book ii. Thus he, like they, may often offer suggestive parallels and patterns but they rarely apply to all of *Sartor* and are hardly so exclusive in application as claimed by their advocates. John Clubbe in "John Carlyle in Germany and the Genesis of *Sartor Resartus*" (in *Romantic and Victorian: Studies in Memory of William H. Marshall*, ed. E. P. Elledge and R. L. Hoffman, 1971) carefully documents every possible influence Carlyle's brother's letters from Germany in the late twenties might have had on the genesis of *Sartor*. He concludes with other students of *Sartor* that this influence was minimal in regard to philosophy, but he shows that it was somewhat greater than has been thought in regard to milieu and setting used by Carlyle.

The intellectual burden of Carlyle's work has attracted attention in its own right from Bernhard Fehr's "Der deutsche Idealismus in Carlyles *Sartor Resartus*" (*GRM*, 1913) and Lafcadio Hearn's "On the Philosophy of *Sartor Resartus*" in *Interpretations of Literature* (1915) to Surendra Nath Agnihotri's "The Philosophy of Carlyle as Revealed in *Sartor Resartus*" (*The Aryan Path*, 1961). These are all negligible, except perhaps Fehr, who stresses the intellectual indebtedness of *Sartor* to Kant and Fichte as opposed to Goethe and Jean Paul. The most impressive separate study of the philosophic dimensions of *Sartor* is Knut Hagberg's *Thomas Carlyle: Romantik och Puritanism i* Sartor Resartus (1925). Hagberg sees the polarities of *Sartor* as expressive of Carlyle's own deep-seated personal and philosophic inclinations, on the one hand his native puritanism and on the other a kind of Scottish cum German Romanticism of the blood. Some of the arguments about sources are not convincing, but the stress on the interaction of the two drives frequently illuminates the peculiar tension of *Sartor*. Emma S. Richards' dissertation "Romantic Form and Doctrine in *Sartor Resartus*" (Lehigh 1967) attempts to ascertain formal patterns in *Sartor* as consequences of certain Romantic precepts such as the unconscious and the relation of the spiritual life to historical cycles.

Style in Carlyle is always central and in *Sartor* it is overriding in importance. Otto Lincke in *Über die Wortzusammensetzung in Carlyles* Sartor Resartus (1904) approached the matter by compiling lists of compounds to show how Carlyle formed his words. Also statistical is Liselotte Eckloff's *Bild und Wirklichkeit bei Thomas Carlyle* (1936), which seeks to understand in this way Carlyle's imagery and metaphorical style. German and English authors are levied upon for parallels as is the Bible, but Eckloff still finds Carlyle's method uniquely his own.

Recent stylistic criticism is more mindful of the unity in *Sartor* between style and structure and less concerned than earlier studies with specific words or verbal techniques in isolation. The focus has been on structure, pattern, and point of view. Daniel P. Deneau in "Relationship of Style and Device in *Sartor Resartus*" (*VN*, 1960) discerns two voices, sometimes merging, but varying in tone to give different emphases. John Lindberg (*VN*, 1960) goes further and notes a dynamic tension between editor and Teufelsdröckh and between the forms of the novel and biography, out of which an artistic unity arises. Alvan S. Ryan in "The Attitude toward the Reader in Carlyle's *Sartor Resartus*" (*VN*, 1963) gives further study to the editorial voice as a corrective to Roellinger's earlier study of Carlyle's style. All these studies have contributed to the now general awareness of the variety in point of view that Carlyle achieved with a minimal cast of characters in *Sartor*.

Not only are we now aware of several voices artistically deployed in *Sartor*, we have also learned from recent criticism that the total structure of *Sartor* is more coherent than earlier criticism recognized. Leonard J. Deen in "Irrational Form in *Sartor Resartus*" (*TSLL*, 1963) tries to show that the work is "expressionistic art," a way of working out a conflict to achieve an answer to skepticism. Deen's study offers insights rather than a technique for analyzing *Sartor*, but George Levine in "*Sartor Resartus* and the Balance of Fiction" (*VS*, 1964) and in *The Boundaries of Fiction* (1969) concentrates fruitfully on Carlyle's use of fictional and semifictional techniques in works nominally factual. Levine still finds the result "static," which is not the dominant modern view, and he persistently analyzes Carlyle's psychology from the "evidence" of his works, but there is much of practical value in his consideration of Carlyle and fiction and in the acuity of his critical perceptions.

Three dissertations continue the contemporary interest in style and structure of *Sartor*: Joseph T. Sigman's "Idea and Image in Thomas Carlyle's *Sartor Resartus*" (Pennsylvania 1968), Gerry H. Brookes's "The Rhetorical Structure of *Sartor Resartus*" (California, Berkeley 1968), and Stephen C. Zelnick's "The Pursuit of Conviction in *Sartor Resartus*: The Meaning of Its Style and Structure" (Illinois

1969). Sigman sees the imagery as flowing from Carlyle's philosophical orientation; Brookes sees the structure as that of the "persuasive essay," organized rhetorically; and Zelnick sees the structure as issuing from Carlyle's "desperate pursuit of conviction." Brookes's study has just been published as a book (1972). Rowland Douglas McMaster's "Criticism of Civilization in the Structure of Sartor Resartus" (*UTQ*, 1968) is less structure oriented than its title implies and actually argues for an organization around three chief symbols—the labyrinth, the Satan-Prometheus figure, and the phoenix—which operate complexly but organically to unify the work and give a vantage point for Carlyle's critique of society. McMaster's view is not satisfactory for the whole of Sartor, but it manifests again the inexhaustibility of the work for generating complex verbal and allusive patterns. Even more arresting is Walter L. Reed's "The Pattern of Conversion in Sartor Resartus" (*ELH*, 1971), which builds on existing criticism of Sartor to argue that a pattern of secular conversion underlies the structure and the dynamics of the book. He also sees the pattern as leading to Carlyle's social and more outward-looking concerns of the years following Sartor. Ultimately, in Reed's view, conversion leads to revolution, and Carlyle's pattern marks an important stage in the development of the Victorian sensibility.

Because Sartor is so protean in allusion and structural pattern, it has brought forth a wealth of short specialized studies of words and passages. The best of these, like Heinrich Kraeger in "Carlyle's Sartor Resartus" (*Anglia Beiblatt*, 1899) on an obscure German reference to *Teusinke*, are incorporated into the notes of the good annotated editions. A few are too extensive for that and there has been no fully annotated edition since Harrold's in 1937, so later notes must be consulted directly. Such is John J. Parry's good annotation of "Baphometic Fire-Baptism" and the name Teufelsdröckh in "A Plea for Better Anthologies" (*CE*, 1944), Keith Rinehart's (*Expl*, 1953) on the meaning of the title, and William B. Toole's (*Expl*, 1959) on the implications of an expression from the "Everlasting Yea." Another level of allusion in Teufelsdröckh's name is uncovered by Patrick Brantlinger (*ELN*, 1972).

Carlyle's denial of eighteenth-century philosophy is, in the view of Olle Holmberg in *David Hume in Carlyle's* Sartor Resartus (1934), frequently a specific attack on David Hume who operates as Teufelsdröckh's "invisible opponent." Holmberg considers Carlyle's whole response to the eighteenth-century world view and includes discussion of "Wotton Reinfred" and its philosophical implications, but the study remains a sidelight on Sartor. Willis D. Jacobs in "Carlyle and Mill" (*CEA*, 1959) argues somewhat implausibly that the reference to "Mill of death" in Book II is a pun on John Stuart Mill and his philosophy. It would be more likely that at that time Carlyle was slashing at James than at John Mill. An arresting but not wholly convincing piece on the lack of organic structure in Book III of Sartor is Alvan S. Ryan's "Carlyle, Jeffrey, and the 'Helotage' Chapter of Sartor Resartus" (*VN*, 1965). Ryan does make good use of biographical circumstances concerning Francis Jeffrey's 1830 visit to Craigenputtock to clarify Carlyle's views on Malthusianism.

With all the existing Sartor criticism, one is constrained to say that scholars could more profitably direct attention elsewhere in the future, and in the main this is true. Other works have languished while Sartor received exceptional attention. But Sartor is certainly Carlyle's most enduring work, and it has often proved to be the seed field for subsequent critical studies. What is now needed is for some of the serious and capable critical attention directed to Sartor and some of the techniques developed in modern *Sartor* and general Carlyle criticism—as in the works of Holloway, Tennyson, Levine, LaValley, and others—to be directed to other Carlyle works.

LIFE OF SCHILLER (1825). Despite Goethe's direct involvement in it, there are few studies of *Schiller* outside the treatments in larger works and critical biographies. Max Batt (*MP*, 1904) offers a brief textual note showing the additions to the biography between serial and book publication. These turn out to be chiefly translations in verse. Paul Raabe tells how *Schiller* was made available in Germany and of Goethe's support for it in "Ein Beitrag Goethes zur Weltliteratur: Zur Entstehungsgeschichte von Carlyles Schiller-Biographie" (*Imprimatur*, 1954–55). G. B. Tennyson in "Carlyle's Earliest German Translation" (*AN&Q*, 1963) finds it to be a passage on Gustavus Adolphus from Schiller's *Thirty-Years' War*. *Schiller* is frequently considered in studies of the evolution of Carlyle's style because of its supposed Johnsonian stylistic characteristics. These studies should be examined in considering *Schiller*. The full study of the work has not yet appeared.

SHOOTING NIAGARA (1867). No separate study. See Levine's "Use and Abuse of Carlylese."

LIFE OF JOHN STERLING (1851). Two early notices of the work still bear consideration: Emile Montégut's "Thomas Carlyle et John Sterling" (*RDM*, 1852) and George Brimley's piece in his *Essays* (1858). Brimley complains of Carlyle's apparent lack of Christianity, but still likes the work. Stanley Thomas Williams considers *Sterling* in his *Studies in Victorian Literature* (1923), praising it for its sweetness of tone and also for the valuable light it casts on the crosscurrents of Victorian doubt. Williams astutely describes the work as "a biography of a man of talent by a man of genius." An anonymous editorial note "John Sterling as Hero" (*TLS*, 23 Sept. 1944) compares Sterling to Edward King and Arthur Henry Hallam, and thus implicitly Carlyle's book to *Lycidas* and *In Memoriam*. The work, says the *TLS*, exhibits a "pellucid style" and is blessedly free of Carlyle's "adulation of power and force." The writer also notes that Sterling himself has a "genius for discipleship." Like other critics, the *TLS* writer sees Sterling as a type of Victorian doubt, as does Samuel C. Burchell in "The Approaching Darkness: A Victorian Father to His Son" (*YULG*, 1953).

The most important work on *Sterling* has been that of William Blackburn and Anne K. Tuell. Blackburn's "Carlyle and the Composition of *The Life of John Sterling*" (*SP*, 1947) makes use of Carlyle marginalia in the Duke University Library copy of Sterling's own *Essays and Tales* and on Hare's *Memoir* of Sterling's life, and he argues that Carlyle evolved his own approach to Sterling's biography through his study of Hare's. It is a good article. Anne Kimball Tuell has studied Carlyle's marginalia in a Harvard copy of *Essays and Tales* (*PMLA*, 1939), and she has intelligently considered *The Life of Sterling* in her *John Sterling: A Representative Victorian* (1941). There is also a good treatment of the work in LaValley.

WILHELM MEISTER (1824, 1827). This work has not been studied in recent years though there is a paperback edition of *The Apprenticeship* by Victor Lange (1962). The only study of the whole work is Olga Marx's *Carlyle's Translation of Wilhelm Meister* (1925), which has done service faute de mieux for many years. Marx is strong on listing errors in the translation and passages Carlyle softened for British reception, but short on critical evaluation of the purport and effect of the work. A. R. Hohlfeld's "The Poems in Carlyle's Translation of *Wilhelm Meister*" (*MLN*, 1921) is valuable chiefly for pointing out that there is a textual problem in Carlyle's *Meister* in that changes and additions were made by Carlyle and perhaps others in later editions. Since Hohlfeld there has been no textual study of *Meister* and the text in use is probably corrupt. But then, so probably is the text of most other Carlyle works. In connection with *Meister*, and the later Victorian novel, students should not forget Susanne Howe's *Wilhelm Meister and His English Kinsmen* or Tennyson's "The *Bildungsroman* in Nineteenth-Century English Literature," and should perhaps add for completeness Hans Wagner's *Der englische Bildungsroman* (1951).

WOTTON REINFRED (1828, 1892). The work is frequently referred to in general studies especially as a forerunner of *Sartor* but not much examined in its own right. Heinrich Kraeger did so in "Carlyles deutsche Studien und der Wotton Reinfred" (*Anglia Beiblatt*, 1898) and then expanded the study to "Carlyles Stellung zur deutschen Sprache und Literatur" (*Anglia*, 1899), which indicates the approach he takes to the work, namely an instance of Carlyle trying to translate his German literary and philosophical findings into fiction. This has been the general focus of criticism of *Wotton*, but it is best done in Moore's "Thomas Carlyle and Fiction." There is an interesting note on this work by Ian Campbell (*ELN*, 1972).

As could be expected, studies of individual works are spotty. The vagaries of scholarly interest account for some of the unevenness, Carlyle's fluctuating reputation probably accounts for much more.

VIII. CARLYLE'S REPUTATION

Nothing would illustrate with greater clarity the curious fate of the Victorian prophet than a full-length study of Carlyle's reputation. No such study exists; however, many individual studies have appeared, and scarcely an essay on any aspect of Carlyle can avoid some mention of his rise and fall. Hostile critics have been assuring us for decades that Carlyle is rightly dead, and sympathetic critics have been equally insistent that Carlyle is coming back or shortly will. At times both have been right, but in the long run it seems that Carlyle will survive for the simple reason that he cannot be spared.

Without returning to the Victorian chroniclers of Carlyle's reputation or to those who alternately resuscitated or interred him in the Froude controversy and its aftermath, we can remember the extensive testimony of Carlyle's contemporaries scattered through Victorian reminiscences and memoirs. Late to appear but not to be overlooked among them is Leslie Stephen's recollection of Carlyle's reputation at Cambridge in the 1850's in *Some Early Impressions* (1924). More in the tradition of modern assessments are the studies by H. L. Stewart, certainly a sympathetic critic, who sought to restore Carlyle's reputation in "Carlyle and His Critics" (*NC*, 1919) and the "Declining Fame of Thomas Carlyle" (*Trans. of the Royal Soc. of Canada*, 1920). While Stewart's views will not be shared unreservedly by all readers, his setting forth of the variations of Carlyle's nineteenth-century reputation and his analysis of the effects of war psychosis (World War I, of course) still bear consideration. Fifty years after Carlyle's death several commentators sought to assess his position. Henry W. Clark (*ConR*, 1931) claims that Carlyle's central thought was the "dominance of right" and that his pessimism, "strange humors," and inconsistencies often obscured that message. Egon Friedell (*Living Age*, 1931) gives a German laudatory statement on Carlyle as "hero as thinker." Charles Sarolea in "The Tragedy of Thomas Carlyle: A New Interpretation" (*Eng. Rev.*, 1931) seeks to explain why and how Carlyle habitually went astray but is nevertheless more timely today than in his own time. The explanation for this bizarre thesis is apparently that Carlyle succumbed to all the wrong influences, such as German literature, and did all the wrong things, such as leave Scotland. Therefore he "lost all his battles" but for that reason he is great, and Froude has kept him alive. Sarolea's article says relatively little of critical value but its existence itself perhaps testifies to Carlyle's vitality.

Isaac W. Dyer in "Carlyle Reconsidered" (*SR*, 1933) attempts to correct Carlyle's own self-confessions of temperament and morbidity by citing his many personal kindnesses and the abundant testimony of his contemporaries of all kinds. Nevertheless, by the time of World War II, critics and readers asked again with Henry Cook, "Has Carlyle Still a Message?" (*Baptist Q.*, 1940). Cook thought he did if we could salvage the early Carlyle and jettison the later, a not uncommon position throughout twentieth-century Carlyle criticism. Eric Bentley, in "The Premature Death of Thomas Carlyle (1795–1945): An Obituary and a Footnote" (*ASch*, 1945), appended to later editions of *A Century of Hero-Worship*, took back some of the harsh judgments in his book, but only after assessing Carlyle as of 1945 as "a nullity" in terms of reputation and as "morally dangerous, aesthetically boring or repellent, and personally a neurotic" whose fame had always been personal and moral, never literary. What Bentley did allow, however, was that there was another side entirely to Carlyle—the positive element, the emphasis on questions rather than answers, the closeness to fact and experience. These have turned out to be some of the dimensions that recent critics have been willing to count in Carlyle's favor, plus, of course, the conviction, despite Bentley, that Carlyle is a great literary artist.

W. A. Munford in "Carlyle and the Twentieth Century" (*Lib. Rev.*, 1946) sought to pronounce on which Carlyle works were still serviceable and which not. The choices appear to be his own preferences, but these are commonplace enough to stand for the preferences of many. Again it is the early Carlyle over the later, with *Cromwell* and *Frederick* most specially rejected. Similar but harsher sentiments are expressed by W. R. Davies in "Can Carlyle Be Resurrected?" (*Saturday Night*, 1953), with the addition of ponderous animadversions on the evils of Carlyle's Germanism (to Carlyle, says Davies, "the Holy Ghost was a German Imperial Eagle"), aspersions on Carlyle's sexuality, and the assertion that Carlyle was a prophet "of a faith which cast out love." Somehow Davies concludes that *The French Revolution* is worth saving. Davies' essay certainly is not. Nor is there much of special value in A. J. P. Taylor's book section leader article "Was Carlyle a Great Writer?" (*New Statesman*, 1953). Taylor thinks Carlyle seriously flawed, especially in the post-*Cromwell* works, but still a great writer whose "genius was unique." Pieter Geyl considered the matter in "Carlyle zijn betekenis en reputatie" (*De Gids*, 1953).

The most recent attempt to assess Carlyle's present position is Sydney Mendel's "Carlyle: Notes towards a Revaluation" (*ESA*, 1967), but it is superficial, even though it strives for a kind of modernity by comparing Carlyle to Sartre. John Gross's *The Rise and Fall of the Man of Letters* (1969) gives something of the impact of Carlyle on the idea of the man of letters in the age, yet this readable but breezy treatment misses the opportunity for a serious evaluation of what that concept really meant to Carlyle and how he impressed it upon his contemporaries. Gross follows the common view of praising the early and deploring the later Carlyle, which is supported by his noting that Carlyle's influence on "advanced opinion" faded sharply after 1850 and *Latter-Day Pamphlets*. The most substantial documentation yet provided for any study of Carlyle's reputation is Jules Paul Seigel's *Thomas Carlyle* (1971) in the Critical Heritage series. This costly volume contains most of the well-known Victorian statements on Carlyle as well as some lesser-known ones. It is organized chronologically and by major works and the introduction gives a useful overview of the nineteenth-century response to Carlyle.

While there is, apart from Seigel, little serious scholarship on Carlyle's English reputation, there is a good deal on his American one. Starting with Frank Luther Mott's "Carlyle's American Public" (*PQ*, 1925), there are several serious examinations of how Carlyle's fared in the United States in his own day. Mott's study shows that Carlyle's fame spread outward from New England and suffered a setback during the War between the States. Mott notes many sources of American response to Carlyle and even cites some American attempts at Carlylese; he does not, however, find many references one way or another to Carlyle in writing from the South, but he is surely negligent here. William S. Vance in "Carlyle in America before *Sartor Resartus*" (*AL*, 1936) concerns himself exclusively with the reputation Carlyle enjoyed as a result of *Schiller* and *Meister* and his essays on German literature. But George Kummer in "Anonymity and Carlyle's Early Reputation in America" (*AL*, 1936) retorted that Carlyle's pre-*Sartor* or pre-Emerson reputation was more diffuse than Vance claimed because his works, though known, were anonymous and many American readers, including Emerson, were unaware that a single author was responsible for all the German essays and translations. The American reputation also occupied Howard D. Widger in "Thomas Carlyle in America: His Reputation and Influence" (Diss. Illinois 1945), and it was treated again by John Paul Pritchard in *Literary Wise Men of Gotham* (1964). Pritchard claims that Carlyle's style provoked more annoyance than delight and that "only *Sartor* found any favor" from the reviewers. However, they responded favorably to much of Carlyle's doctrine, especially his emphasis on the content of literary works as opposed to form. An article edited by Kenneth Walter Cameron, "Carlyle Evaluated and Criticized" (*Amer. Transcendental Q.*, 1970), reprints an 1850 review of *Latter-Day Pamphlets* from the New York *Tribune* and thus throws light on Carlyle's American reputation. One should also consult the studies on Carlyle and Emerson and Whittier for evidences on the state of Carlyle's reputation in America in the nineteenth century. All these studies even taken together do not add up to an exhaustive examination of Carlyle's American reputation, but they constitute a more thorough body of material than is available for his English reputation.

Curiously, the most thorough of all studies of Carlyle's reputation is for France and Latin countries: Alan Carey Taylor in *Carlyle: Sa première fortune littéraire en France (1825–1865)* (1929), which was continued and concluded by the same author's *Carlyle et la pensée latine* (1937). Taylor expressly undertook the topic because Carlyle had not penetrated deeply into Latin countries and he sought to examine the effect of Carlyle's "very British spirit" in the Latin world. It turns out to be greater than one might suppose, even if Friedrich Baldensperger's comment that a French Carlyle would be difficult to imagine must be counted true. Still, French readers of Carlyle are not so difficult to imagine. Taylor shows that Carlyle gained attention in 1848–51 and again in 1864–65, then reached a new summit after his death and up until World War 1 when he plunged again. He came later to Spain and Italy, although Mazzini lent him support in Italy as early as the 1840's. At the time of his writing Taylor speculated that Carlyle was coming back in Italy. Certainly he did so in Spain, if Unamuno's considerable interest is any indication. Throughout, Taylor seems to equate Carlyle's fortunes in Latin countries with the popularity of his political and social views rather than with his philosophy or style. Taylor has an excellent bibliography especially rich in works about Carlyle in Latin tongues and with impressive lists of translations of Carlyle into French, Italian, Spanish, Rumanian, and Portuguese.

It might seem curious to conclude a review of research on Carlyle with a work on his reputation in Latin countries, but in many respects it is a very proper conclusion, for it can stand as a beacon to comparable studies in areas where the challenge is greater. Few topics so need investigation as Carlyle's reputation, in his own day and in ours. Even the Germans, of all people, have been behindhand in this matter. Yet what else could offer the dissertation challenge of Carlyle's reputation in Germany? Some groundwork has been done with American reputation, and even a little with Canadian in the work of Stewart. References and materials lie in terrifying abundance for a study of Carlyle's reputation in Britain. Even now a study of the Froude controversy and of the question of Carlyle and Nazism will reveal that much of the scholarship turns on Carlyle's reputation. As I pointed out earlier, it has of necessity been a dimension in the recent interest in Carlyle's relation to his own age. The present study itself is a document in an understanding of Carlyle's position today. But the critic who can bring all this together with scholarship and insight will make an invaluable contribution to an understanding of the nineteenth century and to an understanding of our own and we will all then better comprehend why Carlyle cannot be spared.

JANE WELSH CARLYLE

•

G. B. Tennyson

Jenny kissed me when we met,
Jumping from the chair she sat in;
Time, you thief, who love to get
Sweets into your list, put that in;
Say I'm weary, say I'm sad,
Say that health and wealth have missed me,
Say I'm growing old, but add,
Jenny kissed me.

—LEIGH HUNT

One reason that Jane Welsh Carlyle leapt from her seat to kiss Leigh Hunt is said to be that Hunt had brought news that publishers had accepted a work of Carlyle's. Another version has it that Hunt had just recovered from an illness and Jane was glad to see him. Both versions tell us something completely in character for Jane Carlyle. On the one hand she was intensely loyal and devoted to Mr. Carlyle, on the other she possessed an irrepressible gaiety that expressed itself in impulsive gestures of this kind. Jane was always Mrs. Carlyle and she was always Jane.

Jane Carlyle is well known for having been the first to recognize the genius of *Sartor Resartus* and almost as well known for having, close to a decade earlier, been the first to recognize the genius of Thomas Carlyle. Indeed, it is a commonplace to say that Jane married for fame, not for love, and that she got more of the former and less of the latter than she ever expected. Alexander Carlyle tried to dispel such notions with the publication of the love letters of the two Carlyles, but the story that Jane endured a sad and loveless life, albeit with much fame, will not die. One thing is certain: Jane would have been the first to denounce the posthumous attacks on Carlyle as man and thinker and to denounce also the portraits of her life as blighted by her marriage. The fact is that Jane Carlyle got what she bargained for and she got it in spades; had she married Edward Irving she would have fared much worse. Jane will, as subject, always be a biographical satellite of Thomas, but she will also remain one of the rare Victorian literary wives who are of literary interest in their own right. To have been with considerable success the wife of Thomas Carlyle is distinction enough for any woman; to be remembered further as one of the great letter writers (in some opinions, her husband's superior) of the nineteenth century is glory beyond the dreams of avarice.

The matter of Jane Carlyle clearly resolves itself into the two main themes of biography and correspondence. Students of Jane Carlyle will, of course, want to consult parallel sections of the Carlyle chapter, but they may well be surprised by how much material exists on Jane in her own right. Further acquaintance with her, however, will make clear that the attention is fully justified and that more is needed. Perhaps Jane, unlike Thomas, could be spared, but only the ruthless and the humorless would ever want to do so.

I. CORRESPONDENCE: MANUSCRIPTS, BIBLIOGRAPHIES, EDITIONS

Since Jane's work lies almost wholly in correspondence, the important manuscripts are letters, most of which are in the National Library of Scotland in Edinburgh. Charles Richard Sanders reports it holds some 1,380 of Jane's letters. In all Sanders has located almost 3,500 letters by Jane in various repositories, the other important ones being those in the collections cited for Thomas Carlyle's letters. Some of Jane's letters have been published many times, but the Duke-Edinburgh edition of the correspondence of the two Carlyles will be the first to publish all known letters, for up to now only about 800 of Jane's letters have been published. The new volumes will therefore become the single most important source for scholarship on Jane.

Other source materials for Jane Carlyle are her diary and miscellaneous papers in the National Library of Scotland, Geraldine Jewsbury's memoir of Jane also in the National Library, materials printed in Carlyle's preparation of the *Letters and Memorials* (1883), in his *Reminiscences* (1881), and in an 1853 story by Jane published by Alexander Carlyle under the title "A Story from Real Life" (*Cornhill*, 1920), and the various materials in other editions of letters. There is little else available. Some of the hitherto unreleased Carlyle material in Carlyle family hands may also contain documents by Jane.

There is, of course, no separate bibliography for Jane Carlyle. She is often included in bibliographies devoted to Thomas, but most commonly intermixed rather than listed separately. Such is the case in the *NCBEL* (1969) and to a lesser extent in Dyer's bibliography of Carlyle (1928), but Dyer has a good index and should be consulted for the pre-1930 material. Bibliographies are also usually appended to editions of the letters and to biographies. The best of these is in the Hansons' biography.

Other source material on Jane is the early biographical contributions of her contemporaries, the reminiscences, memoirs, and correspondence of such as David Masson, Charles Gavan Duffy, John Forster, Harriet Martineau, Francis Espinasse, Henry James, Sr., Mrs. Gaskell, and the like. There are also a few periodical memoirs containing firsthand accounts of Jane, those by Mrs. Oliphant (*Macmillan's*, 1881; and *ConR*, 1883) and Henry Larkin (*Brit. Q. Rev.*, 1881) being the most important.

As with Carlyle's letters, the Duke-Edinburgh edition will eventually render most previous collections of Jane's correspondence out of date. But until it does, we must continue to use the existing editions. The premier edition of Jane's letters is that prepared by Carlyle himself and edited by James Anthony Froude, *Letters and Memorials of Jane Welsh Carlyle* (3 vols., 1883). In a kind of replay of the imbroglio surrounding the *Reminiscences*, Alexander Carlyle issued *New Letters and Memorials* (2 vols., 1903) to correct omissions and distortions in Froude and thus further exacerbated the Froude controversy, but the result is still two substantial collections of Jane's letters and some other materials, such as parts of her journal in the *New Letters*. Thus the Froude and Alexander Carlyle editions constitute the main published works by Jane Carlyle.

Four other collections round out the major materials: the letters up to 1840 edited by David G. Ritchie, *Early Letters of Jane Welsh Carlyle* (1889); Alexander Carlyle's edition of *The Love Letters of Thomas Carlyle and Jane Welsh* (1909); Leonard Huxley's *Jane Welsh Carlyle: Letters to Her Family, 1839–1863* (1924), consisting mainly of letters to Jane's cousins in Liverpool; and Townsend Scudder's edition of *Letters of Jane Welsh Carlyle to Joseph Neuberg, 1848–1862* (1931). The love letters were translated into German by Lucy H. Ernst and the Huxley edition into German by Adele Benedikt (1931).

There are many additions in periodical articles to the book-length collections and no complete listing will be attempted here, but the important article supplements to Jane's correspondence are: Reginald Blunt, "Letters of Jane Welsh Carlyle to Her Housemaid" (*Cornhill*, 1901); Alexander Carlyle, "Eight New Love Letters of Jane Welsh" (*NC*, 1914) and "More New Letters of Jane Welsh Carlyle" (*NC*, 1914); Reginald Blunt, "Jane Welsh Carlyle's Unpublished Letters" (*Forum*, 1921–22); and Leonard Huxley, "Letters from Jane Welsh Carlyle" (*Cornhill*, 1926). Recently a new find of Jane letters to a former suitor was reported by E. B. Chalmers in "Mrs. Carlyle's Letters to John Stodart" (*TLS*, 25 June 1971). Extensive citation is provided in the article from these letters from Jane in the 1850's and 1860's.

The only selected edition of Jane's letters, Trudy Bliss's *Jane Welsh Carlyle: A New Selection of Her Letters* (1950; British paperback ed., 1959), contains a Jane chronology and a note on the furor at the time of Froude's publication of the letters. Bliss also edited a selection of letters *to* Jane, *Thomas Carlyle: Letters to His Wife* (1953).

II. BIOGRAPHIES

Of the three main biographies of Jane Welsh Carlyle, Elizabeth Drew's *Jane Welsh and Jane Carlyle* (1928), Townsend Scudder's *Jane Welsh Carlyle* (1939), and Lawrence and Elisabeth Hanson's *Necessary Evil: The Life of Jane Welsh Carlyle* (1952), the Hansons' is the best. Drew's biography, popular rather than scholarly, is capable and not thesis-ridden, although she firmly believes that Jane and Thomas loved each other and illustrates this conviction throughout in a sane and balanced manner. Scudder's biography is based on reliable source materials but is regrettably written in what the author calls "the idiom of the Carlyles and those who knew them." This idiom as Scudder presents it makes often for rather gushy reading and verges frequently on the novelistic, apparently an irresistible urge for those who take up Jane's biography. The Hansons' life, despite its regrettable title, is the most extensive and thorough. Based on a careful reading of Jane's published and unpublished correspondence, it succeeds in presenting a sympathetic portrait of Jane without going to the extreme of making Thomas an adversary. The authors relegate the vexed question of the sexual relations of the Carlyles to an appendix and try to reach an undogmatic and rational conclusion.

John Stewart Collis' *The Carlyles* (1971) treats Jane and Thomas together as do many other biographies, but it is strictly of the lurid school and clearly not the product of scholarly research.

Other studies of Jane's life include the early biography by Mrs. Alexander Ireland, *Life of Jane Welsh Carlyle* (1891), and Osbert Burdett's *The Two Carlyles* (1930), which is strongly pro-Froude except for a welcome mitigation of anti-Carlyle bias. Marion Lochhead's "Jane Welsh Carlyle" (*QR*, 1960) is a recent sympathetic treatment but too anecdotal. On the impotence issue Lochhead is very sensible. Lucy Poate Stebbins in *London Ladies: True Tales of the Eighteenth* [sic] *Century* (1952) includes among its romanticized treatments an "evocation" of the Jane-Thomas-Edward Irving triangle. It adds nothing of critical or scholarly value. Some other sketchy evocations of no value are Barine Arvède's *Portraits des femmes* (1909), Philip Guedalla's "Jane Welsh Carlyle" (*Good Housekeeping*, 1928), and the same author's "Bonnet and Shawl" (*Mentor*, 1929).

SPECIALIZED ASPECTS OF LIFE. Many treatments deal with particular aspects of Jane's life, especially her relations with particular persons or circumstances. Perhaps the most popular specialized area is that of Jane's domestic life, with its attendant illnesses and servant problems, and the atmosphere of mid-nineteenth-century Chelsea. Reginald Blunt, the chronicler of Chelsea, must be mentioned first in this connection for his *The Carlyles' Chelsea Home* (1895), still a mine of information about the appearance and appointments of No. 5 Great Cheyne Row. More domestic in focus but also highly readable and entertaining is Thea Holme's *The Carlyles at Home* (1965). This is the best source for seeing how Jane coped with servants and for day-to-day insights into the Carlyles' domestic life. Holme based her research on Jane's correspondence and she writes with wit and gaiety of the Carlyle domestic world. The National Trust also published a nicely illustrated brochure titled "Carlyle's House" (1966), as it is today, restored to its previous Victorian charm.

The Carlyles' Chelsea life is also the subject of G. H. Stevenson's "Little House" (*FortR*, 1934); Filson Young's "Round the Carlyles' House" (*Listener*, 1934); Hilda S. Primrose's "Jane Welsh Carlyle: Her Chelsea Home and Her Music Books" (*Musical Times*, 1938), from which we learn that Jane preferred to play and sing Scottish airs; and Joanna Richardson's "The Carlyles of Cheyne Row" (*Listener*, 1960), containing information on the original furnishings. C. W. Parish's obscure "Mrs. Carlyle Discovers Rottingdean" (*Sussex County Mag.*, 1949) reveals that Jane was enchanted with the little Sussex village long before Kipling, but failed ever to rent the seaside cottage she yearned for.

Jane's relations with Thomas are not as such a special category, rather they form the substance of the biographies, but there are a few articles more narrowly concerned with the matter. Joseph J. Reilly in "Jane Carlyle Looks at Thomas" (*CathW*, 1928; rpt. in *Of Books and Men*, 1942) seeks to show that Jane never forgot that Thomas was a mere mortal even while the rest of the world revered him as a prophet. Walther Fischer in "Thomas und Jane Carlyle im Spiegel der Briefe Amely Böltes an Varnhagen von Ense" (*Eng. Studien*, 1929) adds little to existing general knowledge but supplies details on the relationship of about 1850 when Amely Bölte, a German governess, resided for a time with the Carlyles. An editorial, "The Two Carlyles" (*TLS*, 30 Dec. 1949), and N. Brysson Morrison's "When Thomas Carlyle Met Jane Welsh" (*Scots Mag.*, 1952) are both conventional, the former emphasizing Jane's letter writing, the latter biographical aspects.

Jane's relations with others occasionally receive separate treatment. Mabel Davidson in "The Record of a Broken Friendship" (*SAQ*, 1925) traces Jane's increasing estrangement from Carlyle's brother, Dr. John Carlyle. She had contempt for him as a physician and despised his indecision. For his part, he ministered to her rather unsympathetically in an illness in 1864 and opined that she had too much leisure and read too many French novels. End of friendship. Charles Platt's "Development of an Attitude: The Carlyles and Their Good Friend Froude" (*Century*, 1928) is an anti-Froude piece that draws frequently on Jane's letters to weaken Froude's views in the biography. Virginia Woolf wrote "Geraldine and Jane" (*Bookman*, 1929) on the Jane-Geraldine Jewsbury relationship, but added nothing of value. Susanne Howe in *Geraldine Jewsbury: Her Life and Errors* (1935) is more informative, but she does not consider one of Geraldine's errors to be her allegations about the Carlyle sexual relationship. Here she relies too heavily on Froude. She furthermore advances her own quasi-Freudian notions about a sexual attraction Geraldine felt for Jane which, if true, hardly encourages one to believe what Geraldine might later have to say about Jane's sexual unfulfillment with Carlyle. Howe, moreover, does not correct Geraldine's own conflicting testimony on Jane at death, testimony at the time that Jane looked serene, testimony years later that she looked anguished. Despite Howe, Geraldine Jewsbury appears to have been a most addled woman. Mrs. Alexander Ireland edited *Selections from the Letters of Geraldine Endsor Jewsbury to Jane Welsh Carlyle* (1892), which contains a monograph on Geraldine. There was also a leader article "Geraldine and Jane" (*TLS*, 28 Feb. 1929) of very minor interest.

Jane is a principal figure in the Ashburton relationship which is studied most extensively in Iris Origo's "The Carlyles and the Ashburtons: A Victorian Friendship" (*Cornhill*, 1950; rpt. in *A Measure of Love*, 1957). Grace J. Calder in "Erasmus A. Darwin: Friend of Thomas and Jane Carlyle" (*MLQ*, 1959) offers information on another interesting Jane association. Sir Philip J. Hamilton Grierson in "Mrs. Carlyle's Claim to Descent from John Knox" (*Trans. of Dumfries Natural Hist. Soc.*, 1920) casts doubt on the celebrated claim of Jane's descent from the Scottish reformer, claiming that Jane actually descended from an elder brother of the man who married Knox's daughter, hence was not descended from Knox at all. Ronald Pearsall in "The Death of Jane Welsh Carlyle" (*Hist. Today*, 1966) gives a conventional treatment of Jane's last days and of her letter writing excellence.

FICTIONALIZED TREATMENTS. Jane Carlyle enjoys, with Elizabeth Barrett Browning, the curious distinction of encouraging a novelistic or quasi-fictional approach in her biographers and, even more curious, of having stimulated several historical plays and stories based on her life. The first of these is L. Housman's "Fire-lighters: A Dialogue on a Burning Topic" (*London Mercury*, 1929), a play about the Carlyles and Mills and the burning of the manuscript of *The French Revolution*. O. W. Firkins wrote the one-act "Two Passengers for Chelsea" (in *Two Passengers for Chelsea and Other Plays*, 1928), a comedy about the Carlyles, including such characters as Alfred Tennyson, Giuseppe Mazzini, and Richard Monckton Milnes. Part of the excitement is provided by a scene in which Jane takes a puff from Tennyson's pipe to the horrified disapprobation of Lady Harriet Baring who speaks to Tennyson in this wise: "Mr. Tennyson, at my earnest entreaty, you will have the goodness to remove your pipe from the mouth of Mrs. Carlyle." Nevertheless, Jane triumphs and keeps Carlyle at the close. Glenn Hughes wrote *Mrs. Carlyle: A Historical Play* (1950), rendering the domestic life of Thomas and Jane, also with a concluding scene involving Lady Harriet Baring. Elsie Thornton-Cook wrote a novel called *Speaking Dust* (1938) based on the courtship and married life of the Carlyles. It was translated into German (1939) by H. Böhmer.

Jane's biography, then, is a much-cultivated field. Some further light might be cast on individual relationships, but this will probably occur as new correspondence is published.

III. CRITICISM

If Jane is the commanding letter writer that her partisans claim her to be, there should be more serious literary criticism of her work than there is. Although there are numerous articles, most of them are superficial and often are review articles which take the occasion of reviewing a volume of Jane's correspondence to make various claims for her genius as a writer. There is need for a more serious approach to this subject, and it will no doubt come forth in connection with the publication of the Duke-Edinburgh edition of the letters.

Lord Ernle in "Mrs. Carlyle and English Letter-Writing" (*QR*, 1924) tries to define the essence of good letter writing and Jane Carlyle's place in the history of English letter writers. He claims that her best letters are early rather than late for the later letters complain too much and lack her earlier buoyancy. A. Koszul in "Nouvelles lettres de Jane Welsh Carlyle" (*RAA*, 1924–25) in reviewing Huxley's edition of Jane's letters acclaims them as "lettres admirable, vrais chefs-d'œuvre de l'art epistolaire." Gabrielle Reuter in "Jane Welsh Carlyle" (*Die Literatur*, 1931) is favorable to Jane but contributes little of critical value. Lyn Irvine in *Ten Letter Writers* (1932) includes Jane and lauds both her letter writing and the sophistication of her mind which he says "has probably never been surpassed by that of any woman." Irvine also makes a few of those rare literary observations about Jane's letter writing that one wishes there were more of. He notes, for instance, that the Scottish dialect gave added fiber to Jane's style and made her aware of idiomatic subtleties. He says her style makes use of proverbs and possesses a vivid picturesque simplicity.

Nothing comparable to Irvine's study, slight though it is, came along for some time. Eston Everett Ericson's "A Scotch Dialect Contraction" (*Anglia Beiblatt*, 1936) is a brief note on a Jane expression. R. Chapin's "Warm, Witty, and Courageous Woman" (*Christian Sci. Monthly Mag.*, 1950) reviews favorably Trudy Bliss's selection of letters. Lord David Cecil, however, in *The Fine Art of Reading* (1957) devotes an essay to "Some Women Letter-Writers" and includes Mrs. Carlyle. He calls her "brilliant" and "cantankerous" and one of the best of women letter writers. V. S. Pritchett considered Jane in "Books in General" (*New Statesman*, 1950) as a result of the Bliss selection but remained largely anecdotal, noting, however, that Jane lacked "that messiah-producing and soulful inner glumness of the pregnant artist," which is one reason why she didn't become a novelist like Jane Austen.

The capable Jane biographer Elizabeth Drew offers as good criticism on Jane as a letter writer as is available anywhere in *The Literature of Gossip: Nine English Letter Writers* (1964). She discusses again much of the biographical background, including the Ashburton relationship, from which she thinks Jane though hurt recovered sufficiently and concludes that Jane is "the most unaffected of letter-writers; so gusty and vivid, 'splashing off' whatever she has to say, with much natural vitality and phrasing." It is a good judgment, though again one would like more literary rigor in arriving at it.

The other contributions to criticism on Jane are almost all very lightweight or highly specialized. In the latter category, H. L. Creek in "The Opinions of Jane Welsh Carlyle" (*SR*, 1926) has culled the letters for a fascinating assemblage of Jane's remarks on her contemporaries. Joseph J. Reilly in "Jane Carlyle Appraises Her Contemporaries" (*CathW*, 1944) has done much the same thing. These two gatherings prove that Jane was almost Thomas' equal in pithy summations of friends and acquaintances. Mabel Davidson in "The Religion of Mrs. Carlyle" (*SR*, 1927) argues that Jane never became a mystic and was never strongly religiously inclined but remained an agnostic.

As stated above, the criticism does not by its weight or power prove the case for Jane as perhaps the greatest letter writer of her age. Of course the correspondence itself must do that, but the criticism that should attend on the work for which so much is claimed is unduly thin. Jane is not too badly served by biographies; she has been and is being well served by editions of her correspondence; criticism can now address itself to her literary achievement. To be sure, in the final analysis Jane will always be filtered through the genius of her husband, but it was he who claimed for her "a soft invincibility, a clearness of discernment and a noble loyalty of heart, which are rare." These are the qualities that shine through the letters maintaining just the right balance between Mrs. Carlyle and Jane.

JOHN HENRY NEWMAN

·

Martin J. Svaglic and Charles Stephen Dessain

MAN AND HUMANIST

•

Martin J. Svaglic

I. BIOGRAPHICAL MATERIALS

The death of Cardinal Newman on 11 August 1890 called forth a great chorus of public tribute of which Dean R. W. Church's obituary in *The Guardian* (rpt. in his *Occasional Papers*, II, 1897) is a good example: "we lose in him not only one of the very greatest masters of English style, not only a man of singular purity and beauty of character, but the founder, we may almost say, of the Church of England as we see it." Among other tributes were an affectionate memoir by William Lockhart, whose conversion to Rome well before Newman's was one of the scandals of the Oxford Movement: *Cardinal Newman: Reminiscences of 50 Years Since by One of His Oldest Living Disciples* (1891); a brief *Life* by "John Oldcastle" (Wilfred Meynell, 1890); a long obituary in the *Spectator* (1890) by its literary editor R. H. Hutton, whose account of the Kingsley controversy had been of inestimable value in winning Newman a sympathetic hearing; and a warmly appreciative biographical and critical study by Hutton, *Cardinal Newman* (1891), which he had been preparing for the Leaders of Religion series at the time of the Cardinal's death.

Hutton's book concentrates on Newman's Anglican career, accepting the account in the *Apologia*, which it amplifies with brief analyses and criticism of Newman's major works, Roman Catholic as well as Anglican. There are perceptive contrasts between the style of the Anglican and Roman years; and in general Hutton credits Newman with a "singular command of imaginative eloquence, of the most rare and delicate pathos, and of a satire finer at once in its point and in its reserve than any satire of this generation." He finds "hardly any other instance in our literature of so definite and remarkable a literary genius being entirely devoted, and devoted with the full ardor of a brooding imagination, to the service of revealed religion."

Among those disturbed by such tributes to the dead Newman was his younger brother Francis William, Emeritus Professor of Classics at University College, London, who had been virtually separated from John Henry for sixty-six years, during which in familiar Victorian fashion he had turned against organized religion in favor of an intense moral idealism and a vague theism. His bête noire was sacerdotalism, to which he felt that his famous brother had given a most baleful impetus. Accordingly, to warn Protestants against the speciousness of John Henry's pleadings, he wrote a little book called *Contributions, Chiefly to the Early History of the Late Cardinal Newman* (1891), an argumentum ad hominem, with little analysis of Newman's thought; indeed, some of the remarks make the reader wonder if he ever bothered to read his brother closely: for example, as regards the crucial Tract 90, "I was so sick of the whole subject, that I never took the trouble of getting the tract to read."

The portrait of Newman that emerges is of an imperious and conceited person who could not bear "the coarseness of the vulgar," who insisted always on having his own way, who could be personally generous (as to Frank himself), but who was also an authoritarian, some of whose poems like "Persecution" and "Private Judgment" in the *Lyra Apostolica* show him to have been long a concealed Romanist though not perhaps a Papist, there being little or no distinction for Frank between Catholicism and Romanism. For him the *Apologia* does not tell the true story. He even describes the verdict against Newman in the Achilli trial as "quite just" and deplores "the wild violence of my brother against Mr. Kingsley." Despite its obvious rhetorical bias, *Contributions* remains of value for its insights into the Newman family and certain undeniable traits of at least the early John Henry Newman.

A more scholarly and thorough attempt to deflate Newman's reputation was Edwin A. Abbott's *The Anglican Career of Cardinal Newman* (2 vols., 1892), probably still the locus classicus of the anti-Newman position. Abbott was a Broad Church clergyman and a distinguished educator of the Thomas Arnold type, who in *Philomythus* (1891) had already attacked Newman for credulity in his views about miracles. Now in the wake of the funeral elegies, he feared that Anglicans might be tempted to ask, "If Newman was right, are not we wrong?" Accordingly, he set out to show that the *Apologia* was "by no means so accurate in its representation of facts as it is delightful in its literary style." Newman's conversion he characterized as a "Soul's Tragedy," a drama of spiritual involution in which Reason was sacrificed to achieve the peace of Faith, "or what seemed Faith." Abbott was noted for instilling in his pupils a devotion to fact, and he was shocked by Newman's tendency to rely heavily in thinking about religion on presumption, signs, antecedent probabilities, and so on. Like Thomas Arnold, Archbishop Whately, and F. W. Newman, he is severe on Newman's *Elucidations* of Dr. Hampden's Bampton Lectures, which he regards as a culpable misrepresentation. He believes that Newman's imagination dominated his reason and that this conclusion is substantiated by a comparison with the original text of the revisions Newman made in the second edition of the *Apologia* to render his ultimate decision more rational in appearance than it actually was. Abbott was so harsh with Newman that his book evoked many protests: for example, R. H. Hutton's in an appendix to the second edition (1892) of his biography. Nevertheless, his views have influenced many subsequent works on Newman.

The most famous and in some ways most perceptive early study of Newman was probably Henri Bremond's *Newman: Essai de biographie psychologique* (1906), translated by H. C. Corrance in 1907 as *The Mystery of Newman*, the mystery presumably being Newman's combination (like Bremond's own) of such ordinarily antithetical traits as faith and skepticism. Bremond attempted to steer a path between the apotheosizers and the calumniators of Newman, a thing difficult to do even today since, as an unusually compelling spokesman for what some consider eternal verities and others regressive myths, Newman continues to attract or repel most readers quite strongly, with the result that disinterested writing about him is relatively rare. Bremond's book is not a straightforward biography but rather a study of various aspects of Newman's life and thought such as his all-important first conversion, his sense of the invisible, the nature of his preaching, and so on. The author had the uncommon advantage of possessing both a religious and an artistic sensibility which gave him many insights into Newman's writing: for example, his interpretation of "the documents of the past in the light of his own history." He finds Newman's ruling qualities to be "psychological realism" and "supersensuous realism," the latter being the power of making the invisible present and palpable through the accumulation of detail, as in the sermon "Worship, A Preparation for Christ's Coming" (*Parochial and Plain Sermons*, v) or what Bremond in company with many nineteenth-century critics regarded as the "marvellous" *Dream of Gerontius*. He distinguishes Newman's egocentricity from "a vulgar self-esteem," saying that he exalted the value of his soul "only to impose on himself in consequence a loftier and stricter moral rule."

Although so respected a critic as Charles Du Bos regarded Bremond's study of Newman as his best work, it must be acknowledged that the book does have serious weaknesses: it greatly exaggerates Newman's skepticism, "autocentrism," and detachment, it being sheer ignorance to say that among his equals, Newman's was "the most detached, the least inquiring mind which the last century has known" and that "What is called contemporary thought interests him less than the history of ants." And although Bremond defends Newman against Abbott's charge of credulity by arguing that the disposition of a Christian to believe would naturally color his inquiries into miracles and that Newman was not credulous but highly skeptical, the net effect is with Abbott, who was one of his principal sources, greatly to simplify and so distort Newman's empirically grounded and analogous theory of belief. It is unfortunate that Bremond did not know more about the life and thought of a man he admired so greatly—Wilfrid Ward's biography had not yet appeared when he wrote, nor had any letters beyond those of the two-volume Anne Mozley edition.

In 1912 appeared the standard and still on the whole the best biography, *The Life of John Henry Cardinal Newman Based on His Private Journals and Correspondence* (2 vols.), by Wilfrid Ward, son of William George Ward, onetime disciple of Mill and then of Newman. Relying by Newman's own desire on the *Apologia* and the Mozley letters for the Anglican years, to which he devoted only a long chapter, Ward concentrated on the Roman Catholic life of Newman. Like his subject, he was a cultivated, well-balanced, and progressive-minded Catholic whose book, predicted the *TLS* reviewer, "was likely to take its place at once among the great biographies, not so much because of its literary qualities—though these are good—as because of its obvious truthfulness." This early judgment has recently been echoed by A. O. J. Cockshut, who ranks the book with Boswell's *Johnson* and Froude's *Carlyle* as one of the "truly great biographies" that "in the discussion of a great and complex personality . . . give the sense of a 'lifetime burning in every moment' " (*Essays and Poems Presented to Lord David Cecil*, ed. W. W. Robson, 1970). Feeling that Newman's life was "in the main" that of "a writer and thinker," Ward concentrates on ideas and allows Newman to speak for himself when possible. Not the liveliest of writers, he tells nevertheless an engrossing story of Newman's struggle against unbelief and for an enlightened Catholicism in the face of sometimes timid and uncomprehending, sometimes hostile and reactionary opposition of leaders of the Roman Church in England and Ireland who almost turned his life into a tragedy. Ward has been accused of overdramatizing Newman's life and concentrating too much on its sad aspects; but the fact is that Newman himself constantly saw life in dramatic terms, and much of the narrative now reads like a prophetic anticipation of the principal issues raised by the second Vatican Council.

Ward's biography was later supplemented for the Anglican years by his daughter Maisie's *Young Mr. Newman* (1948), a well-illustrated book not intended for scholars, however, and only imperfectly documented, the author fearing "a rash of footnotes disagreeable to the eye." Despite its overly chatty and protective tone, the book is in many ways quite informative, especially about the Newman family, thanks to a skillful use of the Mozley family letters and of Harriet Newman's *Family Adventures* and *The Fairy Bower*. It is uneven in tracing Newman's intellectual development, saying little about the influence of Butler and Keble, for instance, but providing good material on the Evangelicals, on Dr. Hampden, and on Froude's *Remains*.

In 1952 Seán O'Faoláin's lively account of the Anglican years, *Newman's Way: The Odyssey of John Henry Newman*, also inadequately documented, brought to light further information about the family background, on which the Newmans were inclined to maintain a genteel reticence. Thus, in his Autobiographical Memoir prefixed to Anne Mozley's edition of his correspondence, John Henry says only that his father was a London banker "whose family came from Cambridgeshire." The full story, according to O'Faoláin, is that his grandfather was only a poor grocer. Similarly, Harriet spoke of her ancestors as "small landed proprietors"; but they were very small indeed, and their land had come from a William Newman, an early eighteenth-century tailor. O'Faoláin also presents what was then the fullest account available of the second and virtually unknown Newman brother, the eccentric Charles, whom he describes as "the family plague for fifty years."

In 1962 the most elaborate biography of Newman thus far appeared, a twelve-hundred-page work by Meriol Trevor in two volumes entitled *Newman: The Pillar of the Cloud* and *Newman: Light in Winter*. (In New York the second volume was published in 1963.) Trevor's is the first biography to be written out of an extensive knowledge of the immense amount of material in the archives of the Birmingham Oratory; and for the facts of Newman's life, it is now the indispensable source. It contains much important information even about the Catholic years that is not to be found in Wilfrid Ward including the first detailed account of the quarrel between the Birmingham and London Oratories; and it would certainly have superseded Ward except that it is much less the biography of a writer and thinker, more that of Newman as a person. In this respect it is often very good indeed, as in its clarification of Newman's frequently misrepresented views about virginity. It suffers, however, from a partisanship that makes the author too defensive about Newman, too uncritical, and too unfair to his opponents, who are melodramatized. There is still room for a disinterested critical biography of Newman, man and thinker, set in the richer context of his age as brought to light by recent scholarship in the religious history of the Victorian era. The difficulty is, as Geoffrey Tillotson remarked in another connection, that writers of sufficient breadth to do justice to the many sides of Newman are rare indeed.

Among other works deserving attention are two rather slight but quite literate biographical and critical studies, with emphasis on Newman as a man of letters: William Barry's *Cardinal Newman* (1904; rev. 1927) and especially Bertram Newman's *Cardinal Newman* (1925). The latter is concerned with Newman's status as an English classic. He thinks that beginners in Newman should start with the "University Sketches" (*Historical Sketches*, 1); like Hutton, he credits Newman with astonishing powers of satire, as in parts of *Loss and Gain*; he regards the *Development of Christian Doctrine* as a model of subtle argument, lucid eloquence, and orderly arrangement: "undoubtedly Newman's greatest though not his most attractive work"; he describes the *Apologia* as a "striking instance of what can be effected by sheer power of style working upon materials not obviously promising"; and he thinks that the passages by which Newman "has chiefly enriched our literature are those where there is no question of enforcing an argument or refuting an opponent, where deep feeling finds simple utterance, and a perfect naturalness is seconded only by the fastidiousness of a scholar and the ear of a musician": for example, the endings of the *Apologia*, the *Essay on Development*, and the sermon called "The Parting of Friends."

Among the many books and articles elicited by the centenary of the Oxford Movement in 1933, two biographical studies are outstanding. The first is *John Henry Newman*, by Frank Leslie Cross. Putting special emphasis on Newman's Anglican writings, his temperament, and his motivation, Cross makes two claims to originality: first, the stress he lays on Newman's moralism (hinted at but not developed by Yngve Brilioth and Clement Webb), his "absolute faith in the finality of the data of the moral consciousness" which is at the root of his interpretation both of religion and of philosophy; and second, the application to Newman of Nietzsche's theory of *ressentiment*. According to Nietzsche, says Cross, the slave-moral Christian, "who had forbidden himself to meet his foe in the face, contented himself with a victory over him in the imagination." Such types are rare among Christians, but Newman was one of the exceptions, combining an aristocratic Pelagianism in some aspects of his behavior with an Augustinian sense of self-distrust that made him look for support outside himself: to his bishop, for example. "Newman's refusal to proceed with schemes in the face of opposition" caused him subsequent mental torments, a sense of injury or feeling of grievance. "Unable to secure a victory where he had sought it, he contented himself with a pseudo-victory in the consciousness that he had done his utmost." Hence his conversion, the *Apologia*, his behavior toward Roman Catholic authorities, and so on. The *Apologia*, "probably the greatest autobiography in the English language," gives "a distinctly misleading account" of Newman's chief motives, which were primarily psychological, only secondarily moral or intellectual: "Newman's temperament was far too distrustful of reason ever to have been led to such a radical change on primarily intellectual grounds."

Passing over the obviously too broad generalization about Newman's refusal to proceed in the face of opposition, one might say at least two things of all such interpretations based on some theory of resentment on Newman's part, which have periodically recurred from Bishop Wilberforce's *Quarterly* review of the *Apologia* to Walter Houghton's *Art of Newman's* Apologia: there may well be an element of truth in them, Newman himself admitting in the *Apologia* that it was the recent acts of bishops in the Tract 90 affair that had given inquiry "its force and its edge"; but second, that in *Development*, the *Apologia*, and elsewhere, he himself, noted for his introspective powers, denies the primacy of such motivation, saying he wished to be guided chiefly by his reason. As it happened, he reasoned virtually all his adult life, thanks to the influence of Aristotle and Butler, by the cumulation of "probabilities" often involving the employment of analogy and parallel cases; and the *Apologia* supplies the cases decisive for him: "the Fathers made me a Catholic." It would seem that by adducing evidence, one might legitimately argue that Newman's method of reasoning was faulty in itself or in its application to the events cited in the *Apologia*; but that it is mere assertion, for which there is no solid evidence in Newman's later life or letters (rather the contrary), to affirm with confidence that Newman's principal motives in reaching his crucial decision were other than those he adduces in the *Apologia*.

The second psychobiography of distinction published in 1933 was Geoffrey Faber's *Oxford Apostles*, a vivid array of sparkling character sketches with emphasis on Newman. Faber was the grandson of Newman's friend Francis Faber, older brother of the convert Frederick Faber, who later became head of the Brompton Oratory. It was his grandfather's letters to Newman that kindled Geoffrey Faber's interest in the Tractarians, with whose religious and ascetic tendencies he had even less sympathy than Charles Kingsley. His point of view is clear from his remark that in those days psychology "had not yet taught men to look for the roots of spiritual ideals in their animal nature. Love, therefore, was not an object of suspicion. But psychology lies between us and them." With Faber the psychology is Freudian. Although he asserts that we "cannot, without risk of self-deception, treat a Newman as if he were a patient in the consulting room of a psychologist," he confidently proceeds to set him down as one who met a dogmatic system under a friendly guide at the receptive time of puberty, a system that satisfied his own egocentric and aloof nature so that the rest of his life became a struggle to protect the citadel where his infant self lay entrenched. Newman's friendship with Hurrell Froude is interpreted as at least subconsciously homosexual, with Newman as the feminine element. At times Faber can be not only simplistic but downright crude and vindictive, as when he explains Pusey's holding firm to his Anglicanism: "He had experienced the essential human passions. He was, in fact, what Newman never was—a man. Let Newman, with his escort of hermaphrodites, succumb to these alien, imperious fascinations."

In one form or another Faber's interpretation, which concentrates on the feminine and simply ignores the masculine side of Newman's character, has proved quite influential, turning up with more sophistication in later studies of Newman. Although Faber was not a scholar—his knowledge of Newman was very limited, his book is badly documented, and he depended heavily on E. A. Abbott for much of his ammunition—he does make the Oxford Movement come alive, and he undoubtedly has genuine insights to offer which make *Oxford Apostles* still worth reading.

Other biographers of Newman include F. A. D'Cruz (Madras, n.d.), Gaius Atkins (1931), J. M. Flood (1933), John Elliott Ross (1933), John Moody (1945), Robert Sencourt (1948), J. A. Lutz (1948), Eleanor Ruggles (1948), Louis Bouyer (1952), William Robbins (1966), and Charles Stephen Dessain (1966). The last three are most likely to repay the attention of Victorian specialists.

Bouyer's *Newman: Sa vie, sa spiritualité* (1952; trans. J. Lewis May, 1958) was written, according to Henry Tristram, out of a feeling that Abbé Bremond had travestied Newman. Bouyer's psychobiography, two-thirds of which is devoted to the Anglican years, stresses Newman's sanctity, the evidence for which is based especially on the spiritual journal that he kept during the retreat before his conditional ordination in Rome in 1847. Bouyer was the first to print this important journal (Latin and English versions first appeared in their entirety in the *Newman Autobiographical Writings* of 1956). A onetime Lutheran minister turned Catholic priest, Bouyer also stresses the contemporary significance of Newman as apologist to the unbeliever and irenicist who through such works as *Lectures on Justification*, which Bremond made light of, set forth an "advance pattern, a model" of an ecumenical theology to bring all Christians together. Highly analytical and interpretive, Bouyer is quite rewarding on such matters as the influence of Hawkins on Newman, Mary Newman's death, Newman's illness in Sicily, and his good common sense as clergyman and educator, so hard to reconcile with the view of him as a delicate neurotic. His book would be more impressive and convincing, however, if it were not so one-sided and protective of Newman, who in his journals was far readier to admit his own failings than Bouyer ever is. A pointed discussion of some of Bouyer's weaknesses and a spirited if somewhat irascible defense may be found in A. Dwight Culler's review of the book in *Renascence* (1959) and in Justus George Lawler's "Newman: Biography or Psychography" (*Ren*, 1961).

Insofar as William Robbins' *The Newman Brothers* (1966) is an attempt to show that Francis William Newman was more than the "faddist and crank" he gained the reputation of being through some of his eccentricities and through the verdicts of Matthew Arnold and Lionel Trilling, it is a useful book, providing a good outline of Frank Newman's admirably many-sided life and conscientious spiritual development. Its subtitle is not "an essay in rehabilitation," however, but "An Essay in Comparative Intellectual Biography," and on this level the book is unsatisfactory, not because John and Frank do not represent opposite types of mind, but because the comparison is made in terms loaded against the former and simplistic to a high degree. The informing dialectic is Karl Popper's distinction in *The Open Society and Its Enemies* between "the Platonizing idealist (often authoritarian) on the one hand, and the 'social engineer' on the other, with his piecemeal empirical constructions." Frank is the open society; John is its enemy. To arrive at so pat a conclusion, Robbins has Platonized the latter out of all proportion, something that can be done only by ignoring his work as educational theorist and administrator and testimony by such contemporaries as James Anthony Froude that Newman had a "world-wide" mind, "interested in everything which was going on in science, in politics, in literature." (See "The Oxford Counter Reformation" in Froude's *Short Studies in Great Subjects*, IV, 1881.)

Charles Stephen Dessain's *John Henry Newman* (1966) concentrates not on personalities and background but on Newman's work in religion, the book having been written for a new Leaders in Religion series. It makes better use than anyone else of primary sources like the *Parochial and Plain Sermons* to indicate Newman's spiritual ideas. There are also good chapters, equally marked by fresh quotation from primary sources, on the Oratory, on the Irish University, on the defense of the laity and the *Apologia*, on Newman's relation to Catholic extremists in education and doctrine, and on *A Grammar of Assent*. All of this is accomplished in 169 pages, and there is also an excellent brief bibliography, slightly enlarged in the second edition (1971). Dessain, curator of the Newman archives at the Birmingham Oratory and editor of Newman's letters, almost certainly has greater familiarity with every aspect of Newman's life than anyone else; and his brief intellectual biography, together with the article on Newman by Joseph Bacchus and Henry Tristram in the *Dictionnaire de théologie catholique* (1931), provides the best introduction to Newman now available.

In addition to the biographies, there have been several articles on important aspects of Newman's life. "The School-Days of Cardinal Newman," by Henry Tristram (*Cornhill*, 1925), is a good account of Newman's "first and only school," Great Ealing, and of his life there—his reading in classics, his acting in Terence, the periodicals he conducted, the influence of the twenty-six-year-old Evangelical Walter Mayers, who regretted the time devoted to teaching as "injurious to his spiritual state and no less prejudicial to his ministerial usefulness." Dessain's "Newman's First Conversion" (*Studies*, 1957) collects all the passages in which Newman speaks of the crucial change that occurred in him between 1 August and 21 December 1816. Dessain is informative on the influence of Walter Mayers and Thomas Scott, on the meaning of Newman's famous phrase about resting "in the thought of two and two only supreme and luminously self-evident beings"—an echo of the whole Christian ascetical tradition—and on the differences between Newman's and the typical Evangelical conversion.

Martin J. Svaglic's "Newman and the Oriel Fellowship" (*PMLA*, 1955) is a detailed account, based on Newman's Private Journals and "Personal and Family Letters" in the Birmingham Oratory, of Newman's election to a Fellowship on 12 April 1822, an event he called "the turning point of his life and of all the days most memorable." The article includes the first complete publication of Newman's English essay on diffidence, which played an important part in the Oriel examination and reveals at an early date the psychological insight for which he became famous and the strong influence on him of the *Nicomachean Ethics*.

Howard B. Slavin's "Newman's Illness in Sicily: A Review and an Interpretation" (*Wiseman [Dublin] Rev.*, 1964) is a fascinating clinical analysis by a Washington physician of all the symptoms of the famous illness that began in Sicily in late April 1833 and lasted about a month. It is based especially on "My Illness in Sicily," Newman's own graphic account which Anne Mozley expurgated and which first appeared in its entirety in the *Newman Autobiographical Writings* of 1956. Citing medical authorities and his own experience with patients, Slavin concludes that Newman's symptoms were not those of cholera or brucellosis but almost certainly of typhoid fever. According to Slavin, "My Illness in Sicily" is "without question one of the most penetrating personal accounts of prolonged febrile delirium ever written and, perhaps, the best."

Three articles by Vincent Ferrer Blehl, S.J., all based on letters and documents hitherto unpublished, make other episodes in Newman's life much clearer. "Newman on Trial" (*The Month*, 1962) gives a good account of the origin of the Achilli libel suit and of the actual trial (21–24 June 1852), which Newman himself was too busy in Dublin to attend, so that there are no lively descriptions of the event in his letters. "Newman and the Missing Miter" (*Thought*, 1960) shows that it was chiefly Archbishop Cullen of Dublin who dissuaded Pius IX from his earlier acceptance of Wiseman's suggestion that Newman be made a bishop in order to deal on equal terms with the Irish hierarchy in administering the affairs of the new Catholic University, Cullen arguing that the enterprise should first get under way, that the people might complain about the expense involved, and that Irish nationalistic feeling might be provoked. "Newman's Delation: Some Hitherto Unpublished Letters" (*DubR*, 1960) gives us two letters and part of a third to the Secretary of the Congregation of Propaganda in Rome in which Bishop T. J. Brown of Newport delated Newman for heresy in his July 1859 *Rambler* article "On Consulting the Faithful in Matters of Doctrine." Brown felt that Newman was actually putting forth arguments against the authority of the Church commonly espoused by her enemies, and he shows some animus against the new convert clergy, especially Newman's and Faber's Oratorians.

"Charles Newman and His Brothers," by Svaglic (*PMLA*, 1956), gives the most detailed account of the sometimes comic, more often pathetic, life of the second Newman brother, the little-known antiestablishment agnostic socialist Charles Robert, whom John and Frank supported for much of his long life. The article is based principally on Newman's twelve-page "Memorandum" consisting for the most part of fragments of Charles's letters (thus exemplifying Newman's own theory of biography), a document tucked away at the end of the second MS volume of "Personal and Family Letters" in the Birmingham Oratory.

II. AUTOBIOGRAPHICAL MATERIALS

The primary sources for Newman's autobiography are the *Autobiographical Writings*, the letters, and the *Apologia pro Vita Sua*. *John Henry Newman Autobiographical Writings* (1956) is a collection of seven groups of documents: an autobiography in miniature; two autobiographical sketches originally intended for reference works; the complete text of the Autobiographical Memoir abridged by Anne Mozley in her edition of the letters; "My Illness in Sicily," the franker parts of which Mozley had omitted; three journals covering the years 1804–26, 1821–28, and 1838–47, the last of which contains Newman's retreat notes before his ordination at Rome; a journal for 1859–79, much of which is familiar from Wilfrid Ward's biography; and a "Memorandum about My Connection with the Catholic University." The last item is introduced by Dessain, the rest by Henry Tristram, the principal editor, who died in 1955 before the book was completed. These indispensable documents, which concentrate on the earlier and later years of Newman's life before and after the *Apologia*, contain Newman's frankest self-revelation.

The principal collections of Newman's letters, of which more than 20,000 are believed to exist, are *Letters and Correspondence of John Henry Newman during His Life in the English Church, with a Brief Autobiography*. Edited, at Cardinal Newman's Request, by Anne Mozley (2 vols., 1891); and *The Letters and Diaries of John Henry Newman*, edited by Dessain (assisted in Vols. xiv and xv by Vincent F. Blehl and in Vol. xxi by Edward E. Kelly), a continuing series which began in 1961 with Vol. xi, covering the first year (1845–46) of Newman's Roman Catholic life, and by 1972 had reached Vol. xxii (1865–66). Mozley's edition is as yet indispensable for Newman's Anglican years, but the letters are erratically edited and often incomplete. Eventually her edition will be superseded by the magisterially edited *Letters and Diaries*, the plans for which were outlined by Dessain in "The Newman Archives and the Projected Edition of the Cardinal's Letters" (*CHR*, 1960) and under a slightly different title in the *Dublin Review*, 1960. These letters deal largely with education and religion in a world moving toward unbelief. Though often repetitive and burdened with the minutiae of administrative detail, they compel interest in revealing Newman's devotion to his cause in the face of difficulties that might well have staggered most men; the extraordinary range of his abilities; a deep knowledge of human nature frequently manifested in pungent aphorisms of which a gathering ought to be made; and a personality of great complexity, now proud, sensitive, fastidious, and reserved, now affectionate, hardheadedly practical, and down-to-earth.

The next most important collections of Newman's letters are *Correspondence of John Henry Newman with John Keble and Others, 1839–45*, edited at the Birmingham Oratory, 1917; and Gordon Huntington Harper's *Cardinal Newman and William Froude, F.R.S., A Correspondence* (1933). The Keble correspondence is an excellent supplement to the Anglican letters, concerned as it is with the crucial years of the Oxford Movement and throwing much light on the question of Newman's motivation. The Froude correspondence, a rehearsal in effect of *A Grammar of Assent*, is a fascinating exchange of letters over a period of forty years (1838–79) on the possibility of attaining a legitimate certitude, especially in matters of religion.

Of more recent collections of letters, the most important is *Newman Family Letters* (ed. Dorothea Mozley, 1962), an attractive book with charming sketches from the family collection. It is dominated by the letters of the spirited Harriet Newman, the acute minor novelist so very like her brother John, to whom at one time she was closest but whose conversion so incensed her that she permanently estranged herself from him. *The Letters of John Henry Newman* (ed. Derek Stanford and Muriel Spark, 1957) provides a concise biography of Newman drawn from letters of the Anglican and Catholic periods. Though virtually all of the 110 letters have been previously published, it is useful to have them in one place. However, the book is badly edited, especially in Stanford's Anglican section.

Apologia pro Vita Sua has been published in a great many different editions, of which the following are the most useful for specialists: Wilfrid Ward's Oxford Edition (1913), long out of print and without annotation but valuable for its ingenious (if difficult to read) combination of the 1864 and 1865 texts, its inclusion in an otherwise disappointing Introduction of notes on Oxford and on the Church of England which Newman wrote for a French edition of 1866, and its reprinting of both Newman's and Kingsley's pamphlets; Maurice Nédoncelle's French edition (1939), the first annotated edition of the *Apologia* (trans. L. Michelin Delimoges) with an excellent Introduction stressing Newman's influence on modern thought and the significance of his personalism; C. F. Harrold's edition (1947), attractively printed and well introduced though in minor matters not always sound in text; the Modern Library edition (1950), introduced by Anton C. Pegis, which like the Image Books edition of Philip Hughes (1956) prints the 1864 text and includes Newman's and Kingsley's pamphlets; the Riverside edition (1956), edited by A. Dwight Culler, helpfully annotated and with a thoughtful and sensitive Introduction unfortunately marred by the editor's stressing of only the feminine side of Newman's personality and his oversimplification of important aspects of Newman's thought: for example, Newman did not hold "that deduction is good and induction in matters of religion bad"; the World's Classics edition (1964), convenient and attractive though the Introduction by Basil Willey is slight and disappointing; the Oxford English Text edition (1967), edited by Martin J. Svaglic, extensively annotated and containing all variant readings including those omitted by Wilfrid Ward; and the annotated Norton Critical Edition (1968), edited by David J. DeLaura, especially useful for its collection of scholarly essays on the *Apologia*.

In "Newman's *Apologia* and the Burthens of Editing" (*MLQ*, 1971), Justus George Lawler argues that from "the standpoint of comprehensive attention . . . to text or contents, the *Apologia* has not been well served by its editors." Wilfrid Ward is given no credit whatever. Henry Tristram is dismissed as "the perpetrator of an undying strain of erroneous judgments and factual distortions"; Dwight Culler is said to have "advanced the state of *Apologia* studies precisely to the degree that he proved himself dependent not only on Tristram but also on Nédoncelle," himself dependent on Tristram; and of Svaglic's Oxford English Text edition, to which most of Lawler's attention is devoted, we are told that for the goal of coming to a real knowledge of the *Apologia*, "more would seem to be required than the mere fleshing out of the paradigm of earlier editions," and this more "Svaglic fails to provide." Some of Lawler's criticism is correct and salutary; some of it is marred by omission, distortion, and gratuitous assertion; and all of it is one-sided. If Lawler is to be believed, no editor of the *Apologia* has made any serious contribution to the elucidation of Newman's masterpiece.

The origin and background of the *Apologia* are treated not only in most of the editions cited but also in several articles. T. L. Robertson, Jr., in "The Kingsley-Newman Controversy and the *Apologia*" (*MLN*, 1954), raises the question of whether Newman deliberately published the Kingsley correspondence in order to stir up Kingsley's violent reply, as Wilfrid Ward seemed to think, and thus give himself the opportunity to tell his own story in full. Robertson's conclusion is that this might be true only if the author were "a man of little emotion and scheming tendencies." It is impossible to answer the question with certainty, but the probability that Newman did deliberately force Kingsley's hand and for perfectly understandable reasons is advanced with documentation from Oratory letters by Svaglic in "Why Newman Wrote the *Apologia*" (in *Newman's* Apologia: *A Classic Reconsidered*, ed. F. X. Connolly and V. F. Blehl, 1964, and in the Norton Critical Edition of the *Apologia*).

In "The *Apologia* and the Ultramontanes" (in *Newman's* Apologia: *A Classic Reconsidered*), Edward Kelly, S.J., shows how the Manning-Ward-Talbot group reacted against Newman's remarks in his fifth chapter on papal infallibility and in his "Notes" on the position of the Church of England, the former of which particularly they felt were directed against them. The article is especially informative on the Newman-Manning estrangement. Some of this material is treated also in Kelly's "Newman's Catholic History as Background of the *Apologia*" (*Personalist*, 1965), which otherwise covers ground already familiar from Wilfrid Ward's biography and other works.

The fullest treatment of the immediate and ultimate reasons why Kingsley attacked Newman is to be found in Svaglic's Introduction to the Oxford English Text edition of the *Apologia*. G. M. Young's "Sophist and Swashbuckler," in his *Daylight and Champaign* (1937), offers a good analysis of the anti-Catholic temper of the Victorian age and of Kingsley himself as "very nearly the central man of that period of swift change which sets in soon after 1845 and was consummated about twenty years later." Young feels that "in their clumsy way Kingsley and the public were right. . . . what is one to make of a man, especially of a preacher, whose every sentence must be put under a logical microscope if its full sense is to be revealed? In the end one is as sorry for Kingsley as one is for the Jesuits to whom Pascal replied."

What the Kingsley-Newman controversy ultimately represented—"the fundamental clash, both then and now, between Protestant Liberalism and Christian Orthodoxy, whether Roman Catholic or Evangelical"—is penetratingly examined by Walter E. Houghton in "The Issue between Kingsley and Newman" (*Theol. Today*, 1947; rpt. in *Victorian Literature, Selected Essays*, ed. Robert O. Preyer, 1967, and in the Norton Critical Edition of the *Apologia*). Houghton outlines Kingsley's theological position, a kind of disguised naturalism owing much to both Carlyle and Maurice, the drift of which, "what may be called the dead-end of Liberal Protestantism," is to be seen in such sermons of Newman as "The Religion of the Day" and especially "Nature and Grace." Raymond Chapman's *Faith and Revolt* (1970), a study of the literary effect of the Oxford Movement, suggests that among Kingsley's reasons for attacking Newman was that he equated clerical celibacy with the homosexuality he feared he had discovered in his brother Henry.

The critical reception of the *Apologia* is treated briefly by V. F. Blehl in "Early Criticism of the *Apologia*" (in *Newman's* Apologia: *A Classic Reconsidered*; rpt. in the Norton Critical Edition of the *Apologia*), a survey of some fifty early reviews which show that Wilfrid Ward was inaccurate in saying that the enthusiasm of such journals as the *Saturday Review* and the *Spectator* was echoed almost universally. Blehl's conclusion is that the reaction was "not at all uniform but exceedingly complex, subtle, and nuanced." Mary James McCormick's "Newman's *Apologia pro Vita Sua*: Its Origin, Composition, and Critical Reception" (Diss. Fordham 1965) covers much the same ground more intensively and also studies "selected highlights" in critical reaction to the *Apologia* between 1865 and 1945.

The changes that Newman made from time to time in the text of the *Apologia* are considered in "The Revision of Newman's *Apologia*" (*MP*, 1952) by Svaglic, who concludes that the later versions are not only less controversial but clearer, more exact, less egotistical, so to speak, less colloquial and more dignified, yet also more dramatic. In view of the disagreement of critics to this day about Newman's motives for conversion, it is noteworthy that in revision he added the letter of 16 November 1844, explicitly discounting such interpretations as undue passivity, disappointment, or irritation.

The most thorough study of the *Apologia*'s literary roots is Walter E. Houghton's monograph *The Art of Newman's* Apologia (1945), which examines the "theories of rhetoric, conceptions of man and the psychology of faith, ideas about the art of style and the nature and methods of biography" lying dormant and unrelated in Newman's mind but "capable potentially of combining for action, let the right stimulus occur." Houghton's is a genuinely creative and illuminating book, marred only by too heavy a reliance in the question of Newman's motivation on the views of Wilberforce and Cross discussed above.

Houghton's book was probably the chief stimulus to the examination of the *Apologia* as a work of literature. In recent years the rhetoric, structure, style, and literary status of Newman's masterpiece have been widely studied. Leonard W. Deen's "The Rhetoric of Newman's *Apologia*" (*ELH*, 1962; rpt. in the Norton Critical Edition of the *Apologia*) argues that Newman "obviously considered his defense against Kingsley a problem of rhetorical means and ends" and in solving it used "both the principles and particular devices of classical rhetoric" though "he did not want to persuade by them alone or think them sufficient. The effectiveness of the *Apologia* depends on Newman's using the basic principles of classical rhetoric in a way that virtually transformed them." But since the principles of classical rhetoric, like the notes of a scale, are capable of infinite variation in treatment, all this really means is that Newman was a rhetorician of extraordinary skill. Deen correctly sees that the important question about the *Apologia* is "not the validity but the sincerity and intelligibility of Newman's beliefs" and concludes that Newman succeeds in demonstrating these qualities.

In "A Rhetorical Analysis of Cardinal Newman's *Apologia pro Vita Sua*" (Diss. Notre Dame 1962), Mary Baylon Lenz examines each chapter for examples of logical, ethical, and pathetic arguments and also studies various aspects of style: the "dramatic elements" of imagery, rhythm, sentence patterns, tone, and personalization. Her apparatus is more thorough and more germane to Newman than Deen's, but she does not employ it as acutely. Her article "The Rhetoric of Newman's *Apologia*" (in *Newman's* Apologia: *A Classic Reconsidered*) surveys the first four chapters of the book for examples of the ethical argument whereby Newman maintained his loyalty to Anglicanism as an answer to the belief common in 1864 that he had been for some years before his conversion a concealed Romanist. While she is undoubtedly correct, she often seems to be stressing what is already obvious. However, both her work and Deen's are somewhat pioneering efforts in a mode of analysis that has only recently come back into favor. Few good rhetorical analyses of prose texts are available, and few scholars today have the grounding in classical rhetoric that Newman and many of his contemporaries possessed. Whatever else one may think about Newman, he was unquestionably one of the greatest rhetoricians in our language; and valuable criticism remains to be written about his techniques by someone properly equipped.

Although it is not directly concerned with rhetorical analysis, Eric M. Zale's "The Defenses of John Henry Newman" (Diss. Michigan 1962) is relevant here, arguing that the *Apologia* is only one of a series of defenses of his views brought on by traumatic experiences in 1838, 1841, and 1845, as well as by his apparent failures as a Catholic. Thus, Tract 90, the *University Sermons*, and the *Development of Christian Doctrine* are "preliminary defenses," the foundation for a lifelong series of apologias beginning with *Loss and Gain* and *Callista*, "both far more revealing autobiographically" than the defense of 1864. Anne Mozley's edition of the letters and Wilfrid Ward's *Life* were also intended by Newman himself as defenses, and Zale finds this defensiveness continuing in the work of his disciples and scholars, though here his evidence is too brief, selective, and outdated.

The way Newman ordered his material has been the subject of several articles. Svaglic (*PMLA*, 1951; rpt. in *Victorian Literature: Modern Essays in Criticism,* ed. Austin Wright, 1961, and in the Norton Critical Edition of the *Apologia*) views in analogical terms the structure of the *Apologia* as determined by Newman's dramatic conception of the spiritual life as warfare and of conversion as a conquest by "the force of truth." Complementary to this view is Robert A. Colby's "The Poetical Structure of Newman's *Apologia pro Vita Sua*" (*J. of Religion*, 1953; rpt. in the Norton Critical Edition of the *Apologia*), which argues that Newman gave greater magnitude to his work through plot structure and characterization usually associated with tragedy and epic. Colby (*DubR*, 1953; rpt. in the Norton Critical Edition of the *Apologia*) maintains that Newman arranged the parts of his story to cohere "*dramatically* as the beginning, middle, and end of an action; *genetically* as the stages of a life cycle of spiritual birth, growth, decline, death, and rebirth"; and "*logically*" as the stages of attaining certitude along the "graduated scale of assent" to which Newman refers in Chapter i. Because its concerns are an extension of Colby's, mention should be made here of a book discussed in Dessain's essay,

Thomas Vargish's *Newman: The Contemplation of Mind* (1970). Vargish considers Newman's *Grammar of Assent* his greatest book and attempts "to demonstrate the relevance of Newman's epistemology to his attacks on liberalism, his theories of education, and his novels and autobiography."

George Levine's "The Prose of the *Apologia pro Vita Sua*" (*VN*, 1965) analyzes the style of such passages as the last three paragraphs of Chapter i and the famous sentence in v, "To consider the world in its length and breadth, . . ." to conclude that, though Newman was sensitive to the particular and concrete, "Experience comes through his prose as through a filter. Explicable and inexplicable alike reveal themselves as under the direction of Providence, which alone can account for everything. We live through his language not the experience described but the feelings of a reserved, sensitive, and dignified man, whose mind is made up and who can, therefore, transmute the particular into the generalized language which itself becomes a principle of providential order." There is undoubtedly some truth to this view, though it needs a good deal more qualification since much of Newman's writing does show a striking commitment to the particular. In "Newman: Non-Fiction as Art" (*Style*, 1969), Levine attempts to show how even the most trivial details of the language of the *Apologia* are "expressive of essential aspects of Newman's selfhood," such as his distrust of the "material world." Levine isolates for examination Newman's use of the form "not this, but that," parallel series, and "quiet" diction. It is an interesting study much influenced by the approach of Richard Ohmann in *Shaw: The Style and the Man* and elsewhere; but it seems less inductive than Levine appears to think it, since the inferences made (e.g., from Newman's use of clearly stated transitions, reflecting what Levine terms "an almost compulsive need to find order") seem to result as much from a conception of Newman already formed as from a disinterested analysis of the syntax itself.

In "The *Apologia*: History, Rhetoric, and Literature" (in *Newman's* Apologia: *A Classic Reconsidered*), Francis X. Connolly argues that the book is "an autobiography whose place in literature should be judged by its success or failure as personal revelation." It is universally recognized as a "classic," not so much because of its historical or rhetorical value, as because "it is the artistic representation of the growth of a soul instinct with the universal emotions of hope and fear, sadness and joy; because it communicates to those who read it the shape and the meaning of man. These are the values that, I believe, the historian of literature ought to point out with decisive emphasis." In a similar vein in the same commemorative volume, William E. Buckler admits in "The *Apologia* as Human Experience" that it is a difficult book repugnant in subject matter to today's students and offers advice on how the professor can help them read it "with that understanding which constitutes the essential condition for a significant literary experience." John Coulson argues that the criteria appropriate to the evaluation of works like Wordsworth's *Prelude* or Dante's *Comedy* "are alone those which can help us to an adequately theological response to the *Apologia*. . . . the response required must always be to resonance, tone, and subtle verbal precisions," and the book must be seen more as a clash of traditions than of personalities (in *Newman: A Portrait Restored*, by Coulson, A. M. Allchin, and Meriol Trevor, 1965).

Judging the *Apologia* as autobiography, Roy Pascal (*Design and Truth in Autobiography*, 1960) finds that though it is "substantially true to the facts" and "written with superlative skill," it has nevertheless a "fatal fault": "Its rounded finality, the controlled suggestivity of the writing in all its details, evokes a certain distrust, and this distrust is reinforced by the absence of a full account of the child and young man." While Newman "represents the great decision as taking place in these few years," a "true decision of this type must be rooted deep in the man, and from an autobiography we need to find it already pre-fashioned in the earlier life, and affecting the total man, his personality and mode of life." Since Newman explicitly denies that he is writing an autobiography—the *Apologia* is a work of rhetoric—it is unfair to judge the book by Pascal's criteria. In any event, it is misleading to say that Newman represents his decision as taking place in a few years. The remarkable thing about the *Apologia* is that every detail, from the earliest characteristics of his childhood (e.g., being superstitious and loving the *Arabian Nights*), has a bearing on Newman's final decision.

A challenging view of the significance of the *Apologia* today is DeLaura's "Newman as Prophet" (*DubR*, 1967, and in a slightly altered version in his Norton Critical Edition of the *Apologia*). DeLaura contends that almost all of "Newman's claims upon the modern reader—personal, literary, philosophical, theological, prophetic—converge in the *Apologia*," and that the book is successful not merely because it brings us "for a while," as John Holloway says, to a living understanding of Newman's need, but because it brings before the reader as live possibilities "a more permanent and committed understanding, vision, and experience," and can still change his fundamental attitude toward religion and life in general.

III. INTRODUCTIONS AND ANTHOLOGIES

A good brief introduction to Newman is J. M. Cameron's *John Henry Newman* (1956), in the Writers and Their Work series prepared for the British Council and the National Book League. For a pointed account of virtually all of Newman's works, including a masterful study of *A Grammar of Assent*, there is nothing to compare with the article on Newman by Henry Tristram and Francis Bacchus in the *Dictionnaire de théologie catholique*, XI (1931), the English version of which should be reprinted as a pamphlet. Tristram's "On Reading Newman" (in *John Henry Newman: Centenary Essays*, 1945) offers an excellent brief survey of Newman's works. Charles Frederick Harrold's *John Henry Newman: An Expository and Critical Study of His Mind, Thought and Art* (1945) is a four-hundred-page book that provides biography, bibliography, a detailed study of Newman's thought on the development of doctrine, the nature of education, and the logical cogency of faith, and a briefer survey of his work as Anglican theologian, Roman controversialist, historian, and man of letters. It is an intelligent, lucid, and fair-minded guide that is now virtually the standard introduction to Newman for students of literature.

Over the years there have been many anthologies of Newman. Two of the best are *A Newman Treasury* (ed. C. F. Harrold, 1943) and *The Essential Newman* (ed. V. F. Blehl, S.J., 1963). Harrold's excellent Introduction was a kind of rehearsal for his *John Henry Newman*, and his selections stress the same major themes: development of doctrine, the problem of belief in a rationalistic age, and humanistic education. There are also six sermons, selected passages on various subjects, some of the *Apologia*, and a collection of Newman's aphorisms. Blehl's attractive and useful anthology manages to live up to its title, presenting key passages well introduced from Newman's four chief works, selections from the

Tracts and Anglican sermons, and a group of passages illustrating the contempora-
neousness of Newman on such subjects as "The Church and the Modern World,"
"The Role of the Laity in the Church," and "Christian Perfection." Two brief,
useful anthologies edited by Henry Tristram are *The Living Thoughts of Cardinal
Newman* (1948), which emphasizes Newman's opposition to doctrinal liberalism;
and *The Idea of a Liberal Education* (1952), which contains an excellent Preface
summarizing Newman's approach to education.

The increasing attention that has been paid in recent years to Newman as a
literary artist is well exemplified in Geoffrey Tillotson's anthology *Newman: Prose
and Poetry* (1957). Calling him "one of the supreme geniuses of nineteenth century
England. And a supremely literary genius," Tillotson goes on to stress this aspect
more than the theological or philosophical side of Newman. He reprints complete
works only, including the *Apologia*, the Dublin *Discourses on the Scope and Nature
of University Education, Loss and Gain* (which he shares Hutton's high opinion
of), "The Tamworth Reading-Room," four Anglican sermons, and a few letters and
poems. Other anthologies include W. S. Lilly's *Characteristics* (1874; rpt. with
an introd. by Henry Tristram, 1949), offering a comprehensive summary of
Newman's "ultimate judgments on the most important matters of which he has
written"; Floris Delattre's *La Pensée de J. H. Newman* (1914), the selections in
which are arranged chronologically; Joseph J. Reilly's *The Fine Gold of Newman*
(1931), collecting "from every phase of Newman's many-sided writings some of his
noblest, wisest, and most perfect utterances"; and Connolly's well-introduced and
remarkably comprehensive *A Newman Reader* (1964).

IV. FRIENDS AND CONTEMPORARIES

Although Newman is often described as reserved and shy, he had more than an
average share of close and lasting friendships, many of which are commemorated in
the dedications of his books. In *Newman and His Friends* (1933), Henry Tristram
has provided a charming series of biographical sketches tracing Newman's relationships with the subjects of these dedications. On Newman's closest and most significant friendship, that with R. H. Froude, there are informative dissertations by Sister
M. Regina (Loyola, Chicago 1961) and Bernard C. O'Halloran (Columbia 1965),
both using unpublished Oratory material. The latter credits Froude with undermining Newman's belief in the theory of the Via Media and argues that Newman's
conversion can be attributed "in major part" to Froude's influence. A good brief
study of the nature of this influence is Herbert Clegg's "Froude's *Remains*" (*CQR*,
1966), which stresses that (as Newman himself was aware) Froude anticipated
both the Tract 90 view of the Thirty-Nine Articles and Newman's idea of the
development of doctrine.

Similar work should be done on Newman's friendship with John Keble, a
subject still virtually untreated at any length, even in Georgina Battiscombe's *John
Keble: A Study in Limitations* (1963). As for the less decisive but still very
important friendship with Dr. Pusey, there is a brief popular sketch, "Newman and
Pusey," by Robert Sencourt (*DubR*, 1945); but the best, if still inadequate, sources
are probably H. P. Liddon's four-volume *Life of E. B. Pusey, D.D.* (1893–97) and
Meriol Trevor's biography of Newman.

Two of Newman's important Oxford friendships with younger followers have been studied, the first briefly by Christopher Hollis in "Cardinal Newman and Dean Church" (*John Henry Newman: Centenary Essays*, 1945), which dispassionately outlines the views Church shared with Newman and the reasons he did not follow him in 1845; and at some length in Bernard A. Smith's *Dean Church: The Anglican Response to Newman* (1958), which sees Church as a Newmanite to the end in everything "which concerns the devotion to God of a moral personality in fear and trembling" but celebrates his "emancipation" from the Newman who "as if by instinct, contracted out before the arrival in full force of intellectual ordeals which most Christians, except Roman Catholics, had to face for themselves." Some interesting comments by Newman on a draft that Church had sent him of his *Oxford Movement* have been published by R. W. Hunt (*BLR*, 1969). Newman's relationship with Henry Wilberforce is briefly treated in *The Wilberforces and Henry Manning: The Parting of Friends* (1966), by David Newsome, whose attitude toward Newman is rather like Smith's.

Two more of Newman's Oxford friendships, with C. P. Golightly and J. R. Bloxam, both former curates of his, have been well studied from original MS material, the first briefly by Robert William Greaves (*JEH*, 1958), who shows how Golightly became the relentless foe of the Tractarians after the publication of Froude's *Remains* and then Tract 90; and the second at length by R. D. Middleton in *Newman and Bloxam: An Oxford Friendship* (1948), which stresses the consolidation of the Via Media as Newman's chief accomplishment and contains an appendix of letters between Hawkins, Pusey, and Newman relative to Pusey's edition of Tract 90 in 1866.

Among the friends of Newman's later years, Father Faber is the subject of a biography by Ronald Chapman (1960), which throws light on the *other* side of the quarrel between the Oratories. Dessain's " 'Heart Speaks to Heart': Margaret Mary Hollahan and John Henry Newman" (*The Month*, 1965) traces the development of Newman's friendship with the poor Irish orphan from the East End of London who became the foundress of the English Dominican Sisters and to whose convent Newman directed many of the Tractarian ladies on their conversion to Roman Catholicism. Though the outlines seem clear, the full story of Newman's mixed feelings and growing disillusionment about Manning may never be known as, fearing that they might come into the wrong hands, Newman destroyed Manning's and others' letters to him after the death of Ambrose St. John in 1875. In *Essays* (1911), Henry Ignatius Dudley Ryder, Superior of the Oratory after Newman's death and a nephew of Manning, provides an interesting but too circumspect discussion of Edmund S. Purcell's *Manning* (1896), a book that charged its subject with duplicity in his treatment of Newman. Meriol Trevor's biography of Newman and Edward Kelly's "The *Apologia* and the Ultramontanes" (in *Newman's* Apologia: *A Classic Reconsidered*) should also be consulted on this subject. As more of Newman's letters are published, there will be opportunities for further study of his important friendships. If enough material can be found, the friendship with Ambrose St. John, for one, is a subject that should throw a great deal of light on Newman's personality.

Among his contemporaries Newman has often been compared to Coleridge. An early discussion of their similarities, perceptive but too general and with little documentation, is W. R. Castle's (*SR*, 1909), which argues against the view that had Newman known German, his spiritual progress would have been different, on the ground that Coleridge knew German and yet came to many of the same positions as Newman. Both men were immersed in the concrete, both asserted personality as the mainstay of religion, and to both "it was essential first to recognize will, then to bring that will into accord with the divine will, represented in conscience." In "Was Newman a Disciple of Coleridge?" (*DubR*, 1945), H. Francis Davis answers that he was not, for he first read Coleridge in 1835, by which time he had already taken up his own distinctive positions. Davis points out that both men were influenced by Bishop Butler, however, and suggests that further research might show a common stimulus here. Though Newman did not agree with Coleridge on such questions as the divine authority of the Church, Davis shows that both thought the deeper foundations of religion should be laid in men's consciences, both admitted a responsibility of the will in the search for truth, both believed in the Aristotelian principle that one must be content with the kind of proof afforded by a given subject matter, and both recognized the validity of an implicit or informal reasoning process.

A more detailed illustration of the similarities between Newman and Coleridge is to be found in *The Romantic Comedy* (1948), by D. G. James, who maintains that the "cardinal doctrine" of both is that "through obedience to conscience alone . . . we come to know what is real in the spiritual world." Drawing on Newman's essays "The Mission of St. Benedict" and "The Benedictine Schools" (*Historical Sketches*, ii) to picture a Newman who "longed for the life of the Benedictine monks in full escape from the burden of civilization," James contrasts the two by arguing that though "Newman's romanticism . . . does not yield to Coleridge's in its sense of the supernatural which over-arches the human, in its perception of the unseen, in what must remain mysterious and undisclosed, . . . it differs profoundly from it in its lowliness, its quietness, its revulsion from power, its abandonment of claim." In these respects James finds Newman more like Wordsworth. But this is to overromanticize Newman, who was at least as involved in the world as Coleridge. Mention should also be made here, though it is discussed in Dessain's essay, of John Coulson's *Newman and the Common Tradition* (1970), described as a study in the language of church and society and arguing that the language proper to religious insight is similar to that of poetry. Coleridge, Newman, and F. D. Maurice are all considered on the tensions between the church as it is in itself and as it is institutionally manifested in a given society. Coulson is illuminating on the relevance of Maurice and Newman today.

Although with his usual contempt for anyone attempting to patch up Hebrew old clothes Carlyle utterly dismissed Newman as a man with the intellect of a moderate-sized rabbit, there are important similarities between them, as Jefferson B. Fletcher pointed out (*AM*, 1905). Fletcher argues that a common belief in unconscious or implicit reason leads to resemblances all along the line, though ultimately the differences are greater. Both men stressed the importance of personal influence, the revelation of divinity especially in the most intimate of His works, the conscience, and the importance of the elect. At the same time, it is Newman who asks the shrewder questions about the testimonials of heroes, according to Fletcher. In "Two Leaders—Newman and Carlyle" (*Cornhill*, 1928), Henry Tristram, reflecting on Swinburne's calling both men childless children of the night, argues that though this might be true of Carlyle, who had little constructive to offer, it was not true of Newman, who besides his religious legacy has left us the way of the humanist, "the right attitude toward the vital issues of life and literature . . . a spirit tenacious of the past, alive to the needs of the present, and sensitive to the hidden forces that are molding the future." The fact is that Tristram did not know enough about Carlyle, whom Newman had considerable respect for, to do justice to him; and the subject of the resemblances between the two men could stand further examination.

We know by his own proud admission that Matthew Arnold was deeply influenced by Newman, but precisely how and to what extent has until recently been largely a matter of conjecture. In "Newman and Matthew Arnold" (*Cornhill*, 1926), Henry Tristram points out that Newman preceded Arnold by a decade in his assaults on Philistinism, though he did not use the term; and that in *The Idea of a University* he maintained the ideal of culture for its own sake and anticipated Arnold's message that the "Apostolic Succession" in culture was to be traced through Rome to Greece. At the same time, Tristram prudently cautions that "it is well-nigh impossible to lay a finger on this or that point, to specify this or that principle, and to say that Arnold was here writing under Newman's influence." In "Newman's Influence on Matthew Arnold's Theory of Poetry" (*N&Q*, 1958), however, Denis Butts lays a finger on a passage in Newman's 1839 essay "Prospects of the Anglican Church" and finds it not merely anticipatory of but "more than likely . . . the origins of Arnold's own lofty conception of the high destiny of poetry." It is Newman's remark that "the taste for poetry of a religious kind has in modern times in a certain sense taken the place of the deep contemplative spirit of the early Church. . . . Poetry then is our mysticism." It is well to remember, however, that Newman was talking about the kind of poetry that can "draw men away from the material to the invisible world," which was not precisely Arnold's concern; and that the idea of the high destiny and moral function of poetry would have been familiar to Arnold from such other sources close to him as Wordsworth and Keble.

The first attempt in depth to trace Newman's influence on Arnold is DeLaura's remarkably thorough "Matthew Arnold and John Henry Newman: The 'Oxford Sentiment' and the Religion of the Future" (*TSLL*, 1965; rpt. with slight alteration in his *Hebrew and Hellene in Victorian England*, 1969). DeLaura seeks "to define the mechanics of the process by which the substance of dogmatic Christianity was transformed, within one or two generations, into the fabric of aestheticism." Attempting to explain what Arnold meant in telling Newman that he had learned from him "habits, methods, ruling ideas, which are constantly with me," DeLaura concludes "that Newman was more central and more essential to Arnold's development than is generally believed. The precise weight and tone of Arnold's attitude toward a number of crucial matters—criticism and the qualities of the critic [urbanity, delicacy, the historical role of an elite, the mutual exclusiveness of the moral and intellectual spheres, disinterestedness], culture, Liberalism, Philistinism, religious 'development,' the Oxford Movement, the Roman Catholic Church; the relation of religion to poetry—cannot be caught without reference to Arnold's relation to Newman." DeLaura also argues that the common view that Newman was one of the fathers of *Culture and Anarchy* but had little to do with Arnold's religious theorizing is decidedly incorrect, Arnold frequently taking ideas and arguments from works like Newman's *Development of Christian Doctrine* and turning them to his own quite different use. DeLaura is quite aware of the charges that can with some justice be made against his work: the detail is rather "stupefying," the effect "somewhat scattered," and the "fallacy of the unique source" a clear and present danger. From time to time DeLaura succumbs to this danger in not making sufficient allowance for the fact that the "Oxford sentiment" almost certainly filtered through to Arnold from many sources, as it did to Newman himself. Nevertheless, DeLaura's argument as a whole seems convincing and often, as with reference to Arnold's ambivalent use of Newman's religious thought, brilliantly perceptive.

DeLaura's "Pater and Newman: The Road to the 'Nineties" (VS, 1966; rpt. in his *Hebrew and Hellene in Victorian England*) takes off from T. S. Eliot's remark in "Arnold and Pater" (1930) about "a direction from Arnold through Pater, to the nineties, with, of course, the solitary figure of Newman in the background." De-Laura sees both Arnold and Pater as attempting to preserve for the future "the European past—mind, imagination, devotion . . . apart from belief, through refine-ment of taste and the pursuit of a self-regarding culture." Aestheticizing the idea Arnold associated with Newman of "a spiritual and intellectual elite who are alone the privileged bearers of truth," Pater makes "the language of religious doctrine a vindication of the life of pure aesthetic apprehension." In *Marius the Epicurean*, his "most sustained engagement with Newman's thought," the central arguments of his theology are those he had found in Newman's writings, especially *Loss and Gain*, *The Idea of a University*, and, above all, *A Grammar of Assent*: "on the nature of religious 'assent' and the role of will and personality in belief; on the inadequacy of a religion of mere 'taste'; on the authority of a great religious-humanistic tradition in possession of the Western mind." DeLaura also points out that Pater looked to Newman's ideas about literature for a "personalist" doctrine of style "which would be the adequate vehicle of his favored religious-aesthetic consciousness." The essay is a thorough and convincing demonstration of a hitherto undiscussed literary influence, even less open to question than DeLaura's study of Arnold and Newman. If the extent of Newman's influence on Pater has been almost unsuspected until now, however, it is only because most students of English literature are not very familiar with books like *A Grammar of Assent*.

In "Gladstone and Newman" (*DubR*, 1967), based in part on unpublished Oratory letters, J. Derek Holmes discusses the relations of two men who were never really close but maintained a friendly interest in one another till the end. Glad-stone's attitude was somewhat ambivalent. He thought Newman with Butler (and surpassing Hooker) one of "the two greatest Theologers" to come from Oxford, likened his *Dream of Gerontius* to the *Purgatorio* and *Paradiso*, and shared many of his attitudes toward the ultramontanes. At the same time he thought that New-man had been too influenced by the Evangelicals, that his *University Sermons* were unsafe in philosophy, and that there was a gulf between his theological method and "that taught by the historic sense," of which Döllinger was "an absolutely normal example." Francis Herrick's "Gladstone, Newman, and Ireland in 1881" (*CHR*, 1961) offers a brief but interesting correspondence in which Gladstone sought Newman's help in influencing the Pope to curb Irish clerical supporters of the Land League. Newman declined to involve himself and expressed the opinion that Glad-stone overrated the Pope's power in practical matters.

Henry Tristram's "The Correspondence between J. H. Newman and the Comte de Montalembert" (*DubR*, 1949) is based on a disappointingly thin series of letters mostly from the sixties. Newman admired Montalembert's memoir on Lacordaire. Both men stood against the ultramontanes for more freedom in the Church, but Montalembert seems to have gone further than Newman in the direction of accept-ing the modern pluralistic state based on liberty of conscience rather than mere expedience. Tristram's "Cardinal Newman and Baron von Hügel" (*DubR*, 1966), a 1945 essay hitherto available only in German in a festschrift for Erich Przywara, attempts to explain why Von Hügel, for all his acknowledged debt to Newman, found his few visits to him somewhat depressing. According to the Baron, Newman never surmounted "his deeply predestinarian, Puritan, training"; and Von Hügel found him lacking the deep sign of joy that Benedict XIV regarded as a distinguishing mark of Catholic sanctity. Of course, as Tristram says, von Hügel made very few visits to Newman and was his junior by fifty years.

William Barry's "Cardinal Newman and Renan" (*Nat. Rev.*, 1897), about two influential men in the same field of activity who never met nor were acquainted with each other's writings, provides an interesting contrast between two very different sensibilities somewhat along the line of Newman's comparison between Pascal and Montaigne in *A Grammar of Assent*; but the essay is too moralistically biased in favor of Newman. A comparison at a deeper level, showing how Newman resembled in temperament Lacordaire rather than Renan, is to be found in Wilfrid Ward's essay "Newman and Renan" (*Problems and Persons*, 1903). A student of letters will also find much of interest in Erich Przywara's "Kierkegaard—Newman" (*Newman Studien*, I, 1948).

Brian Vickers' "Hopkins and Newman" (*TLS*, 3 March 1966; cf. also letter of W. H. Gardner, 15 Sept. 1966) notes an apparent borrowing in "Carrion Comfort" from Part I of *A Dream of Gerontius*. This is one of the few attempts (see also Wendell Stacy Johnson's *Gerard Manley Hopkins: The Poet as Victorian*, 1968) to point out a specific example of what almost certainly was the profound influence that Newman exerted on the work as well as the life of Hopkins, who at one time wished to prepare an annotated edition of *A Grammar of Assent*. A detailed study of this fascinating subject remains to be made.

Barry Ulanov's "Newman and Dostoevsky: The Politics of Salvation" (in his *Sources and Resources: The Literary Traditions of Christian Humanism*, 1960) sees both men as turning against "Liberalism" toward faith and as prophets of and battlers against the infidelity of the future.

V. NEWMAN AS EDUCATOR

Newman's principal concerns in life were, of course, religion and education, and much has been written about his work as educator, principally in connection with *The Idea of a University*, the book whose fame among Newman's works is second only to that of the *Apologia* and whose readership is now probably wider. Three editions of the *Idea* are especially useful to specialists: that by C. F. Harrold (1947), valuable for reprinting Discourse v of the first edition, which Newman omitted after 1852; the Image Book edition by George N. Shuster (1959), which contains the essays "Elementary Studies" and "University Preaching" not included in the Harrold text and also a valuable index; and the Rinehart edition by Svaglic (1959), which is the only annotated edition and also contains the complete text. In "Dublin Discourses: Rhetorical Method in Textual Revisions" (*Ren*, 1968), Richard W. Clancy outlines the changes in the various editions of the *Idea*, concentrating on the differences between the edition of 1852 and the final version of 1873, into which all major revisions in the 1859 edition had been absorbed. He finds that Newman "dropped any references, whether theological or educational, which might annoy a general reader or might freeze his discourses in the Dublin context of their first delivery. He tightened his argumentative consistency by emphasizing the epistemological view of the necessary correlation of the sciences. In this way he argued the place of theology, he strengthened his essential thesis of the primarily intellectual end of a university, and he carefully distinguished the relation of theology and the Church to the university."

Of the many books and articles inspired principally by *The Idea of a University*, some are concerned with historical background, some with analysis of the text, some with Newman's day-to-day work as educator and administrator, a few with all three aspects of the subject. In "Liberal Studies and Moral Aims: A Critical Study of Newman's Position" (*Thought*, 1926), T. Corcoran, S.J., argued that what Newman had set himself to do in the *Idea* was "to formulate a philosophy of education that would afford a justification of the actual academic position of Oxford in his own times" when, thanks to the decline of theology and the professions in the schools, "the preliminary or language section of the historic faculty of arts . . . had assumed to itself the entire functions and scope of a university." The result was a philosophy of "severance" between intellect and virtue that contrasts sharply with "the traditional doctrine of Christian Europe" which underlay the 1854 Brief of Pius ix on the opening of the Catholic university. Newman's "bare idea" of a university, according to Corcoran, "intrinsically repels all possibility of the university's becoming an instrument of the Church at all." Corcoran's views, which he also expressed elsewhere, were challenged repeatedly: for example, by Fernande Tardivel in *J. H. Newman éducateur* (1937), by Michael Tierney ("Catholic University" in *A Tribute to Newman*, 1945), and by John E. Wise in "Newman and the Liberal Arts" (*Thought*, 1945), who points out that when Newman calls knowledge an end in itself, he is speaking of knowledge as the formal object of a university, as salvation is the object of the Church; and that Newman, well aware of the spiritual dangers of mere intellectualism, gave the Church an important role in maintaining the "integrity" of the university.

W. F. P. Stockley's *Newman, Education, and Ireland* (1933), a rather discursive assessment of Newman's achievement, has been largely superseded; but its insights into individuals like Cardinal Cullen give it some value still. Paul Sobry's *Newman en zijn* Idea of a University (1934) is valuable for its analysis of the text and its historical background and for a list of Newman's writings and sermons from 1824 to 1852 which supplied themes for the *Idea*. Fernande Tardivel's *J. H. Newman éducateur* provides a good account of Newman's entire career as educator and a brief but sensible analysis of his writings on education. Thus on the oft-debated status of Newman's gentleman, taken by some as an ironic sketch, she says simply and cogently: "La nature est une réalité, la grâce en est une autre; l'œuvre la plus achevée de la première est le 'gentleman,' mais la parfaite action de la seconde produit le saint. Du reste, Newman ne pense pas du tout que ces deux courants de valeurs soient inconciliable, il tend même à prouver qu'ils peuvent s'unir et se rendre mutuellement efficaces." Roger McHugh's "The Years in Ireland" (in *A Tribute to Newman*) is a brief but informative essay on the Irish political background since 1845, on Newman's audience for the discourses, on the physical properties of the university, and on contemporary reactions to Newman's work as rector.

J. F. Leddy's "Newman and Modern Educational Thought" (in *American Essays for the Newman Centennial*, ed. John R. Ryan and Edmond D. Benard, 1947) is disappointingly meager in view of its ambitious title, but perhaps inevitably so in view of the situation in 1945: "On visits to several university libraries I have examined the standard books on the history and on the philosophy of education, and in very few of them is Newman even mentioned. . . . I am further informed by several educators whose views seem to be typical that Newman has nothing for us today, and that he represents an extreme and outmoded intellectualist position." Where there is a reference, he adds, "it is almost always the same, to the very first lines of the preface of *The Idea of a University*, in which Newman states that in his view a university is a place of *teaching* universal *knowledge*, and not of research. The usual comment on this leaves one with the painful feeling that these eminent authors have read no further and have taken no trouble to understand Newman's full and subtle opinion."

W. M. Conacher's "Newman and Liberal Education" (*QQ*, 1947–48) is an intelligent and humane if rather elementary commentary on Newman's purpose in the discourses. More searching and critical is Culler's "Newman on the Uses of Knowledge" (*J. of Gen. Educ.*, 1950), an attempt "to examine the meaning and assess the validity" of "the most famous and characteristic assertion of the *Idea of a University*"—that knowledge is "its own end" and may be pursued "for its own sake." Culler traces the Aristotelian source of this idea, attempts to show that Newman's religious position was also necessary to him "simply as the answer to an intellectual problem" raised by the disjunction in modern philosophy "between the mind and its object," and considers objections to the idea of pursuing knowledge for its own sake such as: "it seems quite impossible to realize a spiritual end which we consciously pursue" and if we pursue knowledge "as a kind of mental gymnastic," we run the danger of sacrificing the power knowledge has of placing us in communion with reality.

In "Newman and Education" (*Cambridge J.*, 1950–51), G. H. Bantock finds Newman's position far subtler and richer than that of the Benthamites and Cambridge rationalists like Leslie Stephen and Henry Sidgwick. Newman "manages to combine passion and reason in a unity that enables him o seek for fact and knowledge in realms the utilitarians never dreamt of." Opposing to "Locke's ideal of how the mind ought to act . . . the acceptance of how it does act," Newman developed what for the nineteenth century was an "unusually complex" appreciation of the bases of understanding, and this "enabled him to conceive the various fields of knowledge in terms of their ends, the coalitions and distinctions which marked the disparity in unity, and the unity underlying separateness which characterizes the mental construction of man, in a way unusual since the middle ages."

For the history of Newman's university in the concrete and his work as administrator, two thoroughly and freshly documented studies are of great value. The first is Fergal McGrath's *Newman's University: Idea and Reality* (1951), the purpose of which is thus indicated: "The reading of his [Newman's] University essays leaves many with the impression that they emanated from a mind keen and balanced when dealing with abstract principles, but somewhat unaware of the needs and demands of the changing world in which he lived. The history of his actual government of the University shows that there was hardly an administrative problem of living interest today which he did not resolutely face, and for which his solution has not been vindicated by the experience of a century." The second such work is Frank V. La Ferrière's "A Documentary History of the Catholic University of Ireland, 1851–1858" (Diss. California, Los Angeles 1965), which uses material unknown to McGrath such as Newman's "University Journal" (3 Nov. 1853 to 29

March 1856) to throw much light on Newman's collegiate and tutorial system, the *Catholic University Gazette* and the *Atlantis*, professional studies in the university (medicine and science), the Faculty of Philosophy and Letters, the examination system, and so on.

Michael Tierney's "Newman's Doctrine of University Education" (*Studies*, 1953) is a sensible, well-balanced essay providing background material on the university, indicating Newman's main works on education, and discussing such questions as whether Newman's educational philosophy was one of "severance." On this matter he comes to an interesting if debatable conclusion: "We are not, I think, misinterpreting Newman when we suggest that in his view the main function of Liberal Knowledge is to train in the virtue of prudence, which is merely the Latin for Aristotle's *phronesis*." Tierney's and four lectures delivered at University College, Dublin by other faculty members to commemorate the centenary of Newman's 1852 *Discourses on the Scope and Nature of University Education* (on faith and reason, on the medical school, on literature, and on science) were published in the 1953 volume of the Irish journal *Studies* and in book form in 1954 in Dublin under the title *Newman's Doctrine of University Education*.

In the three parts of *The Imperial Intellect: A Study of Newman's Educational Ideal* (1955), Culler tells with an abundance of fresh documentation the story "of Newman's education, of his work as educator of others, and of his educational thinking as expressed in the *Idea of a University*." The first part studies Newman at Oxford and shows in detail the influence of people like Whately, for instance, who taught that a student should aim at an elementary rather than a superficial knowledge—the same Aristotelian distinction Newman himself was to make in Discourse VI of the *Idea*; the second part examines Newman's work in Dublin as a liberal and efficient university administrator who went beyond the Oxford reforms of 1854; and the third part is an uneven but stimulating expository and critical discussion of *The Idea of a University*. Although Culler's study of the educational influences on Newman is incomplete and therefore somewhat unbalanced—for example, there is no attempt to discuss the important influence of the Alexandrian Platonists—*The Imperial Intellect* remains the best single work on its subject.

For the educational influence of at least some of the Fathers of the Church, two articles are useful: C. F. Harrold's "Newman and the Alexandrian Platonists" (*MP*, 1939–40), which is more philosophically oriented; and Blehl's "Newman, the Fathers, and Education" (*Thought*, 1970), which outlines the influence of the Fathers, especially Clement and Origen, on Newman's educational theory: "First, there is set forth as an ideal the development of man's rational powers—his reason, imagination, and taste—or what Newman calls the philosophic habit of mind. Secondly, the unity of knowledge which Newman places as the underlying principle of the University is analogously that of Clement. Knowledge and truth may be found in every system, because each truth is a reflection of the *Logos*; but Christianity provides a center of unity. It is capable, therefore, of assimilating all these truths to itself."

Disagreeing somewhat with Culler's remark that *The Idea of a University* "deliberately omits any consideration of means and concentrates exclusively upon ends," H. Francis Davis attempts to show in "Newman and Educational Method" (*DubR*, 1957) that Newman had very specific and quite modern ideas on such topics as the errors in common methods of teaching and on the importance in teaching of the proper use of language. In *Newmans Idee einer Universität: Prob-*

leme hoeherer Bildung (1958), Wolfgang Renz offers a well-documented study of the Oxford background of the *Idea* and of Newman's views on the sciences, theology, the aim of a university, and its relations with the Church. His book is also useful for a close study of textual changes in the 1852, 1859, and 1873 editions of the *Idea*.

J. H. Whyte's important article "Newman in Dublin: Fresh Light from the Archives of Propaganda" (*DubR*, 1960) makes good use of hitherto unpublished Roman documents to show that Cardinal Cullen was almost certainly the principal influence holding back the appointment of Newman to the bishopric which Wiseman had urged in Rome in 1853; and also to indicate Cullen's objections to Newman's rectorship as the years went by.

A brief but perceptive article by John M. Gill, "Newman's Dialectic in *The Idea of a University*" (*QJS*, 1959), argues that Newman's "organic technique is essentially to dichotomize: his own statements emerge only through the hypothetical questions of his listeners or the quoted propositions of his opponents. He achieves his thesis only through its antithesis." This view, though here overstated, is basically sound, for the dialectic informing virtually all of Newman's work is that between nature and grace. This is a major aspect of Newman's writing that should well repay further study.

Fergal McGrath's *The Consecration of Learning: Lectures on Newman's* Idea of a University (Dublin, 1962; New York, 1963), which relates Newman's book to some contemporary educational problems, maintains that Newman's "fundamental theme" is that "without religion, there can be no unity or order among the various branches of knowledge" and that the "secondary theme" is "the imparting of true or philosophically comprehensive knowledge" as "the principal aim of a university education." In "Newman's *The Idea of a University*: The Dangers of a University Education" (*VS*, 1972), P. A. Dale goes even further and, in reaction against modern commentators who praise the book for illustrating the humanist idea of a liberal education, insists rather that it is "from beginning to end primarily a defence —first in intellectual and then in moral terms"—of religious exclusiveness and Church control of university education. "Much as one may want to make it into something more liberal and 'enlightened,' it remains just as Newman intended it should be, a profoundly conservative statement about the ends of a university education and a classic pièce de résistance to the contemporary glorification of knowledge." Dale reads and reasons well; and his article is a useful corrective, though like most correctives it goes too far on the other side: for example, in maintaining that the famous Discourse v, "Knowledge Its Own End," is "hardly to be characterized as . . . even a justification of liberal knowledge." Newman's work as Rector, his letters, and such essays of his as "Christianity and Scientific Investigation" in the here ignored second half of the *Idea* make quite clear that Newman's educational interests and aims were a good deal broader and more liberal than Dale seems willing to acknowledge.

John R. Griffin's "In Defense of Newman's 'Gentleman,'" (*DubR*, 1965) is an attack on the ironic or derogatory interpretation of Newman's gentleman evident in Culler and McGrath and most obviously in William Buckler's remark that "the 'gentleman,' which is education's best end product, is a figure with which no man of truly imaginative vision would allow himself willingly to be identified." In rebuttal Griffin cites such passages as that at the end of Discourse v of the *Idea*: "Liberal education makes not the Christian, not the Catholic, but the gentleman. It is well to be a gentleman"; and he maintains that Newman could hardly have made so complete a change in his meaning by Discourse VIII as would be involved in accepting the currently popular ironic interpretation.

Newman's reasons for refusing to get involved in Manning's ill-fated plan in 1872 for a Catholic college to be affiliated with London University are made clear in "Newman and the Kensington Scheme" by Derek Holmes (*DubR*, 1965), who rejects the view of Vincent A. McClelland in *Cardinal Manning, His Public Life and Influence* (1962) that Newman's attitude was provoked by Manning's refusal to help him in Dublin. Manning's administration was to be in clerical hands, and Newman feared an atmosphere of restraint. "The Archbishop is not contemplating a real University education for young Catholics," he wrote, "but wishes to do just as much as will stop the present clamour, and take off the edge of the evident injustice of forbidding Oxford and substituting nothing for it."

In "Newman's Universe of Knowledge: Science, Literature, and Theology" (*DR*, 1966), Harold M. Petitpas describes that universe as at once both a unity (the circle of sciences) and a hierarchy (the degrees or levels of knowledge), the subject matter or branches of knowledge all connected as being "the acts and work of the Creator," with the three principal areas of investigation (Nature in science, Man in literature, God in theology) subordinated one to another in that order. This is basically a sound essay though much of it is merely an explication of fairly obvious passages in the *Idea*, there is too easy an assertion of Coleridge's influence and too little of Aristotle's and Bacon's, and the nature of Newman's "philosophy" needs further clarification.

Newman's attitude toward science and its place in university education has been the subject of several articles and at least one dissertation in recent years. In "Newman and Science" (*A Tribute to Newman*, 1945), P. J. McLaughlin says that "Newman viewed science from a point between the liberalism of Lord Brougham and the conservatism of Cardinal Cullen," pointing out that Newman's impressive call for freedom of inquiry, "Christianity and Scientific Investigation," though written for the school of science in Dublin and approved by theological censors, was not delivered "on account of the prevailing temper on matters theological and the views of Dr. Cullen." Newman recommended "not only the candid acceptance of modern scientific theories in all their degrees of probability, but a bold change of policy. . . . By strenuous intellectual effort the larger-minded theologians and the Christian men of science would reach a way of intellectual life that would be sound and honest, and better than a cheap brand of apologetics which fails to carry conviction to the people of a new age, because it ignores that it is a new age, and takes no account of new outlooks and new problems."

T. S. Wheeler's "Newman and Science" (*Studies*, 1953) outlines Newman's views on the place of pure science, of scientific research, and of applied science in university education. The development of a good school of science was one of his foremost objectives, but he felt that science should be taught "only to students who had received a basic liberal education. He believed in the need for stressing principles, and rejected the criterion that utility should be the basis of what is taught." Although he would not give research the primacy over teaching and appears to neglect research in the preface to the *Idea*, he did in fact foster research in his university, founding a scholarly journal *The Atlantis* and calling for a university press to print scientific registers and literary work. He also had a scheme for an Institute of Applied Research, and his chemistry laboratory was equipped "to meet

the wants of those requiring a knowledge of chemistry for practical purposes, as for example, mining, metallurgy, the various chemical manufactures, bleaching, dyeing, tanning, brewing, distilling, sugar-boiling, and paper making." William Doolin's "Newman and His Medical School," in the same issue of *Studies*, is a good brief account and something of a supplement to Wheeler's article. Joseph Francis Hosey's "Physical Science in Newman's Thought" (Diss. Pennsylvania 1954) germinated in an attempt to analyze the imagery of *A Grammar of Assent*, which contains many allusions to science. Ultimately the author decided to study Newman's interest in science during his student years and show how this interest had a distinct effect on the development of his ideas and hence on his literary work, especially the *Idea* and the *Grammar*.

A good summary of Newman's position, based principally but not wholly on *The Idea of a University*, is "Newman's Idea of Science," by Petitpas (*Personalist*, 1967), which considers the distinctions Newman established between science and theology with respect to their subject matters, their proper methodologies, and their developmental character. The twentieth-century scholar might object, according to Petitpas, that Newman's thought "is too dependent upon the idea of science fostered by the Baconian and Newtonian natural philosophy tradition—that it is too clearly indebted to the British empirical tradition; that it establishes too sharp a cleavage between inductive and deductive ways of reasoning; that it does not make sufficient allowance for the role of analogies in scientific discovery; that it does not allow for the application of the experimental method to the study of group human behavior." The modern scholar should concede, on the other hand, "that science, that is, the scientific method, is most properly and most effectively adapted to the study of the physical universe, to the Buberian It-world; that the 'truths' discovered by science are necessarily probable, tentative—that science is *per se* developmental in character; that science, despite its indifference to such alliances in the universe of knowledge, is inextricably related to and dependent upon certain philosophic assumptions about the cosmos . . . that . . . in advocating a reconciliation between the rival claims of science and theology . . . Newman rendered a remarkably liberal judgment upon the contemporary antagonist to the traditional religious philosophy."

VI. NEWMAN AS LITERARY ARTIST

Although Newman's stature as one of the masters of English prose was firmly established in his own lifetime, the subject matter and the direction of his writing in an increasingly secular age inevitably narrowed his audience, so that until fairly recently, of his forty volumes, only two, the *Idea* and the *Apologia*, were widely read outside of theological circles. As a result, the range, subtlety, and power of his artistry remained almost unexplored by literary critics with few exceptions like R. H. Hutton. A pioneer work in winning for Newman broader recognition as an artist was Joseph J. Reilly's *Newman as a Man of Letters* (1925), a study of Newman as man, preacher, novelist, poet, historian, and controversialist, with emphasis on the writer's skill more than on his subject matter. Although a good deal of Reilly's book is by current standards quite elementary and too effusively impressionistic as criticism, there are many sound observations along the way. Reilly credits Newman with a threefold literary endowment: mastery of rhetoric, a perfect style, and psychological insight, the last being Newman's special gift, as steady as Thackeray's, as subtle as Browning's.

A more thorough and penetrating study, well documented from his letters and books, of the elements that contributed to Newman's development as a writer is Fernande Tardivel's *La Personnalité littéraire de Newman* (1937), originally a Sorbonne dissertation under the direction of Louis Cazamian. Tardivel examines Newman's natural gifts (keen sensibility, an extraordinary memory, an intellect geared to the concrete) as well as the influences on him of Oxford and Alexandria; and on the whole her conclusions still hold up even though much new material has come to light since she wrote: for example, "Newman attache plus de prix à la réalité resaisie dans le passé qu'à l'expérience du moment présent, et c'est pourquoi sa mémoire a pu être pour lui un merveilleux instrument de travail littéraire." She is fascinated by the paradoxes of Newman: apostle of authority but also of free inquiry; detractor of reason but exalter of intelligence; subtle logician trusting especially to intuition; realist and mystic, scarce believing in the world he studies so closely, aesthete and ascetic, tender and yet detached. Yet she sees, more clearly than Bremond, that Newman assimilates them all "en restant toujours cohérente."

Another dissertation carefully traces the gradual change in Newman's view of literature, originally very Romantic: Alvan S. Ryan's "Newman's Concept of Literature" (Iowa 1940), a shorter version of which appears in *Critical Studies in Arnold, Emerson, and Newman* (Univ. of Iowa Humanistic Studies, vi, 1942). Ryan's work serves as a corrective to those studies which see Newman in wholly Romantic terms: for example, Sister Mary Kiener's *John Henry Newman, the Romantic, the Friend, the Leader* (1933). His conclusion is that "Newman is neither classical nor romantic in any strict sense, but rather a subtle blend of the two . . . the ruling idea of his work is the Christian conception of man. . . . He tried . . . to work out a view of literature expressive of what has been called [by Norman Foerster] 'the blended might of humanism and religion.' "

Jeremiah Hogan's "Newman and Literature" (*Studies*, 1953), another of the University College, Dublin lectures on the centenary of the *Discourses*, studies Newman as a writer and theorist of literature. Newman is said to excel "in what might be called the *unliterary* essentials of good prose. He had great knowledge, and a powerful and well-trained mind; the gifts of ordonnance, distinction, analogy, harmony, were his." If his doctrine of style, with its insistence that he use words only "to explain clearly and exactly his meaning" might seem to militate against his being an artist, says Hogan, "there is far less disparagement of style than there might seem to be; because Newman's *meaning* is not that of a geometrician or abstract reasoner, but a much finer, subtler thing, greatly dependent on the colour and accent of its expression, and on the personality of the man." Hogan is undoubtedly correct here, though he is mistaken about Newman's disparaging a *copia verborum*. He also points out that Newman anticipated several of the ideas in T. S. Eliot's "What Is a Classic?" and that he "never looked on modern literature with contempt or thought that the study of English must be, in the famous words of an Oxford don in 1887, merely 'chatter about Shelley.' He set up a chair of English when there were none in these islands except at Scotland and at Kings' College, London."

In "Newman on the Imagination" (*MLN*, 1953), Merritt E. Lawlis focuses on one aspect of Newman's literary theory, pointing out that although he praises imagination in the 1829 essay on poetry in terms that have suggested Coleridge and

Shelley, in theological and philosophical discourse he views imagination in the light of Addison—a faculty of mind "that, like a reservoir, stores up sense impressions; very closely allied with memory, it is a passive agent, acted upon rather than acting"—and especially of Samuel Johnson, as in Chapter xliv of *Rasselas* on "The Dangerous Prevalence of Imagination."

Newman's tastes in literature clearly proclaim him a Romantic, according to Stanley T. Williams ("Newman's Literary Preferences," *SR*, 1920; rpt. in his *Studies in Victorian Literature*, 1923). "It is perhaps true to say that Newman seldom cared for books whose general trend was not to make the will of God prevail. But it is equally true that there are notable cases of his liking books whose only appeal could have been their romance. A book which lacked both of these qualities could not hold him. Thus the realism and the agnosticism of George Eliot repelled him doubly; he could not endure the novels of natural fact. On the other hand, although he condemned Byron, he was unable to resist his ecstatic romances." On the whole, Williams is probably correct, though Newman's fondness for Crabbe, Miss Mitford, Mrs. Gaskell, Thackeray, and Trollope would indicate that some qualifications are in order.

In "Cardinal Newman—The Literary Aspect" (*DubR*, 1955), Hugh Dinwiddy maintains that Newman was happiest "showing the truth, which he knew himself, to others, and showing it in such a way that it is living, growing, and in every aspect real . . . showing it to those simple enough in heart to feel imaginatively with him. . . . And the showing for Newman is the literary aspect, the making real in words the truth he has himself experienced in life and in study; while his 'preparation of heart' [the error of the world being to think itself a Judge of religious truth without preparation of heart] lies in the fullest possible acceptance of experience."

One of the most glowing and yet discriminating assessments of Newman as an artist is Geoffrey Tillotson's "Newman the Writer" (in *Mid-Victorian Studies*, by Geoffrey and Kathleen Tillotson, 1965), a slightly revised version of his Introduction to the Reynard Library anthology *Newman* (1957). For all Newman's detestation of "the mere literary ethos," argues Tillotson in gentle reply to Henry Tristram's "On Reading Newman," the necessity that drove him to write not only to order and clearly but also beautifully was that of one "born to be a writer"—he was not merely "one of the supreme geniuses of nineteenth-century England" but "a supremely literary genius." He may have been only an occasional writer, but he "consciously laid himself open" for many of the occasions. He may have had a Platonic distrust of the reality of material phenomena, but "he handled earthly things *as if* they were real," seeming "as thoroughly at home among things as Chaucer or Shakespeare or Pope or Dickens." He is "constantly keen . . . not just because of his free speech [as in the earthy account of the Sicilian tour] . . . but because his mind is sensuous." He is "also a writer in his matter . . . as alert to the trivial round as Wordsworth or Hardy; as alert as Matthew Arnold to the urgent public matters of the day—e.g., cholera, mesmerism, the goldfields . . . as alert as a novelist to the personal characteristics of everybody he met." Many students of literature who might willingly grant that Newman is "one of the shining demonstrations that the style is the man" will yet be surprised to hear that "the ease with which he can be brilliantly witty," as in the *Difficulties of Anglicans*, "seals him of the tribe of the Henry Jameses and Oscar Wildes." But then how many students of literature are likely t ave read the *Difficulties of Anglicans*?

Theodore N. Hong's "Cardinal Newman as a Literary Critic" (Diss. Minnesota

1958) argues that just as in Newman's religious life there is what Vincent Reade has called "a persistent identity of inner life amidst notable outward change," so both his early and late literary views illustrate what may be called a sacramental view of literature. Hong may be right, depending on how one defines the terms, that Newman "could not grant that the arts should have an existence independent of religion and have a morality of their own. This was precisely the kind of fragmentation which liberalism led to." Nevertheless, the attitude toward literature that he takes in the *Idea*, where it is defined as the life and remains of the natural man, is surely far more "liberal" than the attitude toward poetry taken in the 1829 essay, the 1846 essay on Keble, and the 1849 lecture on poetry. What seems probable is that Newman's conception of poetry in the narrow sense remained more "sacramental" or Platonic than his conception of literature in general.

A provocative essay which insists that art is not, for Newman, "to be identified with morality and religion" and that "Newman recognized that the primary end of art is pleasure and not instruction" is Petitpas' "Newman's Idea of Literature: A Humanist's Spectrum" (*Ren*, 1964). The article succinctly outlines Newman's views in relation to the artist, the work of art, the universe, and the audience: for example, his primary critical focus is on the artist, and when he discusses a work, his primary interest is in language as "the faithful expression of the author's intense personality." Petitpas, who relies for his material primarily on the 1829 essay on poetry and on the lectures on literature in the *Idea*, does not indicate any change in Newman's views over the years.

In "Newman and the Novelists" (*Cornhill*, 1927), Henry Tristram discusses Newman's attitude toward Scott, Disraeli, and particularly Thackeray and Trollope, his special favorites among his later contemporaries. Dickens never won his affection to the same degree, though he admired *David Copperfield*. "Trollope's pictures of clerical life reproduced in their vivid realism the tone and atmosphere of the ecclesiastical circles into which he had been plunged by the Tractarian campaign." M. S. Bankert's "Newman in the Shadow of *Barchester Towers*" (*Ren*, 1968) makes clear that Trollope's own sympathies were with "the moderate high Churchman who was addicted neither to the exuberances of Roman ritualism nor to the strenuous ascesis of Geneva" and sees the Rev. Francis Arabin, the waning Tractarian, as "a compound of the young Arnold and Isaac Williams."

On 24 December 1856, Newman wrote a letter to young Thomas Arnold making suggestions about a syllabus Arnold had presented to him for a pioneering survey course in English literature at the Catholic University in Dublin. The letter was later presented to the Pierpont Morgan Library by Arnold's daughter, Mrs. Humphry Ward, and was first published by J. Connop Thirlwall in "Cardinal Newman's Literary Preferences" (*MLN*, 1933). Besides illuminating Newman's strong partiality for Addison, it makes clear what for him constituted the hierarchy of English literature: "Must not you confine the two years to three to six chief classics? If so, they must be Shakespeare, (Milton?) Pope, Clarendon (?) Addison, Johnson. Or who? Then for the next two years you might take Spenser—Bacon—Milton—the Novelists." Thirlwall points out that Newman was here concerned with the "classics" of literature; and as he had explained in his lecture on "Literature," "By the classics of a national Literature I mean those authors who have the foremost place in exemplifying the powers and conducting the development of its language."

In a charming essay "The Classics" (*A Tribute to Newman*, 1945), Tristram says that Mark Pattison was right in suggesting that Newman's knowledge of the classics was quite limited in extent if not in depth, there being no evidence that he "ever thought of enlarging the range of his classical reading beyond the point it had reached when he took his degree." Like most of his contemporaries before "the star of Jowett" had risen, he never read the works of Plato, for instance. And yet, as Tristram shows, what Newman did read he absorbed deeply, not merely notionally but really, with the result that throughout his life he could quote the classics as appositely as he quoted the Bible. One favorite passage of his is especially revealing. "I have," Newman wrote in 1855, "an enormous dislike to puffing. . . . From a child a description of Ulysses' eloquence in the *Iliad* seized my imagination and touched my heart. This is the only way in which I have done anything." And in 1858, thinking presumably of the end of his university rectorship, he made his point clearer: "Recollect, and let me myself recollect, that from the first it has been my fortune to be ever failing, yet after all not to fail. When I was a boy, I was taken, beyond anything in Homer, with Ulysses seeming like a fool or an idiot, when he began to speak,—yet somehow doing more than the others, as St. Paul with his weakness and foolishness. I think that this was from some presentiment of what was to happen to me."

Two articles by Charlotte E. Crawford explain the genesis of Newman's novels. "The Novel That Occasioned Newman's *Loss and Gain*" (*MLN*, 1950) bears out the reviewer in *Fraser's Magazine* of 1848, who saw in Newman's tale of a convert an answer to the brief anonymous novel *From Oxford to Rome and How It Fared with Some Who Lately Made the Journey*, By a Companion Traveller (1847). The author was soon identified as Elizabeth Furlong Shipton Harris (1822–52), who had become a Roman Catholic in 1846, been disillusioned, and was now writing to keep Anglicans in their own church, while looking toward eventual reunion of Anglican and Roman Catholicism. In the 1847 Preface to the sixth edition of *Loss and Gain*, Newman explained that in the summer of 1847 a "Tale, directed against the Oxford converts to the Catholic faith" had been sent to him at Santa Croce in Rome; and he, feeling a direct notice of the book inappropriate, had chosen to reply in a novel written from the point of view of one of the Oxford converts. Newman did not identify the novel, but certain internal as well as the external evidence points to the work of Elizabeth Harris.

According to Crawford's "Newman's *Callista* and the Catholic Popular Library" (*MLR*, 1950), *Callista* was a volume in a series of books for laymen, the Catholic Popular Library, published by Burns in two series from 1854 to 1861. The project was inaugurated with Wiseman's *Fabiola*, which was probably intended to correct the picture of Church history in Kingsley's *Hypatia* (1853) that had offended Roman Catholics and High Churchmen alike. Wiseman's preface suggested appropriate sequels such as a tale of the Church of the Catacombs, of the Basilicas, of the Cloister, etc. Newman had done some preliminary sketches for *Callista* in 1848 but had put them aside until 1855, when he took them up and expanded them for publication in 1856. It was, like Wiseman's, a tale of fourth-century Christians but not one of the sequels; and Newman's preface says it was "the nearest approach which the author could make to a more important work suggested to him from a high ecclesiastical quarter."

Joseph E. Baker's *The Novel and the Oxford Movement* (1932) contains a chapter on "Newman as Novelist," which anticipates perhaps the major point of George Levine's later studies: "A naturalistic novel as a study in mundane cause and effect," writes Baker, "makes the background a part of the story, almost one of the actions, that could not be removed without breaking a link in the sequence of events. Newman's supernaturalism allows him to write without achieving that intimate fusion of setting and plot. We feel that the subjective study has been worked out first, the frame fitted rather awkwardly around it. The social and physical world never emerges into convincing reality." Baker seems less aware than Hutton, Tillotson, or Levine, however, of Newman's strength as a novelist.

Newman's novels are discussed briefly and sensibly, if too uncritically, by Margaret Maison in *The Victorian Vision: Studies in the Religious Novel* (1961), published also in a paperback called *Search Your Soul, Eustace*. Maison credits Newman with being "the only eminent Victorian who could write a confessional novel of spiritual biography in high spirits as well as high seriousness" and notes that a reviewer in *Fraser's* was rather shocked by the "jokes," "gossip," and "levities" of *Loss and Gain*, "a somewhat undignified vehicle for the opinions of one who has long been revered as a prophet and a saint." She also observes that *Callista* gives Newman an opportunity "to express much of his feminine sensibility" and that the chief stages in Callista's spiritual growth "bear no little resemblance to Newman's own."

In "Newman's Fiction and the Failure of Reticence" (*TSLL*, 1966), George Levine argues that since in Newman's view "men make decisions not by weighing according to some moral calculus the alternative possibilities but by an act of will that gives direction to a large number of subtle—perhaps subliminal—movements of mind and feeling," we should expect from him "a detailed view of the minute but important causes which operate on the mind and feelings; in the fiction, however, we find only the barest dramatic embodiment of this view." Levine illustrates his point by comparing the treatment of Newman's self-imposed celibacy in the *Apologia*, where the discussion has "just the right air of valorous though reticent confrontation of an ungentlemanly and insidious libel," with its treatment in *Loss and Gain* and *Callista*, where Newman's failure to move much beyond the reticence of the *Apologia* is clearly a defect, "especially for a post-Freudian audience," since a novelist is "committed to an exploration of a character's inner life." In *Loss and Gain* so much of the explanation of Reding's celibacy and the conversion itself is given in terms which, if "antirationalist," are nonetheless "thoroughly intellectual," that it suggests not merely an inadequate dramatization of Newman's "theory of the way in which people decide on grounds not conventionally regarded as rational," but also that the theory itself "does not really come to grips with irrational forces, but is essentially directed at the rational and conscious, though what is rational and conscious may not be conventionally articulable."

Callista is more revealing, according to Levine, perhaps because its setting in a pagan world allowed Newman more freedom to employ the disguises of fiction. In any event, in a passage about Agellius contemplating a proposed marriage to Callista, there is revealed "an essential distrust of the living busy world, of self, and of anything outside of self" which on the subject of Newman's attitude toward celibacy "is much more to the point than theological arguments about what St. Paul meant, and probably approaches far more closely to the true source of the attitudes." And what Levine thinks the "true source" is may be inferred from his remark that the "revulsion from the flesh and the fear of self in Newman is [sic] so deeply rooted that the very texture of *Callista* renders the sense of it."

In "Newman and the Threat of Experience," Levine combined his various articles into one and joined them with studies of Macaulay and Carlyle in a book called *The Boundaries of Fiction* (1968), which argues that "Newman's openness to experience was . . . restricted, as even the greatest Victorian art frequently was, by attitudes toward social order ingrained in the very meaning of the word gentleman, and made even more intense by an otherworldliness which saw all the activities of this life as secondary to that of the next." This seems true enough; and Levine is likewise fair and correct in adding: "Of course, Newman was no more guilty of conscious distortion than Carlyle or Macaulay—perhaps less. Each in a different way remained open to some of the complexities of experience, but each tended to shape the experience into a pattern which existed before he knew the facts."

What is both curious and regrettable in Levine's criticism is the expense of intelligence and sensitivity in taking Newman to task, however gently, for "failures" he shared with most of his contemporaries before the novel had turned to psychology and before the appearance of a Zola or a Freud. "It seems to me," he writes, "that one important objection to Newman's theory of belief is not that it is excessively irrationalist but that it is not irrational enough. Newman's irrationalism is curiously rational; he seemed to assume, though in a peculiarly complicated way, that man's nature is rational." But of course! It is Levine, not Newman, who evinces a "commitment to irrationalism," who knows the "true source" of Newman's attitude toward celibacy, who knows that the modern novel and autobiography are "essentially secular forms," with a "commitment to raw experience and to the minute investigation of particular injustices and sufferings." In other words, Newman does not fit Levine's "pattern" of experience. At the same time, he is so remarkable a writer and person, as Levine is acutely aware, that there is always a danger, as he cautions his readers, of allowing oneself "to become so deeply involved with Newman that one could see nothing except from his point of view." One of these days another critic may find himself writing an essay called "Professor Levine and the Fear of Newman."

The best brief study of the relations of his novels to Newman's own life is A. Martin's "Autobiography in Newman's Novels" (*The Month*, 1960), which argues that "Newman is the central figure in his own novels" and that in Callista, much more than in Reding, "we feel the feminine sensitiveness of the author; her craving for sympathy, her desire for perfection . . . everything in Callista recalls Newman. She certainly provides the best portrait of his conversion; his own experiences have given him powers of insight into the convert soul. Newman projects on to her his own tormented soul in its every aspect, enlightened by a subtle and sure illative sense."

In a highly useful dissertation (Yale 1967), Mary Paton Ryan has provided a critical edition in two volumes of Newman's *Callista*, "one of the few books about which so much information is available" and "a kind of metaphorical mirror for the speculations advanced by Newman in his greater books." Volume 1 contains an introductory section on the writing of the novel, its verbal texture, and its setting in the context of Newman's nonfictional prose, as well as an appendix containing Newman's notes (annotated by the editor) preparatory to writing the novel; diary entries with the first sketches for *Callista*; fragmentary MS versions from 1848 and 1855; a bundle of miscellaneous notes of about 50,000 words containing plot sketches, descriptive passages, information gathered from travel literature, and the names of books to be consulted for information about early Christian and secular life in Africa. Volume ɪɪ provides a critical edition of the text based on the collation of a MS and eight corrected editions. (There is a bibliographical description of the editions published in Newman's lifetime.) Ryan argues convincingly that *A Grammar of Assent* provides almost a gloss to *Callista*.

"The Biographical Writings of John Henry Newman" (Diss. Fordham 1970), by Carole Ann Ganim, concentrates on such earlier works as *Primitive Christianity* and *The Church of the Fathers* and later essays like those on Theodoret and St. John Chrysostom in order to assess Newman's merits and defects as a biographer. The conclusion is that, though he lacked historical objectivity and a sense of chronology and was affected by the nineteenth-century conventions hampering the freedom and artistry of the kind of biography that reached its apex in Boswell, Newman did bring to his biographical sketches artistic selection and acute psychological insight into character which were unusual for his times.

Another valuable dissertation provides us with the only critical edition of Newman's poems: Elisabeth A. Noel's "An Edition of Poems by John Henry Cardinal Newman" (Illinois 1956). The work contains an Introduction, with a good account of all MSS, and the text of all the poems known to have been written by Newman—about 200, including seven hitherto unpublished—briefly annotated and with variant readings.

Newman's reputation as a poet has always been a minor one, with the result that most critical attention has been focused on his only widely known poems, "Lead, Kindly Light" ("The Pillar of the Cloud") and *The Dream of Gerontius*; and there have been few attempts to consider his work as a whole. One of the earliest is "The Poems of John Henry Newman" (*Blackwood's*, 1870), the author of which is identified in the *Wellesley Index to Victorian Periodicals* as Elizabeth Hassell, a prolific critic of the day. In Newman's *Verses on Various Occasions* (1868) she singles out "the presence of these three indispensable requirements in the poet . . . an antique singleness of thought and simplicity of diction . . . a due preference for the concrete to the abstract; nor though their themes exclude the ordinary sources of passion in poetry, and though their writer's severe self-restraint may look cold to a superficial glance, shall we find them otherwise than the expression of genuine and strong feeling."

Catherine A. Burns's "A Study of the Poetry of John Henry Newman" (Diss. Iowa 1922) shows that "in general, Newman continued throughout life to turn to verse-writing for the expression of his emotional life," and that his poems in many respects resemble his prose, especially in the sermons. She also analyzes Newman's revisions and metrical technique, shows the deep influence on him of Keble's *Christian Year*, and the influence on *The Dream of Gerontius* of the Fathers and of such Roman devotional books as the Breviary.

In "Newman as Poet" (*Thought*, 1945), a rather elementary but useful survey, John K. Ryan argues that Newman is "like Wordsworth in that he is to be judged by the best that he wrote, not by the poorest and most awkward. The best includes such sonnets as 'Substance and Shadow,' 'The Progress of Unbelief,' 'Messina,' 'Angelic Guidances,' and 'Memory,' all of which can stand high in a literature rich in sonnets. It includes *The Dream of Gerontius* and 'The Pillar of the Cloud.' It includes a series of poems that always win respect because of the complete candor and humility with which an earnest heart and troubled mind are laid bare." Hans Dennerlein's "Newman als Dichter" (*Newman Studien*, ɪ, 1948) attempts to make Newman's poems better known to German readers, and includes an uncritical but informative introduction, and good translations into German of twelve of Newman's poems, with a brief commentary on each.

In "Newman the Poet" (*Ren*, 1956), John Pick offers a sensitive assessment of the strengths and weaknesses of Newman's poems, which he finds often severely beautiful in their dignity and restraint, but often also too restrained, too lacking in lyrical ardor, pictorial power, and sharply focused imagery, too marked by poetic diction and clichés, the tendency toward generalization and the personification of abstractions, too prosaic, wooden, and moralistic. Newman had a weak critical sense in poetry, he points out, but a very strong one in prose; and Pick attempts to explain this fact by the low state of English verse when Newman was writing most of his poetry and by some of the ideas expressed in Newman's 1829 essay on poetry, with its Platonic rejection of the world of the senses and its view of poetry as a free and unfettered effusion of genius.

John C. Thirlwall's "John Henry Newman: His Poetry and Conversion" (*DubR*, 1968) is a reverential article tracing Newman's spiritual life in his poetry but making Newman anticipate too much, as when "The Cruel Church" is said to prove "that in 1835 Newman's heart was striving to find his spiritual haven in Rome" or the early "Eucharist" that "he was unconsciously preparing himself for the doctrine of Transubstantiation."

An excellent article for the centenary of what in 1881 J. A. Froude called the most popular hymn in the English language is Henry Tristram's "Lead, Kindly Light—June 16, 1833" (*DubR*, 1933). Newman, of course, never intended it as a hymn and preferred to hear Faber's "The Eternal Years" on his own deathbed, thinking his poem too much the voice of one in darkness for such an occasion. When in 1879 Newman was asked for an explanation of the last two lines, he politely refused on the ground that poets were not bound to be critics or give a sense to their own words, and that it was pointless for him to try to explain a mood of half a century ago. Tristram attempts to explain the lines against the background of Ham, Grey Court, of which Newman used to dream as a boy as if it were a paradise peopled with angels, and also of his illness in Sicily.

Paull F. Baum's "The Road to Palermo" (*SAQ*, 1956), in effect a supplement to Tristram's essay, is a good discussion of the meaning of the poem, which he finds both incoherent at times and yet powerful, "the impulsive impromptu of an undisciplined muse." In the third stanza, for instance, the "moor" and "fen" "are obviously English landscape, the 'crag and torrent' curiously Sicilian; and the 'night' is both those feverish nights when he prayed for strength to reach Palermo and the night of past pride and perplexed unfaith."

There is an annotated edition of *The Dream of Gerontius* "with some words on the poem and its writer" by W. F. P. Stockley (1923), but the introduction is excessively laudatory and uncritical. An early and sensible discussion of the work appears in F. H. Doyle's *Lectures on Poetry* (1869), indicating how seriously the poem was once taken in England, where almost 30,000 copies were sold in the two decades after Newman's death, where it is still occasionally performed in Elgar's Oratorio version, and where as recently as 1951 it was performed as a dramatic poem with music by Fernand Laloux. Doyle, Arnold's successor as Professor of Poetry at Oxford, describes *Gerontius* as "grave and subdued as to tone, somewhat bare of ornament, but everywhere weighty with thought. It is written also with Dr. New n's usual mastery over the English language, and moves along from the beginni g to the end with a solemn harmony of its own. I am here referring to the blank verse; the speeches rather. The lyrical portions . . . are, in my judgment, less successful. The strains as they flow forth from the various ranks of angels are not differentiated by any intelligible gradations of feeling and of style, and indeed, do not move me much more than those average hymns which people, who certainly are not angels yet, sing weekly in church."

In "*The Dream of Gerontius* and the Fall of Man" (*DubR*, 1945), Abbot Horne notes that the picture of the Fall given by Newman is rather different from the ordinary one—"man going back to a very low type of savage life, little removed from that of the beasts of the field among whom he dwelt, and remaining in this state for long ages" before being gradually restored to manhood. Horne, whose article first appeared in the *Downside Review* for May 1932, asked whether Newman had ever written elsewhere in this fashion about the Fall. The *Dublin Review* version of his article adds a note written by Newman in September 1864 when, according to its supplier Francis Bacchus, "J.H.N. was speculating a good deal on evolution." Newman suggests that "the progress of which men boast so much just now is nothing beyond the recovery of physical nature, from the effects of losing Paradise at first."

In " 'Gerontion' and *The Dream of Gerontius*" (*Furioso*, 1948), William Van O'Connor notes the similarity in titles between T. S. Eliot's poem and Newman's, the fact that Eliot did read Newman and that both poems have advanced age as a common subject. But though he notes "some few similarities in phrases and symbols"—Gerontius finds that in the House of Judgment "The sound is like the rushing of the wind" and Gerontion feels himself "an old man, / A dull head among windy spaces"—they are not impressive; and the critic has little choice but to conclude that the poems are "in no sense identical even though each is concerned with the Christian mysteries and with salvation. Gerontius lives among believers. Their voices fade behind him as he approaches judgment. His faith is secure. Gerontion lives among non-believers. For his time there is no life-giving faith."

That Newman must have been either directly or indirectly familiar with "the great and terrible eleventh-century hymn of St. Peter Damian, the *De die mortis rhythmus*" is the fairly persuasive argument of Esther R. B. Pese in "A Suggested Background for Newman's 'A Dream of Gerontius' " (*MP*, 1949). Both Newman and Damian concentrate on the particular rather than the general judgment, she points out, adding: "The portrayal of the moment of death; the journey; the passages about the demons that bar the way; the final note of divine aid, not only mercy but divine effort on the soul's behalf—these are the points in common, and they are the focal points of both poems." At the same time, she finds the "relation in emotional quality between Newman and Damian" to be "the relation between tepidity and white heat," with "the watered-down Victorian spiritual sensibility" a poor substitute for the "violent realism of the medieval imagination."

In "Source of an 'Inspiration': Francis Newman's Influence on the Form of 'The Dream of Gerontius' " (*VN*, 1961), David J. Mulcahy prints a fascinating letter of F. W. Newman to John dated 15 October 1864, offering reflections on his brother's wish to do "*some one* great work" and expressing the belief that "you were naturally made for a great *poet* or a great *musical composer*." He goes on to suggest that Newman could help to create a noble Catholic literature in English, a possibility for others that John himself had discussed in *The Idea of a University*, and adds: "The form of literature which I would suggest is Tragedy, varied by scenes half comic, not coarse as in Shakespeare, but veiled as in the Orestes and the Persae."

Helen G. Hole, in "A New Look at Newman's *The Dream of Gerontius*" (Diss. Indiana 1970), provides a survey of the rise and decline of the poem's reputation as well as a study of the development of the religious beliefs synthesized in the poem and of Newman's techniques for appealing to the emotions and the intellect which make *The Dream* still worthy of appreciation despite its weaknesses.

Much attention has been paid in recent years to Newman's 1829 essay for the *London Review*, "Poetry with Reference to Aristotle's Poetics." A good exposition of and commentary on the essay is Geoffrey Tillotson's "Newman's Essay on Poetry," first published in *Newman Centenary Essays* (1945), later revised and expanded in *Perspectives of Criticism* (ed. Harry Levin, 1950), and finally revised slightly again in Tillotson's *Criticism and the Nineteenth Century* (1951). Describing Newman's as an essay that exists "to effect a dematerialisation of poetry," Tillotson shows how Newman Platonized Aristotle's concept of the poet as discovering the general in the particular by making poetry concern itself "not with the world in general . . . but with that part of the world which is capable of matching the 'eternal form of beauty and perfection' that exist in the poetic mind, and which is therefore capable of responding to grace, purity, refinement, and good feeling." Like Keble, Newman "placed most value on those manifestations of life which are gentlest, most intimate and commonplace," preferring the lyrical and, among lyrics, homely lyrics—the "quiet kind of poetry which Keble had written his essay on sacred poetry to commend."

In *English Poetic Theory 1825–1865* (1950), Alba H. Warren, Jr. offers an illuminating analysis of Newman's essay as "a good example of Early Victorian criticism. Its serious, combative, and yet persuasive tone, its point of view, independent and disrespectful of old authority, its enthusiasm for originality, imagination, emotion, its preference for these to formalism of any kind, its confusion of Aristotelian and neoplatonic theory, its tendency to assimilate all poetry to the quality of the lyric are all representative."

In "Newman on Rousseau: Revisions in the Essay on Poetry" (*N&Q*, 1954), Stephen M. Parrish shows that in the 1871 reprint of *Essays Critical and Historical*, several sentences apparently altered by the editor, Blanco White, now stand as Newman first wrote them: for example, Newman wrote that "Rousseau, it may be supposed, is an exception to our doctrine" that a right state of heart is the formal condition of a poetical mind; whereas in 1829 the sentence read, "Rousseau is not an exception to our doctrine for his heart was naturally religious." White reversed Newman's sense and added the latter clause if Parrish is correct, and the connectives in the following sentence appear to indicate that he is.

Examining Newman's marginal notes of 1820 and especially of 1827–28 in his copy of Aristotle (trans. Thomas Tyrwhitt, Oxford, 1817), Robert A. Colby finds what "amounts to a first draft" of Newman's essay. Critics quoted include Horace, Longinus, Bacon, Hurd, Dacier, Voltaire, and Johnson; and Colby concludes: "It seems obvious that [Newman] went at Aristotle not only more predisposed towards other kinds of critics but with the aid of interpreters who distorted him, like Hurd" ("Newman on Aristotle's *Poetics*," *MLN*, 1956).

Luca Obertello's "Il 'Saggio sulla Poesia' di Newman" (*Rivista di Estetica*, 1964) is a well-informed essay pointing out that Newman is not so much explicating Aristotle as using him to support his own Romantic definition of poetry. Obertello notes many similarities between Newman's thought and that of his contemporaries, and concludes: ". . . il vero significato del *Saggio* si deve ricercare

negli accenni alla volenza artistica del 'sistema morale' e della religione, e all'origi-
nalita dell'immaginazione creativa; sopratutto per questi elementi, esso e un note-
vole esempio del clima romantico alla sua maturità."

In a searching and stimulating essay called "Newman, Aristotle, and the New
Criticism: On the Modern Element in Newman's Poetics" (*PMLA*, 1966), Norman
Friedman considers Newman's essay as an example of the tendency of nineteenth-
century and modern critics to write off through a misunderstanding of his method
Aristotle's conception of plot as responsible for a mechanical, predetermined notion
of poetic form, while praising Aristotle as lending support to the belief that poetry
deals with a "higher" kind of truth, a notion derived from misunderstanding his idea
that poetry is more philosophical than history, dealing in universals rather than
particulars. Newman reminds one of John Crowe Ransom or E. M. Forster in his
belief that "it is not in the plot, but in the characters, sentiments, and diction, that
the actual merit and poetry of the composition is placed," an assertion that according to Friedman is based on the assumption "that texture is poetical and structure is
not."

In arguing that "poetry is ultimately founded on correct moral perception,"
Newman resembles no modern, however, save perhaps Yvor Winters or F. R.
Leavis. According to Friedman, Newman could see that science, rhetoric, and
psychology were subordinate to art in the sense that the poet's aim is to make an
effective whole "rather than to display his knowledge," but "he cannot see that the
same applies to morality and religion." The modern critic who reads Chapter ix of
the *Poetics* interprets the truth of poetry not in a moral so much as in a metaphysical
or epistemological sense, poetry giving us the truth not only of the fact but of the
fact plus its value, not only of the idea but of how it feels to have the idea. The
modern critic adds wit, irony, and the world of the commonplace to Romantic-
Victorian transcendentalism: both conceive of poetry as giving in some sense a
higher kind of truth.

Friedman's essay is really a polemic in favor of Aristotle as a genuine modern,
the "one true pioneer" of those who are looking for formal criticism since he "sees a
play as organized after its own inner logic rather than . . . according to some
mechanical and 'rational' plan—a conception which Newman and the moderns
mistakenly attribute to Aristotle." Friedman's ideas are those of the "Chicago
school" of criticism, and they are expressed with the old familiar assurance that is
so enviable and exhilarating if not invariably convincing: for example, on the
question of whether *any* notion of type at all is implied in Aristotle's assertion in
Chapter ix that the poet is more philosophical than the historian. Friedman does
not seem to be aware that Newman himself later had second thoughts about his
essay on poetry; and he is more than a little unfair in a comparison he makes
between Newman and J. S. Mill which implies that for Mill but not for Newman
morality meant doing things "for their own sakes, rather than merely for the
rewards they might bring." But whatever its defects, his essay is well worth pondering.

In "Newman and Aristotle's *Poetics*" (*Ren*, 1968), Edward A. Watson concerns himself with "the implicit meaning of Newman's theory." He finds the 1829
essay "an admixture of romantic theory and an argument from analogy in which
great poetry represents a visible sign of an inward and divinely granted spiritual
grace. This view of poetry which subscribes to the idea that the poet is divinely
inspired (not in the generalized Romantic terminology but in the sense that man is

further endowed with powers to achieve salutary acts) led Newman to conclude that poetry was based on correct moral perception. The poem is, in itself, an affirmation of the spiritual reality of God, and, in this respect, capable of conveying the truth about natural phenomena." This is a thoughtful article, but no evidence is supplied that in 1829 Newman knew much about or was concerned with such doctrines as actual grace.

Although there have been a few studies of Newman's rhetoric in the *Apologia*, as we have seen, there has been no general study of Newman as a rhetorician. The closest thing to such is probably John Holloway's *The Victorian Sage* (1953), in which Newman is considered one of a group of writers (Carlyle, Disraeli, George Eliot, Matthew Arnold, and Thomas Hardy) who exposed a view of "the world, man's place in it, and how he should live," a wisdom "acquired and confirmed in a distinctive manner," exposition becoming proof "of a knowledge that is somehow both elusive and simple, that cannot even be formulated unless by a well-ordered and healthy mind, and that ultimately is known by a special sense, an intuition." According to Holloway, the sage "has a special problem in expounding or in proving what he wants to say. He does not and probably cannot rely on logical and formal argument alone or even much at all. His main task is to quicken his reader's perceptiveness; and he does this by making a far wider appeal than the exclusively rational appeal. He draws upon resources cognate, at least, with those of the artist in words. He gives expression to his outlook imaginatively. What he has to say is not a matter just of 'content' or narrow paraphrasable meaning, but is transfused by the whole texture of his writing as it constitutes an experience for the reader."

One major difficulty in subsuming Newman under such a description is, of course, that as Holloway admits, on opening his pages at random, one is likely to get the impression "that Newman is not a sage at all," for he does rely to a considerable extent on logical and formal argument. Nevertheless, in examining Newman's view of the world and of the course of things, the personality and tone that suffuse his work, some of his typical forms of argument, his illustrations and his imagery, Holloway makes many perceptive observations; and one can fully agree that his methods "do not merely state Newman's outlook, but they display it," while his techniques "steadily tend to make the controversial non-controversial, so that we are not coerced by any 'smart syllogism' into accepting Newman's conclusions in the abstract, but brought imperceptibly to a living understanding of his creed. The continuous texture of his work modifies our receptivity until we find ourselves seeing the world as he sees it . . . the impact is not that of a formal argument, but in its fullness and vividness more resembles that of a work of art, something which can make the reader find more in his experience, see it with new eyes, because for a while it constitutes his whole experience."

The apparatus and terminology, and hence to some extent the results, of Holloway's criticism are somewhat impoverished, however, by a neglect of the resources of classical rhetoric, which Newman and many other Victorian writers knew quite well. Newman was and proclaimed himself to be a rhetorician; and Holloway's "sage" is simply a rhetorician who like all of his tribe employs *in varying degrees* not only logical but also ethical and emotional or pathetic appeals expressed with all the possible resources of diction, imagery, and composition, as in the fifth chapter of the *Apologia*. Holloway writes as if he were breaking new ground, thinking so perhaps because the old lay so long untilled. Newman himself had thought long and deeply about the art of persuasion; and his remarks, scattered through many works, may be found summarized in Mariella Gable's "The Rhetoric of Cardinal Newman's Sermons" (Diss. Cornell 1934) and in James H. Loughery's "The Rhetorical Theory of John Cardinal Newman" (Diss. Michigan 1951), which contains chapters on Newman's ideas about rhetoric in general, invention, arrangement, style, meaning, and delivery. Much useful work remains to be done in the application of such ideas to analyses of Newman's work and that of the other great Victorian rhetoricians. Cecil Chesterton's "The Art of Controversy: Macaulay, Huxley and Newman" (*CathW*, 1917) offers a brief but illuminating comparison of the general technique by which each writer tries to defeat an opponent.

In *The Heeded Voice: Studies in the Literary Status of the Anglican Sermon, 1830–1900* (1959), E. D. Mackerness offers a brief but sensitive and suggestive consideration of Newman's "religious music." He also makes an unfavorable judgment on many of the Roman Catholic sermons except for a few like "Second Spring." In too many of them, he maintains, Newman not merely threw off, in Tristram's words, "the restraint of his Anglican days," but "he voluntarily compromised a part of his primal integrity." The literary merit of Newman's sermons is a subject that would repay much more study.

Remarks on his universally admired style appear in various studies of Newman such as those by Reilly, Tardivel, Harrold, Houghton, and Holloway; but there has been little detailed study of the subject, perhaps because the precise analysis of prose style is both time-consuming and difficult, and there is no general agreement on methodology. In "Prose Poets: Cardinal Newman" (*Aspects of Poetry*, 1882), J. C. Sharp, Doyle's successor as Professor of Poetry at Oxford, says that Newman possessed "the true poet's gift, and could speak the poet's language, had he cared to cultivate it," of which his prose is the best evidence: "It was in his *Parochial Sermons*, beyond all his other works, that he spoke out the truths which were within him—spoke them with all the fervor of a prophet and the severe beauty of a poet. Modern English literature has nowhere any language to compare with the style of these Sermons, so simple and transparent, yet so subtle withal, so strong yet so tender . . . expressing in a few monosyllables truths which would have cost other men a page of philosophic verbiage . . . reading to men their own most secret thoughts better than they knew them themselves."

In another warm appreciation (*Res Judicatae*, 1892), Augustine Birrell writes of Newman's "stern accuracy and beautiful aptness," his oratorical rush ("He writes as an orator speaks, straight at you"), and his humor, "largely, if not entirely . . . playful," *The Present Position of Catholics in England* being "one of the best humoured books in the English language." Praising his style as "pellucid . . . animated . . . varied," aiming always at effect and never missing it, Birrell suggests a course of reading in Newman beginning with the *Present Position* and *The Idea of a University*: "If after [the reader] has despatched these volumes he is not infected with what one of those charging bishops called 'Newmania,' he is possessed of a devil of obtuseness no wit of man can expel."

Perhaps the most discerning appreciation of Newman's style is Lewis E. Gates's "Newman as a Prose Writer" (*Three Studies in Literature*, 1899), which argues that "for the trained student of literary method much of the surpassing charm of Newman's work is due to the possibility of finding in it, on analysis, a continual victorious union of logical strenuousness with the grace and ease and charm of a colloquial manner and idiom. This victory is so easily won as to seem something by the way; but the student and analyst knows that it is the result of rare tact, finely disciplined instinct, exquisite rhetorical insight and foresight, and extra-ordinary luminousness and largeness of thought." According to Gates, Newman took many hints from another great rhetorician, De Quincey, as can be seen in a later sermon like "The Fitness of the Glories of Mary." This is a possibility worth further exploration.

George Saintsbury's *A History of English Prose Rhythm* (1912), describing Newman as "one of the greatest masters of quietly exquisite prose that the world has ever seen," scans a passage from *A Grammar of Assent* ("Let us consider, too, how differently young and old are affected by the work of some classic author"), finding that in it "the possibilities of standard style, slightly but marvellously 'super-rhythmed,' are seen almost at their perfection." Saintsbury also finds echoes of Newman in Pusey, Thackeray, J. A. Froude, Pater, and others.

In "Newman and the Problem of Critical Prose" (*VN*, 1957), Francis G. Townsend, though praising *The Imperial Intellect* highly for its first section, objects to Culler's discussion of Newman's argument in *The Idea of a University* as obscuring "the aerial clarity of Newman's work by raising objections and suggesting alternatives which Newman sometimes mentioned, sometimes ignored, and some-times knew nothing about." Arguing that in Culler's words "a great expository work is its own best exposition" and in his own that the canons of the New Criticism are "perhaps more applicable to the essay than to poetry," Townsend offers his own method for the analyst of prose: "In the face of the essay, the scholar can trace the development of the internal formulation; this is his proper work. By showing the roots of an essayist's thought in the events of his life and in the circumstances of the society around him, by demonstrating the human drama of the essayist's strug-gle to comprehend the world about him, the scholar can win for his subject the tolerance of readers and perhaps, eventually, the respect and admiration that the Victorian sage deserves."

"To what extent . . . linguistic choices act out and express more pervasive psychological strategies" is the special interest of Norman N. Holland in "A Psy-choanalytic Approach to Non-Fiction" (*The Art of Victorian Prose*, ed. George Levine and William Madden, 1968). In this type of analysis, figurative language is said to provide "the nearest thing to a royal road to unconscious content." Consid-ering the passage from Discourse VIII of the *Idea* beginning "It is well to be a gentleman" and ending with the famous aphoristic challenge, "Quarry the granite rock with razors," Holland does not "get at all the feeling of balance and reassur-ance" he does from Arnold: "Newman's style feels to me like a protesting too much, or perhaps more accurately, like a self-directed *Schadenfreude*—he seems to court his own defeat." He adds that behind "such a fear of defeat, I sense a wish for it, for every man's fear is also his deepest wish—so clinical experience says." It is perhaps pointless to evaluate rationally a type of analysis based so heavily on the critic's personal feelings except to say that it should be possible to produce a less surprisingly reductive example of it.

This is perhaps the place to mention two articles dealing with aesthetic aspects of Newman's temperament that left their mark on his style. One is Covelle New-comb's "Newman and Nature" (*CathW*, 1939), which traces a love that expressed itself in childhood "in sheer ecstasy over color and scent and interest in the forms of nature," later "motivated his meditations on grief and death and on the passing of all things with time," and finally "discovered for him a perpetual mirroring of its own moods in the temper of man," so that he can become as lavishly poetic as De

Quincey while differentiating between the Church Fathers Basil, Chrysostom, Gregory, and Athanasius in terms of the four seasons of the year. Newman shared Southey's view that nature is "calculated to expand the soul."

The second is a pamphlet of fifty pages, Edward Bellasis' *Cardinal Newman as a Musician* (1892), reprinted with additions and musical examples from *The Month* of September 1891. It collects Newman's remarks on music scattered throughout his works, discusses his violin-playing and composition of hymns, and indicates his opinions of various composers. "And just as Blanco White would seem to have thoroughly initiated Mr. Newman into the mysteries of Beethoven, so did Dr. Newman lead on his boys (as they would say) 'to swear by' that master. They might start with Corelli, and go on to Romberg, Haydn, and Mozart; their ultimate goal was Beethoven, and round would come the 'Father Superior' with ancient copies of the quintet version of the celebrated septet, and arrangements from the symphonies; nor were the first ten quartets, the instrumental trios, the violin sonatas, and the overtures forgotten. The 'Dutchman,' with his force and depth, his tenderness and sweetness, was the Cardinal's prime favourite."

VII. HISTORIAN AND POLITICAL THINKER

A good deal of Newman's work from *The Arians of the Fourth Century* through the various pieces finally collected in *Discussions and Arguments* and in the three volumes of *Historical Sketches* is concerned with history and, to a certain extent, politics; and in the past twenty-five years especially, his talents and contributions in these fields have received considerable attention. Aubrey Gwynn's "Newman and the Catholic Historian" (*A Tribute to Newman*, ed. M. Tierney, 1945) offers a brief survey of the state of historical writing when Newman began his work shortly before the rise to fame of German scientific history; of Newman's reading: "Scripture and the Fathers of the Church; the Anglican divines of the seventeenth century; the great ecclesiastical historians of Italy and France before the Revolution; these were the texts that he knew best, the masters from whom he learned in his Oxford years"; and of his relations with Acton's group and his attitude toward the problems facing the Church at the time.

The best brief critical survey of Newman's historical writings is probably C. F. Harrold's in his *John Henry Newman* (1945), a disinterested assessment of Newman's strengths and weaknesses: "His psychological insight, his philosophic spirit, his concern with great historical figures, his sense of the mystery of man's actions," which make the *Historical Sketches* "one of the finest portions of Newman's entire work"; but also the lack of a "time sense," a lack of interest in "the outward show and drama" in favor of the philosophy and psychological insight that animate his "psychographies" of a Chrysostom or a Theodoret. Harrold is probably right also in saying that "Newman always approaches history with his mind made up and solidly established on principles which, for him, throw light on everything and are indeed truer and more real than historical facts. Thus he explains the facts in accordance with a philosophy which appears to him much clearer than the facts themselves."

In "John Henry Newman's Use of History in His Anglican Career" (Diss. Illinois 1950), Gibbon Francis Butler compares the treatment of history in the two essays on miracles, "The Miracles of Scripture" (1825) and "The Miracles of

Ecclesiastical History" (1842–43), concluding that in the former, while the criteria of antecedent probability for the occurrence of miracles are not decisive, they do relegate historical evidence to a subordinate position; whereas in the latter, the criteria of judgment are based so heavily on antecedent probability and considerations of piety and faith as practically to deny the relevance of historical criticism. Butler also attempts to show that in the gradual development and then rejection of a Via Media Anglican theology based on the appeal to antiquity, Newman's works between 1833 and 1845 exhibit a development similar to that between the first and second essays on miracles. In view of the influence on Newman of such events as the Council of Chalcedon and of the nature of a book like the *Development of Christian Doctrine*, this is a harder position to sustain. Butler admits that in the *Development* Newman did not reject the witness of history nor the claim of Christianity to be a historical religion but says that neither did he base his position ultimately on the testimony of history, subscribing instead to an authority superior to historical evidence.

A more comprehensive study is Thomas S. Bokenkotter's *Cardinal Newman as an Historian* (1959), which concludes: "Without doubt, there is no question of numbering him among the masters of scientific history during the last century. But even though he was self-taught in the field, he did succeed in assimilating some of the fundamental requirements of the historical method and deservedly occupies a place of esteem among the historians of Christian antiquity who lived in the last century." Bokenkotter is quite informative on Newman's reading of history at Oxford, on history itself as the key to his conversion, on his historical writings as a Catholic, on his use of primary sources, and on his methods of historical criticism. His examination of Newman's second essay on miracles, though well aware of its weaknesses, also provides a needed corrective to such extreme attacks as Abbott's *Philomythus. An Antidote against Credulity*, which Bremond and some others since have uncritically accepted.

The central theme of Hugh A. MacDougall's *The Acton-Newman Relations* (1962) is indicated by its subtitle: "The Dilemma of Christian Liberalism." It is an engrossing study of how similarly and how differently two eminent Catholic intellectuals, one thirty-three years older than the other, reacted to the basic Victorian problem of reconciling old beliefs with various new challenges: "Catholic education, the Italian revolution, the decline of Liberal Catholicism, the Vatican Council and its aftermath, these were the main topics that united or divided Catholics in the 60's and 70's. And it is with these subjects that the first phase of the Acton-Newman relations is principally concerned. The large measure of sympathy existing between them throughout this period has never been given due recognition. But by the 1880's, Acton, the earlier champion of Catholicism and friend of Newman, is found condemning the Papacy in terms reminiscent of Luther, and rejecting Newman's thought as a system of infidelity." Acton had come to believe that the historian was guardian of "the conscience of mankind," with a duty to promote the cause of liberty; whereas too many Churchmen, he thought, Newman included, were willing to sacrifice the truth and even tolerate the idea of or at least justify past persecution in the interest of promoting religious doctrine.

In "Newman and History" (*VS*, 1964), Josef L. Altholz praises Newman as "a worthy exemplar of the critical school of the early nineteenth century (represented by such men as Niebuhr in Germany and Grote and Thirlwall in England) which did not seek new sources but rather reworked the old in a new and more critical spirit." His "most striking contribution to theology was the introduction of the dimension of time in the study of doctrine," and of the *Development of Christian Doctrine* "one might say that no work has done more to elevate the status of history." After this study had led him to submit to an ecclesiastical authority, however, "henceforth Authority, not history, was the source of his religious certainty."

Altholz, who had earlier covered the same ground more dispassionately in *The Liberal Catholic Movement in England* (1962), then tells pretty much from the disillusioned Acton's point of view the story of the Newman-Acton break in 1861 over Newman's objections to Richard Simpson's treatment of St. Pius v ("an abrupt, unmeasured attack upon a Saint"), concluding that Newman "quailed before the massive impartiality and dangerous independence of scientific history" and that "his commitment to religion was too profound to allow him to submit to the rival discipline of history." The fact is that history was never *the* source of Newman's religious certitude. The position which as Altholz later correctly says "Newman held to the end of his life" was that indicated in Discourse IV of the *Idea of a University*: "The evidence of History, I say, is invaluable in its place; but, if it assumes to be the sole means of gaining Religious Truth, it goes beyond its place."

In a reply to Altholz (*VS*, 1965), Derek Holmes contends that "Acton and (insofar as he shares his views) Altholz seem to have too high an opinion of history and too low an opinion of historians. The historian cannot divorce himself from his background, his politics, or his beliefs" but must seek to achieve "an adequate balance between fact and interpretation in the narration of his personal insights into the past." Newman, he says, "adopts an essentially balanced position, clearly distinguishing the sphere of theology from that of history, and while striving to be objective, recognising the natural limitations of the historian. Theological beliefs, no more than political or philosophical beliefs, of themselves limit a thinker or an historian; they *may* do so but do not *necessarily* do so." To which Altholz replied: "Acton, whatever his faults, at least pursued the ideal of objectivity. Newman did not. I do not think that Newman as an historian ever sat down before the facts as a little child or discovered, as true researchers do, that the facts would often tell their own story if only the historian would let them."

In "Cardinal Newman and the Study of History" (*DubR*, 1965), Derek Holmes stresses three aspects of Newman's achievement: first, before the new German approach to scientific history had begun to influence England, he educated himself to a more critical attitude toward history than was common at the time in England; second, although he interpreted history in the light of Christian teaching, "he is careful to distinguish between history and theology"; and third, his "attitude toward the process of knowledge prevented him from demanding from history or from historians what they are unable to give." In this latter respect he "had a much better grasp of the problems involved in the study of history than Lord Acton had, and a deeper appreciation of the nature of historical research."

Newman's many insights into politics and political theory, though scattered throughout his writings, are especially evident in such works as "Who's to Blame?" (in *Discussions and Arguments*), on the Crimean War; and the "Letter to the Duke of Norfolk" (in *Difficulties of Anglicans*, II), prompted by Gladstone's accusation that the Pope's sovereignty and infallibility made it impossible for a British subject to be both a loyal citizen and a good Catholic. According to Harold Laski (*Studies in the Problem of Sovereignty*, 1917), "The *Letter to the Duke of Norfolk*, the *Apologia* apart, was Newman's masterpiece. Its profound psychology, its subtlety, its humour, its loyalty to his friends, its whimsical castigation of his enemies, place it in a class by itself. But it is more than a piece of ephemeral argument. It remains with some remarks of Sir Henry Maine and a few brilliant dicta of F. W. Maitland as perhaps the profoundest discussion of the nature of obedience and sovereignty to be found in the English language. . . . Newman, even apart from his theology, was an able political thinker who had devoted the twelve years of his connexion with the Oxford Movement to the study of the problem of sovereignty in its acutest phase—that of Church and State." The background of the argument is well outlined by Humphrey J. T. Johnson in "The Controversy between Newman and Gladstone over the Question of Civil Allegiance" (*DubR*, 1945); and there is an edition prepared by Alvan S. Ryan of the relevant texts by both men in *Newman and Gladstone: The Vatican Decrees* (1962).

In "The Development of Newman's Political Thought" (*Rev. of Pol.*, 1945), Ryan shows how Newman early came to fear political as an ally of religious liberalism—he liked Lamennais' anti-Erastianism, for instance, but not his democratic tendencies; and he distrusted O'Connell for combining with the liberals. The Irish University campaign gave him more sympathy for Irish democratic aims, however, and for the role of a laity confronted by a reactionary hierarchy; and he eventually came to a recognition that a practical solution to Church-State problems in England, at least, involved an acceptance of "liberal principles" of pluralism. "It is well to emphasize, however, that Newman does not make a universal of this solution, nor does he call for a 'Free Church in a Free State' as did Montalembert. He feared the tyranny of unregulated State power but also disliked radical democracy. Yet in no wise did he move toward that authoritarianism and contempt for ballot-boxes and Parliaments that vitiates much of the later work of Carlyle and Ruskin."

Russell Kirk's "The Conservative Mind of Newman" (*YR*, 1952) was later incorporated into his *The Conservative Mind: From Burke to Santayana* (1953), a book that attempts to indicate a system of ideas common to England and the United States that "has sustained men of conservative instincts in their resistance against radical theories and social transformation ever since the beginning of the French Revolution." Kirk sees Newman as "a consistent Tory, devoted to the principle of aristocracy and the concept of loyalty to persons." He uses "The Tamworth Reading Room" as a framework for the exposition of the "conservative concepts" whereby Newman maintained the view of Hooker and Burke that society subsists upon faith, "the ancient religious view of society," against "grim utilitarian expediency." "The Tamworth Reading Room" is, however, an early work of Newman dealing with the insufficiency of a wholly secular education. It gives no indication of the extent to which Newman's political attitudes were liberalized by "expediency," as recounted by Alvan Ryan and Terence Kenny.

Kenny's *The Political Thought of John Henry Newman* (1957) makes clear that though Newman's attitude toward society was fundamentally conservative, he realistically came to an "acceptance of the modern democratic, secular, tolerant State," one which "must come and ought to come in a civilised society." His stress on conservatism, on the value of tradition and the wisdom of the ages, "did not exclude a large measure of a kind of liberalism, which was ultimately made necessary by the very theory of development which is at the basis of his conservatism." The kind of liberalism he especially objected to in politics was that involved with the views on human perfectibility of the Benthamites.

An essay that stresses Newman's "profound collectivism" more than the individualism so commonly associated with him is Werner Stark's "The Social Philosopher" (*Newman Centenary Essays*, 1945), arguing that Newman has much to contribute to "the main task of sociology," described by the author as understanding "the vital bond which forms many independent individuals into one body social." Newman thought that in practice "the unity of historical societies is always guaranteed by their social soul, by their super-individual mind. Individuals are only too strongly tempted to break away, but the community as such, the bulk of the community, will preserve what is essential of the common possession," as in the age of the Fathers.

VIII. REPUTATION AND INFLUENCE

No study of Newman's reputation has yet been published. However, there have been many essays on Newman through the years which attempt to assess his significance and thus provide some of the primary materials for so desirable a study. Those concerned almost wholly with Newman's contribution to theology and philosophy are noted elsewhere in this volume by Dessain. Naturally, however, religion enters to some degree in almost every assessment of Newman.

A very warm appreciation of his character by an eminent Scottish divine who drew many Protestants to Newman is Alexander Whyte's *Newman: An Appreciation in Two Lectures: With the Choicest Passages of His Writings Selected and Arranged* (1901). Whyte's only regret is that Newman's sermons put too much stress on works and not enough on the "healing evangelical truth" of a saving faith. From a literary point of view, however, according to W. J. Dawson (*Makers of English Prose*, 1916), Newman as a sermon writer "has no superior in the English language, either for range or style. He combined in the most felicitous degree two qualities seldom combined, simplicity and profundity." He is indeed "the greatest religious writer whom England has produced."

In two articles for the *Fortnightly Review*, "Cardinal Newman and the Newer Generation" (1904) and "Last Words on Cardinal Newman" (1918), W. S. Lilly, who knew Newman for eighteen years, singles out his "largeness of mind" as the characteristic that struck him most. Though praising his work in the terms that Archdeacon Manning applied to the *Development of Doctrine* (it "exhibits an intellectual compass and *movement* belonging to an order of minds which live in a region above the reach of all except a few"), Lilly adds: "He was one of those great souls of whom it may be said, as Vittoria Colonna said of Michael Angelo: 'Those who know only his work know the least part of him.' "

Paul Elmer More epitomizes the humanism he shared with Irving Babbitt in his assertion that "our reservation in the praise due to Newman's beautiful life [must be] that he stopped short of the purest faith." Newman was born in an age "when the old faith in an outer authority based on an exact and unequivocal revelation could be maintained only by doing violence to the integrity of the believer's mind. . . . he might have accepted manfully the sceptical demolition of the Christian mythology and the whole fabric of external religion; and on the ruins of such creeds he might have risen to the supreme insight which demands no revelation and is dependent on no authority, but is content within itself. Doing this he might possibly, by the depth of his religious nature and the eloquence of his tongue, have made himself the leader of the elect out of the long spiritual death that is likely to follow the breaking-up of the creeds" ("Cardinal Newman," in *The Drift of Romanticism*, 1913). More apparently found it impossible to follow his own prescription, however, and eventually became an Anglo-Catholic.

In the Lowell Lectures for 1914 (included in his *Last Lectures*, 1918; rpt. 1967), Wilfrid Ward, having in mind critics who praised Newman for his artistry but somehow separated it from and even deplored his religion, argued that the chief motive force giving unity to Newman's work was "the intense desire to defend Christianity in view of the incoming tide of infidelity"; that the sources of his much praised style were his ideas, his theology—his style arose "from his simple and earnest desire to communicate to others the experience of his own life, which moved him to deep feeling"; that in philosophy he anticipated modern emphasis on the unconscious ("implicit" reason), pragmatism, and evolutionary thinking; that his apologetic is "kindled and intensified" by appeals to the whole man—his conscience, affections, and imagination; and that he possesses, as is generally agreed, extraordinary psychological insight into the strengths and weaknesses of various types of men: the man of learning, the man of letters, the narrow mind (*University Sermons*, pp. 307–08), the victim of prejudice (*Present Position of Catholics*, pp. 239–40), the national character (*Discussions and Arguments*, pp. 33–38).

In what was originally a review of Ward's *Life of Newman* (rpt. in *Outspoken Essays*, 1920), Dean W. R. Inge, linking Newman to Modernism because of the differences between his and traditional Catholic apologetic, thus summed up a view on the whole quite sympathetic: "All cultivated readers, who have formed their tastes on the masterpieces of good literature, are attracted, sometimes against their will, by the dignity and reserve of his style, qualities which belong to the man, and not only to the writer. Like Goethe, he disdains the facile arts which make the commonplace reader laugh and weep. . . . Like Wordsworth, he might say, 'To stir the blood, I have no cunning art.' There are no cheap effects in any of Newman's writings. . . . That his life is for the most part a record of sadness and failure is no indication that he was not one of the great men of his time."

In 1926 a critic and literary historian influenced by the New Humanists, Robert Shafer, asserted in *Christianity and Naturalism* that Newman "is now recognized as the greatest figure in English religious life of the nineteenth century, not alone because he exerted a profound and abiding influence upon both the Anglican Church and the Catholic, but also because his character was at once manly and saintly, while it had as its ready instruments a rich imagination and a powerful intellect." Attributing to him "a knowledge of human nature and of life, of its real problems and issues, which for subtlety and depth few men in any age have rivalled," Shafer credited Newman with "single-hearted and life-long devotion, in a way whose significance may not even yet be fully apparent, to what is central and abiding in human nature. It may or may not be right or possible to follow the whole way in the path which he took, but this cannot impair, and should not obscure, the importance and significance of his life and work. We at least cannot disregard the fact that a brilliantly gifted and keen-minded man of the nineteenth century, a man whose character was at once saintly and manly in the full sense of both words, did utterly revolt from the materialism of his day and stood uncompromisingly for the reality and primacy of man's spiritual nature and destiny." Shafer's view is quite similar to that taken by DeLaura in his previously mentioned "Newman as Prophet" (*DubR*, 1967).

An indication of the Mozley family view of Newman may presumably be found in two articles by J. F. Mozley, "Newman's Opportunity" and "Newman in Fetters" (*QR*, 1926). Even before his conversion, Newman was "surrendering himself to the idea that Christian humility is simply passivity and submission," and Rome was for him a relief from "the burden of responsibility in religion." It was not his "true self" ("bold, strong, and fearless . . . ever urging him forward") that spoke of his perfect peace and contentment with Rome. His weaker self, his passivity, had mastered him, with the result that "Newman never won his way into freedom; he grew to be distrustful of himself and of his powers, afraid of his call, afraid of being presumptuous and taking too much upon himself; he never accomplished his full work, and the whole world has been the loser."

A view quite opposite to that of Wilfrid Ward in *Last Lectures* was taken in "Was Newman a Failure?" (*NC*, 1933), by L. A. G. Strong, who argues that Newman failed not as a man but "as a writer. . . . The tragedy of Newman was that he was not born a Catholic. He was a predestined Catholic, and—again from the purely artistic point of view—a great deal of valuable time would have been saved had he been born one. . . . Newman's genius was taken up with apologetics, which is another way of saying that the greater part of his work is rhetorical. The rhetorician has to be always mindful of his audience, for his business is to convince. The poet minds no one but himself. Such genius as Newman had was meant for better work than advocacy." Reasoning like this would condemn to "failure," however, not only Newman but virtually all of the great Victorian prose writers.

In an influential article called "Newman and His Age" (*DubR*, 1945), originally an address to the first National Newman Congress in England, the historian Philip Hughes praised Wilfrid Ward for making known to Englishmen the treasure they have in Newman but asserted that in his biography he stressed the dark shadows in Newman's life. What was needed, he said, were both a new life of Newman "where none should speak but himself" and the publication of all the Cardinal's letters and papers. Hughes also pointed out that the full history of the Catholic University had not yet been written, so that few people realized all that Newman stood for and accomplished as an educator. To a considerable extent all of these needs have since been or are being met. Hughes sees Newman as "the Christian prophet to the Liberal Age."

In "Newman and the Modern Age" (*Newman Centenary Essays*, 1945), commenting on the gradual displacement of theology prophetically delineated by Newman in "A Form of Infidelity of the Day," Douglas Woodruff sees Newman as a continuing challenge to the secularization of education, to the habit of judging everything favorably or unfavorably by a social criterion. To those who take it for granted that this means progress, "Newman is a voice from the immediate past observing that the great question is being begged; if the revelation previously believed is untrue, indeed the secularism has not gone far enough, but if it is true then the secularism has gone very much too far. It has already produced a generation hardly able to consider the issues involved because it has grown up in so deep and deliberate an ignorance of both the content and apologetic of revelation."

Another centenary essay, Joseph J. Reilly's "The Present Significance of Newman" (*Thought*, 1945), reflecting on such work as *Development*, the *Grammar*, and *The Idea of a University*, argues that Newman possesses the two essentials of a great writer: "lasting significance in what he says, and power and beauty in the way he says it"; and that "it may be said of him as of Coleridge that among his chief claims to permanence is his seminal mind." Still another centenary essay, "John Henry Newman: His Prophetic Sense" (*CathW*, 1946), by Robert Wilberforce, sees its subject as the great prophet of contemporary secularist infidelity.

In "Newman and Our Time" (*A Newman Symposium*, 1952), Svaglic notes a gradual improvement in Newman's reputation as a thinker since the turn of the century, sees him as representing a via media between the older rationalism and the newer forms of irrationalism, and suggests that his works most relevant to the modern mind are *The Idea of a University*, the sermons, and especially *A Grammar of Assent*.

Roger Aubert's "Actualité de Newman" (*RevN*, 1955) is primarily a survey of post-1945 Newman scholarship, principally European. "The Significance of Newman," by the Abbot of Downside (*DubR*, 1959), concentrates on the importance of the theory of the development of doctrine. John Beer's "Newman and the Romantic Sensibility" (in *The English Mind: Studies in the English Moralists Presented to Basil Willey*, 1964) sees Newman as belonging to the Romantic tradition of "the sensibility reaching toward permanence," like Wordsworth longing "for a repose that ever is the same." Beer finds an element of the "given" in Newman's thinking "not subjected to the questioning of thought," and says that he had "little feeling for" the "more vitalistic" Romantic tradition represented by Blake, the early Coleridge, and Keats, which, "seeing man as a child of the earth and an involuntary disciple of his own imagination, sought to use those resources for the renewal of humanity." In consequence Newman seems "a great but isolated individual" whose "extraordinary balance of intellect and emotion" and "play of sensibility within a firm but formal intellectual structure draws us near in respect but not home in acceptance."

In *Newman and the Modern World* (1968), Christopher Hollis offers a kind of biography of Newman with the highlight of each episode related to problems or to solutions accepted by the modern Church, of which Newman is seen as a forerunner. "He pleaded, and almost got himself condemned, for his championship of the apostolate of the laity which now is officially proclaimed. Catholic policy is increasingly stamped by his ideas on education. He championed what we today consider the accepted rights of the scholar in biblical interpretation. He found, in short, the Church at one of the lowest moments of its history a servile society and turned it into a free society. It would be hard to find any other character in the Church's history who has so totally transformed the nature of Catholic apologetics."

Few even limited studies of Newman's influence and reputation have appeared. W. E. Collin's "Cardinal Newman and Recent French Thought" (*Trans. of the Royal Soc. of Canada*, 1937) offers only "notes" on four French philosophers "whose hearts and minds have been touched by those doctrines which for our purpose may be reduced to three or four, viz., the inner life, anticipation, organic growth and development, and real assent." The four are Denys Gorce, Georges Sorel, Ramon Fernandez, and Maurice Blondel. M. Benoit Holahan's "Newman in France" (Diss. Illinois 1944) concentrates on the period between Newman's correspondence with the Abbé Jager (1837) and 1914, "when Modernism ceased to be an issue." It was written without access to the documents at the Birmingham Oratory but is useful nevertheless for its description of the work of various French writers on Newman whose subject matter is by and large outside the province of the present article.

Two notes in *The Month* (1922), the first signed W. J. C. and the second E. P. (probably W. J. Courtney and Erich Przywara), briefly describe "The Newman Movement in Germany," with emphasis on the pioneering work of M. Laros in making Newman's work known to German readers. P. Simon's "Newman and German Catholicism" (*DubR*, 1946) asserts that Newman never came into his own in Germany till the perid of Modernism, but there is little documentation.

Sr. Maria Serafina's "Newman in Italy" (*A Newman Symposium*) concludes that "Newman's philosophical and theological writings have not been at all prominent in Italy since the passing of Modernism," but also that his "writings of general interest are being noticed by the Italian reading public," thanks to the work of scholars like Giuseppe De Luca. Her "Summary of a Chronological Bibliography of Newman Literature in Italy" from 1840 to 1951 provides titles of books on Newman, lists of translations, and indications of the number and location of articles in periodicals. Her work on this bibliography was still in progress at the time of publication, and it is not complete.

The Rediscovery of Newman: An Oxford Symposium (1967), edited by John Coulson and A. M. Allchin, contains brief articles on Newman in France (B. D. Dupuy), Germany (Werner Becker), the Low Countries (A. J. Boekraad), and England (H. Francis Davis). Anne Fremantle's "Newman and English Literature" (*A Newman Symposium*) is a brief, quite selective, and rather chatty survey of the attitude toward Newman taken by various writers of the nineteenth and twentieth centuries.

Evidence that Oscar Wilde had been reading a good deal of Newman at Wandsworth Prison in 1895 and 1896, including the *Apologia*, leads Jan B. Gordon to suggest that Wilde's "most notorious letter, the *De Profundis*, written between January and March of 1897, while disguised as a sincere *cri de cœur*, exhibits certain formal and stylistic features common to the *apologia* in general, and Newman's in particular" (*Ren*, 1970). The idea is not improbable, and the essay is fairly interesting; but Gordon's comparisons often seem rather loose and fanciful.

J. S. Atherton's "Cardinal Newman in *Finnegans Wake*" (*N&Q*, 1953) notes allusions to a small paragraph in the *Apologia* which Joyce had probably copied into his notebook. In "Newman and T. S. Eliot on Religion and Literature" (*A Newman Symposium*), Alvan S. Ryan makes an illuminating comparison between the views of both men that "literature is not a substitute for religion" and that "the classics should be studied in some relation to Christianity." Ryan points out differences in their views as well and does not suggest that Eliot, who had Arnold and Babbitt in mind, was influenced in these matters by Newman. The fact is, however, that there are several echoes of Newman in Eliot; and the tone of his few direct references to Newman, as in the tribute paid him in his essay on the *Pensées* of Pascal, implies an influence of some depth that might repay further exploration.

On the other hand, H. L. Weatherby argues in "Newman and Victorian Liberalism: The Failure of Influence" (*CritQ*, 1971) that because of his affinities with the skepticism and idealism of a Carlyle, Arnold, Tennyson, or Pater, Newman has not exerted much influence on modern Christian writers: "he failed to bring to modern letters what he, as a Catholic, was in a unique position to offer—namely a Thomist (a realist) metaphysics and epistemology which would be capable of giving philosophical and theological justification to the things of the real world." Hence a Hopkins or an Eliot, for instance, was forced to seek in the Middle Ages and Renaissance for modes of thought and utterance which the nineteenth century had not provided. This is a stimulating article, but there is too easy an assumption of Newman's lack of influence, a subject which requires much more investigation; and there is little or no recognition of the side of Newman stressed by Geoffrey Tillotson.

To this day the name of Newman appears in the catalogs of some famous book dealers only under the heading of theology. The serious study of Newman as a major figure in the literature of England may almost be said, with occasional exceptions like the work of R. H. Hutton and Lewis E. Gates, to have begun only about thirty years ago. It was abetted by the Victorian revival in general but even more by the growth of ecumenism on the one hand and of religious indifferentism on the other, both of which attitudes have made possible a more disinterested and scholarly approach to a writer all too often hitherto the victim of partisanship and special pleading by admirer and detractor alike. The result of this freer approach has been that Newman's reputation today, both as thinker and as artist, is probably higher and more widespread than it has ever been, even among those who regard his long struggle against "liberalism" as either inevitably or deservedly a lost cause.

Among the present desiderata of Newman scholarship are studies of his influence on other writers (e.g., Hopkins and the major figures of the Catholic Revival); studies of the influence of other writers on him: e.g., Bacon, Addison, Butler, Crabbe, Hume, and Gibbon; a history of his reputation, especially in England; more thorough and sophisticated examinations of his rhetorical technique and literary style; a new and more critical biography based on a knowledge of all his books and extant letters, something very few writers on Newman have ever possessed; and perhaps, above all, critical editions of most of his major works.

NEWMAN'S PHILOSOPHY AND THEOLOGY

•

Charles Stephen Dessain

During Newman's lifetime and for more than half a century after his death there were comparatively few studies of his philosophy and theology. The reviews of such works as *The Development of Christian Doctrine* and *A Grammar of Assent* either were merely out to controvert or else misunderstood Newman's purpose. This hindered Anglican writers of that period, even High Church ones who had great personal respect for Newman, from evaluating all his teaching correctly. (Apart from the case of *Apologia*, little research has been done on the reception in England of Newman's works, except for an excellent 1964 London Univ. thesis by Nina Burgis on *The Tamworth Reading Room*.) One reason, at least in the English-speaking world, for the absence of books on Newman's thought was that his own books were there for all to read. It still remains true that the best way to understand Newman's philosophy and theology is to read and reread his own writings. He published no work of importance until he was over thirty, and by then his main principles were settled, both the unified philosophical ideas which underlay all his thinking, and his theology in which he strove to submit himself to revealed religion. Hence there have always been those who have steeped themselves in his writings, and understood him, without needing a guide to his thought.

What is undoubtedly still the most satisfactory and complete general introduction to his teaching is the article "Newman" by the two Birmingham Oratorians, Francis Joseph Bacchus and Henry Tristram, translated into French for the eleventh volume of the *Dictionnaire de théologie catholique* (1931). (The English original is still unpublished.) Each of the works is considered separately, and there is a special study of *A Grammar of Assent*. Unfortunately there is lacking an assessment of the theology contained in *Lectures on Justification*. The authors remark, "L'Angleterre n'apporte guère de contribution à l'étude de la philosophie et de la théologie de Newman." This was not true of the continent of Europe, and their article forms a kind of watershed in Newman studies. Its masterly and authoritative exposition made impossible, or at least inexcusable, those misunderstandings of Newman that had been so widespread in France a generation earlier. Besides this work, Bacchus, who helped and encouraged other scholars, wrote two short articles, "Newman's Oxford University Sermons" and "How to Read the 'Grammar of Assent'" (*The Month*, 1922, 1924), which have in their way proved decisive. He was also responsible for *The Correspondence of John Henry Newman with John Keble and Others, 1839–45* (1917), full of extremely useful explanatory matter as to the road Newman followed from the Anglican to the Roman Church.

Three other English commentators, all long before the Bacchus-Tristram article, must be mentioned on account of their authoritative expositions of Newman's teaching. William George Ward, who in theology differed widely from Newman, had a clear understanding of his philosophy. His *Essays in the Philosophy of Theism* (1884) includes "Explicit and Implicit Thought" and "Certitude in Religious Assent" (*DubR*, 1869, 1871). His son, Wilfrid Ward, gave an excellent general picture of Newman's characteristics as a thinker in the first half of *Last Lectures by Wilfrid Ward* (1918). This comprised the six Lowell Lectures on "The Genius of Cardinal Newman" that discuss the unity of Newman's work, his philosophy, and his psychological insight. These were to some extent a corrective of Ward's two-volume biography. Instead of the sad portrait, which those who had known him found unrecognizable, the stress was laid on Newman's lifelong "passionate concentration of extraordinary and varied gifts on one great enterprise," the service of the Christian religion. Richard Holt Hutton, in *Cardinal Newman* (1891, 2nd ed., 1892; with an appendix on Edwin A. Abbott's attack, *Philomythus*, 1891: "He is tilting at imaginary hypotheses of his own"), one of the first biographies, devoted most of his space to Newman's teaching, which he described as unified by his championship of revealed religion. Hutton wrote an earlier sketch, in the *Contemporary Review* (1887), included in *Essays on Some of the Modern Guides to English Thought in Matters of Faith* (1888), and a long obituary article in the *Spectator* (1890), included in *Criticisms on Contemporary Thought and Thinkers* (1894). "He could justify theoretically the potent implicit reason of man. . . . He could show how much more powerful was the combination of humility, trust, imagination, feeling, perception in apprehending the revealed mind and will of God, than the didactic and formal proofs." Hutton, who corresponded with Newman for over twenty years, also defended him against Fairbairn's charge of skepticism (*ConR*, 1886).

I. FRENCH FANTASY AND GERMAN UNDERSTANDING

Before describing the new era in Newman studies ushered in by the Bacchus-Tristram article, and which, ever since World War II, has made itself manifest by its continuous stream of works and articles on Newman, two earlier Newman movements require consideration. In France at the turn of the century, Newman's thought was not studied in its context and with the scholar's detachment. He was invoked in their support by the Modernists, and protagonists on both sides in that controversy were ready to portray as a species of Modernist the champion of the "dogmatic principle" and the lifelong opponent of "liberalism in religion."

Already in 1880 Léon Ollé-Laprune, in his *De la certitude morale*, had made known correctly *A Grammar of Assent*, although the book itself was not translated into French until 1907. Bergson was one of Ollé-Laprune's pupils, and both Wilfrid Ward, in *Last Lectures*, and Fernande Tardivel, in *La Personnalité littéraire de Newman* (1937), have drawn attention to Newman's influence on him. Very different was the presentation by Auguste Sabatier in his *Esquisse d'une philosophie de la religion d'après la psychologie et l'histoire* (1897), who claimed Newman's support for his subjective theory. He was answered at once in *Le Correspondant* by Eudoxe I. Mignot, in "L'Evolutionnisme religieuse," republished in *L'Eglise et la critique* (1910). Others, however, were led astray, among them Alfred Loisy, who in 1896 had been sent by Friedrich von Hügel the chief works of Newman. Loisy published in 1898 a number of articles, the one most directly concerned with Newman being "Le Développement chrétien d'après le Cardinal Newman," under the pseudonym A. Firmin (*Revue du Clergé Français*, 1898). Loisy appreciated the scientific quality of Newman's historical work, but confused his teaching with that of Sabatier. His earlier articles were answered by Léonce de Grandmaison in *Etudes* (1898; rpt. in *Le Dogme chrétien*, 1928).

It was, however, from Henri Bremond, through his *Newman: Essai de biographie psychologique* (1906; rpt. 1932; English trans., *The Mystery of Newman*, 1907), and through his volumes of selections, that French readers derived their knowledge of Newman. Bremond had not yet found his true métier, and Wilfrid Ward, for example, described him as presenting "a largely fictitious Newman" (*Last Lectures*). In accordance with the views he himself held, he portrayed Newman as an anti-intellectual and a fideist. Newman's was a religion of the heart merely, he was an English Schleiermacher. Bremond interpreted Newman's key teaching about conscience ("an authoritative voice," "an impulse of nature") as though it were simply his name for religious feelings. Thus Newman, the defender of objective faith and a visible Church, was held up as a teacher of that particular aspect of Evangelicalism that he had decisively rejected. Deriving his knowledge solely from Bremond, E. Baudin in a series of articles on "La Philosophie de la foi chez Newman," in *Revue de Philosophie* (1906), was critical and described Newman as a pragmatist and intuitionist. This view was accepted by such men of weight as Léonce de Grandmaison, who wrote of Baudin, "Sur le fidéisme de Newman je n'ai rien lu en français de plus net," and Jules Lebreton, "Son jugement est sévère mais je le crois dans son ensemble, définitif."

The picture of Baudin and Bremond after a while ceased to be taken seriously and was given the coup de grace by Louis Bouyer in *Newman sa vie, sa spiritualité* (1952; English trans., 1958). This accurate and moving biography was based on a full documentation, much of it not available half a century earlier. For a half-hearted plea in defense of Bremond see Maurice Nédoncelle's "Newman selon Bremond, ou le procès d'un procès," in Jean Dagens and Maurice Nédoncelle, *Entretiens sur Henri Bremond* (1967). An account of the whole controversy will be found in the article by B. D. Dupuy in *The Rediscovery of Newman* (ed. John Coulson and A. M. Allchin, 1967), and more fully in Roger Aubert, *Le Problème de l'acte de foi* (1945), who reaches the balanced conclusion that the various misinterpretations prepared the way for a truer understanding of the nature of faith as an act not merely of the reason but of the whole man.

In England, George Tyrrell understood his Newman far better than the French Modernists. H. Francis Davis has remarked, although Tyrrell "saw so clearly that Newman was by all his tastes and conscious tendencies cordially opposed to every form of modernism," yet he was "determined to drag him into it." The story of the effort to implicate Newman in the condemnation of Modernism may be followed in the *Times* and the *Tablet* (1907–08), but is only indirectly connected with the study of Newman himself. A defense of him was written by Edward Thomas Dwyer, Bishop of Limerick, *Cardinal Newman and the Encyclical* Pascendi Domini Gregis (1908). See also H. Francis Davis, "The Catholicism of Cardinal Newman," in *Centenary Essays* (1945), edited by Henry Tristram, and J. Derek Holmes, "Newman and Modernism" (*Baptist Q.*, 1972). As interest in the Modernist movement increases, no doubt this aspect of it will tempt a historian.

The story of the Newman movement in Germany is very different from that in France. It began only after World War I. Newman's earlier works had been known and read, but *A Grammar of Assent* remained untranslated. See the article in *The Rediscovery of Newman* (1967), "Newman's Influence in Germany," by Werner Becker, who states that "Between 1920 and 1940 there took place among German Catholics a general spiritual and intellectual awakening." The interest in Newman was first aroused by Matthias Laros, parish priest of Geichlingen near the Belgian border, and one of the promoters of ecumenism in Germany. He began translating some of Newman's works, and besides a stream of articles and lectures, published a small book, *Kardinal Newman* (1921), in the Religiöse Geister series, in which he gave a bird's-eye view of Newman's teaching and emphasized its relevance for the times. Erich Przywara, the outstanding German Newmanist of this period, wrote of the new German translation of the *Apologia, Ausgewählte Werke*, 1 (1922), "In his introduction, as well as in notes which he added, Dr. Laros points out, against the misrepresentations of the modernists, the undoubtedly Catholic spirit of Newman, but also hints at an affinity of his ideas with those of Max Scheler . . ." (*The Month*, 1922). Independently of Laros, Theodor Haecker at Munich translated *A Grammar of Assent* (1921) and *The Development of Doctrine* (1922). Haecker was a keen admirer of Kierkegaard, whom he also translated. "In the epilogue to his translation of the *Grammar* he traces a similarity between Newman and Edmund Husserl . . ." (*The Month*, 1922). Haecker republished the epilogues of his two translations in *Christentum und Kultur* (1927). Thus he, as well as Laros, saw parallels between Newman and leading phenomenologists.

With the writings of the German Jesuit Erich Przywara, Newman studies took a decisive step forward. *Newman Christentum, Ein Aufbau aus seinen Werken* (1922) consisted of eight volumes, the first three being selections to show the approach to Christian faith, apologetics, and the last four selections to show the religious demands of Christianity, ascetical teaching. These were translated into German with the help of Otto Karrer. The fourth volume, entirely by Przywara, *Einführung in Newman, Wesen und Werk*, was intended to serve as an introduction to the rest. The translated volumes were published in English as *A Newman Synthesis* (1931), reprinted as *The Heart of Newman* (1962), but *Einführung* has never been translated. Tristram ("A Newman Synthesis," *Clergy Rev.*, 1931) described it as "the most exact and the most comprehensive contribution to the study of Newman hitherto made." It was the first examination of Newman's thought for its own sake, trying neither to harness it to some alien movement nor to criticize it as dangerous to Catholic thought. It was concerned, however, less with Newman's philosophy as a whole than with his philosophy of religion, and of that its treatment was masterly. In *Religionsbegrundung, Max Scheler—J. H. Newman* (1923), Przywara discussed further Newman's importance for philosophy as such, in reference to current German trends.

Tristram remarks, "In claiming Newman as an immanentist the French writers went wrong, just because they had failed to grasp what he was driving at; it redounds to Przywara's credit that, with the same evidence before him, he succeeded in avoiding the same pitfall." Przywara now turned to Bacchus for guidance, and his side of the correspondence has been preserved. Bacchus sent him copies of various unpublished papers so that he could see Newman's purpose in his *University Sermons* and *Grammar*, which was to justify the faith of ordinary people. In an 1860 paper Newman wrote: "If religion is consequent upon *reason* and at the same time for *all* men, there must be reasons producible sufficient for the rational conviction of every individual." Tristram reported (*Clergy Rev.*, 1931) that "When this paper was brought to Przywara's notice he wrote the essay on 'J. H. Newman's Problemstellung,' which is included in *Ringen der Gegenwart* (1929), and which ought to be read as a supplement to the *Einführung*." Przywara was writing when the Thomist revival was at its height, and although not misinterpreting, he was inclined occasionally to overharmonize, and thus sometimes failed to bring out Newman's originality of thought and entirely different method.

Nonetheless, Przywara had far more accurate ideas about Newman than the few contemporary English-speaking writers, who were too inclined to measure him by a scholastic yardstick and to impose on him alien categories. Martin D'Arcy devoted three chapters to *A Grammar of Assent* in *The Nature of Belief* (1931; new ed., 1958). It is not unfair to say that he underestimated Newman as a philosopher and appeared to judge him from too narrowly conceptualist a standpoint. For a severe criticism see Edward Sillem in the *Clergy Review* (1963), and the reply of D'Arcy, who confessed that his appreciation of Newman had developed with the years. An American, John Francis Cronin, in *Cardinal Newman: His Theory of Knowledge* (1935), gives a more sympathetic if not a profound enough exposition of the subject. He set Newman in his historical context, and showed how modern trends in philosophy were giving increased importance to his ideas, and his hope was that Newman would make a contribution to the Scholastic system. Cronin says of D'Arcy that, in spite of his criticism, "When he comes to give his own solution of the problem, he offers nothing but a re-phrasing of Newman's thought. Global apprehension and 'the unity of indirect reference' add nothing to the *Grammar* or the *University Sermons*."

II. NEWMAN STUDIES AFTER 1945

With the end of World War II a new era opened in Newman studies. His greatness and his originality were generally recognized. There was no longer the same attempt to force him along beaten paths that were not his. From more objective study and the desire fully to understand Newman there resulted a new agreement among Newman scholars. It was remarked at the first Oxford Newman Conference in 1966, whose proceedings were published as *The Rediscovery of Newman*, how harmonious the discussions were. Differing theological allegiances or philosophical opinions were no hindrance to the general consensus as to Newman's meaning, and indeed his relevance. Newman had been so often misrepresented in the past that this agreement was even suspected as being due to mere idolatry. In fact it was the result of a new critical understanding which resulted in a new appreciation. Newman always used to say that time was his best friend, and it was not until half a century after his death that his teaching came fully into its own.

Most of those who wrote on Newman after the second war began by acknowledging a debt to the personal guidance of Henry Tristram. He wrote more on Newman than his master Bacchus, and although the bulk of his articles was literary, some such as "J. A. Möhler et J. H. Newman" (*RSPT*, 1938) or "In the Lists with the Abbé Jager" (*Centenary Essays*, 1945) were of theological importance. To this latter volume, which Tristram edited, he also contributed an article "On Reading Newman." England was still behindhand. Tristram wrote an introduction to Philip Flanagan's *Newman, Faith and the Believer* (1946), the best account until that date in English of Newman's psychology of faith. It was still too much concerned with vindicating Newman from past attacks and did not quite bring out the richness of his theory of knowledge. Its worst defect was the misinterpretation of his teaching on Conscience, almost as though it led men to God by syllogistic argument. This was the opposite extreme to Bremond. A far more authoritative guide was and is H. Francis Davis, some of whose numerous articles (which ought to be collected into one volume) will be mentioned in their place. In the United States, Charles Frederick Harrold in his *John Henry Newman, An Expository and Critical Study of His Mind, Thought, and Art* (1945) gave a straightforward account and summarized the best earlier writing on his subject. He began a new edition of Newman's works, with perceptive introductions, and his early death in 1950 was a severe loss to Newman and Victorian scholarship.

The new understanding was far from being confined to what may be called professional students of Newman. His teaching is neither esoteric nor written in technical jargon. There is a valuable comparison of the teaching in the *University Sermons* with that of Coleridge in the latter part of D. G. James's *The Romantic Comedy* (1948; paperback ed., 1962). John Holloway in *The Victorian Sage* (1953) thoroughly appreciates Newman's method while rejecting what he has to say. Criticism of this attitude will be found in the appendix to Walgrave's study, mentioned below, and in David J. DeLaura's essay, "Newman as Prophet" (*DubR*, 1967, rpt. at the end of his edition of the *Apologia*, 1968). The force of Newman's defense of Christian faith is drawn out in the chapter on him in Basil Willey's *Nineteenth-Century Studies* (1949).

Since the 1950's new books on Newman have been regularly discussed in *Philosophical Studies*, published annually by the National University of Ireland and edited by James D. Bastable.

III. INTRODUCTIONS TO NEWMAN'S PHILOSOPHY

The fact that from France after World War II there came a distinguished introduction to Newman's philosophy was proof that a new era had dawned. Maurice Nédoncelle's *La Philosophie religieuse de John Henry Newman* (1946) was first published as the preface to a collection, *Œuvres philosophiques de Newman*

(1945). Nédoncelle brought out the deep personalism of Newman's thought, explained the part played by conscience in man's relation to God, discussed his psychology of faith and his theory of development, and in a final chapter on the *Idea of a University* described his Christian humanism. Nédoncelle's book was a turning point, and almost all that can be said by way of criticism is that the different aspects of Newman's thought might have been more closely linked. Already in 1939 he had published the first fully annotated edition of the *Apologia*, and he now began to edit French translations of Newman's works. His preface to the *University Sermons*, which completes *La Philosophie religieuse*, is mentioned below.

Meanwhile in Germany the movement led by Przywara gathered new strength. During the war Heinrich Fries was preparing his *Die Religionsphilosophie Newmans* (1948), a worthy companion to Nédoncelle's book, although, as the title suggests, more limited in scope. He shows that Newman was not a professional philosopher, solving problems in the abstract, but one who dealt with the difficulties of persons and their religious beliefs. Fries rendered further service by founding, with Werner Becker of the Leipzig Oratory, the "Cardinal Newman Curatorium," which since 1948 has published nine volumes of *Newman Studien*, containing important bibliographies, articles, and treatises by Newman scholars in various countries, by no means all written in German. There have appeared further works by Fries on Newman's theology, and a study on Newman's "Personalism" by Gunter Rombold, "Das Wesen der Person nach John Henry Newman" (*Newman Studien*, IV, 1960). The treatment by Alfred Läpple, *Die Einzelne in der Kirche, Wesen-Züge einer Theologie des Einzelnen nach Cardinal Newman* (1952), laudable in intention, is defective in its account of conscience, where besides Newman's two elements, "a judgment of reason and a magisterial dictate," a third is introduced—"moral instinct." See the appendix to Walgrave's book, now to be described.

A third excellent introduction to Newman, first published in Flemish during the war, was that by the Belgian Jan H. Walgrave, revised and extended for the French edition, *Newman, le développement du dogme* (1957; English trans., *Newman the Theologian*, 1960). Walgrave showed the organic connection between Newman's psychology of knowledge and his doctrine of development. It was an introduction also to Newman's theology, and contained critical assessments of other work on Newman. Like Nédoncelle and Fries, Walgrave was concerned primarily to discover and expound what Newman really thought, and while being himself a distinguished Dominican theologian, never tried to force him into categories that were not his. Further discussion of Walgrave's book is to be found in B. P. Dupuy's "Bulletin d'histoire des doctrines: Newman" (*RSPT*, 1961) and in Nicholas Lash, "Second Thoughts on Walgrave's 'Newman'" (*DownR*, 1969). Dupuy has another useful "Bulletin d'histoire des doctrines: Newman aujourd'hui" (*RSPT*, 1972). From the Low Countries came two other studies of Newman's philosophy, A. J. Boekraad's *The Personal Conquest of Truth According to J. H. Newman* (1955) and Dr. Zeno's *John Henry Newman, Our Way to Certitude* (1957). Using *A Grammar of Assent* and unpublished material Boekraad draws out Newman's personal, phenomenological way of thinking, and shows its metaphysical basis. Zeno had already published in Dutch a study of the illative sense, *Newman's Leer over het Menselijk Denken* (1942). Both his volumes are accurate and complete, but suffer from an overdesire to harmonize Newman and St. Thomas.

Another short and straightforward introduction to Newman's philosophy deserves special mention, *Philosophical Readings in Cardinal Newman* (1961), edited by James Collins. He contributes an initial chapter, and also introduces the various sections of his anthology. He shows Newman's relevance, and how our appreciation of him depends on our learning "gradually to walk at his own pace and along his own path." Collins has also provided an excellent survey of Newman's philosophy of mind in the article on him in *The Encyclopaedia of Philosophy*, v (1967).

However, the fullest introduction and one that was able to profit by all the first fruits of the new era in Newman studies is that by Edward Sillem, "General Introduction to the Study of Newman's Philosophy," which fills the first volume of his edition of *The Philosophical Notebook of John Henry Newman* (1969). Although Sillem's style is inclined to be repetitious, he provides a clear initiation for the beginner and full information for the scholar. Newman is shown as deliberately rejecting the secular liberal philosophy, the last effort of rationalism, and choosing to be the great outsider who makes a completely new start in philosophy. "Like the Phenomenologists Newman sought a new method of philosophizing, and one that would help him to avoid the Scylla and Charybdis of Empiricism and Idealism. He tried to lay the foundations of a metaphysics of being by investigating existent things as they stood revealed in the prism of his mind, or as they appeared in the certitudes he had reached concerning them in and through his total experience of them."

Sillem has a packed chapter on Newman's sources, a subject on which nonetheless further research is needed. He shows Newman's debt to Aristotle, which has been one-sidedly stressed in Franz M. Willam's *Aristotelische Erkenntnislehre bei Whately und Newman* (1960), on which Rombold's study, mentioned above, should be consulted. On the influence of the Alexandrians Sillem is brief. Louis Bouyer has written on "Newman et le platonisme de l'âme anglaise" (*Revue de Philosophie*, 1936; English trans., *Monastic Studies*, 1963). There are also articles by Jan G. M. Willebrands, "Het Christelijk Platonisme von Kardinaal Newman" (*Studia Catholica*, 1941), C. F. Harrold, "Newman and the Alexandrian Platonists" (*MP*, 1940), and Vincent F. Blehl, "Newman, the Fathers, and Education" (*Thought*, 1970). Sillem has given full attention to Newman's relation to Butler and to his reaction to Locke: "I cannot find one single passage of his writings in which he states an opinion of Locke to say expressly that he accepts it as his own." On the other hand it can hardly be disputed that Newman thinks and writes from within the English tradition, as James M. Cameron maintains in articles mentioned below. John Coulson has worked this point out in *Newman and the Common Tradition* (1970), with special reference to Coleridge, whom Newman, however, did not discover until 1835, when his own doctrine was formed. See H. Francis Davis, "Was Newman a Disciple of Coleridge?" (*DubR*, 1945). Sillem draws attention to various other influences on Newman, and describes his reaction to Kant's teaching as he found it in 1859 in the pages of H. M. Chalybäus' *Historical Development of Speculative Philosophy from Kant to Hegel* (English trans., 1854).

Sillem's study is directed to the *Philosophical Notebook* now first published, which, he maintains, reveals a new dimension in Newman's philosophy. It should be insisted, as Newman insisted, that the *Notebook* was very tentative and not meant for publication. Newman's *Letter on Matter and Spirit* is printed as an appendix to the *Notebook*.

IV. *A GRAMMAR OF ASSENT* AND *SERMONS PREACHED BEFORE THE UNIVERSITY OF OXFORD*

These two works are discussed in the general books listed above, and Bacchus' earlier contributions have also been mentioned. It is worth noting that, according to Frederick E. Crowe, "*A Grammar of Assent* had a profound influence on Lonergan's developing epistemology" (*Bernard Lonergan Collection*, 1967). In "Newman and Logic" (*Newman Studien*, v, 1962), Brian Wicker has pointed out how Newman's assumption that Formal Logic treats of mental acts is rejected by logicians today, but he goes on to show that Newman's main argument is not weakened, rather the contrary, if his psychological theory of logic is eliminated. That is to say, if logic is not in fact a description of how the mind works in ideal conditions, the ground is left more than ever clear for Newman's defense of certitude, which he bases on the facts of experience, on our psychological processes. As he explains in the *Grammar*, most of the certitudes on which we rightly base our lives we have not and cannot prove scientifically.

The chief difficulty for the ordinary reader who embarks on *A Grammar of Assent* is the total absence of any introduction explaining Newman's purpose. An account of this and therefore a kind of introduction to the book is supplied by a chapter in Dessain's *John Henry Newman* (1966; 2nd ed., 1971), which is a concise outline of Newman's thought rather than a biography. See also Dessain's article, "Cardinal Newman on the Theory and Practice of Knowledge: The Purpose of the *Grammar of Assent*" (*DownR*, 1957). The illative sense gives certainty and is a purely intellectual faculty. The prolonged attempt Newman made to convince his scientific friend William Froude that certainty was attainable exhibits the arguments in the *Grammar* being tested beforehand. This may be studied in Gordon H. Harper, *Cardinal Newman and William Froude, A Correspondence* (1933), and in *The Letters and Diaries of John Henry Newman* (xix, 1969, ed. Dessain). There is an excellent exposition of *A Grammar of Assent* in Italian by Luca Obertello, *Conoscenza e persona nel pensiero di John Henry Newman* (1964). His evaluation should be compared with that of Sillem. He fully understands Newman's place in the English tradition. Another valuable Italian work is the thesis of Alberto Bosi at the University of Turin on Newman as a philosopher (1968).

Quite recently English philosophers have given attention to *A Grammar of Assent*: John Hicks, in *Faith and Knowledge* (1967), and H. H. Price, in his Gifford Lectures, *Belief* (1969). Price discusses with great respect and at considerable length the first part of the *Grammar*, whether there are degrees of assent (which Newman firmly denied), and the distinction between real and notional assents, but does not go outside that book in his search for Newman's meaning. Price's account of the part played by moral dispositions in the attainment of truth is in the closest harmony with Newman's ideas. Indeed, his witty and urbane lectures belong to the same class as the *Grammar*. David Pailin in *The Way to Faith, An Examination of Newman's* Grammar of Assent *as a Response to the Search for Certainty in Faith* (1969) considers the background and Newman's earlier writings on the same theme, including unpublished material, some of which he prints in an appendix. He fails, however, in his grasp of Newman's argument.

The best short introduction to Newman's philosophy of religion and Christian apologetic is the clear and well-balanced study by Thomas Vargish, *Newman: The*

Contemplation of Mind (1970). After describing Newman's debt to the Evangelicals and the Empiricists, Vargish shows why Newman was a lifelong opponent of "liberalism in religion," and how he applied his doctrine to secular society, to education, and to conversion.

The two most elegant introductions to Newman's *Oxford University Sermons* are undoubtedly Nédoncelle's preface to the French translation (1955) in his collection of carefully edited *Textes Newmaniens*, and James M. Cameron's essays, which conclude *The Night Battle* (1962). Nédoncelle shows that Newman had no use for a mere religion of the heart, the "warmth of a corpse," and explains how he could disparage "reason" and yet have a reasonable or rather intellectualist explanation of credibility and belief. For Newman even the word "feeling," which he uses once, includes for him an intellectual grasp of truth. The implicit reasons most men have for their beliefs are opposed to explicit, not as unrealized to realized but as real to notional, or better, as personal to impersonal. Cameron in "The Logic of the Heart" and "Newman and Empiricism" brings out to the point of exaggeration the tension between mere reason and religious understanding. D. M. Mackinnon, in the introduction to a reprint of *Oxford University Sermons* (1970), has continued the discussion of Newman's openness to the empiricist temper and tradition.

Giovanni Perrone, the theologian with whom Newman became friends in 1847, had his objections to Newman's views, which the latter tried to explain. Henry Tristram published the explanations, "Cardinal Newman's Theses de Fide and His Proposed Introduction to the French Translation of the University Sermons" (*Gregorianum*, 1937).

V. NEWMAN'S THEOLOGY: CONSCIENCE AND FAITH

In the article "Conscience," in *A Catholic Dictionary of Theology* (1967), J. H. Crehan writes, "Newman may be termed the *doctor conscientiae* as others were termed 'subtle doctor' or 'irrefragable' in the Middle Ages." After explaining further, Crehan adds, "Newman thus supplied the best answer to Kant. Where Kant had tried to account for the phenomena of moral activity without allowing for any intuitions by man of his own acts . . . Newman took his reader into the sanctuary of conscience, and asked: 'Do you see what I see?'" For him conscience is the link between natural and revealed religion. The natural conscience leads to belief in God, and those who follow it will be on the lookout for a revelation. "It inspires in them," remarks Newman, "the idea of authoritative guidance, of a divine law; and the desire of possessing it in its fullness, not in mere fragmentary portions or indirect suggestions." Once a revealed religion is accepted as from God, it will rule a man's conscience. When Newman speaks of drinking to Conscience first and the Pope afterward, he is not considering the Pope as one of the means by which revealed truth is made certain, but as a legislator and as the governor of a divine society.

Conscience is the bridge between Newman's philosophy and his theology, although the two disciplines are interlocked as they are in the writings of the Fathers, who were his models and his authorities. Thus many of the works already mentioned deal with conscience. Walgrave is at his most effective, both in the body of his book and in the appendices, on this part of Newman's teaching. The same is true of Boekraad and Fries, who show the necessity of moral dispositions for the conquest of truth. The former has also published *The Argument from Conscience to the Existence of God According to J. H. Newman* (1961), and has included in it unpublished papers, among them a section from the *Philosophical Notebook*, "Proof of Theism." D. Duivesteyn has worked out some of the implications of Newman's teaching in "Reflexions on Natural Law" (*Clergy Rev.*, 1967). There is also an interesting and workmanlike thesis by Eugene F. Lauer, *An Historical-Analytical Comparison of Newman's Concept of Conscience and Tertullian's Testimonium Animae* (Gregorian Univ. 1966).

Conscience leads on to faith. There is a masterly article by H. Francis Davis, "Newman on Faith and Personal Certitude" (*J. of Theol. Stud.*, 1961), and a more technical discussion in Roger Aubert's *Le Problème de l'acte de foi* (1945). The latter has also written "Newman, une psychologie concrète de la foi et une apologétique existentielle" (*Lumen Vitae*, 1952). The depths of Newman's teaching on faith have still to be explored. It includes the acceptance of propositions, but it is first of all the loving dutiful adherence to a Person, who is revealed in history. See also Dessain, "Cardinal Newman Considered as a Prophet" (*Concilium*, 1968).

Fries has written on "Newman's Bedeutung für die Theologie" (*Theologische Quartalschrift*, 1946; rpt. in *Newman Studien*, 1, 1948) and also "Newman und Grundprobleme der Heutigen Apologetik" (*Newman Studien*, 111, 1957). In this latter work he shows Newman as the apologist in action, "doing the truth in love," and insisting on the necessity of right dispositions, a good conscience, if argument is to convince. Fries shows how Newman's approach is perennially valid. There are a number of studies on Newman's apologetics, including Sylvester Juergens, *Newman on the Psychology of Faith in the Individual* (1928), Borghild Gundersen, who analyzes Newman's method in *Cardinal Newman and Apologetics* (1952), and on special subjects, J. D. Folghera, *Newman Apologiste* (1927; English trans., *Newman's Apologetic*, 1928), and J. Richard Quinn, *The Recognition of the True Church According to John Henry Newman* (1954). Bacchus and Tristram discuss Newman's *Essays on Miracles*. For a defense against the attacks of Dr. Abbott in *Philomythus*, see the second edition of Richard Holt Hutton's *Life*, and Henry Ignatius Dudley Ryder, *Essays* (1911). General, but somewhat dated, is Edmond Darvil Benard, *A Preface to Newman's Theology* (1945).

Much work remains to be done on Newman as an apologist, on such points as his method and presuppositions, the uselessness of discussion until first principles are agreed upon, the fair presentation and even overstatement of the opposing case, the sense of mystery always preserved. Then Newman's attitude to atheism and to non-Catholic religions must be examined. For an excellent exposition of the former topic see Jean Guy Saint-Arnaud, *Newman et l'incroyance* (1972). There is a famous passage in the review of Milman's *Latin Christianity*, which Newman quoted again in *The Development of Doctrine*. It shows how he regarded religious truths as scattered everywhere, "wild plants indeed but living," and finding fulfillment and balance in Christianity. Then there is his realization that Christianity must be adapted not only to different ages but to different places. Thus *The Development* has been justly described as a "manual of missionary adaptation." What he has to say on the conversion of the heathen is systematized in Willi Henkel, *Die religiöse Situation der Heiden und ihre Bekehrung nach John Henry Newman* (1967). Men need to be prepared gradually to accept the truth. Newman's pastoral use of "reserve" or economy in communicating it forms the subject of a brilliant thesis by Robin Selby (Oxford 1972), and is discussed in the book on abuses in the Church by Richard Bergeron, mentioned later. For an opposite procedure on Newman's part, see Piers Brendon, "Newman, Keble and Froude's *Remains*" (*EHR*, 1972).

VI. THE DEVELOPMENT OF CHRISTIAN DOCTRINE

The best general account of the genesis and scope of Newman's view on development is undoubtedly the fourteen columns devoted to the subject in the article by H. Francis Davis, "Doctrine, Development of," in *A Catholic Dictionary of Theology* (1967). Davis shows Newman's originality, and how he was led on to the subject thanks to his controversy with Renn D. Hampden, who wished to limit all authentic Christian doctrine to what could be expressed in the actual words of Scripture. Relying on the last of the *University Sermons*, "The Theory of Developments in Religious Doctrine," which is indispensable for understanding the theory, Davis writes, "Newman's theory of development is affected by four factors: (a) We have no direct contact with our sources; (b) the object of revelation is basically one, Jesus Christ; (c) human language can express a simple, unified object only in complex language, with multiple words and phrases; (d) there are no especial difficulties, inherent in the attempt to express supernatural truth in earthly human language." Davis attaches less importance to the *Essay on Development*, which, however, prepared the way for Newman's entry into the Catholic Church by convincing him that her doctrines were legitimate developments caused by a vivid realization of the original deposit. There is also an earlier article by Davis, "Newman and the Psychology of the Development of Doctrine" (*DubR*, 1945). The best account of the way in which *Development* came to be written is Owen Chadwick's learned and sparkling *From Bossuet to Newman* (1957). He shows how Newman's theory was the result of his historical studies and how it linked the teaching of the Church with history. He agrees, against Acton, that the theory did not "emancipate Newman from history." Chadwick thinks, however, that Newman's theory involves continuous new revelation. Newman himself did not think so, as Davis points out in his article in *A Catholic Dictionary of Theology*, and also in a review of Chadwick (*DownR*, 1958). See also Davis' "Is Newman's Theory of Development Catholic?" (*Blackfriars*, 1958), and B. D. Dupuy, "Bulletin d'histoire des doctrines: Newman" (*RSPT*, 1961). Another excellent work, which traces the progress of Newman's thought during the Oxford Movement, by Jean Stern, *Bible et tradition chez Newman, aux origines de la théorie du développement* (1967), agrees with Davis. Stern writes: "Malheureusement Chadwick sous-estime le caractère intellectuel de la saisie laquelle, pour Newman aboutit à une connaissance véritable, quoiqu'implicite." This point Newman had clarified in a paper of 1868, but only published after Chadwick's book: by Dessain, "An Unpublished Paper by Cardinal Newman on the Development of Doctrine" (*J. of Theol. Stud.*, 1958), also by Hugo M. de Achaval in *Gregorianum* (1958).

Walgrave's study of Newman and development has already been described. Since then, in a long preface to a French translation by Luce Gérard, *J. H. Cardinal Newman: Essai sur le développement de la doctrine chrétienne* (1964), Walgrave considers the influence of Newman's theory in the controversies concerning Revelation since his day, and especially at the present time. Walgrave discusses the paper of 1868, unknown to him when he wrote earlier, and shows how it confirms the view that Newman's doctrine excluded the possibility of additions to Revelation. See also Walgrave's *Unfolding Revelation* (1972). Further studies will be found in *Newman Studien*, vi (1964), including another by Walgrave, "L'Originalité de l'idée Newmanienne du développement," and two on the later history of the doctrine: B. D. Dupuy, "L'Influence de Newman sur la théologie catholique du développement dogmatique," and Dessain, "The Reception among Catholics of Newman's Doctrine of Development." Of the contemporary Anglican criticisms, Newman felt that none came to grips with him, or forced him to alter what he had written. See C. C. Brown, "Newman's Minor Critics" (*DownR*, 1971). For Newman's own explanation of his meaning in Rome in 1847, see T. Lynch, "The Newman-Perrone Paper on Development" (*Gregorianum*, 1935). Many of the notes Newman made while writing *The Development of Doctrine* have been most perspicaciously used and interpreted by Chadwick, and will be invaluable for the preparation of a fully critical edition of Newman's work.

The literature on Development is immense. There is a full account by Johannes Artz, "Entstehung und Auswirking von Newmans Theorie der Dogmenentwicklung" (*Tübinger Theologischen Quartalschrift*, 1968). Among recent works are Herbert Hammans, *Die neueren Katholischen Erklarungen der Dogmenentwicklung* (1965), and a chapter by Karl Rahner and Karl Lehmann in Johannes Feiner and Magnus Lohrer, *Mysterium Salutis, Grundriss Heilsgeschichtlicher Dogmatik*, i (1965). Jacques Chevalier discusses Development from a more philosophical standpoint in *Trois conférences d'Oxford* (1933), and Jean Guitton in *La Philosophie de Newman* (1933) analyzes *The Arians of the Fourth Century*, the *Via Media*, and the *Development* showing the connection between them. Nicholas Lash, in "Faith and History: Some Reflections on Newman's 'Essay on the Development of Christian Doctrine'" (*Irish Theol. Q.*, 1970), shows how Newman was guided by facts, not by theory.

VII. HOLY SCRIPTURE

Newman's devotion to Holy Scripture is described in Jean Stern's *Bible et tradition chez Newman* (1967), where he makes one or two criticisms of the exhaustive work of Jaak Seynaeve, *Cardinal Newman's Doctrine of Holy Scripture According to His Published Works and Previously Unedited Manuscripts* (1953). Some of the manuscripts are printed, not entirely accurately, and there is much more work to be done on them, on Newman's ideas as to the senses of Scripture, and on Scripture generally. The passage dealing with the Galileo case is printed in Vincent Ferrer Blehl, *The Essential Newman* (1963). Stern, who is master of his subject, also treats of the relations between Scripture and tradition in an article on the controversy with Abbé Jager in *Newman Studien*, vi (1964). Tristram has a factual account "In the Lists with the Abbé Jager" (*Centenary Essays*, 1945), and Louis Allen has prepared an edition, as yet unpublished, of the various letters that passed between the two antagonists. Heinrich Fries has contributed a valuable study, "J. H. Newmans Beitrag zum Verständnis der Tradition," in *Die mundliche Ueberlieferung* (1957), edited by Michael Schmaus. Gunter Biemer's

Überlieferung und Offenbaring, Die Lehre von der Tradition nach John Henry New-
man (1961; English trans., *Newman and Tradition*, 1967) contains useful material
but is inaccurate and attributes to Newman a work written in 1857 by Manning.

Catholic suspicions of Newman lingered longest in regard to his teaching on
the inspiration of Holy Scripture. The second Vatican Council in this as in other
matters has spoken in a way consonant with his point of view. The essays he wrote
in his old age have now been edited by J. Derek Holmes and Robert Murray, *On*
the Inspiration of Scripture, John Henry Newman (1967). The full introductory
matter by the editors provides the necessary guidance and describes the part played
by Newman in the development of the Catholic doctrine of Inspiration. See also
J. Derek Holmes, "Newman's Attitude towards Historical Criticism and Biblical
Inspiration" (*DownR*, 1971). There is a short account also in James Tunstead
Burtchaell, *Catholic Theories of Biblical Inspiration since 1810* (1969).

VIII. THE CHURCH, THE PAPACY, THE LAITY

Considering how central the Church was both in Newman's life and in his
doctrine, it is surprising how little his teaching on the subject has been studied.
Apart from the first part of Alf Härdelin's book on the Eucharist to be mentioned
later, there is as yet no study of Newman's sacramental view of the Church or of
the Church regarded as a Communion, aspects so much stressed by him, and
brought to the fore since the second Vatican Council. His idea of the Church, apart
from the question of the Papacy, was complete in all its essentials many years
before he left the Anglican Church, and was then only added to, not substantially
altered. W. H. Van der Pol wrote, while still a Dutch Protestant, *De Kerk en Het*
Leven en Denken van Newman (1936; German trans., 1937), which, following
Newman's course, aims at bringing out the supernatural reality of the Church and
promoting ecumenical understanding. Norbert Schiffers, in a more systematic work,
Die Einheit der Kirche nach John Henry Newman (1958), makes the Church
central in Newman's teaching. His view of it as the authorized guardian of revelation is described, and its place in salvation history. It continues to exercise the three
offices of Christ, those of Priest, Prophet, and King. Stanislas Jáki, in *Les Ten-*
dences nouvelles de l'ecclésiologie de Newman (1957), has some pages on Newman's teaching concerning the spiritual character of the Church. "Pour Newman la
structure sacramentelle de l'Eglise et le sens religieux personnel ne sont pas deux
choses isolées l'une de l'autre, mais sont deux facteurs également indispensables
pour mener à la perfection de la vie surnaturelle." Jáki insists that all the modern
themes of ecclesiology are to be found in Newman, "des passages saisissaints sur le
rôle des laiques, sur le rapport entre les religions naturelles et l'Eglise, sur l'engagement d'une Eglise sainte dans le domaine profane, sur le signification dogmatique de
l'histoire de l'Eglise, sur la piété catholique et sur l'aspect eschatologique de l'Eglise."

The position in the Church of bishops, whom Newman held in high honor, has
been little studied. There is an article by H. Francis Davis, "Le Rôle et l'apostolat de
la hiérarchie et du laicat dans la théologie de l'Eglise chez Newman" (*Revue des*
Sciences Religieuses, 1960; rpt. in the symposium *L'Ecclésiologie au dix-neuvième*
siècle, ed. M. Nédoncelle). There is also a comprehensive Munich thesis by

Paul Misner, "John Henry Newman on the Primacy of the Pope" (1968), but much remains to be done. Romuald A. Dibble, *John Henry Newman: The Concept of Infallible Doctrinal Authority* (1955), is based on a certain amount of unpublished material, but is not always a reliable guide to it. Dessain has collected much of what Newman has to say in his contribution to *The Infallibility of the Church, An Anglican-Catholic Dialogue* (1968), "What Newman Taught in Manning's Church." J. Derek Holmes has a fuller account, "Cardinal Newman and the First Vatican Council" (*Annuarium Historiae Conciliorum*, 1969). Damian McElrath examines *A Letter to the Duke of Norfolk* in *The Syllabus of Pius IX, Some Reactions in England* (1964). He also discusses the Ward-Ryder controversy on the scope of infallibility, on which Newman has left papers, which, after Ryder's entry into the breach against the extreme Ultramontanes, he did not need to use. There are in B. D. Dupuy's French translation of *A Letter to the Duke of Norfolk* (1970) an outstanding introduction and notes. Gary Lease, *Witness to the Faith* (1971), gives a historical account of Newman's views on the teaching authority of the Church, but does not sufficiently clarify the role of the hierarchy.

More attention has been devoted to Newman's teaching on the place of the Laity in the Church and on the "sensus fidelium" as a source of dogma, a matter in which Newman anticipated the second Vatican Council. His article "On Consulting the Faithful in Matters of Doctrine" (*The Rambler*, 1859) has been reprinted with an excellent introduction by John Coulson (1961). This was utilized by Jean Guitton in *L'Eglise et les Laics* (1963). Newman's letters during the period of his editorship of the *Rambler* with much collateral matter bearing on the subject of the Laity will be found in *The Letters and Diaries of John Henry Newman* (XIX, 1969, ed. Dessain). Useful comment will be found in Yves Congar, *Jalons pour une théologie du Laicat* (1953; English trans., *Lay People in the Church*, 1957).

Newman also discussed the "Prophetical Office" in the 1878 Preface to the *Via Media*. There and elsewhere he adumbrated a theology of abuses in the Church. The Preface has been discussed by John Coulson, "Newman on the Church—His Final View, Its Origins and Influences," in *The Rediscovery of Newman* (1967), and by Nédoncelle in a comprehensive article, "Newman, théologien des abus de l'Eglise" (*Oecumenica, Jahrbuch für ökumenische Forschung*, 1967). Since then the full-scale treatise by Richard Bergeron, *Les Abus de l'Eglise d'après Newman* (1971) has appeared. There has been no proper treatment yet of the freedom and free discussion in the Church, which Newman thought of such importance, as the final chapter of the *Apologia* emphasizes. Fries has an interesting comparison of Newman and Döllinger in *Newman Studien*, II (1954). Further material will be found in Jacob W. Gruber, *A Conscience in Conflict, The Life of St. George Jackson Mivart* (1960), and in Hugo M. de Achaval's study of the same subject in *Newman Studien*, VI (1964). On Newman's appeal to history there is a valuable article by J. Derek Holmes, "Newman, History and Theology" (*Irish Theol. Q.*, 1969).

Newman's importance for ecumenism was one of the themes of *The Rediscovery of Newman*, and was introduced there by A. Michael Ramsey, Archbishop of Canterbury, in "The Significance of Newman Today." Dessain has collected various passages in "Cardinal Newman and Ecumenism" (*Clergy Rev.*, 1965). The correspondence with Ambrose de Lisle, in E. S. Purcell, *Life and Letters of Ambrose Phillipps de Lisle* (1900), in R. D. Middleton, *Newman and Bloxam* (1947), and in *The Letters and Diaries of John Henry Newman*, XVIII (1968), edited by

Dessain, is of importance here. Indeed, so is Newman's correspondence generally. Owen Chadwick in his contribution to *Anglican Initiatives in Christian Unity* (1967), "The Church of England and the Church of Rome from the Beginning of the Nineteenth Century to the Present Day," places Newman beside the Bible and the Fathers as the three areas offering common ground between Anglicans and Catholics. For Newman's views on Anglican Orders, see *Essays Critical and Historical*, II; *The Letters and Diaries*, XXIV (1973); and Placid Murray's introduction to his *Newman the Oratorian* (1969) as well as his letter in the *Clergy Review* (1965).

Newman's view was that "the Church must be prepared for converts, as well as converts for the Church," and the ecumenical importance of his life and work was long ago recognized in Germany by Laros, Werner Becker, and others. See also Johannes Artz, "Newman als Brucke zwischen Canterbury und Rom" (*Una Sancta*, 1967).

IX. GRACE, JUSTIFICATION, THE SACRAMENTS

Although Newman lived always in the world and defended the Church as a visible society, "the concrete representative of things invisible," no one emphasized more that her most important work was invisible. Since the new era in Newman studies it has been recognized that he was no abstract thinker or solitary, but always a pastor. From the time of his Anglican ordination, all his activity had some apostolic purpose. Doctrine was there not for speculation but to be lived. It is not surprising, then, that he had a vivid understanding of the New Testament teaching on the Indwelling of God in the soul, the "partly realized eschatology" of which the Church is the instrument. The more important passages are quoted and comparison made with modern theological discussion of the subject in Dessain's articles, "Cardinal Newman and the Doctrine of Uncreated Grace" (*Clergy Rev.*, 1962) and "The Biblical Basis of Newman's Ecumenical Theology" in *The Rediscovery of Newman* (1967). There is an account of how Newman gradually arrived at the doctrine of baptismal regeneration, based on the study of unpublished early papers, by Thomas L. Sheridan, *Newman on Justification* (1967). It contains a description of Evangelicalism, which Newman met for the first time during his last year at school. There was also a Louvain University thesis by John E. Linnane, *The Evangelical Background of John Henry Newman, 1816–1826* (1965), which relies on secondary sources. Dessain has tried to make the event of 1816 understandable in modern terms in "Newman's First Conversion" (*Newman Studien*, III, 1957; also in *Studies*, Dublin, 1957). Newman always insisted that his had been an intellectual process, and so was not a typical Evangelical conversion.

Much more research is needed into what is really Newman's greatest theological work, *Lectures on Justification*, before which Sheridan stops short. Yngve Brilioth discusses Newman's treatise sympathetically in *The Anglican Revival* (1925). Mention should be made here of C. de Vogel's *Newman's gedachten over de rechvaarding* (1939), which was highly praised when it appeared, but which few people have read because nearly all the copies were destroyed during the war. De Vogel's autobiography, which contains some pages on the subject of Newman and Justification, has been published in a French translation, *Du protestantisme orthodoxe à l'église catholique* (1956). Newman's emphasis on the connection between justification and the Paschal Mystery is one more forgotten truth that has been "rediscovered" in the mid-twentieth century. There is an unpublished Trier thesis by James T. Meehan, "The Easter Theme in the Preaching of John Henry Newman" (1969), and Dessain also calls attention to it, but there is much more to be said on this topic and on the related one of baptism, so important for Newman. There is an excellent study on the Eucharist, based on printed and unprinted sources, by Alf Härdelin, *The Tractarian Understanding of the Eucharist* (1965), while Placid Murray in *Newman the Oratorian* traces the continuity of Newman's eucharistic belief and practice. The same two writers also discuss Newman's views on the liturgy, which is otherwise a field largely unexplored. There is much to prove, notably, in as-yet-unpublished Anglican sermons, how deep an insight he had into the true nature of liturgical worship. This eminent preacher rated it higher than preaching. Murray touches on Newman's preaching. There are also worthwhile theses on the subject: Gerald L. Potter, "The Idea of Preaching According to John Henry Newman" (Gregorian Univ. 1963) and Roger G. O'Brien, "The Theology of Preaching in the Parochial and Plain Sermons of John Henry Newman" (Louvain 1968). Josef Mann's *John Henry Newman als Kerygmatiker, der Beitrag seiner anglikanischen Zeit zur Glaubensverkundung und Unterweisung* (1965) gives a clear and systematic account. See also the excellent introduction by W. D. White to a selection of the sermons, *The Preaching of John Henry Newman* (1969).

On Our Lady there is the very thorough work, Francis J. Friedel, *The Mariology of Cardinal Newman* (1928), and "La Mariologie de Newman," by H. F. Davis, in *Maria*, III (1954). To it may be added Jean Stern's article, "Le Culte de la vierge et des saints et le conversion de Newman au Catholicisme" (*La Vie spirituelle*, 1967), and Michael O'Carroll's "Our Lady in Newman and Vatican II" (*DownR*, 1971). Newman's eschatology has had no book written on it. There was "development" in regard to Purgatory, of which *The Dream of Gerontius* is the conclusion.

X. NEWMAN'S SPIRITUAL TEACHING

Newman's teaching on the spiritual life is to be found in many places for he never separated it into a special compartment. Much is to be gleaned from the almost unworked mine of his letters. These include some letters of direction, but revealing remarks are to be found in many others not concerned with spiritual matters. The first book on the subject as such was that of William R. Lamm, *The Spiritual Legacy of Newman* (1934), which expounded the chief themes of *Parochial and Plain Sermons*. As has been said, a decade earlier Przywara was drawing attention in Germany to Newman's ascetical teaching. The sermons were directed not at specialists (members of religious orders), but at ordinary Christians. Thus Newman provided spiritual teaching for the baptized, for those living in the world. This is emphasized by Dessain in the *Clergy Review* (1960), in "Newman's Spirituality and Its Value Today" (rpt. in *English Spiritual Writers*, ed. Charles Davis, 1961).

Louis Bouyer was the first to write a life that laid stress on Newman's holiness, which he did very effectively, correcting many misunderstandings, in his *Newman:*

Sa vie, sa spiritualité, dedicated to Henry Tristram. Tristram himself has a valuable essay, "With Newman at Prayer," in *Centenary Essays* (1945), and at the same time another Birmingham Oratorian, Francis Vincent Reade, who like Tristram had imbibed the tradition from Newman's companions, described the picture thus formed in his mind, in "The Spiritual Life of John Henry Newman" (*DubR*, 1945). He speaks of Newman as "treating sardonically, and almost with amusement the notion that the Catholic faith stood for or was exhausted by a paradigmatic theology, a geometrical planning out of the unseen world, a clockwork sanctification of souls." Two recent lives of Newman devote considerable attention to his spiritual life: Jean Honoré, *Itinéraire spirituel de Newman* (1963) and Louis Cognet, *Newman ou la recherche de la verité* (1967). There is also Hilda Graef's *God and Myself, The Spirituality of John Henry Newman* (1967). She finds the Anglican Newman pessimistic. Others would dispute that as a verdict on the Sermons, and concerning Newman himself, the picture that emerges from his letters is one of serenity and cheerfulness. This is also the testimony of Reade and Tristram. See the former's "The Sentimental Myth" in *Centenary Essays* (1945), and the latter's "Newman and Baron von Hügel" (*DubR*, 1966). *Newman Mystico* (1964), by Giovanni Veloci, tries to fit Newman into the categories of the theologians of mysticism.

The Oratory and the humanist St. Philip Neri, its sixteenth-century originator, played a paramount role in Newman's life as a Catholic. His papers on the history and nature of the Oratory, the result of careful study, and many of the Chapter Addresses delivered to his Oratorian community in Birmingham have been published, with a long introduction on the priesthood and the religious life, by Placid Murray, *Newman the Oratorian* (1969). These papers, with the editor's explanations, throw a new light on Newman and his vocation. They also provide a kind of realistic spiritual reading, well suited to the late twentieth century, and they have a much wider scope than might be imagined in their explanations of what is meant by living in a community.

Meriol Trevor, who in her biography gave a vivid account of Newman the Oratorian, has shown his relevance as a spiritual teacher in her introduction to a new edition of the posthumous *Meditations and Devotions* (1964). She draws attention to the value of the "Meditations on Christian Doctrine," which Placid Murray would rate as the Catholic counterpart to *Parochial and Plain Sermons*.

In the course of the foregoing pages various suggestions as to further areas of research in Newman's philosophy and theology have been hazarded. Clearly more examination of his sources and the influences that affected him is needed, which will show his place in the English tradition without thereby diminishing our sense of his originality. Thomas M. Parker has already, in his contribution to *The Rediscovery of Newman*, proved how late in the day Newman studied the Caroline divines. It will be of great interest, also, to examine and account for the influence which, unlike most of his contemporaries, he continues to exercise today. Where and why is he felt to be so relevant? A practical difficulty, which efforts are being made to overcome, is the absence of critical editions of his works. As to unpublished material, there is a short account by Dessain of the archives at the Birmingham Oratory in *Newman Studien*, III (1957), also in the *Dublin Review* (1960–61), and in the *Catholic Historical Review* (1960). Much has been published in recent years, and a further collection in three volumes of Newman's philosophical and theological papers is in preparation. After that almost the only manuscripts by

Newman remaining will be his unpublished sermons. The more Newman is studied for his own sake as he really was, and in his own setting, the more he will be understood. It has been the merit of the studies of the last quarter of a century to give to the world the real Newman. Undoubtedly one of the best ways to come to know not only Newman but also his philosophy and theology is to read his letters, which correct false impressions and answer criticisms based on insufficient knowledge. A review of one of the volumes of *The Letters and Diaries of John Henry Newman* begins: "A lesser man than Newman would undoubtedly be diminished by the publication of his complete letters in a 30 volume series, each running to more than 600 pages. But as this series grows"—Volumes xi to xxiv inclusive have now appeared—"Newman's true stature becomes apparent" (*Times Educational Supp.*, 1968).

JOHN STUART MILL

·

John M. Robson

In the last hundred years, John Stuart Mill (1806–73) has been generally accepted as a major and representative exponent of British empiricism, liberalism, and classical economics. As a result, it is impossible in a guide of this sort to deal with the discussions of Mill and his works that appear in virtually every general and many specialized histories of the thought and life of the period. The student who wishes to place Mill in the context of a discipline or tradition should, therefore, first consult the main encyclopedias, histories, and reference works dealing with particular areas of thought, taking care to recognize the difficulties and distortions, too often passed over, that result when one isolates aspects of Mill's thought from one another.

In fact, the main problem facing anyone who wishes to see Mill whole lies in the breadth of Mill's interests, and in the immense volume of writings dealing with those interests. He wrote on a vast number of subjects, from logic to botany, from women's rights to defenses of the East India Company, from Irish land reform to psychology, and often combined his varied interests in one work. The best example is his collection of essays, *Dissertations and Discussions*, which, because it includes essays on French historians, currency, franchise reform, literary theory, etc., has never attracted attention as a unified body of writings, as have the collections of such of his contemporaries as Arnold, Carlyle, and Macaulay.

The result has been a proliferation of specialized critiques, typically in article form, appearing in the *Scottish Bankers' Magazine, Philosophy and Phenomenological Research, Moneda y Crédito* (Madrid), *Historical Studies: Australia and New Zealand*, and all places in between. As will be seen, few critics have been tempted to read all his works or to consider secondary sources in a comprehensive way; there are comparatively few general studies, and the body of detailed comments is too large and diverse for systematic summary.

It appears most practicable and useful, therefore, after a discussion of the mercifully less complicated tale of bibliography and editions, to give a survey of the critical response to Mill's writings during his lifetime and since, and then to comment on biographical and related writings, organized according to certain well-marked periods in Mill's life, before discussing the specific areas of most critical interest, philosophy, economics, and literature.

I. BIBLIOGRAPHY, RESEARCH MATERIALS, AND EDITIONS

The establishment of the Mill canon is much easier than for most other writers of his range and fecundity because he kept a record of his publications, made available in the edition by Ney MacMinn, John R. Hainds, and James M. McCrimmon, *Bibliography of the Published Writings of J. S. Mill* (1945; rpt. 1970), which, with its editorial apparatus, gives an almost complete and generally reliable record. Slight additions are made in Jacob Viner's review of MacMinn's edition (*MP*, 1945) and in John M. Robson's "A Note on Mill Bibliography" (*UTQ*, 1964). A breakdown of the material in MacMinn into subject classifications, useful though not always clear or accurate, is found in Volume III, Part IV, of Keito Amano's *Bibliography of the Classical Economists* (1964).

Apart from letters, there is very little unpublished material by Mill now extant (and probably there never was much). Excluding correspondence, almost all of that little is made up of journals of walking tours and debating speeches, some of which were published by Harold Laski in various periodicals (*MNL*, 1965). One journal, made up of Mill's letters to his father from France in 1820, has been published by Anna J. Mill in her *John Mill's Boyhood Visit to France* (1960), with extracts from a notebook taking the account to 1821. Of the other unpublished materials, the most interesting are an early draft of the *System of Logic* and a "Traité de logique" (both in the Pierpont Morgan Library) and a set of lecture notes on logic (in the Mill-Taylor Collection, British Library of Political and Economic Science); the latter two of these date from the same trip to France, when Mill was fourteen years old, covered in Anna Mill's book, where the notes of one of the lectures are printed. There are also five unpublished translations, with notes, of dialogues of Plato, written at the same time as the four published in the *Monthly Repository* (1834–35), in the Berg Collection of the New York Public Library. Other known materials are mainly manuscript fragments in the Mill-Taylor Collection, and a few scattered notes relating to revisions of published works.

There are also few extant manuscripts of published works; the most important are the press-copy manuscripts of the first volume of the *Principles of Political Economy* (Pierpont Morgan), of the *System of Logic* (British Museum), and of the *Autobiography* (John Rylands). Two other manuscripts of the *Autobiography* also exist: the holograph from which the defective press-copy manuscript was copied (Columbia); and the "Early Draft" in Mill's hand (Univ. of Illinois). All manuscripts are being used in the preparation of the *Collected Works* (see below), and the manuscripts of the *Autobiography* are described in the introduction to Jack Stillinger's edition of *The Early Draft of John Stuart Mill's* Autobiography (1961).

The main repositories of manuscript material, consisting, as already noted, principally of letters, are in the Mill-Taylor Collection, the Yale Library, the Brotherton Library (Leeds), the National Library of Scotland, the Johns Hopkins Library, and the British Museum. An account of the most important of these is given by Frederick A. von Hayek and Francis E. Mineka in *The Earlier Letters of J. S. Mill* (*Collected Works*, xii, xiii), and by Mineka and Dwight N. Lindley in *The Later Letters* (xiv–xvii).

There was no English collected edition of Mill's works during his lifetime, though Theodor Gomperz, a disciple of Mill, brought out a German edition, *Gesammelte Werke*, in twelve volumes (1869–80), which includes the works published by Mill in volume form during his lifetime. A cheap edition published by Routledge early in this century was discontinued after five volumes that have no textual authority. Not until after the work of Hayek and MacMinn, partly reflecting and partly initiating a new interest in Mill, did it seem feasible to plan a Collected Edition. This was initiated at the University of Toronto with F. E. L. Priestley as General Editor; John M. Robson is now General Editor. Of some twenty-five projected volumes, the following have appeared: *The Earlier Letters*, edited by Mineka (2 vols., 1963); *Principles of Political Economy*, edited by Robson, with an introduction by Vincent Bladen (2 vols., 1965); *Essays on Economics and Society*, edited by Robson, with an introduction by Lord Robbins (2 vols., 1967); *Essays on Ethics, Religion, and Society*, edited by Robson, with introductory essays by Priestley and Douglas P. Dryer (1969); *Later Letters*, edited by Mineka and Lindley (4 vols., 1972). The volumes next scheduled are *A System of Logic* and *Essays on Politics and Society*; the edition should conclude about 1980 with an index volume and bibliography.

Mill published only two collections of his writings: one minor, *Chapters and Speeches on the Irish Land Question* (1870), a gathering of chapters from the *Principles of Political Economy* and speeches in the House of Commons; one major, *Dissertations and Discussions* (2 vols., 1859; 2nd ed., 3 vols., 1867; 3rd ed., 4 vols., 1875), a gathering of what Mill thought to be his most significant and enduring articles, mainly from the leading reviews. Prior to the *Collected Works,* *Dissertations and Discussions* has served as the principal supplement to Mill's major works for critics wishing to cover a broad area of his thought.

Some of Mill's periodical and newspaper writings not republished by him have been made available in editions that deserve notice because of their merit and/or the uses critics have made of them. A good deal of comment has resulted from Hayek's edition of five articles Mill wrote for the *Examiner* in 1831, *The Spirit of the Age* (1942). As yet less attention has been given to Bernard Wishy's *Prefaces to Liberty: Selected Writings of John Stuart Mill* (1959), a very useful collection of newspaper and periodical writings bearing on individual freedom. Ruth Borchard's *Four Dialogues of Plato* (1946) reprints the translations and notes, mentioned above, that Mill published in the *Monthly Repository*. There are also two reprints of economic materials, *John Stuart Mill on the Protection of Infant Industries*, with a preface by Hugh Elliot (the first editor of Mill's letters, 2 vols., 1910) and an introduction by James Bonar (1911); and Jacob Harry Hollander's *John Stuart Mill: Two Letters on the Measure of Value* (1936), which brings together Mill's first published writings and the comments of Robert Torrens on them.

A curious item that deserves special mention is Dorothy Fosdick's edition of *On Social Freedom* (1941). She reprinted the essay from the *Oxford and Cambridge Review* (1907), where it was attributed to Mill, the manuscript having been bought at the Avignon sale of Mill's effects in 1905. The incompatibility of the argument in this work with that in *On Liberty* led to some hesitation among Mill scholars, who were generally gratified when it was proved not to be by Mill in John C. Rees's *Mill and His Early Critics* (1956); see also Maurice Cranston's review of Rees, "Illiberal Tract Proved Spurious" (*Manchester Guardian*, 9 June 1956). But references to the work continue to appear in Mill criticism, it having been argued that Mill should have written such a work, and also that reading it against *On Liberty* reveals more about the genuine work. (And many library catalogs continue to list *On Social Freedom* as by Mill.)

The earliest anthology of Mill's writings was J. W. M. Gibbs's *Early Essays by John Stuart Mill* (1897), which first brought to critical attention Mill's reviews of Tennyson's *Poems* and Carlyle's *French Revolution* (neither included in *Dissertations and Discussions*), and his "Remarks on Bentham's Philosophy" which had been buried as an appendix to Bulwer's *England and the English*. Two widely used anthologies with valuable introductions are Alexander Dunlop Lindsay's *John Stuart Mill: Utilitarianism, Liberty, and Representative Government* (1910, with many reprintings) and R. B. McCallum's *On Liberty and Considerations on Representative Government* (1946). Harold Laski's edition of the *Autobiography* (1924, with many reprintings), though its text (that of the first edition) is now superseded, still gives the most available form of six of Mill's debating speeches.

In more recent years there has been a flood of anthologies, demonstrating the new interest in Mill and the forms that interest takes. Gertrude Himmelfarb's *Essays on Politics and Culture* (1962) reflects its title and its editor's interests in concentrating on the tension between conservative and liberal elements in Mill's thought; it has special textual interest in that it prints the earlier rather than the later version of essays that Mill revised for *Dissertations and Discussions*, with selected variants. A similar focus is found in Maurice Cowling's *Selected Writings of John Stuart Mill* (1968). The introductions of both contain significant comment on Mill's social and political views. Max Lerner's *Essential Works of J. S. Mill* (1961) and Albert W. Levi's *Six Great Humanistic Essays of John Stuart Mill* (1963) concentrate on the main texts and have no special merit. Jerome B. Schneewind's edition of *Mill's Ethical Writings* (1965) has a perceptive introduction, and brings together some less frequently cited sources that are now attracting attention from philosophers. The most satisfying textual work is shown in Jack Stillinger's edition of the *Autobiography and Other Writings* (1969; Stillinger's introd. with the text of the *Autobiography* was published separately at the same time); this edition supersedes, by correcting the readings of, John J. Coss's edition (1924) of the Columbia holograph manuscript of the *Autobiography*, and gives reliable readings of *On Liberty* and some other essays. Robson's *John Stuart Mill: A Selection of His Works* (1966) brings together with some of the major texts a selection from his lesser works that bear upon the central issues dealt with in the introduction. Of special interest to literary students are Edward Alexander's *John Stuart Mill: Literary Essays* (1967) and Schneewind's *Mill's Essays on Literature and Society* (1965), which have similar contents and good introductions. It is to be regretted that so many of these anthologies, prepared by some of the most prominent Mill scholars, should have overlapped in contents and in time, for cooperation would have made it possible to reprint in inexpensive format other important essays by Mill.

There have been, of course, many reprintings of single works. In general, these need not be mentioned, but, partly because interest in one work appears likely to increase, reference should be made to Alice S. Rossi's edition of *The Subjection of Women*, which appears in *John Stuart Mill and Harriet Taylor Mill: Essays in Sex Equality* (1970), with two early comments by Harriet Taylor and Mill on marriage and divorce (rpt. from Hayek's *John Stuart Mill and Harriet Taylor*) and Harriet Taylor's "The Enfranchisement of Women." Rossi's hastily researched introduction is less informative and instructive than that of Wendell Robert Carr, in his edition of *The Subjection of Women* (1970), which dwells more on the content and intellectual context.

In the *Collected Works*, Textual Introductions, with headnotes for the separate items, discuss the texts. (The procedures are outlined in Robson's "Principles and Methods in the Collected Edition of John Stuart Mill" in *Editing Nineteenth-Century Texts*, 1967.) Before the Collected Edition, there was almost no careful study of Mill's texts, the major exceptions being Stillinger's precise and masterful work on the *Autobiography* (see his "The Text of John Stuart Mill's *Autobiography*," *BJRL*, 1960, and his introd. to the *Early Draft of John Stuart Mill's* Autobiography), and Anna J. Mill's detailed presentation of the text in *John Mill's Boyhood Visit to France*. An interesting preparatory study of the textual variants in the *Principles of Political Economy* by Miriam A. Ellis (*Econ. J.*, 1906) led to the preparation of the deservedly well-known edition by W. J. Ashley (1909, and reprints), which records many of the most significant variants; this work is discussed by Robson in his Textual Introduction to the *Principles* (rpt. in O M Brack, Jr. and Warner Barnes, eds., *Bibliography and Textual Criticism: English and American Literature 1700 to the Present*, 1969). In his *Development of Mill's System of Logic* (Illinois Studies in the Social Sciences, 1932), Oskar A. Kubitz, though he terminates his study with the first edition, presents valuable work toward a textual study, which has, however, not yet been done. John B. Ellery (Diss. Wisconsin 1954) gathers the majority of Mill's speeches, but both the text and the commentary leave much to be desired, and a large number of speeches are omitted.

II. SURVEY OF CRITICAL RESPONSE

The easiest way to assess the extent and areas of the published response to Mill's writings is to consult the chronological listing in the *New Cambridge Bibliography of English Literature*, III, edited by George Watson (1969). As will be seen, during Mill's lifetime the most consistent response was prompted by his *Logic* (1843), though his *Examination of Sir William Hamilton's Philosophy* (1865) produced more, and more hostile, comment. Both these works, in editions subsequent to the first, include Mill's answers to his critics, and, with his ethical writings, may be considered as embodying his attack, from a utilitarian and empirical basis, on intuitionist and a priori philosophies, representatives of which (esp. Whewell and Ward) responded to the attack. His *Principles of Political Economy* (1848), which like the *Logic* became a standard textbook, was comparatively less attacked, as is indicated by the relatively fewer answers to critics in the revised editions. Other works that later received much attention, especially *On Liberty* (1859) and *Considerations on Representative Government* (1861), while they were widely read and appreciated, did not for a time receive much attention except in reviews; *On Liberty* was attacked on specific points, particularly by advocates of temperance who were annoyed by Chapter v. The main response to such works as *Auguste Comte and Postivism* (1865) and *The Subjection of Women* (1869) was from specially interested individuals. But by the time of their publication, as a result of the publicity attendant on his parliamentary career (1865–68), and especially on his election in 1865 and his defeat in 1868, Mill was becoming recognized as the major British philosopher of his time. The consequent interest in his works and life prepared for the wide and warm response demonstrated after his death in 1873 in obituary notices and surveys. (It should be noted that the generation of writers and public figures coming into prominence in the seventies, many of whom had met Mill, had, in the universities and elsewhere, read widely in his work.)

After a few years, the normal revisionism set in, as new speculations in philosophy and political economy challenged Mill's views; a glance at the *NCBEL* will show how much more attention was given to Herbert Spencer in the closing years of the nineteenth century. Still, Mill's works continued in print, and there was a strong academic concern with his philosophy in Europe, particularly in Germany. At the time of the centenary of his birth, in 1906, and with Hugh Elliot's edition of the *Letters*, in 1910, there were flurries of interest, and through these years the Fabians, who claimed him as a forerunner, kept up his reputation in Britain. With the general repudiation of Victorianism, however, during and after World War I, Mill's stock declined still further; discussions of his thought, mainly concentrating on his political philosophy, appeared frequently, but were usually condescendingly critical.

In the mid-twenties, the London School of Economics acquired the bulk of Mill's extant papers from the sale of the estate of Mary Taylor, his step granddaughter. (The level of interest in Mill may be gauged by comparing the ridiculously low prices obtained for his papers with the inflated prices got for Carlyle's at the same Sotheby's sales. Even now Carlyle's letters sell for considerably more than Mill's, but the narrower margin may be taken to reflect the comparative literary value of their letters.) The material at the London School of Economics, now called the Mill-Taylor Collection, provided the basis for modern Mill scholarship, which may be said to begin with Harold Laski's interest. Laski, who knew some of those who had been directly influenced by Mill, such as John Morley, bought the manuscripts of Mill's debating speeches at a Sotheby's sale, and, as already noted, prepared them for publication in various journals (he planned but never produced an edition for the Fabian Society), and published six speeches in his edition of the *Autobiography*. (See also his letters to Holmes, which reveal, as did his teaching and his voluminous writings, his concern with Mill.)

In the mid-thirties James McCrimmon found in the Mill-Taylor Collection the bibliography of published writings prepared by Mill, eventually published in 1945. Early in the 1940's Hayek emerged as the main force in Mill scholarship, as, basing his work on the Mill-Taylor Collection and on the other collections deriving from Mill's estate at the Brotherton Library (Leeds), Yale, and Johns Hopkins, he began work toward the publication of Mill's correspondence. He edited two important volumes, *The Spirit of the Age* (1942) and (a crucial document in recent Mill studies) *John Stuart Mill and Harriet Taylor: Their Friendship and Subsequent Marriage* (1951; the American ed. is mistakenly subtitled *Their Correspondence and Subsequent Marriage*). Hayek's work led to further biographical study, capped by Michael St. J. Packe's *The Life of John Stuart Mill* (1954).

Since then there has been a constantly increasing interest in Mill's life and thought, witnessed already in the discussion of editions above, and demonstrated in more detail in the following sections of this chapter.

III. BIOGRAPHICAL AND RELATED STUDIES

Packe's biography may be taken as the standard, though not fully definitive, work on Mill's life as a whole, superseding the slighter prior studies by William L. Courtney (1889) and Mary A. Hamilton (1933), as well as going beyond the subsequent studies by Ruth Borchard (1957), Maurice Cranston (1958), and John B. Ellery (1964). Borchard's book in some ways supplements Packe's, but should be read with caution as to interpretation; Ellery's in the Twayne English Authors series brings in some detail from his work on Mill's speeches, but is shot through with errors; Cranston's short study, in the series of supplements to *British Book News* (available also in Vol. II of Bonamy Dobrée's *British Writers and Their Work*), is, within its narrowly defined limits, a valuable preliminary guide.

Apart from Packe's *Life*, only one discussion of Mill's whole career still merits close attention: Alexander Bain's *John Stuart Mill. A Criticism: With Personal Recollections* (1882), which should be read with his *James Mill: A Biography* (1882) and his *Autobiography* (1904). Bain, Mill's younger philosophical ally, and in many respects his closest disciple, did much original research for his *James Mill*, which is still the only comprehensive treatment of a man too much neglected. As its subtitle indicates, Bain's *John Stuart Mill* is a much less full treatment, possibly because Bain's relations with Mill's stepdaughter and heir, Helen Taylor, were permanently ruptured shortly after Mill's death, and he was cut off from sources that he knew to exist and be important. (One of the great losses to Mill scholars, it should be noted, is the mass of material in Bain's hands when he wrote these works; numerous inquiries have led to no finds of importance, though some of Bain's papers are in the library of King's College, Aberdeen.) All three of Bain's books remain important because, though Packe uses them for detail, Bain's appreciative but not adulatory views are based on an intimacy with Mill's thought and career that cannot now be matched.

Packe's *Life* draws on a wide acquaintance with the manuscript sources not available to earlier biographers, and on a good survey of other materials. Its main outlines are firm, and while his desire to draw together themes results in occasional vagueness concerning dates, the tale is in general reliably and pleasantly told. The interspersed discussions of Mill's thought are not so valuable, especially when they reflect one of Packe's main themes, Mill's reliance on his wife's practical and theoretical guidance, which gives the work a romantic flavor only partly justified by the evidence. Some new biographical data have come to light since Packe's book appeared, but as yet its place is secure as the best account of Mill's life.

When one turns to more circumscribed biographical discussions, the view is clouded by the intermixture of life and thought that properly characterizes most studies of Mill. Therefore the best approach for the student of literature and the history of ideas is to survey the criticism in groups based on the chronology of his career.

Early Life to 1826

For a variety of reasons, including the account in his *Autobiography*, the early gossip and wonder about his education, and the importance in British political life of his early associates, a great deal of interest has been shown in Mill's relations with the Philosophic Radicals, who are discussed in all accounts of the background of the great Reform Bill of 1832. The main influences on him in these years were those of his father, the historian of British India, economist, philosopher, and propagandist for the Philosophic Radicals, and of Jeremy Bentham, legal philosopher and reformer, whose writings, almost as diversified as those of the younger Mill, define the practical aspects of early utilitarianism. For the movement, and John Mill's place in it, one should consult Elie Halévy's magisterial *La Formation du radicalisme philosophique* (3 vols., 1901–04; trans. Mary Morris as *The Growth of Philosophic Radicalism*, 1928; rpt. 1952) and Leslie Stephen's three-volume *The English Utilitarians* (1900; rpt. 1950) the final volume of which, *John Stuart Mill*, is the first major study of a wide range of Mill's thought. Other studies retaining value are C. B. Roylance Kent's *The English Radicals* (1899); Andrew Seth Pringle-Pattison's *The Philosophical Radicals* (1907); Robert S. Dower's "John Stuart Mill and the Philosophical Radicals," in *The Social and Political Ideas of Some Representative Thinkers of the Age of Reaction and Reconstruction, 1815–65*, edited by Fossey John Cobb Hearnshaw (1932; rpt. 1949); and S. Maccoby's *English Radicalism, 1832–1852* (1935). The most recent study, Joseph Hamburger's *Intellectuals in Politics: John Stuart Mill and the Philosophic Radicals* (1965), moves beyond the early years of Mill, as do most of the other studies mentioned above, and gives much the fullest record of the group's activities in the 1830's. Hamburger's discussion of the role of ideology in the movement, which had prompted some rebuttal, reflects current thought on the subject, as well as providing detailed analysis of the activities of the Philosophic Radicals. (It should be read with Hamburger's *James Mill and The Art of Revolution*, 1963.)

Mill's relations with his father, dealt with in Halévy, Stephen, and Hamburger, are more fully covered in Bain and Packe, and are further illuminated in other biographies dealing with prominent Philosophic Radicals, such as Graham Wallas' *Life of Francis Place* (1898; rpt. 1919), or R. E. Leader's *Life and Letters of John Arthur Roebuck* (1897). Interesting detailed information is given in Anna Mill's *John Mill's Boyhood Visit to France*. A fascination with James Mill's educational experiment on his son has been in evidence since the publication of the *Autobiography*. Most of the early accounts are merely summaries of Mill's own description, interspersed with exclamations of wonder or horror. Given the terms of that experiment, it is difficult to estimate just how great Mill's undoubted intellectual abilities were; it is interesting, but hardly conclusive, to find him ranked by Catherine M. Cox, in *The Early Mental Traits of Three Hundred Geniuses* (Genetic Studies of Genius, 1926), at the very top, with an estimated IQ of about 200. A fairly comprehensive review of the evidence concerning Mill's education, not however departing from the standard interpretations found in biographies, may be seen in Ian Cumming, *A Manufactured Man: The Education of John Stuart Mill* (Auckland Univ. Bull., No. 55, 1960).

Discussions of Bentham's relations with John Mill, in the works on Philosophic Radicalism cited, have mainly concentrated on the intellectual inheritance

(Bentham and James Mill explicitly claimed the younger Mill as their philosophic and political heir); references to the problem of Mill's adherence to, or departure from, Bentham's views will be found below in the sections dealing with philosophy and politics. One valuable discussion may be mentioned here, though: Jacob Viner's "Bentham and J. S. Mill: The Utilitarian Background" in his *The Long View and the Short: Studies in Economic Theory and Policy* (1958), which goes beyond the title in coverage. So far as the personal relations between Bentham and Mill are concerned, the fullest account to date is in Robson's "John Stuart Mill and Jeremy Bentham, with Some Observations on James Mill" in *Essays in English Literature from the Renaissance to the Victorian Age, Presented to A. S. P. Woodhouse* (ed. Millar MacLure and Frank W. Watt, 1964).

Mill's relations with the other Philosophic Radicals have not received the attention they deserve, but material will be found in biographies of George Grote, Edwin Chadwick, William Molesworth, Albany Fonblanque, and other associates, as well as in those of Place and Roebuck already mentioned. The initially close association between Mill and Roebuck has received separate attention in Francis E. Hyde's "Utility and Radicalism, 1825–37: A Note on the Mill-Roebuck Friendship" (*Econ. Hist. Rev.*, 1946), but, like other such associations (esp. those with Grote and Chadwick, which were lifelong), needs more study.

Another matter needing more study is Mill's brush with authority resulting from his distribution of birth-control literature in the early 1820's. The fullest account of the episode, exact details of which are not known, is in Peter Fryer's *The Birth Controllers* (1965); two articles by Norman E. Himes, "The Place of John Stuart Mill and of Robert Owen in the History of English Neo-Malthusianism" (*Q. J. of Econ.*, 1928), and "John Stuart Mill's Attitude towards Neo-Malthusianism" (*Econ. Hist.*, 1929), give contextual focus. More evidence, especially bearing on the effect of the episode, which was common gossip in the clubs, on Mill's social relations is discussed in Mineka's "John Stuart Mill and Neo-Malthusianism, 1873" (*MNL*, 1972). Here one finds reference to the acrimonious exchanges after his death, resulting from the *Times*'s obituary (10 May 1873) by Abraham Hayward, whose dislike for Mill went back to the days of the London Debating Society in the late 1820's. William D. Christie's *John Stuart Mill and Mr. Abraham Hayward, Q.C.: A Reply about Mill to a Letter to the Rev. Stopford Brooke* (1873) provides one side of this dispute, which led to Gladstone's withdrawal of his name from the committee seeking a Westminster Abbey burial for Mill.

Middle Years, 1826–40

Since the publication of Hayek's studies increasing attention has been paid to the middle period of Mill's life, from the time of his mental depression (1826–27) and subsequent revaluation of his inheritance and personal powers, till the publication of his essay on Coleridge (1840) and the completion of his *Logic*.

Probably the most frequently discussed episode in Mill's life is his "mental crisis," as critics have tried to explain the causes and effects of this turning point in his career. (See his own classic account in the *Autobiography*, on which all other accounts are based.) Early discussions of the causes emphasized overwork and the sterility of the Benthamite philosophy, but with the first discussion of the Early Draft of the *Autobiography* by Albert William Levi, attention has turned to a psychological explanation, based on Mill's subconscious rebellion against his father.

The basic account is in Levi's "The Mental Crisis of John Stuart Mill" (*PsyR*, 1945); a further discussion of interest is in Lewis S. Feuer's *Psychoanalysis and Ethics*, 1955. Himmelfarb, in her introduction to *Essays on Politics and Culture by John Stuart Mill*, adds an interpretation of the effect of James Mill's death in 1836 on his son's emotional and practical life. Further examinations of the effect of the crisis on Mill's thought have mostly taken his recognition of the need for poetic and emotional culture as their departure point, and so are mentioned in the section on literature below.

In the years surrounding his crisis, Mill took part in organized discussions and debates in a variety of groups, including the Mutual Improvement Society, the Utilitarian Society, the Co-operative Debating Society, the London Debating Society, and the Society of Students of Mental Philosophy that met at Grote's house for discussion. More is known of the last two of these than of the others, and only concerning the London Debating Society is there anything approaching a record of Mill's contributions. The main body of his debating speeches derives from the meetings of that society; a list of these, which have as yet received only incidental treatment, is given, with publication data, in the above-mentioned article by Britton and Robson (*MNL*, 1965). Since then one more manuscript has been discovered and published; see "On the Character of Catiline," edited by Michael Laine (*MNL*, 1972). The debating speech of most literary interest is treated in Britton's "J. S. Mill: A Debating Speech on Wordsworth" (*Cambridge Rev.*, 1958); and Britton considers a related matter in "J. S. Mill and the Cambridge Union Society" (*Cambridge Rev.*, 1955). Mill's acquaintance with Wordsworth is outlined in Anna J. Mill's "John Stuart Mill's Visit to Wordsworth, 1831" (*MLR*, 1949), based on one of Mill's journals of walking tours in these years with his friends (including Henry Cole, William Ellis, and Horace Grant). Dr. Mill, who is editing these journals for the *Collected Edition*, deals with an episode from one of them in "Another of J. S. Mill's Reticences" (*MNL*, 1968), and on Mill's early relations with Cole (*MNL*, 1969), supplying inter alia new evidence of his musical interests.

Given his developing passion for artistic and cultural matters, and his acquaintance through the London Debating Society with many of the most important young men in London society and literature, it is not surprising that Mill became known to Wordsworth, Coleridge, Southey, and other members of their circle in the early 1830's. But his movement into a wider social group than that of the early utilitarians was frustrated by the rumors and rebukes, extremely distasteful to him, resulting from his meeting and falling in love with Harriet Taylor, a young married woman with three children. While he did not disappear from public view, he saw much less of his early associates, and moved for a few years (roughly 1830 to 1834) into association with the Unitarian group, including Harriet Taylor and her husband John, centering on William Johnson Fox; he wrote extensively for Fox's *Monthly Repository*, while still keeping his more orthodox radical contacts through the *Examiner* newspaper. This period is most interestingly covered in Hayek, and in Mineka's *The Dissidence of Dissent: The* Monthly Repository, *1806–38* (1944).

The influence on Mill exercised by Harriet, whom he married in 1851 after her husband's death in 1849, has taken a place of unusual importance in many comments. Mill is himself responsible for the fascination with this question, for he praised her so highly during her life and after her death in 1858 that critics have felt compelled to question his judgment. Those who knew her (and they were few, for after their marriage as well as before they saw little company together) were sure that Mill exaggerated both her powers of intellect and her role in his work. Bain summarizes such judgments, but he himself never met her. Desultory comment, some of it strongly adverse, from the publication of the *Autobiography* (1873) until the 1940's, focused on the strength of Mill's attachment, without new evidence by which to test his statements. Examples are S. E. Henshaw's disapproving "John Stuart Mill and Mrs. Taylor" (*The Overland Monthly*, 1874); Elbert Hubbard's *John Stuart Mill and Harriet Taylor* (1906), which deserves to be remembered if only because of the title of the series in which it appeared, Little Journeys to Homes of Great Lovers; M. Ashworth's "The Marriage of John Stuart Mill" (*Englishwoman*, 1916); and Guy L. Diffenbaugh's "Mrs. Taylor Seen through Other Eyes than John Stuart Mill's" (*SR*, 1923). Of special interest, though biased and far from conclusive, are Mary Taylor's comments in "A Note on Mill's Private Life" in Elliot's edition of the *Letters*, and "Mrs. J. S. Mill: A Vindication by Her Granddaughter" (*NC*, 1912). With the publication of Hayek's *John Stuart Mill and Harriet Taylor* in 1951, new epistolary and other evidence changed the terms of the discussion. Hayek's assertion that she had a very great influence on Mill, especially in returning him to rationalism from romanticism, was amplified by Packe, who argued that her influence was even greater than Mill said it was. This contention has not satisfied others. H. O. Pappé (*John Stuart Mill and the Harriet Taylor Myth*, 1960; see also John Rees's review, *Pol. Stud.*, 1962), Jack Stillinger (introd. to *The Early Draft*), Francis E. Mineka ("The *Autobiography* and the Lady," *UTQ*, 1963), and John M. Robson ("Harriet Taylor and John Stuart Mill: Artist and Scientist," *QQ*, 1966) have all challenged this view, arguing that the evidence is not sufficient to justify either Mill's own or Hayek's and Packe's claims, and that other explanations of Mill's belief in her abilities are more persuasive than the attempted proofs that she had the abilities he ascribes to her.

Two other associations made in these years have also received considerable attention: those with the Saint-Simonians and with Thomas Carlyle. Both are dealt with in Richard Pankhurst's *The Saint Simonians, Mill and Carlyle* (1957), but are more carefully analyzed in Lindley's "The Saint-Simonians, Carlyle, and Mill: A Study in the History of Ideas" (Diss. Columbia 1958). On the Saint-Simonians one should also consult Hill Shine's "J. S. Mill and an Open Letter to the Saint-Simonian Society in 1832" (*JHI*, 1945), with a reply by J. R. Hainds, "John Stuart Mill and the Saint-Simonians" (*JHI*, 1946), and Lindley's "John Stuart Mill: The Second Greatest Influence" (*VN*, 1957). Concerning Carlyle, most of the major studies of Mill have something to say (see also below, Literature), but the major study is still Emery Neff's *Carlyle and Mill: An Introduction to Victorian Thought* (1926; the first ed., 1924, was subtitled *Mystic and Utilitarian*). Carlyle's side of his extensive correspondence with Mill is found in Alexander Carlyle's edition of *Letters of Thomas Carlyle to John Stuart Mill, John Sterling, and Robert Browning* (1923). A slight but pleasant comparison is in Anna J. Mill's *Carlyle and Mill: Two Scottish University Rectors* (1966).

Two other important influences on Mill in the thirties, those of Alexis de Tocqueville and Auguste Comte, have attracted similar attention. The former, especially in recent years, has been looked at carefully by students of de Tocqueville as well as of Mill. The best accounts are in H. O. Pappé's "Mill and Tocqueville" (*JHI*, 1964) and in Jack Lively's *The Social and Political Thought of Alexis de Tocqueville* (1962), both of which bring out the mutual respect and influence of the two great commentators on democratic tendencies. Also of value are Jacob-

Peter Mayer's *Alexis de Tocqueville* (1960) and T. H. Qualter's "John Stuart Mill, Disciple of de Tocqueville" *WPQ*, 1960). The correspondence is in Volume VI of Mayer's edition of de Tocqueville's *Œuvres* (1954).

The relations between Mill and Comte, on the other hand, have not aroused nearly so much interest in recent years. The early comments, however, retain much interest, as they generally were prompted by strong distaste among Comte's disciples at Mill's criticisms of the "founder of sociology." The earliest is Hippolyte Taine's generally laudatory *Le Positivisme anglais, étude sur Stuart Mill* (1864; trans. T. D. Haye, 1870). The publication of Mill's *Auguste Comte and Positivism* (1865) brought forth Emile Littré's *Auguste Comte et Stuart Mill* and G. Wyrouboff's *Stuart Mill et la philosophie positive* (bound together, 1866), John H. Bridges' *The Unity of Comte's Life and Doctrine: A Reply to Strictures on Comte's Later Writings, Addressed to J. S. Mill* (1866), and George Henry Lewes' "Comte and Mill" (*FortR*, 1866). Thomas Whittaker's *Comte and Mill* (1908; rpt. in his *Reason: A Philosophical Essay with Historical Illustrations*, 1934) is contentious, and the judgments of Frederic Harrison, for example in his *On Society* (1918), are valuable because of his intimate knowledge of the thought of both men. Robson devotes a section of his *The Improvement of Mankind: The Social and Political Thought of John Stuart Mill* (1968) to Comte (as well as sections to Carlyle, the Saint-Simonians, Coleridge, and de Tocqueville). David H. Lewisohn has some interesting comments on a central question in "Mill and Comte on the Methods of Social Science" (*JHI*, 1972). Mill's lengthy and detailed letters to Comte are, of course, in *Earlier Letters*, while both sides of the correspondence may be found in *Lettres inédites de John Stuart Mill à Auguste Comte*, edited by Lucien Lévy-Bruhl (1899); a translation would be useful for many students.

The influence on Mill of the French thinkers mentioned above, and of contemporary French history, especially the revolutions of 1830 and 1848, is given comparative treatment in Iris W. Mueller's *John Stuart Mill and French Thought* (1956). She argues that French influence can be placed second only to Benthamite influence in establishing the main lines of Mill's thought, and presents cogent evidence to establish her case. Still more might be adduced, for her coverage of the French historians on whom Mill wrote important essays (see *Dissertations and Discussions*) is not full enough, and in other places the account is slightly hasty. Nonetheless, her work is an important contribution in an understudied area.

One other work dealing with this middle period of Mill's life is essential reading, not least because it provides a rare insight into one of Mill's closest friendships, that with John Sterling, which is very meagerly documented elsewhere. This is Caroline Fox's *Memories of Old Friends*, edited by Horace Pym (1882), which gives an intimate record of Mill's talk and behavior during the time when his beloved younger brother, Henry, was dying.

Maturity and Fame, 1840–73

Discussions of Mill's thought relate mainly to the years after the publication of his first book, the *Logic*, and as already indicated they tend to focus on specific areas of his work; they are therefore outlined in the sections on his philosophy, economics, and literary criticism. Some topics more closely related to biography have, however, been treated by critics, though most of them require more examination which should be greatly facilitated by the publication of the *Later Letters*.

Mill's career in the East India Company, for example, has not called forth much comment, though he worked for the Company from 1823, when he joined his father in the Examiner's office as a clerk, until 1858 when he retired, on the Crown's taking over the Company, as Chief Examiner. There are some references in Eric Stokes's *The English Utilitarians and India* (1959), and a chapter in George B. Bearce's *British Attitudes towards India, 1784–1858* (1961), but the best treatment is in Abram L. Harris' "John Stuart Mill: Servant of the East India Company" (*CJEPS*, 1964).

Work still remains to be done on Mill's support for the North in the American Civil War, separately treated in John D. Waller's "John Stuart Mill and the American Civil War" (*BNYPL*, 1962). In this context it might also be mentioned that the correspondence of John E. Cairnes with Mill (in the Mill-Taylor Collection) contains much on this subject, which is, of course, mentioned in the biographies.

One curiously underexamined area is Mill's parliamentary career, 1865–68, the period of the Second Reform Bill, when he gave his support to many unpopular causes, such as woman suffrage (which he brought into serious parliamentary discussion for the first time), and when he expanded his knowledge of working-class ideas and motives. Again the biographies give the outlines, and John Vincent's *The Formation of the Liberal Party, 1857–68* (1966) has some extended comment. But much still may be gleaned from contemporary sources, including the campaign article written by William Dougal Christie, "Mr. John Stuart Mill for Westminster" (*Macmillan's*, 1865).

During this period Mill took a leading part in the agitation against Governor Eyre of Jamaica, who ruthlessly suppressed a Negro revolt in the island. The strength of feeling on this issue, which brought into conflict the prominent liberals and conservatives, may be seen in the contemporary account by a strong Eyre supporter, William F. Finlason, in *History of the Jamaica Case* (2nd ed., 1869), in which Mill plays a villainous role. More recent and sympathetic discussions will be seen in George H. Ford's "The Governor Eyre Case in England" (*UTQ*, 1948) and in Bernard Semmel's *The Governor Eyre Controversy* (1962).

Other subjects that need examination are his part in the movements for women's education and enfranchisement (Constance Rover's treatment in *Women's Suffrage and Party Politics in Britain, 1866–1914*, 1967, is, even given the book's prime focus, seriously deficient), his role in the Land Tenure Reform Association (see Vol. v of the *Collected Works*), and, of less significance, his lifelong career as an amateur botanist.

Mill bought a house in Avignon after his wife's death there in 1858, and henceforth spent about half of each year in the south of France, almost always with his stepdaughter, Helen Taylor, who came to occupy a place in his regard close to that of her mother. Their life there is treated by Packe in some detail, and although there is no separate study in English, several short French accounts are useful, Louis Rey's being the most significant: *Le Roman de John Stuart Mill* (1913; trans. in *NC*, 1913); *John Stuart Mill en Avignon* (1921); and "Souvenirs sur J. Stuart Mill" (*Annales de l'Ecole Palatin d'Avignon*, 1922). Further accounts include Marc de Vissac, "John Stuart Mill" (*Mémoires de l'Académie de Vaucluse*, 1905); Alfred Dumas, "Stuart Mill et Mistral" (*Mémoires de l'Académie de Vaucluse*, 1927); Jules Véran, "Le Souvenir de Stuart Mill à Avignon" (*RDM*, 1937); and, in connection with Mill's friend, the naturalist Fabre, Jules Charles-Roux, *J.-H. Fabre en Avignon* (1913).

A promising area for at least brief examination lies in Mill's contact with and influence on the generation coming to maturity in the years when his great works appeared, many of whom came to know him. The group includes Alexander Bain, Herbert Spencer, Henry and Millicent Fawcett, Charles Dilke, John Morley, Thomas Hare, Leslie Stephen, John Cairnes, and Lord and Lady Amberley. It is impossible to list all the quarries from which information might be mined, but various kinds of ore will be found in such sources as these: Leslie Stephen, "Some Early Impressions" (*Nat. Rev.*, 1903); George O'Brien, "J. S. Mill and J. E. Cairnes" (*Economica*, 1943); Jerome Hamilton Buckley, "The Revolt from Rationalism in the Seventies" (in *Booker Memorial Studies*, ed. Hill Shine, 1950); and Bertrand and Patricia Russell, *The Amberley Papers* (2 vols., 1937). In connection with the last named, one should also look at the judgment by the godson of Mill and Helen Taylor, the Amberleys' son, Bertrand Russell, in his *Portraits from Memory and Other Essays* (1956); Russell is of course of a later and more critical generation, but his reactions and tributes are significant not only because of his own eminence in fields cultivated by Mill, but also because of the familial association. (On this last matter, see Ann P. Robson, "Bertrand Russell and His Godless Parents," *Russell*, 1972.) One of the relations with a younger disciple has received separate treatment in Adelaide Weinberg's *Theodor Gomperz and John Stuart Mill* (1963), containing personal as well as intellectual details.

As a guide to Mill's reputation at his death—there has been no study of obituary notices—a gathering of commissioned articles in the *Examiner*, edited by Henry Richard Fox Bourne as *John Stuart Mill: Notices of His Life and Works* (1873), is of considerable interest; it includes discussions of many phases of his life and thought, by such friends and associates as William Thomas Thornton, Spencer, Cairnes, Fawcett, and Harrison.

IV. PHILOSOPHY

While Mill, as a representative of the British empirical school, and more especially as a representative of the ethical (utilitarian) and political (democratic) aspects of nineteenth-century empiricism, finds a major place in histories of British philosophy, there have been relatively few discussions of his philosophy as a whole. For a general view of Mill's place and reputation in the eyes of modern philosophers, the quickest and most reliable guide will be found in *The Encyclopaedia of Philosophy* edited by Paul Edwards (8 vols., 1967), in which not only the main essay on Mill (by Schneewind) but also the index and the bibliographies attached to the articles give a comprehensive guide to the literature. Also of value for their range and insight are John Passmore's *A Hundred Years of Philosophy* (2nd ed., 1968), Volume ii of John Herman Randall, Jr.'s *The Career of Philosophy* (1966), Volume viii of Frederick Copleston's *A History of Philosophy* (1966), and M. H. Carré's *Phases of Thought in England* (1949).

The range of coverage and the light cast on Mill's reputation by some of the early works on him give them continued value. The most general is the third volume of Leslie Stephen's *The English Utilitarians*, which covers the dominant, and many less central, themes; also of interest, especially in their comments on Mill's metaphysics, which is of less concern to more recent critics, are William George Ward's

The Philosophy of Theism (1884), the first volume of which contains Ward's numerous reviews of Mill's writings; William Leonard Courtney's *The Metaphysics of John Stuart Mill* (1879); Charles Mackinnon Douglas' *John Stuart Mill: A Study of His Philosophy* (1895); James McCosh's *An Examination of John Stuart Mill's Philosophy* (1866; 2nd ed., enl., 1877); and John Grote's *Exploratio Philosophica* (2 vols., 1865, 1900).

The four recent works of most value, dealing specifically with Mill, are Richard Paul Anschutz' *The Philosophy of John Stuart Mill* (1953), Karl Britton's *John Stuart Mill* (1953), Alan Ryan's *John Stuart Mill* (1970), and H. J. McCloskey's *John Stuart Mill: A Critical Study* (1971). Anschutz treats Mill's philosophy in general, with particular emphasis on the *Logic*, using an analytic approach that assumes a knowledge both of Mill and of the subjects treated. Pointing, like most other philosophers, to inconsistencies in Mill, he contends that realism and experientialism are mixed in his thought because he desired to promote practical reform and to oppose the intuitionists. Britton's book is wider ranging than Anschutz', being designed for a broader audience (it begins with a chapter on Mill's life), and incorporates a more sensitive and appreciative (though not exculpatory) reading of Mill. McCloskey's work, in the Philosophers in Perspective series, specifically designed for students, also has a brief (and somewhat inaccurate) summary of Mill's life, and devotes chapters to the major areas of Mill's philosophy. While providing a useful survey of topics of central interest to contemporary students, it is generally unsympathetic, attributing "strange" arguments to Mill. All three works are to be recommended, especially Britton's for the nonphilosopher, though none can stand against Ryan's more complete and sustained study, which, while it concentrates more closely than Britton's on purely philosophical questions, is based on a broad examination of questions contributing to, and growing out of, Mill's central philosophic concerns. Like Anschutz and Britton, Ryan discusses, but more fully than they, the metaphysics and psychology of Mill, and through a sharp but sympathetic reading in context, demonstrates the coherence, if not the consistency, of Mill's thought, and also makes more readily apparent the areas in that thought most relevant to contemporary philosophers.

This comparatively short list does not, of course, give a true view of the critical interest in Mill's philosophy. Such a view can emerge only after one has isolated the specific areas of concern.

Politics and Sociology

For nonphilosophers as well as for political philosophers, this is probably the most interesting area of Mill's thought, including as it does his most widely read work, *On Liberty*, as well as *Considerations on Representative Government* (still a useful guide to the subject), and other well-known essays. Because Mill is generally taken as the prime embodiment of nineteenth-century liberal thought and (more recently) ideology, surveys and discussions of the political and social philosophy of the period normally give considerable space to his writings. Representative summary treatments will be found, for example, in John Bowle, *Politics and Opinion in the Nineteenth Century* (1954); C. Crane Brinton, *English Political Thought in the Nineteenth Century* (1933; rpt. 1949); John Bagnell Bury, *A History of Freedom of Thought* (1913); George Catlin, *A History of the Political Philosophers* (1939); William L. Davidson, *Political Thought in England: The Utilitarians from Bentham to Mill* (1915, and later reprints); Hans Kohn, *Prophets and Peoples: Studies in Nineteenth-Century Nationalism* (1946); the first volume of Robert H. Murray's *Studies in English Social and Political Thinkers of the Nineteenth Century* (1929); George H. Sabine, *A History of Political Theory* (1937, and later eds.); and D. C. Somervell, *English Thought in the Nineteenth Century* (1929, and later eds.).

All these may be taken as standard surveys; other works giving considerable attention to Mill's political and social thought in special contexts include Angadipu-ram Appadorai, *Revision of Democracy* (1940); Christian Bay, *The Structure of Freedom* (1958); Albert V. Dicey, *Lectures on the Relationship between Law and Public Opinion in England during the Nineteenth Century* (1905; 2nd ed., 1914); Peter Winch, *The Idea of a Social Science* (1958); and Sheldon S. Wolin, *Politics and Vision* (1960).

Valuable early comparative studies by men directly in contact with Mill's ideas include Frederic Harrison's generally favorable *Tennyson, Ruskin, Mill* (1899); John MacCunn's *Six Radical Thinkers* (1907); and John M. Robertson's *Modern Humanists* (1895), which should be compared with his *Modern Humanists Reconsidered* (1927). Early negative criticisms that had wide influence will be found in David George Ritchie's *Principles of State Interference* (1891), which deals also with Spencer and Green, and Bernard Bosanquet's *Philosophical Theory of the State* (1899), a very strong attack.

Those who wish a fuller treatment of Mill's political and social views will find rich fields of comment, generally including the relations between his ethical and his political thought, and often touching on the relevant parts of his *Logic*, especially Book VI, "The Logic of the Moral Sciences." Robson's *The Improvement of Mankind* attempts to trace the development of Mill's ideas through the various periods of his life, drawing on a wide variety of his writings, and also to give clues to a comprehension of his thought as a whole. Ryan and Leslie Stephen cover the main points, Ryan more incisively; his discussion of *On Liberty* is especially rewarding. Apart from Robson, Ryan, and Stephen, the fullest treatment of the whole area is Levi's *A Study in the Social Philosophy of John Stuart Mill* (1940), which pioneers some aspects of the discussion of Book VI of the *Logic*. More recently two full discussions have appeared: Sobhanlal Mookerjea's *The Political Philosophy of John Stuart Mill* (1965) and Maurice Cowling's condemnatory *Mill and Liberalism* (1963), about which more in a moment.

The clearest and most concise account of Mill's views at different stages in his career, with considerable detail and careful attention to the qualifications he introduced into his advocacy of democracy, is J. H. Burns's "J. S. Mill and Democracy, 1829-61" in *Mill: A Collection of Critical Essays*, edited by Schneewind (1968). Other useful brief accounts, neither so widely nor biographically based, are Maurice Cranston's "J. S. Mill as a Political Philosopher" (*Hist. Today*, 1958) and Jacob S. Shapiro, "John Stuart Mill, Pioneer of Democratic Liberalism in England" (*JHI*, 1943).

In the more recent works cited, especially those by professional political philosophers, a concentration on analysis rather than summary leads to certain crucial issues, almost all centering on *On Liberty*. This concentration is justified by Mill's own attitude to the work; he expected it to be more enduring than his other writings because of the importance of individual liberty, which he believed to be increasingly threatened by social and political changes just beginning in the 1850's when he composed *On Liberty*. That his expectation has been fulfilled is borne out by the mass of critics who have commented on the theme, beloved of instructors, "the value of *On Liberty* today." Such comments are imbedded in most discussions of Mill's political thought, but some instances must be cited to demonstrate the point: Robert C. Binkley, "Mill's Liberty Today" (*Foreign Affairs*, 1938); Parley A. Christensen, "On Liberty in Our Time: Milton and Mill" (*WHR*, 1952); Harry W. Jones, "Freedom and Opportunity as Competing Social Values: Mill's Liberty and Ours," in *Liberty, Nomos* IV, edited by Carl J. Friedrich (1962; rpt. 1966); James D. Marwick, "John Stuart Mill and Liberty, and the Need for the Application of His Ideals in the Present State" (*Scottish Bankers' Mag.*, 1948); A. W. Levi, "The Value of Freedom: Mill's *Liberty* (1859–1959)" in *Limits of Liberty: Studies of Mill's* On Liberty, edited by Peter Radcliff (1966), which reflects a centennial view, as do Harry A. Holloway's "Mill's *Liberty*, 1859–1959" (*Ethics*, 1961; a reply to Levi); Emory K. Lindquist's twenty-four-page *John Stuart Mill's Essay on Liberty: A Centennial Review* (1959), and R. B. McCallum's "The Individual in the Mass: Mill on Liberty and the Franchise," a fine article in a fine book, *1859: Entering an Age of Crisis*, edited by Philip Appleman et al. (1959).

This sense of contemporary relevance colors discussions of Mill's defense of liberty because practice is (as Mill would agree it ought to be) closely allied to theory for most critics. From the first strong attack by James Fitzjames Stephen in his *Liberty, Equality, Fraternity* (1873; rpt. 1967), to those by such modern critics as Cowling and Willmoore Kendall ("The 'Open Society' and Its Fallacies" in Radcliff's collection), there has been an attempt to show the perniciousness of excessive demands for individual freedom and eccentricity. At the same time there has been a parallel, though not so strongly expressed, criticism of Mill for not stressing adequately the values of freedom from social control; this is seen in comments by George Grote quoted by the biographers and, in recent times, is implied in Henry D. Aiken's writings, including "Mill and the Justification of Social Freedom" in the *Nomos* IV volume and "Utilitarianism and Liberty: J. S. Mill's Defense of Freedom" in his *Reason and Conduct* (1962). Actually this strain is also seen in Cowling, who varies between attacks on Mill for being too liberal and for being not liberal enough. A similar tension is seen in Shirley R. Letwin's account in her *The Pursuit of Certainty: David Hume, Jeremy Bentham, John Stuart Mill, Beatrice Webb* (1965) which, though much more dispassionate than Cowling's, finds similar problems in Mill's attempts to reconcile his "puritan" inheritance with his desire to "contain the whole world in a single theory."

The most constant element in discussions of Mill's social views is the argument about his attempt to distinguish between self-regarding conduct (which should be free from legal and social restraint) and other-regarding conduct (which is properly liable to such restraint). Hardly a single commentator on *On Liberty* fails to deal with this distinction; and those who wish to evaluate current attitudes will find the issues debated from a wide variety of viewpoints in three recent collections, all cited above, those of Schneewind, Freidrich, and Radcliff. Schneewind's volume contains essays on many aspects of Mill's thought, especially concentrating on ethical issues, but it includes some essays, mentioned below, of special value on Mill's political and social views. *Liberty, Nomos* IV, the volume edited by Friedrich, concentrates more narrowly on the issues raised by *On Liberty*; it includes Arnold Brecht's "Liberty and Truth: The Responsibility of Science"; Andrew Hacker's "Freedom and Power: Common Man and Uncommon Men" (a broadly based comment on the tension between "aristocratic" and "democratic" principles in Mill); Frank H.

Knight's "Some Notes on Political Freedom and on a Famous Essay" (a strong attack on what Knight sees as Mill's failure, historically and analytically, to penetrate to the key questions); Albert A. Mavrinac's "Freedom, Authority, Conscience, and Development: Mill, Acton, and Some Contemporary Catholic Thinkers"; and Margaret Spahr's "Mill on Paternalism in Its Place" (taking issue in part with Aiken's essay in the same volume, and going on to discuss education, "backward societies," and the enfranchisement of women). One of the most useful essays in the volume is William Ebenstein's "John Stuart Mill: Political and Economic Liberty," which works through the problem of reconciling positive (or democratic) freedom with negative (or individual-social) freedom; sensitive to terms and attitudes, Ebenstein touches many points outside *On Liberty* in concluding that Mill's ultimate adherence is to negative freedom. The other is David Spitz's "Freedom and Individuality: Mill's *Liberty* in Retrospect," an able defense, beginning with citations of the strongest denunciations of Mill, and proceeding to demolish the worthless and to consider carefully the more valuable.

The least broad of the three collections, Radcliff's *Limits of Liberty*, is nonetheless useful in making readily available Stanley I. Benn and Richard Stanley Peters' "The Philosophical Problem of Liberty" from their *Social Principles and the Democratic State* (1959; rpt. as *Principles of Political Thought*, 1965); Isaiah Berlin's "The Notion of 'Negative' Freedom" from his *Two Concepts of Liberty* (1958), which should be read in conjunction with his *John Stuart Mill and the Ends of Life* (1960) and the essay by Ebenstein cited above; and H. L. A. Hart's "Paternalism and the Enforcement of Morality" extracted from his *Law, Liberty, and Morality* (1963). In Radcliff's volume one essay stands out for its value to the general discussion of Mill's political views: John C. Rees's "A Re-reading of Mill on Liberty" (rpt. from *Pol. Stud.*, 1960, with a "Postscript [1965]"). Here Rees, generally one of the most able commentators on Mill, deals with criticism of the self- and other-regarding distinction, claiming that critics have failed to give careful enough attention to Mill's wording, and particularly to his use of the term "interests" with reference to other-regarding conduct. On this matter one should also consider the views of R. J. Halliday, whose "Some Recent Interpretations of John Stuart Mill," in the Schneewind volume, deals primarily and intelligently with the interconnection of self- and other-regarding conduct; Halliday bases his discussion on what he considers the deficient accounts of Rees and Cowling.

The other issues in *On Liberty* central to modern concerns also emerge in a reading of these collections. They may be summarized as elitism and justification of freedom. Concerning the former, some commentators concentrate on isolating Mill's claims for the "clerisy" (Coleridge's term), the moral and intellectual elite, as properly leaders of the masses, necessary to progress and stability. Cowling, whose indictment is phrased in slightly more measured terms in his introduction to *Selected Writings of John Stuart Mill* and in the revised extracts from his *Mill and Liberalism* included in the volume edited by Schneewind, may be taken as the extreme proponent of this view of Mill; the critics of Cowling, especially Rees (see his "Was Mill for Liberty?" *Pol. Stud.*, 1966, and "The Reaction to Cowling on Mill," *MNL*, 1966), find distortion in his reading of Mill, particularly in his failure to bring together and reconcile the need for liberty and equality with that for good government. Attempts to deal with this problem are found in Ebenstein and others of the authors just cited, and more extensive treatments will be seen in the books by Robson and Ryan. A very significant contribution to the discussion is

Richard B. Friedman's "An Introduction to Mill's Theory of Authority," in the Schneewind volume, which hits at one of the basic points in the arguments of those who find elitist views at the base of Mill's thought. Such critics have argued that *The Spirit of the Age*, representing Saint-Simonian influence on Mill, and hence a departure from utilitarian notions of authority, is explained either as being incompatible with *On Liberty* or as showing that the later Mill was not so libertarian as is frequently thought (Friedman lists the proponents of these explanations). He counters them by an acute exposition of John Austin's orthodox utilitarian discussion of authority in his *Province of Jurisprudence Determined* (1832, based on lectures that began in 1829), which is compatible with both the *Spirit of the Age* and Mill's later writings. (Mill attended the lectures, and reviewed the work on its publication; he also contributed his lecture notes for the revised version of Austin's work published in 1861.) Friedman's discussion has special relevance because Austin's influence has been very little examined, and also because much of the recent discussion has turned on interpretations of Mill's view of liberty at different stages of his life. Cowling finds Mill comparatively consistent, but elitist; Gertrude Himmelfarb, in her introduction to *Essays on Politics and Culture*, argues for a more complicated development, locating an early, relatively conservative Mill, who reasserted himself in later life, after a middle period (1840–59) when the liberal Mill, dominated by Harriet Taylor, emerged. Both these views are countered ably by C. L. Ten, in "Mill and Liberty" (*JHI*, 1969), who concludes that "to reject, or radically modify, the traditional picture" of Mill "as the great liberal . . . would be a grave error."

The other central issue, Mill's justification of freedom, is also well explored in the three collections cited. The problem is that Mill in *On Liberty*, while eschewing any support from "natural rights," argues that individual liberty is a good because it contributes to the utilitarian summum bonum, general happiness, and also because it is an integral element in human self-development. Of the separate treatments of this question, the most useful is another essay by Friedman, "A New Exploration of Mill's Essay *On Liberty*" (*Pol. Stud.*, 1966), in which he asserts that while Mill uses inherited notions of liberty as freedom from interference, he (like de Tocqueville) also looks to the dangers of a society in which people do not desire to be free. In the one case, individual values are in question, and Mill's argument is specially concerned with, and directed to, the minority who continue to value freedom as a means to self-development; in the other case, the argument is directed to society as a whole, and here the basic element is the justifiable appeal to the greatest happiness which is furthered by individual liberty.

While the writings cited to this point cover the field, a more detailed survey should not overlook the following articles, each of which has its distinctive approach and contribution through analysis: Donald G. Brown, "Mill on Liberty and Morality" (*PhR*, 1972); John Patrick Day, "On Liberty and the Real Will" (*Philosophy*, 1970); Hilail Gildin, "Mill's *On Liberty*," in *Ancients and Moderns*, edited by Joseph Cropsey (1964); R. Lichtman, "Surface and Substance of Mill's Defense of Freedom" (*Social Research*, 1963); Henry M. Magid, "Mill and the Problem of Freedom of Thought" (*Social Research*, 1954); A. D. Megill, "J. S. Mill's Religion of Humanity and the Second Justification for the Writing of *On Liberty*" (*J. of Pol.*, 1972); H. J. McCloskey, "Mill's Liberalism" (*PhQ*, 1963, with a reply by Ryan, *PhQ*, 1964, and a rejoinder by McCloskey, *PhQ*, 1966); Rees, "A Phase in the Development of Mill's Ideas on Liberty" (*Pol. Stud.*, 1958); James P. Scanlan,

"J. S. Mill and the Definition of Freedom" (*Ethics*, 1958); Koenraad W. Swart, " 'Individualism' in the Mid-Nineteenth Century" (*JHI*, 1962) (on Mill and Carlyle); and Frank Thilly, "The Individualism of John Stuart Mill" (*PhR*, 1923).

Though the title of Mill's *Considerations on Representative Government* is known almost as well as that of *On Liberty*, the work itself has attracted far less direct and detailed comment. It is, of course, mentioned in all studies of the development of Mill's political thought, and is drawn on in all descriptions or criticisms of that thought, but in this mass of material it is hard to find anything, apart from such a slight comment as Enid Lakeman's "Centennial—Mill: *Representative Government*" (*ConR*, 1961), solely devoted to what is an important work in its own right. As it deals with the relations between individual citizens, their representatives, and political government as a whole, it naturally calls for comment by those primarily interested in *On Liberty*, and many of the articles cited on that work contain references to, and brief comments on, *Representative Government*. For the fullest discussions, however, one must look to the major studies of Mill's thought, already cited, such as Ryan and Robson.

Specific social and political issues, indicated by the titles of the works, are treated in the following, most of which stand alone: William Anderson, "John Stuart Mill and the Model City Charter" (*Nat. Municipal Rev.*, 1922); George Davy, "L'Explication sociologique et le recours à l'histoire, d'après Comte, Mill, et Durkheim" (*RMM*, 1949); R. Leroux, "Guillaume de Humboldt et J. Stuart Mill" (*EG*, 1951, 1952); Fritz Hippler, *Staat und Gesellschaft bei Mill, Marx, Lagardee* (1934); H. L. A. Hart and A. M. Honoré, "Philosophical Preliminaries," in their *Causation in the Law* (1959); Paul B. Kern, "Universal Suffrage without Democracy: Thomas Hare and John Stuart Mill" (*Rev. of Pol.*, 1972); Fred Kort, "The Issue of a Science of Politics in Utilitarian Thought" (*Amer. Pol. Sci. Rev.*, 1952); Kenneth E. Miller, "John Stuart Mill's Theory of International Relations" (*JHI*, 1961); Karl R. Popper, "The Autonomy of Sociology," in the Schneewind volume (extracted from *The Open Society and Its Enemies*); Susan M. Power, "Democracy, Representation, and John Stuart Mill" (*SUS*, 1965); Herbert Speigelberg, " 'Accident of Birth': A Non-Utilitarian Motif in Mill's Philosophy" (*JHI*, 1961); Richard H. Powers, "John Stuart Mill: Morality and Inequality" (*SAQ*, 1959); and Gordon A. Welty, "Mill's Principle of Government as a Basis of Democracy" (*Monist*, 1971).

Ethics

Mill's ethical thought has attracted nearly as much attention as his political thought, for here again he stands as a main figure in the principal British tradition, utilitarianism. Valuable early assessments of his thought, placing him in that tradition and relating his ethical thought to his philosophy generally, are to be found in John Grote's *An Examination of the Utilitarian Philosophy* (1870); in Charles M. Douglas' *The Ethics of John Stuart Mill* (1897), which combines a selection from Mill's writings with a long introductory essay; in Simon S. Laurie's *Notes Expository and Critical on Certain British Theories of Morals* (1868); in Leslie Stephen's book on Mill; and in Ernest Albee's *A History of English Utilitarianism* (1902), which argues that while utilitarianism is the most characteristic ethical theory in England, it is not as important as that represented by Bishop Butler. Also of continuing interest are the criticisms of Mill found in the major later Victorian ethical philosophers, such as Francis Herbert Bradley, *Ethical Studies* (1876); Henry Sidgwick, *The Methods of Ethics* (1874); and Thomas Hill Green, *Prolegomena to Ethics* (1883). As already indicated, the books by Anschutz, Britton, McCloskey, Robson, and especially Ryan place Mill's ethical thought in relation to other philosophic aspects of his work; and a concise, often harsh, and historically illuminating discussion is given by John Plamenatz in his *The English Utilitarians* (1949), which includes the text of *Utilitarianism*.

As Plamenatz among many others points out, the terms of ethical discussion altered with the work of George Edward Moore; most modern discussions of Mill, therefore, refer to, or implicitly take account of, Moore's *Principia Ethica* (1903; rpt. 1959), the first and third chapters of which are important for an understanding of contemporary criticism of Mill's ethics. Unfortunately for the student interested generally in Mill's thought, the modern concentration on conceptual analysis results in an isolation of various passages in Mill, especially in *Utilitarianism*, and thus in noncontextual evaluations of the concepts therein dealt with. This is not to say that the criticism is uniformly negative; in fact many of the numerous recent discussions are very favorable to Mill, stressing the inadequacy of Moore's critique. Perhaps the most careful of the analytic accounts is that of D. P. Dryer, in his introductory essay to Volume ten of the *Collected Works*. Three recent collections of essays demonstrate the range and complexity of these discussions: Schneewind's *Mill: A Collection of Critical Essays* (noted above as containing essays also on nonethical matters); *Mill's Utilitarianism: Text and Criticism*, edited by James M. Smith and Ernest Sosa (1969); and the special Mill issue of *Philosophy* (1968). Smith and Sosa, in addition to selections from Mill and extracts from Bentham, Moore, and Bradley, include five essays on Mill's ethics; there are also five in the special issue of *Philosophy* (one of which is more concerned with *On Liberty*); and seven in Schneewind's collection. There is overlapping among the volumes, worth mentioning here only as calling attention to clearly significant essays: Jean Austin's "Pleasure and Happiness" appears in all three, and the perceptive essays by J. O. Urmson ("The Interpretation of the Moral Philosophy of J. S. Mill") and J. D. Mabbott ("Interpretations of Mill's *Utilitarianism*") appear in Smith and Sosa, and in Schneewind. Further elucidation is to be found in another collection edited by Schneewind, *Mill's Ethical Writings*, where the editor's intelligent and broad selection from Mill is supplemented, as already noted, by his introductory summary of Mill's position and of critiques of that position, and by a useful bibliography (similar to the one he contributed to the *Encyclopaedia of Philosophy*).

In general, it may be said, the essays in these collections (which are genuinely representative of the varieties of recent comment) center on specific passages in the most significant, though certainly not the sole, expression of Mill's ethical thought, that is, *Utilitarianism*. (The most notable exceptions are Schneewind, and G. W. Spence in *Philosophy*.) The specific passages so frequently cited are those bearing on the "proof" of utility and on the distinction between "quantity" and "quality" of pleasures. The first of these, in particular, comes into the current discussion of the distinction between, and relative merits of, "act" and "rule" utilitarianism (sometimes referred to as "extreme" and "restricted" utilitarianism), which involves debate about such concepts as justice and obligation; related discussions of the nature of moral discourse and logic also bear upon the "naturalistic fallacy" ascribed by Moore to Mill. Students who wish to go beyond the articles cited above on these issues will find some twenty more listed in the bibliography in the *Mill News Letter*.

To avoid the distortions entailed in this brief summary, those interested in contemporary assessments of Mill's place and value in ethical philosophy should consult more general works that take some account of Mill. These include Alexander Chalmers MacIntyre's controversial *A Short History of Ethics* (1966), John Hosper's *Human Conduct: An Introduction to the Problems of Ethics* (1961), Richard B. Brandt's *Ethical Theory* (1959), and William K. Frankena's short and accessible *Ethics* (1963). More technical and less immediately relevant to Mill, but very influential expositions of attitudes to contemporary utilitarianism are David Lyons' *Forms and Limits of Utilitarianism* (1965); Jan Narveson's *Morality and Utility* (1967); and David Hargraves Hodgson, *Consequences of Utilitarianism* (1967).

Logic

Mill's political and ethical views are expounded not only in central and well-known works such as *On Liberty* and *Utilitarianism*, but also in many subsidiary essays that need examination if a full analysis is desired; his logical thought, however, is given expression in one work only, his great *System of Logic*, though many related topics are treated in his *Examination of Sir William Hamilton's Philosophy*. The only closely relevant essay is his early (1828) review of Whately's *Logic*, and its place in the growth of Mill's logical ideas is treated in the only—and fortunately good—study of that growth, Oskar A. Kubitz' *Development of J. S. Mill's System of Logic* (1932). Kubitz, who admits ambiguities and inconsistencies in the work without dwelling on them, and who also intentionally omits evaluation from a modern point of view, attempts to unravel and explain the stages in Mill's logical thought from 1825 to 1843. (Comments on the development after 1843, as revealed in the correspondence and the textual variants in the second to eighth editions, will be found in the Textual Introduction to the *Logic* in the *Collected Works*.) Given the limitations on the detailed knowledge of Mill in the 1930's, when he did his work, Kubitz' acuteness and diligence in expounding the biographical context, and relating it to the historical context, is all the more admirable, and at this date his remains probably the most interesting study of Mill's *Logic* for the humanist.

The best exposition of the ratiocinative aspects of the *Logic* is Reginald Jackson's *An Examination of the Deductive Logic of J. S. Mill* (1941), which clarifies many of the issues. The phenomenological cruces, brought into sharp focus when the *Examination of Sir William Hamilton's Philosophy* is considered with the *Logic*, are treated by Leslie Stephen, Anschutz, Britton, and Ryan. Levi's *A Study in the Social Philosophy of John Stuart Mill* also has useful things to say, from a humanistic viewpoint, on such topics as freedom of the will, sociological method, and the logic of practice.

The study of logic is now very different from what it was in Mill's time, and it might be said, in explanation as much as in defense, that his work is on the philosophy of logic rather than on logic itself. Recent logical texts give little place to Mill, beyond a discussion of his four experimental methods.

H. L. Stewart's "Mill's *Logic*: A Post-Centenary Appraisal" (*UTQ*, 1947), though it gives erroneous details about the composition of the *Logic*, presents a useful general explanation of its enthusiastic reception and adoption as a textbook; Stewart, without giving the detail that Kubitz does, shows how vacant of rivals the field was, and how impressive, in contemporary terms, Mill's achievement was. He also reveals, in arguing that Book VI is both more original and more enduringly valuable than Book III (which deals with induction, including the experimental methods), how fluctuating fortune is, even for logicians.

Confirmation of the dominant recent view will be found in Curt J. Ducasse's chapter on Mill's *Logic* in Ralph M. Blake et al., *Theories of Scientific Method: The Renaissance through the Nineteenth Century* (1960; rpt. 1966); and in Ernest Nagel's introduction to his widely used selection from Mill's writings (including major portions of the *Logic*), *John Stuart Mill's Philosophy of Scientific Method* (1950; rpt. 1963). With these may be compared the treatment of Mill in Morris Raphael Cohen and Ernest Nagel, *An Introduction to Logic and Scientific Method* (1934, and subsequent eds.), and Carl M. Boegholt, "Examination of Cohen and Nagel's Reply to Mill" (*JP*, 1936).

Other assessments of Mill's logical thought, their subjects again adequately indicated by their titles, cover specific areas of interest to contemporary philosophers: Karl Britton, "The Nature of Arithmetic: A Reconsideration of Mill's Views" (*Proc. of the Aristotelian Soc.*, 1948); R. Jackson, "Mill's Treatment of Geometry—A Reply to Jevons" (1941), in Schneewind's *Mill: A Collection of Critical Essays*; Charles Whitmore, "Mill and Mathematics: An Historical Note" (*JHI*, 1945); Robert McRae, "Phenomenalism and J. S. Mill's Theory of Causation" (*PPR*, 1948); John H. Randall, "John Stuart Mill and the Working-out of Empiricism" (*JHI*, 1965); and Gilbert Ryle, "The Theory of Meaning," in *British Philosophy in the Mid-Century*, edited by Cecil Alec Mace (1957).

Because modern discussions turn so commonly on specific topics, it is useful to turn to the older discussions, where one can sense the growth and change in logical conceptions resulting in part from Mill's work and the criticisms of it. Of these, the most important are Thomas Hill Green, "The Logic of John Stuart Mill," in the second volume of his *Works*, edited by Richard Lewis Nettleship (1886); F. H. Bradley, *Principles of Logic* (1883); John Venn, *The Principles of Empirical or Inductive Logic* (1889); and William Stanley Jevons, "John Stuart Mill's Philosophy Tested," reprinted from the *Contemporary Review* (1877–79) in his *Pure Logic* (1890). (The immediate reaction to Jevons' onslaught may be seen in articles by George Croom Robertson and Robert Adamson with replies by A. Strachey and Jevons, *Mind*, 1878.) For more particular study of special topics having modern relevance, one might also refer to Gottlob Frege, *The Foundations of Arithmetic: A Logico-Mathematical Enquiry* (1884), edited by John L. Austin, with parallel German and English texts (1950), Chapters i and ii; and John Maynard Keynes, *A Treatise on Probability* (1921), Chapter xxiii.

The close relation between Alexander Bain and Mill gives special significance to Bain's "Mill's Theory of the Syllogism" (1878), in his *Dissertations on Leading Philosophical Subjects* (1903). Also worthy of reference is the first review, or rather eulogy, of the *Logic*, by Bain in the *Westminster Review* (1843). With it may be compared William Whewell's *Of Induction, with Especial Reference to Mr. J. Stuart Mill's System of Logic* (1849), reprinted with alterations in his *Philosophy of Discovery* (1860); Mill, who acknowledged a considerable debt to Whewell, also saw him as his chief opponent in many ways: see G. Buchdahl, "Inductivist *vs.* Deductivist Approaches in the Philosophy of Science as Illustrated by Some Controversies between Whewell and Mill" (*Monist*, 1971); Edward W. Strong, "William Whewell and John Stuart Mill: Their Controversy about Scientific Knowledge" (*JHI*, 1955); and H. T. Walsh, "Whewell and Mill on Induction" (*Philosophy of Sci.*, 1962).

V. ECONOMICS

Obituary notices, as well as contemporary accounts and reviews, and the acceptance of his *Principles of Political Economy* and *System of Logic* as textbooks show that Mill was primarily thought of as a political economist and logician in his lifetime. Subsequently, in economics as in logic, his reputation was inevitably lowered as new and usually more specialized works replaced his. Generally, economic textbooks and surveys published in the late nineteenth and early twentieth centuries took his ideas, particularly those reflecting his education as a classical economist of the school of Ricardo, as a starting place, and went on to controvert or amplify specific points. After Keynes and the advent of a more strictly quantitative economic analysis, attention has tended to focus on topics of special interest to the writer concerned, rather than on Mill's economic thought as a whole. As a result it is even more difficult in this area than in philosophy for the nonprofessional to make connections (or even to understand the discussions), and so the following outline should be taken as much less complete and specific than the literature warrants.

The areas of Mill's economic thought that have received most attention over the past hundred years are his view of the method of political economy, his position on questions relating to economic development (theories of production and capital), his attitude to distribution (as more subject to human desires than production), his theories of value and international trade, his monetary theory, and his ideas on general problems of economic policy, with reference to the relations between government and society, and the powers of government. As economists have recently turned their attention increasingly to questions of economic growth and the effects of government action on development and distribution, there has been an interest in Mill's views on these matters, as well as in his theory of international trade. Historians of economic thought have also considered anew his attitudes to money and value, and there is still an interest, though less obvious, in his thoughts on method.

The literature being so diverse, and much of it being so technical, one should consult Amano's *Bibliography* for specific topics. Noneconomists interested in Mill's thought generally will find enlightening treatments in most of the standard textbooks. The best expositions, linking Mill to the Classical School and to the main topics of interest to contemporary economists, are those of Lionel Robbins in his *The Theory of Economic Development in the History of Economic Thought* (1968), his *The Theory of Economic Policy in English Classical Political Economy* (1952), and his introduction to Mill's *Essays on Economics and Society* (*Collected Works*, IV and V, 1967). Other valuable assessments are in the introductions to Mill's *Principles* by William James Ashley (1909) and Vincent Bladen (*Collected Works*, II and III, 1965). Recent discussions include the chapters on Mill in Wesley C. Mitchell, *Types of Economic Theory* (1967), and W. J. Barber, *A*

History of Economic Thought (1967), and the summary view of economic thought to 1870 n the first chapter of Terrence W. Hutchison's *A Review of Economic Doctrines, 1870–1929* (1953). George J. Stigler gives a sprightly and effective account of Mill's originality as an economist (he is generally considered primarily as an expositor and synthesizer) in "The Nature and Role of Originality in Scientific Progress," in his *Essays in the History of Economics* (1965).

In the third edition of his *Principles* (1852), Mill made major changes in his discussion of the merits of socialism and came to see himself as "a qualified socialist." The exact definition of his position has proved somewhat elusive, though there is widespread agreement with the position best set forth in Lord Robbins' discussions, that Mill in general adhered to a laissez-faire position, modified by his belief in the moral, educative, and economic gains to be expected through an expansion of cooperative ventures, and also by his view of the inequities of unearned income from landed property. Discussions of various aspects of the question —which of course bears intimately on Mill's views of political liberty—may be seen in Henry G. Abel, "John Stuart Mill and Socialism" (*FortR*, 1938); Max Beer, *History of British Socialism* (1920), II, Ch. ix; L. S. Feuer, "Mill and Marxian Socialism," with comment by Jacob S. Schapiro (*JHI*, 1949); in three discussions by Abram L. Harris, "John Stuart Mill: Liberalism, Socialism, and Laissez-Faire" in his *Economics and Social Reform* (1958), "John Stuart Mill's Theory of Progress" (*Ethics*, 1956), and "J. S. Mill on Monopoly and Socialism" (*J. of Pol. Econ.*, 1959); and in three articles in the *Mill News Letter* by L. E. Fredman and B. L. J. Gordon (1967), Pedro Schwartz (1968), and William H. Hughes (1972). Schwartz's *La "Nueva Economia Politica" de John Stuart Mill* (1968), published in translation as *The New Political Economy of John Stuart Mill* (1972), also has extended intelligent comment on Mill's socialism, and Robson devotes a section of his *Improvement of Mankind* to the question.

While it seems certain that Mill neither met Marx nor knew of his economic writings (which were generally unread in England until after Mill's death), Marx knew and criticized Mill's work, and Marxists have since devoted some space to critiques of Mill's views; an example will be seen in Maurice Dobb's *Political Economy and Capitalism* (1945; rpt. 1950). Short comparative studies, some of which find similarities between Mill and Marx, include Bela A. Balassa, "Karl Marx and John Stuart Mill" (*Weltwirtschaftliches Archiv*, 1959); Vincent Bladen, "The Centenary of Marx and Mill" (*J. of Econ. Hist.*, Supp., 1948); Bernice Shoul, "Similarities in the Work of John Stuart Mill and Karl Marx" (*Science and Society*, 1965); and Angus Walker, "Karl Marx, the Declining Rate of Profit and British Political Economy" (*Economica*, 1971).

One of the clearest accounts of closely related issues is J. Bartlet Brebner's "Laissez Faire and State Intervention in Nineteenth-Century Britain" (*J. of Econ. Hist.*, Supp., 1948), which places Mill closer to the tradition of "Benthamite interventionism" than to laissez-faire attitudes. An interesting glance into the Political Economy Club, of which Mill was a lifelong member, is seen in Adelaide Weinberg's "A Meeting of the Political Economy Club" (*MNL*, 1966), based on a diary of Cairnes.

Mill's influence on the Fabians and on the Labour movement generally was as much through his social and political views as his economic thought; this is again one of the subjects on which more work remains to be done, but there are some interesting points made in the following: Margaret Cole, *The Makers of the Labour*

Movement (1948); Julius West, *John Stuart Mill* (Fabian Society Tract No. 168, 1913); William Irvine, "Shaw, the Fabians, and the Utilitarians" (*JHI*, 1947); and Mary P. Mack, "The Fabians and Utilitarianism" (*JHI*, 1955).

In brief and thus distorted summary of the aspects of Mill's economic reputation and thought that students should be aware of, one may say that the important elements are the Ricardian core of his work (the combined forces of diminishing returns, population pressure, and the rising costs of production of wages goods, leading to a diminished real rate of profit; and reassessments of Say's law concerning overproduction); and his ability to combine in exposition post-Ricardian views (e.g., his discussion of the interest rate in relation to abstinence, and the role of demand in determining prices). There is disagreement as to how far Mill moved from the Classical position, but in one respect, demonstrated in his placing in his *Principles* the discussion of distribution before that of value (contrary to subsequent practice), there is general agreement that he failed, with the Classical School, to recognize the place of distribution analysis in the general theory of value. His attitude to economic policy puts him, despite his favorable comments on some aspects of socialism, clearly in the "reformist" camp, relying on checks on the rights of private property without ruling it out or minimizing the profit motive. At the same time, his repeated emphasis on the need for population control, reflected in his discussion of various policy questions (such as trade unions, the competitive price mechanism, cooperation, and education), gives his work contemporary interest for discussions of underdevelopment.

VI. LITERATURE

Mill's only direct contribution to literature was through his review articles; a few of these, almost all deriving from his response to the Romantic poets in the early 1830's, have a minor place of their own in the history of literary criticism. But it is the importance of Mill on other grounds, including his significance for an understanding of the cultural life of the Victorian period, that gives his criticism its value. Contextual study of his literary essays is therefore imperative, though too often slighted.

A major help in an understanding of Mill's views is *The Literary Criticism of John Stuart Mill* (1967), by Francis Parvin Sharpless, the first extended study of this aspect of Mill's thought, which summarizes all the major relevant documents, traces the development of Mill's attitudes, and gives background information on Benthamite literary theory. Interesting and informative throughout, Sharpless' argument is based on a distinction among three stages in Mill's career: the first, up to about 1828 (i.e., until after his "mental crisis"), marked by a Benthamite concern for only the political and moral content of literature, and a disparagement of feeling; the second, between 1828 and 1837, marked by an attempt, through establishing an experientialist justification for poetry, to synthesize philosophic and literary truth; the third, subsequent to 1837, marked by an insistence more on the pragmatic utility of literature than on its empirical truth. Given that Sharpless is not trying to write a full history of early utilitarian critical theory, but to explain the atmosphere in which Mill's first criticism emerged, the account of the first stage elucidates usefully the narrow view of the utility of literature that informed the polemics of the Philosophic Radicals. Concerning the second stage of Mill's development, on which more has been written—as noted, almost all the major documents date from these years—Sharpless' summary and exposition are again clear and illuminating, though his comment lacks an appreciation of how much Mill's views reflect not just his own experience and creation but also current Romantic attitudes. The discussion of the third stage draws on Mill's psychological views, as expressed in his notes to his father's *Analysis* (2nd ed., 1869) and his review of Bain, and also in his important account, in his review of Grote's *Plato*, of the stages in Plato's career, which Sharpless finds interestingly similar in key respects to Mill's own. The discussion of this third stage is less persuasive than those of the earlier two, partly because there is less direct evidence, partly because the distinction between the second and third stages is too firmly established (and perhaps in the wrong place), and partly because Sharpless, though he draws on a wide reading of Mill's work, does not give due weight to the implicit attitudes as well as explicit doctrines of Mill's major nonliterary works, which give a better framework for his mature view of literature than do his isolated later comments on literary matters. Nevertheless, Sharpless' book has earned a central place in any further discussions of Mill's literary criticism.

Two other book-length treatments should be mentioned, the first, J. R. Hainds's "John Stuart Mill's Views on Art" (Diss. Northwestern 1939), because it contains valuable discussion; the second, Thomas Woods's *Poetry and Philosophy: A Study in the Thought of John Stuart Mill* (1961), because the promise of its title is not at all fulfilled in its pretentious, if somewhat pleasant, text. Only a few other critics have been interested in relating Mill's literary views to his attitudes in general. Of these, one may mention the introductions in the anthologies edited by Edward Alexander, *John Stuart Mill: Literary Essays* (1967), and J. B. Schneewind, *Mill's Essays on Literature and Society* (1965), and Alexander's "Mill's Theory of Culture: The Wedding of Literature and Democracy" (*UTQ*, 1965). Robson attempts a wider synthesis in his *Improvement of Mankind*, in which he partly incorporates his "J. S. Mill's Theory of Poetry" (*UTQ*, 1960).

As suggested above, those concentrating specifically on Mill's literary essays have perforce dwelt on his early years when, having imbibed the early utilitarians' contempt for "feeling," he feared at the time of his "mental crisis" that he was devoid of emotion. In casting about for cures for his desolation, he found no help in Byron, but found in Wordsworth the healing power to which many other Victorians testify. Within a few years he had analyzed his response, and having encountered Harriet Taylor's enthusiasm for Shelley, and Carlyle's for Goethe, embodied his thoughts in articles on poetic theory. The most important of these will be found in the two anthologies just cited, whose contents overlap; lesser cognate pieces, with comment, are reprinted in Hainds's "J. S. Mill's *Examiner* Articles on Art" (*JHI*, 1950). All these will eventually be gathered in the *Collected Works*, along with the debating speeches, many of which have related interest.

The essays that have occasioned most discussions are "What Is Poetry?" and "The Two Kinds of Poetry" (conflated in *Dissertations and Discussions* as "Thoughts on Poetry and Its Varieties"). Meyer H. Abrams, in *The Mirror and the Lamp* (1953), provides the best literary context for the essays, identifying them as illustrative of "expressive" Romanticism, and indicating how they attack the great commonplaces of critical tradition in elevating the lyric above other genres, in denigrating mere imitation of the natural world, and in arguing that conscious attempts to affect an audience reduce poetry to eloquence. Abrams also calls attention to passages that anticipate in detail elements in the criticism of Hulme, Eliot, and Richards.

The distinction between the truth values of poetry and logic, a matter dwelt on by Mill in his letters to Carlyle, is treated briefly by Abrams. The point is seized on by Séamus Cooney in his "'The Heart of That Mystery': A Note on J. S. Mill's Theory of Poetry" (*VN*, 1962), where he argues that Mill's interest in reconciling the two kinds of truth waned, with his interest in poetry, as he grew older. In an earlier and similarly hostile article ("Mill, Poets, and Other Men," *VN*, 1960), Cooney argues that the special kind of mental association Mill attributes to lyric poets reflects only his own need for personal reassurance; like Walter J. Ong ("J. S. Mill's Pariah Poet," *PQ*, 1950), Cooney finds little critical value in Mill's views. Concerning influences on Mill, Cooney (citing Alba H. Warren) calls attention to Thomas Brown; others, including Robert Preyer ("The Utilitarian Poetics: J. S. Mill," *UKCR*, 1953), note the background against which Mill was working; Sharpless, in his "William Johnson Fox and Mill's Essays on Poetry" (*VN*, 1965), presents evidence that Mill drew upon and enlarged Fox's ideas; as yet there has been no major comment on the influence of James Martineau, whose article in the *Monthly Repository* in 1833 is explicitly cited by Mill, in his *Logic*, as having influenced him.

Other discussions based on these early articles, such as Alba H. Warren's in his *English Poetic Theory, 1825–1865* (1950) and Robert Langbaum's in his *Poetry of Experience* (1957), derive interest from their relational value, but add little to an understanding of Mill.

As indicative of nonliterary interest in literary aspects of Mill's life in these years, one may cite three essays viewing his "mental crisis" in the light of his development: John Durham, "The Influence of John Stuart Mill's Mental Crisis on His Thought" (*AI*, 1963; Durham anticipates Gertrude Himmelfarb's comment on the effect of James Mill's death on his son); Robert Cumming, "Mill's History of His Ideas" (*JHI*, 1964); and Karl Britton, "J. S. Mill: The Ordeal of an Intellectual" (*Cambridge J.*, 1948).

Mill's critical comments on the two most important Victorian poets, Tennyson and Browning, have received special attention, more because of their subjects than their content. His review (1835) of Tennyson's first two volumes of poetry is discussed by William D. Paden in *Tennyson and the Reviewers (1829–35)* (Studies in English, Univ. of Kansas Publications, Humanistic Series 6, 1940), and by Edgar Finley Shannon in his *Tennyson and the Reviewers* (1952), with primary reference to Tennyson's early reception; Shannon also indicates a few revisions that were perhaps prompted by Mill's comments among others.

Mill's remarks on Browning have led to more discussion, oddly enough, for they were part of a proposed review that never appeared. In 1833, on the suggestion of W. J. Fox, Mill and Harriet Taylor read and annotated a copy of Browning's *Pauline*; after failing to place a review in the *Examiner* and *Tait's Edinburgh Magazine*, Mill returned the copy to Fox, who in turn, rather incautiously, gave it to Browning. Taking the criticisms to heart, Browning made some further marginal comments, and determined to give his poetry a less personal and more dramatic tone. The annotated copy, now in the Victoria and Albert Museum, was noticed by Anna B. McMahon in *The Dial* (1901), and the incident has taken its place in the standard biographies of Browning, beginning with William Hall Griffin and Harry

Christopher Minchin, *The Life of Robert Browning* (1910), and of Mill (see Hayek, *John Stuart Mill and Harriet Taylor*, and Packe, *Life of Mill*). The text of the main comment (from the flyleaf) is given, with some inaccuracies, in Griffin and Minchin, and in Hayek, and has been dignified as an essay in *Robert Browning: A Collection of Critical Essays* (1966), edited by Philip Drew. Separate discussions, in the main centering on the effect of the criticism on Browning, are found in M. A. Phillips, "John Stuart Mill and Browning's *Pauline*" (*Cornhill*, 1912); William L. Phelps, "Notes on Browning's *Pauline*" (*MLN*, 1932), with a list of the marginalia; William C. DeVane, *A Browning Handbook* (1935; rev. ed., 1955); Lewis F. Haines, "Mill and *Pauline*: The 'Review' That 'Retarded' Browning's Fame" (*MLN*, 1944); C. N. Wenger, "Sources of Mill's Criticism of 'Pauline'" (*MLN*, 1945); Masao Miyoshi, "Mill and *Pauline*: The Myth and Some Facts" (*VS*, 1965); O. P. Govil, "A Note on Mill and Browning's *Pauline*" (*VP*, 1966); and in Sharpless' *The Literary Criticism of John Stuart Mill*. Sharpless' account does more to relate the comments to Mill's poetic theory than any other, while Miyoshi gives much the best account of the importance of the incident to Browning.

Apart from his essays on poetry, some of Mill's other writings have received what may be called a literary treatment. Of most importance, of course, are attempts to assess his *Autobiography* generically and as a literary work in its own right. The former attempt will be seen in the following studies, whose titles indicate their theses: John N. Morris, *Versions of the Self: Studies in English Autobiography from John Bunyan to John Stuart Mill* (1966); Wayne Shumaker, *English Autobiography: Its Emergence, Materials, and Form* (1954); and Herbert N. Wethered, *The Curious Art of Autobiography: From Benvenuto Cellini to Rudyard Kipling* (1956). No separate major study of the *Autobiography* on its own merits has yet appeared; the most useful discussions are those by Jack Stillinger in his introductions to his editions of the *Early Draft of John Stuart Mill's* Autobiography (1961) and of the *Autobiography* (1969). One may also consult William Thomas' "J. S. Mill and the Uses of Autobiography" (*History*, 1971); Keith Rinehart's "John Stuart Mill's *Autobiography*: Its Art and Appeal" (*UKCR*, 1953); and John M. Robson, "Mill's *Autobiography*: The Public and the Private Voice" (*CCC*, 1965).

Mill's essays on Bentham and Coleridge, brought into new prominence by F. R. Leavis' edition (1950; rpt. 1962), have been subject to some rhetorical and literary analysis: separate treatment will be seen in Norman N. Feltes's "'Bentham' and 'Coleridge': Mill's 'Completing Counterparts'" (*MNL*, 1967); the strategy of the two essays in relation to Mill's other periodical writings on ethics and society is discussed by F. E. L. Priestley in his introduction to Volume x of the *Collected Works* (1969); and for a different emphasis, one should see Raymond Williams' treatment in his *Culture and Society* (1958). Two short treatments of *On Liberty* are also worth mention as indication of this recent literary interest in his works: John Grube's "*On Liberty* as a Work of Art" (*MNL*, 1969) and David R. Sanderson's "Method and Metaphor in Mill's *On Liberty*" (*VN*, 1968). Nels Juleus, in "The Rhetoric of Opposites: Mill and Carlyle" (*Pa. Speech Annual*, 1966), concentrates on Carlyle's and Mill's antagonistic articles on the Negro Question (available in Crofts Classics, ed. Eugene August, 1970) and their rhetorical addresses at Edinburgh and St. Andrews. (Juleus' thesis, "The Rhetorical Theory and Practice of John Stuart Mill," is abstracted in *Speech Monographs*, 1964.) A further excursion into Mill's rhetoric, more provocative than precise, is seen in Alan Donagan's "Victorian Philosophical Prose: J. S. Mill and F. H. Bradley," in *The Art of Victorian Prose* (1968), edited by George Levine and William Madden.

Mill's early acquaintance with another Romantic tradition is discussed in Anna J. Mill's "John Stuart Mill and the Picturesque" (*VS*, 1970), which deals with the landscape descriptions in one of his walking-tour journals. And finally, in this context, one should consult the lexicographic detective work by Roland Hall on Mill's diction (seen in a series in *N&Q*, beginning in 1959 with "A Virtually Untapped Source for Dictionary Quotations," and continuing with "The Diction of John Stuart Mill" in 1964, 1965, and 1970). One may anticipate some computerized analyses before long, and one of the major desiderata in Mill studies is a full examination of his rhetoric.

Yet another relatively understudied area is Mill's relation with the periodical press. He wrote extensively for quarterlies, monthlies, and newspapers (some 500 items), and had an intimate connection with several of them. He was one of the most important contributors to the *Westminster Review*, from its beginning in 1824 to 1828; he founded the *London Review* (later the *London and Westminster*) in 1835, and edited it until 1840; and, to mention only the most important of his other connections, he had at various times a significant part in the *Examiner*, the *Morning Chronicle*, the *Monthly Repository*, the *Reader*, and the *Fortnightly Review*. While there has been no separate study of his career as editor and contributor, his relations with some of these periodicals have been commented on in C. Marion Towers, "John Stuart Mill and the *London and Westminster Review*" (*AM*, 1892); Edwin M. Everett, *The Party of Humanity: The* Fortnightly Review *and Its Contributors* (1939); Francis E. Mineka, *The Dissidence of Dissent: The* Monthly Repository, *1806–38* (1944); George L. Nesbitt, *Benthamite Reviewing: The First Twelve Years of the* Westminster Review, *1824–36* (1934); and in John F. Byrne's "*The Reader*: A Review of Literature, Science and the Arts, 1863–1867" (Diss. Northwestern 1964).

In spite of the extensive interest in Mill's education, there has been no serious study of his reading. The Bibliographic Appendices in the separate volumes of the *Collected Works* are designed in part to facilitate such study by giving information about all works cited by him, including his possession of copies. Books from his collection given to Somerville College, Oxford were noticed in Rose Sidgwick's "The Library of John Stuart Mill" (*Cornhill*, 1906); further detail about the history of his library is given in Hayek's Introduction to Volume XII of the *Collected Works*. Though not a confirmed annotator, Mill left some marginalia apart from that in the Browning volume mentioned above, of which the only considerable notices are in Hayek's editing of Mill's notes on Senior's *Political Economy* (*Economica*, 1945) and Edward Alexander's "Mill's Marginal Notes on Carlyle's 'Hudson's Statue'" (*ELN*, 1969).

Except for Rees's *Mill and His Early Critics* (1956), a study of the immediate periodical response to *On Liberty*, no important work has been done on the reception of Mill's works. Nor, to reiterate in part, have there been any special studies of such promising areas as his contact with workingmen, his parliamentary career, his activities as a proponent of land reform, or—most surprisingly—his part in the women's suffrage movement. (Again, these will be facilitated by the publication of the *Later Letters*.)

There have been, however, a number of comparative studies of Mill and his well-known contemporaries, especially of Mill and Carlyle. In addition to those mentioned above, one may cite the earliest, Edward Jenks's *Thomas Carlyle and John Stuart Mill* (1888), which throws more light on nineteenth-century Cambridge than on Mill or Carlyle; and such special studies as Richard Paul Anschutz' "J. S. Mill, Carlyle, and Mrs. Taylor" (*Pol. Sci.*, 1955); Peter E. Martin's "Carlyle and Mill: The 'Anti-Self-Consciousness' Theory" (*Thoth*, 1965); Henry Ebel, "'The Primaeval Fountain of Human Nature': Mill, Carlyle, and the French Revolution" (*VN*, 1966); and Iva G. Jones, "Trollope, Carlyle, and Mill on the Negro: An Episode in the History of Ideas" (*J. of Negro Hist.*, 1967).

Of other studies of Mill and his famous contemporaries, the most interesting deal with men Mill did not know intimately, Matthew Arnold and John Ruskin. The fullest is Edward Alexander's *Matthew Arnold and John Stuart Mill* (1965), which ably demonstrates the similar approaches to contemporary problems taken by Arnold and Mill, despite the few rather disparaging comments Arnold made about Mill, and the apparent conflict between *Culture and Anarchy* and *On Liberty*. A shorter account, similar in its conclusions, is found in Robson's "Mill and Matthew Arnold: Liberty and Culture" in *Of Several Branches* (1968), edited by Gerald S. McCaughey and Maurice Legris.

Kate Millett's "The Debate over Women: Ruskin versus Mill" (*VS*, 1970, adapted from her *Sexual Politics*, 1970) is less informative about but much more sympathetic to Mill than to Ruskin; it is polemical, and represents another aspect of the "relevance of Mill" theme. That Ruskin, who took Mill's definition of wealth as a starting point for his criticism of heartless political economy, was mistaken in his reading of Mill is demonstrated in John T. Fain's "Ruskin and Mill" (*MLQ*, 1951) and "Ruskin and the Orthodox Political Economists" (*Southern Econ. J.*, 1943). (Ruskin's annotated copies of *On Liberty* and *Principles of Political Economy* are in the British Museum. They, like other annotated copies of Mill's works, such as Leslie Stephen's fourth edition of the *Logic*—also in the British Museum—provide interesting evidence of reaction to Mill. One valuable study has appeared, Sydney Ross's "Sir John Herschel's Marginal Notes on Mill's *On Liberty*, 1859," *JHI*, 1968.)

Mill being seen by so many as epitomizing nineteenth-century liberalism, especially in politics, it is surprising that only recently have studies of his influence on various countries begun to emerge. The title of an earlier work, George Morlan's *America's Heritage from John Stuart Mill* (1936), is misleading, for it contains not a study of influence, but a plea for the adoption of some of Mill's ideas and the rejection of others in the United States of the 1930's. Future full studies of Mill's international influence will draw upon the more detailed examination found in such articles as R. S. Neale's "John Stuart Mill on Australia" (*Historical Studies, Australia and New Zealand*, 1968); E. D. Steele's two articles on Mill and the Irish question in the *Historical Journal* (1970); James P. Scanlan's "John Stuart Mill in Russia: A Bibliography" (*MNL*, 1968); and the section on Canada in Joseph Hamburger's *Intellectuals in Politics*.

Ignoring some small matters, details of which students will find in the bibliographies mentioned at the beginning of this chapter, one may isolate one final literary quest of significance, though the ultimate findings are not likely to be staggering. Not a writer of fiction, and not intimately acquainted with any of the leading novelists of the period, except Bulwer-Lytton, Mill nonetheless had some influence on the novel. Being so closely identified with utilitarianism, he inevitably has been, with his father, seen as providing material for Dickens' satiric attack in *Hard Times* on political economists of a utilitarian cast. This view, found in Edgar Johnson and F. R. Leavis, has been effectively countered by Edward Alexander in "Disinterested Virtue: Dickens and Mill in Agreement" (*Dickensian*, 1969), where it is shown that Mill actually criticizes narrow utilitarianism on the same grounds as Dickens; Alexander's article supersedes K. J. Fielding's "Mill and Gradgrind" (*NCF*, 1956), where similar evidence is cited, but with the implication that Dickens was, therefore, not attacking utilitarianism. William J. Baker, in "Gradgrindery and the Education of John Stuart Mill: A Classification" (*WHR*, 1970), emphasizes the difference between the two. (On what little evidence there is, it may be remarked that Mill was not an enthusiastic reader of Dickens, objecting especially to *Bleak House*, with its onslaught on pretentious women.) It seems likely that similarities in ethics and philosophy between Mill and George Eliot will be examined further than they are in the two useful discussions by George Levine, "Determinism and Responsibility in the Works of George Eliot" (*PMLA*, 1962), and by Larry M. Robbins, "Mill and *Middlemarch*: The Progress of Public Opinion" (*VN*, 1967). Four other articles on different novelists' use of Mill's thought illustrate in their titles the kind of interest that he has aroused in critics of fiction: Lewis F. Haines, "Reade, Mill, and Zola: A Study of the Character and Intention of Charles Reade's Realistic Method" (*SP*, 1943); Charles J. Hill, "Theme and Image in *The Egoist*" (*UKCR*, 1954); William J. Hyde, "Theoretic and Practical Unconventionality in *Jude the Obscure*" (*NCF*, 1965); and Donald Pizer, "The Ethical Unity of *The Rise of Silas Lapham*" (*AL*, 1960).

It is appropriate to remark, in closing this chapter, that in spite of the vast literature on Mill, there are many interesting and important matters still meriting close attention. Many of these have been mentioned; hints toward others will be found also in studies that do not concentrate on Mill but contain valuable insights on his thought. There is probably no modern critic—the present writer certainly is not—competent to deal with the full range of Mill's writings and the often highly specialized treatments of them by commentators; consequently an account such as the foregoing almost inevitably errs in omission and commission, and apologies are due to those whose work is slighted or misrepresented.

JOHN RUSKIN

·

Francis G. Townsend

I. EDITIONS AND SELECTIONS

Ruskin scholarship began where most scholarship ends, in a monumental edition. Between 1903 and 1912 Sir Edward T. Cook and Alexander D. O. Wedderburn published *The Works of John Ruskin* in thirty-nine handsome volumes. The effect was curious. The monumental Library Edition, instead of promoting scholarship, seemed to inhibit it, because the conventional lines of investigation known at the time had all been pursued with the utmost diligence: for example, the errors in the earlier Thomas J. Wise bibliography were quietly noted and corrected. There are flaws in the edition, but its reputation for accuracy withstood challenge for almost fifty years.

There are numerous editions of selected readings from Ruskin, interesting because they represent the judgment of distinguished scholars as to what is enduring in those thirty-nine volumes. Especially valuable are the introductions to John D. Rosenberg's *The Genius of John Ruskin: Selections from His Writings* (1963) and Kenneth Clark's *Ruskin Today* (1964). Another noteworthy collection is Peter Quennell's *Selected Writings of John Ruskin* (1952). In her introduction to *The Lamp of Beauty: Writings on Art by John Ruskin* (1958) Joan Evans found it lamentable that moderns are so ignorant of Ruskin when we owe to him so much of what we take for granted in our own aesthetic views. Robert L. Herbert's *The Art Criticism of John Ruskin* (1964) and Harold Bloom's *The Literary Criticism of John Ruskin* (1965) are other efforts to demonstrate our debt to Ruskin.

Aside from *The King of the Golden River*, single titles of John Ruskin are seldom reprinted. Exceptions are Kenneth Clark's *Praeterita* (1949) and Joseph Gluckstein Links's abridged edition of *The Stones of Venice* (1960).

II. BIOGRAPHIES AND BIOGRAPHICAL STUDIES

Modern Ruskin scholarship begins in 1933 with Reginald H. Wilenski's biography, *John Ruskin: An Introduction to Further Study of His Life and Work*. The foundations had already been firmly laid in the basic biographies by Sir E. T. Cook and William G. Collingwood, in the massive Library Edition of Cook and Alexander Wedderburn, and in the aesthetic critique of Henry Ladd. But even those excellent works seemed unsophisticated after the Wilenski study. A generation of subsequent study has tended to confirm what might have seemed at the time a highly speculative psychological analysis.

Cook's *The Life of John Ruskin* (2 vols., 1911) stands as a superb example of the way in which meticulous accuracy about some facts combined with extraordinary reticence about others can create a gap between the truth and the whole truth. Although Collingwood in his *The Life and Work of John Ruskin* (1893; rev. 1900) maintained the same Victorian reserve, he did not mislead, because he did not disarm the reader with an imposing array of information. The impression of accuracy and candor is still more dangerous in the Library Edition, where a profusion of facts, all honestly adduced, screens the fact that we learn almost nothing about Ruskin's courtship and marriage.

Wilenski gave a motion and a spirit to the mass of details in Cook and Collingwood. Far from destroying Ruskin, Wilenski made him a tragic figure, and threw his works into a new perspective. As Wilenski makes clear, Ruskin had small chance of a normal life. He was the son of first cousins. His paternal grandfather had gone mad in 1815 and committed suicide in 1817. The next year his father, John James Ruskin, having at last achieved financial success, married his cousin, Margaret Cox, to whom he had been engaged for nine years. In 1819 there was born to the thirty-eight-year-old bride and to her thirty-four-year-old husband-cousin a son, their only child. They were overly solicitous of him, of course, and far too strict. As a child he had few friends of his own age. As an adolescent he fell madly in love with Adèle Domecq, daughter of his father's partner, but since he had no experience in such matters, he botched the affair. When he went to Oxford his mother took rooms in town and he had tea with her every day. When he traveled through Europe, he went with his parents; not until 1845 did he travel alone. As Wilenski tells the story, Mrs. Ruskin decided in 1847 that her son should marry, there was a convenient guest at Denmark Hill, an attractive young lady named Euphemia Chalmers Gray whom John had met some years before and for whom he had written *The King of the Golden River*, and in 1848 he married her. He never had sexual intercourse with her because, as he told his doctor, he did not love her and therefore had no right to consummate the marriage.

In 1854 Effie secured an annulment on the grounds of his impotence. At first Ruskin seemed relieved, but within five years he had lost his religion and with it the puritanical fear that pleasure was a guilty thing and then he fell in love with a ten-year-old girl who seemed to remind him of Adèle. The rest of his life was a frantic attempt to recapture the past, which he had squandered in his time. Hence from 1858 on his life assumes a repetitive pattern which becomes more and more obvious as the years pass; he loves little girls, but after puberty they do not charm him. Nevertheless he moves toward marriage, as he should have in his youth. He believes that his parents had ruined him, but he has to retrace the old roads he traveled with them in his youth. When infirmity prevents him, he hires others to sketch the old scenes, thus reliving them vicariously. He is a man trying to live his life over again.

The John Ruskin who thus emerges from the Wilenski analysis is a man who was never really sane, who was doomed to a life of unbearable tension by both heredity and environment, whose whole life was a desperate fight to establish his own sanity, or at least to persuade others that he was sane. Such an interpretation has its danger, in that it can induce such a repugnance to Ruskin that his work cannot be evaluated with proper objectivity. On the other hand, it can lead to a depth of sympathy and understanding which was simply impossible to earlier scholars. It makes biographies like those of Amabel Williams-Ellis, *The Tragedy of John Ruskin* (1928), and David Larg, *John Ruskin* (1932), although competently written, seem superficial and outmoded.

Like any revolutionary biography, Wilenski's led to a new way of looking at Ruskin's works, although its full implications were not immediately apparent. He observed that in order to get at what Ruskin had to say we have to rewrite his works for him, discarding much of what he says on a given subject at any given time because much of it is a rationalization of his own weakness, although remembering that what he wrote drove always in one direction, and furthermore, that nearly every page he wrote is truly original and worth heeding, even when it appears to have been inspired by someone else. I have condensed Wilenski's judgment to heighten the paradox, but paradoxical or not, the judgment is the best contribution yet made to the understanding of its subject. Thus the portrait of Ruskin most fruitful to later scholars has been that of a man endowed with extraordinary physical awareness and profound analytical power, whose natural gifts were flawed by psychological tensions, which, however, gave him new and revealing ways of looking at the supposedly obvious, while at the same time undermining his ability to convey his vision in a sustained artistic performance. What we find in Ruskin is not a readily organizable set of statements but a direction. For example, "The Nature of Gothic" remains one of the treasures of world literature, but only down to the point where it meanders into irrelevant brilliance, interesting for its own sake but not germane to the issue.

The second major breakthrough in Ruskin biography came in 1947 with the publication of *John Ruskin and Effie Gray: The Story of John Ruskin, Effie Gray and John Everett Millais Told for the First Time in Their Unpublished Letters*, edited by Admiral Sir William James, Effie's grandson. Despite the bumbling amateurishness of the editor, the excerpts from the letters were a revelation. Wilenski had done surprisingly well at exposing the true John Ruskin, but he lacked the evidence that James made available. For example, Wilenski thought it possible that John Ruskin might have had normal relations with a woman, say around 1858, just before the onset of the Rose La Touche affair, a surmise which now seems unlikely. For another example, Wilenski accepted the story circulated by Ruskin's admirers: he thought John had been pushed into a marriage arranged by his parents.

The James letters called forth an angry rebuttal, J. Howard Whitehouse's *Vindication of Ruskin* (1950), noteworthy only because it contained Ruskin's statement about the marriage, dated 27 April 1854, and turned over to his solicitor. Although it is true that Admiral James reflected the pent-up bitterness of the Millais family, certainly a revision of the record was long overdue. As Peter Quennell said: "Around the whole subject of his marriage, Ruskin himself, his friends, and his official biographer agreed in later years to draw heavy curtains of silence and obscurity. What information they provided was deliberately designed to mislead, and a report was put about, to be sedulously propagated by the Ruskinian faithful, that Ruskin had married 'to please his parents,' who 'saw in a marriage with Euphemia the means by which they might gain a daughter and not lose a son.'" James tore down the curtains, however clumsily.

The chapter "Affection Rampant" leaves little doubt about Ruskin's infatuation; that he loved her in the odd, bashful way of a man who knows nothing about women is clear enough. Equally clear, and a little sobering, is his own awareness of his desperate need for help: ". . . how absolutely and without need of comparison fortunate I am in winning you yet so young when it is still time, I hope—to recover by your kind influence that morbid tendency in me which has come upon me by being without such a hope so long." Since there are passages in these letters that make one wonder exactly what Ruskin meant by the "morbid tendency" from which Effie might yet save him, the James letters cried out for interpretation; Peter Quennell perhaps supplied as good an explanation as any in a series of articles in the *Cornhill* and the *Atlantic Monthly* during 1946 and 1947, and in his biography *John Ruskin: The Portrait of a Prophet* (1949). Quennell argued that John Ruskin was sexually excited by Effie Gray, a highly attractive young woman, but that he recoiled from the consummation of their love. Partly it was that Ruskin was the victim of a rather common masculine delusion: he was in love not with a real woman, but with an ideal woman who was his own creation. Partly it was that Ruskin had a Puritan's fear of pleasure, especially sexual pleasure. "Between imagination and passion, between spiritual and sensual love, there existed a disastrous dichotomy which, although it did not kill desire, reduced his faculties to impotence." Quennell felt that the whole century was torn between this attraction and repulsion.

The scholars of twenty years ago were highly critical of James and Whitehouse. Commenting on the former, Charles Frederick Harrold said: "Out of 633 letters of Ruskin and Euphemia Chalmers Gray, the editor, Effie Gray's grandson, has chosen a comparative handful with which to vindicate the memory of his grandmother. The result is as distorted a picture as the reader can well imagine; there is, of course, no attempt at explaining Ruskin's conduct. The value of such a publication as this is virtually nil" (*MP*, 1948). And in "Controversy over Ruskin: A Review Article," Karl Litzenberg argued: "The real question at issue is: How far can one go (or how far does one need to go) with the biographical investigation of a thinker and still contribute to an understanding of his thought—or, for that matter—to an understanding of his place in posterity?" (*JEGP*, 1951).

Derrick Leon's *Ruskin the Great Victorian* (1949) was not open to the same strictures as James and Whitehouse. It was old-fashioned even when it appeared. Written before the end of World War II and published posthumously, it assumed the necessity of filling in the social background, albeit sketchily and eclectically. This defect, however, was more than compensated for by the wide knowledge of Victoriana that Leon brought to his task. Unfortunately the documentation is faulty, probably because the work was left incomplete. Ruskin partisan though he was, Leon had few illusions about his hero. He called attention to Ruskin's suppressed savagery, a side of his nature most biographers pass over lightly, although no critic can afford to ignore its intrusion into his writings, especially since in a recent article, "John Ruskin: Radical and Psychotic Genius" (*PsyR*, 1969), Robert J.

Joseph rejects the manic-depressive diagnosis, contending instead that Ruskin was a severely sadomasochistic character whose defenses gradually crumbled, revealing his schizophrenic psychosis.

Leon also gave the first reasonably full account of the Rose La Touche affair, contenting himself with the facts and arguing very little for any particular interpretation. His major contribution to our understanding of this bizarre courtship was his publication of generous portions of the letters written by Ruskin, Rose, and her mother to John James Ruskin, Mrs. Cowper-Temple, and George Macdonald.

Perhaps the most satisfying of all the biographies is Joan Evans' *John Ruskin* (1954). What is impressive about her work is the balanced judgment and the sense of tact with which she selects the best suggestions of other scholars and passes the rest in silence. The Introduction is exceptionally valuable, because in it she gives a brief evaluation of the principal items of Ruskin scholarship.

Although she acknowledges our permanent indebtedness to Cook and Wedderburn for the editorial labors which provided such a massive store of information, she notes with mild disapproval Cook's Victorian reserve. She accepts in the main Wilenski's diagnosis of Ruskin's mental illness as a case of manic-depressive psychosis. She does not quarrel with Quennell's interpretation; she incorporates most of it into her own. In her account of Ruskin's marriage and Effie's elopement she employs with telling effect two Millais drawings of 1853, one of a meeting between a man and a woman who looks like Effie, another which is a macabre fantasy of the wedding at Bowerswell, complete with the ghost of Ruskin's grandfather. (See also Joan Evans, "Millais' Drawings of 1853," *Burlington Mag.*, 1950.) She admires Leon's encyclopedic fullness without adopting his extravagant evaluation of Ruskin's importance: very few, she thinks, will ever again read many of the thirty-nine volumes. She succeeds, however, in painting a remarkably warm and honest portrait which brings the man alive before us in all his grandeur and folly. Satisfying though it is, there is very little originality about her interpretation except its quiet sanity and the felicity of its wording.

Since 1955 there has been no full-length biography of Ruskin, but one biographical study deserves special mention, Helen Gill Viljoen's *Ruskin's Scottish Heritage: A Prelude* (1956). Viljoen announced in her introduction that this was to be the first volume of a multivolume definitive biography. Since no second volume has appeared, the prelude remains a study of Ruskin's ancestry, a study that ends with John James and Margaret beginning their honeymoon. The publication of this book raised a number of questions which are still pertinent.

Does the fact that a man produced a certain quantity of literature justify study of his genealogy? Certainly his heredity is important. If it is out-of-bounds for the literary scholar, how do we justify environmental studies, which quite possibly are less important in explaining the genesis of literary art than chromosomal arrangement? In such questions our practical rule is that the latitude allowed is in direct proportion to the fame of the artist. Certainly in Shakespeare's case almost anything goes. In this particular case some judged that Viljoen had stepped out-of-bounds. Ruskin's merit does not justify such an excursion into the cultural history of the lower-middle class in Scotland. But we recall that Harrold and Litzenberg cried "Hold, enough!" when James, Quennell, and Whitehouse were publishing in 1947–50, and yet without their efforts there could have been no Joan Evans. Sir E. T. Cook gave us the conventional facts, but an itinerary of Ruskin's travels and a calendar of his social appointments provide no entry into his mind.

Leaving this controversy aside, there is very little doubt about the value of Viljoen's contribution to Ruskin studies, a value that does not in the least depend on whether or not her projected biography is ever finished. She proved her point: she marshaled more than enough evidence to convince anyone that the Library Edition must be used with caution. Before 1956 biographers popular and scholarly seemed so dazzled by its splendor that they tended to take it on faith. Viljoen overstated her case, to be sure, but if the Library Edition must still be regarded as one of the most reliable editions in the field of Victorian prose, then the implications for scholarship are sobering.

Viljoen also demonstrated the danger of accepting Ruskin's autobiography, *Praeterita*, as an accurate record. Ruskin did not deliberately deceive but his emotions colored his memories of events long past. The Margaret Ruskin of *Praeterita* is not the mother Ruskin knew as a child, according to Viljoen, but a Ruskin creation. The real Margaret was a sensitive spinster with feelings of inferiority, who suffered much from her uncle, whose son she at last married when she was in her late thirties.

Viljoen charged that Cook and Wedderburn assembled evidence to support the accuracy of *Praeterita* and to give a favorable picture of Ruskin and his parents. "And never once since they produced that long array of volumes has any biographer failed to found his work upon *Praeterita* as though in it one finds the Ruskin gospel, to be read verbatim and uncritically accepted, as though one were an Evangelical turning to his Bible." Again, the case may be overstated, but there is truth in it.

Growing dissatisfaction with the text of *Praeterita* in the Library Edition was underscored by Samuel E. Brown's examination of the manuscript, "The Unpublished Passages in the Manuscript of Ruskin's Autobiography" (*VN*, 1959). In their critical apparatus Cook and Wedderburn added about ninety pages to the original text, at times with unhappy results which suggest that Ruskin's rejection of the passages was sound. On the other hand, some interesting passages do not appear in their edition.

John Lewis Bradley's *An Introduction to Ruskin* (1971) is the best work of its kind, a short biography with sound comments on the individual works. The bibliography is carefully selected and annotated.

III. LETTERS, JOURNALS, AND OTHER BIOGRAPHICAL MATERIALS

Unfortunately we are still awaiting the remaining volumes of Viljoen's biography. In the meantime she has produced three other items: a catalog, *Ruskin's Backgrounds, Friendships and Interests as Reflected in the F. J. Sharp Collection* (1965); an edition, *The Froude-Ruskin Friendship as Represented through Letters* (1967); and most important, *The Brantwood Diary of John Ruskin, Together with Selected Related Letters and Sketches of Persons Mentioned* (1971). Of particular interest are the disjointed entries during the onset of madness in 1878, competently analyzed and annotated by Viljoen. If it is distressing to read of the madman's violence, it is some recompense to discover that he retained the respect of the physicians who tended him, Sir John Simon and George Parsons. Parsons had little money, but in 1878 he contributed to the fund to purchase the "Pass of Splugen" for his patient.

The most important new materials published since Cook and Wedderburn are *The Diaries of John Ruskin*, selected and edited by Joan Evans and John Howard Whitehouse in three volumes (1955–59). Most of what was valuable in these diaries from the purely factual viewpoint had already been explored by Cook and Wedderburn, and Joan Evans had already used them to excellent effect in her biography. Later works like John D. Rosenberg's *The Darkening Glass: A Portrait of Ruskin's Genius* (1961) have been much enriched by their availability. Despite their obvious value, these volumes must be used with caution, because after all they are selections. It is difficult to single out, as specially significant, individual features of a work of more than a thousand pages that has already contributed significantly to the exegesis not just of an important writer but of a whole age. But to cite just two such features, first, there is the account of the very real raptures of the lad on first beholding the Alps, a healthy corrective to Samuel Butler's story about going up to the monastery to see the dogs. Our century having seen the dogs, the twenty-first may find hypocrisy irresistibly attractive. Second, there is Ruskin's openness to a wide range of intellectual interests during his Oxford years, and, in the years when he was composing *Modern Painters*, I and II, a similar openness to sensual impressions. The two in combination led to the brilliant beginning of Ruskin's career.

Another edition of considerable importance is John Lewis Bradley, *Ruskin's Letters from Venice 1851–1852* (1955). Most of the 278 letters had never been published before; the record of prior publication is painstaking and apparently complete. Especially noteworthy is the introduction, in which Bradley evaluates the various collections of Ruskin letters edited before 1955. He points out that in both the Norton and the James editions there are numerous excisions, many on the grounds of decorum, and thus, possibly, we are deprived of the precise passages that would be most illuminating. By all means, Bradley argues, Ruskin's correspondence should be edited in its entirety. "From the foregoing, it should be apparent that the editing of Ruskin's letters has not been on as high a plane as is desirable. . . . It is to be hoped that effort will be made by future scholars to edit his correspondence fully and competently, so that the old antipathies and ghosts of Victorian propriety may be finally banished from Ruskin biography."

Bradley pursued his labors in another fine, well-annotated edition, *The Letters of John Ruskin to Lord and Lady Mount-Temple* (1964). Although this correspondence spans the period 1856–88 and touches on a wide range of Ruskin's concerns, the important letters are those which reveal what Ruskin thought, or said he thought, about Rose. Bradley shrewdly observes that despite the sheer bulk of what Ruskin wrote about Rose, she "seems singularly wraithlike when one tries to imagine the sort of person she was." The letters bear out Bradley's judgment. They reflect a habit of mind that Joan Evans identified in some of the James letters. Ruskin never put Effie before himself either consciously or unconsciously; when he wanted to please her, he described how he felt when she pleased him.

By 1964 one might well have asked if there was any point in examining more letters by and about Ruskin. We already knew more about him and his relatives and friends than we do about most Victorians. Then in 1965 came Mary Lutyens' fascinating *Young Mrs. Ruskin in Venice: Unpublished Letters of Mrs. John Ruskin Written from Venice between 1849–1852*, and two years later her *Millais and the Ruskins*. These two volumes are biographical studies in the form of letters quoted in whole or in part, some familiar to scholars, some hitherto unpublished, combined by means of a running commentary into a coherent, unified account of the Ruskins and their intimates between 1848 and 1854, with adequate prologue and epilogue. Together they compel an adjustment of received opinions. If we could know as much as we knew about Ruskin on such mountainous evidence as we had in 1964, and if two volumes could enable us to know what we know so much more clearly, then we have to wonder just how much we really know about the major literary figures of earlier times. And the question raised by many concerning Viljoen's book on the Scottish heritage has been answered: the "facts" about a man's life are infinite, and new facts do change old views, no matter how well grounded they were.

John James Ruskin seems more than ever the major culprit, as Viljoen had argued, and for the reasons that she set forth. He was a merchant on the make, worried by his lack of social standing, anxious to win it for his son, ready to reprimand Mr. Gray for his lack of business sense, piously smug about the misfortunes of others, disappointed that John could not marry better, shrewd at penetrating the poses of Effie and her family, but obtuse when it came to the trinity of Denmark Hill. His letter to Mr. Gray, 16 February 1854, is a marvel which every Victorian scholar should know (*Millais and the Ruskins*). Despite all that had been written about him before 1965, he lacked a third dimension, which these books provided. Margaret Ruskin seems even more repelling than before, but she remains shadowy. It is wise to remember that we see her almost entirely through Effie's eyes.

Effie Gray is a major surprise. It has always been easy to dismiss her as empty-headed: in that case, it is hard to explain how she managed to give such a superb picture of Venice in the early 1850's when local society was dominated by the Austrian occupation forces. Perhaps if she had tried, she would have failed, but rambling on, transferring her own gossip to paper, she was an artist. Never questioning the values of society, always observing every detail with intense interest, she wrote directly without the inhibitions of a trained intelligence.

Lutyens gives us as much information about the sexual relationship between John and Effie as we are ever likely to have. She also gives an absorbing account of Effie's flight which answers many questions but raises still more. Far too many people knew what was afoot to keep it a secret; it was known to the Grays, their friends the Cheneys, the obstetrician Dr. Robert Lee, the lawyers retained by the Grays, Sir Charles Eastlake and Lady Eastlake, Murray the bookseller, Millais, Rawdon Brown, and even John Ruskin's servant Crawley. Given this list, it seems reasonable to assume that there were others. Was it really a secret? Crawley left with Effie, then returned to his job with Ruskin, and years later became the curator of the drawing school at Oxford.

Mary Lutyens acknowledges her deep indebtedness to Helen Gill Viljoen, and regards these two volumes as slight compared with Viljoen's promised biography. If her estimate is just, then that will indeed be a book worth waiting fifteen years to read.

Other fruits of Lutyens' research are "The Millais-LaTouche Correspondence" (*Cornhill*, 1967) and "Millais's Portrait of Ruskin" (*Apollo*, 1967). The former is the first publication of the whole correspondence, including a hitherto unknown exchange two years before the famous letter of 1870. The latter is an account of the painting of the picture and its subsequent history. Still another item of major interest for an understanding of the marriage manqué is Joseph G. Links, *The Ruskins in Normandy: A Tour in 1848 with Murray's Handbook* (1968), a combination narrative and commentary based on the letters of John and Effie, plus the diary of John Hobbs, the servant whom they called "George" because there were already too many John's in the family.

However tangled the story of Ruskin's marriage, the biographer needs no more than a reasonable share of patience, candor, and charity to tell it well, so great is its inherent interest. The Ruskin-Whistler controversy is another episode which almost invariably promotes good narration, as in H. Montgomery Hyde's *Their Good Names* (1970), a legal study of famous suits for libel. Francis L. Fennell argues in "The Verdict in Whistler v. Ruskin" (*VN*, 1971) that the jury performed commendably, and would have found in favor of Ruskin had not Sir John Holker botched the defense and had not Baron Huddleston confused the issues in his charge to the jury. The girls' school at Winnington is another matter. "But what, I here ask myself, was Miss Bell about to permit and encourage these proceedings?" as R. H. Wilenski observed and after giving the Cook and Wedderburn answer, he concluded: "Perhaps that was the whole story. Perhaps not." The best account is Van Akin Burd's edition of *The Winnington Letters: John Ruskin's Correspondence with Margaret Alexis Bell and the Children at Winnington Hall* (1969). This edition inspired a sensitive and sympathetic review article by V. S. Pritchett, "Ruskin and the Girls" (*New Statesman*, 1970).

From these biographies and editions it is relatively easy to compile a checklist of letters, their locations, and their peregrinations. Bradley, Lutyens, and Viljoen are especially helpful. Also useful are Charles T. Dougherty, "John Ruskin" (*VN*, 1958) and Charles Richard Sanders, "Carlyle's Letters to Ruskin: A Finding List with Some Unpublished Letters and Comments" (*BJRL*, 1958). The John Rylands collection is described in an article by Robin Skelton, "John Ruskin: The Final Years. A Survey of the Ruskin Correspondence in the John Rylands Library" (*BJRL*, 1955).

Part of this correspondence was studied by Margaret Spence, "Ruskin's Friendship with Mrs. Fanny Talbot" (*BJRL*, 1960) and later edited under the title *Dearest Mama Talbot: A Selection of Letters by John Ruskin to Mrs. Fanny Talbot* (1966). Spence has written three important articles on other parts of this collection. "The Guild of St. George: Ruskin's Attempt to Translate His Ideas into Practice" (*BJRL*, 1957) is a sympathetic account of the St. George experiment, based on MSS in the John Rylands. Spence's point is one that has long cried for attention. "While it is true to state that Ruskin did in fact build up a National Store in so far as he set up a museum in which were uncut gems, rare texts, and works of art, and he also secured several plots of land, he did not seriously at any time ever envisage the practical realization of his Utopian vision." Peter Quennell had formed the same judgment on much less evidence.

The second article, "Ruskin's Correspondence with Miss Blanche Atkinson" (*BJRL*, 1959), is still another depressing revelation about his later years. In March 1873, the twenty-six-year-old unmarried daughter of a rising Liverpool soap merchant, vastly dissatisfied with her father's business associates and desirous of making something worthwhile of her life, sent Ruskin a subscription to *Fors* and a note of appreciation. She wanted to be a servant of St. George's Guild but he fended her off. To her insistent demands that he give her something useful to do he responded by sending her new books—she was to cut the pages. Eventually she helped him keep track of his enormous correspondence. He wrote her one hundred and forty letters in a period of about thirteen years. They met exactly three times.

In the last of the three articles, "Ruskin's Correspondence with His God-Daughter Constance Oldham" (*BJRL*, 1961), Spence tells how in 1878 Constance Oldham requested some very specific information from Mrs. Severn concerning Ruskin's breakdown. Constance's brother had suffered a similar illness shortly before. Some of her specific questions might well have been quoted but they were not. We do learn that Constance cut passages from some letters Ruskin wrote at the time of the Olander affair.

This, the last and most depressing of Ruskin's loves, is the burden of Rayner Unwin's *The Gulf of Years: Letters from John Ruskin to Kathleen Olander* (1953). Young Kathleen had high hopes of becoming his secretary and restoring his faith in orthodox Christianity, but by 1888 he had other ideas. Even after Kathleen heard about his "marriage" she wanted to be his wife, but by the end of this year Joan Severn was intercepting her letters.

There are other melancholy memorials of those last years. Oliver Ferguson's "Ruskin's Continental Letters to Mrs. Severn" (*JEGP*, 1952) shows the confused mental state of Ruskin on the last tour, 1888. He seemed to be all right until he left Chamouni and headed for a meeting with the Alexanders, Francesca, and her mother. Charles T. Dougherty's "Ruskin and Manning: Some New Ruskin Letters" (*Manuscripta*, 1966) is interesting only as evidence of Ruskin's confusion in 1883. Roger Fulford's brief but interesting letter, "Ruskin's Notes on Carlyle" (*TLS*, 16 April 1971), is a discussion of Ruskin's marginalia in his copy of the Charles Eliot Norton edition of Carlyle correspondence. In 1967 James Dearden edited *The Professor: Memoir of John Ruskin by Arthur Severn*, which tells us more about the shortcomings of Severn than about Ruskin. The best recent account of Ruskin's slow decay is in Sheila Birkenhead's *Illustrious Friends: The Story of Joseph Severn and His Son Arthur* (1965), which makes abundantly clear how difficult the old man was, and how much he owed to Joan Severn, who saw him through to the end. To these must of course be added Viljoen's edition of the Brantwood diaries.

In addition to his work on Arthur Severn's memoir, James Dearden has contributed several other items of biographical and bibliographical interest. "John Ruskin's Bookplates" (*BC*, 1964) contains a useful caution concerning the origin of certain bookplates reading "Ex libris / John Ruskin / Brantwood." This article should be read in conjunction with another of the same name (*BC*, 1969). In "John Ruskin's Poems (1850)" (*BC*, 1966) Dearden announces an attempt to account for the copies of this rare edition. A subsequent report is in "The Production and Distribution of John Ruskin's *Poems* of 1850" (*BC*, 1968). "*Ruskin's Politics* by Bernard Shaw" (*BC*, 1971) recounts the origin of this curious pamphlet, which was not a successful publishing venture. In an important series of three articles and a note, all under the title "Wise and Ruskin" (*BC*, 1969 and 1971), Dearden examines at full length the whole subject of the infamous Ruskin forgeries. John Carter's "Wise Forgeries in Dove's Bindings" (*BC*, 1968) and Simon Nowell-Smith's "Wise, Smart & Moody" (*BC*, 1969) are notes on the same subject. From these recent studies the Cook and Wedderburn bibliography emerges with honor though not without error. It is pleasant to record that Jean Halladay, in "Some Errors in the Bibliography of the Library Edition of John Ruskin's Works" (*PBSA*, 1968), finds very few errors in the listing of reviews, testimony to the astonishing accuracy of this massive bibliography.

Dearden's "John Ruskin, the Collector: With a Catalogue of the Illuminated and Other Manuscripts Formerly in His Collection" (*Library*, 1966) contains a catalog of MSS once in Ruskin's possession, as complete as scholars can make it at the present time. It does not include literary MSS such as those of four Scott novels which once belonged to Ruskin. His collection was once quite large. He gave many items to his friends, either intact, for which we admire his generosity, or in part, for which we deplore his vandalism. After his death the Severns sold many valuable items. Dearden's "The Ruskin Galleries at Bembridge School, Isle of Wight" (*BJRL*, 1969) is a descriptive catalog of MSS and letters. "John Ruskin's Art Collection —A Centenary" (*Connoisseur*, 1971) is a general account of the collection which took seventy years to build, and which was scattered over the earth after his death. A Turner which hung over a fireplace at Brantwood recently sold for £31,000. Some of these articles have been reprinted as part of Dearden's *Facets of Ruskin* (1970), a miscellany, as the title suggests.

IV. CRITICISM

Retrospect

Turning to the general criticism of Ruskin's work, we note certain trends since Wilenski in 1933 gave a clear, if arguable, summary of Ruskin's aesthetic and social criticism. From 1933 to the end of World War II little was added to our knowledge but the twilight memories of late Victorians, illuminating at times and always interesting, but otherwise not very useful. After 1945 Ruskin again became the object of serious study in the field of art by Van Akin Burd, and in the field of economics by John T. Fain. The work of these scholars is on the whole sympathetic though not uncritical, and nearly always informed and objective. In general, from 1933 to 1961 the received view was patronizing toward Ruskin's aesthetics, but politely favorable toward his economics, although for no reason more compelling than sentimental socialism. Then, in 1961, with the publication of John D. Rosenberg's *The Darkening Glass: A Portrait of Ruskin's Genius*, a new dimension is added to Ruskin scholarship. The scholarly work of the last decade is impressive, earlier work suffers by comparison.

A few of the early testimonies to Ruskin's influence still deserve careful attention, among them G. B. Shaw's *Ruskin's Politics* (1921), William R. Inge's thoughtful lecture of 14 February 1934, "Plato and Ruskin" (*Essays by Divers Hands*, Trans. of the Royal Soc. of Lit., XIV, 1935), and John W. Mackail's chapter on Ruskin in *Studies in Humanism* (1938). Charles A. Beard paid a touching tribute in "Ruskin and the Babble of Tongues" (*New Republic*, 1936). He recalled that in 1899 the economics taught at Ruskin College, Oxford, were the economics of the future, thanks to the man for whom the college was named.

Benjamin E. Lippincott's *Victorian Critics of Democracy: Carlyle, Ruskin, Arnold, Stephen, Maine, Lecky* (1938) has permanent value as an example of the methodology of a generation ago. It is very careful, more thorough than some later work, but defective by recent standards. He found fault with Ruskin because, like Carlyle, he believed that the sins of the society were the sins of individuals and he looked to individuals for reform. Obviously Lippincott's conclusion is at least questionable, although it can be supported by numerous citations. The error is the result of trying to reconstruct the system of an unsystematic thinker by quoting indiscriminately from works written over a period of twenty-odd years. Much the same shortcoming mars another painstaking study, Hilda B. Hagstotz, *The Educational Theories of John Ruskin* (1942). The best summary of Ruskin's influence on British social thinkers of the late nineteenth and early twentieth centuries is Frank Daniel Curtin's essay, "Aesthetics in English Social Reform: Ruskin and His Followers" (in Herbert Davis, William C. DeVane, and Robert C. Bald, ed., *Nineteenth-Century Studies*, 1940). Mature thinkers rejected Ruskin's fantasies; they were not so distracted by his eccentricities that they missed his very real importance.

Just a year before Wilenski's book appeared, the standard study of Ruskin's art theories was Henry Ladd's *The Victorian Morality of Art: An Analysis of Ruskin's Aesthetic* (1932), which remained until 1971 the best systematic exposition of Ruskin's theories, arranging them as logically as possible with due recognition of qualifications and contradictions. In retrospect, however, it does seem a static analysis of a man whose ideas were constantly changing, and it suffered by the accident of preceding Wilenski by one year. Wilenski showed how much of Ruskin's thought had to be discarded as psychic vagary in order to find those constants which give his art criticism its permanent value. They are scattered through *Modern Painters, The Seven Lamps of Architecture,* and *The Stones of Venice*; little of importance was added in later works. Wilenski's abstract of these constants has its own lasting value, inasmuch as recent criticism seems to reinforce rather than supersede it.

According to Wilenski, Ruskin believed that since great art is in some sense a revelation of God, it cannot be produced by aesthetic means alone, and therefore only a man who is on balance a good man can produce great art. The Aesthetic Man is as much an absurdity as the Economic Man. The great artist is a phenomenon of nature, extraordinarily sensitive to the world around him and able to see life clearly. He delights in his material and he is influenced by it. The technique he evolves as a means of expression is itself valuable. He is never concerned with illusionist imitation. All great art is invention. It is in a way and to a degree conventional and abstract. In the hands of an artist who is metaphysically bad, abstraction becomes geometric art, which is dead; in the hands of a great artist abstraction produces organic art which contains the fullness of life. The noblest art is that which reveals most about life, and thus expresses the greatest number of great ideas. After 1858 two things destroyed even the semblance of unity in Ruskin's theory. First, he based his criticisms on the existence of a transcendent order; when his faith was shaken, so was his aesthetic, bluster how he might. Second, Ruskin was too honest to his own impressions to maintain any consistency; when he liked what his theory excluded he enlarged the theory to include the object.

On Ruskin as a critic of society Wilenski was stimulating but uneven. *John Ruskin: Social Reformer* (1898), by the distinguished though unorthodox economist John A. Hobson, had provided a sound foundation for further study. Nevertheless Wilenski was misleading in his exposition of Ruskin's economics, because he did not know the status of that science in the 1860's. Inevitably, therefore, he overrated the significance and the effectiveness of Ruskin's attack on the Economic Man. More valuable was his characterization of Ruskin's social theories as an application to the world at large of the microcosm on Denmark Hill with its paternalism and stratification intact. That society was in some ways exemplary and in others sadly lacking, like the orderly world that John Ruskin envisioned.

The first substantial article to employ Wilenski's insights effectively was Robin Ironside's "The Art Criticism of John Ruskin" (*Horizon*, 1943). Although Ironside's scholarship was unreliable in detail, his judgments were illuminating. He conceded that Ruskin frequently lapsed into "laughable, sometimes touching, puerilities of phrase and thought," but that was excused by its cause, a voracious sensibility and a willingness to share his reactions. From a man of such exposed emotions we should expect "chordal variety" in his utterances, a baffling inconsistency as he responds to the emotion of the moment, so that he can write like a prude and then defend Swinburne. He can demand photographic accuracy and deny the importance of realism. To try to unify his work by regrouping his dicta is to miss the point: ". . . it is in the passages of rhapsody, in the subtle analyses of his own conflicting emotions, that his spirit is today most alight. Compared with these, recent art criticism in England is an affair of flat balanced notions . . . which come near to reducing the importance of the subject to that of an amenity recommendable on rational grounds to all; . . . Ruskin at least leaves us in no doubt that he is dealing with a passionate issue, momentous to anyone able to grasp its inspiring breadth."

Three other articles of the war years are still worth noting. In "Ruskin's Relation to Aristotle" (*PhR*, 1940), Katherine Gilbert noted that Ruskin was both repelled and attracted by Aristotle, repelled because he disliked system, attracted because he sympathized with the inductive approach to art. In "The Relationship of Wordsworth's 'Ode on the Intimations of Immortality' to Ruskin's Theory of the Infinite in Art" (*MLR*, 1941), Douglas R. Angus pointed out that the image of light in the distance is basic to the great ode and that such images are types of infinity in *Modern Painters* II. In "The Reception of *Modern Painters*" (*MLN*, 1942), Lester Dolk surveyed the reviews and memoirs which record reactions to the first volumes. Dolk concluded that Ruskin's success with the general public was immediate but that he failed to change the opinions of qualified judges.

Economics and Social Reform

Richard Jennings was probably expressing the common view in "A Victorian Prophet" (*NC*, 1946) when he said that, although as an art critic Ruskin seemed capricious and unjust, as a social critic he seemed a major prophet. This received view was modified by John T. Fain in a series of articles which culminated in *Ruskin and the Economists* (1956). After a preliminary article, "Ruskin and His Father" (*PMLA*, 1944), in which he rehearsed John James's attempts at censorship, Fain outlined the main points of his studies in "Ruskin and the Orthodox Political Economists" (*Southern Econ. J.*, 1947).

According to Fain, Ruskin's attack was based on three positions: (1) orthodox economics scorned Christian morality; (2) although it professed to be a science of humanity in one set of relationships, it ignored all human characteristics except the brutish; and (3) even considered as no more than a commercial science, it was obviously false. At the heart of the matter lay the distinction between "value in use" and "value in exchange," which originated with Adam Smith and came down intact to Marshall. For more than a century and a half British economists of the "orthodox" variety (Senior, J. S. Mill, Cairnes, Bagehot) ignored the use and concentrated on the exchange. Methodologically speaking, they were right to do so, but ignoring the real harm caused by certain forms of production and consumption led to the ideological abuses of various business interests. Ruskin's attack on the economists was ignorant and unjustifiable, but if certain interests resorted to perversion of the theorists, then in all fairness it would seem that Ruskin was entitled to attack the perversion.

In the second part of this major article, Fain pointed out that literary students are seldom informed about economics: therefore they rely on passing comments by equally uninformed literary critics, or at best on Hobson's book, the only full-length study of Ruskin by a professional economist. Unfortunately Hobson, although professionally competent, was a foe of orthodox economics and on the same grounds as Ruskin. Fain outlined the thought of several eminent Victorian economists on the key point selected by Ruskin for attack. Nassau Senior, for example, defined wealth in terms of exchange, consciously and explicitly. Mill specified that his economics dealt only with man as a being who sought wealth and warned that economic theory could not be applied without reinstating the actual man in place of the economic abstraction. Cairnes admitted that the "economic man" was an abstraction but he felt, like many distinguished theorists, that the abstraction was necessary to investigate certain phenomena.

Thus one of Ruskin's main points was conceded. Was he, therefore, justified in belaboring it? Yes. The economists strove for objectivity in describing commercial transactions and they did not offer advice, but the practitioners of business chose to treat their abstract analyses as advice, and Ruskin was right to attack the perversions of applied economics. "In so far as Ruskin's indictment applies to the work of the best exponents of nineteenth-century orthodox political economy, it is false. In so far as his indictment applies to the prostitution of that economy by politicians and industrialists, it is sound."

Two other Fain articles were devoted to individual economists. "Ruskin and Mill" (MLQ, 1951) explained how Ruskin was the victim of his own rhetorical strategy. He liked to feign ignorance in order to ask embarrassing questions with beguiling innocence. Thus at times he seems to misread Mill deliberately, as when he ridiculed Mill's distinction between productive and unproductive labor. Ruskin "complained bitterly that contemporary economists gave him no sympathetic understanding. He should have tried to give a little himself" (p. 154). The other article, "Ruskin and Hobson" (PMLA, 1952), underscored Hobson's identification of Ruskin's main contribution to economic theory as his development of the concepts of social utility and social cost.

Of course it is possible to argue that here as in the field of aesthetics the attempt to construct a Ruskinian system is futile, as Gaylord C. LeRoy did in two articles, "Ruskin and the Condition of England" (SAQ, 1948) and "John Ruskin: An Interpretation of His 'Daily Maddening Rage'" (MLQ, 1949). In the first, LeRoy rejected as useless any attempt to erect a Ruskinian economics and attempted instead to bring his ideas into focus by identifying and discarding those which are the product of psychopathology. We have to reject every Ruskin effort to erect his whims into cosmic laws, for example, declaring waterpower right and steam power wrong. Such things we can easily identify and put aside. In many ways he was out of touch with the best thought of his own time and irrelevant for ours, but he can startle us with insights into "the humbug that passes for sanity."

In the second article LeRoy contended that Ruskin went mad for reasons he did not understand, but on the conscious level he thought he was going mad because he could not influence the course of events. His reaction is more than an individual matter because it is a symptom of the malaise of the century: (1) he doubts the ability of reason to affect events; (2) he assumes that civilization is on the decline and becomes a philosophical pessimist; (3) abandoning reform in despair, he retreats into art for art's sake; and (4) he advocates a basic reconstruction of society. LeRoy reinforced the basic contentions of these two articles with an interesting psychological analysis in his chapter on Ruskin in *Perplexed Prophets: Six Nineteenth Century British Authors* (1953). In short, Ruskin could compare an imagined state of national well-being with the actual state of Great Britain, but he could not construct a system.

Holbrook Jackson in *Dreamers of Dreams: The Rise and Fall of 19th Century Idealism* (1948) offered a brief but perceptive judgment. Primarily Ruskin welded aesthetics and ethics into a set of social, as opposed to financial, values. Concerning his contradictions, Jackson observed that they were natural changes of mind, whims and fancies such as most writers experience but keep to themselves.

Since 1945 there has been very little study of Ruskin's educational theories. Aside from incidental commentary, the only substantial addition to the literature was Francis X. Roellinger, "Ruskin on Education" (*J. of Gen. Educ.*, 1950). A few articles on specific issues are still noteworthy. George H. Ford's "The Governor Eyre Case in England" (*UTQ*, 1948) gave a balanced judgment of Ruskin's role in the affair. He had supported Mill and Thomas Hughes for Parliament, but he went against them on this issue which split the reformers into Tories and radicals. An interesting sidelight on Ruskin's Alpine irrigation project is in Hans W. Haüsermann, *The Genevese Background: Studies of Shelley, Francis Darby, Maria Edgeworth, Ruskin, Meredith, and Joseph Conrad in Geneva, with Hitherto Unpublished Letters* (1952). In "Ruskin as Utopist" (*N&Q*, 1956), W. H. G. Armytage gave a brief account of the Totley Farm experiment near Sheffield and of Edward Carpenter's account of it in *My Days and Dreams* (1916).

In a provocative article, "The Debate over Women: Ruskin versus Mill" (*VS*, 1970), Kate Millett compares "Of Queen's Gardens" with *The Subjection of Women*, because, she argues, the whole range of Victorian thought on the subject is compressed within these two statements. "Ruskin's lecture is significant as one of the most complete insights obtainable into that compulsive masculine fantasy one might call the official Victorian attitude." After picturing the domesticated female who is queen in her garden, Ruskin holds her responsible for morality in the world. "The salvation of the world which, he is assured, should come from its subject women is a concoction of nostalgic mirage, regressive sexuality, religious ambition, and simplistic social panacea."

In view of all the casual tributes to Ruskin as a critic of society, it is curious indeed that so little has been said about this side of his work in the last fifteen years, especially when we think of poverty and pollution. Ruskin's instinctive fear of new and artificial sources of energy was long regarded as an eccentricity, certainly reactionary, perhaps pathological in origin. Now it appears prophetic. Edward Alexander's "Ruskin and Science" (*MLR*, 1969) compels a reevaluation of a seldom read book. According to Alexander, Ruskin drew a clear distinction—about as good as any since—between the truth of science and the truth of art. Science got at the truth of essences, whereas art aimed at the truth of appearances, including the emotions of the beholder in the presence of the object. But eventually Ruskin became disillusioned by the destructiveness of science. Technology had made war unthinkable and threatened to ruin life on earth by polluting the air and the water. The shift toward disillusionment is the burden of *The Eagle's Nest*, which attacked not science itself, but rather the abuse of science by those who made it a law unto itself. Like every other part of human life, science had to prove itself useful or beautiful, life-giving rather than death-dealing. In another article, "Art amidst Revolution: Ruskin in 1848" (*VN*, 1971), Alexander traces the growing sense of guilt which beset Ruskin as he became more and more aware of the social evils around him. Was his occupation worthwhile? Like Newman, he argued that the apparent uselessness of art did not destroy its importance, because there was a profound utility in its refining and ennobling effects on the members of society. In *Ruskin Today* (1964) Clark writes that according to some of his Chinese acquaintances, "Mao was thinking of Ruskin when he organized Chinese Communism." What Clark implies here is profoundly important for the understanding of Ruskin. For his day he was extraordinarily sophisticated in matters of symbolism and semantics, fanciful yes, but there was method in his madness, though at times garlanded with wild flowers. It is entirely too easy to think of St. George's Guild as a matter of costume and coinage, thus missing some rather grim meanings.

John O. Waller's "Ruskin on Slavery: A Semantic Controversy" (*VN*, 1965) is a lesson on the difficulty of interpreting Ruskin even at the surface level. The difficulty in this case arises because Ruskin did not object to forced labor any more than Carlyle did. Waller finds seven senses of the term slavery in Ruskin's works. Does it make sense to interpret Ruskin's Utopian pronouncements literally? Did he really think St. George's Guild was a practical solution to England's problems? Peter Quennell and Margaret Spence have surmised that he did not, and their position is not at all untenable.

Art and Aesthetics

Since World War II there has been a very slow shift of opinion toward Ruskin's aesthetics. In general, increased knowledge and the perspective of time have led to a more favorable view of him both as artist and as critic. The first sign of this shift was Sir Richard W. Livingstone's lecture "Ruskin" (*PBA*, 1945). Livingstone found that by the end of World War II Ruskin's erratic economics seemed almost a set of truisms, but that between 1920 and 1940 his work on art had seemed hopelessly outmoded by art for art's sake. Now, he contended, a reaction had set in. Livingstone compared art for art's sake to a plea for cancer, which is the uncontrolled growth of a part of an organism without regard to the welfare of the organism as a whole. Art is just one more special interest of mankind demanding complete independence. "In his own time his insistence, now universally approved, on the claims of moral and spiritual ideals in the realm of economics was deeply resented; his insistence on their importance in the field of art, which his contemporaries rejected, is equally unfashionable to-day. I believe that in both art and economics he was right." According to Richard Jennings, Kenneth Clark, in a review of Livingstone's lecture, predicted a Ruskin revival. Jennings, however, appraised informed opinion as still favorable to Ruskin on economics, unfavorable to Ruskin on art ("Ruskin Revival" and "A Victorian Prophet," *NC*, 1946).

When Clark took his place as Slade Professor he paid tribute to his great predecessor in *Ruskin at Oxford: An Inaugural Lecture* (1947). He found marked similarities between the conclusions of those "two great critics," Fry and Ruskin, who apparently differed so widely. Perhaps because they came of Puritan stock, they came "to the same conclusion: that the most fatal defect in a work of art is for the artist to be more interested in displaying his own skill than in conveying the idea. As a result, both placed a high value on what used to be called primitive art; and for luxury art, art designed for the gratification of rich people, they reserved their most severe condemnations." With the perspective of a great scholar, Clark concluded his address: "And if we pause to reflect on his opinions on art, so often alarmingly at variance with our own, how often do we find that we have been the dupes of intellectual fashion, as incomprehensible, it may be, as the economic fantasies of our grandfathers. All the tortures of conscience, all the pressure of his rigid moral sense, could not numb those marvelous powers of perception which allowed Ruskin to penetrate farther into the core of certain kinds of art than any critic before or since."

There followed modest contributions by Jared Moore, "The Sublime, and Other Subordinate Aesthetic Concepts" (*JP*, 1948), singling out Ruskin as the first to recognize the sublime as a particular kind of beauty, and by Robert B. Shaffer, whose "Ruskin, Norton, and Memorial Hall" (*HLB*, 1949) was an offbeat article, readable and permanently valuable for its insight into the problems of architects, circa 1870. By the end of the century there was a reaction against literary buildings like Memorial Hall at Harvard; people had forgotten that the Gothic Revival was in its day a dominant intellectual movement, far more solidly based in philosophy than later revivals. At the midpoint of our century Grace Banyard remarked that Ruskin's influence was pervasive but went unrecognized; people held his ideas without knowing it, because they did not read his works ("Ruskin," *FortR*, 1950).

In a monograph, *Ruskin and the Landscape Feeling: A Critical Analysis of His Thought during the Crucial Years of His Life, 1843–1860* (1951), Francis G. Townsend examined *Modern Painters* not as an organized system of aesthetics, but as the external record of a mental process. As Ruskin's faith weakened, he could no longer write with conviction of the beauty of God revealed in nature: at the same time, as he grew more sophisticated he no longer hoped to improve the world through art. Because art was the product of society, it was necessary to improve the society in order to produce good art, not vice versa. Townsend succeeded in making it possible to read Ruskin's masterpiece as connected, rational discourse, but only by sticking to the conscious level and resolutely avoiding any symbolic entanglements.

In 1953, there appeared the first of a series of four articles by Van Akin Burd; together they constitute a substantial study of how Ruskin's defense of Turner came into being. "Another Light on the Writing of *Modern Painters*" (*PMLA*, 1953) compared what happened to Ruskin in 1842 with Ruskin's account of what happened in *Praeterita*. Cook and Wedderburn had relied on *Praeterita*, noting that there was no diary for this key period. Others, including even Derrick Leon, followed the editors in accepting the account in *Praeterita* at face value. But Ruskin had given the missing diary to C. E. Norton in 1872, and eventually Mr. and Mrs. Arnold Whitridge donated it to the Yale Library, for which see Charles Beecher Hogan, "The Yale Collection of the Manuscripts of John Ruskin" (*YULG*, 1942). *Praeterita* celebrates the epiphany at Fontainebleau, when a single aspen showed Ruskin the art which surpasses art: there is no record of the epiphany in his diary. *Praeterita* states that he was oppressed by the flat country between Fontainebleau and Chartres: the diary says it was an interesting ride. On the day when Ruskin should have been enraged by the *Blackwood's* attack on Turner, there is a note on lizards. Forty years later, Turner and Wordsworth loomed large in his memory, but they did not figure much in his diary.

"Ruskin's Quest for a Theory of the Imagination" (*MLQ*, 1956) is another comparison between episodes in *Praeterita* and the records Ruskin made at the time, in this case his letters to his parents during his Italian tour of 1845. Burd concluded that the Library Edition had been "carefully pruned." Instead of the sentimental pathos of the autobiography, the letters reflect the happiness and enthusiasm Ruskin felt on this, his first trip alone. As we might expect, the tomb of Ilaria made no such impression on the young Ruskin when he saw it, as the old Ruskin recalled in *Praeterita*, at least none that he thought worth mentioning in his letters home.

"Ruskin's Defense of Turner: The Imitative Phase" (*PQ*, 1958) is a prudent inventory of the intellectual equipment which the graduate of Oxford brought to his task. According to Burd, the juvenilia bear witness to Ruskin's orthodox religious views, his admiration for Renaissance painters, and his respect for Sir Joshua Reynolds as both painter and critic. In the years 1836–43, certain qualities developed rapidly. His real and deep love for natural beauty and his appreciation of Turner matured into a largeness of vision which freed him from the tyranny of the conventional.

In "Background to *Modern Painters*: The Tradition and the Turner Controversy" (*PMLA*, 1959) Burd examined the aesthetic milieu of the years preceding the first volume. In general the prevailing view of art was that of Reynolds' *Discourses on Art*, delivered at the Royal Academy between 1769 and 1790, in which he revivified the Renaissance idea of generalized form. The academy lectures down to 1847—by Barry, Fuseli, Opie, Phillips, and Henry Howard—perpetuated Sir Joshua's theories while avoiding discussion of contemporary painters who were not safely dead. Even after 1830, the reviewers for the *Literary Gazette*, the *Athenaeum*, and *Blackwood's* hewed to the academy line. They claimed that Turner was extravagant and false because they saw only what earlier painters had taught them to see. Ruskin saw in 1842 that they could be overthrown by a direct appeal to the evidence of the eye. He also saw that Reynolds had known his business, but that his principles had been misunderstood and misapplied by theorists and practitioners like Beaumont.

These four articles together comprise a major study of the composition of *Modern Painters* I and II, and of *Praeterita* as well. Whether Ruskin knew what he was doing or not, his autobiography makes the discoveries of his youth more startling than they seemed at the time. Indeed, the years before 1843 assumed heroic proportions and dramatic qualities that the man who lived them knew not of until it was too late. If that is the case, then *Praeterita* is a literal lie and a symbolic truth. Or perhaps the sage of Brantwood is telling us how the Don Quixote of Denmark Hill should have felt but did not, in which case we begin to understand what Proust saw in Ruskin.

A common source of confusion is Ruskin's distinction between truth and beauty, which is closely related to such matters as the choice between representational and abstract art. In a fine article, "Ruskin's Views on Non-representational Art" (*Coll. Art J.*, 1955), Charles T. Dougherty offered a succinct solution. The beauty of a work of art, according to Ruskin, lies in its formal qualities, while the truth lies in its grasp of external reality. Roger Fry once argued that a man's head is no more important than a pumpkin for purposes of art, to which Ruskin's response would have been, according to Dougherty, that an artist who sees no more in a man's head than in a pumpkin has never really seen a man's head, whatever he may perchance mean by his vision. Another favorable critique on similar grounds was "Ruskin on the Pathetic Fallacy, or on How a Moral Theory of Art May Fail" (*JAAC*, 1955), in which Bertram Morris argued that Ruskin's moral theory consists of an insistence that there is a reality outside of art greater and more important than art, and existent whether man likes it or not. The artist must come to terms with nature, which is a moral act, and the movement of the future must be to bring man and nature into harmony again.

Still a third article on the same subject was Dougherty's "Ruskin's Moral Argument" (*VN*, 1956), probably the best short exposition of the vexed question of whether or not Ruskin said that a bad man can produce good art, and if he said it what he meant by it. Ruskin did indeed so argue, but by 1860 he knew that it was impossible to tell how moral a man is, so he tended to argue backward, from the bad art to the immoral in its creator. Ruskin, argued Dougherty, is best understood as the culmination of eighteenth-century aesthetics. He contended that man's intellect was engaged by the truth of art, while his "feelings" and senses were engaged by beauty. By "feelings" he meant the nonrational, nonsensory part of man which moralists called the "will," and a certain poet called "a passion and an appetite," and Ruskin called "taste." If morality resides in the will, then there is such a thing as moral, or immoral, art. Great artists have always died for the truth outside; bad or immoral artists have turned inward in their pride.

Despite many fine studies, Ruskin as an art critic continued to be viewed with reserve, if not active hostility, in many quarters during the fifties. V. S. Pritchett said: "He is the most solitary of the Victorians, a man living in the intellectual paradise and personal hell of visual egotism. Only the prospect pleased, only man was vile" ("The Most Solitary Victorian," *New Statesman*, 1956). In "Ruskin on English Contemporary Artists" (*Connoisseur*, 1959), Ralph Edwards said that despite innumerable eloquent passages *Modern Painters* developed an aesthetic theory which had long ceased to command assent. Still, as Joan Evans had pointed out in her biography, even after conceding the validity of the common charges against Ruskin, it is obvious that never had there been art criticism of such value before, and very seldom since. No one, she argued, who has ever read *Modern Painters* 1 can look at a Turner without feeling the influence of Ruskin.

She also called attention to the value of his drawing. Her "John Ruskin as Artist" (*Apollo*, 1957) is a delicate appreciation, beautifully illustrated. The significance of Ruskin's drawings as an index to his thought was suggested by a major article, Paul H. Walton's "Seven Ruskin Drawings in the Fogg Art Museum" (*HLB*, 1960). The seven, which date from 1842 to 1856, show Ruskin's indebtedness to Turner, the travel illustrators, and the Picturesque tradition. Late in his career, Turner began to use watercolor to transcribe his vision of color, light, form, and space as an absolute unity. Perhaps, Walton speculated, this same perception was what came to Ruskin at Fontainebleau. At any rate, in 1845 he began to model his drawing on the *Liber Studiorum*, and the effect on his criticism was to give it a historical and moral attitude toward subject matter which has rendered it unpalatable for our tastes. Nevertheless, his emphasis helped to break up the Picturesque tradition and to turn attention toward abstract pictorial quality, at the same time that it raised his own pictures "to a high rank among landscape drawings of their time."

Walton followed this article with another fine study, "A Water-Colour by John Ruskin" (*Burlington Mag.*, 1962). There are two Ruskin drawings of Amalfi, one a highly imitative work of 1841, the other a highly imaginative work of 1844, obviously the product of Turnerian influence. These two drawings, one on either side of *Modern Painters* I, reveal Ruskin's discovery of the ambiguity inherent in imitation, which can lead either to undisciplined fantasy or to self-effacing realism. In a wider context, these two drawings "present an interesting and revealing analogy, not only with the antithesis between truth and beauty that recurs so often in his criticism, but also with the split between observation and expression that was to characterize art in the second half of Ruskin's century." Another testimony to the growing respect for Ruskin's drawing is the short account of his Venetian studies in Denys Sutton's "The Pleasant Place of All Festivity" (*Apollo*, 1971).

Those inclined to say loosely that Ruskin condemned the pathetic fallacy should take careful note of a later article by J. D. Thomas, "Poetic Truth and the Pathetic Fallacy" (*TSLL*, 1961). What Ruskin said was that poets of the first order seldom produce a pathetic fallacy, although poets of the second order frequently do. But by poets of the second order he meant such masters as Wordsworth, Keats, and Tennyson.

By 1961 it was apparent that Joan Evans had done her work well. There was a new interest in Ruskin which was more than biographical. Then came John D. Rosenberg's *The Darkening Glass: A Portrait of Ruskin's Genius* (1961). Rosenberg made no major discovery: rather what he did was to sum up, in a fine literary style and with exquisite scholarly tact, what had been said by others. He based his psychological analysis on Wilenski, quietly tempering his predecessor's wilder flights of fancy, and adding with careful discrimination some of the insights gained from the work of Evans and Whitehouse. On Ruskin's shift from aesthetics to social criticism he adopted Townsend's outline, while recognizing that it was oversimplified and introducing the necessary qualifications. He followed, as everyone must, Clark on the Gothic Revival and *The Seven Lamps of Architecture*. For economics he avoided Wilenski's untempered adulation by utilizing the findings of John T. Fain, although he took exception to Fain's defense of the classical economists because he felt that Nassau Senior, Mill et al. should have guarded against the prostitution of their theories by commercial interests.

But perhaps the most valuable section of *The Darkening Glass* is the patient, sympathetic handling of the years of growing madness. Rosenberg shows remarkable balance when he discriminates between hallucination and perception, between futile rage and effective rhetoric in works like *Fors Clavigera* and *Time and Tide*. He grasps the peculiar importance of *The Storm Cloud of the Nineteenth Century*: there is an almost mythological quality about the marriage of madness and prophecy in these lectures. Rosenberg pursued his literary analysis in "The Genius of John Ruskin" (*VN*, 1963), in the introduction to *The Genius of John Ruskin: Selections from His Writings* (1963), and in "Style and Sensibility in Ruskin's Prose," his distinguished contribution to *The Art of Victorian Prose* (1968), edited by George Levine and William Madden. Since these studies by Rosenberg sum up and evaluate what has gone before, they are the starting point for future Ruskin scholarship.

For example, there is a new understanding in even a short article by Georges LeBreton, "La Folie de Ruskin" (*Mercure de France*, 1963). LeBreton notes that there was a very real darkening of the sky near the end of the century, and that

Mont Blanc did indeed change in appearance during Ruskin's lifetime, observations which he owed to *The Darkening Glass*. Ruskin may have been mad, but it is dangerous to challenge his observation of a fact.

And a monograph like Quentin Bell's *Ruskin* (1963), intended only as an introduction for the general reader, can give an informed and judicious appraisal of Ruskin's sexual behavior and its effect on his work. Bell enters a thoughtful demurrer to the opinion, widely held since Wilenski, that the Oxford lectures added little of value to the theories that Ruskin had propounded in his early books. Bell thinks that in some of these lectures defending early Italian painters Ruskin was working toward a justification of modern art. Unfortunately, just when Ruskin was beginning to think in new terms, he happened to write an angry passage about Whistler, and the man and the moment did not meet.

There is a higher level of interpretation in a fine paper by Charles T. Dougherty, "Of Ruskin's Gardens," in *Myth and Symbol: Critical Approaches and Applications*, by Northrop Frye, Lionel C. Knights et al. (1963). As Joan Evans had noted, *Modern Painters* v is like nothing before it. Dougherty attributes the change, first, to Ruskin's abandonment of his Evangelical religion in 1858, and second, to his work on the Turner Bequest in 1857–58, which led him to examine 19,000 sketches by the artist he had set out to defend fifteen years before. He had employed symbols effectively as far back as *The King of the Golden River*, in which a fertile valley is turned into a wasteland by greed and then restored by love. It was written for a little girl whom he later married. Now he had met another little girl, and the symbols that engrossed him were the garden and the woman. In the apocalyptic passages on Turner, chaos and death triumph over harmony and life, a nightmare vision of what Ruskin saw happening in society. *Modern Painters* v is written in a new dimension, which is carried forward into *Sesame and Lilies* and *The Queen of the Air*. In a 1967 review of Hélène Lemaître's monograph *Les Pierres dans l'œuvre de Ruskin* (1965), William K. Wimsatt said: "The assimilation of the physical object and its catalogues to mythopoeic visionary purpose begins nowadays to make Ruskin a strong candidate for the main succession of British prophets with the American mythopoeic critics" (*MLR*). John Rosenberg contended in an essay-review ("The Geopoetry of John Ruskin," *EA*, 1969) of the same monograph that Ruskin had brilliantly employed the typological mode of exegesis a full century before Northrop Frye revived it.

And always there is the uncomfortable feeling that even in his madness and confusion Ruskin could see what remains invisible to others. There is an example of his uncanny critical intuition in Robert F. Gleckner, "Ruskin and Byron" (*ELN*, 1965). In *Fiction Fair and Foul* Ruskin analyzed a passage from Byron's poem, *The Island*, the MS of which is now in the University of Texas Humanities Research Center. Ruskin sensed strain and uncertainty precisely where the MS revisions suggest that Byron was having trouble, not just with conveying meaning, but also with deciding what he meant.

Attitudes toward Ruskin were changing, partly because of a general shift in fashion noted in an unsigned article, "John Ruskin Returns to Verona," in the September 1966 issue of the *Connoisseur*. "A generation that has turned to Art Nouveau, that finds Neo-Classicism exciting, and that thronged the Beardsley Exhibition at the Victoria & Albert Museum is now rediscovering John Ruskin." According to another unsigned article in the *Times Literary Supplement*, "the special attraction that Ruskin has for us today is precisely his vulnerability. This kind of single-mindedness—following his enthusiasms and ideas wherever they led, without regard for modesty or decorum or commonsense in the expression of them, and with more scant regard for objectivity than we have come to demand—makes him an easy target, yet makes him too a kind of figure that our own literary and intellectual scene is sadly lacking in." And that is why "the exhibition 'Ruskin and His Circle' held recently in London proved to be one of the most successful shows of its kind that the Arts Council has put on in its gallery" ("Follies But No Fool," 5 March 1964).

But there is another reason for the revival of interest in Ruskin, namely, that his place in the history of criticism is coming into better perspective. John Arthos, in his article "Ruskin and Tolstoy: 'The Dignity of Man'" (DR, 1962), finds that Tolstoy is ultimately destructive of all values. Not so Ruskin. Ruskin found in nature a sense of harmony, order, growth, and proportion, in which man could share, and in which he achieved his true happiness.

Even when scholars are extremely critical of Ruskin, they now respect his achievement and understand the reasons for his failure. A good example of current attitudes is Solomon Fishman, The Interpretation of Art: Essays on the Art Criticism of John Ruskin, Walter Pater, Clive Bell, Roger Fry, and Herbert Read (1963). Fishman says that Ruskin was treated unfairly during the first part of the century, but that there is now a feeling that he should receive more sympathetic treatment. Fishman doubts that Ruskin will ever be fully rehabilitated. His difficulty in holding readers is twofold. First, his mental problems made it impossible for him to conduct a sustained rational discourse. Second, historically he came at the end of the long line of development from Early Renaissance to Romantic, and at the beginning of the movement toward Modern Art. Thus his work combines outmoded judgments and astonishing prescience; a demand for slavish imitation of nature suddenly turns into an attack on representational art. With all his faults he is an important figure in the history of art because he made a tremendous effort to situate art in the totality of human experience. He is often foolish, never trivial.

In The Heaven of Invention (1963), George Boas arrived at a similar conclusion. The chapter "Functionalism" is a detailed analysis of The Seven Lamps of Architecture, for the most part sharply critical, but in the end favorable. According to Boas, Ruskin insisted on seeing the artist as a complete man in a total environment. He was not the kind of art critic who "skims off" colors, shapes, and sounds, and ignores substance. It seems that a new consensus is forming. Ruskin's importance as an art critic lies in his unrelenting opposition to any view of art that ignores its total context. A generation ago he was praised as the destroyer of that abominable abstraction, Economic Man; now he is beginning to win respect as the implacable foe of the Aesthetic Man.

Since 1966 there has been a flood of articles which seek to re-create the art world of Victorian England in an effort to study Ruskin's criticism in its native habitat. It becomes increasingly clear that the colossal confusion which has always made him an inviting target is also a function of his strength. According to Wendell Stacy Johnson in his article "'The Bride of Literature': Ruskin, the Eastlakes, and Mid-Victorian Theories of Art" (VN, 1966), Ruskin's contemporaries attacked him effectively for confusing literature and art, but that was only a part of a larger confusion. His criticism was simultaneously mimetic, pragmatic, and expressive; he demanded that art tell the truth, inculcate morality, and honestly express the artist's personality or the culture as a whole. In short, Ruskin forced people to examine their ideas and commit themselves.

In a major article, "Ruskin and the Adequacy of Landscape" (*TSLL*, 1967), Donald Wesling explores the significance of Ruskin's attitude toward landscape, and how his thought is related to that of other writers. Herbert Read says of nineteenth-century landscape painting that it is a disillusioned version of the pastoral, full of the sense of something lost, the old rural tradition, the old social bonds, now yielding to industry and scientific knowledge. Wesling argues that writers as diverse as Wordsworth, Ruskin, and Lawrence had an instinctive aversion to the pollution of the environment and instinctively connected it with society's forms. Ruskin saw that the modern artist had been cut off from the tradition that found value in nature, and therefore the outer fact and the inner emotion had become separated. The function of the artist in modern times was to restore spiritual value to the world around him, and that was what Turner had done in his time. Hopkins, Hardy, and Lawrence all read *Modern Painters* and all regarded sketching and writing as complementary.

In "Letters Pro and Con [John Ruskin and Herbert Read]" (*JAAC*, 1968), George P. Landow points out that in *The Meaning of Art* Herbert Read cited Croce twice and Ruskin seven times; his debt to Ruskin is clear elsewhere. In "Ruskin and Baudelaire on Art and Artist" (*UTQ*, 1968) Landow argues that both critics set out to defend a major artist, in one case Turner and in the other Delacroix, and in the process each transferred the theory of Romantic poetry to painting. In "Ruskin's Versions of 'Ut Pictura Poesis' " (*JAAC*, 1968) Landow traces Ruskin's theories to the eighteenth-century analogy between painting and poetry which Turner also accepted, judging from his unpublished lectures. Ruskin held that as long as poetry was mimetic, its analogy was painting, but when poetry became expressive its analogy was music. Thus his aesthetic was bifurcated, the mimetic leading to Typical Beauty, the expressive leading via mind and mood to Vital Beauty.

In still another article, "Ruskin's Refutation of False Opinions Held concerning Beauty" (*BJA*, 1968), Landow contends that Ruskin tried to establish an objective basis for beauty in a metaphysical order based on the existence of God, in order to avoid tracing Beauty to psychological association as Alison and Jeffrey had done. When Ruskin's belief faltered, so did his theory, and he based his new aesthetic on human values. In "J. D. Harding and John Ruskin on Nature's Infinite Variety" (*JAAC*, 1971) Landow examines the relationship between Ruskin and his old drawing masters, whose *Principles and Practice of Art* was published in 1845. Although there are many similarities, Harding relied on a mimetic theory, while his pupil advanced into the nineteenth century when he developed a theory of art as statement, a kind of language for expressing visual aspects of nature. In "Ruskin's Revisions of the Third Edition of *Modern Painters*, Volume I" (*VN*, 1968), Landow shows how Ruskin profited from the criticism of the second volume, and how he shifted the emphasis from the defense of a specific painter to the development of a general theory of art.

Landow's work culminated in *The Aesthetic and Critical Theories of John Ruskin* (1971), which must now be regarded as the standard commentary. Exploiting to full advantage the scholarship of his predecessors, and adding his own superior knowledge of the Victorian art world and Evangelical homiletics, Landow was able to ask certain key questions about *Modern Painters* II and to provide satisfactory answers. In this volume Ruskin tried to give a systematic exposition of his views: as a result it furnishes a remarkable number of familiar quotations. Yet it was not often reprinted and Ruskin was dissatisfied with it. Landow traces the difficulty to the original distinction between Typical Beauty and Vital Beauty, the first dependent for its validity on Evangelical theology, the other capable of surviving a crisis of faith. The concept of Vital Beauty led inevitably to social criticism. Another way of apprehending the significance of the distinction is to connect Typical Beauty with the quest for objective standards, and Vital Beauty with the shift toward subjective standards based on nothing more authoritative than human emotions. Or looked at in still another way, Typical Beauty is rooted in the classical past, while Vital Beauty leads toward Romanticism and the future.

All of these studies by Landow, Johnson, and Wesling tend to put Ruskin in a much larger perspective and a more sympathetic light than he has enjoyed heretofore. Several other articles during the last decade have explored Ruskin's relationship with half-forgotten issues and controversies. Of these the most important is Herbert L. Sussman, "Hunt, Ruskin, and the Scapegoat" (*VS*, 1968). Holman Hunt was very clear about the informing principle of Ruskin's criticism. The central problem of Victorian art was to use accurate imitation of the phenomenal world in order to produce symbols of the transcendental order beyond. The possibility of a solution was the point at issue in the controversy over Hunt's "The Scapegoat." W. M. Rossetti stated flatly that the goat in the picture was a symbol of exactly the same sort as the goat in the Bible. In other words, the viewer had to interpret a religious picture à la private judgment, like a good Protestant, in order to find its "true" meaning, like a higher critic. Ruskin was simply the greatest of the many voices expounding that theory, which, however, was fast becoming untenable. The *Athenaeum* pronounced the goat a goat, and not an allegorical animal. Sussman concludes: "once the natural fact is no longer felt to have a metaphysical correspondence to a specific spiritual fact, then any physical object can serve equally well as a counter for any spiritual principle or emotional state and the way is open for the private mythologies that characterize the art and literature of the nineteenth and twentieth centuries."

In "A Note on the Ruskin-*Blackwood's* Controversy" (*VN*, 1966), Kenneth W. Davis tells how John Blackwood solicited a harsh review, "Mr. Ruskin's Works," for the September 1851 issue and how the reviewer, William Henry Smith, originally reluctant, was glad to oblige, but only after he became convinced of Ruskin's irrationality. In "Ruskin and Stillman" (*ELN*, 1966), George Monteiro cites a Ruskin letter, probably written early in 1861, as evidence that there was no hard feeling between the two artists at the time, although each looked back on the summer of 1860 with distaste. John Unrau's "A Note on Ruskin's Reading of Pugin" (*ES*, 1967) is a sharp attack on Ruskin's denial of any debt to Pugin except two facts about buttresses and ironwork. Ruskin admitted having read two items by Pugin, but not *True Principles of Pointed or Christian Architecture*, where Pugin does discuss buttresses and ironwork. Unrau recalls Graham Hough's judgment that Ruskin was a pathological liar when his self-esteem was threatened. Geoffrey Grigson makes a similar judgment in his reaction to the 1964 Ruskin exhibition of the Arts Council: "Why does he, at all periods, young, middle-aged, old, affect one as a writing liar?" (*New Statesman*).

Along the same line, a most revealing article is M. J. H. Liversidge, "John Ruskin and William Boxall" (*Apollo*, 1967). While he was preparing to write *Modern Painters* ii, Ruskin was with Boxall in Venice. Later, when he was struggling with his review of Eastlake's *Materials for the History of Oil Painting*, he sought Boxall's help on technical matters. In his letter of 13 September 1847 he asked Boxall to keep this matter secret.

Mary Lutyens traces the history of two famous pictures in "Millais's Portrait of Ruskin" and "Portrait of Effie" (*Apollo*, 1967, 1968). Van Akin Burd successfully dates another well-known likeness in "Ruskin, Rossetti, and William Bell Scott" (*PQ*, 1969), an article which includes a less familiar photograph which William Downey made on the same day. Luke Hermann gives an account of an important part of Ruskin's work as Slade Professor in *Ruskin and Turner: A Study of Ruskin as a Collector of Turner, Based on His Gifts to the University of Oxford; Incorporating a Catalogue Raisonné of the Turner Drawings in the Ashmolean Museum* (1969). In "Ruskin and Turner: A Riddle Resolved" (*Burlington Mag.*, 1970), Hermann identifies the Mrs. Cooper from whom Ruskin acquired the nucleus of the Turner collection he donated to Oxford in 1861. In "Turner, Ruskin and Constable at Salisbury" (*Burlington Mag.*, 1971), Selby Whittingham suggests that Turner's watercolor of the cathedral, once a part of Ruskin's collection, was inspired by his less successful rival's preoccupation with the same subject.

According to Harold I. Shapiro, "*The Poetry of Architecture*: Ruskin's Preparation for *Modern Painters*" (*Ren. & Mod. Stud.*, 1971), Ruskin in 1837–38 thought of architecture as part of the landscape. While writing this series of articles he became aware of the deficiencies of picturesque theory, and for the next ten years the term has little importance in his writing. James Dearden's "Ruskin's Tour to the Lake District in 1837" (*Connoisseur*, 1968) is an examination of Ruskin's drawings from which grew *The Poetry of Architecture*; he was beginning to see architectural detail with great clarity. Dearden's "The Cunliffe Collection of Ruskin Drawings" (*Connoisseur*, 1969) is a beautifully illustrated account of the extensive holdings of Robert Cunliffe, who died in 1902. Dearden's "Edward Burne-Jones— Designer to John Ruskin" (*Connoisseur*, 1969) has little of interest except for its illustrations. Tim Hilton defends Ruskin's remarks on Dürer against the strictures of a *Times* reviewer (*TLS*, 17 Dec. 1971).

The imagery in Ruskin's prose and poetry has at long last begun to receive the analysis it deserves. As Norman N. Feltes observes in "The Quickset Hedge: Ruskin's Early Prose" (*VN*, 1968), Ruskin used the metaphor of the hedge to express the vitality of Gothic ornament as opposed to the "sapless thicket" of Roman Renaissance; Feltes uses the same metaphor to express the arborescent quality of Ruskin's early prose, which celebrated the unity of man with nature under eternal law. Earlier, when Ruskin seemed to be trying to assess the roles of restraint and release, he used a different metaphor. Gerald Levin's "The Imagery of Ruskin's 'A Walk in Chamouni'" (*VP*, 1967) is a study of a poem first published in 1844 and reprinted in 1891, possibly as an illustration of *Praeterita*.

There is nothing new about the sexual interpretation of Gothic architecture, what with lancets and rose windows, and it was inevitable that *The Stones of Venice* should attract such treatment, as it does in David Sonstroem's "John Ruskin and the Nature of Manliness" (*VN*, 1971). At this point in his career Ruskin admired Gothic because to him it suggested sexual potency; when he turned to social criticism, his ideal of manliness became the father rather than the lover. Pierre Fontaney, in "Ruskin and Paradise Regained" (*VS*, 1969), gives a Jungian analysis to the vision of the Rhone at Geneva, one of the most highly charged passages in *Praeterita*, and demonstrates that it is a complex tapestry of archetypal symbols.

Studies of Ruskin's Influence

Since 1945 there have been several studies of Ruskin's influence in France. In a pamphlet, *Ruskin et Bergson: De l'intuition esthétique à l'intuition metaphysique* (1947), Floris Delattre pointed out that Bergson praised Ruskin and annotated copies of some of his works. Jean Autret contributed an examination of the most important literary relationship in *L'Influence de Ruskin sur la vie, les idées et l'œuvre de Marcel Proust* (1956). Autret's *Ruskin and the French before Marcel Proust* (1965) contains a good but brief survey of early French criticism. This monograph consists mainly of passages from Ruskin translated into French by various scholars who antedated Proust. Autret collaborated with William Burford on a translation and edition, *Marcel Proust: On Reading* (1971); this essay was the preface to Proust's translation of *Sesame and Lilies*. Frank D. Curtin, in "Ruskin in French Criticism: A Possible Reappraisal" (*PMLA*, 1962), evaluated French attitudes from Milsand through Proust and Bergson to Delattre. The French have not spent much time on Ruskin's biography, nor have they made the mistake of overrating him, but they appreciated his great merits and since Milsand's *L'Esthétique anglaise: Etude sur M. Ruskin* (1864), they have recognized the close connection between his merits and his faults. Pierre Fontaney's "Ruskin d'après des livres nouveau" (*EA*, 1960) is a review of recent publications.

Francis G. Townsend, in "The American Estimate of Ruskin, 1847–60" (*PQ*, 1953), examined the periodical literature of the time and concluded that by 1856 Ruskin was accepted as a literary master. Americans objected to his dogmatism and intemperate language, and they noted his habit of contradicting himself, but they admired his high moral tone, his enthusiasm, and his originality. Almost unanimously they welcomed his early books as a stimulus to the development of art in America. On the other hand, Richard P. Adams, "Architecture and the Romantic Tradition: Coleridge to Wright" (*AQ*, 1957), attributed less to Ruskin's influence. Roger B. Stein's *John Ruskin and Aesthetic Thought in America, 1840–1900* (1967) is almost a model of its kind. Stein pursued his research into organizations and carried his study down to the early career of Frank Lloyd Wright. Michael Lloyd in "Hawthorne, Ruskin, and the Hostile Tradition" (*EM*, 1955) traced much Anglo-American hostility toward Italy to two factors: the Italians had rejected the Reformation, and they had closed their society to the flood of English-speaking bourgeois tourists. Albert Bush-Brown in " 'Get an Honest Bricklayer!' The Scientist's Answer to Ruskin" (*JAAC*, 1958) pointed out that American scientists in the late nineteenth century were against traditional architecture because they were for progress and regarded Gothic as a relic of Catholic superstition. Charles H. Kegel's "Ruskin's St. George in America" (*AQ*, 1957) is an account of the Ruskin Cooperative Association in Tennessee during the nineties. Although the members hailed Ruskin's attacks on the economic system, they favored machinery, democratic processes, and a classless society.

As for Ruskin's influence on American literature, Miriam Allott in "A Ruskin Echo in *The Wings of the Dove*" (*N&Q*, 1956) suggested that James used the Britannia of the marketplace to describe Mrs. Lowder. The title "The Pound-Ruskin Axis" (*CE*, 1955) is a little misleading. Louis B. Salomon did not argue for a Ruskinian influence; rather he tried to illuminate Pound by comparing him with the revered Victorian. In "Joyce and Ruskin" (*N&Q*, 1953), Charles T. Dougherty traced a passage in *Portrait of the Artist* to a *Fors Clavigera* letter of 1873.

John D. Jump's "Ruskin's Reputation in the Eighteen-Fifties: The Evidence of the Three Principal Weeklies" (*PMLA*, 1948) followed the line of investigation that was opened by Wilenski and pursued in Dolk's article of 1942. Jump found that the *Spectator* was highly favorable as long as W. M. Rossetti was its critic, the *Athenaeum* gave Ruskin no less than eighty-seven notices during the decade, thus acknowledging his importance even when most critical of him, and the *Saturday Review* at the outset treated him with respect, then turned against him when he exposed his heterodoxy in economics. The three great weeklies gave clear proof that Ruskin had great influence on the dominant middle class, whether or not he carried weight in art circles. In the supplementary article, "Ruskin Satirized" (*PMLA*, 1949), Jump cited an 1857 pamphlet about "Buskin" and others. It indicates that Ruskin was well known to the cultured public and readily identifiable as the prophet of the Pre-Raphaelites.

The most important postwar study of Ruskin's influence in Great Britain was Graham Hough's *The Last Romantics* (1949). Although only the first chapter is devoted specifically to Ruskin, actually the whole book is a tracing of symbolism in English literature to Ruskin's effort to educate his countrymen, to free them from convention, so that they could see what was before them. "Ruskin is the earliest (perhaps the only) English writer of first-rate intellectual power to devote himself mainly to the visual arts." A true product of Puritanism, Ruskin was bound to see art as expressive of the lives of the artists and hence inextricably bound up with moral issues. Ruskin and those whom he influenced are the natural enemies of the idea that art comes from an aesthetic faculty, or of any other idea which would separate art from life. Art must discharge a religious function, indeed becomes a new religion. As Hough said: "I became interested in the genesis of Yeats's ideas from those of the small poetic circle with whom he associated in the nineties. They in turn seemed to owe almost everything to Pater and the Pre-Raphaelites, and from them I was inevitably led back to Ruskin. At this point I came to a stop. The new ideas about the arts and their relations to religion and the social order all seemed to originate somewhere in the dense jungle of Ruskin's work."

Probably the most provocative piece of Ruskin scholarship since Wilenski is "Overtures to Wilde's *Salome*" (*TriQ*, 1969), in which Richard Ellmann interprets Wilde's version of the story as psychic autobiography. Salome is Pater, all virginal sensuality, and Iokanaan is the prophetic John, all renunciation, while Herod is the tertium quid, Wilde himself, attracted to both. Ellmann's analysis of *The Stones of Venice* as concealed sexual drama is well worth reading. Why did Ruskin give an exact date for the fall of Venice, namely, 8 May 1418? He said it was the deathday of Carlo Zeno, but no other historian believes Zeno is that important. Ellmann suggests—in his own words, at the risk of having his sanity questioned—that the date is exactly four hundred years before Ruskin's conception. Ruskin's fear of sensuality and his growing distaste for his gregarious wife emerge as the decline of Venice from spiritual idealism to Renaissance corruption.

Gerard Manley Hopkins admired Ruskin without being blind to his follies. In "Ruskin's Ploughshare and Hopkins' 'The Windhover'" (*ES*, 1962), William D. Templeman points out parallels in the way the two Victorians thought of ploughs and furrows. Donald R. King, in "The Vision of 'Being' in Hopkins' Poetry and Ruskin's *Modern Painters* I" (*Discourse*, 1966), finds similarities in the way the two men saw landscapes. These similarities are real enough but their significance remained doubtful until the publication of Patricia M. Ball's illuminating study, *The Science of Aspects: The Changing Role of Fact in the Work of Coleridge, Ruskin and Hopkins* (1971). Her theory is that Ruskin's insistence on the importance of the objective fact was a healthy corrective to the excesses of Romantic subjectivism. Hopkins knew *Modern Painters* and his poetry combines Coleridge's introspection with Ruskin's close attention to every detail of the object itself. *Modern Painters*, Ball maintains, is not an eccentric bypath, but a necessary step in the progress of nineteenth-century criticism.

In "Ruskin and George Eliot's Realism" (*Criticism*, 1965), Darrel Manson, Jr. argues that George Eliot's theory of realism was based on *Modern Painters* III, which she and George Lewes read with delight and admiration. In "Ruskin and His Master" (*VN*, 1967), Donald R. Swanson notes the difference between work in Carlyle and Ruskin: the former thought that it was a duty, the latter that it should be a joy.

In "Ruskin and Browning: The Poet's Responsibility" (*SLitI*, 1969), William E. Colburn compares Browning's bishop ordering his tomb with Ruskin's passages on Renaissance pride in *The Stones of Venice*. This well-known literary parallel is traced to its source by Robert A. Greenberg in "Ruskin, Pugin, and the Contemporary Context of 'The Bishop Orders His Tomb'" (*PMLA*, 1969), a superb article which finds striking similarities among the three Victorians, even to individual images, some of them suggestive of later developments. We are especially indebted to Greenberg for his exposition of the metaphor of the talisman with which Ruskin concluded his analysis of Browning's poem. Indeed the metaphor is, as Greenberg says, remarkable and it has escaped notice, an interesting phenomenon in view of the dawning appreciation of Ruskin's seemingly random creativity.

William M. Johnston's *The Formative Years of R. G. Collingwood* (1967) is an account of the education and early career of the eminent philosopher whose father was Ruskin's first biographer. R. G. Collingwood especially admired two qualities of Ruskin's thought: first, he had a synthetic mind, a mind that saw the unity of things; second, he did not hesitate to contradict himself, believing as he did that contradiction was the only road to truth. In "Ruskin and Exuberance: Control in Literature" (*OL*, 1968), E. San Juan, Jr. reexamines Ruskin's concept of the pathetic fallacy and finds that it has permanent value in literary criticism. The dialectic between passion and dispassionate objectivity is seen as the precursor of T. S. Eliot's "objective correlative."

MATTHEW ARNOLD

•

David J. DeLaura

I. BIBLIOGRAPHY*

Thomas Burnett Smart's *Bibliography of Matthew Arnold* (1892; rpt. 1968), with its "synoptical index" to the various editions of Arnold's poetry, remains the standard bibliography. Its republication in *The Works of Matthew Arnold*, xv (1904) allowed a few more items to be added, but this later version lacks the valuable list of "Criticisms and Reviews of Matthew Arnold's Writings." The chapter on Arnold in *Bibliographies of Twelve Victorian Authors*, edited by T. G. Ehrsam and R. H. Deily (1936; rpt. 1968; supplemented by J. G. Fucilla, *MP*, 1937), though incomplete and sometimes inaccurate, is invaluable in listing reviews of Arnold's volumes and a large body of later critical comment. But the discovery in recent years of numerous primary items by Arnold, as well as the near flood tide of modern commentary on Arnold, have made an up-to-date, annotated bibliography a major desideratum of Arnold studies.

Marion Mainwaring's "Notes toward a Matthew Arnold Bibliography" (*MP*, 1952) points out deficiencies in Smart and adds new items. Her list of Arnold's Oxford lectures, and E. K. Brown's in *Matthew Arnold: A Study in Conflict* (1948), are corrected and completed by R. H. Super (*MLN*, 1955). Fraser Neiman, in "Some Newly Attributed Contributions of Matthew Arnold to the *Pall Mall*

---

* The present chapter for the most part omits notes concerning sources and parallels, as well as bibliographical information about editions, textual variants, and manuscripts, now accessible in Kenneth Allott's edition of *The Poems of Matthew Arnold*, R. H. Super's edition of *The Complete Prose Works*, and A. K. Davis, Jr.'s *Descriptive Checklist* of Arnold's letters. Frederic E. Faverty's chapter on Arnold in *The Victorian Poets* (2nd ed., 1968) has made it possible to concentrate on the more important critical studies of the poetry.

Gazette" (*MP*, 1957), using unpublished notebooks at Yale, identifies ten new items. Super adds four more in "Arnold's Notebooks and Arnold Bibliography" (*MP*, 1959). R. L. Brooks confirms four of Neiman's attributions in "Matthew Arnold and the *Pall Mall Gazette"* (*MP*, 1961) and corrects another in "'A Deptford Poet': An Addition and a Correction to the Matthew Arnold Bibliography" (*PQ*, 1962). Brooks has discovered three other Arnold items: "'A Septuagenarian Poet': An Addition to the Matthew Arnold Bibliography" (*MP*, 1960); "'A Few Words about the Education Act': A Signed, Unrecorded and Uncollected Article" (*MP*, 1969); and a newspaper account of a speech, "Matthew Arnold and the National Eisteddfod" (*N&Q*, 1961). S. O. A. Ullmann records "A 'New' Version of Arnold's Essay on Wordsworth" (*N&Q*, 1955), and J. R. Atkin takes note of "An Unpublished Report on Roman Catholic Schools by Matthew Arnold" (*N&Q*, 1962). Fraser Neiman's attribution to Arnold of an 1879 review of Joseph de Maistre (*MLN*, 1959) is confirmed by Roger Brooks's publication of five letters from Arnold to William Smith, editor of the *Quarterly* (*HLQ*, 1967).

Apart from the restoration of twenty-four lines of "The River," now incorporated in Kenneth Allott's edition of the *Poems* (1965), few additions to the canon of Arnold's poems have recently appeared. Allott has also published a Latin poem, "A Birthday Exercise by Matthew Arnold" (*N&Q*, 1958), written when Arnold was two months short of thirteen, and a piece of "Tennysonian pastiche" written in 1866 (*TLS*, 25 Feb. 1965). Roger Brooks, in "The Story Manuscript of Matthew Arnold's 'New Rome'" (*PBSA*, 1964), explains the subtitle of the poem and gives some new variants. William Leigh Godshalk, in "Autograph Fragments of Two Arnold Poems" (*PMLA*, 1970), offers new but minor manuscript variants in "The Buried Life" and the elegy for Edward Quillinan.

The indispensable source of factual information regarding the poems is *The Poetry of Matthew Arnold: A Commentary*, by C. B. Tinker and H. F. Lowry (1940). But it is more a handbook than an interpretation, and only infrequently does it convey a sense of the movement of Arnold's poetry or his poetics. The notes in Allott's edition of the *Poems* constitute a more critically alert updating of the *Commentary*, though the latter should still be consulted. The special strength of Tinker and Lowry was their access to unpublished materials in the magnificent Arnold collection at Yale University. From the collection came Tinker's article, "Arnold's Poetic Plans" (*YR*, 1933), based on Arnold's list of projects for the year 1849. Of prime importance is Kenneth Allott's "Matthew Arnold's Reading-Lists in Three Early Diaries" (*VS*, 1959), which shows that from 1845 to 1847 Arnold submitted himself to an extensive course of philosophical reading. Roger L. Brooks (*PBSA*, 1971) adds twenty-four titles to the list of known works in Arnold's library. Most Arnold scholars seem unaware, however, that a large proportion of the Yale collection remains unpublished. David G. Osborne's dissertation, "Matthew Arnold, 1843–1849: A Study of the Yale Manuscript" (Rochester 1963), points out that Tinker and Lowry used only a small percentage of the notes and poetic fragments in the Yale MS, not to mention the unpublished diary material.

The publication history of Arnold's poetry has never been fully told, though Roger L. Brooks has made a good beginning in several articles: "The Publication of Matthew Arnold's Early Volumes of Poetry" (*VN*, 1962), "The Strayed Reveller Myth" (*Library*, 1963), "A Census of Matthew Arnold's 'Poems' (1853)" (*PBSA*, 1960), "A Neglected Edition of Matthew Arnold's Poetry and a Bibliographical Correction" (*PBSA*, 1961), "Matthew Arnold and Ticknor & Fields"(*AL*, 1964), and "An Unrecorded American Edition of the Selected Poems of Matthew Arnold" (*Library*, 1961). See also R. H. Super's "American Piracies of Matthew Arnold" (*AL*, 1966). Similar facts regarding the prose can be culled from William E. Buckler's *Matthew Arnold's Books: Toward a Publishing Diary* (1958). Buckler, in "An American Edition of Matthew Arnold's *Poems*" (*PMLA*, 1954), shows that various changes still attributed to the 1881 English edition of Arnold's poems—notably in "The Church of Brou" and "Resignation"—were in fact first published in 1878. In "Studies in Three Arnold Problems" (*PMLA*, 1958), Buckler discusses "The Evolution and Text of *Culture and Anarchy*" and gives a history of Arnold's unfinished "Guide to Greek Poetry." Brooks's revealing compilation, "Some Unaccomplished Projects of Matthew Arnold" (*SB*, 1963), lists twenty-one items, in both poetry and prose, ranging from 1846 to 1888. J. D. Jump ("Matthew Arnold and 'Enoch Arden,'" *N&Q*, 1954) discusses Arnold's toying with the idea of reviewing Tennyson. T. J. Wise's forgery of the first edition of *Alaric at Rome* is discussed by R. Baughman (*HLQ*, 1936), anonymously in *CLQ* (1953), and by R. H. Super (*HLQ*, 1956). One of the few extant manuscripts of a prose work by Arnold, his "Common Schools Abroad," is discussed by Neda Westlake (*LC*, 1959).

Stephen Maxfield Parrish's *Concordance to the Poems of Matthew Arnold* (1959) is a notable addition to Arnold studies, though little critical use has been made of it so far. Finally, Frederic E. Faverty's chapter on Arnold in *The Victorian Poets* (2nd ed., 1968), a critical and descriptive bibliography, is a wise and discerning commentary on the whole range of Arnold scholarship and criticism.

II. EDITIONS

Apart from the letters, Arnold's works have been well served by his modern editors. The fifteen-volume *Works of Matthew Arnold* (1904), edited by G. W. E. Russell, has doubtful textual authority and for the most part need no longer be consulted. *The Poetical Works of Matthew Arnold* (1950), edited by C. B. Tinker and H. F. Lowry, is the standard edition and supersedes earlier Oxford editions of 1909 and 1942. It is the basis for Parrish's *Concordance* (1959). Kenneth Allott's splendid edition of *The Poems of Matthew Arnold* (1965), praised above for its apparatus, prints only "significant" textual variants (adding some to the Oxford edition). Students should note that Allott modernizes spelling and punctuation; as a result, in scholarly work Allott's readings must be verified against those of Tinker and Lowry. This edition, which includes juvenilia, unfinished poems, and fragments, is the most nearly complete collection of Arnold's poetry. Allott's chronological arrangement of the poetry (though some dates have been challenged) is far more useful than Tinker and Lowry's acceptance of Arnold's classification of his poems.

In *Studies in the Text of Matthew Arnold's Prose Works* (1935; rpt. 1969), E. K. Brown, by skillfully exploring the significance of textual changes in such works as *Culture and Anarchy* and "Literature and Science," made evident the need for a critical edition of the prose. The number of inaccuracies and misreadings discovered in Brown, however, suggests that the book should be used with some caution. The need for a modern edition has been met by Super's monumental edition of *The*

Complete Prose Works of Matthew Arnold, which reached Volume VIII in 1972. The "Textual Notes" follow "Critical and Explanatory Notes" that summarize much of modern scholarly and critical work on Arnold and make numerous independent contributions to our knowledge of the publication history of Arnold's prose. Super's edition will eventually incorporate the contents of K. Allott's *Five Uncollected Essays of Matthew Arnold* (1953) and Fraser Neiman's *Essays, Letters, and Reviews by Matthew Arnold* (1960). Merle M. Bevington's edition of Arnold's *England and the Italian Question* (1953) retains some value by its inclusion of Fitzjames Stephen's reply, "Matthew Arnold and the Italian Question." John Y. Simon has reprinted Arnold's "General Grant" with Mark Twain's rejoinder (1966) and offers interesting remarks on the interrelations of Arnold, Grant, and Twain. Two of Arnold's books have had separate modern editions. J. Dover Wilson's introduction to *Culture and Anarchy* (1932) is still valuable, and an edition by Ian Gregor appeared in 1968. Sister Thomas Marion Hoctor's edition of *Matthew Arnold's Essays in Criticism, First Series* (1968) includes textual and explanatory notes, contemporary reviews, and an introduction concentrating on Eliot's attacks on Arnold.

The Note-Books of Matthew Arnold (1952), edited by H. F. Lowry, K. Young, and W. H. Dunn, includes and identifies the thousands of literary items in Arnold's notebooks from 1852 to 1888. Material is most abundant from the mid-1860's onward. Unfortunately, most studies of Arnold since 1952 have not sufficiently exploited the riches of the *Note-Books*, not only for the sources of Arnold's ideas but for the subtle shifts in Arnold's intellectual sympathies. Richard C. Tobias (*PQ*, 1960) dates the two "General Note-books" included by Lowry, Young, and Dunn, the first from the early sixties, the second between 1876 and 1888, mostly after 1880. Unfortunately available only in microfilm is William Bell Guthrie's dissertation, "Matthew Arnold's Diaries: The Unpublished Items" (Virginia 1959). Guthrie provides a mass of miscellaneous material not used in the *Note-Books* that the careful student of Arnold should not overlook.

Two modern one-volume collections of Arnold's poetry and prose, notable for their scope, are John Bryson's *Matthew Arnold: Poetry and Prose* (1954) and A. Dwight Culler's *Poetry and Criticism of Matthew Arnold* (1961)—the latter graced by an exceptionally thoughtful introduction. An unusual item is William E. Buckler's republication of *Passages from the Prose Writings of Matthew Arnold, Selected by the Author* (1963; original, 1880). As Buckler points out, "exactly half of the book is made up of passages under the heading 'Philosophy and Religion.'"

III. LETTERS

The greatest remaining impediment to the study of Arnold's biography and of his intellectual development is the lack of a complete edition of the letters. Checklists of Arnold letters compiled by T. H. V. Motter (*SP*, 1934) and by Marion Mainwaring (*MP*, 1952) were greatly expanded in three articles by Roger L. Brooks (*SP*, 1959; *MP*, 1962; *SP*, 1963). A major stage toward the goal of a complete edition was the publication in 1968 of *Matthew Arnold's Letters: A Descriptive Checklist*, by Arthur Kyle Davis, Jr. The *Checklist* describes more than 2,600 printed or manuscript letters to 506 different correspondents. Some errors and omissions, even in well-known sources, have been detected, but the work will prove invaluable to serious students. A continuing source of mischief in Arnold scholarship is Arnold Whitridge's assigning a date of 1853 to Arnold's important "fragments" letter to his sister Jane (*Unpublished Letters*, 1923, p. 18). E. K. Chambers in 1947 and E. K. Brown in 1948 both saw that the correct date is 1849. The Davis *Checklist* enters the letter under *both* 1849 and 1853. It is welcome news that Cecil Y. Lang has recently undertaken the editorship of the Arnold letters.

Two recent articles not listed by Davis are Jan B. Gordon's "Matthew Arnold and the Elcho Family: A Record of Correspondence" (*N&Q*, 1967) and Joseph O. Baylen's "Matthew Arnold and the *Pall Mall Gazette*: Some Unpublished Letters" (*SAQ*, 1969). Among them, four articles appearing in the July 1971 *Notes & Queries* present four unpublished Arnold letters as well as a new letter from Clough to Arnold, and change the date of an early Arnold letter. Although most of Arnold's letters are less than revealing regarding his inner life or his intellectual development, two articles deserve mention for the light they shed on Arnold's dealings with contemporary intellectuals. W. H. G. Armytage, in "Matthew Arnold and T. H. Huxley: Some New Letters: 1870–80" (*RES*, 1953), reveals an Arnold eager for Huxley's approval. The evidence would suggest that whereas Arnold was to some extent conforming his ideas to the limits imposed by Huxley, Arnold himself may have had a share in complicating the last phase of Huxley's religious thinking. The relationship deserves further exploration. In "Matthew Arnold and *The Academy*" (*PMLA*, 1953), Diderik Roll-Hansen ably illuminates a little-known aspect of Victorian thought by publishing five of Arnold's letters to Charles Edward Appleton, a Hegelian philosopher and editor of the *Academy*.

Though it is the standard edition, *Letters of Matthew Arnold, 1848–1888* (2 vols., 1895), edited by G. W. E. Russell under the direction of the Arnold family, is defective by reason of its frequent excisions, its scanty annotation, and its lack of an index. William S. Peterson, in "G. W. E. Russell and the Editing of Matthew Arnold's Letters" (*VN*, 1970), using unpublished letters of Mrs. Arnold and Russell, places most of the blame on the Arnold family. Because the *Letters* was repaginated for a one-volume edition in 1900, and then again (with further deletions) for inclusion in the *Works* (1904), any reference should include the date of the letter. *Unpublished Letters of Matthew Arnold* (1923), edited by Arnold Whitridge, is lightly annotated and has no index. The study of Arnold was transformed by the appearance of H. F. Lowry's masterful edition of *The Letters of Matthew Arnold to Arthur Hugh Clough* (1932), which for the first time made available indispensable information regarding Arnold's early poetry and the development of his poetics. William E. Buckler's *Matthew Arnold's Books*, already mentioned, is primarily valuable for establishing the publication history of Arnold's works, but it also contains valuable incidental information regarding his literary plans.

IV. BIOGRAPHY

The materials for an account of Matthew Arnold's first thirty years remain frustratingly scanty. The Davis *Checklist* (1968) records only a handful of letters before 1848. The chief and indispensable source for Arnold's development after that date remains *The Letters of Matthew Arnold to Arthur Hugh Clough* (1932).

The Arnold family background can be assessed in several studies of Thomas Arnold, above all in the classic *Life and Correspondence of Thomas Arnold,* first published by A. P. Stanley in 1844. Some facts about Matthew Arnold's career at Rugby and Oxford are presented in J. P. Curgenven's "Matthew Arnold in Two Scholarship Examinations" (*RES,* 1946) and R. H. Super's "Matthew Arnold's Rugby Prizes" (*N&Q,* 1955). Mrs. Humphry Ward, daughter of Arnold's brother Tom, presents much information about the Arnold family (including letters of Matthew Arnold) in her two-volume *A Writer's Recollections* (1918). Kathleen Tillotson, in "Dr. Arnold's Death and a Broken Engagement" (*N&Q,* 1952), provides information regarding Matthew's favorite sister, Jane. The bibliography of L. Bonnerot's *Matthew Arnold, poète* (1947) is rich in items concerning Arnold's family and friends.

Materials regarding Arnold's younger brother Tom, perhaps Clough's closest friend in the forties, have accumulated. Tom Arnold's *Passages in a Wandering Life* (1900) and W. T. Arnold's "Thomas Arnold the Younger" (*Century Illustrated Monthly Mag.,* 1903) are worth consulting. Kenneth Allott's "Thomas Arnold the Younger, New Zealand, and the 'Old Democratic Fervour'" (*Landfall,* 1961) captures the spirit of the Arnold-Clough circle in the late forties. In 1967, James Bertram edited *New Zealand Letters of Thomas Arnold the Younger: With Further Letters from Van Diemen's Land and Letters of Arthur Hugh Clough, 1847–1851.*

Attempts to locate the "secret" of Arnold's early life and poetry have not usually been successful. William S. Knickerbocker, in "Matthew Arnold and Oxford" (*SR,* 1927), found the Arnold family's "inherited tendency to heart failure" to be "the hidden cause" of the melancholy of Arnold's poetry. Knickerbocker is more convincing in reading the letters to Clough as revealing a "widening of the chasm" between the two men ("Semaphor: Arnold and Clough," *SR,* 1933). Frequently cited in Arnold studies is Alan Harris' "Matthew Arnold: The 'Unknown Years'" (*NC,* 1933), which draws on Arnold-Clough letters and "unpublished documents" in the hands of "numerous owners." Harris finds that Arnold became "the predominanting partner," even intellectually, in the friendship with Clough, and detects the "strain of ruthlessness" in Arnold's personal relationships. Lady Katherine Chorley, in *Arthur Hugh Clough: The Uncommitted Mind* (1962), is penetrating on the pluses and minuses of the Arnold-Clough relationship. David J. DeLaura, in "Arnold, Clough, Dr. Arnold, and 'Thyrsis'" (*VP,* 1969), shows that as late as 1865 Arnold did not know certain essential facts regarding Clough's early life.

Any information regarding Arnold and his Oxford circle in the 1840's is especially welcome. Not listed in most bibliographies is William Knight's *Principal Shairp and His Friends* (1888), which renders the tone of Oxford in the forties exceptionally well. The two-volume *Correspondence of Arthur Hugh Clough* (1957), edited by F. L. Mulhauser, is a mine of information not yet fully worked by Arnold scholars. The 740 Clough letters omitted from the edition may be worth consulting in manuscript. *The Life and Correspondence of John Duke Lord Coleridge* (1904), edited by E. H. Coleridge, is valuable for the Arnold letters it contains, especially those concerning his poetry. Another of Arnold's Oxford friends is the subject of John Curgenven's "Theodore Walrond: Friend of Arnold and Clough" (*DUJ,* 1952). Kathleen Tillotson, in "Rugby 1850: Arnold, Clough, Walrond, and *In Memoriam*" (*RES,* 1953; rpt. in *Mid-Victorian Studies,* 1965), discusses a semifictional portrait of Arnold at Rugby in the late forties and gives rich detail regarding the Arnold circle during and after the Oxford years. Patrick J. McCarthy's *Matthew Arnold and the Three Classes* (1964) fills a major gap in Arnold biography by providing a full account of Arnold's early political and social attitudes and their background.

The Marguerite "problem" continues to absorb the attention of students of Arnold's poetry; the topic is discussed with the appropriate poems later in this chapter. Here may be mentioned Louis Bonnerot's "La Jeunesse de Matthew Arnold" (*RAA*, 1930), which attributes much in Arnold's later career to the effects of the Marguerite experience. Later readings are sounder in suggesting that the Marguerite episode, though crucial and even decisive, merely confirmed already fully developed tendencies of Arnold's mind and personality. Isobel Macdonald's *The Buried Life: A Background to the Poems of Matthew Arnold, 1848–1881* (1949), a novelized version of the experience reflected in Arnold's first two volumes, is surprisingly tactful regarding Marguerite and Francis Lucy Wightman and bases most of its statements on known sources. Kenneth Allott, in "Matthew Arnold and Mary Claude" (*N&Q*, 1969), implicitly reopened the Marguerite question by identifying a friend of Arnold's for whom he may have had a "romantic passion" in the 1840's. Park Honan ("A Note on Matthew Arnold in Love," *VN*, 1971) sums up further, and admittedly inconclusive, evidence for the view "that Mary Claude was Arnold's original model for Marguerite."

Patrick McCarthy throws light on a little-studied aspect of Arnold's life in "Mrs. Matthew Arnold: Some Considerations and Some Letters" (*HLB*, 1969) and "Mrs. Matthew Arnold" (*TSLL*, 1971). The details of "The Death of Matthew Arnold" have been recently debated and clarified by R. H. Ronson, J. P. Curgenven, Kenneth Allott, and W. S. Peterson (*TLS*, 10 Oct., 17 Oct., 24 Oct. 1968; 28 Aug., 11 Sept. 1969).

The only modern attempt at a biography, in the limited sense, E. K. Chambers' *Matthew Arnold: A Study* (1947; rpt. 1964), should be used with caution. Though the production of a distinguished scholar, the book must be considered a failure by reason of its lack of all references and its numerous errors of fact. Eschewing virtually any interpretation, the book is especially inadequate on the poerty and gives largely bald summaries of the prose. A final chapter devoted to Arnold's "personality" is merely a catalog of the impressions of some of Arnold's friends and conveys nothing of Arnold's "literary" personality.

V. GENERAL STUDIES

Before the appearance of the letters to Clough in 1932 and the Tinker and Lowry *Commentary* in 1940, Arnold criticism, and what little scholarship there was, went in hobbles. The great bulk of such discussion was plagued by the confused chronology of the composition of Arnold's poems, especially those of the 1867 volume, and by lack of precise knowledge of the shifts in Arnold's poetry and poetics in the 1840's and 1850's. Only in recent years have recurring simplicities and errors concerning Arnold's early development been put firmly aside, and a fuller and more just portrait put in their place. As a result, only a limited number of earlier commentators deserve attention.

Earlier book-length surveys have been almost entirely superseded. The fault-finding in George Saintsbury's *Corrected Impressions* (1895) was somewhat mitigated in his *Matthew Arnold* (1899), still readable for its flashes of insight and lively writing. Herbert Paul's *Matthew Arnold* (1902) is a negligible effort, as is G. W. E. Russell's reverential book of the same title (1904), except for the inclusion of fragments of unpublished Arnold letters. Stuart P. Sherman's *Matthew Arnold: How to Know Him* (1917), an attempt to capture Arnold for the New Humanist movement, seemingly is the first study to find a clear pattern in Arnold's poetry: "A gradual spiritual pilgrimage through disillusions to ennui and despair, thence to resignation and stoical endurance, and ultimately to a new kind of courage and hope, denoting a pretty complete moral recovery." Sherman reveals the perplexities of such a moralist's reading of Arnold; obliged to respect the Preface of 1853 and the later "moral" poems, he admits "that as the discipline of [Arnold's] feelings approached completion there was relatively little feeling left to discipline." Hugh Kingsmill's *Matthew Arnold* (1928) is probably too much neglected by students of Arnold for its unrelentingly harsh tone. Even without the evidence of the letters to Clough, Kingsmill reverses the premises of Sherman: "Is his rejection of 'Empedocles,' and in this busying himself with action, Arnold was escaping from life under the pretense of entering more deeply into it. His way into life lay through the despair of Empedocles, not through the sword-play of Sohrab and Rustum." Kingsmill anticipates recent judgments in speaking of Arnold's "divided impulses" and "the personal bias, the lack of disinterestedness" in his criticism. The book has done much mischief, however, in elaborating the still popular and simple view that Thomas Arnold was the villain of Matthew's career—a view probably picked up from Lytton Strachey (see C. R. Sanders, *Lytton Strachey: His Mind and Art*, 1957).

H. F. Lowry's extended introduction to *The Letters of Matthew Arnold to Arthur Hugh Clough* (1932) has some value in defining certain essential Arnoldian qualities. Though Lowry was the first critic in a position to explore Arnold's early poetics in its complexity, he did not apply that new knowledge critically until his 1941 lecture, *Matthew Arnold and the Modern Spirit*: "in the passing away of his poetic activity there was some principle of renouncement on his part, as if his poetry had been almost a weakness in his character." Virtually no insights will be discovered in Charles H. Harvey's *Matthew Arnold: A Critic of the Victorian Period* (1931), an adulatory summary of Arnold's writings. Carleton Stanley's *Matthew Arnold* (1938), despite its sympathetic tone and its lively surface of incidental opinions, also offers little to the student.

Lionel Trilling's *Matthew Arnold* (1939) is the most distinguished general study, and still by far the best attempt to place Arnold in the nineteenth-century spiritual and intellectual situation. Interested in Arnold more as a thinker than as an artist, Trilling is less successful in handling the poetry than Arnold's social and political views. The book has thus enforced the still not uncommon view that Arnold's "Greek" and secular humanism of the sixties is the true center of his career. Trilling's discussion of Arnold's relationship with his father is more judicious and informed than most.

In his introduction to the Penguin anthology of Arnold's poetry (1954; rpt. in Robert O. Preyer, ed., *Victorian Literature: Selected Essays*, 1966), K. Allott speaks of Arnold's special ability to express a "time-ridden sensibility and the disenchantment that it produces, our own disenchantment." Developing similar hints in his pamphlet, *Matthew Arnold* (1955), Allott is remarkably successful in capturing the elusive "quality" of Arnold's poetry: for example, "his vocation was to sing of melancholy and indecision, to express the sad confusion of desires which find no sufficient object, to create for us the self-conscious animal whose thinking runs ahead and undermines his present experience of happiness." Allott sees that "when Arnold discovered how dark were his gifts as a poet, he stopped writing poetry," and he accepts the view of W. H. Auden (in "Matthew Arnold," 1940) that because of his father Arnold "thrust his gift in prison till it died." But he complicates the Kingsmill view by insisting, "he did it out of love." Less satisfying is J. D. Jump's *Matthew Arnold* (1955), which follows F. R. Leavis in severely indicting Arnold, especially in the Oxford elegies, for indulging in evasion and escape. Like Leavis, Jump has few reservations about Arnold's criticism. A reliable and scholarly introduction to the whole range of Arnold's activities is Fraser Neiman's *Matthew Arnold* (1968), which makes a number of shrewd observations concerning the early poetry. Michael Thorpe's *Matthew Arnold* (1969) is generally safe and often perceptive, but is hampered by a tone adapted to its presumed younger audience. Douglas Bush's survey, *Matthew Arnold* (1971), is also part of a series, but his surer grasp of the major problems of Arnold's career, as well as his mastery of recent comment and scholarship, make his the preferable book.

William Madden's important book, *Matthew Arnold: A Study of the Aesthetic Temperament in Victorian England* (1967), is intellectually distinguished though it verges on special pleading. Taking the second of the two possible directions T. S. Eliot saw in Arnold's thinking—Religion is Morals, Religion is Art—Madden offers the most sustained argument yet made for Arnold's native "aesthetic" temperament as the controlling factor of his entire career. In doing so, he overcompensates for the familiar "moral" reading of Arnold by playing down, or totally neglecting, the genuinely moral and religious dimension in Arnold's thought. In effect, he reconstructs Arnold in the pattern of the Pater who selectively chose from Arnold this unquestionably central line in Arnold's thought.

VI. ARNOLD'S POETRY

About the reception of Arnold's writings in his own lifetime, we lack mature studies of the sort that have illuminated the careers of Tennyson and Dickens. Of the various dissertations that have canvassed parts of the subject, there may be mentioned: Josephine G. Rickard's "The Reputation of Matthew Arnold as a Poet, 1849–1869" (Cornell 1945), Charles T. Wilkins' "The English Reputation of Matthew Arnold, 1840–1877" (Illinois 1959), and Roger L. Brooks's "Matthew Arnold's Poetry 1849–1855: An Account of the Contemporary Criticism and Its Influence" (Colorado 1959).

Swinburne's enthusiastic review of Arnold's 1867 *New Poems* (collected in *Essays and Studies*, 1875), at once gratifying and embarrassing to Arnold, is an important document in Arnold criticism and immensely readable. R. H. Hutton's discussions, now more readily identifiable in R. H. Tener's checklist (*VPN*, 1972), are the fullest and most clear-sighted that Arnold's poetry received before Trilling. Though hostile to Arnold's religious writings, he was the first to make important points about the poetry, including Arnold's numerous links with Wordsworth as well as "his fundamental rejection of him." He defined the various kinds of duality in Arnold and established him as the greatest English elegiac poet. He saw that

Arnold's melancholy is always countered by a "buoyancy" and "elasticity," and insisted that Arnold was wrong to say that "Empedocles" offers no resistance to despondency. Hutton knew that the 1853 Preface "was a condemnation of every successful poem [Arnold] has written," and that Arnold's distresses and consolations are best reconciled in precisely "the elaborate delineation of his own poetic individuality." He reads the "digressions" that close several of the major poems as "parables" and "analogies" that solve no problem but lighten the burden of the mystery.

Apart from occasional insights, criticism in succeeding decades is disappointingly thin and impressionistic. E. C. Stedman, in *Victorian Poets* (2nd ed., 1887), identified Arnold's most ideal trait as "the subtility with which he responds to, and almost expresses, the inexpressible—the haunting suggestions, the yearnings of man and nature—the notes of starlight and shadow, the evasive mystery of what we are and 'all that we behold.' " Two of the better extended readings of Arnold occur in Stopford Brooke's *A Study of Clough, Arnold, Rossetti and Morris* (1908) and Hugh Walker's *The Greater Victorian Poets* (1895). Some interest still attaches to John Dewey's essay of 1892, "Matthew Arnold and Robert Browning," collected in *Characters and Events* (1929). Two of Arnold's friendly enemies have written about him: Frederic Harrison, generously, in *Tennyson, Ruskin, Mill and Other Literary Estimates* (1900), and Leslie Stephen, rather querulously, in *Studies of a Biographer* (1898). T. Herbert Warren, in *Essays of Poets and Poetry* (1909), and A. C. Benson, in *The Leaves of the Tree* (1911), offer two of the period's few balanced judgments of Arnold's achievement. More typical is Sir Walter Raleigh's hostile and inaccurate essay of 1912, reprinted in *A Collection of Literary Essays, 1896–1916* (1923).

Arnold criticism enters a new phase after 1920, as T. S. Eliot and I. A. Richards begin their elaborate engagement with Arnold, as Arnold becomes a central issue in the debate over the New Humanism, and as Arnold's achievement is depreciated in the widespread rejection of all things Victorian. The first two topics are discussed below as part of Arnold's role in the critical tradition; as for the third, Arnold is implicitly caught up in the indictment of the Romantics and the Victorians for (in Eliot's influential formula) their disunified sensibility: "they thought and felt by fits, unbalanced; they reflected. . . . Tennyson and Browning ruminated" (*Selected Essays*, 1932).

A. Clutton-Brock (*Essays in Literature & Life*, 1926) is nearly unique in this period for his sympathetic penetration of the "conflict" in Arnold and those "few moments of victory and delight . . . won through a myth, a dream from which he soon awakes." "The process of poetry carried him unawares into that dream, into that wish-fulfilment, which was his inspiration": Keats could surrender to that dream, whereas, "to Arnold it was something dangerous, the siren-song that a part of him sang to the other part." A similar point was made, briefly and more harshly, by John Middleton Murry (*Discoveries: Essays in Literary Criticism*, 1924). (Murry's later, more sympathetic view of Arnold in *Looking Before and After*, 1948, is worth reading for its emphasis on the centrality of religion in Arnold's work.) Most other treatments are either desultory or condescending. G. R. Elliott, in *The Cycle of Modern Poetry* (1929), comments with some success on the sources of the Arnoldian melancholy. H. W. Garrod dismissively presents Arnold as given to "a kind of spiritual *fussiness*" and as "more of a gentleman than a poet has any right to be" (*Poetry and the Criticism of Life*, 1931). Even more disappointing is Sir Edmund Chambers' Warton lecture on Arnold (*PBA*, 1935). W. S. Knickerbocker, in "Thunder in the Index" (*SR*, 1939), makes casual comments about Arnold's movement from his early "vacillation" to his later "oscillating dialectic." In 1940 F. L. Lucas could judge that Arnold's criticism is respected but dated; it is "by his poetry that Arnold lives to-day" (*Ten Victorian Poets*, 1940). An upturn in the quality of Arnold studies is heralded by Kenneth Muir's compressed survey of the poetry in "Matthew Arnold and the Victorian Dilemma" (*Penguin New Writing*, No. 31, 1947). Muir comments intelligently on Arnold's relations with his father, the suicide in "Empedocles," the deficiencies of "Sohrab and Rustum" and "Rugby Chapel," and the use of pastoral in the Oxford elegies.

The continuing insecurity of Arnold's reputation as a poet is revealed by the tone of Geoffrey Tillotson's "Matthew Arnold in Our Time" (*Spectator*, 2 April 1954; rpt. in *Mid-Victorian Studies*, 1965). He patiently explains that Arnold is "one of the really powerful emotional forces" in English poetry, whose subjects are "aching hearts, longing, frustration, the depths of blankness and isolation," and a man "marvellously gifted in the expression of sorts and shades of emotion." A similar tone of preaching important news to an uncomprehending generation pervades Lionel Stevenson's "Matthew Arnold's Poetry: A Modern Appraisal" (*TSL*, 1959). Stevenson interestingly describes Arnold as everywhere expressing "the dilemma of the modern intellectual, who can find satisfaction neither as a recluse in a cloister nor as a participant and policy-maker in public affairs." But Jonathan Middlebrook ("Sunshine Supermen," *CE*, 1969) will have none of this. Cheerfully celebrating contemporary popular poets who "take the sun as the real light of the world" and sing of "self-knowledge and joy," Middlebrook finds Arnold's moonlit landscapes and nostalgia part of the discarded past, his ideal of "rational calm" a delusion, and his emotions "debilitating." Even distinguished students of the period question Arnold's status. John Rosenberg (*The Genius of John Ruskin*, 1963, p. 11) flatly declares Arnold to be a "bad" poet, and Robert Langbaum (*JEGP*, 1967) finds most of the elegies "pretty bad poems" and questions whether Arnold "can maintain his position among the Big Three of Victorian poetry." Despite the great bulk and generally high quality of Arnold studies in recent years, then, Arnold's claims as an artist in verse and as the spokesman in his poetry for an essential aspect of the modern experience are even now not secure beyond debate.

Arnold is not precisely an unpopular poet, however, and his sympathetic modern critics are in general not as defensive as, for example, the Cloughians. But since doubts persist regarding both Arnold's significance and his artistry, it is worth noting that the major achievements of the past two or three decades are works of descriptive rather than evaluative criticism. Trilling aside, the modern study of Arnold's poetry begins impressively with Louis Bonnerot's *Matthew Arnold, poète: Essai de biographie psychologique* (1947). It is less a "life" than the mapping out of Arnold's "rhythme intérieur," a double movement of expansion toward the external world of nature and contraction toward the interior world of morality. Bonnerot finds the key to Arnold's psychology in a pathological state of doubt, manifested in inquietude, anguish, obsession, and above all oscillation. Bonnerot anticipates later readers in stressing the losses Arnold incurred by his self-discipline of action and morality, and claims that Arnold's best poetry is a victory for the imaginative and contemplative side of his personality that he consciously sought to suppress. It is regrettable that the book was not translated and its thesis widely tested by later Arnold critics, since it raises problems of methodology that remain unsolved.

E. D. H. Johnson, in his influential *The Alien Vision of Victorian Poetry*

(1952), also presents Arnold as a figure of double awareness: "two worlds in conflict, an inner and private one of individual consciousness, and an outer and public one of shared experience." While correctly outlining the "*volte-face* in aesthetic intent" by which Arnold moved from the near aestheticism of 1849 to the new moralism of 1853, Johnson is perhaps too free in assigning Arnold's shifts of perspective to a persistent rationalization on his part. He finds in Arnold, as in Tennyson and Browning, a "curious ambivalence": "the expressed intent [of the poems] has a dark companion, its imaginative counterpart, which accompanies and comments on apparent meaning in such a way as to suggest ulterior motives." The evidence presented for Arnold suggests that he fits such categories less than comfortably. A too-little-noticed study by G. Müller-Schwefe, *Das persönliche Menschenbild Matthew Arnolds in der dichterischen Gestaltung* (1955), presents an even more negative psychological portrait of a "divided" Arnold. Rejecting outer reality, Arnold's poems remain abstract, unable to embody poetically his inner reality. Everywhere the poems present an isolated figure torn by inner conflict.

W. Stacy Johnson's *The Voices of Matthew Arnold: An Essay in Criticism* (1961), developing ideas in his "Matthew Arnold's Dialogue" (*UKCR*, 1960), is more rewarding than some critics have allowed in its close reading of several of Arnold's important poems. Johnson shows that Arnold is weakest when speaking as oracle, lecturer, or prophet, and at his best when expressing "the dialogue of the mind with itself" in a dramatic situation, a tension or conflict between attitudes. H. C. Duffin's *Arnold the Poet* (1962) is a late variant of the "genial" criticism of the last century; it will offend some readers by its "Victorian" objections to Arnold's alleged pessimism and "morbid outlook." But the book has a handful of surprising insights and will do little harm.

The chapter on Arnold in J. Hillis Miller's *The Disappearance of God: Five Nineteenth-Century Writers* (1963) deserves the closest attention from any student of Arnold. The book has been vigorously attacked for its inattention to chronology and its failure to read poems as aesthetic wholes. But Miller's exceptional literary perceptiveness generally surmounts any incoherence in his controversial methodology, a difficult combination of formalist attention to style and existential or structuralist concern for the "organizing form" in the consciousness of the author. Critical resistance to the Arnold chapter may proceed from Miller's bleak conclusion that "Arnold's ultimate experience is negative." After exploring Arnold's views of time, space, society, love, and passion, Miller finds that "no way will work, and whichever way Arnold turns he is thrown back on himself, and on his usual state of isolation and fluctuation." Miller, not quite happy with Arnold, allows only a small rift in the clouds: though Arnold accepts the absence of God, he nevertheless awaits "the future return of the divine spirit." Miller's argument cannot be easily refuted. It was partially anticipated in a remarkable but little-known essay by J. C. Powys (*Enjoyment of Literature*, 1938), who sympathetically views Arnold as betraying "a cold and weary distaste, a fastidious shrinking, a magnetic *repulsion* from the rough-and-tumble of human intercourse."

Erik Frykman's "*Bitter Knowledge*" and "*Unconquerable Hope*": A Thematic Study of Attitudes towards Life in Matthew Arnold's Poetry 1849–53 (1966) schematically divides positive from negative themes in the early poetry. The book disappointingly concludes that Arnold's most persistent theme is "the quest of the true self."

A. Dwight Culler's *Imaginative Reason: The Poetry of Matthew Arnold*

(1966) is by far the most authoritative study of Arnold's poetry. Though he moves back and forth between the life and poems with a less than clear methodology, Culler's full grasp of the biographical sources and his interpretative power combine to present the most intimate tracing of Arnold's movement from the near-aestheticism of the late forties to the moral poetics of the 1853 Preface. His three-part scheme of Forest Glade, Burning Plain, and Wide-Glimmering Sea, along with their symbolic personae, for the first time established the imaginative unity of Arnold's poetry, even if some poems are ill served by the landscape framework. Although especially penetrating on the elegiac quality of Arnold's best poems, Culler is less successful in showing that the later poetry is indeed the adequate culmination of what is implicitly a "progressive" view of Arnold's poetic career.

G. Robert Stange, in *Matthew Arnold: The Poet as Humanist* (1967), eschewing any metaphoric unity in Arnold's poetry, defends it as poetry of ideas. He nonetheless finds that Arnold saves his poetry from overabstraction by "either building an image out of the objective situation of a poem, or dramatizing the process of thought itself." Arnold's poetry, and sometimes unfortunately individual poems, are distributed among the ruling "Ideas": those of Poetry, Nature, Self, and Love. Though the larger meaning and movement of Arnold's poetry remain difficult to grasp, Stange's patient reading of a number of Arnold's poems makes this an important book.

Looking back beyond the Romantics, Alan Roper's novel strategy in *Arnold's Poetic Landscapes* (1969) is to examine landscape poems in the light of the practice of Thomson, Gray, and Collins. He concludes that in Arnold's best poems, the setting provides "metaphors and terms with which to identify the situation of the subject," and that Arnold thinks "in terms of the landscape, . . . trying to understand or trying to explain why he thinks and feels as he does in such a setting." Although Roper's limited thesis does not allow him to rise to a convincing statement of Arnold's total significance, he is more successful than anyone but Culler in explaining *how* Arnold operates within his poems. Roper's arguments do not derive from the less well-mapped "symbolic landscape" laid out in his earlier article, "The Moral Landscape of Arnold's Poetry" (*PMLA*, 1962).

A group of shorter studies of special themes in Arnold's poetry deserves mention. Apart from the running comments in several of the books already discussed, and the studies of Arnold and the Stoics, there are surprisingly few discussions of the philosophical and religious implications of Arnold's poetry. Joseph Warren Beach, in *The Concept of Nature in Nineteenth-Century English Poetry* (1936), presents Arnold as a defector from the "nature-faith" of the Romantics and aligns him with Tennyson and Hardy in his "suspicion of nature as pagan and immoral." Almost none of the poetic quality of Arnold's handling of external nature survives this treatment. An excellent and compact survey of Arnold's attitudes toward nature is W. Stacy Johnson's "Matthew Arnold's Sea of Life" (*PQ*, 1952). He not only defines the tension in Arnold between a naturalistic monism and "a hopeful faith in the spiritual essence of life," but also explains the breakdown by the sixties of Arnold's search for an imaginative symbol "of some adequate source and ground of human existence." The least inadequate discussion of Arnold's "Stoicism" is by John Hicks (in *Critical Studies in Arnold, Emerson, and Newman*, 1942), who finds stoicism everywhere in Arnold's thought and temperament. Though alert to Arnold's increasing insistence on "joy" in the sixties, Hicks, lacking the evidence of the *Note-Books*, plays down the Christianization of Arnold's ethics and the signs of dissatisfaction in the Marcus Aurelius essay of 1863. The three chapters on Arnold in Evelyn A. Hanley's *Stoicism in Major English Poets of the Nineteenth Century* (1964) simplify Arnold's career even more drastically. Far more authoritative because of its use of the Yale MS is David G. Osborne's discussion of Arnold's "rigorous teachers" of the forties, in his dissertation, "Matthew Arnold, 1843–1849: A Study of the Yale Manuscript" (Rochester 1963). He claims that by 1847 Arnold's search for a "rational and naturalistic substitute for a disintegrating religious faith and traditional ethic"—aided by the *Gita*, Lucretius, Sénancour, and others—had failed. Only Spinoza survived as a guide as Arnold turned from an attitude of withdrawal and escape to one of "joyful activity" and "humanism." Hoxie Neale Fairchild, in *Religious Trends in English Poetry*, iv (1957), betrays the irritation of the dogmatist at finding in Arnold's poetry only "abortive religious hankerings." James Benziger, though intellectually less rigorous, is more sympathetic in exploring the hints of transcendence in Arnold's poetry, in *Images of Eternity* (1962).

Robert A. Donovan ("Philomela: A Major Theme in Arnold's Poetry," *VN*, 1957) discusses the pain and isolation Arnold sees as inseparable from the poet's office, the cause being the poet's necessary loss of illusions about the world and even the loss of his own identity. Since poetry itself is sometimes associated with "illusion" in Arnold, the relationship between loss of illusion, writing poetry, and possessing one's own soul is left less than clear. But the subject is important and deserves further attention.

The legitimacy of ascribing a "tragic" quality to Arnold's poetry—and indeed to Victorian poetry as a whole—deserves further study. W. S. Johnson, in *The Voices of Matthew Arnold* (1961), remarks on the Arnoldian mood of "all but tragic acceptance" and Arnold's experience of "the pain of incompleteness and of isolation in time." In a suggestive article, "Of Time, Rivers, and Tragedy: George Eliot and Matthew Arnold" (*VN*, 1968; included in *George Eliot's Early Novels*, 1968), U. C. Knoepflmacher finds the early George Eliot like Arnold in finding the only catharsis in "an acceptance of the ineluctable flux." But George Eliot, he argues, later went beyond Arnold by adapting her "tragic vision to the moderation of ordinary life."

Curtis Dahl, in "The Victorian Wasteland" (*CE*, 1955; rpt. in *Victorian Literature: Modern Essays in Criticism*, ed. Austin Wright, 1961), contrasts the wasteland imagery in Arnold and T. S. Eliot. John M. Wallace, in "Landscape and 'The General Law': The Poetry of Matthew Arnold" (*BUSE*, 1961), attempts to mitigate the emphasis on conflict and alienation in modern studies of Arnold, claiming that the oppositions in Arnold are not incompatible, "but merely elusively disunited." The point is an important one, but the article is marred by a habit of sweeping and unsupported generalization. In a more careful study of Arnold's search for "a point of balance between activity and repose" ("Equilibrium in the Poetry of Matthew Arnold," *UTQ*, 1960), Allan Brick concludes that Arnold's poetry communicates, not a balance of attitudes, but "the necessary futility of activism braving an alien reality." Melvin Plotinsky ("Help for Pain: The Narrative Verse of Matthew Arnold," *VP*, 1964) suggests that whereas Arnold's best poetry deals with the divided mind, his narratives fail by attempting to resolve or mitigate division. But Plotinsky interestingly subverts his apparent point by finding faint undertones in the four narratives chosen—"The Sick King in Bokhara," "Tristram

and Iseult," "Sohrab and Rustum," and "Balder Dead"—indicating Arnold's faith-
fulness to his perception of "incurable alienation." M. G. Sundell, in "Arnold's
Dramatic Meditations" (*VN*, 1967), is original in showing that the speakers in
"Dover Beach," "Stanzas from the Grande Chartreuse," and "Heine's Grave" are
dramatically differentiated. The speakers "provide form for the poems they ostensibly
speak," while also demonstrating the elusiveness and complexity of truth. The
evidence of ambiguity and ambivalence in Arnold's poetry is interestingly surveyed
in Masao Miyoshi's *The Divided Self: A Perspective on the Literature of the
Victorians* (1969). John R. Reed, in "Matthew Arnold and the Soul's Horizons"
(*VP*, 1970), usefully collects the "sight" and "vision" passages in Arnold's poetry
and concludes, unsurprisingly: "the means to controlling life aesthetically, overcom-
ing passion and business, clearing mists and dreams, is to find in the broad visual
horizons around us emblems of the 'soul's horizons' where past the limits of time
and space man can find freedom from the brazen prison of existence."

The close study of Arnold's poetic artistry—especially his prosody and diction
—is disappointingly scanty, perhaps reflecting a persistent modern doubt concerning the authenticity and authority of Arnold's poetic impulse. Christopher Ricks
(*VS*, 1968) chides recent readers for neglecting to ask whether Arnold's poems are
"well written," and implies doubts about Arnold's "verbal achievement." He points
out that Arnold's poetry, far from being consistently plain, "is full of Miltonic and
Romantic diction which repudiates simplicity and directness." His is the challenge
that future critics of Arnold's poetry must meet. The only extended discussion of
Arnold's metrics is to be found in the perceptive but impressionistic remarks in
George Saintsbury's *A History of English Prosody* (1910). John Drinkwater (*VP*,
1923) found in Arnold's poetry "the hard, jade-like, quality in a phrase" that we
associate with the seventeenth-century lyricists. Bernard Groom (*On the Diction of
Tennyson, Browning and Arnold*, 1939) saw in Arnold's reflective verse a similar
quality, and for the first time described Arnold's characteristic word-forms with
some precision. Interesting though narrower in approach is Hans-Werner Ludwig's
discussion (*Die Self-Komposita bei Thomas Carlyle, Matthew Arnold und Gerard
Manley Hopkins*, 1963) of Arnold's "self-compounds" as reflective of both "the
height and dignity of individual freedom and independence" and the nineteenth
century's "depth of self-consciousness and self-isolation."

The continuing dissatisfaction with Arnold the stylist can be traced most
directly to F. W. Bateson and F. R. Leavis in the 1930's. Bateson, in *English Poetry
and the English Langauge* (1934), indicted all mid-Victorian poetry, Tennyson's
excepted, as "badly written." He accuses Arnold of vagueness of diction and loose-
ness of thought. Some of Leavis' similar remarks will be encountered below. A
more fruitful approach is that of G. Müller-Schwefe (*Das Persönliche Menschenbild Matthew Arnolds in der dichterischen Gestaltung*, 1955), who describes the
poetic effect of the Arnoldian locutions already listed by Groom, such as italics,
foreign words, negative prefixes, and compounds including "self." Park Honan
("Matthew Arnold and Cacophony," *VP*, 1963) engages the bogey directly by
claiming that in Arnold's "discordant sonnets" of 1849 and 1867 the "harsh or
cacophonous verses" provide "a sound-metaphor for the spiritual temper of the
age," while the more euphonious verses provide "a style-metaphor for the noble
character of the poet who was to instruct that age." The argument verges on the
fallacy of imitative form. Too little note has been taken of Josephine Miles's
remarks on Arnold as a representative of "the classical mode," with its "balance of

phrasal and clausal structures," in her pioneer work, *Eras and Modes of English Poetry* (1957; 2nd ed., 1964), and more briefly in *Style and Proportion: The Language of Poetry and Prose* (1967). William T. Going's "Matthew Arnold's Sonnets" (*PLL*, 1970) is practically the only study of Arnold's use of a particular poetic form, but the value of its mildly interesting remarks on the formal elements in Arnold's twenty-nine sonnets is made dubious by the fact that little of Arnold's best poetry can be found in them.

Arnold and Romanticism

In recent years, probably the most significant advance in understanding Arnold's poetry has been the establishment of his relationship to the English Romantic poets. A major issue is the description and evaluation of the nineteenth-century poetic tradition, still imperfectly conceptualized. Following the sweeping dismissals made earlier by T. S. Eliot, F. R. Leavis, in *New Bearings in English Poetry* (1932) and *Revaluation: Tradition and Development in English Poetry* (1936), condemned the entire "nineteenth-century idea of the poetical" and especially the Victorian view "that the actual world is alien, recalcitrant and unpoetical, and that no protest is worth making except the protest of withdrawal." Leavis' charges against Arnold, in particular, of withdrawal, evasion, and escapism, are essentially moral in character. Arnold can then be described, pejoratively, as a "Victorian Romantic" who characteristically "slips away to moonlight transformation," and for whom "the iron time dissolves into wistful, melodious sentiment." This simple polemical view of the nineteenth-century tradition and of Arnold continues to hold the field for some critics (e.g., Jump in *Matthew Arnold*, 1955). The view neglects two complicating facts: first, the recurrent note of moral "stiffening" injected into Arnold's melancholy, noted much earlier by R. H. Hutton; and second, the complexity of Arnold's inheritance from the Romantics.

More sympathetic and more useful is the treatment of Arnold by Douglas Bush in *Mythology and the Romantic Tradition in English Poetry* (1937; rpt. 1963) and *English Poetry: The Main Currents from Chaucer to the Present* (1952; rpt. 1963). Bush details the conflicts in Arnold's poetry and finds them to be "his version of Keats's dilemma, of 'sensations' versus 'thoughts,' of the artist's 'negative capability' versus the moralist's attainment of 'identity,' of 'a soul.'" Of course, as Bush notes, Arnold did not know the fact, and he and Keats move toward the center from opposite emotional poles. George Ford (*Keats and the Victorians*, 1944) also holds that when reading Keats in 1848, Arnold was unaware "that Keats was groping in directions not dissimilar to those he himself projected." Despite Arnold's disapproval of Keats's influence and the "anti-Keatsian" style of the poems written in accordance with the theory of the 1853 Preface, Ford finds the theme and style of some of Arnold's best poetry Keatsian in inspiration.

A serious if somewhat debatable attempt to defend Arnold as not the Oxford classicist but "a highly romantic poet" is made by John Heath-Stubbs (*The Darkling Plain*, 1950). But only in "The Strayed Reveller" did Arnold attain "to an intensity of imaginative creation which transcends the limitations imposed upon him by his time and the inner conflict of his personality." The rest of Arnold's career is simply a gradual falling away of that initial experience of "the intensity of the act of imaginative vision itself." R. A. Foakes, in *The Romantic Assertion: A Study in the Language of Nineteenth Century Poetry* (1958), is even more severe in finding Arnold's "failure of language in the rhetoric of assertion and the rhetoric of love" to be a sign of "the disintegration of the Romantic vision." He indicts Arnold for pathos and "clumsy vagueness" in his language, and for escaping into either a nostalgic past or "unsubstantial assertions of hope or faith."

Three book-length studies have been devoted to Arnold and the Romantics. Two of them, William A. Jamison's *Arnold and the Romantics* (1958) and D. G. James's *Matthew Arnold and the Decline of English Romanticism* (1961), do not treat at any length Romantic influences on Arnold's poetry, and will be considered with studies of Arnold's criticism. The James book, it may be noted, offered in exaggerated form what by 1960 had emerged as a nearly consensus view of Arnold's poetic career: Arnold "failed to apprehend the spiritual resources of Romanticism" and unfortunately rejected "the Romantic doctrine of the autonomy of the imagination." Arnold's "failure to trust the genius of poetry and its power of truth" led to the "drying up within him of the sources of poetry." Easily the best study of the subject is Leon Gottfried's *Matthew Arnold and the Romantics* (1963), which is objective enough to accept "the bankruptcy of Romanticism" as resulting from causes other than Matthew Arnold's personal deficiencies. His summary of the Romantic elements in Arnold shows impatience with the Romantic tradition as much as with Arnold: Arnold's blindness to certain aspects of the English literary tradition; his tendency to "romanticize" the literatures of the past; his narrowing of the range of emotion to "the exalted, the solemn, the melancholy, or the pathetic"; and "his inability to construct a new style adequate to his demands on poetry." As such a listing suggests, Gottfried's judgment of Arnold's poetic achievement is fairly negative; Arnold's poetry is part of a "literary" Alexandrian tradition running (presumably downhill) from Wordsworth to Oscar Wilde.

By pointing to numerous parallels, Gottfried could describe Arnold's "Resignation" as in effect "a conscious reply" to Wordsworth's "Tintern Abbey." A notable extension of this approach is made in Knoepflmacher's "Dover Revisited: The Wordsworthian Matrix in the Poetry of Matthew Arnold" (*VP*, 1963). Knoepflmacher examines several of Arnold's poems as inverting the premises of Wordsworth's faith in nature and perceptively contrasts Wordsworth's "transcendent and symbolic" vision with Arnold's more "analytical and allegorical" method. His most original point is that Arnold's poetry represents, not "a mere negation of Wordsworth's vision," but "a definite effort at conservation." Arnold attempted, paradoxically, to "engender feeling by bemoaning the loss of feeling" and to "preserve Wordsworth's emotional core." The point deserves expansion and debate. Herbert R. Coursen (" 'The Moon Lies Fair': The Poetry of Matthew Arnold," *SEL*, 1964) argues more simply that Arnold's poetry unsuccessfully revisits the Wordsworthian scene in order "to find there the transcendent significance which revealed itself to Wordsworth." But the Wordsworthian background is scanty here, and the otherwise interesting analyses of Arnold's moonlit landscapes are not a sufficient vehicle for his conclusions. The questionable view that Arnold's poetry changes very little from 1849 to 1867 is bolstered by the untenable assumption that "Dover Beach" is a late poem.

M. G. Sundell (" 'Tintern Abbey' and 'Resignation,' " *VP*, 1967) tries to modify the views of Gottfried and Knoepflmacher, arguing that Arnold's poem is not a "quarrel" with Wordsworth's poem but an attempt "to write the same kind of poem about a similar experience." But this conclusion is hard to square with Sundell's description of how precariously the speaker's final "philosophical" view is held, a view in any case very different from Wordsworth's. His most original point is to examine the "new genre" of Arnold's poem, with origins in Wordsworth, Coleridge, and Byron, as it employs new devices: "sharp changes in speaking voice and point of view, division of focus between narrator and story, and use of self-dramatizations as characters in larger contexts." Sundell's remarks on the Romantic prototypes of the form of Arnold's meditative poetry were anticipated briefly in two important earlier articles: Irene H. Chayes's "Rhetoric as Drama: An Approach to the Romantic Ode" (*PMLA*, 1964) and M. H. Abrams' "Structure and Style in the Greater Romantic Lyric" (*From Sensibility to Romanticism: Essays Presented to Frederick A. Pottle*, ed. F. W. Hilles and H. Bloom, 1965).

Once free of the Leavisite rejection of nineteenth-century poetry as a whole, recent views of Arnold's relations with the Romantics have tended to polarize around those defenders of the Romantic tradition (such as D. G. James and R. A. Foakes) who see in Arnold a chief defector from the Romantic faith, and those students of the Victorian period who more sympathetically see Arnold as inhibited by his time, his personality, and the demands of intellectual integrity. Both sets of views see the course of Arnold's poetry as a movement toward the repression of the Romantic elements in his poetry and his personality. The recent books by A. Dwight Culler and G. Robert Stange seek to escape this polemical dialectic by resisting the "disaster" reading of Arnold's career. William A. Madden (*Matthew Arnold*, 1967), though no defender of Arnold's poetry, inverts the fundamental premise of almost all previous studies by minimizing the element of conflict in Arnold and by insisting that it is precisely the Romantic doctrine of the autonomy of art and of the imagination that is the central clue to Arnold's career at all stages. All three of these books, however, like much recent work by professional Victorianists, are in varying degrees vitiated by a lack of feeling for and understanding of the Romantic experiment.

An excellent antidote for these simplifications is Patricia Ball's *The Central Self: A Study in Romantic and Victorian Imagination* (1968). She discerningly shows that "Empedocles" represents Arnold's penetration into the heart of the Wordsworthian "egotistical imagination" and that it "does not flinch from its desperation, nor wish its discoveries unmade. The poetry of experience is vindicated not dishonoured by the decision of Empedocles." Arnold's stress on the "self" leads to the essential modern irony that "self-consciousness equals self-alienation"; the Preface of 1853 thus represents a rejection of *both* Romantic modes of self-involvement in the poetic art, the "chameleon" as well as the "egotistical."

Arnold and the Classics

Arnold's attitudes toward classical civilization and his use of the classics in his poetry are topics not easily detached from that of Arnold and the Romantics, since both subjects involve controversy over the meaning of past cultures and over the movement of Arnold's career. Two of the best earlier studies—Ruth I. Goldmark's *Studies in the Influence of the Classics on English Literature* (1918) and Ralph E. C. Houghton's *The Influence of the Classics on the Poetry of Matthew Arnold* (1923)—suffer from the lack of a "clue" to Arnold's poetic development. Working with the conception of Greek "naturalism" as involving "beauty, sensuousness, harmony of life," and objecting to Arnold's moralism, Goldmark concludes: "The effect of the Greek upon [Arnold's] poetry is . . . varied, but academic, and not profound." Houghton, less severely, finds throughout Arnold's poetry the "gentle melancholy that prevails in most classical literature." Frederic Faverty (*The Victorian Poets*, 1968, p. 210, n.) lists a number of earlier discussions, mostly concerning Arnold's classical sources. To these may be added two articles in the *Classical Journal* (1939) by H. C. Montgomery and G. L. Hendrickson, and brief treatments in two books by J. A. K. Thomson: *The Classical Background of English Literature* (1948) and *Classical Influence on English Poetry* (1951). J. P. Sullivan, in "Matthew Arnold on Classics and Classicists" (*Arion*, 1963), offers a selection of Arnold's more provocative opinions on the classics and their later relevance. Douglas Bush's *Mythology and the Romantic Tradition in English Poetry* (1937) is apparently the only detailed treatment before Trilling to get the inner proportions of Arnold's poetic career right. Bush finds that "Arnold's dreams of a primitive mythical world of simple joy and harmony" are a corrective for modernity and a refuge, but that they do not create a "mere poetry of escape." He sees the ambiguous implications of Arnold's "classicism": his failure to win serenity "made him a poet"; his later "partial victory" made him "a journalist and a classicist." Bush is surprisingly uncritical of the classical doctrine of the 1853 Preface and later, but he anticipates later verdicts in finding the classicism of *Merope* "almost entirely factitious and synthetic."

Warren D. Anderson, in his important *Matthew Arnold and the Classical Tradition* (1965), comprehensively surveys Arnold's treatment of classical figures and themes, and suggests, from the point of view of an informed twentieth-century classical scholar, the subjectivity and highly variable authenticity of Arnold's Apollonian classicism. Anderson conveys less successfully the totality of Arnold's "Hellenism," its origins in German art and thought of the eighteenth and nineteenth centuries, and its relationship to the broader currents of nineteenth-century intellectual conflict. For Anderson, "The Strayed Reveller" is Arnold's "one close approach through the classical to a difficult and more direct experience," while "Empedocles" marks "the beginning of his classicism." The process of Arnold's poetic career is a "disengaging action," "a planned withdrawal from the risks of intimate contact with the disturbing, unpredictable, many-faceted classical experience." In *Victorian Essays: A Symposium* (1967), Anderson summarizes the stages of Arnold's involvement with the classical experience, but adds interesting juxtapositions with Tennyson and Browning.

H. A. Mason ("Arnold and the Classical Tradition," *Arion*, 1962) found Arnold "radically inadequate" in his conception of translation in the Homer lectures; the reason is Arnold's "limited standard of simplicity." Arnold's irony and "vivacity" are "the mask hiding Arnold's embarrassment over failure to expose himself to Homer and discover himself." Henry Ebel's response to Mason (*Arion*, 1963) was the basis of his major article, "Matthew Arnold and Classical Culture" (*Arion*, 1965). Ebel finds Mason's view that Arnold saw the Greek classics "fixed in god-like calm" too simple; as late as 1857, Arnold was "still struggling between the desire to place a positive valuation on modernity, on his own culture, and a desperate nostalgia for the imagined conditions of Greek society." Strikingly, and perhaps too paradoxically, Ebel concludes that, again and again, "Arnold undertook . . . the quixotic, courageous, disjunctive and surely tragic task of rejecting himself." In a similar vein ("A Discreet Vote for Apollo," *Arion*, 1966), Ebel finds the history of Arnold's relations with the classical "a colossal failure, one of the great wrong turnings in the history of ideas." Ebel's "Matthew Arnold and Marcus

Aurelius" (*SEL*, 1963), largely a paraphrase of the 1863 essay, finds parallels between Arnold's version of Marcus Aurelius and the Empedocles he rejected in 1853; indeed, Marcus Aurelius is virtually Arnold himself.

Arnold's *Merope* has been a touchstone for the authenticity of Arnold's classicism; almost all modern readers have rejected it. What could be said in its defense was said long ago by John Bailey (*Poets and Poetry*, 1911). In the best recent reading of the drama, Gabriel Pearson ("The Importance of Arnold's *Merope*," in *The Major Victorian Poets*, ed. Isobel Armstrong, 1969) sees Arnold's distrust of the truth revealed by poetry as springing from the post-Romantic problem of the status of the "imagination": "Is the imagination socialisable, or is its essential nature anarchic and disruptive?" *Merope*, Pearson concludes, "is Arnold's last fling. It is the act by which he apparently assumed the paternal, authoritative role, stationed himself on his elevation and, like Polyphontes, took on 'the stern, repressed attitude of rule.' " Almost the climax in recent severe readings of Arnold's poetry, Pearson judges that Arnold "fudged" "life's basic, existential issues."

Arnold's Homer lectures (1861–62) have in recent years received mostly incidental comment, in such broad-ranging works as Gilbert Highet's *The Classical Tradition* (1949) and Albert Cook's *The Classic Line: A Study in Epic Poetry* (1966).

Major Formative Influences

Some of the best recent work on Arnold has been in the area of the early formative influences on his poetry and thought. Mention has already been made of Arnold's relations to classical culture, the Stoics, and the English Romantic poets. William Robbins (*The Ethical Idealism of Matthew Arnold*, 1959) provides an excellent chapter giving brief summaries of Arnold's debts to Newman, Carlyle, Sainte-Beuve, Wordsworth, Goethe, Thomas Arnold, Bishop Butler, Coleridge, the Cambridge Platonists, Emerson, the Stoics, Renan, and George Sand. Robbins' treatment of Arnold and Spinoza is the best we have. R. H. Super, in *The Time-Spirit of Matthew Arnold* (1970), throws numerous new lights on Arnold's thought in its contemporary context, working out illuminating parallels and contrasts with Emerson, Carlyle, Goethe, Newman, Mill, Dr. Arnold, Burke, and Spinoza. In almost every instance, however, the precise degree of Arnold's assimilation and rejection of such influences remains unsettled, and further work is obviously in order. The influences on Arnold's later religious thought will be considered below, under that topic.

The "native" influences may be considered first. Kathleen Tillotson's important lecture, "Matthew Arnold and Carlyle" (1956; rpt. in *Mid-Victorian Studies*, 1965), deftly re-creates the atmosphere at Oxford in the 1840's, when Carlyle's influence was at its height, and suggests the reasons for his short-lived appeal. She finds the closest connection with Carlyle in Arnold's "Empedocles" and the "Grande Chartreuse." David J. DeLaura, in "Arnold and Carlyle" (*PMLA*, 1964), turns to Arnold's prose of the sixties, in which he repeatedly finds "a peculiar psychological mechanism whereby Carlyle will be rejected with expressions of scorn, distrust, or condescension, while the surrounding text will, in a variety of ways, reveal its substantive debt to Carlyle's writings." He attributes the "persistent ambivalence" in Arnold's view of Carlyle to a "personal aggrievement": "We often have conveyed to us a bitter sense of high youthful hopes dashed and betrayed."

Turning to the important question of Carlyle's possible influence on Arnold's aesthetic views, Lawrence J. Starzyk ("Arnold and Carlyle," *Criticism*, 1970) attributes to Carlyle a decisive role in the moralization of Arnold's poetics and Arnold's later emphasis on the social and religious function of poetry. But in its neglect of other probable sources such as Wordsworth and the Goethe mediated by Carlyle, and in its frequent violation of the canons governing the attribution of "influences," the article is to be read with caution.

A number of ties between Arnold and John Henry Newman were suggested by Henry Tristram in "Newman and Matthew Arnold" (*Cornhill*, 1926). A monograph-length study by David DeLaura (*TSLL*, 1965, Supp.) appeared in revised form in his *Hebrew and Hellene in Victorian England: Newman, Arnold, and Pater* (1969). Drawing on unpublished correspondence and concentrating on Arnold's critical and religious writings, DeLaura claims that "Newman comes to occupy a startlingly central position in Arnold's idea of human perfection; he is at once the embodiment of intellectual refinement and a model for the conduct of public debate, as well as perhaps the clearest exemplar Arnold knew of the temper of Jesus, which he recommended, and the tragedy of Jesus, which he found so affecting." His strongly worded conclusion, that "No other figure in Arnold's development—not Goethe, or Wordsworth—is so frequently found at the center of Arnold's total humanistic vision," deserves debate.

Darrel Abel, in "Strangers in Nature—Arnold and Emerson" (*UKCR*, 1949), misuses his interpretative power in order to extol Emerson at Arnold's expense. Arnold, a "combination of misanthropy and overweening morality" and a figure of "mistrust and alienation," could not be, like Emerson, "a benign and potent influence on his country's life." Much more solid is "Emerson and Arnold's Poetry" (*PQ*, 1954), by Super, who skillfully marks out the "large areas of correspondence" between the two men while remaining aware of "the fundamental difference" between the two minds.

V. L. Romer, in "Matthew Arnold and Some Poets" (*NC*, 1926), briefly suggested not only the similarities but the important differences between Arnold and Sénancour. Such balance does not mark Iris Esther Sells's *Matthew Arnold and France: The Poet* (1935). Sells declares that up to 1855 "the influence of Obermann overshadows all others," and she finds numerous parallels in their thought. Though obviously exaggerated, her claims have never been subjected to extended analysis. Florence L. Wickelgren ("Matthew Arnold's Literary Relations with France," *MLR*, 1938) begins the task by giving the more scholarly background to Arnold's relations with George Sand, "Marguerite," and Sénancour, and by gently correcting some of Sells's excesses. A modest but discriminating study of a later "influence" on Arnold is G. Thomas Fairclough's *A Fugitive and Gracious Light: The Relation of Joseph Joubert to Matthew Arnold's Thought* (1961).

In 1872, Arnold said that Sainte-Beuve was one of four men from whom he had "learnt habits, methods, ruling ideas, which are constantly with me." The external evidence is gathered in Louis Bonnerot's *Matthew Arnold, poète* (1947) and in Super's "Documents in the Matthew Arnold–Sainte-Beuve Relationship" (*MP*, 1963). The anonymous author of "The Prince of French Critics? Sainte-Beuve Reconsidered" (*TLS*, 31 July 1937) granted to Arnold "a freer intelligence" and superiority as an analyst, though he lacked the assurance of "a living tradition" to which Sainte-Beuve could appeal. Arnold Whitridge ("Matthew Arnold and Sainte-Beuve," *PMLA*, 1938), though conceding affinities of temperament, tellingly contrasts Sainte-Beuve's essential skepticism with Arnold's commitment to conduct and righteousness. Despite Arnold's professions of discipleship, Ruth Z. Temple (*The Critic's Alchemy*, 1953) goes so far as to declare that "Arnold's criticism has no real resemblance in theory, in spirit, or in practice" to that of Sainte-Beuve. David DeLaura (*Hebrew and Hellene in Victorian England*, 1969) suggests that the influence extends to "habits" and "methods" rather than to the larger "ruling ideas" of Arnold's career. The relationship awaits a definitive treatment.

Even less settled is the matter of Arnold's indebtedness to Ernest Renan. The subject was well begun in the short but solid "Renan and Matthew Arnold" (*MLN*, 1918) by Lewis F. Mott, who found Arnold's "most definite obligations" to Renan in the Celtic lectures. J. W. Angell ("Matthew Arnold's Indebtedness to Renan's *Essais de morale et de critique*," *RLC*, 1934) adds virtually nothing to Mott. The most adequate study so far is by Sidney M. B. Coulling (*Renan's Influence on Arnold's Literary and Social Criticism*, Fla. State Univ. Stud., 1952), who finds that Arnold's "obvious similarities to Renan have obscured his essential dissimilarities." He concludes that although Arnold read Renan closely, "he was never, in any important sense, under Renan's influence." Joan Harding, in "Renan and Matthew Arnold: Two Saddened Searchers" (*HJ*, 1959), comes to the interesting if somewhat tendentious conclusion that Arnold failed to realize "how easily morality, divorced from faith in Absolute values, degenerates into universal hedonism," and that Renan's "imaginative dissolution" of religious belief was merely the logical conclusion of Arnold's own efforts in the seventies. Rose Bachem in "Arnold's and Renan's Views of Perfection" (*RLC*, 1967) uncritically finds the two men alike in their joining of Hebraism and Hellenism, the latter defined as classical antiquity "diluted" by contact with Christianity. She finds that Arnold and Renan, more than any other thinkers of their age, resemble the humanists of the Renaissance.

The dangers of basing a complex rereading of a text on a conjectural "source" are illustrated in Flavia M. Alaya's " 'Two Worlds' Revisited: Arnold, Renan, the Monastic Life, and the 'Stanzas from the Grande Chartreuse' " (*VP*, 1967). The author attempts to attribute Arnold's increase in sympathy for monasticism between "To Meta" (ca. 1849) and the "Grande Chartreuse" to his reading of an essay of Renan published in January 1855. But the arguments against her hypothesis are nearly insuperable: Arnold's poem was published in April 1855, and was thus finished no later than March; the composition of this elaborate poem almost certainly began as early as 1851 or 1852; and the evidence is continually forced to make the poem a direct reflection of Renan's views, which are not verbally close to the poem. The article's recurrent confusions as to the identification of various speakers (e.g., equating Christianity with the party of "grief") prove, in passing, how far we still are from a satisfactory reading of the poem. Alaya's study, "Arnold and Renan on the Popular Uses of History" (*JHI*, 1967), extends a wider net. She convincingly aligns the two men in their "religious" conception of the human future, while perceptively contrasting Renan's attraction to uncertainty and flux with Arnold's aversion to "thought without form."

Unsettled too is the extremely important question of not only the depth but the precise nature of Goethe's influence on Arnold's career. Ludwig Lewisohn ("A Study of Matthew Arnold, II. Formative Influences: The Influence of Goethe," *SR*, 1902) was one of the first to point out similarities, especially in formal qualities shared by the poetry of the two men. Helen C. White ("Matthew Arnold and Goethe," *PMLA*, 1921) summarized the familiar "Goethean" ideas in Arnold's conception of criticism and culture. James Bentley Orrick, in his impressive "Matthew Arnold and Goethe" (*PEGS*, 1928), sought to overthrow the earlier simplicities by arguing, in reaction, that Goethe was not even "a primary influence" on Arnold. What did influence Arnold greatly was the "quite illusory" conception of Goethe, mediated by Carlyle, as a "physician, moralist, and high priest." Arnold, in Orrick's view, saw Goethe primarily as a thinker and not as "an artist, a liver of the creative life"; whereas Goethe goes to Greek art precisely "for an escape from the 'moral interpretation' which Arnold sees in him and in the Greeks alike."

More recent readers of Arnold have been disturbed by this sweeping judgment. William Robbins (*The Idealism of Matthew Arnold*, 1959) agrees that Arnold overemphasizes the moral element in Goethe, but insists on "the modern and naturalistic Goethe" as the source of Arnold's ideals of cultural totality and the critical examination of all established beliefs. For William Madden (*Matthew Arnold*, 1967), Goethe is "the writer to whom [Arnold] was perhaps most deeply indebted," and the central line of Arnold's poetics derives from the "Weimar classicism" of Goethe and Schiller. An important strength of G. Robert Stange's *Matthew Arnold: The Poet as Humanist* (1967) is his discovery of a number of Goethean models for certain of Arnold's poems. He argues that three of the four major "organizing" ideas of Arnold's poetry seem to be "conscious extensions of Goethe's insights." But in the opinion of David DeLaura ("What, Then, Does Matthew Arnold Mean?" *MP*, 1969), Madden and Stange allow such evidence to imply too simply that Goethe's "humanism" is the model of Arnold's. Neither critic offers "any coherent discussion of what Goethe characteristically stands for and whether Arnold did in fact absorb Weimar classicism and aestheticism integrally." DeLaura suggests elsewhere (*Hebrew and Hellene in Victorian England*, 1969) that "Arnold's Hellenism —and certainly his Hebraism" often seem closer to the ethical strain of Herder's Humanität than to Goethe's classicism. Similarly, Kenneth Allott (*E&S*, 1968) finds that Arnold read Goethe as a sage and not primarily as a poet. The topic requires a more comprehensive and authoritative treatment than it has yet received.

Considering that Heinrich Heine is the major source for both Arnold's term "Philistine" and his Hebraism-Hellenism antithesis (see Super, *Complete Prose Works*, III, 436; v, 435–36), little effort has been made to explain Heine's role in Arnold's evolving thought. Walter Fischer ("Matthew Arnold und Deutschland," *GRM*, 1954) deftly but briefly suggests the limitations of Arnold's understanding of Heine. Sol Liptzin, in *The English Legend of Heinrich Heine* (1954), offers mostly a paraphrase of Arnold's influential essay of 1863 and his poem, "Heine's Grave." Elsie M. Butler, in a lively if too easily dismissive article ("Heine in England and Matthew Arnold," *GL&L*, 1956), finds Arnold's sketch of Heine taking on Goethe's "mantle" laughable: "granted that there was a deep influence, it took the form of a passionate reaction against Goethe's classicism and his latter-day Olympianism and conservatism." She attributes Arnold's failures with Heine (as Orrick did in the parallel case of Goethe) to his "heavy-handed Anglo-Saxon morality." Far better is Charles D. Wright's "Matthew Arnold on Heine as 'Continuator' of Goethe" (*SP*, 1968), which points out that Heine, in his "intrepid application of the modern spirit to literature," *was* consciously following one main line of Goethe's effort, the aspect of Goethe most significant to Arnold. For Heine, however, the really significant Goethe was the artist: "Goethe was a kind of artistic counter-weight to Heine's passionate involvement in the issues of his epoch." The dilemma, that of Art versus Propaganda, was also Arnold's. The most complete study of the relationship, Ilse-

Maria Tesdorpf's *Die Auseinandersetzung Matthew Arnolds mit Heinrich Heine* (1971), shows a full awareness of the differences separating the two men.

Arnold and History

Arnold's views of history deserve special mention because of the centrality of this concern in his entire career. But the subject has received attention only belatedly. In 1953, Gaylord C. LeRoy in *Perplexed Prophets* noted in Arnold a "philosophy of history . . . impressive in its comprehensiveness and inner consistency." But Arnold's notion of "a dialectical advance" avoiding "the crude view of progress" received largely rhetorical formulation: "Arnold's account of the 'perfect society' towards which the dialectical movement of history is aimed remains as one of the noblest embodiments of the reaches of the human spirit in the nineteenth century." In the same year John Holloway, in *The Victorian Sage*, more effectively contrasted "the apocalyptic quality of Carlyle's historical determinism" with Arnold's view that the "course of history is not grand, simple and mysterious, but neat and orderly, now one thing and now another, according to time and place." The topic was treated with admirable perceptiveness in Fraser Neiman's "The Zeitgeist of Matthew Arnold" (*PMLA*, 1957; incorporated into his *Matthew Arnold*, 1968). Though the evidence was restricted to the recurrence of only one key term, Arnold's entire intellectual development was illuminated by Neiman's conclusion that in the period of the letters to Clough *Zeitgeist* meant "the temper of the times, with the additional idea that time is a local, changeable phenomenon opposing eternal values," while in the period of Arnold's religious writings the term "signifies a cosmic spiritual power that wills the development of human reason and that reveals development in the sequence of historic time."

Paul W. Day, in a monograph *Matthew Arnold and the Philosophy of Vico* (1964), resolutely but unconvincingly attempts to attach Arnold's recurrent "backward-looking tendency" and his interest in the "heroic" past to a slender connection with Vico's *Scienza Nuova*—namely, that Thomas Arnold mentioned Vico once! But Duncan Forbes (*The Liberal Anglican Idea of History*, 1952) is much more cautious in speaking of the role of Vico in Thomas Arnold's view of history, and Day for the sake of his thesis is forced to discount all other eighteenth-century "primitive" theories of history, as well as Wordsworth's. Committing the fallacy of the unique source in a case with virtually no direct evidence, Day has to conclude lamely that as part of the "floating intellectual currency" of his times, "Arnold, along with many other nineteenth-century thinkers, absorbed Vico's philosophy in its broad outlines, in his earliest years, and retained it as a shaping force in his own most characteristic expressions of belief." Edward Alexander (*Matthew Arnold and John Stuart Mill*, 1965) is more reliable in discussing at length the conflict of absolute values and historical relativism in the two men. But his treatment suffers from the lack of a meaningful setting in nineteenth-century historiography. Flavia Alaya ("Arnold and Renan on the Popular Uses of History," *JHI*, 1967) claims that Renan's "continuous opposition of menace and love, authority and unction, energy and calm" constitutes "a series of spiritual antitheses that profoundly affected Arnold's treatment of religious history."

An important addition to our understanding of Arnold's view of history in his earlier poetry was made by R. A. Forsyth in " 'The Buried Life'—The Contrasting Views of Arnold and Clough in the Context of Dr. Arnold's Historiography" (*ELH*,

1968). Complicating the views of Paul Day, and relying on the image of the River of Life in Thomas Arnold's prose and in a poem first published by Allott (*The Poems of Matthew Arnold*, 1965), Forsyth shows that Thomas Arnold took a more optimistic view of man's ability to learn from history than either Vico or his own son did. Matthew Arnold's pessimistic view that the "genuine self" is buried through "the cultural atrophy of the 'religious' sensibility resulting from the unnatural latter-day predominance of the intellect" is probingly contrasted with Clough's more Christian and "absolute" view of "man's real self as the immortal and immutable soul whose nurture and protection continue to be supremely difficult in a world of distractions and temptation." After Forsyth, Charles R. Moyer's "The Idea of History in Thomas and Matthew Arnold" (*MP*, 1969) is disappointingly thin. Also relying on Thomas Arnold's poem, Moyer perceives that his river image suggests a greater willingness on the father's part "to accept and redeem the busy life of the crowded cities of the plain," but concludes weakly that, "by elucidating the similarity between apparently dissimilar periods of history, his father helped him toward his method of imaginatively exploring and giving form to his sense of himself and his situation." Even less light is shed by the superficial discussion of "historical periodicity" in Charles Mohan, "Matthew Arnold's Concept of History" (*Stud. in the Humanities*, 1969–70).

The most rewarding recent discussion of Arnold's "use" of history is to be found in two exceptionally able articles by John P. Farrell. In "Matthew Arnold's Tragic Vision" (*PMLA*, 1970), Farrell finds Arnold rejecting the classical tragic view in favor of a post-Romantic tragic figure who is not an offender but a victim of "revolutionary" historical change. The pattern for this autobiographical figure, wandering between two unacceptable worlds of value, is found in Arnold's "Falkland" (1877), and was worked out in "Empedocles," "Balder Dead," *Merope*, and the unfinished *Lucretius*. Arnold's attempt to find in history those unchanging values that survive the "historical audit" and the erosions of the rational intellect is the subject of his "Matthew Arnold and the Middle Ages: The Uses of the Past" (*VS*, 1970).

Individual Poems

Early Poems

Apart from readings in the books by Culler, Madden, Stange, and Roper, surprisingly few of the poems in Arnold's 1849 volume have received close attention. G. Thomas Fairclough ("The Sestet of Arnold's 'Religious Isolation,'" *N&Q*, 1962) defends the poem against Trilling's charge of incoherence. Edmund Bergler ("Writers and Ulcus," *AI*, 1953) reads "The Sick King in Bokhara" as about a "repressed masochistic wish to suffer." Albert Van Aver adds little to our understanding of Arnold's "In Harmony with Nature" (*Personalist*, 1967) by accusing Arnold of an "indecisive attitude toward nature." James G. Nelson, in *The Sublime Puritan: Milton and the Victorians* (1963), suggests in passing the Miltonic quality of Arnold's early sonnets. In "Matthew Arnold's Mournful Rhymes: A Study of 'The World and the Quietist'" (*VP*, 1963), Robert A. Greenberg finds great significance in the poem, which he reads as different from Arnold's other early "quietist" poems in being not merely a confession of alienation but a justification for "the writing of poetry that is the consequence of alienation," Arnold's "debating poetry." "In

Utrumque Paratus" receives a close reading from W. Stacy Johnson (*Expl*, 1952), who concludes that "the only way one can be 'in utrumque paratus' is by balancing the stringent morality demanded by the personal conscience of idealism with the natural sympathy suggested by materialism." The overelaborate argument of Jan B. Gordon's "Disenchantments with Intimations: A Reading of Arnold's 'In Utrumque Paratus'" (*VP*, 1965) is further impaired by the uninformed view that the shattering of the "Wordsworthian intimations" of the poem's opening represents "a unique inversion" of the "Wordsworthian matrix" in Arnold's poetry.

Considering its inherent merits and its importance in Arnold's development, "Resignation" has received very little close analysis, the best being that in Stange's *Matthew Arnold: The Poet as Humanist*. The Wordsworthian background of the poem has been considered above in connection with Arnold and Romanticism. Paull F. Baum (*Ten Studies in the Poetry of Matthew Arnold*, 1958) offers a close paraphrase of the poem but is harsh in his judgment of its success. The other major poem of the 1849 volume, the even more difficult "The Strayed Reveller," has recently fared somewhat better. Warren Anderson's comments in *Matthew Arnold and the Classical Tradition* have already been noted. Leon Gottfried (*Matthew Arnold and the Romantics*) finds the poem ironic, and makes the epithet "strayed" the key to interpreting the poem as an anti-Keatsian allegory. A. Dwight Culler's exceptionally penetrating section on the poem (in *Imaginative Reason*) is part of his exposition of Arnold's search in his early poetics for a "middle way between the superficial pictorial vision of the gods and the agonized probing of the poets." A similar framework for the explication of the poem is employed by M. G. Sundell in "Story and Context in 'The Strayed Reveller'" (*VP*, 1965). Sundell is one of the few to make clear that the Reveller in his "joyful eagerness" is not of the class of poets who experience "a powerful ecstasy" but have "no joy in perception or creation." Alan Roper (*Arnold's Poetic Landscapes*) is like Gottfried in finding in the poem "a tacit reproach" for the Reveller's "intoxicating loss of feeling." He tries to correct Sundell by finding the Reveller's "choice" to be not "that between actual and vicarious experience," but "between the gods' unimpassioned objectivity and the poet's painful subjectivity, and between the revels of art and the revels of divine worship." Norman Friedman, in "The Young Matthew Arnold 1847–1849: 'The Strayed Reveller' and 'The Forsaken Merman'" (*VP*, 1971), judges that both poems fail to resolve the problems they raise. Though the author shows little sense of the development of Arnold's poetry, and his "ultimate interest" is in large notions like Romanticism, Victorianism, and Modernism, he intelligently raises critical points that deserve further discussion.

Arnold's Shakespeare sonnet presents perhaps unresolvable problems of interpretation and, partly as a consequence, has become a kind of touchstone for judging Arnold's quality as a poet. As part of his campaign against Arnold's poetry, F. R. Leavis turned his full artillery on the poem in *Education & the University: A Sketch for an 'English School'* (1943; rpt. 1948). Finding in line 5 ("Planting his steadfast footsteps in the sea") "a ludicrous suggestion of gigantic, ponderously wading strides," Leavis ends by convicting the poem of "general debility" as a result of the "dead conventionality of the phrasing" and "the lack of any vital organization among the words." A series of seven articles in *Notes and Queries* (1942) established a range of possible interpretations of the two cruxes of the poem: the "hill" and "brow" imagery and the meaning of lines 12–14. Equally important are the suggestions made in *The Explicator* (June, Dec. 1946; Oct. 1947). Paull Baum (*Ten Studies in the Poetry of Matthew Arnold*) reads "All pains . . . " as referring to Shakespeare's experiences; thus the poem is about Shakespeare's own aloofness, and "Resignation" becomes the best commentary on the sonnet. Tom J. Truss comments (*Expl*, 1961), rather obscurely, on the poem's balancing of pictorial effect and personification. More impressive, but not less problematical, is the reading by Robert A. Greenberg ("Patterns of Imagery: Arnold's 'Shakespeare,'" *SEL*, 1965), who reads the "loftiest hill" not as Shakespeare but as the hill of further awareness that Shakespeare had climbed, beyond common knowledge. Against Baum, Greenberg sees Arnold as congratulating Shakespeare for having achieved the difficult balance needed by the poet: *sharing* in human experience "while at the same time possessing an inner coherence that secured him from fragmentation." J. W. Frierson ("The Strayed Reveller of Fox How," *VP*, 1967) finds a not very significant "source" for the poem's mountain-cloud-brow imagery in Stanley's *Life and Correspondence of Thomas Arnold*.

Though admired from the time of its first publication in 1849, "The Forsaken Merman" has received little critical attention. Against the view of W. S. Johnson (*The Voices of Matthew Arnold*) that the poem is written from Margaret's point of view, Howard W. Fulweiler argues ("Matthew Arnold: The Metamorphosis of a Merman," *VP*, 1963) that "the sea . . . represents freedom, beauty, love, and the deepest mysteries of life, yet paradoxically it also represents moral responsibility to others, as in the care of the children. The land represents imprisonment by convention, insensitivity to the deepest moral values, and monotonous, mechanical, incessant activity." Kenneth Allott ("Matthew Arnold's 'The Neckan': The Real Issues," *VP*, 1964) rejects Fulweiler's reading of the "Merman" as an allegory of Arnold's personal crisis about "art, love, and faith," and points out that the flowering staff episode in "The Neckan," which Fulweiler sees as a sign of recovery, was in Arnold's original source. Unconvinced, Fulweiler replies (*VP*, 1964) that the new source substantiates his own reading. Fulweiler earlier had noted interesting parallels between Arnold's "Merman" and two of Tennyson's early poems, "Merman" and "Mermaid" (*VN*, 1963), but declines to call them "sources."

Poems of 1852

The contents of *Empedocles on Etna and Other Poems* (1852) represent Arnold's period of Sturm und Drang, after the comparative serenity and detachment of the 1849 volume. The extremely complex biographical and literary problems involved in this period of Arnold's greatest personal and creative crisis have been handled in masterly fashion by Culler in *Imaginative Reason*.

A satisfactory understanding of the inner proportions of "Empedocles on Etna" has only recently emerged as a result of a number of intensive readings. For nearly a century, the centrality of the poem in Arnold's development remained obscured by the absence of any convincing theory of Arnold's development between 1849 and 1852. A single shaft of light comes from A. Clutton-Brock (*Essays in Literature & Life*, 1926): "Is not Empedocles the myth of a divided personality, the inner truth about Arnold himself, which, as soon as he told it, he wished to suppress because it was indeed a conflict in himself to which he could see no solution?" Bush (*Mythology and the Romantic Tradition in English Poetry*, 1937), one of the first to profit from the evidence of the Arnold-Clough letters, also suggests that Arnold suppressed "Empedocles" because "he had said the opposite of what he believed he ought to have said." Bush reads the entire poem as "an anti-intellectual affirmation on the side of simple feeling, sensuous intuition. But Arnold cannot, as Keats sometimes can, surrender wholly to one part of himself; the dilemma remains a dilemma." The function of Callicles' songs is by implication and contrast to "supplement and feed the nostalgic regret of Empedocles." Thus Bush seems to imply that the songs are a contributory cause of the suicide. All recent readings of "Empedocles" are aware of T. Sturge Moore's claim (*E&S*, 1938) that "*Empedocles* more and more seems the most considerable poem of a comparable length by a Victorian."

The understanding of "Empedocles" was greatly advanced by the nearly eighty-page introduction to Louis Bonnerot's translation, *Empedocle sur l'Etna* (1947)—though most later critics seem curiously unaware of its existence. His reading is somewhat hampered by the limitations of the dualistic thesis which, in the same year, dominates his *Matthew Arnold, poète*. Bonnerot judges that "Empedocles" ends "à une mort qui ne contient même la promesse de l'Union parfaite avec l'Univers." It is precisely Arnold's lack of the imaginative faith that sustains the myths of the great Romantics, which leads Bonnerot to conclude severely that Arnold's poem lacks "l'élan poétique" as well as unity of tone and structure. The most valuable passages are the shrewd comparisons and contrasts of Arnold's "antiheroic" hero ("une originalité négative") with a wide variety of other literary figures: Hamlet, Faust, Clough's Dipsychus, Manfred, and Browning's Paracelsus.

Joan Harding ("The Poetry of Matthew Arnold," *ConR*, 1952) is in line with other recent readers in judging that Arnold suppressed his "experiment" when "it had not yielded him what he wanted." But she is closer to Arnold's contemporaries in approving his willed removal from the "dismay and isolation" of "the void for which he was heading." Correct in describing Arnold's moral hesitancies, this view overlooks the damage done to the sources of his creativity by decisions culminating in the Preface of 1853. A powerful antidote to such moralism is the influential reading of the poem by Frank Kermode (*Romantic Image*, 1957), who sees Arnold's solitaries—Obermann, Guérin, and especially Empedocles—as so many examples of the nineteenth-century "alienated" artist. "A certain act," Kermode generalizes, "a violent process of life, is possible to the contemplative and to the artist; but the cost is extinction." Unable or unwilling to repeat his rather Pyrrhic victory, Arnold chose "poetic extinction." Kermode's discussion of Arnold's "dissociation" of the figure of the Romantic poet in Empedocles and Callicles deserves close attention. Kermode concludes that the answer to Arnold's problem as an artist—if not as a man—"lay in the cruel effort and continued self-expenditure of a series of Empedoclean victories, not in the carefully qualified betrayal, the compromise of life and art, action and inaction, which his Mask as Critic represents."

The well-known essay by Walter E. Houghton, "Arnold's 'Empedocles on Etna'" (*VS*, 1958), clearly analyzes the structure of the poem and admirably defines those elements of the modern intellectual's experience summed up in the figure of Empedocles. The major question regarding his reading lies in his finding a dominant note of "moral victory" in the suicide: depression is not "the direct or immediate cause," and Empedocles dies in a "strange mood of exaltation, even of triumph." But the evidence for this judgment is in fact largely negative, as even Houghton's emphasis on Empedocles' "glad realization that he is not *wholly* dead, not *all* enslaved to the mind or to the world" suggests. The "tone" of Empedocles' final action and its motives—whether it is Kermode's cruel "victory" that is really "extinction" and "self-destruction," or Houghton's less ambiguous "victory" that brings "the very pulse of life"—remain unresolved problems of Arnold criticism. Houghton's version would carry greater weight if it had put "Empedocles" into relationship with the rest of Arnold's poems and discussed its place in the development of his poetics.

Several attempts have been made to identify philosophical and literary sources for "Empedocles." S. Nagarajan ("Arnold and the *Bhagavad Gita*: A Reinterpretation of *Empedocles on Etna*," *CL*, 1960) does not establish his thesis that "the intellectual frame of reference" of the poem is "substantially derived" from the *Gita*. Still, the evidence in David Osborne's thesis suggests the depth of Arnold's interest in "Eastern" religious thought during this period, and thus indirectly strengthens the case. Nagarajan undercuts a reading of the suicide like Houghton's by noting that (by the standards of the *Gita*) Empedocles' desire to die before his exaggerated intellectuality "utterly estranges him from the truth of truth" is "hardly a solution: a temporary release from the ego sense is confounded with the annihilation of the ego." Fred L. Burwick, in "Hölderlin and Arnold: Empedocles on Etna" (*CL*, 1965), is even less successful in finding sources in Hölderlin's drama on the same topic. External evidence is entirely lacking, and the verbal echoes, parallel themes and images, and similarities in structure can be accounted for in the use of identical sources. Quite different is K. Allott's "Arnold's 'Empedocles on Etna' and Bryon's 'Manfred' " (*N&Q*, 1962), which shows that the setting, as well as 'the form and general evolution of Arnold's poem," show the influence of *Manfred*.

Donald J. Gray ("Arthur, Roland, Empedocles, Sigurd, and the Despair of Heroes in Victorian Poetry," *BUSE*, 1961) points out that Empedocles' failure is more complete than that of other heroes of the period, including Arnold's own; it anticipates the late Victorian abandonment of "hope in the efficacy of individual will." Though too ambitious for its length, Charles Berryman's article (*VN*, 1966) is a shrewd reading of the "dramatic" qualities of the poem, especially the hero's lack of certainty. Though the point is denied by other critics, Berryman shows that Arnold's intended theme, "refusal of limitation," explains much in the poem, especially the alternatives of unworthy compromise and suicide in "negation" and "despair." Though Arnold thereafter sought "a positive alternative beyond Empedocles," Berryman says, "The genuine despair of Empedocles is better than the forced emotion of Sohrab."

In many ways the culmination of the recent studies of the poem, K. Allott's "A Background for 'Empedocles on Etna' " (*E&S*, 1968) explains with mature critical insight and a wealth of detail the significance of the poem in Arnold's career. Allott shows that Arnold's problem in the forties, when he read Goethe, Lucretius, and the *Gita* for enlightenment as well as "spiritual reassurance," was to salvage an attitude of "reverence" from the collapse of his orthodox religious beliefs. "Empedocles" can then be read as "Arnold's most comprehensive attempt to '*solve* the Universe' by bringing into unity the fragments of his thought, but paradoxically it is the failure of this intention that is responsible finally for the artistic success of the poem." The true meaning of "the rejection of subjectivity" in the 1853 Preface is, then, Arnold's "décision to hold back something of himself in the act of creation."

Two recent readings throw light on "Empedocles" by paying special attention to Callicles. Meredith B. Raymond ("Apollo and Arnold's 'Empedocles on Etna,' " *REL*, 1967) reads the poem as a conflict between harmony (identified with Apollo and the lyre) and "mind." Empedocles, though in many ways sympathetic, is guilty of "intellectual pride," "lack of balance," and "egotism," and as a result fails "to recognize pride in Typho, Marsyas, and in himself." Thus Raymond attempts to argue away the evident "disparity between the advice to Pausanias in Act i and the soliloquy in Act ii"; in both uses Empedocles is dominated by an "intellectual self sufficiency" which becomes the motive of his "despair and destruction." But she underplays Arnold's obvious near identification with Empedocles and reads back into 1849 a new theory of poetry which did not take its final form (and that only painfully) until 1853. More convincing, if novel, is the balance of motives found by Linda Lee Ray, in "Callicles on Etna: The Other Mask" (*VP*, 1969). Callicles, she shows, is not merely a young Empedocles, but one who speaks in "the condemning voice of the moralist and critic." Arnold's attitude remains "ambivalent . . . because while objectively he must condemn Empedocles' Promethean defiance, emotionally he sympathizes and pities him." Improving on the Raymond thesis, Ray sees Arnold as admiring and pitying Empedocles while resenting that the cosmic order, associated with Apollo, "is what it is." The paradox then is that the philosophical Empedocles is the spokesman for "the romantic, perplexed Arnold associated with the poetry," while the poet Callicles anticipates "the moralizing Arnold associated with his later prose." The case is not easily refuted.

A final note of caution on the solemnity of recent Arnold criticism may be in order. Arnold's enthusiastic modern readers, who would take offense at Samuel Chew's judgment that the ending of "Empedocles" is "faintly ridiculous" (*A Literary History of England*, ed. Albert C. Baugh, 1948), may be referred to George Meredith's impish view of Arnold's "heels in air" philosopher ("Empedocles," 1892). More seriously, Bush (*Pagan Myth and Christian Tradition in English Poetry*, 1968) challenges Culler and Raymond by claiming that the affirmation in Callicles' final lyric, though attractive, is part of Arnold's "nostalgic primitivism" and, like the views of the English Romantics, inadequate for modern man.

"Tristram and Iseult" has proved, of all of Arnold's major poems, one of the most resistant to close analysis. Three short notes on special topics are Lyman Cotten's "Matthew Arnold's Pronunciation of the Name Iseult" (*MLN*, 1952), Guy Battle's "Heine's *Geoffroy Rudèl und Melisande von Tripoli* and Arnold's *Tristram and Iseult* and *The Church of Brou*" (*MLN*, 1950), and Roger L. Brooks's "Matthew Arnold's Revisions of *Tristram and Iseult*: Some Instances of Clough's Influence" (*VP*, 1964). Paull Baum (*Ten Studies*) examines the sources closely, and Jon R. Russ (*VP*, 1971) adds another possibility. One of the few earlier critics to make poetic sense of the Merlin and Vivian story is T. Sturge Moore ("The Story of Tristram and Isolt in Modern Poetry," *Criterion*, 1922).

Four recent and probing essays, surprisingly similar in their conclusions, study Arnold's poetic strategies closely in order to define the poem's elusive point of view. J. L. Kendall ("The Unity of Arnold's *Tristram and Iseult*," *VP*, 1963) finds that the poem does not adopt the attitude of Iseult of Brittany; each of the two kinds of love in the poem is presented as an alternative to "death in life." The poem's general theme of man's predicament "as a self-conscious creature ruled by forces he does not understand" is also the truth symbolized in the tale of Merlin. Hence Arnold's sudden shifts in viewpoint are appropriate to "the problem of disequilibrium between inspiration and sanity." M. G. Sundell ("The Intellectual Background and Structure of Arnold's *Tristram and Iseult*," *VP*, 1963) has less confidence in the moralistic narrator's judgment, but even he suggests "the superiority of imaginative to physical truth" and even to the "actual reality" of Tristram's vision. Instead of settling the questions raised in the poem, "We sense that for a man like Tristram love, vision, and creation enforce absolute isolation; yet we cannot be sure even of this in a work in which all is questioned." In the end, "the nature of reality becomes unclear" in Arnold's "multiple vision."

Robert A. Greenberg ("Matthew Arnold's Refuge of Art: 'Tristram and Iseult,'" VN, 1964) reads the poem as an allegory in which "Arnold enacts the drama of Europe's dying hour." Using "a narrative voice not his own" to express Tristram's difficulties, "which are also the dilemmas of Arnold and of modern man," Arnold "groups" and "disposes" his material in a combination of narrative and dramatic modes. The wayward element in the article lies in Greenberg's use of "Memorial Verses" for a key to the poem's interpretation. He correctly sees the poem as rejecting both Byron and Wordsworth as, in different degrees, unsatisfactory. But to say that through the image of Goethe (*"Art still has truth, take refuge there!"*) "Arnold projects his own stance and method" is to overlook Arnold's implicit criticism of Goethe as too detached and analytical to serve as a model. Masao Miyoshi ("Narrative Sequence and the Moral System: Three Tristram Poems," VN, 1969) is at one with these other recent readers in finding that with "its medley of narrative modes, its broken sequence and its many thicknesses of obscurity," the poem "expresses Arnold's own dilemma and his poetic means of avoiding it." The poem "recommends a program of disinterestedness to the reader" and "teaches avoidance of ultimate questions and practice of a serene art."

The "Marguerite question" hovers over Arnold's 1852 volume, occupying the borderland between biography and criticism. Earlier views, the best being Baum's (*Ten Studies*), are summarized by Frederic E. Faverty in *Victorian Poetry* (1968). A. Dwight Culler (*Imaginative Reason*, 1966) assigns a severely pruned list of poems to Marguerite and associates *Faded Leaves* with Mrs. Arnold G. Robert Stange, in *Matthew Arnold: The Poet as Humanist* (1967), rather startlingly, finds "the historical Marguerite" nearly irrelevant. He carefully charts the history of the texts and their sequence, finding in the ultimate *Switzerland* grouping a "lyric poem cycle" after the manner of Heine. The major effect of the rearrangements, Stange finds, "is to make the hero a more serious figure, and Marguerite a lighter one."

Kathleen Tillotson's "'Yes: In the Sea of Life'" (*RES*, 1952; rpt. in *Mid-Victorian Studies*, 1965) is a critically sensitive examination of parallels and possible sources of Arnold's universal theme, as distant as Horace, as close to home as Thackeray and Carlyle. John Bourke ("The Notion of Isol tion in Matthew Arnold," *N&Q*, 1953) tries to complicate the theme by showing that isolation also attracted Arnold "as a source of strength; a state to be cultivated, not deplored." Wendell Stacy Johnson ("Arnold's Lonely Islands," *N&Q*, 1954) sees Clough as the most immediate stimulus of the poem. Two possible sources for lines in Arnold's "Memorial Verses" have been suggested: one in Hazlitt, by Paul Turner (*N&Q*, 1947); the other in Gray, by Peter Ure (*N&Q*, 1968). Arnold's "A Summer Night," not generally a favorite with recent readers, is declared by G. Robert Stange ("The Victorian City and the Frightened Poets," *VS*, Supp., 1968) to be "the only English poem of the time which invests the city with the symbolic depth and richness of Baudelaire's Paris." "The Buried Life," despite its occasional plangencies, has not fared well at the hands of recent critics. Baum (*Ten Studies*) finds it ill-made: "the confusion of the poem is the confusion in Arnold's mind." Alan Roper's judgment (in *Arnold's Poetic Landscapes*) that "the poem provides no conceptual equivalent" for its landscape features and that the poem's naturalistic solution is not congruent with the problem of "the metaphysical definition of life" deserves close attention.

Later Poems

To suggest that Arnold's *Poems* of 1853 begin his "later" phase is merely to acknowledge the decisive shift in his poetics represented by the famous Preface. That document is treated below as part of Arnold's criticism.

The major showpiece of Arnold's new view of the poetic office, "Sohrab and Rustum," has received relatively little criticism, most of it hostile. In a Jungian analysis, Maud Bodkin (*Archetypal Patterns in Poetry*, 1934) approves the ending of the poem as expressive of "a death-craving akin to that of an infant or neurotic for the mother, but in synthesis with the sentiment of a man's endurance." Kenneth Burke (*A Rhetoric of Motives*, 1950) finds the "self-abnegatory attitude" of Empedocles part of "the same motivational cluster" as his attitude toward his father, expressed more accurately in the later poem "in the imagery of a son 'unconsciously' killed by his father, and *in the name of* his father." J. B. Broadbent ("Milton and Arnold," *EIC*, 1956) indicts "Sohrab and Rustum" for a wide variety of literary sins: "inert language" and "inert ideas," unfunctional similes, and an ending that not only does not derive from the poem's action but is sentimental and even callous. John Holloway ("Milton and Arnold," *EIC*, 1957) does not so much defend the poem as shift the grounds of the condemnation: lacking "a great action," the poem offers "no more than a timid hint as to how this special event illuminates life's general fabric," and Arnold's "treatment of its social and as it were dynastic import . . . is feeble." A. Dwight Culler defends the poem (in *Imaginative Reason*, 1966) as "a unified work of art," but concedes damagingly: "Limpidity, placidity, complacency pervade it from the very beginning." Roger L. Brooks (*PQ*, 1963; *ELN*, 1967) finds a source for some of Arnold's details in Hugh Murray's edition of *The Travels of Marco Polo*. Iran Jewett (*OS*, 1967) reveals the complicated process of Arnold's borrowings from an acknowledged source, Malcolm's *History of Persia*. Warren S. Walker, in "Burnes's Influences on *Sohrab and Rustum*: A Closer Look" (*VP*, 1970), gives further parallels from another known source.

"The Scholar-Gipsy" continues to present problems of interpretation as complex as those in "Empedocles," and the valuations attached to the later poem are even more varied. Stuart P. Sherman (*Matthew Arnold: How to Know Him*, 1917), from his own special moral height, took offense at Arnold's uncustomary appearance, in the two Oxford elegies, "of dallying by the wayside, of digressing, of indulging in a moral holiday." "The Scholar-Gipsy," especially, betrays Arnold's "poetical sympathy with an impulse which in his own conduct he severely checked —the impulse to drift and wander irresponsibly." E. K. Brown, in "The Scholar Gypsy [sic]: An Interpretation" (*RAA*, 1935), counters that the descriptive stanzas display exactly the "calm, aloofness and intimacy with nature" by which the Scholar "achieves unity of purpose in life." Brown is one of the few readers who have found the Tyrian Trader's flight "exactly analogous" to the Scholar's flight before the denizens of Oxfordshire. Laurence Perrine (*Expl*, 1957) argues that the Scholar-Gipsy, as the symbol of a life dedicated to the search for truth, "is a quester, not an irresponsible drifter or escapist." Misinterpretations of the poem stem from Arnold's inability to choose between "striving" and mere "wandering," a discrepancy reflected in the use of words suggesting passivity and drifting.

Quite similar to Sherman's complaint in wording and tone is F. R. Leavis' now-famous attack on "The Scholar-Gipsy." As early as 1936, in *Revaluation*, Leavis had said: "What it was that the Scholar Gypsy [sic] had that we have not, Arnold doesn't, except in the most general terms, know." The Scholar "was happy loitering about the countryside . . . for an eternal week-end as Arnold could not have been." George Orwell, in "Inside the Whale" (1940), also viewed the poem as an example of "irresponsibility," in its railing against modern life and its final "magnificent defeatist simile," and as expressive of the prevailing literary attitude of the past century. When Leavis renewed the attack in 1952 in *The Common Pursuit*—claiming that the Scholar in his "drifting" is a symbol of Victorian poetry, "relaxed, relaxing and anodyne"—the critical climate was more favorable to a defense. G. Wilson Knight replied ("The Scholar Gipsy [sic]: An Interpretation," *RES*, 1955) that the Scholar, far from being weak, guards Oxford from its own too exclusive intellectualism. The poem confronts the Apollonian legacy of the West with hints of a wisdom "of eastern affinities" that nourishes man's "central powers." The most complete, and probably the most convincing, reading of the poem is J. P. Curgenven's "The Scholar Gypsy [sic]: A Study of the Growth, Meaning and Integration of a Poem" (*Litera*, Turkey, 1955, 1956). "Fundamentally," he says, "Arnold's myth stands for unity, stability and permanence in a world of flux and change, and for freedom and creativity in a world of lassitude, frustration and stagnation." The article is especially cogent in showing the integration of landscape and "meditation," the fusion of complaint and diagnosis. Accepting Knight's Apollonian-Dionysian antinomy, Curgenven draws on the evidence of "Empedocles" and Arnold's interest in the *Gita* and other sage-literature to illustrate his rejection of unaided intellectuality as a means "to deal with the complexity of life." The poem is Arnold's highest poetic achievement in that it summarizes the Romantic cult of inwardness and negative capability, while avoiding "the disruptive consequences of a tendency to split personality."

A. E. Dyson, in "The Last Enchantments" (*RES*, 1957), argues, against Knight, that "Arnold never commits himself to the gypsy," who in fact "embodies . . . the optimistic but chimerical hopes of an earlier age." Against Leavis' charge of intellectual debility, however, Dyson sees Arnold's contrast of the Scholar's serenity with the perplexities of the modern world not as a renunciation of the nineteenth century but as Arnold's admirable "stoic acceptance of unpalatable realities." To sustain his reading, Dyson is forced to darken Arnold's portrait of the Scholar: because he lacks *both* Hebraic and Hellenic virtues, he does not stand for culture but for doing what one likes. Not only are "Time and the Zeitgeist . . . in alliance against the gipsy," but "The reality of the scholar gipsy is *death*" and he is "a potential enemy." The doubt Dyson injects into the modern discussion of Arnold's attitude toward the Scholar-Gipsy was anticipated long ago by T. Sturge Moore (*Criterion*, Oct. 1922), who found in the last two stanzas a "sudden revulsion of feeling" against the rest of the poem. The "young light-hearted masters of the wave" resemble the "jaded moderns" only in being fled from "by those whose conception of life was less adequate." The young "masters" had "the brilliant future of Greece before them," just as in Arnold's view there was a more brilliant future before modern thought than before the Scholar-Gipsy.

V. S. Seturaman, in "*The Scholar Gypsy* [sic] and Oriental Wisdom" (*RES*, 1958), attempts to refute Dyson by noting that images of death are applied only to the Victorian age. He returns to the position of Knight and Curgenven, finding that Arnold endorses a state of consciousness, such as that taught in the *Gita*, "which transcends all dualisms." The conclusion that the poem presents "an integrated vision" rather than "a stalemate" logically follows, but Seturaman leaves out of account the fact that, except as an object of desire, the speaker does not participate in the ideal—not even "in hope." Paul Edwards ("Hebraism, Hellenism, and 'The Scholar-Gipsy,'" *DUJ*, 1962) attempts further refinements in explaining Arnold's "Hellenism," a crucial matter in several recent readings. It is precisely the fault of the *Gita*'s influence that when Arnold needed "a symbol of intellectual vigour," he instead gives "a symbol of physical lethargy and intellectual passiveness." Reading back Arnold's intellectual ideal of the 1860's into a poem of 1853 (as others do), Edwards claims that Arnold's Hellenism "is in fact close to the doctrine of the *Bhagavad-Gita* in setting knowing above doing." But Arnold could not finally reject action and its fruits, and the more adequate figure of the Tyrian Trader may reject the Greeks not out of Arnold's oriental wisdom so much as his "Hebraic" seriousness and his yearning for "activity." Therefore the poem fails to reconcile the two sides of Arnold: the Hellenist and lover of Hindu literature and religion on the one hand and the Hebraic moralist on the other. Arnold cannot decide between the two ideals.

In a subtle and probing essay centering on "The Scholar-Gipsy," "Poetry in an Age of Prose: Arnold and Gray" (*In Defense of Reading*, ed. R. A. Brower and R. Poirier, 1962), Neil H. Hertz makes good use of Arnold's portrait of Gray and of parallels in Keats's odes to discuss Arnold's persistent attempt, and failure, to find images for "the inner life as an activity with clear consequences in the outer world." After so many careful studies, George Roppen's essay in *Strangers and Pilgrims: An Essay on the Metaphor of Journey* (1964) will seem comparatively unsatisfactory. Roppen refuses to judge: though the Scholar's wanderings "appear to be just as much a flight as a quest," and he "keeps his freedom and aloofness, instead of immersing himself in the destructive element, the ordinary life," still, his is "not the life of a weak man, but of a dedicated man who lives by his choice." Philip Drew's "Matthew Arnold and the Passage of Time: A Study of *The Scholar-Gipsy* and *Thyrsis*" (*The Major Victorian Poets: Reconsiderations*, ed. Isobel Armstrong, 1969) suffers from rhetorical inflation, as when Drew claims Arnold's two elegies provide "the most serious scrutiny of the meaning of Time since the Mutability cantos." Specific contours fade as the two poems are lumped together: the melancholy in the poems represents "not a symptom of the failure of poetic control or the lack of moral fibre" but "the feelings of a man at the passage of time, the fear that life is no more than an inevitable process of decay and disintegration." In a stimulating but disconcertingly elliptical article, "The Argument of 'The Scholar-Gipsy'" (*VP*, 1969), Roger B. Wilkenfeld finds the flaw in Arnold's contrast between the scholar's life and that of "mortal men" to lie in his argument "that the difference between constancy and flux, freshness and fatigue, firmness and doubt is the difference between the immortal and the mortal life." But Arnold's virtue, Wilkenfeld claims, lies in his *not* leaping easily "from the shattering of his happy vision to the assertion of the sought condition"; instead, he laid bare "the involuted exercise that moved him from despair to joy."

Deserving of special attention for its lucidity and penetration is David L. Eggenschwiler's "Arnold's Passive Questers" (*VP*, 1967), which treats both of the Oxford elegies. Analyzing the structure of "The Scholar-Gipsy" with a keenness matched only by Curgenven, Eggenschwiler sees the poem as "a dramatic lyric in which the speaker explores the nature of an emotional ideal and comes to a fuller understanding of himself." Unsuccessfully attempting to define "a paradoxical state of consciousness" in which "the quest is its own fulfillment, and activity is psychological rest," Arnold concludes, with J. S. Mill, that "happiness cannot be achieved if it is pursued directly." In one of the most successful attempts to show the place of "Thyrsis" in Arnold's development, Eggenschwiler attributes the relative weakness of the later poem to the fact that "Corydon chooses the way of the gipsy and reaffirms faith in himself, but he does not explain how modern man can successfully perform the quest." The "weakly justified" hope of the final stanzas shows a Corydon "trying to create fact out of desire through a self-delusion similar to that which the speaker of 'The Scholar-Gipsy' practiced, discovered, and rejected." In short, "the price of affirmation is illusion"; only in the prose works was Arnold to show his readers "the way to animated nobility." As will be evident in the section on Arnold's religion, many readers have questioned whether, even later, Arnold succeeded in locating the "joy whose grounds are true."

Some recurring problems in "The Scholar-Gipsy" have received special attention. The identity of the "one" on "the intellectual throne" remains in some doubt. The claims of Tennyson, the leading contender, are summed up by W. S. Knickerbocker (*Expl*, 1950); those of Goethe, by C. K. Hyder (*Expl*, 1950); and those of Leopardi, by J. C. Maxwell (*RES*, 1955). Sources for the imagery of the final two stanzas have been suggested: in Thucydides, by R. H. Super (*N&Q*, 1956); in Ezekiel, by E. E. Stevens (*VN*, 1963); and in Herodotus, by Kenneth Allott (*TLS*, 18 Oct. 1963). David R. Carroll's view of the Tyrian Trader (*MLR*, 1969) as Arnold's successful embodiment of "a form of activity which aptly combines action upon society with withdrawal from it" will seem unexceptionable if too familiar in the current lively discussion of the poem. But his finding a source in Grote's treatment of the Phoenicians and Greeks, in the *History of Greece* (1846), is less convincing, requiring as it does a reversal of Grote's judgments. Finally, Paull Baum (*Ten Studies*) is unique in the fullness of his discussion of metrics and rhyme in both Oxford poems.

Once among Arnold's most admired poems, and often treated simply as a companion to "The Scholar-Gipsy," "Thyrsis" has suffered in the growing sense that the poetry of the sixties is seriously defective. Culler (in *Imaginative Reason*) treats the poem helpfully but, hampered by the requirements of his thesis regarding Arnold's development, draws back from the problem of the poem's quality. As long ago as 1923, Robert Bridges ("Poetic Diction in English"; rpt. in *English Critical Essays, Twentieth Century*, ed. P. M. Jones, 1933) criticized the poem precisely for its "'rational' diction" and its "exclusion of conventions." The effect is one of insincerity; compared with "Lycidas," Arnold's elegy "lacks in passion, as if it were a handling of emotions rather than a compelling utterance of them." The most satisfying and complete reading of the poem is by J. P. Curgenven (*Litera*, Turkey, 1957, 1958, 1959). "The Scholar-Gipsy," like all of Arnold's best poetry, is "about the principle of duality at the heart of life" and it explores "stress, division and integration." "Thyrsis," looser in structure, exploits "ideality, aspiration, verticality and transcendence." Curgenven finds the concluding stanzas unconvincing, since the goal and its path are not clear: it is "more of a hope, or a memory from inspired times, than a presently beheld object; and, if seen, glimpsed at intervals rather than held steadily." This study should be read in conjunction with Eggenschwiler's (*VP*, 1967), noted above.

The highly generalized thesis of Richard Giannone's "The Quest Motif in

'Thyrsis' " (*VP*, 1965) is that "Corydon's acceptance of Thyrsis' death draws heavily from his recognition of a universal need to search out the meaning of human life even if the answers are not forthcoming." The reader's confidence in the author's precision is not strengthened when he identifies the quest for "truth" in the poem with "the universal commitment to intellectual ideals." Jerome L. Mazzaro's suggestion ("Corydon in Matthew Arnold's 'Thyrsis,' " *VP*, 1963) that the name Corydon carries homosexual overtones is not convincing. Roger L. Brooks (*RES*, 1963) has worked out the long history of the poem's composition. DeLaura (*VP*, 1969) presents a letter of Arnold's dated 4 December 1865 indicating that Arnold read Clough's *Letters and Remains* during the final stages of the poem. The book may have influenced Arnold's awkward attempt to make a hopeful statement in the finale.

The problems of dating "Dover Beach"—written in two parts and not published until 1867—continue to vex the critics. Earlier sources—Thucydides, the historical Empedocles, Sénancour, Carlyle in "Characteristics," or Newman in an 1839 sermon, "Faith and Reason"—present few critical difficulties. John Robert Moore (*SR*, 1922) offered interesting but inconclusive parallels with William Lisle Bowles and Coleridge. More exactly contemporary sources are another matter. The possible role of Clough, especially, has interpretive consequences. W. Stacy Johnson ("Parallel Imagery in Arnold and Clough," *ES*, 1958) is the most convincing exponent of the view that Arnold and Clough are in their poetry carrying on "a kind of correspondence or debate." Paul Turner (*ES*, 1947) had seen the immediate source of Arnold's night battle in Clough's *Bothie* (1849) and found Arnold "replying" to Clough's unwarranted optimism. Buckner Trawick (*PMLA*, 1950) found less convincing further parallels in the *Bothie*, but avoided adding a gloss. D. A. Robertson (*PMLA*, 1951) sought to further the process by arguing that Clough's "Say Not the Struggle Nought Availeth" was meant as a response to, and corrective of, "Dover Beach." But this was to claim that the first 28 lines of "Dover Beach" were written before mid-October 1849. In reply, Paull F. Baum (*MLN*, 1952; and *Ten Studies*) argued for 1851, especially on the basis of similarities to other poems of that period. The parallel with a pensée of Sainte-Beuve first published in 1851 has been noted many times (see Baum, *Ten Studies*, p. 91, n.; misleadingly noted there only as written in 1839).

Even later dates have been suggested. Burton R. Pollin (*VN*, 1969) finds parallels in Browning's "Andrea del Sarto," first published in 1855. J. C. Maxwell (*N&Q*, 1967) offers an interesting parallel in Walter Bagehot's 1862 essay on Clough. Super (*N&Q*, 1967) argues that Arnold's failure to publish the poem in the 1855 collection indicates a later completion of lines 1–28. Michael Thorpe (*N&Q*, 1967) returns to the case for the early fifties on the basis of resemblances to "Human Life," first published in 1852. The debate has been brought full circle, for the moment, by K. Allott (*N&Q*, 1967), who replies to Super that Arnold did sometimes delay publication of completed poems and that he may have withheld "Dover Beach" as both too personal and too "black" not to be distressing to his wife and others. He convincingly reassembles the evidence for late June 1851 as "a sober and rational conjecture." He might also have stressed that claims for a "late" dating have to meet the objection that no poem of Arnold's after 1855 adopts a tone approaching that of "Dover Beach." It should be noted that Allott (*N&Q*, 1969) has found significant errors of transcription committed by Tinker and Lowry.

"Dover Beach" continues to be read by some as a poem virtually devoid of hope. For example, William I. Thompson, in "Collapsed Universe and Structured Poem: An Essay in Whiteheadian Criticism" (*CE*, 1966), finds that the division between a meaningless universe and human values, between "man's knowledge and his emotion," renders human values "insignificant." But the two most impressive readings of the poem, by Murray Krieger and William Cadbury, succeed in complicating our sense of the poem's mood. Krieger, in "'Dover Beach' and the Tragic Sense of Eternal Recurrence" (*UKCR*, 1956; rpt. in *The Play and Place of Criticism*, 1967), claims that the poet not only rises above the "death-in-life," the nonpurposiveness of the modern view of nature through his personal love, but asserts his humanity "primarily in his insistence on realizing fully the sense of its loss, in his refusal to be ignorant of it." This view of a possible existential sense of "freedom" even in a naturalistic universe is furthered in Cadbury's difficult but rewarding essay, "Coming to Terms with 'Dover Beach'" (*Criticism*, 1966). Cadbury goes so far as to claim paradoxically that the poem is "cheerful" and that it "makes us accept bondage among the ignorant armies as a kind of release." The narrator, by his "gratuitous acts" of understanding and love and in despite of an indifferent nature, "creates for us a perfect image of human worth."

Sidney Feshbach's "Empedocles at Dover Beach" (*VP*, 1966) makes strong claims for the influence of Empedocles' *On Nature and Purification* on "Dover Beach." "Empedocles' philosophy of nature and man gave to Arnold a *cosmology* which is at once materialistic and moral (manifesting love and strife), a psychology of the senses which retains and rationalizes disparities in perception, a philosophy which finds a proper place for the coexistence of the 'true' illusion of love and the 'truer' reality of strife, and finally a dynamics of man and nature which is conceived in images of rhythmic cycles." In the absence of fully convincing verbal parallels (though Baum had pointed out the parallel with Fragment 121) the case must be considered conjectural, although it does deepen our apprehension of the poem. Richard Gollin's richly researched "'Dover Beach': The Background of Its Imagery" (*ES*, 1967) presents even more difficult problems of method. Gollin reads "Dover Beach" as a virtual allegory criticizing the illusions of almost all of Arnold's contemporaries concerning "the infallibility of conscience as a guide to religious and social reform." Arnold is suggesting, Gollin claims, that Dr. Arnold, Clough, and Froude are "cruelly self-deceived" in their stress on the need "to submit utterly to their conscience in the service of an historical providence." The poem is, then, about the dangers of retaining even vestiges of such a faith in a world "already dark, random, and void of guidance or purpose." Even apart from the difficulty of accepting this as a description of the poem's actual mood, the reader is left suspended between the apparent and the "real" meaning of the poem.

The strain between explicit and implicit meanings is characteristically greatest in psychoanalytic readings. In a witty parody of modern schools of criticism, Theodore Morrison long ago ("Dover Beach Revisited," *Harper's Mag.*, 1940) presented a Freudian portrait of Arnold as a lover lacking in aggressiveness and "the normal joy of conquest and possession," endangered by passion, and in search of "a protective love, sisterly or motherly." Norman Holland's very similar reading ("Psychological Depths and 'Dover Beach,'" *VS*, Supp., 1965) would have profited from some share of the irony that acknowledges the unverifiability of such an approach. Holland reads the poem as a characteristically Victorian concentration on one thing (moral and historical issues) in order to avoid another, in this case Arnold's revulsion against his parents' sexuality. "Dover Beach" is then an attempt "to re-create in the relationship with the lover a simplified, more childish, but more satisfying version of an adult love for another person or the world as a whole." To Wendell V. Harris' spirited refutation, "Freud, Form, and Fights by Night," Holland answers that readings based on conscious and unconscious impulses are not mutually exclusive (both in *VS*, 1966). Gale H. Carrithers' objection in "Missing Persons on Dover Beach" (*MLQ*, 1965), that the two persons in the poem are insufficiently developed as characters, is of doubtful critical significance. John Racin claims ("'Dover Beach' and the Structure of Meditation," *VP*, 1970) that the poem follows the three-part "Ignatian" structure of seventeenth-century religious poetry. The point would have more weight if Racin were aware of Abrams' suggestion that the "meditative" form was mediated and transformed by the Romantic poets, Arnold's obviously direct models.

"Stanzas from the Grande Chartreuse," published in periodical form in 1855 but not collected until 1867, awaits a definitive explication. Several cruxes remain unsolved: for example, whether Thomas Arnold is among the "rigorous teachers," the relationship between the tearful Romantics and the modern "masters of the mind" and the place of the latter group in Arnold's historical scheme, the allusion in Achilles and "The kings of modern thought," and even whether Arnold's two dead faiths are "the Protestant and Catholic forms of Christian orthodoxy" (Baum, Allott) or Christian orthodoxy and Romantic melancholy. Harvey Kerpneck's claim (*MLQ*, 1963) that the Achilles passage is a reference to Newman merely repeats (though Kerpneck does not mention it) a conjecture that Tinker and Lowry took from Chambers. But Kerpneck's suggestion that the reference is specifically to the Achilli trial of 1851–53 and "a salvo fired, only partly in jest, at the unhappy Newman" lacks all probability. James H. Broderick (*MP*, 1968) presents new evidence, based on Mrs. Arnold's letters and the poet's 1851 diary, concerning the honeymoon trip, and interestingly draws out the critical implications of a possible source in Chateaubriand's *Mémoires d'outre-tombe*. Sister Mary Richard Boo (*Expl*, 1965) offers a historical explanation of the "abbey children" as a "tragic parallel" to Arnold's own dilemma.

Frederick Page (*E&S*, 1942) offered an allegorical reading of "Balder Dead" as a comment on "the fortunes and the future of Christianity"; Page admits that his interpretation involves reading *Literature and Dogma* back into a poem of nearly two decades earlier. Clyde de L. Ryals (*VP*, 1966) similarly stresses "correspondences between the Nordic Götterdämmerung and the decline of Christian faith in the nineteenth century." The addition, at the end of the poem, of a new note of hope to Arnold's earlier emphasis on endurance "marks a turning point in Arnold's development." Culler (*Imaginative Reason*) also sees the conclusion as "the first time in Arnold's poetry that the third phase of his myth has been fully and distinctly stated." Roger L. Brooks (*PBSA*, 1962) discusses a Danish translation of the poem. Mary W. Schneider (*N&Q*, 1967) shows that Arnold used, not the 1847 edition of Mallet's *Northern Antiquities*, but one of the two editions by Bishop Percy (1770, 1809). Mallet and Percy stressed the correspondences with Greek myth; if Arnold saw Balder as a Norse Apollo, the theme is close to that of other Arnold poems, "the fate of poetry in a world of daily strife." Kathleen Tillotson's "'Haworth Churchyard': The Making of Arnold's Elegy" (*Brontë Soc. Trans.*, 1967) ably summarizes Arnold's surprisingly full relations with Charlotte Brontë and suggests Arnold's "essential sympathy" for her kind of "imaginative creation." Studies of *Merope* are discussed above, under Arnold and the Classics.

"Thyrsis" is treated in conjunction with "The Scholar-Gipsy." Of the other late poems only "Rugby Chapel" has been extensively discussed. Sources or analogues for the imagery of the poem have been suggested by Lillian H. Hornstein (" 'Rugby Chapel' and Exodus," *MLR*, 1952), Kathleen Tillotson (" 'Rugby Chapel' and 'Jane Eyre,' " *N&Q*, 1948), and William S. Peterson (" 'Rugby Chapel' and *Tom Brown's School-Days*," *ELN*, 1966). Elsewhere (*VN*, 1964), Peterson discriminates two kinds of landscapes, to describe two kinds of people: (1) mountain and snow for those, like the poet, "who achieve only personal salvation"; and (2) stony desert for those, "like his father, who cannot 'alone / Be saved.' " John O. Waller, in "Dr. Arnold's Sermons and Matthew Arnold's 'Rugby Chapel' " (*SEL*, 1969), argues that Arnold, "consciously or unconsciously," constructed much of the poem "from thematic materials preserved in Thomas Arnold's published sermons." Though Waller like Peterson clear-sightedly observes that Arnold places himself outside the world of his father's values, the parallels remain more interesting than persuasive. Harvey Kerpneck's "The Road to Rugby Chapel" (*UTQ*, 1965) raises delicate problems in the use of both internal and external evidence. As support for his view that "Rugby Chapel" is "a kind of summation and, in part, restatement of Arnold's spiritual progress," and a declaration of spiritual recovery even more advanced than "Thyrsis," Kerpneck argues, on inconclusive evidence, that the poem is an answer, not to Fitzjames Stephen's 1858 review of *Tom Brown's School-Days*, but to Stephen's *Saturday Review* article of 3 December 1864. Kerpneck contends that "Rugby Chapel" could not have been begun by the "prostrate" Arnold of the late 1850's; but his case for Arnold's supposed despondency during those years draws on "Isolation" and "To Marguerite—Continued," both poems of 1849! Kerpneck cannot be said to have established "the terminal position" of "Rugby Chapel" in Arnold's development," or a date of 1866.

Kerpneck's judgment that the poem is a "masterpiece" brings up further, more critical questions. Reversing the judgment of his own earlier book, Wendell Stacy Johnson (" 'Rugby Chapel': Arnold as a Filial Poet," *UR*, 1967) also finds Arnold at "his poetic best" in the poem, in the "symbolic balance of personality and world, of self and society." In this paradoxical joining of "peace and action," Arnold for the first time combines his father's life of activity with his own ideal of tranquillity. Such defenses of the poem, like Culler's, somehow fail to meet the objection raised long ago by Edmund Blunden (*The Great Victorians*, ed. H. J. and H. Massingham, 1932): despite the "Excelsior" theme of the poem's ending, "the very bleakness of [Arnold's] tune, the halting pauses of the metre betray the defeatist mood underlying all." More recently, Jonathan Middlebrook (" 'Resignation,' 'Rugby Chapel,' and Thomas Arnold," *VP*, 1970) finds Arnold trying "to make exclamatory fervor disguise the abandonment of his own, on-going criticism of the unthinking active life." The poetic and hence the spiritual quality of "Rugby Chapel" remains moot.

That there may have been a kind of poetic dialogue between Arnold and Browning is an intriguing possibility. A. W. Crawford suggested (*JEGP*, 1927) that the occasion of Browning's "Cleon" was Arnold's "Empedocles on Etna." Richard D. Altick, in "Lovers' Finiteness: Browning's 'Two in the Campagna' " (*PLL*, 1967), finds parallels in language and tone between Browning's poem and Arnold's "Philomela." Altick also compares the mood of isolation, as did W. C. DeVane in *A Browning Handbook* (2nd ed., 1955), to that of Arnold's Marguerite poems. Conrad A. Balliet (*VP*, 1963) develops DeVane's suggestion that Arnold's "Growing

Old" is an answer to Browning's "Rabbi Ben Ezra." John Huebenthal (*VP*, 1965) argues that Tennyson's "Tears, Idle Tears" is a more likely point of departure for Arnold. The sometimes suggested parallels between Browning's early *Paracelsus* and Arnold's "Empedocles" deserve fuller attention.

George W. Polhemus, in "An Additional Variation in Arnold's 'The Terrace at Berne'" (*N&Q*, 1962), offers a unique variant of line 48, dated 1883. K. Allott suggests a new source for an image, in "Matthew Arnold's 'The Terrace at Berne,' ll. 45–8, and the Ramayana" (*N&Q*, 1968). Eugene L. Williamson provides some of the biographical background for Arnold's neglected last elegy in "Words from Westminster Abbey" (*SEL*, 1971).

VII. ARNOLD'S PROSE

To describe and evaluate Matthew Arnold as an artist and thinker in prose involves questions we have scarcely learned to pose, let alone answer. We lack for the Victorians the fine categories and instruments of discrimination that have been developed through decades of study and argument for the Tudor and Stuart prose masters. The development of a true "poetics" of Victorian nonfictional prose remains a prime desideratum of study in the period.

Since, as John Holloway reminds us (*The Victorian Sage,* 1953), Arnold's effort is continually to exhibit a certain temper of mind which is a function of his own self-presentation, and since this temper is brought into connection variously with politics, religion, and literature, the rhetorical categories of content and form are especially inadequate in coming to terms with Arnold's prose. Particularly elusive is Arnold's tone, often matched as it is to a polemical context difficult to recover. Super reminds us, in "Vivacity and the Philistines" (*SEL*, 1960), that much of Arnold's high spirits—progressively eliminated from what originated almost entirely as journalism—is due precisely to its intense topicality. And as Geoffrey Tillotson puts it, Arnold's tone, "so riling at the time for its victims, is for us, who do not find its subject matter so pressing, great comedy" ("Matthew Arnold in Our Time," 1954; rpt. in *Mid-Victorian Studies*, 1965). Even Arnold's earlier readers fell back for explanation on the paradoxes and unresolved tensions now seemingly mandatory in Arnold studies. Leslie Stephen displayed a scar or two of his own when he acknowledged, "I often wished . . . that I too had a little sweetness and light that I might be able to say such nasty things of my enemies" (*Studies of a Biographer*, 1898). Even better is Chesterton's comment that "Arnold kept a smile of heart-broken forbearance, as of a teacher in an idiot school, that was enormously insulting" (*The Victorian Age in Literature*, 1913).

The study of Arnold's "new style," founded as Chesterton saw on "the patient unravelling of the tangled Victorian ideas," was greatly advanced by the lonely pioneering work of Lewis E. Gates (*Three Studies in Literature*, 1899). Gates found in Arnold "some unhappy warring of elements, some ill-adjustment of overtones," which he attributes to Arnold's difficulties in gaining the attention of "a recalcitrant public" as well as to "an ingrained contempt for the 'beast' he was charming." In addition to shrewd observations on Arnold's habits of style, Gates identifies four "distinct manners" in Arnold's style: (1) the severe and exact style of "Democracy" (1861) or of the education reports; (2) Arnold's "most distinctive manner," the affable and colloquial tone of his less controversial essays; (3) "the nonchalant air" of his "cleverly malicious satire," which aroused the greatest prejudice against Arnold; and (4) a more intensely colored, almost lyrical, tone such as is found in the George Sand and Emerson essays.

In the absence of precise studies like those we have for the seventeenth century, attempts to locate Arnold in the larger pattern of nineteenth-century prose have been for the most part unilluminating. In his *Matthew Arnold* (1899), George Saintsbury found Arnold's historical position a fortunate one, since while the best Georgian prose was still the academic standard, Arnold could draw on the freedom and color of the Romantic essayists. The best treatment yet, though largely hints and guesses, is provided in Saintsbury's *History of English Prose Rhythm* (1912; rpt. 1965). Arnold's characteristic method, like "the oratorical style of the eighteenth century," is to arrange "runs of comparatively unaccented syllable-batches, relieved from insignificance by the presence of strongly stressed conclusions in clause and sentence." Saintsbury finds in the prose "an almost stunning clash and jangle." Josephine Miles, in *The Continuity of Poetic Language* (1951; rpt. 1965), rather gnomically finds many eighteenth-century generalized terms in Arnold's prose, but "stirred up by increase and by light to a feeling of activity rather than stability, a force not checked, an intensity more possibly personal than general."

A more promising approach is that of E. K. Brown, in *Studies in the Text of Matthew Arnold's Prose Works* (1935; rpt. 1969). Claiming to study "the textual changes in all of the prose works," Brown is a skillful discerner of tonal changes. He regrets that, in seeking the regularity, precision, uniformity, and balance Arnold admired in prose, he suppressed many lively digressions and topicalities. John Campbell Major ("Matthew Arnold and Attic Prose Style," *PMLA*, 1944), while synthesizing Arnold's views on prose style, fails to suggest what effect these criteria had on Arnold's own style.

Three important modern attempts have been made to isolate those qualities that make up the elusive Arnoldian tone and style. The best is John Holloway's *The Victorian Sage: Studies in Argument* (1953; rpt. 1962). Holloway brilliantly suggests how the "gentle critical reasonableness of mind" which is the substance of Arnold's effort is supported by particular devices: the ad hominem argument, the "value frame" that shapes the reader's response, paradox, authorities, "invented revealing incidents," irony, and self-depreciation—all of which build up a favorable impression of himself and an unfavorable one of his opponents. The other two treatments appear in *The Art of Victorian Prose*, edited by George Levine and William A. Madden (1968). Using the tools of transformational grammar, Richard Ohmann reads Arnold's frequent use of a structure that links noun phrases by "be" as an attempt to bring concepts "into relations of equivalence" and to resolve difficulties "not *through* naming but *in* naming." He even defends Arnold's often-decried repetitions as the mode of "a writer who sees life as exceedingly complex, yet at the same time rationally structured in forms decipherable through the employment of culture and right reason." But Ohmann's conclusion, that in the absence of shared stylistic tendencies among the Victorian prose writers we cannot confidently describe a period style, is made suspect by his evident lack of close familiarity with the Victorian sages and by the simplicity of his criteria. More traditional if leisurely is the approach of Geoffrey Tillotson ("Matthew Arnold's Prose: Theory and Practice"), who astutely indicates the ways in which Arnold designed his personality to be "striking" and conversational. But he ends, sharply, by declaring that Arnold's lack of tact and his posturing were "a big strategical mistake" that deprived him of the effect on English culture that, say, Morris exercised. It is worth noting that Tillotson and Holloway—like almost every commentator from R. H. Hutton, Saintsbury, and Gates to the present—find it necessary to define Arnold's practice in the light of the prose art of Newman, from whom Arnold borrowed many of his polemical strategies.

Tillotson's judgment of Arnold's lack of success in his own time involves questions of fact and rhetorical strategy that we still lack the resources to answer. The charge of failure is at the center of a long debate on Arnold's doctrine of "disinterestedness." The issue was first brought into clear focus by Gates (*Three Studies in Literature*), who attributed Arnold's obtrusive tendency toward "moral suasion" to the influence of his father. Arnold not only lacks detachment, but fails to "regard works of art for the time being as self-justified integrations of beauty and truth." Gates's moderation was thrown aside by Geoffrey Tillotson, in "Matthew Arnold: The Critic and the Advocate" (1942; collected in *Criticism and the Nineteenth Century*, 1951; rpt. 1967), who anticipated the conclusion of his own more careful 1968 essay by attacking Arnold the "salesman," who, so deep were the forces working in him, was offensive to his audience without even knowing it. As soon as he left literary criticism, Arnold "ceased to be disinterested though he did not cease to claim to be disinterested." Disinterestedness is ruled out by Arnold's egotism, which "accounts for the high-pitched conversational tone, the ripple of inspired temporization, the French grace, the lizard slickness." Drawing on hints from Gates and Tillotson, E. K. Brown, in *Matthew Arnold: A Study in Conflict* (1948), finds "a failure in the deepest places of [Arnold's] art and character." The ominous theme of Arnold's "divided mind and spirit" is never developed, but Brown reads Arnold's prose career as strewn with "incoherences" and "artistic disasters," as Arnold first transforms disinterestedness as "a critical faculty or disposition" into a mere "critical strategy," and eventually, as he worked in the practical sphere, abandons the disinterested ideal altogether. Brown's book remains valuable for its close reading of Arnold's local complications of tone and strategy, but his treatment makes heavy weather of a topic which—if complex—is not, in the view of many, simply "contradictory." Brown's attempt to force Arnold onto a very "aesthetic" high ground, above mere "positions," is all the more strange in that he had earlier, in his 1935 study of Arnold's text, deplored Arnold's suppression of those "fervent passages" in which he "discards the toga and writes like a gladiator rather than an elderly senator of criticism."

There have been a few defenders. As early as 1902, W. C. Brownell had approvingly noted, in *Victorian Prose Masters*, that Arnold's "motive is didactic and his method disinterested." Against Saintsbury (and by anticipation, Brown), Everett Lee Hunt, in "Matthew Arnold: The Critic as Rhetorician" (*QJS*, 1934; rpt. in *Historical Studies of Rhetoric and Rhetoricians*, ed. R. F. Howes, 1961), found Arnold's literary essays quite as "hortatory" and "rhetorical" as his political, theological, and social criticism. Displaying a firm grasp of the ancient rhetorical theory that persuasion is "an aspect of character and an instrument of truth," Hunt sees that Arnold's tone of "tolerance, detachment and wisdom" involves no "scientific or even aesthetic detachment"; Arnold's criticism was an act of "earnest, disinterested persuasion." Correcting Brown, K. Allott (*Matthew Arnold*, 1955) argues that "Arnold ordinarily succeeds in finding a third way between a limiting involvement in practical issues and a lack of interest in the social implications of his ideas." And there the question rests for the moment, unless we can say the issue has gone underground, in Norman Holland's comment ("Prose and Minds: A Psychoanalytic Approach to Non-Fiction," in *The Art of Victorian Prose*, 1968) that "Arnold's quite reasonable intellectual position, that criticism should eschew practicality, has unconscious roots in a wish to avoid sexual touchings." Perhaps this is the kind of solution at which Gates and Brown only hinted in their remarks on "failure" and "division" in Arnold.

One final attempt to seize the totality of Arnold's prose deserves mention. Walter J. Hipple, Jr., in "Matthew Arnold, Dialectician" (*UTQ*, 1962), finds Arnold's philosophical method to be "Platonist" and dialectical, though it lacks the highest level of Plato's divided line in the *Republic* and is "a dialectic of becoming rather than of being." Arnold, like many modern philosophers, "finds his first principles in psychology," and the unity of a whole book, like *Mixed Essays*, lies in Arnold's analysis of man's fundamental aspirations and powers. Though in this treatment Arnold is pulled on the one hand toward a Paterian relativism and on the other to a more than Coleridgean organicity (Arnold's "is an organic system, and all Arnold's thought is linked with religion"), the essay is stimulating and original in approach. Edward Sharples' attempt to define "The Holistic Principle in Arnold" (*English*, 1970) is similar in intent but much less successful.

Arnold's Literary Theory
General Treatments

Arnold's achievement in literary theory and criticism remains extremely difficult to describe with objectivity. The value and even the meaning of almost every term or doctrine associated with his name—literature as a criticism of life or as the application of ideas to life, the "grand style," the relationship of style and form or of form and content, the touchstone method, or the relationship of literature to religion—remain matters of controversy.

Attempts to describe Arnold's criticism as a whole are numerous but generally unhelpful for all but the novice. It should be recalled that some have denied Arnold the title of literary critic altogether. Lytton Strachey in 1914 dismissed Arnold's achievement as feeble and insignificant (*Characters and Commentaries*, 1933); and T. S. Eliot, in the Introduction to *The Sacred Wood* (1920), suggested that "In a society in which the arts were seriously studied, Arnold might have become a critic." Still worth reading is Saintsbury's description, respectful if somewhat desultory, in *A History of Criticism and Literary Taste in Europe* (1904; also in *A History of English Criticism*, 1911). H. W. Garrod's chapter on Arnold's criticism in *Poetry and the Criticism of Life* (1931) is disappointingly thin. Though Arnold thinks "too much of the uses of literature, and too little of its pleasures," and though the criticism is "tainted with a certain snobbery and even dandyism," his style remains a source of pleasure. Altogether superior is Edwin Berry Burgum's perceptive article, "The Humanism of Matthew Arnold" (*Symposium*, 1931); for example, he seems to be the first to make clear that Arnold prefers to speak of "style" over "form," because style is closer to rhetoric, which influences conduct, while form "cancels the rhetorical value of style." Quite unsystematic but frequently penetrating are the remarks on Arnold made by H. V. Routh, in *Money, Morals and Manners as Revealed in Modern Literature* (1935), and especially in *Towards the Twentieth Century: Essays in the Spiritual History of the Nineteenth* (1937).

David Perkins' attempt (*ELH*, 1951) to synthesize Arnold's views of literature results in highly abstract conclusions about Arnold's "essentially classical" viewpoint. Even less substantial are an essay by Wayne Shumaker, "Matthew Arnold's Humanism: Literature as a Criticism of Life" (*SEL*, 1962), and the pages devoted to Arnold in Raymond Chapman's *The Victorian Debate: English Literature and Society, 1832–1910* (1968). John Gross, in *The Rise and Fall of the Man of Letters* (1969), offers a comprehensive and fair-minded summary of Arnold's achievement, but fails to suggest how Arnold is part of the tradition about which the book is implicitly written. Though condescending and polemical in tone, the treatment of Arnold by W. K. Wimsatt in his and Cleanth Brooks's *Literary Criticism: A Short History* (1957) is stimulating. He reads Arnold's view of literature as a criticism of life as an "embarrassing" didactic theory, but against those (like Saintsbury and Garrod) who complain of Arnold's ignorance of history Wimsatt counters, "Arnold enjoyed a tall and successful aloofness from the historizing spirit of his times." All of this is fairer and better balanced than Brooks's attack on Arnold's "high seriousness" in Chapter ii of his *Modern Poetry and the Tradition* (1939). René Wellek, in *A History of Modern Criticism,* IV (1965), is comprehensive and painstaking in dealing with Arnold. He sees clearly that Arnold was indeed a historical critic, that disinterestedness never means "Olympian aloofness," that Arnold did not confuse poetry and philosophy, that "high seriousness" is not the equivalent of "churchyard solemnity," and that Arnold was "well aware of the central importance of totality and unity in art." Wellek properly faults Arnold for his didacticism, his lack of clarity on the problem of form and content, and his "feeble grasp of the difference between art and reality." But suggestions that Arnold sees subjects as poetic or unpoetic apart from the poet's treatment, that style for Arnold is somehow independent of or prior to actual use, or that form is "a hard vessel into which the poet pours his content" are more questionable.

Though perhaps not quite so insecure in reputation as his poetry, Arnold's criticism is still occasionally dismissed out of hand. Geoffrey Carnall presents a provocative if insufficiently documented case ("Matthew Arnold's 'Great Critical Effort,'" *EIC*, 1958) that Arnold has been "a bad influence" because "one of the main things he teaches is how to keep complacency intact." If that is not enough, Arnold is "extremely unscrupulous in argument." George Watson, in *The Literary Critics: A Study of English Descriptive Criticism* (1962), while sensibly clarifying some of Arnold's terms, utterly rejects Arnold's "claims to greatness as a critic." In "Arnold and the Victorian Mind" (*REL*, 1967), Watson echoes Carnall, and with as little evidence, in finding Arnold's polemics "remote from any concern with accuracy or fair-mindedness. The love of truth was something he appears simply to have outlived."

The Development of Arnold's Critical Theory

A major defect of most accounts of Arnold's literary theory is a lack of any sense of development in Arnold's thinking. The endless argument over Arnold's terms, for example, is often beside the point because it fails to see Arnold in context, responding to specific challenges or solving special problems in his own literary career. The materials for such a study of Arnold "in context" have gradually accumulated in recent years, though no one has yet put them together and drawn larger conclusions.

Our understanding of the complex shifts in Arnold's early poetics has been greatly enhanced by a number of studies of the Preface to the *Poems* of 1853. Garrod, in "Matthew Arnold's 1853 Preface" (*RES*, 1941), finds the inciting cause of the Preface in Monckton Milnes's 1848 *Life, Letters, and Literary Remains of John Keats*, and sees that in the Preface Arnold "repudiates, in effect, the influences which had gone to make his best poem." J. D. Jump ("Matthew Arnold and *The Spectator*," *RES*, 1949) identified the source of some of the views Arnold was refuting. Alba H. Warren, in *English Poetic Theory, 1825–1865* (1950; rpt. 1966), admirably details the shift in Arnold's view of poetry from "a more or less pure aesthetic object of delight" to "a *magister vitae*, . . . at once regulative, humantistic, and aesthetic." Warren is clearer than most critics in seeing that "this quasi-religious function of poetry" called for in 1852–53 is central to Arnold's poetics, but his view that this is a confusion of religion and art and a basis for the later nineteenth century's "religion of art" needs numerous qualifications. The best of such studies by far is Sidney M. B. Coulling's article, "Matthew Arnold's 1853 Preface: Its Origin and Aftermath" (*VS*, 1964). Coulling not only gives a satisfying account of the complex body of contemporary critical assumptions to which Arnold was responding, but for the first time explains fully in what way the 1857 Inaugural Lecture represents a "significant modification" of the 1853 Preface in the direction of sympathetic involvement with the age. Coulling's alignment of Arnold's "intellectual deliverance" with his later view of criticism as requiring disinterested objectivity and his discrimination of two meanings of "modern" in the 1857 lecture (as doubt and discouragement, and as intellectual vitality) are important contributions to our understanding of Arnold's characteristic terms. To these articles should be added Michael Timko's provocative argument, in "Corydon Had a Rival" (*VN*, 1961), that Clough was the major influence in Arnold's shift from the "Aestheticism" and formalism of the forties to the moralism of 1852–53. Timko claims that the influence, though conjectural, is plausible. The interrelations of Arnold and Clough in this period, and especially their mutual debts in poetry and poetics, remain baffling and unresolved questions.

The difficulty we still experience in defining the shifts in Arnold's poetics up to 1853 derives in part from the simplicity of our categories. The alleged aestheticism and formalism of the forties was from the first carefully "moralized," and was compatible with a rejection of Keats and Tennyson. The supposed moralism of 1852–53 must somehow be squared with the endorsement of "perfection of form" in the letter to Mrs. Forster of September 1858. K. Allott (*E&S*, 1968) sees the rejection of subjectivity as the issue of the 1853 Preface; but where Coulling (*VS*, 1964) reads that rejection as simply anti-Romantic, Warren is more suggestive when he says, "Arnold was himself a 'sick' romantic . . . and the Preface is his desperate—and romantic—escape from the unresolved problems of his personality and his art." The paradox is spelled out by D. G. James (*Matthew Arnold and the Decline of Romanticism*, 1961), who finds Arnold's classical ideal, though directed against Romanticism, a symptom of the Romantic quest for the inviolable and unattainable: "the hunger for the classical in the modern spirit is a useless form of escape from its own nature and destiny." The larger void in our knowledge is the lack of a coherent view of the complexities of the early Victorian critical tradition: the view persists that the Arnold of 1853 is a solid Aristotelian formalist in a turbid sea of debased Romanticism. Two important articles help to complicate our sense of the critical climate. Skillfully using the periodicals, R. G. Cox ("Victorian Criticism of Poetry: The Minority Tradition," *Scrutiny*, 1951) shows that Arnold's criticism of the Romantics (in the letters to Clough, the 1853 Preface, and the essays of the sixties) for weak-mindedness, subjectivity, and formlessness was shared and to some extent anticipated by a significant minority of reviewers. Moving forward to the sixties and seventies, R. V. Johnson ("Pater and the Victorian Anti-Romantics," *EIC*, 1954) finds that the "classicizing" critics continued to reject the tendency of Romanticism "to separate actual life from the world of art." On the other hand, the persistent "Romanticism" of Arnold's own creative personality can be caught in George Ford's *Keats and the Victorians* (1944).

Defining what Arnold was attempting to accomplish in his new role as critic of culture and society in the sixties apparently forces the modern reader back on paradox and even perplexity. William A. Madden, in "The Burden of the Artist" (in *1859: Entering an Age of Crisis*, ed. P. Appleman, W. Madden, and M. Wolff, 1959), reads Arnold's *England and the Italian Question* and Ruskin's *The Two Paths* (both 1859) as motivated not by a rejection of "the direct criticism of art in favor of political and social criticism," but by "a desire to give to art and the artist a new role"—"the burden of saving society"—which eventually, according to Madden, was to drive the artist toward a rejection of social relevance or toward the direct work of criticism. More sympathetically, Edward Alexander, in "Roles of the Victorian Critic: Matthew Arnold and John Ruskin" (*Literary Criticism and Historical Understanding*, ed. P. Damon, 1967), subtly suggests the ways in which Arnold, while attempting "to subordinate his personality to the task of persuasion," reintroduces "his personal experience in a different form from that which it takes in his subjective poetry." The tradition of culture-criticism in which Arnold worked and on which he drew—moving through Burke, Coleridge, Carlyle, and especially Newman—is defined in Raymond Williams' indispensable *Culture and Society, 1780–1950* (1958).

The need to see Arnold's doctrine of criticism and culture as both "evolving" and a response to specific occasions is splendidly met in Coulling's "The Background of 'The Function of Criticism at the Present Time' " (*PQ*, 1963). Coulling shows how Arnold's variously unsatisfactory solutions to the problem of the dissemination of unsettling theological opinions raised by the Colenso controversy issued in the balanced statement of 1864, as Arnold moved toward the larger doctrine of man's perfection he later called "culture." The continuity of Arnold's thinking is further illuminated in Coulling's equally important "The Evolution of *Culture and Anarchy*" (*SP*, 1963), which clarifies the objections Arnold was answering in the "Anarchy and Authority" series. Jump, in "Weekly Reviewing in the Eighteen-Sixties" (*RES*, 1952), suggests Arnold's place in the literary journalism of that decade; he also discusses a particular case, the softening of the *Saturday Review*'s hostility toward Arnold from around 1868, in "Matthew Arnold and the *Saturday Review*" (*RES*, 1946).

The broader "sources" of Arnold's concepts of criticism and culture, in both Newman and the German Hellenists, are explored by DeLaura, in *Hebrew and Hellene in Victorian England* (1969). The more scientific implications of Arnold's "culture" are explored fascinatingly by George W. Stocking, Jr., in "Matthew Arnold, E. B. Tylor, and the Uses of Invention" (*Amer. Anthropologist*, 1963). Arnold's sense of culture as "an inward ideational phenomenon," distinguished from an external "civilization," is closer than Tylor's to its meaning in modern "anthropological relativism." Tylor, a rationalist with an evolutionary and progressivist point of view, is forced into an ethnocentric valuation of Liberal Victorian norms as the culmination of history—a fallacy that the "humanist" Arnold avoids.

Coulling (*SP*, 1963) acknowledges that *Culture and Anarchy* is misshapen, and marred by "an excessive topicality that begins in the immediate and ends in the ephemeral." The charge of disunity might be lodged even more pointedly against Arnold's other books, several of which are collections of independently published essays. Only for *Essays in Criticism* (1865) has the case for unity been discussed at length. Robert A. Donovan (*PMLA*, 1956) finds in the essays a common method of "comparison, as a species of dialectic," which avoids "irreconcilable opposites" and the choice of alternatives in favor of finding value in both sides of a comparison. William E. Buckler ("Studies in Three Arnold Problems," *PMLA*, 1958) retorts that the collection was less "orderly and coherent" than Donovan claims. More fundamental objections might have been raised: the alleged method fits only one essay perfectly, "Pagan and Mediaeval Religious Sentiment"; the evidence has to be blurred to claim that in "Marcus Aurelius" one code is not "preferred" to the other; and in "Joubert," Coleridge and Joubert are not different enough to fit under a "dialectical" scheme. But Donovan's suggestion that by 1870 Arnold had moved beyond the detached intellectualism he admired in Sainte-Beuve and practiced during the years of his professorship, while not beyond debate, may be a clue not only to shifts in Arnold's intellectual orientation, but to still unexplored changes in his methods of argumentation.

In a brilliant tour de force, A. Dwight Culler, applying the topographical method of his own *Imaginative Reason*, argues in "No Arnold Could Ever Write a Novel" (*VN*, 1966) that *Essays in Criticism* tells "the story of a seeker after Truth who left the forest glade of Romantic nature poetry and orthodox Christianity, fought through the wilderness of the modern world, and finally, moving forward from darkness into light, stood at last by the verge of the wide-glimmering sea"—or in other terms, the promised land he was to enter only in *Literature and Dogma*. Culler observes Arnold's "novelistic" use of characters, including his own persona; but the significance of his observation that Arnold's methods change as the later essays in the book end by emphasizing the positive is undercut by the fact that the ordering of essays in the book is quite different from that of their first publication. That is, the effect of such reordering may be more or less conscious in the book, but the question of Arnold's own development in viewpoint is left out of account. In a somewhat similar demonstration, Alan Roper (*Arnold's Poetic Landscapes*, 1969) reads the apostrophe to Oxford at the end of the Preface to *Essays in Criticism* as a "landscape equivalent to a way of life," "a double movement . . . through a series of false images . . . towards the true image of Oxford." Perhaps the closest reading of the techniques employed in a single Arnold essay is Patrick J. McCarthy's interesting "Reading Victorian Prose: Arnold's 'Culture and Its Enemies' " (*UTQ*, 1971). He claims that Arnold's characteristic method is "the way of juxtaposing opposites and striving for a fruitful union"; but in fact his chosen essay better illustrates the permanent "opposition" between "sweetness and light" and "fierceness, narrowness, and machinery" than any "resolution" of these contrary forces. More such close readings of individual essays, from different periods of Arnold's career, are in order.

Arnold's Later Literary Views

Arnold's resumption of his literary and social criticism in 1877, after his nearly eight years in the "wilderness" of religious controversy, presents special, and unsolved, problems in interpretation. Many have passed over the religious books as an awkward interruption and have treated the later literary essays as a rifacimento of

Arnold's doctrines and assumptions of the sixties—a practice supported by Arnold's own rehearsing of his earlier definitions of poetry as "a criticism of life" or as "the noble and profound application of ideas to life." The result has been to treat Arnold's secular "culture" and "Hellenism" of the sixties as the norm of his critical enterprise, and to deny that his later career represents a genuinely new phase, influenced deeply by the insights gained in his "religious" period. The distinctiveness of this period can only be gauged when we accumulate studies of the personal and public matrix of the later essays—especially the crucial series from "Wordsworth" (1879) to "Science and Literature" (1882)—comparable in quality to those we have recently acquired regarding Arnold's thought in the sixties.

In the meantime, discussion of Arnold's terms in those final years continues to fluctuate inconclusively, and Arnold is often condemned in his alleged twentieth-century successors. One way of reducing the tangled lines of argument to some sort of clarity is to see Arnold in these years implicitly pursuing everywhere the question of the relation of poetry and truth—the truth of science as well as the truth claimed by dogmatic theology and philosophy. Particularly vexing are the implications of Arnold's famous prediction, in the opening of "The Study of Poetry" (1880), that "most of what now passes with us for religion and philosophy will be replaced by poetry." As we shall see in treating Arnold and the critical tradition, the point has continued through the twentieth century to divide and confound later critics. Even the primary intention of Arnold's words has been given flatly incompatible readings. On the one hand, William Madden (*Matthew Arnold*, 1967, p. 176), like some of Arnold's contemporaries, accuses Arnold of putting aesthetic experience in the place traditionally claimed by religious worship. On the other, Denis Butts (*N&Q*, 1958), in finding a parallel for Arnold's view in Newman's early statement that "poetry is our mysticism," implies that Arnold's is not the direct assault on Christianity it is often assumed to be. Somewhere in between, George Watson (*The Literary Critics*, 1962) denies that Arnold "sought to substitute poetry for religion": "It is the sham religion of dogmatic assertion which will be replaced by poetry not the true religion of Christian humanism"; poetry and religion are related by analogy.

The "touchstones" brought forward illustratively in "The Study of Poetry" have always been open to the charge of neglecting the larger context of the works they derive from, of negating Arnold's emphasis on action and "architectonicè" in the 1853 Preface, and of being restricted to a narrow range of grim and pathetic emotions. John Eells's *The Touchstones of Matthew Arnold* (1955), though overly long and of highly variable critical quality, is valuable for its careful analysis of the emotional range of Arnold's excerpts and for their relation to Arnold's habitual attitudes. Eells neglects, however, the implications of Arnold's use of the method in his own earlier writings, especially the religious works, and fails to see a basis for Arnold's "need for peace series" (nos. 6, 7, 8), comprising three of the five "new" touchstones, in the "Christianization" of Arnold's later thought. Too seldom has the touchstone method been viewed as directly connected with the problem of poetry's "truth" brought up in the same essay. Against the extreme psychologism of I. A. Richards, Edwin Berry Burgum ("The Humanism of Matthew Arnold," *Symposium*, 1931) counters that in advocating touchstones Arnold was not thinking of emotions but of ideas, for the touchstone does not convey a mood but "utilizes emotion to transfer a moral principle." More moderate than either of these, R. C. Townsend, in "Matthew Arnold, H. M. I., on the Study of Poetry" (*CE*, 1968) turns to a little exploited body of Arnold's thought, his annual school reports, and suggests that the touchstone method advocated in 1880 is the same that governed Arnold's frequent recommendation of short memorized passages in the schools. The method, with its roots in the teaching of the catechism and perhaps in the "constru-ing" exercises of traditional classical education, is meant to civilize and to act as a guide to life, less by the content than by the "spirit" and "temper" of the utterance.

No one of Arnold's critical ideas, or clusters of terms, will lie still for the dissector's needle: each seems to implicate most of the others. Arnold's always inadequate views of the relation of form and content are deeply involved with his central views of the "moral" function of literature. DeLaura ("The 'Wordsworth' of Pater and Arnold: 'The Supreme, Artistic View of Life,' " SEL, 1966) argues that the Wordsworth essay, along with "The Study of Poetry," represents Arnold's condemnation of the formalism and aestheticism recently proclaimed by Pater, while embodying Arnold's "furthest accommodation to the new formalism." Arnold would undoubtedly have been surprised to read John Casey's enthusiastic chapter on "Art and Morality," in his The Language of Criticism (1966), where Arnold's treatment of form and content is made the basis of an "expressionist criticism," which, by concentrating on the analysis of motives, "will tend to cut literature off from questions of truth and falsity, or from assessment of consequences."

The final perspective on these later years will see Arnold's struggles with the nature and function of poetry as a variant of his own lover's quarrel with Romanti-cism. Leon Gottfried concludes his study, Matthew Arnold and the Romantics (1963), by suggesting that Arnold, lacking the energy of the Romantics as well as their faith in the imagination, ended unable to reconcile reason and imagination, or to choose between Christianity and naturalism. A similar and even more powerful attack on the "palpable and pathetic" contradictions in Arnold's theory of poetry is delivered by D. G. James, in his Matthew Arnold and the Decline of English Romanticism (1961), a book unduly neglected for its hostility to Arnold and its special reading of the Romantic premises. James ably discriminates the disparate functions of poetry and religion; he judges that Arnold, meekly submissive to "science," shattered the spiritual unity achieved by the Romantics in his separation of "poetry and science, imagination and thought, knowledge and being."

Small instances help to suggest the balance of elements in Arnold's later struggle to define the nature and function of poetry. Against those who would consign Arnold's views of the "truth" of poetry to an extreme pragmatism or psychologism may be recommended Charles D. Wright's interesting sketch, in "How Matthew Arnold Altered 'Goethe on Poetry' " (VP, 1967), of an Arnold intent on maintaining the importance of "conscious thought and ideas in both the creation and operation of poetry." Though frequently cited throughout the recent Snow-Leavis dispute over our alleged "two cultures," Arnold's "Literature and Science" (1882) has been surprisingly neglected in the continuing debate over Arnold's later critical position. Douglas Cherry's "The Two Cultures of Matthew Arnold and T. H. Huxley" (Wascana Rev., 1966) dismisses Arnold's defense of letters as a rhetorical and theoretical bungle, but shows no real grasp of either Arnold or Huxley.

The two long and probing chapters devoted to Arnold in Vincent Buckley's Poetry and Morality: Studies on the Criticism of Matthew Arnold, T. S. Eliot and F. R. Leavis (1959), undeservedly overlooked in recent Arnold studies, constitute the most nearly adequate treatment of Arnold's view of poetry. Buckley discusses the moral reality or quasi-religious "truth" of poetry as residing, for Arnold, in poetry's capacity for mastering "the oppressive mystery" of life through the attainment of "serenity, detachment, freedom in the contemplation of human destiny." He is unhappy, finally, with Arnold's view of the poet as "the priest of the religion of elevated naturalism: a religion in which any supernatural dimension is simply not available to the imagination." Buckley's premises are thus close to those of William Madden (*Matthew Arnold*, 1967); but he is more successful than Madden in suggesting the variety and strength of Arnold's central insights.

Arnold the Literary Critic

Some—like George Watson (*The Literary Critics*, 1962)—deny that Arnold ever "criticizes" literature at all. The charge, though exaggerated (Arnold looks closely at texts in the lectures on Homer and Celtic literature), is understandable. Much of what little has been done on Arnold's "methods" as a critic can be gathered from a few articles, discussed above, mostly on Arnold's *Essays in Criticism*. Of course Arnold is at one with most of his contemporaries in failing to explicate texts carefully; one of the few who surpassed Arnold in this respect was R. H. Hutton. Gaylord C. LeRoy (*PMLA*, 1941) admirably contrasts the two men: Hutton, superior in "sensitiveness of response," in thoroughness and minuteness of commentary; Arnold, superior in "penetration" because of his greater insight into the instability of contemporary society and its values.

The rest is Arnold's literary opinions, which are very numerous but surprisingly ill surveyed. Most work on Arnold's views of particular authors and periods is weakened by a failure to attend to Arnold's views of history, a subject treated earlier in this chapter. Arnold's views of the classics, including the Homer lectures, and his struggle with the Romantic tradition are also discussed above in separate sections. But his extensive comments on the Romantic poets in the two series of *Essays in Criticism*, well synthesized in William A. Jamison's *Arnold and the Romantics* (1958) and Leon Gottfried's *Matthew Arnold and the Romantics* (1963), deserve special comment. Both Jamison and Gottfried comment interestingly on Arnold's indebtedness to Coleridge, but the topic remains curiously resistant to clarification. It will remain so until the larger topic of the Victorian response to Coleridge is mapped out: the best places to begin now are Charles Richard Sanders' *Coleridge and the Broad Church Movement* (1942) and an Indiana dissertation by Maurianne S. Adams, "Coleridge and the Victorians: Studies in the Interpretation of Poetry, Scripture, and Myth" (1967). Arnold's Wordsworth essay of 1879, a center of controversy from the first, was dismissed by Lane Cooper as "empty bombast" (*Evolution and Repentance*, 1926). J. Dover Wilson, in *Leslie Stephen and Matthew Arnold as Critics of Wordsworth* (1939), finds Arnold's criteria narrow, and his treatment of Stephen both "vicious" and malicious.

Arnold's attitudes toward the eighteenth century are a good test of the still frequently alleged "classicism" of his views. As Oscar Maurer points out in "Pope and the Victorians" (*SEng*, 1944), Arnold was at one with his generation in its "Romantic" patronizing of the eighteenth century. Geoffrey Tillotson, in "Matthew Arnold and Eighteenth-Century Poetry" (*Criticism and the Nineteenth Century*, 1951; rpt. 1967), dismisses Arnold's interpretations of the eighteenth century as having an inadequate basis in the facts and concludes: "For all his humanism, Arnold does not value art." R. C. Churchill ("Gray and Matthew Arnold," *Cri-*

terion, 1938; rpt. in *The Criterion 1922–1939*, 1967) attributes Arnold's misreading of Gray as an isolated poet in an age of prose to his own attraction to the type of the Romantic solitary. In the best study of the topic, "Matthew Arnold and the Eighteenth Century" (*UTQ*, 1940), E. K. Brown also finds the source of Arnold's inability to identify himself with that century's "modes of thought, feeling, living" in Arnold's own Romantic sensibility: "[it] had no power over his imagination, it gave no quickening lift to the life of the Spirit as he understood that life."

Elsewhere ("Matthew Arnold and the Elizabethans," *UTQ*, 1932), Brown shows that Arnold uses the Elizabethan age as the norm against which to measure the aberration that English Puritanism represents. Brown's comments on Arnold's dissatisfaction with Shakespeare are of especial value; for Arnold, Shakespeare is not "relevant to the nineteenth-century mind" as Homer, Sophocles, Wordsworth, and Goethe are. John S. Eells, in *The Touchstones of Arnold* (1955), offers shrewd remarks on Arnold's attitudes toward Shakespeare. But the subject demands a grounding in Arnold's conception—or avoidance—of tragedy, about which very little has been attempted until recently. A related and equally unexplored topic is the attitudes of Arnold, an ardent theatergoer, toward the drama. Arnold's theater letters of the eighties, collected in 1919 as *Letters of an Old Playgoer*, are preceded by an introduction by Brander Matthews suggesting the need for further work on, precisely, Arnold and the theater, tragedy, and Shakespeare.

Arnold's lectures *On the Study of Celtic Literature* have had a long after-history. Andrew Lang (*Blackwood's*, 1897) saw Renan and Arnold as the prophets of the "Celtic Renaissance," and John V. Kelleher ("Matthew Arnold and the Celtic Revival," in *Perspectives of Criticism*, ed. Harry Levin, 1950) shows how closely Arnold's description of "Celtic" qualities was followed, but with every weakness Arnold deplored interpreted later as "a strange characteristic strength." That Arnold's "formula" for the qualities of the Celtic genius has survived a century surprisingly well can be seen in MacEdward Leach's "Matthew Arnold and 'Celtic Magic'" (in *The Celtic Cross: Studies in Irish Culture and Literature*, ed. R. B. Browne, W. J. Roscelli, and R. Loftus, 1964) and Rachel Bromwich's lecture, *Matthew Arnold and Celtic Literature: A Retrospect, 1865–1965* (1965). The more sinister side of Arnold's views of Celticism was what Lang called the "pseudo-scientific ethnological air" of Arnold's racial arguments. Frederic E. Faverty, in his exemplary study *Matthew Arnold, the Ethnologist* (1951), showed that the quasi-scientific views of race that Arnold derived from a number of Continental thinkers affected not only his literary criticism but his religious and social views as well. The shift in Arnold's attitudes toward the "science" of his day, from the relative enthusiasm of the sixties to something like fear in his later career, is excellently shown in Fred A. Dudley, "Matthew Arnold and Science" (*PMLA*, 1942).

Arnold's complex attitudes toward French and German culture and literature are to some extent a function of his relations with Sénancour, Sainte-Beuve, Renan, Goethe, and Heine—discussed above as major influences. E. K. Brown, in "The French Reputation of Matthew Arnold" (*Studies in English by Members of University College, Toronto*, 1931), attributes both the "soundness" and the "meagreness" of Arnold's French reputation to his closeness to the French tradition. But almost all accounts of Arnold as a critic of French literature find him deficient. The most unrestrained attack is that of Ruth Zabriskie Temple in *The Critic's Alchemy: A Study of the Introduction of Symbolism into England* (1953). Temple blames Arnold for his failure in detachment, his lack of a "wide or deep acquaintance" with French literature, his deafness to the music of French verse, and his failure to "anticipate the method of criticism which from the seventies on brought the poetry of contemporary France to sympathetic attention." Temple's uncritical admiration for all things French prevents her from acknowledging that Arnold's tastes were formed too soon to make him fully receptive to mid- and late nineteenth-century French literature and criticism, or that Arnold's advocacy of clarity, openness to ideas, and a Continental point of view did in fact prepare the way for Swinburne's generation. Temple's attack on Arnold's integrity—he deferred to the status quo and to his audience's own "smug satisfaction"—is the central point of Christophe Campos' treatment of Arnold in *The View of France: From Arnold to Bloomsbury* (1965): "Arnold pandered too much to English pride" and "encouraged a complacent form of self-depreciation that is still at large." By far the best balanced treatment is F. J. W. Harding's, in *Matthew Arnold: The Critic and France* (1964). Fully aware of Arnold's deficiencies of vision and taste, Harding nevertheless suggests the role of French literature in Arnold's humanistic program: the French writers Arnold sponsored were to provide "a means of spiritual orientation," and his view of France as "a witness to humanisation in the modern world" was essential to his search for "a way out of the competing claims of rationalism and evangelical morality."

The full extent of Arnold's engagement with German culture has been assessed only twice: in Walther Fischer's short but judicious article, "Matthew Arnold und Deutschland" (*GRM*, 1954), and in an excellent Iowa dissertation by Charles D. Wright, "Matthew Arnold's Response to German Culture" (1963). J. A. Corbett's otherwise unimportant article, "A Victorian Critic in Germany" (*GL&L*, 1938), attempts to rebut Saintsbury's charge that in later life Arnold had surrendered to the charms of Machtpolitik. Wellek, in his *History of Modern Criticism*, IV (1965), judges that Arnold misunderstood not only Goethe and Heine, but the meaning of German Romanticism.

A final word is in order about the need for a study of Matthew Arnold and the novel. Though Geoffrey Tillotson (*Criticism and the Nineteenth Century*) reproaches Arnold for not expecting enough of the nineteenth-century novelist, the fact is that Arnold read a good many contemporary novels—and wrote an elegy on Charlotte Brontë and an essay on Tolstoy.

Arnold and the Critical Tradition

The multitudinous avenues of Arnold's influence on later criticism have received, until recently, surprisingly little detailed attention. A major cause is the grievous lack of a comprehensive study, comparable to M. H. Abrams' *The Mirror and the Lamp*, of the continuity of criticism from the mid-Victorians to, say, the early Pound and Eliot. Marion Mainwaring's Radcliffe dissertation, "Matthew Arnold's Influence and Reputation as a Literary Critic" (1949), is a storehouse of comment on Arnold as both poet and critic, but she does not attempt a larger view of the shifts in the critical situation. E. D. H. Johnson (*The Alien Vision of Victorian Poetry*) suggests at several points that Arnold's early poetics point toward art for art's sake and the cult of the alienated artist, but does not pursue the theme. Culler also remarks in passing (*Imaginative Reason*, p. 75) that Arnold's early poetic theory places him "directly in the line leading into Rossetti, Pater, Swinburne, and Wilde, and it goes a long way towards explaining the sympathy, otherwise rather surprising, which those writers always felt for Arnold." Similar suggestions are made by Frank Kermode in *Romantic Image* (1957) and by William Madden (*Matthew Arnold*, 1967). But the hard work of showing which elements of Arnold's poetry and prose were prized, and by which of his contemporaries and successors, has hardly begun. Louise Rosenblatt, in *L'Idée de l'art pour l'art dans la littérature anglaise pendant la période victorienne* (1931), began the task by judiciously discriminating those Arnoldian doctrines, such as disinterestedness and a universal culture, which appealed to the aesthetes, from those which they ignored, such as the responsibilities of criticism to society. She treats briefly the continuity from Arnold through Pater to Wilde.

A key issue, only recently studied in detail, is Walter Pater's indebtedness to Arnold. For both men, discriminations among periods in their careers are essential. Thinking largely of the themes of criticism and culture, Walter E. Houghton (*The Victorian Frame of Mind, 1830–1870*, 1957) and Graham Hough (*The Last Romantics*, 1947; rpt. 1961) stress, respectively, the "gulf" between Arnold's and Pater's conception of the mind, and the striking differences of emotional tone in their writing. DeLaura, in "The 'Wordsworth' of Pater and Arnold" (*SEL*, 1966) and *Hebrew and Hellene in Victorian England* (1969), explores in detail the ways in which Arnold's "secular" humanism of the sixties is reshaped by the early Pater. Whether Arnold's 1863 portrait of Marcus Aurelius was important in the writing of *Marius the Epicurean* is debated by K. Allott ("Pater and Arnold," *EIC*, 1952), Louise M. Rosenblatt ("The Genesis of Pater's *Marius the Epicurean*," *CL*, 1963), and DeLaura in *Hebrew and Hellene*. The larger theme of the relevance of Arnold's religious views to those of Pater in his last years is explored by U. C. Knoepflmacher (*Religious Humanism and the Victorian Novel*, 1965), who finds *Plato and Platonism* "a latterday equivalent" of Arnold's religious writings. DeLaura, in *Hebrew and Hellene*, sees the deepening of the ethical and religious component of Arnold's thinking in the sixties and the seventies as a virtual model for the central line of Pater's development up through the writing of *Marius*. But beyond Pater lie shoals and rapids. Paul Elmer More, in a perceptive and unduly neglected essay ("Criticism," in *Shelburne Essays: Seventh Series*, 1910), pointed out that while to derive aestheticism from Arnold is to neglect the seriousness of his ethical commitment, nevertheless "the Epicureanism of Pater and the hedonism of Oscar Wilde were able to connect themselves in a disquieting way with one side of Matthew Arnold's gospel of culture." More's tone and phrasing closely anticipate T. S. Eliot's famous passages in "Arnold and Pater" (1930; rpt. in *Selected Essays*, 1932), where "Aestheticism" and "Art for art's sake" are seen as "the offspring of Arnold's Culture." In "Arnold, Pater, Wilde, and the Object as in Themselves They See It" (*SEL*, 1971), Wendell Harris, confining himself to a single idea, throws further light on the critical succession.

Eliot's own multifarious involvement with Arnold, though frequently mentioned, has received surprisingly little comprehensive or authoritative treatment. John Henry Raleigh (*Matthew Arnold and American Culture*, 1957) conveniently surveys the range of Eliot's opinions regarding Arnold, and concludes that "the deep and powerful affinities" between the two men account for their asking the same questions, their answers differing "in degree rather than in kind." As with Pater, periods and emphases in the careers of both Eliot and Arnold must be discriminated. To begin with literature, the Introduction and the essay "The Perfect Critic" in *The Sacred Word* (1920; rpt. 1964) reveal a warily conciliatory Eliot consciously assuming Arnold's mantle. Stanley Edgar Hyman (*Poetry and Criticism: Four Revolutions in Literary Taste*, 1961) reads "Tradition and the Individual Talent," in the same volume, as "an ironic counterstatement" to Arnold's touchstones and high seriousness, but fails to see that Eliot's view of the availability of the European past is obviously indebted to a famous passage near the end of "The Function of Criticism." Emerson R. Marks, in "Pragmatic Poetics: Dryden to Valéry (*BuR*, 1962), sees Arnold's rejection of Shakespeare and Eliot's repudiation of Milton (linked even by verbal parallels) as examples of a recurring, and distorting, process in literary criticism "by which the peculiar virtue of an older poet becomes an occasion for lament." M. L. S. Loring (*SR*, 1935) unconvincingly argues that Eliot's and Arnold's "methods of working are fundamentally opposed in principle": Arnold's excessive "concern for the framework rather than the detail of composition" is contrasted with Eliot's arbitrary imposition of dogma on carefully observed fact. Far more important is Stephen Spender's acute discussion of Arnold as "the unacknowledged legislator of twentieth-century criticism," in *The Struggle of the Modern* (1963). The modern poet-critics like Eliot, Pound, and Yeats did not solve the problem defined for them by Arnold as "the lack of current ideas" available to the poet: "Instead, they made the crisis of poetry, the necessity of criticism, the themes of their poetry."

Some of the attempts to contrast Arnold and Eliot have been both polemical and unexpectedly favorable to Arnold. F. R. Leavis' essay on Arnold in *Scrutiny* (1938; rpt. in *The Importance of Scrutiny*, 1948) refutes Eliot's charges that Arnold was more interested in "greatness" than in the "genuineness" of poetry, and that he neglected poetic style, by arguing that Arnold demonstrated that the moral judgment cannot be separated from "a delicately relevant response of sensibility." The terms of Leavis' defense suggest that Arnold is the chief model of his own critical endeavor. Ian Gregor, in "The Critic and the Age: Some Observations on the Social Criticism of Matthew Arnold and T. S. Eliot" (*DubR*, 1953), finds Eliot's social criticism "peculiarly barren of constructive proposals," while Arnold had a deeper "sense of human possibilities." In "Eliot, Pound, and the Decline of the Conservative Tradition" (*Hist. of Ideas Newsletter*, 1957), R. D. Spector argues, too briefly to clinch the point, that Arnold's "disinterestedness" involved a social concern free of the "despair and rejection" of Eliot's and Pound's views of society. Two essays in *Eliot in Perspective: A Symposium*, edited by Graham Martin (1970), throw new light on the Eliot-Arnold relationship. John Peter, in "Eliot and the *Criterion*," shows that Arnold is the "somewhat unlikely" model for Eliot's editorial commentaries. And Ian Gregor ("Eliot and Matthew Arnold") suggests that in both critical and poetic practice the later Eliot approximates Arnold's position.

Eliot's rejection of Arnold's religious views is discussed in a later section. The remaining issue between them is that most vexing and unresolved question of twentieth-century poetics, the relation of literature to "belief" and to "knowledge" —a question that has not yet attracted even its adequate historian. Central to almost all modern discussions is the opening passage of "The Study of Poetry," declaring that in the collapse of religion and metaphysics, "The future of poetry is immense." That passage was the epigraph of I. A. Richards' *Science and Poetry* (1926), which proposed to set up poetry, now relieved from its "entanglement with belief," as the chief means of making human attitudes and impulses "self-supporting." That Eliot did not simply reject Richards' views (as is often assumed) can be gathered from certain uncollected pieces (e.g., *The Enemy*, Jan. 1927; *The Dial*, March 1927), and such work of the period as "Shakespeare and the Stoicism of Seneca" and the note to the 1929 essay on Dante (both in *Selected Essays*). Matthew Arnold is the conscious object of attack a bit later, obliquely in "Arnold and Pater" (1930), and directly in *The Use of Poetry and the Use of Criticism* (1933): "To ask of poetry that it give religious and philosophic satisfaction, while deprecating philosophy and dogmatic religion, is of course to embrace the shadow of a shade."

The literature-and-belief problem agitated the American New Critics for many years. Arnold and Richards became primal sources of "positivistic" error in Allen Tate's defense of literature as "the complete knowledge of man's experience," "that unique and formed intelligence of the world of which man alone is capable," in "The Present Function of Criticism" (*Reason in Madness*, 1940) and "Literature as Knowledge" (1941; in *The Man of Letters in the Modern World*, 1955). But Francis X. Roëllinger, Jr., in "Two Theories of Poetry as Knowledge" (*SoR*, 1942), concluded that Arnold's view of poetry "in the end . . . is not very much different from Mr. Tate's own theory." Cleanth Brooks, in "Metaphor and the Function of Criticism" (*Spiritual Problems in Contemporary Literature*, ed. S. R. Hopper, 1952), is not unlike Eliot and Tate in finding "Arnold's confusion of the realms of science and religion and aesthetics" a basis for distinguishing two camps in modern poetic theory: "Those who reject Arnold's views that science has disposed of religion, and those who accept it." Richard Foster uses Arnold's famous paragraph as the starting point of his valuable study, *The New Romantics* (1962), concerning the increasingly serious concern with "religion," and broader human issues in the criticism of Richards, Tate, John Crowe Ransom, and R. P. Blackmur. The ambiguities involved in Blackmur's exploration of an Arnoldian view of the relation of poetry and religion are examined with admirable finesse in R. W. B. Lewis, "Casella as Critic: A Note on R. P. Blackmur" (*KR*, 1951).

The controversy over literature and belief, as derived from Arnold and reformulated in the intellectual wars of the 1920's, has subsided somewhat in recent years. Instead, we have opinions en passant: F. W. Bateson ("The Function of Criticism at the Present Time," *EIC*, 1953) accepting the Arnoldian prophecy of poetry's role as far from absurd, and David Daiches (*Some Late Victorian Attitudes*, 1969) rejecting it as in fact "a most erroneous prophecy," neglectful of "the ethical problem." A related controversy of the 1920's was the debate over "poésie pure" in France, where the Abbé Bremond invoked Arnold and other nineteenth-century English authors in his discussion of the analogy of religion and poetry.

It is evident that the continuing controversy over Arnold's role in the modern poetry-religion-philosophy-science entanglement springs, not only from the inherent epistemological conundrums involved, but from a persisting lack of agreement concerning Arnold's original meaning—a debate in itself, considered above. But those who have captured Arnold (whether approvingly or not) for the high-aesthetic line of modern critical theory usually forget that Eliot (in "Arnold and Pater") saw Arnold's religious views as leading to two different conclusions: not only the "Aesthetic" view that "religion is Art," but also the "Humanist" doctrine that "Religion is Morals." John Henry Raleigh notes, all too briefly (*Matthew Arnold and American Culture*), that "The arguments, disagreements, and reciprocity between Arnold's ideas and those of the New Humanists are complex and innumerable." The field of study—starting with the work of Babbitt and More, and with

Eliot as an enigmatic presence—is large and not well mapped. Helpful starting places, besides Raleigh, are the series of articles by W. S. Knickerbocker and Percy H. Houston (*SR*, 1930) and Everett Lee Hunt's "Matthew Arnold and His Critics" (*SR*, 1936). The centrality and complexity of Arnold's role in the New Humanism can be seen in Norman Foerster's *Towards Standards* (1930) and in a number of the essays in *Humanism in America* (ed. Foerster, 1930).

Arnold also plays an important, if much less precise, role in the shifting tides of cultural polemics in the twentieth century. Sometimes, as in Peter Worth's "A Source of Excellence: Two of Matthew Arnold's Terms Adapted" (*Prairie Schooner*, 1967), terms of Arnold's—in this case "natural magic" and "moral profundity"—are expropriated for new purposes. Donald Davie ("The Earnest and the Smart: Provincialism in Letters," *TC*, 1953) skillfully employs Arnold's notion of "urbanity" in criticizing modern demands for "irony." Much more often, Arnold's "criticism" and "culture" are taken as known quantities and defended or, more commonly, attacked. The "nativist" strain in American criticism could lead even Randolph Bourne ("Our Cultural Humility," in *History of a Literary Radical*, 1920) to reject Arnold's culture as passive, external, authoritarian, and "alien." The charge of thinness and vagueness made against Arnold's idea of culture by John Gillard Watson (*QR*, 1956) is mildness itself compared with the strident tone of Herbert Read's pamphlet, *To Hell with Culture* (1941). In an uncollected essay, "Literature and Power" (*KR*, 1940), Lionel Trilling sees Arnold's criterion of adequacy and his view of literature as a civilizing agent as sources for "our culture's exclusive concern with knowledge for the purpose of control." Trilling's careful distinctions would seem irrelevant to Susan Sontag, who in her influential *Against Interpretation* (1966) announces the demise of "the Matthew Arnold notion of culture," with its obsolescent moral, social, and political burdens and its elevation of literature "as the model for creative statement." In its place, we shall have "a new (potentially unitary) kind of sensibility," drawing on the other arts, seeking new "modes of vivacity." In more specifically political and social contexts, Arnold's culture has frequently been reexamined as a counterpoise against contemporary anarchism and unreason. Four thoughtful discussions involving Arnold were published in 1969: James F. Goldberg, "'Culture' and 'Anarchy' and the Present Time" (*KR*); Roy Fuller, "Philistines and Jacobins" (*SR*); Eugene Goodheart, "Relevance and the Authority of Culture" (*CentR*); and Milton Himmelfarb, "Hebraism and Hellenism Now" (*Commentary*).

Where, finally, after such noisy disputes, does Arnold "fit" in the modern critical tradition and what are his distinctive contributions? William Madden's penetrating article, "The Divided Tradition in English Criticism" (*PMLA*, 1958), sees an "unbridgeable gap between the concepts of art as handmaiden and art as savior": one camp has accepted the religious burden Arnold places on poetry and criticism, the other has rejected Arnold's religious views and has "tried to offer some counteraesthetic." Though his reading of Arnold as exclusively "aesthetic," here and in his *Matthew Arnold* (1967), is open to objection, Madden's is one of the few attempts to define the neglected but essential theological underpinnings of modern criticism. Though he has to rely on uncharacteristic texts to prove his point, John Holloway argues ("Matthew Arnold and the Modern Dilemma," *EIC*, 1952; rpt. in *The Charted Mirror*, 1960) that Arnold anticipates Eliot in two cardinal points of modern poetics: "that poetry is an imaginative fusion, and that it fuses not few but many elements into a single complex with an organic unity." Holloway points out that the two errors exaggeratedly attributed to Arnold—that poetry packs an "unusually large number of 'meanings' into a small compass," and that poetry is therapeutic—contain the kernel of two basic truths of modern criticism: "that literature can add something important to the general pattern of life, and that it is an imaginative, not intellectual, synthesis from complex material." Despite his simplification of Arnold's position, Murray Krieger's "The Critical Legacy of Matthew Arnold: Or, the Strange Brotherhood of T. S. Eliot, I. A. Richards, and Northrop Frye" (*SoR*, 1969) sees Arnold's 1853 Preface as a source of Eliot's doctrines of the objective correlative and the unity of sensibility. His most original point is to suggest that *both* Eliot and Richards, following Arnold's lead on the "separation of the poet from ideas," tend to push the "truth" component out of poetry altogether. Probing articles such as Madden's and Krieger's underscore the urgent need for a rewritten history of the relations between nineteenth- and early-twentieth-century criticism.

Arnold's Literary Influence

Arnold's influence on poets and novelists, though almost as various as his critical influence, has been even less closely studied. His authority extends to so major a European figure as Tolstoy. Marion Mainwaring (*NCF*, 1952) revealed not only that Arnold's 1887 essay was virtually the first presentation of Tolstoy to the English public, but that the two men had met in 1861 and that Tolstoy kept close watch on Arnold's critical and religious writings. Victor O. Buyniak (*Wascana Rev.*, 1968) adds even more references to Arnold in Tolstoy's writings. In her article, Mainwaring, drawing on the host of names in her 1949 dissertation, mentions Arnold's influence on such contemporary novelists as Kingsley, Pater, Wilde, Hardy, Howells, Meredith, Gissing, Sarah Orne Jewett, J. H. Shorthouse, Mark Twain, Mrs. Humphry Ward, and Thomas Hughes, as well as such later writers as E. M. Forster, H. G. Wells, James Branch Cabell, and Sinclair Lewis.

Arnold's influence on American poets and novelists divides in accordance with a central division in American culture. John B. Hoben, in "Mark Twain's *A Connecticut Yankee*: A Genetic Study" (*AL*, 1946), shows that Twain's reaction to Arnold's indictment of American culture in the eighties played an important part in Twain's novel. Far different was the reaction of Melville, as Walter E. Bezanson shows ("Melville's Reading of Arnold's Poetry," *PMLA*, 1954). The "despondencies" and the "acute sense of the modern plight" displayed in Arnold's early poetry deeply impressed Melville and influenced the writing of *Clarel*. R. A. Yoder, in "Poetry and Science: 'Two Distinct Branches of Knowledge' in *Billy Budd*" (*SoRA*, 1969), suggests the influence of Arnold's discussion of "Aberglaube" on Melville's later thought. Henry James's deep response to Arnold, from the time of *Essays in Criticism* (1865), deserves a full treatment. Marius Bewley ("The Verb to Contribute," *Spectator*, 24 July 1959) suggests that James is not merely "a fine but attenuated theorist of form," but "Arnold's comrade-in-arms" in his sense of "the relevance of the moral to art, and of art to life." Alwyn Berland ("Henry James and the Aesthetic Tradition," *JHI*, 1962) opens the topic of Arnold's influence, but the article is hampered by a failure to discriminate carefully among the positions of Arnold, Ruskin, and Pater. Far more satisfactory is Edward Engelberg's strikingly thoughtful study, "James and Arnold: Conscience and Consciousness in a Victorian 'Künstlerroman'" (*Criticism*, 1968), which suggests the complexity of James's reaction to certain central terms in Arnold, and in the process provides an excellent model for the study of the ways in which ideas operate in fiction. Other figures might yield interesting results: the melancholy of Arnold's early poetry as part of the background of E. A. Robinson and Henry Adams, or Arnold's religious thought as part of the matrix of Harold Frederic's *The Damnation of Theron Ware* (1896) —though none of the three is mentioned by Raleigh.

At least one effort has been made to define an Arnoldian tradition in English poetry. Rejecting T. S. Eliot's thesis that Pater and the Decadents are Arnold's legitimate progeny, Leonard Brown ("Arnold's Succession: 1850–1914," *SR*, 1934) suggests rather sketchily that the "best minds" after Arnold—Meredith, Hardy, Housman, even Swinburne and Rupert Brooke—share not Arnold's opinions, but his attitudes of "skepticism" and "stoical despair." But the evidence for this interesting thesis is still lacking. Sidney M. B. Coulling's able survey, "Swinburne and Matthew Arnold" (*PQ*, 1970), records the numerous contacts between the two men and Swinburne's critical debts to Arnold, but suggests no influence on the poetry of the young man who had ecstatically read Arnold's poetry as a schoolboy. The evidence for Housman's indebtedness is the most complete, and much can be gleaned from Grant Richards, *Housman, 1897–1936* (1941), Norman Marlow, *A. E. Housman: Scholar and Poet* (1958), and E. H. S. Walde and T. S. Dorsch, "A. E. Housman and Matthew Arnold" (*BUSE*, 1960). Though Hardy remained alert to the various phases of Arnold's career, very little has been done on his poetic debts to Arnold. DeLaura, in "'The Ache of Modernism' in Hardy's Later Novels" (*ELH*, 1967), discusses Hardy's reaction against Arnold's "compromising" theological position, especially as it may have affected the portrayal of Angel Clare in *Tess*. As for the poetry, we have Douglas Bush's "The Varied Hues of Pessimism" (*DR*, 1929), which, while noting interesting parallels in style and theme, claims no direct influence of Arnold on Hardy. James G. Nelson, in *Sir William Watson* (1966), shows that Arnold was a chief influence on the thought and tone of the once well-known Watson. Garrod, in *The Profession of Poetry* (1929), suggests in passing Arnold's influence on the poetry of Robert Louis Stevenson.

With the exception of Pater, treated in the preceding section, Arnold's place in the "other" line, noted by More and Eliot, through Pater and Wilde to the nineties, resists careful definition. Next to nothing has been done on Arnold and the poetry of the nineties, even in such professed admirers as Lionel Johnson and Wilde. DeLaura ("Four Arnold Letters," *TSLL*, 1962) presents a letter from Arnold to Wilde in 1881 and suggests Arnoldian echoes in *De Profundis* and an early poem of Wilde. An interesting article by Jan Gordon, "Hebraism, Hellenism, and *The Picture of Dorian Gray*" (*VN*, 1968), is finally confusing by its failure to see that Wilde's "Hellenism" in the novel is closer to Pater's reshaping than to its Arnoldian original and by its association of Hebraism both with "science" and a "concern with fact" and with unpleasant references to Jews. Two other novelists were deeply in Arnold's debt. Lionel Trilling (*Matthew Arnold*) explained the importance of Arnold's religious ideas in *Robert Elsmere* (1888), by Mrs. Humphry Ward, Arnold's niece. Lou Agnes Reynolds ("Mrs. Humphry Ward and the Arnold Heritage," Diss. Northwestern 1952) shows that Arnold's views in all areas were pervasive in his niece's fiction and thought. Wilfred Stone, in *The Cave and the Mountain: A Study of E. M. Forster* (1966; also in "E. M. Forster et Matthew Arnold," *LanM*, 1968), shows that Arnold's culture was at "the very heart of Forster's esthetic ideal," especially as exhibited in *Howards End*.

That Arnold's direct influence can reach into the mid-twentieth century is evident in Jerome Mazzaro's intriguing if not pellucid "Arnoldian Echoes in the Poetry of Randall Jarrell" (*WHR*, 1969). James Zigerell, in "MacLeish's 'Dover Beach'—A Note to That Poem" (*Expl*, 1959), reads the modern poem as a kind of answer to and reversal of Arnold's original. Apparently no one has yet offered a satisfactory explanation of the implied comment on Arnold's poem in Anthony Hecht's well-known poem, "The Dover Bitch" (*The Hard Hours*, 1967).

Arnold and America

Arnold's relation to Emerson, his influence on the American New Humanists, and his role in the work of several important American writers are considered in earlier sections. Two topics remain: Arnold *in* America and Arnold *on* America. The first has been studied in detail over the years. Roger L. Brooks solved a puzzle of long standing in Arnold studies ("A Matthew Arnold Letter to James Russell Lowell: The Reason for the American Lecture Tour," *AL*, 1959) by proving that Arnold undertook the 1883–84 tour in order to pay his son's Oxford gambling debts. Chilson H. Leonard's 1932 Yale dissertation, "Arnold in America: A Study of Matthew Arnold's Literary Relations with America and of His Visits to This Country in 1883 and 1886" (microfilmed, 1965), for the first time carefully established the chronology and itinerary of Arnold's American visits. Further details of the 1883–84 tour, as well as of the furious press reaction to Arnold, can be gained from James Dow McCallum, "The Apostle of Culture Meets America" (*NEQ*, 1929); E. P. Lawrence, "An Apostle's Progress: Matthew Arnold in America" (*PQ*, 1931); William T. Beauchamp, "Plato on the Prairies (Matthew Arnold at Galesburg)" (*Educ. Forum*, 1941); Harriet R. Holman, "Matthew Arnold's Elocution Lessons" (*NEQ*, 1945); Wayne C. Minnick, "Matthew Arnold on Emerson" (*QJS*, 1951); John P. Long, "Matthew Arnold Visits Chicago" (*UTQ*, 1954); and two notes by George Monteiro, "Matthew Arnold and John Hay: Three Unpublished Letters" and "Matthew Arnold in America" (*N&Q*, 1963, 1966).

Although John Henry Raleigh, in *Matthew Arnold and American Culture* (1957), details the American reaction to Arnold from 1865 on, very little comprehensive work has been done on Arnold's own attitudes toward America—their origins and history. James Bentley Orrick's "Matthew Arnold and America" (*London Mercury*, 1929) is a disappointingly thin survey. John O. Waller, in "Matthew Arnold and the American Civil War" (*VN*, 1962), explains the growth of Arnold's "cold" sympathy for the Northern cause. W. D. Templeman uncritically surveys Arnold's views of America in the eighties, in "Matthew Arnold and the American Way" (*Educ. Forum*, 1957), and discusses one of Arnold's references in "A Note on Arnold's 'Civilisation in the United States' " (*MLN*, 1944). DeLaura ("Matthew Arnold and the American 'Literary Class,' " *BNYPL*, 1966) indicates the extent of Arnold's contacts with the New England literary intellectuals, while suggesting the paradoxical reasons why the "man and the moment . . . did not intersect." Arnold's use of the United States as an exemplum, especially in his later social writings, is a topic that appears in a number of items in the following section.

Political and Social Views

Otto Elias' patient survey, *Matthew Arnolds politische Grundanschauungen* (1931), finds Arnold an annoying mixture of liberal and conservative views, but denies that Arnold hankered after the authoritarian state. A balanced and competent survey of Arnold's social views is presented by B. E. Lippincott, in *Victorian Critics of Democracy* (1938; rpt. 1964). He judges that Arnold understood the democratic movement at least as well as Mill, and that, unlike Carlyle and Ruskin, he "had faith in democracy" and "did not turn to reaction for a solution of the anarchy of individualism." Amplifying notions first developed in "Ambivalence in Matthew Arnold's Prose Criticism" (*CE*, 1952), LeRoy's treatment of Arnold in *Perplexed Prophets: Six Nineteenth-Century Authors* (1953) is stimulating but based on a questionable transference of psychoanalytic terms to the intellectual sphere. Arnold's personal "psychic cleavage," a "sub-conscious or neurotic conflict," leads to his "ambivalent response to the modern world" and his "ineffectual gospel" of culture. LeRoy pursues the theme in "Arnold and Aselgeia" (*BNYPL*, 1963) and describes the history of Arnold's social views as less "a marked shift from the left to the right" than "a continuing ambivalence, first the insurgent then the repressive impulses gaining the upper hand in alternation."

Edward Alexander provides a more reliable summary of Arnold's views in *Matthew Arnold and John Stuart Mill* (1965), linking the two men in their shared concern that "democracy might be wedded to a high ideal of culture." In the end, Alexander's preference for Mill's emphasis on "liberty" leads him to exaggerate Arnold's hankering for authority. John Robson, in "Mill and Arnold: Liberty and Culture—Friends or Enemies?" (*Of Several Branches: Studies from the Humanities Association Bulletin, 1954–65*, ed. G. S. McCaughey, 1968), stresses the similarities between Arnold and Mill, while effectively defining their divergence on the relevance of "traditional and pragmatic sources of authority." One of the most interesting books on Arnold is Patrick J. McCarthy's *Matthew Arnold and the Three Classes* (1964), which draws on out-of-the-way sources and succeeds in illuminating many hitherto obscure passages in Arnold's political and social writings. McCarthy's is probably the most balanced account of Arnold's "reactionary" mood of the 1880's.

The studies mentioned above represent a recent and welcome attempt at even-handed judgment. Far less irenic, and less careful, views are common in the past, though even these are curiously contradictory. Herbert Spencer long ago, in *The Study of Sociology* (1873), treated Arnold at length as an arrant example of "anti-patriotism" deriving from his attempt "to emancipate himself from those influences of race, and country, and locality, which warp his judgment." Far more common in later treatments is the charge that Arnold's vision was distorted by his middle-class point of view (Lippincott) and that he failed in the practical sphere "not because he was too little, but because he was too much, of his age" (LeRoy). But the rejection of Arnold by Spencer, an individualist of the right, is repeated by Leonard Woolf, a libertarian of the left. In *After the Deluge: A Study of Communal Psychology* (1931), Woolf sweepingly dismisses Arnold as a forerunner of the modern "authoritarian, 'democratic' Great State" whose remedy for anarchy is "to abolish liberty." Arnold is not, however, entirely without his earlier defenders. That Irving Babbitt should in an essay of 1917 (in *Spanish Character and Other Essays*, 1940) endorse Arnold's approval of "qualitative and selective democracy" is not surprising. Less expected are the favorable references to Arnold as an advocate of "equality" in R. H. Tawney's *Equality* (1931). Even close students of Arnold may be unaware that, as Reinhard Bendix explains ("The Protestant Ethic—Revisited," *Comparative Studies in Society and History*, 1967), Arnold's views on "the close relation between Protestant dissent and economic enterprise" and on Puritanism's "great emotional and cultural liabilities" were a stimulant in the work of Tawney's German counterpart, Max Weber.

Even Arnold's more recent critics have difficulty describing the pattern of his political and social thinking. N. N. Feltes, in "Matthew Arnold and the Modern Spirit: A Reassessment" (*UTQ*, 1962), presents a balanced account of the majority view; he sees the religious writings of the seventies as the "watershed separating the period of Arnold's approval of the workings of the modern spirit from that of his fear of its evil effects." Concentrating on Arnold's later writings in America, Howard Mumford Jones ("Arnold, Aristocracy, and America," *AHR*, 1944; rpt. in *History and the Contemporary*, 1964) also contrasts Arnold's "reactionary views" of the eighties with his views of the sixties. Without any close attention to the complexities of Arnold's thought, Jones truculently hints at "a working interrelation between the Arnoldian doctrine of culture and the Arnoldian belief in racial snobbery and anti-democratic political action." Far more satisfying is William Robbins' "Matthew Arnold and Ireland" (*UTQ*, 1947), a thorough, discriminating treatment of Arnold's other chief political concern of the eighties. He concludes that, despite Arnold's lack of "prophetic insight" regarding the inevitability of Home Rule, his thinking on the Irish question shows "a rare blend of sound diagnosis, practical remedial proposals, and a balanced historical perspective." A study of Arnold's attitudes toward Ireland throughout his entire career might throw light on the larger pattern of his political and social views.

The severity of Arnold's later illiberality is, then, still in dispute. Those who find the eighties the period of Arnold's repressiveness often forget that it was in the Conclusion to *Culture and Anarchy* that Arnold approved (half jokingly, some say) his father's views on throwing rioters from the Tarpeian Rock—a passage suppressed in later editions. Michael Wolff does not forget it, and in "The Uses of Context: Aspects of the 1860's" (*VS*, 1965, Supp.) he judges that Arnold, George Eliot, and Carlyle, like the literary intellectuals in general, "shared a defensive position before the imminent democracy of their time" and "lined up with the swells and the club blusterers." Such views receive some support in George Ford's fascinating study, "The Governor Eyre Case in England" (*UTQ*, 1948), which in passing discusses Arnold's alarm over the Eyre case and Reform agitation. The contradiction between Wolff's view that "For Arnold . . . the real enemy was liberty" and Allott's insistence (*Matthew Arnold*, 1955) that "It is quite wrong to suppose that Arnold had a sneaking weakness for authoritarianism" can only be resolved by much closer studies relating Arnold's political and social views to the larger movement of his thought. A good example of such a study is Martha Salmon Vogeler's "Matthew Arnold and Frederic Harrison: The Prophet of Culture and the Prophet of Positivism" (*SEL*, 1962), which details the similarity of aim and principle linking these apparently dissimilar figures.

Arnold and Education

The older standard work in the field, Sir Joshua Fitch's *Thomas and Matthew Arnold and Their Influence on English Education* (1898), was superseded by W. F. Connell's admirably thorough *The Educational Thought and Influence of Matthew Arnold* (1950). Connell places Arnold in the full context of nineteenth-century English education and educational debate and suggests the range of Arnold's later influence, with here and there a clear recognition of Arnold's limitations. J. Dover Wilson's essay, "Matthew Arnold and the Educationists" (in *The Social and Political Ideas of Some Representative Thinkers of the Victorian Age*, ed. F. J. C. Hearnshaw, 1933), remains valuable for its deft integration of Arnold's educational views into his larger social goals. Alexander Meikeljohn's sympathetic treatment of Arnold (*Education between Two Worlds*, 1942) makes one telling point: "What [Arnold] never clearly saw was that the breakdown of English education was at bottom a proof of the breakdown of the culture which that education was intended to express."

Interest in Arnold's educational thinking in recent years has been more intense than ever before, though the results are not generally distinguished. A strangely proportioned anthology, *Culture and the State: Matthew Arnold and Continental Education* (1966, ed. Paul Nash), stresses Arnold's pioneering role in "comparative education." This and the better edited anthology by Peter Smith and Geoffrey Summerfield, *Matthew Arnold and the Education of the New Order* (1969), provide extracts from Arnold's almost inaccessible and unduly neglected educational reports. G. H. Bantock's provocative essay, "Matthew Arnold, H. M. I." (*Scrutiny*, 1951), praises Arnold over John Dewey, but attributes the small "apparent carry-over between Arnold the inspector and Arnold the social critic" to Arnold's insufficient interest in people and in "the intimacies of daily life." Bantock's less substantial later essay, "Matthew Arnold and Education" (*J. of Educ.*, 1955), praises Arnold for demonstrating the ability of the literary intelligence "to make vital and important discriminations in the educational field." The same Leavisite point of view governs the treatment of Arnold in William Walsh's argument (*The Use of Imagination: Educational Thought and the Literary Mind*, 1960) in favor of "literary criticism" as an essential "discipline for educating the free intelligence." Heinrich Straumann, in "Matthew Arnold and the Continental Idea" (*The English Mind: Studies in the English Moralists Presented to Basil Willey*, ed. H. S. Davies and G. Watson, 1964), claims to find a "fatal dilemma" in Arnold's educational ideal—"charming indolence" as against "hideous efficiency"—which he then rather facilely compares to the theme of the "divided self" in Arnold's poetry. Two essays of 1952, by N. Hans ("English Pioneers of Comparative Education," *Brit. J. of Educ. Stud.*) and B. Pattison (in *Pioneers of English Education*, ed. A. V. Judges), are laudatory without adding to our knowledge. Fred G. Walcott's *The Origins of "Culture and Anarchy"* (1970) has the merit of reminding us of the close relation between Arnold's educational concerns and his social views, but the book sheds little new light on either area.

Arnold and Religion

As early as 1884, Henry James, who himself had enthusiastically absorbed the secular and aesthetic components of Arnold's writings in the sixties, asserted that a concern for "the religious life of humanity" is at the center of Arnold's vision (*Literary Reviews and Essays*, ed. Albert Mordell, 1957). That Matthew Arnold's nature was "essentially religious" was claimed in 1895 by Arnold's editor, G. W. E. Russell. But Russell also claimed that Arnold's once-disputed theology was "now a matter of comparatively little moment." The religiousness has been acknowledged intermittently. Judgments of Arnold's frequently buried theology continue to be widely divergent. The difficulty, first, of describing Arnold's religious position accurately and, second, of assigning him a place in the history of religious speculation is compounded by the discontinuities of modern theological traditions and by the fact that in recent years the issues raised by Arnold are again the subject of vigorous debate.

The generally hostile press reaction to Arnold's religious writings is summarized in a University of Chicago dissertation by Fabian Gudas, "The Debate on Matthew Arnold's Religious Writings" (1952). That this was the response of merely official, institutionalized Christianity, "fixed in anti-modernist positions," while "Victorian England was not 'religious,' taken as a whole," is the provocative argument developed by John Kent in "The Victorian Resistance: Comments on Religious Life and Culture, 1840–80" (*VS*, 1968). Arnold reflected attitudes widespread among "the more questioning laity"; for this reason Arnold is, in Kent's view, not merely the leading spokesman for a new "non-dogmatic or even sceptical Christianity," but "the most significant Anglican theologian of the nineteenth century." It is not strictly true to say that Arnold's theology had no impact on relatively "main-line" Anglican figures. For example, in *William Temple, Archbishop of Canterbury: His Life and Letters*, by F. A. Iremonger (1948), we find the future Archbishop, on the verge of applying for ordination, praising *St. Paul and Protestantism* for its historical account of "freedom in doctrine" as "the lifebreath of the Church of England." More significant is the fact, apparently unknown to students of Arnold, that Pauline scholars found Arnold's development of the notion of spiritual and moral identification with Christ not only a correction of German rationalism but essentially sound in the light of later scholarship. Starting at least as early as the influential commentary on the Epistle to the Romans by Sanday and Headlam (1895), several scripture scholars, including Bishop Gore, praised the freshness and depth of Arnold's religious insight even while deploring his insistence on "experimental" verification. It is not uncommon to find Arnold's handling of the authorship of the Fourth Gospel, in *God and the Bible*, treated as equally original. The paradoxes might deepen further, and light might be shed on the late nineteenth- and early twentieth-century spiritual situation, if someone were to study the number of Anglican clerics and prelates who responded to the melancholy Stoicism of Arnold's early agnostic poetry, even while deploring his later "reconstructed" Christianity.

Less surprising is what Bernard M. G. Reardon calls Arnold's "marked" influence on English liberal and "modernist" theology, though this too can be elusive. Reardon, whose anthology, *Religious Thought in the Nineteenth Century* (1966), contains lengthy extracts from *Literature and Dogma*, also remarks on Arnold's foreshadowing of "trends in philosophical and theological thinking characteristic of our own day." Arnold's friend, Mountstuart E. Grant Duff (in *Out of the Past: Some Biographical Essays*, 1903), predicted in 1890 that Arnold's conviction—that "A Catholic Church transformed is, I believe, the Church of the future"—will "probably be oftener quoted towards the end of the next century than it is likely to be now." Less conjecturally, that Arnold was a major influence on the chief Roman Catholic "Modernist" in England of that period, George Tyrrell, can be gathered (with further documentation) in John Ratté's *Three Modernists: Alfred Loisy, George Tyrrell, William L. Sullivan* (1967). Arnold's influence on Anglican theology is asserted, approvingly, by Alfred Fawkes (*Studies in Modernism*, 1913) and Percy Gardner (*Modernism in the English Church*, 1926). More elaborate in their praise as well as their criticism are Wilfred L. Knox and Alex R. Vidler (*The

Development of Modern Catholicism, 1933) who stress, as Fawkes had, the importance of Mrs. Humphry Ward's *Robert Elsmere* (1888) in the spread of the Arnoldian gospel.

Arnold's influence and reputation as a religious teacher during the first half of the twentieth century, when little close study of his religious thought was attempted, must be pieced together from a myriad of sources. The reputation of Arnold's religious writings in America—a topic neglected by Raleigh and other surveyors of the American scene—seems to have remained high though relatively uncritical. In 1927, Percy H. Houston ("The Modernism of Arnold," *SR*) suggested the current influence of Arnold on American theology, and W. C. Brownell (*Democratic Distinction in America*) judged that the tenets of Arnold's religious thinking "have very largely become the very texture of the religious thinking and feeling of our time." Garrod's more complex experience may well be paradigmatic of those who came to maturity in England around the turn of the century. Garrod explained in 1931 (*Poetry and the Criticism of Life*) that although Arnold's religious writings had been greatly influential on him as a young man, they are "no longer vital." Garrod's personal rejection had come much earlier, as an interesting essay ("The Theology of Matthew Arnold," *Oxford and Cambridge Rev.*, 1909) reveals.

A distinctive line of criticism was adopted by several historians of nineteenth-century rationalism, including A. W. Benn, *The History of Rationalism in the Nineteenth Century* (1906; rpt. 1962); Janet E. Courtney, *Freethinkers of the Nineteenth Century* (1920); and J. M. Robertson in three works: *Modern Humanists* (1891), *Modern Humanists Reconsidered* (1927), and *A History of Freethought in the Nineteenth Century* (1929). Though all three writers show sympathy for Arnold, the strategy of the dogmatic Benn and Robertson is to treat Arnold as "an anomaly incarnate" who commendably undermined dogmatic religion while inconsistently supporting the historic Church. Arnold's "essential inconsistency" has been similarly attacked by the "organismic" naturalist, Herbert J. Muller ("Matthew Arnold: A Parable for Partisans," *SoR*, 1940).

The theistic critics took a similar approach to Arnold's "self-contradictions," merely inverting the judgment by deploring Arnold's attempt to build a "religious" ethic without a metaphysical basis. This equivalence of analysis between conservatives and radicals, with reversal of judgments, has been characteristic of the debate over "liberal" and "modernist" theology since the mid-nineteenth century (see Basil Willey, *More Nineteenth Century Studies*, 1956). F. H. Bradley's stinging analysis of Arnold's confusion of religion and morality, in *Ethical Studies* (1876; 2nd ed., 1927), has been widely influential. Similar in tone is the more extended treatment of Arnold in Robert Shafer's *Christianity and Naturalism* (1926). Though he accepted Stuart Sherman's view that Arnold was "innately and profoundly religious," Shafer, a disciple of P. E. More, cogently states the case for the failure of Arnold's attempt to "construct a naturalistic theory of life" which would somehow preserve a scale of values derived from traditional Christianity. The assault on the "confusion" of Arnold's theology reaches a climax in the writings of T. S. Eliot, who in 1927 called the critique made by Bradley, one of Eliot's own masters of the mind, "final" ("Francis Herbert Bradley," in *Selected Essays*, 1932, 1951). The attack is pressed further in "Arnold and Pater" (1930; also in *Selected Essays*), and in *The Use of Poetry and the Use of Criticism* (1933), where Arnold's religious writings are judged to be "a valiant attempt to dodge the issue, to mediate between Newman and Huxley."

Thus the reaction to Arnold's theology remained strong but generally hostile and polemical, among otherwise divergent critics, up to about 1930. The lengthy summary of Arnold's religious views in W. H. Dawson's *Matthew Arnold and His Relation to the Thought of Our Time* (1904) shows, despite its title, little sense of even the English intellectual tradition behind Arnold. Trilling's more competent treatment in *Matthew Arnold* (1939) is fair but detached to a fault; he does not sufficiently convey the centrality of Arnold's religious concerns. A shift in the critical winds can be detected in the remarks of T. Sturge Moore (*E&S*, 1938), who saw an essential identity in Arnold's and Bradley's views, and insisted that a doctrine of grace, which Eliot had denied to Arnold, was "the essence of Arnold's doctrine." Ahead of its time in its care and insight is Fred A. Dudley's "Matthew Arnold and Science" (*PMLA*, 1942), which by studying a single important term manages to convey both the unity and the movement of Arnold's thought from the sixties through the religious writings into the later formulation of his religious humanism. Broader in scope than its title suggests, the article explores Arnold's attraction toward, and growing fear of, a naturalistic view of life. Closer and more sympathetic study of Arnold's specifically religious writings, reflecting a change in the intellectual weather at large, begins with Basil Willey's *Nineteenth Century Studies: Coleridge to Matthew Arnold* (1949), which firmly identifies the religious writings as "the corner-stone of Arnold's work." Willey argues that his own "liberal Christianity"—the tenets of which can be gathered from *More Nineteenth Century Studies* (1956) and *Christianity Past and Present* (1952)—is an "authentic development" of the religious liberalism of Jowett and Arnold, improved by modern "eschatological" thinking. It is significant that Arnold's religious writings have for some come into favor again in a climate of "existential" and "demythologized" Christianity which nonetheless abjures the label of "agnostic."

A major event in the study of Arnold's religion was the appearance of William Robbins' *The Ethical Idealism of Matthew Arnold: A Study of the Nature and Sources of His Moral and Religious Ideas* (1959). Robbins shows that Arnold's vulnerable position of "relative absolutism" results from a scarcely acknowledged idealistic strain at odds with his conscious but inconsistent "experiential" method. Robbins seems to regret this transcendental bias, remarking that "A generation later [Arnold] might have been content with an 'as if' formulation on a pragmatic basis." But Robbins, despite his own "immanential" point of view, fairly presents the ways in which, at the emotional and imaginative level, Arnold "goes beyond" both Spinoza and Goethe. Though Robbins discusses the early intellectual influences on Arnold, he nevertheless fails to convey the ways in which the religious writings grew out of a developing context in the sixties, and in the process he blurs the distinctions between culture and religion. Above all, by neglecting the evidence of *Note-Books* (1952), Robbins (whose book grew out of a 1942 dissertation) misses the intensely and increasingly "devout" mood that Arnold displays throughout the sixties, and thus misses some of the authenticity and depth of Arnold's religious concerns. Nevertheless, despite the questionableness of Robbins' attempt to see Arnold's religion as simply part of "a thoroughly secular humanism," his book is the indispensable starting point in the study of Arnold's religious writings.

Paschal Reeves's "'Neither Saint Nor Sophist-Led': Matthew Arnold's Christology" (*MissQ*, 1963), by listing all the doctrines of traditional Christology that Arnold rejects or omits, simply recapitulates the kinds of criticism directed against Arnold in his own lifetime by orthodox theologians. J. Gordon Eaker's "Matthew

Arnold's Biblical Criticism" (*Religion in Life*, 1963) consists largely of summary. Far more penetrating than these is Epifanio San Juan's "Matthew Arnold and the Poetics of Unbelief" (*Harvard Theol. Rev.*, 1964). Frankly relying on I. A. Richards' psychologistic and pragmatic reading of Arnold, San Juan does for the religious writings what Richards did for Arnold's view of the "religious" future of poetry. Though objectionable in failing even to pause over the abundant evidence of the "transcendental" leanings in Arnold that Robbins struggles with, San Juan's essay is almost unique in tying the religious writings to Arnold's later literary position. Invoking the methods of Bultmann, and attributing to Arnold a radical subjectivity verging on self-hypnosis, San Juan sees Arnold attempting "a mythical ordering of human experience through poetic coherence": "In essence, religious experience is equivalent to the poetic experience of equipoise, of psychic harmony." San Juan's reading is compatible with William Madden's more hostile approach (*Matthew Arnold*, 1967) to Arnold's later critical position.

Quite different in point of view is the stimulating chapter on Arnold in A. O. J. Cockshut's *The Unbelievers: English Agnostic Thought, 1840–1890* (1964). Cockshut sympathetically separates Arnold from the high-minded Victorian agnostics by reason of his deep feeling for "the psychological impact of the Christian idea of death and resurrection." Cockshut judges that "Arnold's system really was religious" though not in the historical sense Christian, and finds a "semi-mystical moral vision" to be fundamental in Arnold. Cockshut subtly distinguishes Arnold from the Protestant liberalizers who sought to clear away "the accretions of custom and habit" in order to find "the fundamental truths about God and the human soul"; Arnold is, rather, akin to the later Catholic Modernists, who accepted the whole Christian system but gave it a "symbolic" interpretation.

Recent book-length studies have in general failed to see the importance of Arnold's quest in the forties for a "religious" alternative to Christianity, revealed in the reading lists of 1845–47 and David Osborne's dissertation. Such evidence, which throws light on important poems in Arnold's first three volumes, should eventually invalidate or seriously complicate the industrious attempts to read Arnold as a "Stoic" thinker up into the sixties and beyond. Albert J. Lubell, in "Matthew Arnold: Between Two Worlds" (*MLQ*, 1961), cursorily reads the 1845–47 notebooks as a mixture of "Lucretian naturalism" and "Platonic" idealism, but the reconsideration of Arnold's "religiousness" up to, say, 1863 can scarcely be said to have begun.

As for the specifically religious writings, the relatively few special studies have been hampered by the lack, until recently, of adequate categories for describing Arnold's theology and his place in the theological tradition. The "native" sources are especially significant. Arnold's complex relations with Newman and Carlyle are dealt with above, under Major Formative Influences, but no one seems to have speculated on Arnold's possible indebtedness to the specifically religious component of Carlyle's thought. Studies in the Anglican tradition of the type of David Ranald Steven's dissertation, "Matthew Arnold and Some Anglican Divines: The Influence on Arnold of John Smith, Thomas Wilson, and Joseph Butler" (Texas 1954), are especially welcome. Stevens convincingly qualifies John Hicks's claims for Arnold's "Stoicism" by showing, through Arnold's affinity to the Cambridge Platonists and Bishop Butler, the seriousness of Arnold's quest for "joy" and expansiveness. An intensive study of Arnold's use of other Anglican theologians—including Hooker, the Cambridge Platonists besides Smith, and such Restoration divines as Isaac

Barrow—might further illuminate the tone and intention of Arnold's religious thought. Though he indicts Arnold for "hazy thinking" on the role of "happiness" in religion and shows how much Arnold misrepresents Butler, William Blackburn ("Bishop Butler and the Design of Arnold's Literature and Dogma," *PQ*, 1948) concludes that the two "pragmatic" moralists "are not so far apart as it at first appears." Arnold's reactions to the Oxford Movement and Ritualism, as well as to Newman and the Roman Catholic Church, can be gathered from DeLaura's *Hebrew and Hellene* (1969).

Arnold's relations to "liberal" English theology of the nineteenth century have been studied fairly closely in recent years. Two essays on Coleridge—Huw Parry Owen's "The Theology of Coleridge" (*CritQ*, 1962) and Graham Hough's "Coleridge and the Victorians" (in *The English Mind*, 1964)—make strikingly similar points: Coleridge and Arnold are alike in their approach to Scripture and in their attempt to ground religion on ethical experience, but Arnold's approach represents a dangerous narrowing of the religious perspective. But neither writer attempts the much needed direct study of Coleridge, as "source" and adversary, in Arnold's religious thought. William Blackburn ("Matthew Arnold and the Oriel Noetics," *PQ*, 1946) ably suggests a background for Arnold's distinction between the symbolic language of Scripture and the explicative language of dogma in two Oxford liberals, Richard Whately and R. D. Hampden.

The most important of the Noetics for Arnold was obviously his father, but their relationship has not been closely studied until recent years. The topic was ably opened by Merton A. Christensen ("Thomas Arnold's Debt to German Theologians: A Prelude to Matthew Arnold's *Literature and Dogma*," *MP*, 1957), who placed Thomas Arnold as a follower of those "mediating" German Biblical critics who, relying on Spinoza, "attempted to syncretize, along Kantian lines, the 'barren learning' of the rationalistic critics . . . and the fervor of the less informed Pietists." But Christensen's claim that *Literature and Dogma* is "an extension and elaboration" of this attempt to separate the "spiritual truth" from its temporal expression remained undeveloped. The challenge was accepted by Eugene L. Williamson, in *The Liberalism of Thomas Arnold: A Study of His Religious and Political Writings* (1964), which incorporated his article "Significant Points of Comparison between the Biblical Criticism of Thomas and Matthew Arnold" (*PMLA*, 1961) and added similarities on their conceptions of the role of Church and State. John O. Waller, in "Matthew and Thomas Arnold: Soteriology" (*Anglican Theol. Rev.*, 1962), had also pointed out similarities in the two men, especially their minimizing of dogma, their view of life as a moral struggle, and their stress on "the psychological power of man's affection for Christ" as a mechanism for the moral life. But Waller had implicitly rebuked the essentially uncritical approach of Williamson and even Christensen by firmly noting that Thomas Arnold, however liberal in Biblical interpretation, was an orthodox believing Christian as the modernist Matthew Arnold was not. On the other hand, Waller's own methodology, here and in his article on "Rugby Chapel" (*SEL*, 1969), is open to a serious question that also applies in part to Williamson's work: the rather generalized points of "spiritual" affinity (as opposed to methods of Biblical interpretation) adduced by Waller are in fact not distinctively Thomas Arnold's, but verge on being commonplaces of orthodox piety that Matthew residually accepted but could have absorbed from many sources.

Fundamental category mistakes continue, then, to plague our precise apprehension of Arnold's theological stance and his place in the "liberal" Anglican tradition. A good example is Eugene Williamson's extended petitio principii in "Matthew Arnold and the Archbishops" (*MLQ*, 1963), which, on insubstantial grounds, claims to detect a "surprising degree of consonance between some phases of [Arnold's] thought" and that of four Archbishops Arnold knew, and judges this to be "further evidence of Anglican liberalism in high places between 1850 and 1900." The word "liberalism" achieves the widest imaginable extension in the conclusion that in the primacy of Frederick Temple, "and to some degree that of William Temple, his son, can be seen the triumph of Anglican liberalism in the Church of England"—where a liberal orthodoxy belonging properly to the father (Thomas Arnold) is simply thrust by implication on his unorthodox son. A three-part exchange between K. Allott and Williamson (*VS*, 1960) will stand as a model of the skillful and the unskillful use of "sources" in such hazardous theological waters. Williamson challenged Allott's claim (*VS*, 1959) that by 1841 Matthew Arnold had gone beyond his father's liberalism, and argued, on the basis of specific parallels in theme, that Matthew's liberal views "echoed . . . exactly" his father's. In his reply, Allott notes that, despite Matthew's becoming "papa's continuator" in the sixties, he had moved outside orthodoxy permanently by the time of his arrival at Oxford. Without such fundamental distinctions, mere verbal parallels, such as the one proffered in Williamson's "Matthew Arnold's 'Eternal Not Ourselves . . .'" (*MLN*, 1960), cannot hope to illuminate Arnold's theology.

The significance of Arnold's religious thought can only be understood in a larger European context—through comparison with such figures as Schleiermacher, Ritschl, and Harnack, and with later figures like Bultmann. One of the few such attempts by a competent historian is to be found in Clement C. J. Webb's *A Century of Anglican Theology* (1923). Webb deftly aligns Arnold with Kant in his subordination of religion to morality, but notes that Kant would deny to religion the function of arousing "an emotion which Morality, apart from Religion, would not evoke." Flavia M. Alaya's perceptive study, "Arnold and Renan on the Popular Uses of History" (*JHI*, 1967), suggests similarities of method, while making firm distinctions regarding viewpoint and temperament. An interesting comparison might be made between the religious throught of Arnold and that of such neo-idealists as T. H. Green and Edward Caird—especially since Green was an important influence on Arnold's niece, Mrs. Humphry Ward.

Surprisingly little has been done with the text and the context of Arnold's religious writings, comparable to the work of Coulling on Arnold's earlier prose. William Blackburn, in "The Background of Arnold's *Literature and Dogma*" (*MP*, 1945), usefully relates Arnold's book to three controversies of the early seventies, but with the illegitimate running implication that these were sufficient causes of *Literature and Dogma*, rather than incitements or occasions. Valuable information can be gleaned from three careful articles by Francis G. Townsend: "The Third Instalment of Arnold's *Literature and Dogma*" (*MP*, 1953); "A Neglected Edition of Arnold's *St. Paul and Protestantism*" (*RES*, 1954); and "*Literature and Dogma*: Matthew Arnold's Letters to George Smith" (*PQ*, 1956).

In recent years, Arnold's religious thought, while by no means uncontroversial or always adequately apprehended, is increasingly conceded an importance even when challenged. The validity of Arnold's undogmatic Christianity as a basis for Church unity is argued by H. S. Shelton ("Matthew Arnold and the Modern Church," *HJ*, 1946). William Barrett seeks to complicate Arnold's conception of both Hebraism and Hellenism in the "existential" perspective of his once widely read *Irrational Man* (1958). In *Jerusalem and Albion: The Hebraic Factor in Seventeenth-Century Literature* (1964), Harold Fisch, while criticizing Arnold's confusion of Puritanism with the Hebraic tradition and his excessive detachment from social action, enthusiastically praises Arnold's occasional "revolutionary messianic ardor" for the transformation of society and finds the temper of his Biblical criticism to be close to that of Milton and the Cambridge Platonists.

The seriousness of the approach taken by four recent writers testifies to the enhanced status of Arnold's religious thought. R. B. Braithwaite (*An Empiricist's View of the Nature of Religious Belief*, 1955) explains why Arnold's "keen insight into the imaginative and poetic element in religious belief" made him "a profound philosopher of religion." Calling herself a "modern religious Humanist" in contradistinction to "scientific, naturalistic, anthropological and sociological Humanists," Dorothea Krook, in *Three Traditions of Moral Thought* (1959), treats Arnold as "one of the great prophetic voices of the last age." J. M. Newton, in his insistently paradoxical treatment of Arnold as a "tragic failure" ("Some Notes on Religion, Irreligion and Matthew Arnold," *CQ*, 1969), finds that in the very act of attacking "the crippling Victorian habit of cant" Arnold "was himself another crippled-canting Victorian." Still, he finds Arnold's position a "fundamentally religious" one, and his view of poetry and dogma "very sound." Finally, Arnold's religious thought is illuminated by the lucid account given by Renford Bambrough (*Reason, Truth, and God*, 1969) of Arnold's place in the modern philosophical debate over the contrast between linguistic form and logical content. Though aware of the limitations of Arnold's religious thought, Bambrough sympathetically stresses the "objectively existing power" in Arnold's "Eternal, not ourselves" as well as in his view of literature as "a source and a respository of a moral knowledge and understanding that is found and not fashioned."

Despite the high quality of some of the recent commentary on Arnold's religious thought, fundamental questions have received no generally accepted answers. The questions are as complex as those of "modernist" theology in general; in Arnold's case the answers are further complicated by the multitudinous diversity in the critics' points of view. Perhaps most basically, the metaphysical status of Arnold's "Eternal, not ourselves" resists definition. Earlier critics tended to view Arnold's religion as a devout Stoicism and Agnosticism (F. W. H. Myers, *FortR*, May 1888) or a diluted Positivism (W. H. Dawson)—or a restored Paganism, a State Ritualism without theology (Chesterton, *The Victorian Age in Literature*, 1913). Others, especially more recent readers, tend to find, whether reluctantly (Robbins, Benn) or approvingly (Bambrough), elements of an "ethical" but objective theism in the religious writings. But San Juan reads Arnold's religion as a radically *subjective* "mythic" adjustment of impulses. Most would now agree that Arnold, though genuinely religious, is not Christian in the historical sense because of his "spiritual" treatment of dogma. But does he belong with those antinaturalistic "religious" Humanists who view Christ's gospel as uniquely authoritative (Krook)? Or is he, finally, a Protestant liberalizer (Williamson) or, alternatively, a Catholic modernist possessed of "a semi-mystical moral vision" (Cockshut)? The categories could be multiplied.

The other, related question is that of the relationship of Arnold's Culture of the sixties to his Religion of the seventies—or more particularly, the relationship of *Culture and Anarchy* to *Literature and Dogma*. The virtual identification of religion and culture in Arnold was fixed at least by the time of W. H. Mallock's witty

presentation of "Mr. Luke" in the *New Republic* (1877), and is repeated incau
tiously by the book's modern editor, J. Max Patrick (1950). Scarcely less shaded is
Robert Shafer's assertion that Culture is "Arnold's substitute for traditional Christianity" (*Christianity and Naturalism*, 1926). Eliot's widely influential formulation
—"literature, or Culture, tended with Arnold to usurp the place of Religion" ("Arnold and Pater," 1930)—closely follows Shafer's view. Even the more sympathetic
Basil Willey (*Nineteenth Century Studies*) holds not only (following *Culture and
Anarchy*) that Culture comes to *include* religion, but also, and more enigmatically,
that religion is "the highest form of culture and poetry" or "culture in its most
exalted mood." William Robbins (*The Ethical Idealism of Matthew Arnold*) not
only finds religion "an integral part of culture," but calls the religious writings "a
deepening and modification of his crusade for culture, not a retreat from Greece to
Israel." DeLaura (*Hebrew and Hellene in Victorian England*) also reads *Literature
and Dogma* as a strengthening and deepening of the ethical component of Arnold's
holistic Culture. But he finds that despite Arnold's continued assertion of the "close
relations" of religion and culture, religion emerges as a distinct area of experience
and is assigned a certain paramountcy of value, as Arnold seeks to save man's
religious consciousness not only from scientific naturalism but precisely from the
new aestheticism of the period. The problem appears in a new form in Arnold's
famous prediction of 1880, that "most of what now passes with us for religion and
philosophy will be replaced by poetry." As noted above, William Madden reads this
as the elevation of aesthetic experience to the place traditionally claimed by religious worship, Vincent Buckley presents a more moderate version of the same view,
while George Watson denies that any such confusion was intended.

Such incompatible readings will persist until Arnold's motives are clarified by
closer attention to the crucial texts and to their controversial matrix. A model is
provided by Coulling, in his essay on *Culture and Anarchy* (*SP*, 1963), where he
identifies the attacks by Sidgwick and Greg as sources of, respectively, the "Hebraism and Hellenism" chapter and the first installments of *Saint Paul and Protestantism*. The convergence of such careful studies might allow us better to judge the
intriguing view of Knoepflmacher (*Religious Humanism and the Victorian Novel*)
that Arnold and George Eliot are alike in finally identifying religion and culture,
and that they move to a common position "in their belief in a moral tradition which
could embody an authoritative 'power not ourselves.'" Our present categories do
not easily allow us to express the ways in which, for other readers, Arnold's effort
does in fact encompass areas of thought and feeling sealed off to George Eliot, even
in *Daniel Deronda*.

WALTER PATER

·

Lawrence Evans

Walter Pater is the most subjective of standard Victorian prose writers, the most elusive, and the least secure in the estimation of posterity. He is also without a doubt the most inadequately served by biographers, scholars, and critics; and his image, to the extent that it survives at all in the popular imagination, still resembles that of Mr. Rose, Mallock's languid, leering progenitor of the more provocative divagations of the nineties. But in professional circles, at any rate, Pater's stock is rising. After decades of eclipse, most neatly epitomized by T. S. Eliot's well-known disparagement of Pater, his achievement, and his influence in "Arnold and Pater" (*Bookman*, 1930; rpt. in *Selected Essays*, 1932), the last twelve years have seen a vigorous revival of scholarly and critical interest in him, a revival that may be taken to imply a marked upward revaluation of his work. In this period, Pater has been the subject of six books, and has received substantial attention in five others, while scholarly articles have appeared in profusion. Between 1961 and 1970 twenty-two doctoral dissertations on Pater were completed, nearly twice as many as had been written in the previous six decades combined. Thus, while in 1948 Sir Herbert Read had reason to feel that "no English writer of the nineteenth century stands so much in need of rehabilitation as Walter Pater," today nearly every commentator notes a sustained upsurge of attention, and the bibliography grows and grows.

As later sections of this essay will suggest, however, this "revival" has not been an altogether unmixed blessing for those who value scholarly thoroughness and critical rigor. Far too much recent work on Pater has accepted without question outright misinformation; and far too little has been done to establish fundamental matters of fact—of text, canon, and chronology. More important yet is the failure of many recent writers to bring to bear on Pater's works the kind of rigorous critical discrimination that others have shown in treating Carlyle, Mill, Ruskin, and Arnold. If Pater's most conspicuous detractors from W. H. Mallock to Paul Elmer More to T. S. Eliot have been more often wrong than right, they have nonetheless made some charges that ring true: Pater can be embarrassingly elitist, "precious," and self-indulgent; his prose too easily becomes mannered and obscure; his writings are marked by inconsistencies and evasions not all of which can be excused by ascribing them to his tolerant "humanist" virtues. To accept his works too readily on their own terms, to interpret them only in Pater's own categories will probably produce mere "appreciations," however couched in high-powered contemporary critical jargon and however fully footnoted. To see the object as in itself it really is will require, in the case of Pater, an informed, tough-minded, contextually conscious approach that is yet sensitive and humane. Only so will he be seen in his due place, historically and critically. Only such scholarship and criticism can rightly recognize and make accessible to others the remarkable scope, the often luminous lyricism, the subtlety, wisdom, and pathos of the most important and influential British writer of that so inadequately charted twilight zone between Victorian and Modern.

I. BIBLIOGRAPHY, MANUSCRIPTS, EDITIONS

Before 1960, Pater bibliography was a virtually uncharted wasteland. Pater's friend and editor Charles L. Shadwell offered the public the first author bibliography, with a brief, inaccurate, and decidedly incomplete list of Pater's published works prefaced to the posthumous volume he entitled *Miscellaneous Studies* (1895). (This list has been reprinted in all subsequent editions of *Miscellaneous Studies*. In "Pater's *Appreciations*: A Bibliographical Note," *MLN*, 1950, Edward Killoran Brown made three useful corrections, all of which are incorporated by d'Hangest.) Drawing on Shadwell's account, Thomas Wright provided at the end of the second volume of his *Life of Walter Pater* (1907) a more extensive, but even less reliable, list, including a number of poems from Pater's juvenilia. In *Bibliographies of Modern Authors*, Second Series (1925), Charles A. and H. Winthrop Stonehill gave sound bibliographical descriptions of first English editions and the first (1900–01) collected edition of Pater's *Works*, but ignored uncollected writings and made frequent errors in reference to items first published in periodicals.

With the publication in 1961 of Germain d'Hangest's *Walter Pater: L'Homme et l'œuvre* appeared the first really useful bibliography, both of Pater's own writings and of critical and scholarly studies about him. The bibliographical appendix to his second volume furnishes an admirable and on the whole accurate compendium of all previous bibliographical information, and in addition takes account of some unpublished writings, most importantly Chapters viii to xiii of *Gaston de Latour*. He notes where appropriate the original periodical publication of essays and portraits, and provides also some description of significant textual variations. His work is not, however, exhaustive, even as author bibliography alone: d'Hangest is unconcerned with American editions and with reprintings of the New Library Edition of 1910. His lengthy bibliography of critical and scholarly materials should be supplemented by reference to Ian Fletcher's review of his book (*RES*, 1963), where additional titles and citations are given. For a less extensive but nonetheless helpful bibliography, John Sparrow's contribution to *New Cambridge Bibliography of English Literature*, iii (1969, ed. George Watson) should be consulted.

The most thoroughgoing bibliographical work on Pater is yet unpublished. The manuscript "Walter Pater: A Discursive Bibliography" by Samuel Wright of Bures, Suffolk includes what is for the present a definitive list of all Pater's known writings along with a full bibliography of books, essays, articles, etc. dealing with Pater. Wright provides a chronological list of all published works, followed by an account of presumably "lost" items, unpublished works, and juvenilia. (Wright mentions 5 published but hitherto unacknowledged pieces, all book reviews, that appeared between 1872 and 1887. Two of these items are cited by Lawrence Evans in the notes to *Letters of Walter Pater*, 1970.) This list is followed in turn by another of periodical publications arranged by periodicals in alphabetical order; then a list of books in order of publication, adding collected and selected writings; and finally special notes on those essays published under varying titles. Although this arrangement entails considerable duplication, the plan is particularly useful to the student. Wright's bibliography is professedly "discursive," including some items of mainly anecdotal interest (interviews with persons who knew Pater, tributes and obituary notices, etc.). It is such discursiveness that has apparently stood in the way of publication so far; but the core of this valuable work ought to be made available promptly.

Relatively few manuscripts of Pater's published works have survived; but even those that are accessible have not received due notice. The earliest known manuscript is that of "Diaphaneitè" (1864), at the King's School, Canterbury. The manuscript of "Measure for Measure" (1874) at the Folger Shakespeare Library offers some insight into Pater's intensely personal involvement in his subject and into his efforts to discipline the more lyrical impulses of his prose. D'Hangest calls attention to the manuscript (lecture) version of "Demeter and Persephone" (1875) in the private collection of John Sparrow and quotes some tantalizingly brief extracts that differ in tone from the collected version of the essay, though he does not consider the intermediate and first published text in the *Fortnightly Review* (1876). Manuscripts from the eighties are somewhat more plentiful: "Samuel Taylor Coleridge" (1880), from the first edition of Ward's *English Poets*, at Harvard; "Dante Gabriel Rossetti" (1883), from the second edition of Ward's anthology, in the private collection of Gordon N. Ray; "Sir Thomas Browne" (1886), in the same collection; and Chapters i to v (1888) and vii (1889) of *Gaston de Latour*, in the Berg Collection of the New York Public Library. The Bodleian Library has the manuscript of Pater's last known essay, "Pascal" (1894), a manuscript that should be used, as d'Hangest has seen, to correct errors in the texts printed by Edmund Gosse (*ConR*, 1894) and Shadwell (*Miscellaneous Studies*). At least as late as 1931 the manuscript of "An English Poet" (1878?) was in the hands of May Ottley, when she published the text (part of her inheritance from Hester Pater) in the *Fortnightly Review*. Since Mrs. Ottley's death, however, this item has apparently vanished.

A significant body of unpublished manuscript material remains in two principal collections. John Sparrow has most of Chapters viii to xiii of *Gaston de Latour* (additional pages in the Harvard collection help to fill out Chs. viii & xii); a general description and a suggestive reading of these pages are given by d'Hangest. In 1961 Harvard University acquired the largest known body of Pater manuscripts—all unpublished, and most of them from the last decade of Pater's life. All the items are unfinished, in various stages of composition: some are mere notes, others are nearly complete, in particular two lectures on philosophy and what appears to be another lecture entitled "The Aesthetic Life." There are also portions of two imaginary portraits, "Tibalt the Albigense" and "Gaudioso, the Second," of which a short account is given by Gerald C. Monsman in *Pater's Portraits* (1967). Essays in the Harvard collection treat a wide variety of Pater's interests: Dante, Hobbes, Newman; the history of English literature, especially Chaucer and Shakespeare; Plato, the Parthenon, evil in Greek art; the churches of Troyes; art and religion. Probably the earliest of the manuscript essays is a piece entitled "Arezzo" (1872?), which may have been originally intended to stand between the essays on Luca della Robbia and Michelangelo in *Studies in the History of the Renaissance* (1873). This manuscript, at first titled "Prelude to Michelangelo," is in the hand of one of the Pater sisters, with revisions by Pater himself. Finally, a substantial number of pages comprise exercises in translation, chiefly from Plato and various nineteenth-century French authors.

Many commentators have observed with regret that there is no satisfactory edition of Pater's works. In the absence of such an edition, the ten-volume Macmillan New Library Edition of 1910, variously reprinted, has served as the usual source of scholarly reference. It has recently been reissued in England by Blackwell and in the United States by Johnson Reprint. This edition is not critical, not complete, and—in some cases—not accurate. Twelve short pieces, all but one of them book reviews, omitted both from the New Library Edition and from its predecessor, the *Works* (1900–01), are gathered in *Uncollected Essays* (1903); and six of these, with the 1889 text of "Aesthetic Poetry" and portions of the 1866 essay on Coleridge, were collected in *Sketches and Reviews* (1919). Both these American volumes are out of print and difficult of access. The full 1866 *Westminster Review* text of "Coleridge's Writings," however, can be found in the World's Classics collection of *English Critical Essays of the Nineteenth Century* (ed. Edmund D. Jones, 1916; rpt. 1922). Also missing from the New Library Edition are "An English Poet" and the five short review articles noted by Samuel Wright; and, of course, the unpublished literary remains. For this edition, the volumes published before Pater's death seem to have received at best slight editorial supervision; they normally but not consistently reprint the latest texts published in his lifetime. *Essays from "The Guardian"* was edited by Gosse, and the other three volumes (*Greek Studies, Miscellaneous Studies, Gaston de Latour*) were prepared for the press by Shadwell. A study of Shadwell's editorial malpractice is clearly called for. It could be shown, for instance, that he not only ignores but even denies the existence of revisions made by Pater in 1892 in "The Bacchanals of Euripides" when this essay was printed as part of the introduction to Robert Yelverton Tyrrell's edition of the *Bacchae*. Quite without such a study, however, it is plain that a new critical edition of Pater's works, indicating sources and variant readings, deserves a high priority in the next decade.

Some work has already been done that might contribute greatly to the success of any comprehensive editorial project. The earliest is Bruce E. Vardon's dissertation, "Variant Readings in Walter Pater's *Studies in the History of the Renaissance*" (Chicago 1950). Vardon's thesis provides a well-annotated critical edition of Pater's first book, with both textual and explanatory notes. The groundwork for a critical edition of *Marius* has been laid by Roland G. Frean in his unpublished dissertation, "Walter Pater's *Marius the Epicurean*: Notes and Commentary Preliminary to a Critical Edition" (Toronto 1961). Frean's annotations are explanatory, not textual; only in a few particularly striking instances does he discuss variant readings. But his copious explanatory notes identify passages in *Marius* that appear in quotation marks or in italics, and provide an extensive account of Pater's sources—an achievement especially valuable with a text whose "ponderous allusiveness" Frean demonstrates so well. In his annotations Frean also provides extensive cross-references to other of Pater's works, thereby throwing much light on persistent themes and preoccupations throughout the Pater canon. He incorporates, corrects, and goes far beyond the annotations supplied by Anne K. Tuell and Joseph Sagmaster in their earlier editions (1926 and 1935) of *Marius*. Textual revisions in *Marius* are of considerable interest and importance; and a good discussion and description of them can be found in Edmund Chandler's *Pater on Style: An Examination of the Essay on "Style" and the Textual History of* Marius the Epicurean (1958).

Inexpensive reprints of Pater's works are few in number; and none has any particular textual authority. But at least two paperback editions deserve some notice here. Kenneth Clark's edition of *The Renaissance* (1961; rpt. 1969) contains an impressive introduction, some valuable notes, and (in its 1961 form) some striking illustrations. It also uniquely reprints Pater's essay on "Raphael" (1892) from *Miscellaneous Studies*. A handsome paperback collection of *Imaginary Portraits* (1964), including all the published shorter fiction except "Hippolytus Veiled," was prepared by Eugene J. Brzenk; but unhappily this edition is no longer in print. A reprint of Brzenk's collection along with an inexpensive wide-ranging selection of some of Pater's most effective essays would be useful to college and university students—not to mention scholars—and might help to liberate everyone from the routine selections that have become all but inevitable in anthologies.

II. BIOGRAPHY AND LETTERS

In a letter written not long after Pater's death, Henry James seems more than half to envy "the most exquisite literary fortune" of "faint, pale, embarrassed, exquisite Pater." "He is the mask without the face, and there isn't in his total superficies a tiny point of vantage for the newspaper to flap his wings on." Pater's biographers have made it only too easy, regrettably, to agree with James; and by a curious irony the most *personal* of Victorian prose writers is also the least known and the most inaccurately reported. It might be tempting at this late date to give up as a lost cause, as some writers have already done, the hope of any detailed biographical investigation, were it not that scholarship and criticism seem to require certain facts from the biographer. Much misinformation has been passed from book to book, article to article, because so little has been done to set the record straight. Likewise there are all too many information gaps, particularly in respect to the chronology and intention of Pater's writings, gaps that provoke desperate speculation. Working in an information vacuum, d'Hangest, U. C. Knoepflmacher, and Monsman assume, for example, that *Marius* was begun in 1878 or 1879, even though Pater himself dated his work 1881–84. Resort to the records of his reading at the Brasenose College Library, however, will show that Pater began research for *Marius* in the spring of 1881. This is a single but characteristic instance that should suggest how much more use must be made of these and other unpublished biographical records in future Pater studies.

The root of all—or, rather, most—biographical evils is Thomas Wright's *Life of Walter Pater* (2 vols., 1907). When denied the cooperation of Pater's sisters,

Hester and Clara (who also forbade him to quote from unpublished letters), Wright relentlessly pursued a flock of cousins, associates, and acquaintances, from whose testimonies he compiled his gossipy and trivializing account of Pater's life. Wright seems to have been incapable of evaluating his data and assessing the bias of his sources. As a result, even when his information may be basically correct, the context is often distorted: as one writer has said, he "touched nothing that he did not confuse." Yet in spite of its manifest shortcomings Wright's first volume is the fullest and almost the only source of material concerning Pater's early life; and it also makes some oblique use of a number of early letters now apparently lost. Wright's second volume, however, is an unabashed travesty, dominated by the pathological figure of one Richard C. Jackson, who claimed to have been Pater's closest friend from 1877 on. No one has yet tested Jackson's assertions against the ascertainable facts (though d'Hangest has shown that much of what Jackson passed off as Pater's private conversation consists of phrases culled from the published works); and there is evidence to suggest that Jackson and Pater were never intimate —indeed, may never have met. A careful study of this matter might purge Pater studies of a major legacy of misinformation.

The biographical and critical studies by Ferris Greenslet (1903) and Edward Thomas (1913) are slight and unhelpful; but Arthur Christopher Benson's *Walter Pater* (1906), in the English Men of Letters series, draws on important sources and can almost be taken as an "official" biography. Encouraged by Pater's sisters, Benson won access to most of his subject's surviving literary and academic friends, whose recollections and insights help to document Pater's personal and artistic development from his mid-twenties on. Benson's own understanding of Pater, however, is disappointing. Ever the genteel Edwardian "man of letters," he prefers surface to substance, and repeatedly draws back where candor and psychological insight are needed most. Benson's study is a minor monument of suppression and evasion, as Wright's is of tastelessness and triviality.

The most ample treatment of Pater's life and personality appears in Germain d'Hangest's massive *Walter Pater: L'Homme et l'œuvre* (2 vols., 1961). In this book (to be considered in the next section also as a general critical study), the author has drawn upon numerous sources untouched by and/or unavailable to Wright and Benson. To his material d'Hangest brings considerable intuitive sympathy for his subject; and he is notably not afraid to acknowledge the obvious traces of homosexual feeling in Pater's life and works. But although sensitive to Pater's personality, d'Hangest seems unequipped or unwilling to ask enough of the right questions. He abstracts Pater from his material, social, and cultural environment; and instead of rigorously pursuing the insights he nearly attains, d'Hangest tends to obscure his subject in folds of effusive, "appreciative" rhetoric.

The reader who has slashed his way through the lush undergrowth of d'Hangest's prose can find further useful information concerning Pater's life and character in Lawrence Evans' edition of the *Letters of Walter Pater* (1970). Pater's letters are scarcely notable as literary products; he is certainly the least prolific and probably the dullest correspondent of any major figure treated in this volume. Still, it is curious to find no earlier scholarship on Pater's letters than Evans' preliminary compilation, "Some Letters of Walter Pater" (Diss. Harvard 1961). Though a few letters had been printed in biographies, memoirs, and miscellaneous works, until 1969 there were no articles furnishing checklists and none in which single letters or small collections were published. The first and so far the only article dealing with the correspondence is Warren Herendeen's "Three Unpublished Letters of Walter Pater" (*RES*, 1969). All three of these items are printed in *Letters*. This collection of close to 300 letters gives, at least for the last decade of his life, a clearer picture of Pater's day-to-day existence, and from time to time affords brief glimpses of an anxiety-ridden personality seeking in disengagement and decorum some refuge from the barely tolerable harassments of life. Most valuably, perhaps, the letters, along with the editor's short introduction and annotations, shed new light on Pater's literary career, on his plans and intentions as a writer. Further letters obviously remain to be traced; and if the current revival of interest in Pater continues, the next decade may witness the discovery and publication of some letters as useful as the best printed so far.

Letters confirms the traditional opinion that Pater's life was, by contrast with the careers of other major Victorian prose writers who were engaged in more public controversy, singularly "uneventful"; and the relatively sheltered quality of his life hardly seems to invite traditional full-dress biography. Any would-be biographer begins also with a special handicap in the almost total absence of information about Pater's family and his life before the age of twenty-five. But whatever the obstacles, an interpretive "portrait" at least, an informed reading of the personality half revealed and half concealed in the writings and in the outward pattern of his life, is a prime requisite in Pater studies. The growth of an identity—or perhaps, more accurately, the imperfect quest for an identity—should be studied in its historical context, both cultural and material. The peculiar configurations of perception and response that have been felt for years beg for analysis and interpretation; and to this interpretation psychoanalytic theory, resourcefully and wisely handled, as in the work of Erik H. Erikson, has much to offer. Such study need not be reductionist or debunking; it could organize into a persuasive synthesis some of the real insights that earlier commentators have attained; and it would seem that the time is now ripe for an effort of this sort.

One useful preliminary to a new biography, though it is also a project worthwhile in its own right, would be a thorough Pater chronology (perhaps as a dissertation) along the lines of Mark L. Reed's admirable work on Wordsworth. A good beginning can be made with the *Letters*, but beyond the correspondence there is still a large body of almost unexplored material to document Pater's activities and movements, especially as these bear upon the conception, composition, publication, and revision of his works. No study has been made of Pater's reading (and there are records at three Oxford libraries he used) or of his lectures to undergraduates. Hardly anyone has explored the abundance of allusions to Pater in the (for the most part unpublished) diaries and letters of his friends; yet the papers of Lionel Johnson, Vernon Lee, and Arthur Symons in particular have much to say about his life and literary career after 1880.

A number of particular episodes and elements in Pater's life invite special study. In two recent articles, "Old Mortality at Oxford" (*SP*, 1970) and "Pater, Hopkins, and Fichte's Ideal Student" (*SAQ*, 1971), Gerald C. Monsman provides fresh material concerning Pater's participation during the sixties in an important Oxford essay society, the Old Mortality, and illustrating the early notoriety that Pater attained in conservative Anglican circles there. Some of Pater's principal defeats in Oxford have already been briefly chronicled, that is, his nonelection to the University proctorship in 1874 and his failure to gain first the Professorship of Poetry in 1877 and later the Slade Professorship of Fine Art in 1885. But the full stories have never been told; and very little has been done to document the hostility and opposition Pater faced in Oxford, both within his own College and throughout the University community generally. The name most often heard in accounts of Pater's enemies at Oxford is that of the Master of Balliol, Benjamin Jowett; yet in spite of the pages devoted to Jowett's relations with Pater by the late Sir Geoffrey Faber in his *Jowett: A Portrait with Background* (1958) the matter is far from clear. Faber is both biased (he writes in rebuttal of Benson's hostile account of Jowett) and inadequately informed; and neither he nor anyone else makes mention of Jowett's intemperate marginalia in his copy of *Studies in the History of the Renaissance*.

A study is also needed of Pater's attempt from 1885 to 1893 to live the life of a London "man of letters." The dissipation of already scarce productive energies in extensive book reviewing and social life is a hallmark of this period: why Pater tried this experiment and why he at last gave it up ought to be investigated. Both in Oxford and London, furthermore, Pater was subject to distinct economic pressures; yet the economy of the Pater household, especially as it bears upon the nature and volume of his published work, has had almost no attention. The pattern of his friendships belongs to the general biographer; yet around one particular relationship so much confusion and misinformation and innuendo have gathered that the record must, if possible, be set straight. The course of Pater's friendship with Oscar Wilde, from the early years of Wilde's undergraduate adulation to the marked mutual coolness of the early nineties, should be charted and its implications pursued. A number of biographical essays of the sort suggested here should have, like the longer works here proposed, a bracing impact on the state of Pater studies generally.

III. GENERAL STUDIES

Works treated in this section, ranging from very brief articles to substantial books, are included here because they all profess to deal with the whole of Pater's literary work, instead of focusing primarily upon his career as a critic, or his stories, or his style, sources, influence, etc. Because these distinctions are inevitably to some extent arbitrary, it should be helpful to mention in starting four important studies that might plausibly have been designated as "general" and to indicate where instead they are discussed. Both Knoepflmacher in *Religious Humanism and the Victorian Novel* (1965) and David J. DeLaura in *Hebrew and Hellene in Victorian England* (1969), considering Pater in company with two other Victorian authors, range in the course of their discussions over most of his writings. But the former work deals primarily with the fiction and with *Plato and Platonism*; and it is treated accordingly in Sections v and vi. DeLaura's volume, viewing Pater in the light of two major influences upon his thought and development, will be noticed with other discussions of "influence" in Section vi. Monsman's *Pater's Portraits* gives intelligent attention to *The Renaissance*, *Greek Studies*, and *Plato and Platonism*, as well as the fiction; and like the two volumes previously noted belongs on any basic "reserve book" list. But its chief importance is as a study of the fiction; and it is therefore discussed, at length, in Section v. Finally, the substantial introduction to Frean's dissertation (noted in Sec. 1), though less accessible, should also claim a place as one of the most perceptive overviews of Pater's work.

Readers approaching Pater for the first time are fortunate to find two short general studies of great distinction especially suited to their particular needs—studies that have lasting worth as well for the more advanced investigator. Graham Hough's brilliant chapter in *The Last Romantics* (1949) treats Pater's aesthetic philosophy, especially as developed in *Marius*; his critical theory and practice (see Sec. IV), and finally the "Paterian temperament" that lends a distinctive unity to writings in so many ways diverse. Pater is seen as a pivotal figure in a movement beginning with Ruskin and culminating in Yeats. Gradually severing "art from the interests of common life," this movement—which Hough treats with due seriousness—tended constantly "to turn art itself into the highest value, to assimilate aesthetic to religious experience." But Hough disputes the familiar view that it was principally the "liturgical preoccupations" so bothersome to T. S. Eliot that beckoned Pater toward Christianity; rather he sees instead the traditions of Broad Church theology and Pater's own lonely yearning for community behind his tentative movements toward assent. Hough is always alert to Pater's fluctuations and inconsistencies: he does not force the texts to submit to a thesis they will not sustain. He writes admirably of Pater's rhetorical strategies, as they operate, for example, in the famous "Conclusion." Throughout he is sympathetic but not uncritical; there is no blurring of outline here. If any objection is to be raised, it might be to Hough's downplaying of Pater's development and his exaggeration (subsequently challenged by Milton Millhauser) of Pater's antinomian and "cyrenaic" bent. In any case, this is a classic, indispensable essay, whose "full implications," as one recent writer has observed, "have yet to be worked out."

Ian Fletcher's short monograph in the British Council series (*Walter Pater*, 1959) surveys Pater's literary career in chronological sequence; thus he not unexpectedly gives greater stress than Hough to developments, or at least modifications, within Pater's "philosophy." This is perhaps the best *first* work to recommend to undergraduate, or even beginning graduate, students. Like Hough, whose real distinction he is quick to recognize, Fletcher refuses to oversimplify the complex and ambiguous aspects of his subject; and again like Hough he lays particular stress upon the historical context within which Pater wrote. To Fletcher, as later to Wolfgang Iser, Pater is important for having developed in his writings "a permanently significant symbolical figure: the most complete example, the least trivial, of the aesthetic man." To single out any chief particular excellence in this unobtrusively learned, sensitive, and discriminating study is not easy; but perhaps the careful examination of the essay on "Style" deserves special note. It is surely one of the misfortunes of the current Pater revival that Fletcher has not yet at least chosen to give fuller treatment to an author to whose work he is so intelligently responsive.

In turning from such good work in brief compass to the full-length studies of Pater there is an inevitable letdown. Indeed, to begin with, all general books before 1960 can be dismissed in short order. Ferris Greenslet's *Walter Pater* and Edward Thomas' *Walter Pater: A Critical Study* are as unrewarding as criticism as they are as biography. Benson's *Walter Pater* and Arthur Symons' *A Study of Walter Pater* (1932) are both useful for biographical information, but offer little in the way of rigorous critical insight and interpretation. Lucien Cattan's *Essai sur Walter Pater* (1936) is of interest mainly for the account of unpublished manuscript materials Cattan examined when they were in the possession of Mrs. May Ottley, Hester Pater's legatee. Finally, Federico Olivero's curious and rhapsodic *Il pensiero religioso ed estetico di Walter Pater* (1939) should be noted for its attempt to construct through interminable ecstatic paraphrase of *Marius* a committedly Christian Pater, but also for one real insight, later pursued usefully by Brzenk and others, into Pater's symbolic use of landscapes in his longer fictions.

Since 1960, however, five full-length general books have appeared, all of which have some claim to serious attention. Three of these works argue a thesis, a comprehensive interpretation of the direction and meaning of Pater's writings; the other two more modestly proceed with item-by-item or topic-by-topic exposition. Of the thesis-oriented studies, Wolfgang Iser's *Walter Pater: Die Autonomie des Ästhetischen* (1960) is the earliest and the most tendentious. What is particularly refreshing about this book, for British and American scholars, is its European frame of reference, its Continental philosophical context. Iser's method is phenomenological; his principal categories of interpretation are derived from Kierkegaard. He finds in Pater's writings a preeminent example of what Kierkegaard called the "aesthetic attitude." Rooted in philosophical and religious skepticism, this attitude expresses itself in disengagement, uncommitment, and a plea for unprejudiced receptiveness to the manifold possibilities of experience. When he could not credit any philosophic or religious Absolute, Pater turned to art to supply a kind of ersatz transcendence and justified his "aestheticism" by appeals to history and myth. Iser interprets Pater's principal prose fictions as theoretical exercises or "simulations" in which the author tests out the existential consequences of the aesthetic attitude *Marius* especially is seen as illustrating Pater's awareness of the bitter irony inherent in the "aesthetic life": that experience creates, by its inevitable and pervasive disappointments, a longing for some permanent, transcendental reality; and leaves the aesthetic hero, for all his occasional exquisite moments, not burning with a hard, gemlike flame, but anxious, despairing, and exhausted.

Iser locates the unity of Pater's work not in a permeating "temperament," but in the persistence in both fictional and nonfictional writings of certain compulsive philosophical preoccupations. His reading discloses aspects of Pater's imaginative coloration that other commentators had overlooked or disregarded, but at the price of some serious distortions. Even the science of Tübingen is not immune to thesis-riding. Iser's Pater is a far less various and contradictory figure than the texts allow. Interpretations (especially of *Gaston*) are too often strained; and Pater's tone or intention too frequently eludes the critic. And while his critical doctrine dismisses as irrelevant to this kind of phenomenological study considerations of chronology, Iser himself introduces erroneous chronological implications into the fabric of his argument, as in the suggestion that the treatment of certain issues in *Gaston* (1888–89) and "Apollo in Picardy" (1893) prepares the ground for Pater's presentation of the aesthetic life in *Marius* (1885) and *Imaginary Portraits* (1887). This ambitious and too little noticed study remains challenging and provocative, but is sufficiently out of focus to provoke a lingering distrust.

Like Iser, Anthony Ward in *Walter Pater: The Idea in Nature* (1966) finds throughout Pater's work a constant unifying concern with a central philosophical issue. Here, however, "Pater's aestheticism" is seen as "only a small part of his interest"; Pater's literary career may more usefully be regarded as a search for some kind of coherent pattern in experience, for what Ward calls the (Hegelian) Idea in Nature. As elucidated by Ward, this formula is more liberal than Iser's and permits the critic to relate many aspects of Pater's life as well as of his writings to the thesis presented. "Pater's conservatism, his love for ritual [,] for the principle of authority in church and state, his idealisation of the mother and child relationship, his

III. GENERAL STUDIES · 333

symbolic use of the home-counties as the ideal landscape for art, all point to a
search for security amid the break-up of the traditional framework." As he moved
away from the intransigent repudiation of conventional belief and sentiment that
characterizes the earliest essays, Pater expressed more and more a yearning for
coherence and stability—at the price of intellectual flabbiness: "more than most
authors, [he] employs his imagination to reduce the individual particulars in the
world to a state of blurred outline and confused identity." Ward finds varied and
often telling evidence to substantiate this argument: the presentation of art in "The
School of Giorgione" as a cloistral refuge, the escapism of *Marius*, the generalizing
and idealizing impulse of Pater's prose style, etc. The groundwork of Ward's thesis
is laid out in Part i; while the less satisfactory Part ii presents a succession of
readings in Pater, rather arbitrarily chosen (for instance, nearly all the essays in
Appreciations and all of the shorter "portraits" are excluded) and at times dwin-
dling into little more than stock synopsis-commentary. And although Ward's contention throughout has been that Pater could not satisfactorily reconcile the "Idea"
and "Nature," in his short final chapter he seems to shift direction abruptly and
unconvincingly. Here, in a discussion largely devoted to *Plato and Platonism* ("by
far Pater's most impressive work"), the author claims that in his last writings Pater
achieved through his dialectical method and the essay form the literary resolution
that had hitherto eluded him.

This is a vexing, unbalanced book—one that might have been, with less haste
to publish and more scholarly discipline, very fine indeed, perhaps even the best of
the five books discussed in this section. But in hurrying from dissertation (Cambridge 1964) to literary essay, Ward has retained the common faults of the former
without attaining the poise and stylistic grace of the latter. The reader is confronted
in capricious, often irrelevant, and sometimes ponderously unhelpful footnotes with
a parody of literary scholarship, while genuine scholarly responsibility is abdicated.
Debts to Brzenk, Millhauser, Osbourn, G. Tillotson, Young, and others go unacknowledged; and some basic homework (e.g., d'Hangest, Fletcher, Lenaghan)
apparently was never done. The text abounds in errors: misprints, inaccurate quotations, incorrect dates; and Ward quotes extensively without authorization or
acknowledgment from some of the Harvard manuscripts described in Section i. It
is a shame that a study so often sensitive and even luminous should be in so many
ways professionally irresponsible.

Richmond Crinkley's *Walter Pater: Humanist* (1970) is also organized around
a central thesis; but Crinkley's formula is larger, vaguer, more "liberal," as might be
expected with that most misleading of labels, "humanist," in the title. Pater's
"humanism" here denotes a continuity of interest in whatever has once been the
object of human sympathy; it is expressed not only in the open cultural and moral
relativism of his early essays and in his eclectic idea of the "House Beautiful," but
also, and most significantly, in a persistent fascination with the human image in art
and literature. Pater's "faith" in man, Crinkley argues, is best revealed in his
"favorite metaphor" of life-in-death and death-in-life: the spirit of man prevails,
victorious even in apparent defeat. In evidence are offered not simply the predictable showpieces like the Mona Lisa, but some fresh and subtle readings of such
works as "Denys l'Auxerrois" and the late essays on the monastic church of Véze-
lay and the cathedral at Amiens. Throughout his study Crinkley is especially good
at making clear the rhetorical or strategic element in Pater's essays: he sees how
Pater attempts to interest the reader in the work of art by strategies of evocation

and allusion; he shows how Pater's language can be at once precise and suggestive; he recognizes (though unlike Ward he does not evaluate) Pater's almost constant effort to conciliate and to smooth over distinctions that others might regard as fundamental. He thus finds in *Marius* a public strategy behind the apparent concessions to Christianity: "Pater wrote the book not so much to indicate a change in his philosophy . . . as to cast that philosophy in a mode more acceptable to his contemporaries." Crinkley also gives special stress to Pater's fascination with the corpse—the human image in death—and to the two principal forms of love in his work, the maternal and the homoerotic. ("The former," he observes shrewdly, "is apt to become in Pater a grandiloquent mythic idealization and the latter a kind of uneasy verbal-visual titillation.")

Crinkley's main argument, however, is repeatedly undermined by the very vagueness of the "humanism" he attributes to and obviously admires in Pater. As presented, without historical or philosophical perspective, without what would seem inescapable comparisons with the humanistic doctrines of Comte and Hegel (not to mention Mill), it seems a faith as vague as all unsweet. The only comparison offered to help the reader make more precise his understanding of Pater's viewpoint is with the more prescriptive and magisterial "humanism" of Matthew Arnold. This is not enough. What Crinkley declines to do is to scrutinize rigorously those aspects of Pater's humanism that most sharply differentiate it from the more robust, unromantic, and comprehensive humanistic philosophies of, say, Marx or Joyce. Pater idealizes, as Ward saw: his desperate, insistent idealism blurs or ignores much that has been of deep concern to Western man—let alone to non-Western civilizations. Distinctions deliquesce in the "House Beautiful"; and Crinkley fudges at this point. The inadequacy of his interpretation is most apparent when he discusses Pater's presentation of death. Like Monsman, he offers an "optimistic" Pater, who though focusing "very much on the idea of death, on pain" is yet able to "accept death as a kind of refining process through which the human or the image of the human must go in order to attain a new and fuller being." Certainly there are passages, as Crinkley shows, that demonstrate Pater's *longing* for transcendence; but to assert that he found it is a very different matter. No wonder then that this book never takes up "A Prince of Court Painters," "Sebastian van Storck," or "Hippolytus Veiled"; no wonder that it misrepresents the predominant effect of "Emerald Uthwart" and "Apollo in Picardy"; and no wonder that from Crinkley's *Marius* the pervasive pathos and ultimate irony seem to have been drained away.

The remaining two general books of the last dozen years present accounts of Pater's works not strictly organized in terms of any thesis or leading idea. Germain d'Hangest's ponderous *Walter Pater: L'Homme et l'œuvre* (1961), already noted as a biography, undertakes also an expository reading, in chonological sequence, of nearly everything Pater wrote. Of general studies this is by far the most learned: it synthesizes most of the best that had been known and written about Pater up to 1960 and its often laborious notes accommodate a wealth of useful material. D'Hangest pays attention, for example, to Pater's use of Vasari in *The Renaissance*, to evidences of the influence upon his early art criticism of the critical writings of Swinburne, to his revisions of his texts; and he draws extensively upon materials untouched before him, in particular the unpublished chapters of *Gaston de Latour*. His approach retains a sense of Pater's basic temperament, while at the same time it documents a steady modification in his views. D'Hangest writes well of lingering tensions in Pater's work, especially that between the defiant "aesthetic" commitment of 1873 and traditional moral values; and he observes how Pater seemed increasingly to resolve it in favor of a neo-Christian traditionalism and a longing for inner peace.

Indispensable as this book is in many ways, it has nonetheless some decided shortcomings. It is, as has been noted, tiresomely long: after stretches of protracted paraphrase the eyelids are more than a little weary. For all its learning, it is curiously defective in a sense of historical context: Pater inhabits a vacuum. Little is said about his reading and its influence on his development, or about his place in the history of criticism, or about the state of knowledge in such fields as Venetian painting or Shakespearean texts or classical archeology at the time when Pater addressed himself to these subjects. The relevance of Pater's persistent moral concerns is never developed; nor is there any sense of how social and economic factors may have conditioned his values. Finally, d'Hangest is too willing to take Pater at his own estimation: he prefers "appreciation" to tough-minded discrimination, and in consequence his book is flabby (in more ways than one), defective in rigor, victim of perhaps the least useful lesson of the master.

Gordon McKenzie's posthumous *The Literary Character of Walter Pater* (1967) takes a topical rather than a chronological approach, beginning with "A View of Pater" and proceeding in turn to considerations of mythology and symbolism, philosophy, fiction, and criticism. McKenzie fixes upon Pater's "literary character," by which he means "a slightly different and perhaps even more coherent and understandable personality, related to his own life-personality by circumstances, but much more frequently by idealizations, by desires for what he might have called higher beauties, by motives that in the nature of the situation cannot be discovered." Although he means to avoid biographical issues, evidently in the belief that the historical Pater has been irretrievably obscured by Thomas Wright, McKenzie slips continually into biographical or—more precisely—psychological criticism. He is a psychological critic in spite of himself; and at times quite a good one. Not surprisingly perhaps, in a writer as preoccupied as Pater himself with "personality," McKenzie takes a static or nondevelopmental view of his subject. Few readers will get from this book the impression that Pater ever modified an opinion or revised a text; and McKenzie is nearly as indifferent as Iser to the chronology of Pater's writings and its significance for interpretation. But, at his best, McKenzie is a wise and sensitive reader, particularly of Pater's portraits and the studies in Greek myth. Indeed, he may have anticipated later writers in his emphasis upon their interconnectedness. ("Anticipated" because the manuscript seems to have been largely complete before 1960. This may also account for some striking omissions of reference—as to Chandler, d'Hangest, and Lenaghan.) In both he deals intelligently with Pater's presentation of family relationships; and in the fiction he stresses the anxiety and passivity of Pater's protagonists. McKenzie has at times a real gift for getting beyond the surfaces, so that, for example, he perceives the "narcissistic passivity tinged with paranoia" present in so many of Pater's stories. Still, however, this modest book is erratic in its scholarship and more defective than d'Hangest's in a sense of historical context; above all, it draws back too often just where most seems necessary to be said. If on the whole graceful and undogmatic, it is also unduly tame and evasive.

Among briefer general studies of Pater over the last forty years there are three that deserve particular attention, because all perceive and to some extent elucidate some of the distinctive tensions that inform his principal works. Of these, the earliest and harshest is Edwin Berry Burgum's "Walter Pater and the Good Life" (*SR*, 1932). Though at times crude and misinformed, this essay anticipates much more recent work in its sustained attention to a central conflict in Pater (his "Greek naturalism" against "the uncertainty and fear of paganism in the Victorian temper") to whose nonresolution Burgum ascribes Pater's "reiterated failure" as critic and moralist. "The ill success of [his] attempt to merge and harmonize his two contradictory preferences for spontaneity and control" is evidenced in his inconsistent aesthetic preferences, in the allegedly confused ending of *Marius*, and in some particular qualities or effects of Pater's style. In discerning in so much of Pater's diverse output such insistent reference to certain deeply pondered dilemmas, Burgum laid a groundwork on which for years no one chose to build.

Much the same argument, more sympathetically presented, appears in Robin Ironside's suggestive if all too brief essay, "Walter Pater" (*Cornhill*, 1944). Ironside accounts for some characteristic Paterian effects by postulating a creative tension between inner urgency and a "powerful gift of reserve." "The beatings of his heart are encased in a hard, transparent envelope of thought, an intellectual armour that was a foil, if not positively a warrant, for the dark cluster of sympathies that he really needed to diffuse into the world." This "dark cluster" includes "a sensuousness that extends beyond surfaces to deep, intangible imaginings," a sense of universal pathos—perhaps desperation—underlying his summons to aesthetic sensation, and a rare gift of compassion into which is blended a sadomasochistic "fascination . . . of physical horrors."

Like Ironside, Milton Millhauser lays heavy stress upon "the temperamental dispositions which . . . shaped [Pater's] art." His "Walter Pater and the Flux" (*JAAC*, 1953), written in part at least as a rejoinder to Hough, is the most distinguished general essay on Pater by an American; and it is a testimony to the disarray of Pater studies that it has had regrettably little impact on later work. Millhauser argues that Pater did not simply celebrate, as a moral and aesthetic solvent, the flux he found in nature and consciousness; but rather that he was deeply disquieted by it. Stressing Pater's "almost obsessive consciousness of death" and his "remarkable capacity for imaginative distress and outright physical pain," Millhauser observes in both the fiction and the critical writings an earnest, desperate search for some idea of permanence in a late Victorian world bereft of the consolations and harmonious world view of Christianity. The "portraits"—curiously inconclusive and remote—are read as experiments, explorations in various attitudes that might provide some sort of coherence, some defense against the flux; and in his essays can be seen Pater's efforts to perceive, or create, stasis. "It has been suggested that he tries to find his subject's 'formula'; it is significant that he conceives of it as having one." In his preoccupation with Classical Greece and Renaissance Italy "he studies . . . a series of models for the synthesis his age could not achieve." Both Victorian in his "absolute moral earnestness" and modern in his "disturbing moral originality," Pater is presented as a subtler and more sympathetic figure than he was usually taken to be in the early fifties.

Most of the remaining general essays since the centenary of Pater's birth in 1939 have been, explicitly or implicitly, calls for an upward revaluation of his achievement. Some are extended book reviews in which the reviewer seizes the occasion to speak more generally of Pater; some are public lectures aiming to introduce or reintroduce Pater to an audience of nonspecialists; almost all merit only very summary notice. The centenary prompted a number of essays deploring the neglect into which his work had fallen and inviting renewed attention. An anonymous leader in *TLS* ("Walter Pater: Born August 4, 1839") celebrated his constructive "catholic spirit" and asserted that his work "stands the test of time as no other English prose of the nineteenth century." Both J. H. B. Peel in "Pater and Perfection" (*Poetry Rev.*, 1939) and Benjamin B. Wainwright in "A Centenary Query: Is Pater Outmoded?" (*Eng. J.* 1939) argued rather effectively that Pater is no "mere" or "effete" stylist, but a thinker and critic of rare vigor. The *Fortnightly Review*, to which Pater had once been so distinguished a contributor, lamely offered as its centenary tribute Harry Christopher Minchin's undistinguished "Walter Horatio Pater," an essay notable only for its eccentric suggestion that Marcus Aurelius is the "real hero" of *Marius the Epicurean*.

Richard Aldington's collection, *Walter Pater: Selected Works* (1948), did Pater a better service in its judicious and ample selections than in the compiler's frequently capricious and testy introduction to them. Aldington's anthology, however, provoked from Sir Herbert Read one of the most eloquent and forcible pleas for the rehabilitation of Pater ("Walter Pater," *World Rev.*, 1948; rpt. in *The Tenth Muse*, 1957). Citing "the amazing modernity, the enduring validity of Pater's criticism" along with "his wisdom, his poetry, his subtlety, his gentle humour," Read presents Pater as a more vigorous, even rebellious figure than Aldington had allowed. Sir Herbert was followed shortly by two other illustrious British names, Sir Maurice Bowra and Lord David Cecil. Of the two, Bowra is by far the more impressive. In his urbane reappraisal ("Walter Pater," *SR*, 1949; originally given as a lecture and slightly revised for inclusion in *Inspiration and Poetry*, 1955), he cites as the grounds of Pater's historical importance his "courageous attempt to estimate the place of art in life and of the artist in society." Pater is "a great critic" because he combined "almost a clairvoyant insight into the minds of those whose works he admired" with "a powerful capacity for relating single issues to general problems." Sir Maurice also notes Pater's very British empiricism, the honesty underlying his tentative and carefully qualified judgments, the deep vein of "poetry" that surfaced first in the critical essays and subsequently in the fiction, and the persistent element of self-projection in that fiction. Lord David Cecil's Rede Lecture, *Walter Pater: The Scholar-Artist* (1955; rpt. in *The Fine Art of Reading*, 1957), also evangelizes, using a kind of Paterian formula that balances Pater's "artist's sensibility" against his "academic intellect." But this elegant middlebrow confection has little substance, and even more than Bowra evades some important objections that defenders of Pater must contend with if they are to persuade more widely.

Writing for a more specialized audience, Paul West also calls in "Pater and the Tribulations of Taste" (*UTQ*, 1957) for a careful revaluation of Pater's achievement as a whole. West finds "the display pieces in the anthologies" misleading. If one looks not at isolated "ecstatic" passages, but at the total context, one discovers a writer who achieved "more adequately than Ruskin an intercourse between feeling and thought, between thought and its exposition." A more invigorating approach is taken by Alick West in a chapter devoted to "Walter Pater and Oscar Wilde" in his *The Mountain in the Sunlight* (1958). For this unusually sensitive Marxist critic Pater's early defiant aestheticism appears as an almost revolutionary call for the liberation of the mind from "all fixed forms and abstract absolutes." West not unexpectedly stresses more ably than anyone else Pater's tendency to abstract art "from its social reality," but quite surprisingly does not dismiss Pater as an "effete" bourgeois idealist. Pater is seen as deeply concerned with the situation of modern man, moving from the resigned pessimism with which his "Winckelmann" essay concludes to a humanistic affirmation at the end of *Marius*. The protagonist's sacrificial death "is his recognition that he is part of a world where these things happen. It is his active choice when confronted with the critical issue of his time. He places himself on the side of those to whom, it seems to him, the future belongs, because in them is the true spirit of humanism." It is another curiosity of Pater studies that Alick West's work is almost never noted.

Finally, three extended review essays should be cited for their useful insights into Pater, while at the same time they document the revival of which this essay has spoken so often. Reviewing Edmund Chandler's *Pater on Style* in *Criticism* (1959), Ian Fletcher hopefully discerned the beginnings of a movement toward a more serious appraisal of Pater, as he commented shrewdly on the significance of the 1892 revisions in *Marius* and on Pater's later attitudes generally. When Max Wildi came to review both Iser and d'Hangest five years later (*ES*, 1964), he noted with satisfaction recent progress toward the rehabilitation of Pater "as a serious and original writer who not only explored the nature of art but even had something to say about the nature of man." The most recent and by all odds the most learned review that branches out into a general study is "The Art of the High Wire" (*TLS*, 26 Feb. 1971). This essay begins with the *Letters* and the Blackwell-Johnson reprint of the New Library Edition and proceeds to discuss a number of important textual problems, important because as the authors indicate "the whole question of Pater's development is bedevilled by our total ignorance of what happened to his texts." Chosen for particularly close attention is "Emerald Uthwart," while the "Wordsworth" essay (1874) and *Marius* are also treated.

While such sensitive and learned reviews are always salutary, there is probably no longer any marked need for "rehabilitative" general studies: the trend is, at least in university circles, clear enough. What is needed, as this essay has argued already and will argue again, is more particular scholarly studies, more rigorous appraisals, and more informed attempts to establish some of the many contexts within which Pater's writings will be more fully understood, more deeply felt.

IV. CRITICISM

Ian Fletcher has written that modern scholar-critics are "often suspicious of any work which falls outside fairly strict categories"; for how can they "compare such works with others and 'place' them with a suitable conviction? This difficulty," he adds, "applies to Pater with peculiar force. His work seems to lie in a twilight of categories between criticism and creation; between art and literary criticism, belles lettres, classical scholarship, the *journal intime* and the philosophic novel." If Pater's work as a whole presents such difficulty, he seems hardest to pin down and classify in his role as critic. The fact that he professes to treat as aesthetic objects not only imaginative literature and the fine arts but also landscapes and "fair" personalities "in life or in a book" argues a range that may well intimidate the contemporary specialist. And even if a commentator possesses the credentials and the courage, he may still be insufficiently aware of the context in which Pater wrote, of the critical and philosophical debates of his day, a knowledge of which would certainly clarify many of Pater's emphases, including some of those that seem most annoyingly inconsistent. It is hardly surprising, then, that while a few writers have dealt admirably with his criticism, most discussions of his critical outlook and achievement leave much to be desired. The recent revival of Pater studies, with its special interest in the fiction, has de-emphasized this portion of his work. Perspectives are still confused and issues clouded: commentators disagree about what Pater's aesthetic standards were—or if he had any at all; they seem very much at odds as to what constitutes his ablest and what his least effective critical work; and with dismaying frequency they fail to confront and take specific issue with previous scholarship and criticism. Detailed examination of individual essays is hard to find. There is only one book on Pater's aesthetics or critical theory and no satisfactory extended study of either *The Renaissance* or *Appreciations*. (Albert J. Farmer's *Walter Pater as a Critic of English Literature: A Study of "Appreciations,"* 1931, is rightly dismissed by René Wellek as "little more than a summary.") And there has been surprisingly little notice of how Pater in various ways anticipates several of the most prominent tendencies or schools of twentieth-century criticism.

The most insistent note in studies of Pater as a critic has been the issue, normally the accusation, of "impressionism," that "over-easy and imprecise term," which, as Richmond Crinkley has remarked, "insofar as it is applied to Pater . . . has unfortunate connotations of superficiality and facility." The issue, most fairly stated, seems to be whether, and if so how often and to what degree, his tense subjectivity induces him to misrepresent the objects of his "aesthetic" criticism. Does Pater really "see the object as in itself it really is," or does he re-create the object after his own image? Was Pater, as one of his first reviewers said, "too much of an artist to be a good critic"? In the decades between the wars Pater was often dismissed, under the auspices of Paul Elmer More and the American "Humanist" critics (abetted in England by T. S. Eliot), as a mere "impressionist," an irresponsible aesthete writing on the lintels of the doorpost "whim." Ruth C. Child's "Is Walter Pater an Impressionistic Critic?" (*PMLA*, 1938) made the first sustained attempt to defend Pater against such charges of critical irresponsibility and should be read with the anti-Paterian sentiment of the thirties in mind. Conceding that at times, especially early in his career, Pater does indeed substitute private fantasies for "a judgment or interpretation which will have validity for others," Child proceeds in a quick but sensible survey of his critical essays to show how he normally aims at a communicable account of the unique—"objective"—quality of an artist's work, and that throughout his writing standards of critical judgment are implicit, first in his very choice of subjects for "appreciation," and also in the qualities, both formal and moral, that he chooses to praise in a work of art. With this essay current work on Pater as critic may be said to have begun.

Child renewed and expanded the scope of her defense in *The Aesthetic of Walter Pater* (1940; rpt. 1969). Here she is concerned to show that Pater was no narrow exponent of "art for art's sake," but a critic and theorist "who progressed gradually to a greater and greater emphasis on the ethical function of art." This progress she applauds and—in a prim, moralistic manner—somewhat misconstrues. Pater moves away from the "emphasis on sheer intensity" of *The Renaissance*, with its "admiration for unwholesome beauty" and its "distorted values," to a deeper and richer view of art as an ennobling, "ideal" force in human life. Whether this view in Pater's later writings (or, more accurately, these emphases in what remains an inconsistent attitude) is attained in part at the expense of elements of Pater's original strength and sincerity is not considered. Child's argument was valuable and timely, but her failure to recognize the complexities of the material and her laxity (or misplaced moralistic ardor) in discrimination make this book something less than the definitive study of Pater's critical theory and practice it sets out to be.

The best account of Pater as a critic is that of Graham Hough, in the second section of his essay in *The Last Romantics* (1949). Hough values Pater's critical theory highly ("a continual directive towards sincerity and against irrelevance"), while admitting that in practice Pater's achievement is often inconclusive—suggestive and sensitive to be sure, but not always "vigorous and decisive." A perceptive parallel is drawn between Pater's method and impressionist painting: "In both there is the formal allegiance to science, but behind it an essentially lyrical mood; the same neglect of structure and definition in pursuit of delicate evanescent effects that are felt to be more real and more important, because more immediate." But if "impressionistic" in this sense, Pater is by no means indifferent to moral values in criticism; instead, however confusedly, he is "insistent on the close connection between ethics and aesthetics." Hough calls attention to the interplay between Pater's theory and his tastes, and to the "amateur" stance Pater assumes: "he takes very little notice of literary history, or questions of attribution in painting." It might not be pure hyperbole to suggest that Hough's ten pages are as valuable as all that has been written on Pater as critic in the last twenty-five years.

Geoffrey Tillotson examines Pater's idea of the "aesthetic critic" in his rambling but occasionally insightful "Arnold and Pater: Critics Historical, Aesthetic and Otherwise" (*E&S*, 1950). This essay was revised, expanded, and rechristened "Arnold and Pater: Critics Historical, Aesthetic and Unlabelled" when printed as Chapter iv of Tillotson's *Criticism and the Nineteenth Century* (1951). (All quotations here are from the revised version.) Tillotson argues that Pater's label is ill chosen, as it misrepresents the breadth of his interests and the value of his criticism: his "total response was other than the aesthetic, and being other was deeper—deeper, that is, as depth is measured by mankind as a whole." Pater's ideal "aesthetic" critic is no merely passive "aesthete," but an intensely active being, characterized by kinetic imagery, by "the *power* of being deeply moved." But though Pater recommends to such a critic a historical perspective (in contrast to Arnold's disparagement of the "historic estimate"), Tillotson shows in a striking discussion of his attitude toward the "embrownment" of Renaissance paintings by time and varnish that Pater is hardly a consistently historical critic himself.

René Wellek's discussion of "Walter Pater's Literary Theory and Criticism" (*VS*, 1957; rpt. with slight modifications in *A History of Modern Criticism 1750–1950*, IV, 1965) is a disappointing performance from so eminent a hand. Beginning with what after Child's book are obvious assaults on stock misconceptions, he surveys the more readily apparent features of Pater's aesthetic without probing either their philosophical or psychological foundations. In his estimation of Pater's place in the history of criticism Wellek seems at odds with himself, wavering between qualified eulogy ("a handful of subtle studies, models of the art of the essayist and portraitist") and summary dismissal ("none of Pater's work has escaped the limitations of 19th-century aestheticism").

In *Walter Pater: A Study of His Critical Outlook and Achievement* (1961), R. V. Johnson makes an admittedly "limited and provisional" attempt to reassess Pater's stature as aesthetic theorist and critic of painting and literature. What is distinctive about this modest monograph, in its effort "to show that Pater does perform his critical task responsibly, that he is not merely indulging in camouflaged self-expression," is Johnson's close attention to Pater's actual critical practice in certain selected essays. His scholarly readings of the essays on Botticelli and *Measure for Measure* are particularly balanced, fresh, and incisive. If Johnson's work attains no major innovating insights, it nonetheless states its case well and directs attention usefully to the texts themselves: it can be recommended particularly as an introductory work for the graduate student.

Paul West, in "Pater's Cordial Canon" (*English*, 1963), holds, as does Johnson, that Pater's performance as a critic is markedly uneven. Pater is sometimes "much too personal to be a trustworthy critic; he has no idea of what is irrelevant"; but at his best, when "least autobiographical or . . . most relevantly autobiographical," he shows a rare gift for "translating into words the peculiar sensuous appeal of colour, of form, of composition, and the individual magic with which a particular artist will endow these." This last is well said; and here as in several of his strictures and discriminations West seems to promise a really cogent appraisal; but the promise is short-lived, and the essay remains on the whole muddled and erratic. There is little promise whatsoever in Norman Hidden's "Walter Pater: Aesthetic Standards or Impressionism?" (*Unisa Eng. Stud.*, 1968). Hidden agrees with Child and Johnson (neither of whom he mentions) that throughout his career Pater relies on "certain underlying principles" of critical judgment; but the essay fails to trace and elaborate these principles and thereby fails to resolve the issue it raises.

Two American articles of the late sixties offer sharply conflicting accounts of Pater's viewpoint, and yet are curiously alike in defective scholarship and an overbearing style of argumentation that makes more abrupt distinctions and more sweeping inferences than fairness to Pater's text will permit. By "piecing together" what she calls "touchstone passages," Marvel Shmiefsky in "A Study in Aesthetic Relativism: Pater's Poetics" (*VP*, 1968) tries to prove that Pater's writings do "not reveal the close connection between ethics and aesthetics that some [wholly unspecified] critics say characterizes his ethical theory." She submits in evidence an intimidating pastiche of brief quotations sundered from their moorings; and it comes as no surprise that signs of an ethical awareness in Pater's criticism (e.g., the essay on *Measure for Measure*) are systematically ignored. Belatedly and grudgingly, with a nod to Graham Hough, Shmiefsky acknowledges at least that "Pater's pronouncements . . . are inconsistent"; yet her plodding, procrustean approach has not allowed her to do justice to that so often rich and creative inconsistency. Beverly Gross is fairer in this matter when, in her "Walter Pater and the Aesthetic Fallacy" (*SAQ*, 1969), she maintains that "the same basic aesthetic commitment" can be observed throughout Pater's career, and that "this commitment explains not merely the evolution of Pater's thinking, but even its contradictoriness." The commitment, she writes, is to treating art exclusively for the sake of life, requiring it always to "*provide* something in relation to the demands of living." For Gross, paradoxically, Pater's attitude is not aesthetic enough: he is too concerned with art as "a substitute for life, an escape from life," too *un*concerned with the particular art object itself. (The same argument was made by E. B. Burgum in 1932; but Gross shows no awareness of his essay: see Sec. III.) This is a more perceptive and a more graceful essay than Shmiefsky's, but its coercive rhetoric ("all," "really," "merely," etc.), its neglect of previous scholarship and criticism, and its odd misrepresentation of the important "Winckelmann" essay quicken distrust and undermine confidence in her conclusions.

Generally speaking, Pater's writing on art has received less study than his literary criticism, in part because few professional art historians and critics have turned their attention to him. One distinguished figure among them, however, has written significantly of Pater and contributed importantly to the renewed respect for his work already noted in this essay. In the Introduction to his paperback edition of *The Renaissance* (1961) Kenneth Clark attributes to Pater a seminal position as a critic of painting and views him as an important precursor of some aspects of modern aesthetic theory. By rejecting (in "The School of Giorgione") "literary" approaches to painting, Pater saw clearly what none of his contemporaries recognized: "that what gave an aesthetic experience its unique value is the sensuous or intuitive perception that matter and form are one; and that this unity of perception is most easily achieved in music." A more hesitant version of the same argument is advanced by Solomon Fishman in *The Interpretation of Art* (1963). Like Lord Clark, Fishman points to the Giorgione essay as "an important document in formalist criticism, . . . providing the rationale, if not the means, for the formal analysis of style." Along with the later essay called "Style," it marks a progression, "by no means clear-cut," in Pater's thinking on art, "from the search for specific aesthetic value in the painter's temperament to an identification of aesthetic quality with pictorial (that is, formal) elements." Fishman's essay affords the fullest available account of Pater's criticism of painting. As a strict formalist, however, he faults Pater for being "too much concerned with the spectator's role in the aesthetic transaction . . . rather than with the life and intensity inherent in the work itself." This emphasis upon passive receptivity is connected with Pater's general neglect of contemporary art and with a "cloistered" quality in his own existence.

Fishman sees Pater as a vital link between Ruskin and the twentieth century, arguing that "Pater's visual response to painting was determined by Ruskin" and that his art criticism is "a direct continuation of Ruskin's." These provocative remarks underscore one important area of investigation that remains very much open: a comparative study of Ruskin and Pater that would also consider their criticism of literature, and perhaps tackle the obscure biographical issue of any actual personal relations between them. (Lord Clark, R. V. Johnson, and G. Tillotson all make brief comparisons between passages of Ruskin and Pater; but no one seems to have pursued this line of inquiry much further in print.) More generally, Pater's place in the context of late Victorian art history and criticism needs to be explored, and sources and analogues traced. Although d'Hangest deals briefly with Vasari and although he and others have noted affinities between Pater's early writings on painting and essays by Gautier, Baudelaire, and Swinburne, no one seems to have paid much attention, for example, to his use of Crowe and Cavalcaselle, or of art criticism in British periodicals of the 1860's and 1870's. Here as elsewhere with matters of context there is much to be done.

It should surprise no one that of all Pater's passages on art the familiar (too familiar?) rhapsody on the Mona Lisa has received the most extensive critical and scholarly attention. Donald A. Stauffer suggested forty years ago that Pater superimposed recollections of Dürer's "Melencolia" upon da Vinci's portrait; but his "Monna Melancolia [sic]" (*SR*, 1932) sounds more like a semisatiric jeu d'esprit than a reasoned argument. George Boas puts Pater's interpretation of the Mona Lisa into serious historical perspective in "The Mona Lisa in the History of Taste" (*JHI*, 1940). Pater and Gautier "in apparent independence of each other" initiated a tradition, afterward widely diffused into the popular consciousness, that finds in La Gioconda an enigmatic femme fatale; and Boas proceeds to document something of Pater's extraordinary impact on English-language studies of Leonardo in the later nineteenth and early twentieth centuries. Germain d'Hangest devotes an entire rapturous chapter of *Walter Pater: L'Homme et l'œuvre* to Pater's two paragraphs. The Mona Lisa passage is for him a monumental critical achievement, crystallizing various leading elements in Pater's early writings. Indeed, d'Hangest believes it constitutes the high-water mark of his career before *Marius*: "La Joconde . . . symbolise donc l'humanisme de Pater dans sa morbidité; et par son refus de choisir entre des expériences contradictoires, elle le symbolise aussi dans son aspect esthétique."

Although it was published too long ago for detailed notice in this volume, mention at least should be made of Bernhard Fehr's interesting "Walter Paters Beschreibung der Mona Lisa und Théophile Gautiers romantischer Orientalismus" (*Archiv*, 1916).

One other passage—or, rather, collection of extracts—in Pater's art criticism has been the subject of a sustained study. Max Schoen's "Walter Pater on the Place of Music among the Arts" (*JAAC*, 1942) is an extended gloss upon a few passages in the Giorgione essay, to the neglect of the rest of Pater's aesthetic theory. The focus is not surprisingly upon the now familiar dictum that "all art constantly aspires toward the condition of music." Implicit in the essay, Schoen believes, can be found the outlines of a theory of art not too unlike the aesthetics of John Dewey. For Pater, he suggests, the essential quality of aesthetic experience is abstract, pure feeling; and music is consequently the measure of the arts because its "material"— sound—has about it least of any intellectual element, "because by itself it can have only aesthetic meaning, while that of all other arts can be intellectual."

Finally, there are three studies of *The Renaissance*, all dealing with Pater as a critic of both art and literature, that remain to be noted here. The first is the most ambitious, and the most disappointing. Richard L. Stein's essay, "The Private Themes of Pater's *Renaissance*," published in *Psychoanalysis and Literary Process* (ed. Frederick C. Crews, 1970) undertakes a Freudian reading of the book, with special attention to the essays on du Bellay, da Vinci, Michelangelo, and Winckelmann. Unhappily, Stein's doctrinaire and nervously overinsistent treatment all too often parodies the finest achievements and insights attained elsewhere by the application to literary studies of the approaches and concepts of psychoanalysis. His essay is reductionist in the extreme, leading the reader again and again away from the text and the genuine cultural and intellectual issues it raises to questions of defecation or masturbation, whose connection with the text may be visible only to the "true believer." Nonetheless, Stein has rightly perceived the deeply subjective, almost confessional, nature of *The Renaissance*; and in spite of his perversity and (sometimes) misinformation he shrewdly intuits Pater's distancing or avoidance of erotic elements in the discussions of Michelangelo and Leonardo; he recognizes the defensive impulses behind aspects of Pater's prose style (particularly when Pater deals with the subject of death); and he presents a stimulating and original discussion of the ambiguous meaning of the Latin epigraph (*Et ego in Arcadia fui*) introduced in the third edition to the essay on Winckelmann. Stein has shown successfully that this book will yield to psychoanalytic criticism; but a convincing treatment of *The Renaissance* in these terms awaits maturer hands—perhaps Stein's own, in time.

In "Four Early Studies from Pater's *The Renaissance*: The Aesthetics for a Humanist Myth" (*VN*, 1971), William H. Sullivan occupies himself with Pater's second, third, fourth, and fifth published essays: "Winckelmann," "Poems by William Morris," "Leonardo da Vinci," and "Botticelli." (This essay is derived from Sullivan's frequently suggestive "Walter Pater: Toward a New Literary Form," Diss. Wisconsin 1969. Sullivan is also illuminating when he deals with the symbolic role played in *Marius* by the plague and the Germans.) Reading them as "a document of [Pater's] own aesthetic development," Sullivan observes that, collectively, they "comprise a highly unified statement about the necessity of a humanist myth for the modern artist." Whether or not one reads Pater in terms of any such conscious aesthetic program, it will be hard to find anywhere a better discussion of the essay on Botticelli, especially of the relation between Botticelli's Madonnas and Venus on the one hand and the Mona Lisa on the other. Like Sullivan and Stein, Richard S. Lyons is interested in elements that give more than historical unity to *The Renaissance*. His "The 'Complex, Many-Sided' Unity of *The Renaissance*" (*SEL*, 1972) seeks to show how the "aesthetic, cultural and moral attitudes" he finds in the book both harmonize and clash. The argument is articulate and intelligently developed.

Fresh perspectives on Pater as a critic are very much in order; and here once again a more accurate scholarship, a setting straight of the factual record will be invaluable. A number of special studies, as well as general reexaminations, are needed. No one has yet scrutinized Pater's specific literary preferences to see to what extent his taste and his precepts accord. The two selections of verse he made for Humphry Ward's *English Poets* offer an excellent, ready-made case study, a striking opportunity to compare Pater's critical accounts of Coleridge and Rossetti with his choices from their poetry. One might look also at what appear from his reviews and essays to have been his favorite works and passages to chart his oscillation between the divergent critical positions taken in "Winckelmann" (1867) and "Poems by William Morris" (1868). Such a study would furnish a further context for the right reading of "Romanticism" (1876; later entitled "Postscript") as well. And of course, beyond these more limited efforts, a comprehensive treatment of his whole critical output, theory and practice, investigating his relevance not only for modern formalism but for structuralist, phenomenological, and other schools of contemporary criticism too, remains one of the most useful undertakings that might occupy Pater studies in the 1970's.

V. FICTION

Except for *Marius*, Pater's fictional writings were not especially well regarded even during the twenty years following his death; and with the general eclipse of his reputation around the time of World War I, the fiction passed into even greater neglect than the critical prose—and, when it was noticed at all, was often dismissed as a curious and clumsy diversion from his work as a critic. T. S. Eliot consolidated the general disrepute into which Pater's fiction had fallen by 1930 when he dismissed *Marius* as a "hodge-podge." Since 1960, however, the tide has turned; and the new interest in Pater's stories, frequently coupled with attention to his concern with myth, is the most striking single characteristic of what has been called in this essay the Pater "revival" of the past dozen years. *Marius*, its unfinished sequel *Gaston de Latour*, and the nine shorter "imaginary portraits" have recently evoked widespread interest, in articles, books, and dissertations. Indeed, the claims of Pater's fiction to a central place in the canon have been forcibly and repeatedly urged. Almost every writer who finds the fiction so important also sets out to discern amid the variety of the stories some imagistic or thematic or dramatic "pattern" unifying the whole and significantly embodying Pater's most deeply felt intuitions about man and his world.

Two discussions of this sort are fundamental: Robert Thomas Lenaghan's "Pattern in Walter Pater's Fiction" (*SP*, 1961) and Gerald C. Monsman's *Pater's Portraits: Mythic Pattern in the Fiction of Walter Pater* (1967). Beginning with his recognition of a sustained dialectical movement in Pater's thought, Lenaghan proceeds to derive from his reading of "A Study of Dionysus" (1876) the pattern of a Dionysian-Apollonian tension, which he sees as the informing principle of all Pater's fictional work. The essential meaning of Pater's tales, he argues, lies not in their dramatic action but in certain qualities of the character or temperament of the protagonists. "The presence in this fiction of the Dionysian-Apollonian pattern, manifest abstractly in the terms of the organizing antitheses and concretely in the particular imagery," is documented at length. Apollo and Dionysus represent for Pater two powers, or permanent tendencies of the human spirit; and his stories may be interpreted as a series of experiments in the various oppositions and accommodations of these traits or forces. Apollo is "the concentration of mortal achievement . . . ideal human development"; Dionysus, on the other hand, embodies "the power of a massive vitality external to man and . . . the promise of the continuity of life in nature." Apollo is Dorian, sane, rational, humanistic, centripetal; Dionysus, Ionian, "religious," mysterious, centrifugal. Lenaghan sets out to trace these forces at work throughout Pater's fiction (except for "Hippolytus Veiled" and "An English Poet"); and while he is not so thesis-shackled as to ignore or misrepresent all apparent discrepancies, still in the course of his discussion the key terms are so imprecisely employed that the argument loses much of its original force and clarity. Thus, in *Marius*, the devout Cornelius and Cecilia are Apollonian—but so is the destructive "Apollyon" in "Apollo in Picardy"; the innocent Catholic Christianity of Gaston's childhood is Dionysian—and so, apparently, is the morally ambiguous "Lower Pantheism" ascribed in the same book to Giordano Bruno. Lenaghan's thesis sheds light on the inner logic of "The Child in the House," "Denys l'Auxerrois," "Emerald Uthwart," and (to some degree) *Marius*; but it does not so well accommodate other pieces, in particular "Sebastian van Storck," "A Prince of Court Painters," and "Apollo in Picardy." This sort of effort to read all Pater's tales in terms of a single, restrictive formula or pattern, even by so sober and sensitive a commentator as Lenaghan, is the most persistent shortcoming in recent studies of the fictional works.

Lenaghan deals primarily, as has been noted, with thematic elements manifested in *character*; Monsman, on the other hand, concentrates on the narrative vehicle itself, the story, or, as he perhaps too liberally terms it, the "myth." In tracing out "the conscious, artistic structure of Pater's fiction," Monsman points to the idea of "Renaissance, an intellectual and cultural awakening" as "the subject of historical and imaginary portraits alike." The Paterian protagonist, in many of the critical essays as well as in all of the stories, "is the Dionysian priest of Apollo, and his function is the awakening of art in a barren world." Monsman brings to this reading of the fiction an impressive range of scholarship and many acute and original insights. His scope is greater than anyone else's: he treats not only the published fiction, but the two unpublished portrait fragments, "Tibalt the Albigense" and "Gaudioso, the Second," as well. (Monsman makes no mention, however, of the unpublished Chs. viii to xiii of *Gaston*, an extended account of which was available to him in d'Hangest.) But he is driven to impose on the fiction, throughout, a romantic, "optimistic," Christian interpretation which however ingeniously argued seems to belie the persistent languor, anxiety, and sense of frustration that are so deeply interfused in Pater's most fundamental apprehensions of the world. Concerned as he is with narrative structure, Monsman naturally looks to the endings of Pater's stories for signs of hope—for a "sacrificial death which quickens humanity," for decease ("often") presented "as the consummation of marriage." Death is—too handily—swallowed up in victory. Arguments are advanced that repeatedly evade or underestimate "negative" elements in the denouements of most of the portraits and that thus violate the ordinary reader's sense of the *effect* of Pater's fiction. Monsman's claim to have discovered a consistent pattern of "spiritual victory" and cultural regeneration does not square with the experience of "A Prince of Court Painters" and "Emerald Uthwart" and may seem convincing only with "Duke Carl of Rosenmold" and perhaps also "Gaudioso." The ironic, the provisional, the skeptical elements in Pater's sensibility are inadequately acknowledged; and the result is that though Monsman's thesis is internally consistent, its coherence is achieved at the expense of inverted emphasis: it does not account for the way in which the reader experiences the portraits.

Signs of strain are visible also in Monsman's handling of Dionysian and Apollonian motifs and labels. His interpretations often seem to avoid the obvious, to multiply divinities beyond necessity. For example, he explains the celibacy of almost all Pater's protagonists as owing to the fact that "as gods, they have virtually consecrated their virility to their Great Mother." That as men they might be, like Pater himself, simply uninterested in heterosexual experience is never proposed. But in spite of this oversubtlety and in spite of the relentless overinsistence of the dissertation writer that is visible throughout, Monsman's book is indispensable. He synthesizes the results of the best work before him, and offers able discussions of sources, of imagery, of essayistic elements in the fiction, and of parallels and connections between the "portraits" of historical and imaginary figures. Finally, Monsman's stress on narrative pattern seems the most promising line of approach to Pater's portraits that has yet been taken.

If Lenaghan's is the most stimulating among the relatively few articles attempting to treat the whole range of Pater's fiction, the most sensible, because the freest from forcing of the evidence, is E. J. Brzenk's "The Unique Fictional World of Walter Pater" (*NCF*, 1958). This essay, an outgrowth of Brzenk's dissertation ("The Fictional Technique of Walter Pater," Iowa 1951), surveys some of the chief characteristic features of Pater's stories. Brzenk stresses "the contrast between Pater's works and romantic historical fiction," citing his selective rather than profuse employment of detail, the avoidance of "potentially 'big' scenes," and the relative freedom from nostalgia of tales that however remotely set in time are designed to bear obliquely upon real issues of Pater's own day. There is a good discussion of the journey motif ("always from north to south") in the fiction; and a refreshing restraint when Brzenk sketches the "striking temperamental resemblance" of many of Pater's protagonists. This level-headed piece, along with Brzenk's introduction to his edition of *Imaginary Portraits* (see Sec. 1), is probably the best starting point for the graduate student exploring Pater's fictional work.

After Brzenk, and in spite of his good example, however, the temptation to impose schematic "designs" upon the portraits seems to have been nearly irresistible. Knoepflmacher's "Historicism as Fiction: Motion and Rest in the Stories of Walter Pater" (*Modern Fiction Stud.*, 1963), revised and reprinted in his *Religious Humanism and the Victorian Novel* (1965), is dismayingly simplistic, in both its original and revised versions. Sweeping assertions are repeatedly made about "all" of the portraits, "all" of the protagonists ("are . . . introspective"—Denys? . . . are "pensive young skeptic[s]"—the dogmatist Sebastian? the unreflective Emerald?): such assertions will not bear scrutiny. The best elements in Knoepflmacher's essay are largely derivative, and not always acknowledged as such: like Benson fifty-seven years before him he discusses the replacement of dramatic conflict (between persons) by a clash of temperament and "environment"; and like all readers before Lenaghan and Monsman he recognizes that the results of the "conflict" are almost invariably tragic.

Another attempt to find in, or impose upon, Pater's fiction an overly simple formula or pattern is that of Franklin E. Court in "Change and Suffering in Pater's Fictional Heroes" (*Modern Fiction Stud.*, 1967–68). Viewing the narratives as an oblique expression of Pater's (presumed, not proved) hostility to an unheroic and repressive Victorian society, Court reads them (conveniently omitting four) as tales of unsuccessful, self-afflicting efforts by the protagonists to alter or amend the world they live in. Although Court like Knoepflmacher is at least faithful to the general somber impact of Pater's stories, his discussions of individual portraits continually distort the simple facts and details Pater provides. The same sort of misguided ingenuity, with its suppressions, dodges, and exaggerations, is apparent in Jan B. Gordon's "The *Imaginary Portraits*: Walter Pater's Aesthetic Pilgrimage" (*UR*, 1968). Gordon sees in all of Pater's shorter portraits a "general pattern involving the disappearance of self and a death into art": life is swallowed up in artifice throughout. But while this reading may be plausible in a few instances, especially with the enigmatic "Emerald Uthwart," Gordon, like so many recent commentators on Pater's fiction, is seriously embarrassed by the legerdemain required to make such diverse materials submit to so tidy a formula. His very questionable interpretation of "Sebastian van Storck," like the eccentric reading he gives of the "Conclusion," points up the inadequacy of his thesis. But if Gordon's formula fails in the face of the evidence, he should be credited nonetheless with some insights into the narrative technique of the portraits (Pater's use of framing devices and interpolated documents, in particular) that ought to be pursued further. The relation of theme and technique in the stories has not been adequately treated, and Gordon's observations afford at least a starting point.

Parallels between Pater's critical essays and his fiction have been mentioned by various writers, but apart from Monsman no one has usefully followed up the essayistic elements in the stories or the element of "portraiture" in the essays. The title of John J. Duffy's "From Essay to Portrait: Walter Pater after *The Renaissance*" (*Thoth*, 1965) would appear to promise such a study; but the article itself is little more than an uncritical reiteration of Lenaghan's Dionysian-Apollonian argument.

Among the individual works of fiction, *Marius the Epicurean* (1885) has quite predictably received the most extensive discussion. Scholarship has given considerable attention to backgrounds and sources. Among English influences, the name of Matthew Arnold is frequently heard. In "Pater and Arnold" (*EIC*, 1952) Kenneth Allott tries to show that Arnold's essay on Marcus Aurelius exercised a critical influence over the design of Pater's novel. Allott's argument is recast and impressively amplified by DeLaura in *Hebrew and Hellene in Victorian England* (1969). DeLaura finds Arnold a far more pervasive presence in *Marius* than does Allott, arguing that the book's "very structure . . . reflects Pater's reading of *Culture and Anarchy* and Arnold's religious writings of the seventies." Much is also made of the impact upon Pater of Newman's *Grammar of Assent* (see Sec. VI). One possible English influence, that of Thomas Moore's prose romance *The Epicurean* (1827), is considered and intelligently dismissed by E. J. Brzenk in "The 'Epicureans' of Pater and Moore" (*VN*, 1958).

French influences are given prominence in two articles by Louise Rosenblatt, "*Marius l'Epicurien* de Walter Pater et ses points de départ français" (*RLC*, 1935) and "The Genesis of Pater's *Marius the Epicurean*" (*CL*, 1962). The later essay modifies her earlier argument in the direction of what she calls a "pluralistic hypothesis," incorporating some concessions to Allott as well as considerable new evidence. She argues convincingly that any claims for Arnold's "Marcus Aurelius" as a principal source must allow for the possible influence also of much that was being written in England and France about the Stoic Emperor in the 1870's and 1880's. Her principal effort, however, is directed at showing that Pater "could have derived inspiration" from Ernest Renan's *Les Evangiles* and *Marc-Aurèle*, "not only for setting and philosophic position, but also for certain elements in literary method." Rosenblatt's most tantalizing suggestion is that during the composition of *Marius* Pater was led to his particular denouement by the example of Jules Le-maître's conte *Sérénus* (1883). The parallels she cites are impressive; but, as she is the first to admit, no one yet has produced evidence that Pater knew Lemaître's story before 1886. Further discussion of the backgrounds of *Marius* can be found in d'Hangest; but the most cautious and circumstantial investigation of Pater's reading and research remains that of Frean's dissertation (see Sec. 1).

Marius has been a bone of contention for its various interpreters, but for all their differences of opinion commentators in the past twenty years have demonstrated a remarkable consistency in their principal concerns. There is a repeated effort to establish, in the face of T. S. Eliot's well-known dismissal of the book as "incoherent" and a "hodge-podge," claims for its artistic integrity; and, often intertwined with the preceding, an attempt to chart Pater's theological bearings and implications. Both objectives are pursued in the first important postwar essay, R. V. Osbourn's "*Marius the Epicurean*" (*EIC*, 1951). According to Osbourn, the novel's unifying principle is its presentation of Pater's spiritual autobiography, and its pattern is found in a "cycle of apparent stabilities recurringly failing" before the fact of death, a cycle that culminates triumphantly in the witness of "The Martyrs" (Ch. XXVI). Such a reading, however, leaves Osbourn unable to give a satisfactory account of Marius' death, only on the threshold of assent to Christian revelation (if that). Osbourn is, however, alert to some of the special hazards in interpretation created by Pater's subtlety and indirection, and his candor and modesty, as well as the inadequacies of his reading, should have cautioned subsequent critics more than they appear to have. *Marius* certainly has many traces of an elaborate intellectual structure articulating a philosophical and religious position Pater felt it his "duty" to express: it seems to move toward a somewhat sentimental and self-indulgent "religion of humanity," most fully embodied for a Roman of the second century in the life of the pre-Nicene Church. But it may well be that what Pater felt it his duty to articulate and what his imagination created are not wholly consistent: it is suggested here, at any rate, that many of the problems critics have confronted or evaded derive from an imperfect fusion in *Marius* of "vision" and "design," that the novel is in a profound way "incoherent," though hardly a "hodge-podge." And while none of the commentators here discussed will quite concede this, several of them at times come very close.

What Osbourn calls, in response to Eliot, "the complex but unified structure of the book" is the subject of articles by James Hafley, Jean Sudrann, and Billie Andrew Inman. Hafley (*Modern Fiction Stud.*, 1957) purports to de-emphasize the "ideas" or "philosophy" presented in favor of an attempt to show how aspects of Pater's technique foreshadow qualities in the fiction of Joyce, Lawrence, Proust, and Woolf. But he is soon directly engaged with the question of *theme*, arguing that *Marius* is about "learning to hope," that it unfolds in four stages or "movements" entailing different kinds of hope—a "hope for tradition," a "hope for intelligence," a "hope for pure reason" (i.e., Stoicism), and finally, more or less in Christianity, a "hope for the will and for love." It is not surprising that terms are used loosely, or that Hafley has trouble differentiating clearly between Marius' Cyrenaicism and his exposure (hardly adherence) to Aurelian Stoicism, or that though he sees Marius' death as "intentionally ambiguous" he blurs the issue by failing to make clear just how much affirmation (if any) is given to the claims of Christianity in Marius' last hours. If Hafley's essay is on the whole unpersuasive, he is nonetheless the first to suggest the special importance of the interpolated "Cupid and Psyche" story, which he reads as a kind of parallel action to the main movement of the novel. This notion has been usefully developed and refined by subsequent commentators, especially Monsman.

Jean Sudrann's "Victorian Compromise and Modern Revolution" (*ELH*, 1959) is misleadingly titled, for she explores neither the "Victorian" nor the "modern" elements in *Marius* in any depth. This article is in fact a modest and sensibly argued "new critical" reading of Pater's novel in terms of three central images, by Pater's use of which Sudrann feels *Marius* attains "coherence." The hero's "quest for the vision incarnate" is illuminated by her discussion of the rose, the face of death, and the heavenly city (somewhat confused, perhaps originally by Pater, with the idealized house or home). Because she restricts herself, with new critical determination, to the text of *Marius* alone, she fails to recognize the fuller significance of the symbols she examines: all three are among the most persistent images throughout Pater. She also wants so much to defend the "coherent structure" of *Marius* that she underplays her most telling insight. By calling attention to Marius' sense of exclusion from the ideal community ("He is aware of the vision; he is excluded from it"), she seems to sense a conflict in Pater's denouement; but she fails to follow up the effect this countermovement has on a comprehensive interpretation of the book.

Billie Andrew Inman (*PQ*, 1962) is also eager to argue the novel's claim to aesthetic coherence. For her, however, what holds *Marius* together is simply the consistency of the protagonist's "fundamental character." Pater's descriptions of Roman life and apparent digressions from the main story line are rationalized as projections of aspects of Marius' personality. Inman rightly emphasizes the importance of Marius' skepticism, though her account of his death (this equivocal martyrdom is read as demonstrating that the modern mind "is constrained to preserve its full complexity") illustrates a major weakness in her failure to give sufficient weight to nonideational elements in Marius' history or to allow for possible discrepancies between Pater's intention and his achieved effect. But she does seem to sense that the novel has a strong undertow that works against the apparent progression to the threshold of assent.

Although Bernard Duffey, Martha Salmon Vogeler, and Knoepflmacher concern themselves most directly with the religious bearings of *Marius*, all three carry on the same assumption seen in Hafley, Sudrann, and Inman: that the novel is a coherent artistic whole manifesting Pater's conscious mastery of his own drift. Duffey's argument (*TSLL*, 1960) takes the most extreme position of the three—a position almost as deviant as Olivero's. For Duffey *Marius* stands as a "coherent religious statement," deeply colored by the (insufficiently documented) influence of (John) Frederick Denison Maurice, accepting orthodox Christianity "as both objective and intuitional." But while Duffey rightly recognizes Pater's profound yearning and seriousness, his reading never even tries to confront the ironies and ambiguities most other critics have seen.

Vogeler's essay (*NCF*, 1964) develops a unique and tantalizing but in the end unconvincing interpretation. She finds, like Duffey, a plea for religious faith; but she believes that Pater uses his protagonist as a kind of cautionary example for his contemporaries, who like Marius "were making their definition of faith too narrow." Marius' failure to commit himself overtly to Christianity is seen as conscious irony on Pater's part. ("That Marius dies a Christian in all but his own eyes constitutes the irony of the novel.") But intriguing as Vogeler's hypothesis may seem on first reading, her essay appears more and more simplistic and remote: she never accounts for Pater's extreme empathy with Marius, for his conscious indulgence in pathos, and never takes issue with the more "orthodox" readings of the novel. She does not succeed in reconciling her picture of a too theologically squeamish Marius with what is known of Pater's own religious history.

Knoepflmacher's discussion of "The 'Atmospheres' of *Marius the Epicurean*" in *Religious Humanism and the Victorian Novel* (1965) is often disappointing and contrived (setting up "four materialist systems" against "four idealist systems"), and characterized by a pattern of misleading inferences slipped in at the ends of sentences otherwise quite clear and obvious. But when Knoepflmacher gets to Book IV of *Marius*, he has much of value and interest to offer: his section on "The Christian Death of a Pagan" is probably the best single discussion of the novel's end that has yet appeared. Knoepflmacher almost acknowledges that Pater's control has slipped, or that there are two conflicting and unreconciled impulses at work in these later chapters. He does state boldly and persuasively that "Marius' death remains a convenient escape; it parodies, rather than re-enacts, the myth of the self-sacrificing God common to the religions of Christ and Apollo."

Two other essays on *Marius* deserve attention. Peter Thorslev's "Pater and *Marius*: The Esthetic Stage" (*Grad. Stud. of Eng.*, 1959) looks at the novel much as Wolfgang Iser does, in terms of Kierkegaardian categories. *Marius* is read sympathetically as a sustained testing of "the esthetic attitude, with clarity and honesty" by the course of one man's experience. A much less sympathetic, but in many ways similar argument (including the use of Kierkegaard) is that of James A. W. Heffernan (*VN*, 1969). Heffernan also sees *Marius* as a fictional experiment in the aesthetic life, but finds Pater's apologia "cruelly self-deceptive." He argues quite convincingly that there is much of snobbery and un-Christian pride about certain attitudes in Marius that Pater seems to be inviting his readers to admire; and his discussion of the rarefied, "sanitized" Christianity Pater presents should give future critics occasion for some second thoughts. Heffernan can be crude and unfair, but his most cogent objections stand out the more in the context of most tame and eulogistic discussions of this novel.

One episode in *Marius* has been the subject of several special treatments, just as it has become a main issue in much recent critical commentary. Pater's adaptation of the story of Cupid and Psyche from Apuleius' *Golden Ass* is discussed by E. J. Brzenk (*CL*, 1958) and by Paul Turner (*VS*, 1960). Both essays are valuable in showing some "consistent purpose guiding his selection of materials" (Brzenk), though Turner is more severe upon Pater and his fellow Victorians for their avoidance of realism and humor. Both could be used in studies of Pater's prose style; and both could be used, as Knoepflmacher points out in "Comments and Queries" (*VS*, 1961), in a thematic discussion of *Marius* generally.

The rest of Pater's fiction has had little attention outside the full-length treatments and general articles already discussed. Jan B. Gordon examines the first of the "imaginary portraits" in "The Beginnings of Pater's Pilgrimage: A Reading of 'The Child in the House' " (*TSL*, 1968), but his study is confused and inaccurate—most curiously transforming a cat in the text into a goat in the article. William W. Main's brief note, "Pater's 'Sebastian van Storck' " (*Expl*, 1954), reads this portrait as "a story of man's redemption told in the particular historical context of modern man's futile intellectual isolation in an alien world." Like Monsman, whose discussion is far more ample and subtle, he oversimplifies the story and finds no irony in its effect. The best article on a single portrait is "Pater's 'Apollo in Picardy' and Mann's *Death in Venice*" (*Anglia*, 1968) by Catherine Cox (Runcie). She reads "Apollo" as a *Künstlerroman* in miniature, seeing in the madness and early death of Prior Saint-Jean the sacrifice of the artist "in the service of the merciless beauty of formal perfection." While Cox does not claim to establish any influence of Pater on Mann's novella, the parallels she draws between the two stories are striking and persuasive; and in her hands the work of Mann sheds fresh light on Pater. "Apollo" is also treated by Sloane Frazier in "Two Pagan Studies: Pater's 'Denys l'Auxerrois' and 'Apollo in Picardy' " (*Folklore*, 1970). Frazier seems never to have read standard Pater criticism; but nonetheless the essay points accurately to parallels and differences between the stories, stressing "the strange complicity of polar opposites" in both. Finally, one of Pater's most elusive stories is the subject of Jan B. Gordon's "Pater's Gioconda Smile: A Reading of 'Emerald Uthwart' " (*Stud. in Short Fiction*, 1969). The story is elusive, and it eludes Gordon's grasp in this curiously disjointed and inconclusive article.

Obviously more close studies of the shorter portraits are needed; but in addition, the whole 1887 volume of *Imaginary Portraits* needs to be examined as a unit. Why did Pater print *these* four tales? And why did he arrange them in an order which is neither that of prior publication nor of the periods in which they are set? What interrelationships do they have? How do they illuminate one another? More attention also needs to be given to the stepchild of the Pater canon, the unfinished *Gaston de Latour*. D'Hangest has provided the fullest treatment to date, including a valuable discussion of the unpublished chapters in the Sparrow collection, but much more remains to be done. Particularly useful would be a study that would consider Pater's apparent plan for the work (what would become of Gaston's child?) and the reasons for his having abandoned it. With the fiction, as elsewhere in Pater studies, a search for the facts and their clearer interpretation is long overdue.

VI. SPECIAL STUDIES

The "special studies" noted in this section are works devoted to particular topics that do not lend themselves readily to inclusion under any one of the five rubrics earlier employed. But it should be observed at the outset that some such subjects are inevitably treated in some of the general studies of Section III, above all in d'Hangest; and where these discussions are of unusual value or interest an effort has been made at least to mention them here as well.

SOURCES, BACKGROUNDS, CONTEXTS. Various scholars have attempted to document the sources, backgrounds, and contemporary contexts of Pater's work, either as a whole or in some one of its aspects. Treatments of sources and backgrounds—of "influences"—have suffered from the absence of precise biographical information concerning the nature and scope of Pater's reading from his young manhood on, but it is nevertheless clear enough that Pater was widely read in many fields and greatly affected by certain works in particular. Helen H. Law's "Pater's Use of Greek Quotations" (*MLN*, 1943) provides a handy record of many of his allusions, a useful survey of the extent of his acquaintance with Greek classics, and an approving appraisal of his literary usage of citations from classical texts. R. G. Frean's dissertation impressively documents Pater's indebtedness in *Marius* both to Roman literature and to some nineteenth-century classical scholars and historians. Even more intimately than the classics Pater knew the English Bible and the Book of Common Prayer; and it is curious that no study of his numerous Biblical allusions has yet appeared, all the more so since such a study would illuminate some fundamental elements of his sensibility, for example, the strong appeal for him of passages dealing with motifs of refuge and enclosure.

Pater is said to have won his Brasenose fellowship largely because of his knowledge of German Idealistic philosophy; and it is certainly true that he was widely read in German literature, philosophy, and scholarship from the period of Winckelmann on. Throughout his career he expressed great respect for Goethe; but no one has yet closely investigated Pater's indebtedness to him. Anthony Ward provides some preliminary documentation in *Walter Pater: The Idea in Nature* (1966) and suggests that Pater's view was importantly colored by G. H. Lewes' *Life of Goethe*. Considerably more has been done to establish the extent of Pater's debt to Hegel. Bernhard Fehr first noted Pater's use of the *Aesthetik* in his "Winckelmann" essay in "Pater und Hegel" (*Eng. Studien*, 1916), and his argument has been reinforced by Ward. In "History as Palingenesis in Pater and Hegel" (*PMLA*, 1971), William Shuter further extends and refines Fehr's investigation. He traces Pater's preoccupation with ideas and images of rebirth to Hegel's *Phenomenologie des Geistes* and *Aesthetik*; and even more valuably he demonstrates Pater's indebtedness in the Demeter essays and in *Marius* to Ludwig Preller's *Demeter und Persephone*. Here Shuter has begun to explore some important terrain, and his promised essay on Pater's additional debts to German scholars of the nineteenth century should be of much interest. Shuter is exploring a vein tapped first by John Smith Harrison in his "Pater, Heine, and the Old Gods of Greece" (*PMLA*, 1924), who pointed out Pater's reliance in his treatment of Greek myth upon *Die Dorier* of Karl Otfried Müller. (Harrison's essay is also important as the first to develop at any length the now generally recognized connection between Pater's investigation of Greek myths in the 1870's and at least some of his "imaginary portraits"; it is cited by both Lenaghan and Monsman.)

Pater was also familiar with a wide range of French literature, criticism, and philosophy; and the variety at least of his reading and its pervasive echoes in his writing are documented in part in Arthur Beyer's otherwise plodding *Walter Paters*

Beziehungen zur französischen Literatur und Kultur (1931). Beyer is given to elaboration of the obvious and makes no use of Pater's Oxford reading lists, but nonetheless points valuably to the impact of Michelet (further work here would be especially useful), Rémusat, Fauriel, Sainte-Beuve, Gautier, and Viollet-le-Duc. More needs to be said, however, about Pater's reading in nineteenth-century French fiction, about his indebtedness to Baudelaire's critical writings (d'Hangest has made a beginning here), and—perhaps surprisingly for one who summarily dismissed any "facile orthodoxy of Comte, or of Hegel, or of our own"—about his reading of Auguste Comte, phrases from whose works abound in some of the unpublished manuscripts at Harvard.

That significantly more and better work has been done with British sources and backgrounds is hardly surprising, since most Pater scholarship has been produced by professional students of English literature. Most fully explored among British influences has been the impact of Matthew Arnold. In "The Divided Tradition of English Criticism" (*PMLA*, 1958), William A. Madden briefly treats Pater's use of an Arnoldian vocabulary and his characteristic transformation of Arnold's emphasis —"against duty and high seriousness in favor of intensity, remoteness, and refinement." Arnold's "call for a rationalistic and disinterested study of life and nature resting ultimately on the power of a perceptive tact" becomes "through Pater's mediation, the grounds for a radical cleavage between the poet and society, and for the development of a neoromanticism in which the aspiration for an ideal life satisfied itself in the 'intense' moment of aesthetic passion." But the most impressive work of any kind dealing with influences upon Pater's thought and writing is David J. DeLaura's *Hebrew and Hellene in Victorian England: Newman, Arnold, and Pater* (1969). With an ear tuned to finer frequencies than most scholars can apprehend, DeLaura provides elaborate and generally convincing documentation, especially in certain characteristic rhetorical strategies and phrases, of the pervasive presence of Arnold throughout Pater's literary career. To Arnold, Pater is said to owe a persistent concern with "the dichotomy of Hebraism and Hellenism," though the author is prompt to concede that this formulation has almost two millennia of pre-Arnoldian antecedents. Even more striking than his demonstration of Arnold's impact is DeLaura's wholly original development (originally printed as "Pater and Newman: The Road to the 'Nineties" in *VS*, 1967) of Pater's manifold indebtedness to John Henry Newman (for a fuller description of which see M. Svaglic's chapter on Newman in this volume). *Hebrew and Hellene*, finally, transcends the category of "influence study" and can be read as a significant general account of the course of Pater's productive life.

Other British influences or backgrounds have been less adequately investigated. Something of the probable impact upon Pater's thinking of *On the Origin of Species* is discussed by Philip Appleman in "Darwin, Pater, and a Crisis in Criticism" in *1859: Entering an Age of Crisis* (ed. Philip Appleman, William A. Madden, Michael Wolff, 1959). More attention, however, needs to be given to Broad Church theology, to philosophic writers of the British empiricist tradition (esp. to John Stuart Mill), and to much "minor" controversial prose, theological and philosophical, current in Oxford during Pater's formative years. Among belletristic works, the poetry of Wordsworth has been cited by Mary G. Mason (*HLB*, 1971) as an important influence upon both "The Child in the House" and "An English Poet." From his study of Wordsworth's "poetry of recollection," especially *The Prelude*, Pater "learned much about his own approach to fiction and how he could combine his taste for the philosophical with his desire for concreteness." Certainly Pater, like Ruskin, was deeply penetrated by Wordsworth's poetry, and a study of Pater's Wordsworthian allusions (most conspicuously to the Immortality Ode) might reveal much about his habits of assimilation and about the contours of his imagination generally. Almost nothing has been done with Pater's knowledge of British (and American) fiction, except for a not particularly illuminating exchange on the subject of Pater's reading of *Romola*. DeLaura (*NCF*, 1966) suggests that George Eliot's novel "may well have been the impetus" that led Pater to the writing of *The Renaissance*, and that it may also have exerted a powerful formative influence upon *Marius*. Donald L. Hill (*NCF*, 1968) finds little beyond superficial resemblances between *Romola* and *Marius*, and no convincing proof that *Romola* may have incited the writing of *The Renaissance*; but he agrees with and goes beyond DeLaura in discussing the importance of the figure of Savonarola in Pater's imagination.

Much in Pater's work becomes clearer when some sort of historical context is established, even if no question of "influence" is broached. Pater has often been located in a continuing Romantic tradition in Victorian literature, as by Clyde de L. Ryals in "The Nineteenth Century Cult of Inaction" (*TSL*, 1959) and most perceptively by Graham Hough in *The Last Romantics* (1949). Similarly, it has been a commonplace to consider Pater in the context of the "aesthetic movement"; but since most studies of the movement are so inadequate, little illumination has been shed upon Pater's unique place in it. In *Dark Passages: The Decadent Consciousness in Victorian Literature* (1965), Barbara Charlesworth (Gelpi) struggles with the theme that what links "aesthetes" and "decadents" is the pursuit of heightened sensory experience, ecstatic moments, "enjoyed within the mind outside society." But Pater is more elusive than Charlesworth's general argument will allow, and her treatment of his work is among the less satisfactory chapters in her book.

There is another context, or set of contexts, less obvious but certainly enlightening when pursued: that is, the periodical prose of Pater's own day, especially the controversial prose of the major magazines and reviews of the later Victorian period. A valuable beginning was made by Helen Hawthorne Young with *The Writings of Walter Pater: A Reflection of British Philosophical Opinion from 1860 to 1890* (1933; rpt. 1965), when she examined some themes in Pater's essays and fiction in the context of various philosophical essays published in periodicals of his day, chiefly the *Fortnightly* and the *Contemporary*. She is thus able, for example, to demonstrate the bearing upon *Marius* of the heated late Victorian controversy over vivisection. Though her construction of "philosophical opinion" is so narrow that it somewhat impoverishes her context, Young succeeds admirably in showing how much a sense of context adds to a reading of Pater. Her discussions of such concepts and motifs as "expression," "temperament," "sympathy," the "sentiment of home," and the "divine companion" are particularly helpful. Similarly useful, though more restricted in scope, is James Kissane's "Victorian Mythology" (*VS*, 1962), where Pater is viewed along with Ruskin, Symonds, and Tennyson in the context of various nineteenth-century practices in mythography. What might be called a "negative context" is invoked by R. V. Johnson in "Pater and the Victorian Anti-Romantics" (*EIC*, 1954), as he tries to illuminate Pater's critical theory and practice by a contrast with the position of certain anonymous "anti-romantic" reviewers of his day. The reviews he treats, however, all prove to be the work of one man, William John Courthope; and thus the alleged "context" is radically restricted.

Nonetheless, Johnson gives a useful account of the social and intellectual conditions in later Victorian England that gave rise to the kind of minority culture exemplified by Pater, Swinburne, and Rossetti, and deplored by the conservative Courthope. Johnson, Kissane, and Young have hardly exhausted the possibilities of context studies; and much remains to be done. To cite only one example, much light could be shed upon Pater's "Giordano Bruno" (later included in *Gaston*) by an examination of the interest Bruno excited in England and abroad at the end of the eighties.

INFLUENCE. Pater's impact upon the next two generations of writers, in England and (to some degree) on the Continent, has also been treated by numerous hands. John Pick's "Divergent Disciples of Walter Pater" (*Thought*, 1948) are Oscar Wilde, George Moore, Arthur Symons, and Lionel Johnson. The first three are primly pronounced goats, and Johnson alone a sheep; for, according to Pick, while Wilde, Moore, and Symons never advanced beyond the positions Pater took in the "Conclusion," only Johnson moved "forward" with the master toward a more austere and moralized vision. Pater's influence on Moore is discussed at length by Robert Porter Sechler in *George Moore: A Disciple of Walter Pater* (1931). It is Oscar Wilde, however, of Pick's four "disciples," whose indebtedness to Pater has been most amply documented. Ernst Bendz's monograph, *The Influence of Pater and Matthew Arnold in the Prose-Writings of Oscar Wilde* (1914), illustrates how pervasive in Wilde's early prose are echoes from *The Renaissance* but largely ignores broader matters of ideas and themes. One such broader matter is taken up by Wendell V. Harris in "Arnold, Pater, Wilde, and the Object as in Themselves They See It" (*SEL*, 1971). Both Pater and Wilde sensed a metaphysical muddle behind Arnold's adjuration to "see the object as in itself it really is"; and Wilde, according to Harris, only carried to its extreme conclusion the relativistic construction Pater placed upon Arnold's words. The subtlest examination of Pater's impact upon Wilde is Richard Ellmann's, in "Overtures to Wilde's *Salome*" (*TriQ*, 1969), where the almost heraldic figures of Ruskin and Pater are shown to have haunted Wilde's literary imagination.

A number of commentators have sought to trace Pater's influence upon various major writers of the early twentieth century. Among such figures, the writer most often connected with Pater is, ironically, T. S. Eliot. William Blissett (*UTQ*, 1953) makes the provocative suggestion that early in his career Eliot "was attracted to Pater's works, so strongly indeed that some of the tastes they display, the images they use, the preoccupations they evince" permeate his writing—for all Eliot's public denigration of Pater and his works. Blissett's hypothesis is fortified by Grover C. Smith's identification of some specific Paterian echoes in *T. S. Eliot's Poetry and Plays* (1956). Less persuasive is David J. DeLaura's contention in "Pater and Eliot: The Origin of the 'Objective Correlative'" (*MLQ*, 1965) that a passage in "Sandro Botticelli" stands behind the formulation of Eliot's well-known concept. Various unconvincing parallels are adduced by Robert F. Fleissner in "'Prufrock,' Pater, and *Richard II*: Retracing a Denial of Princeship" (*AL*, 1966), although Fleissner's tracing of one line in "Prufrock" to Pater's "Shakespeare's English Kings" seems eminently plausible.

William Butler Yeats openly invited attention to Paterian influences in his work, not only by his references to Pater in his autobiographies but by reprinting the "Mona Lisa" passage as free verse in his Introduction to the *Oxford Book of Modern Verse*; and Pater's place in the formation of Yeats's sensibility is often alluded to, as notably by Louis MacNeice in *The Poetry of William Butler Yeats* (1941). The only article dealing with this connection is Leonard E. Nathan's "W B. Yeats's Experiments with an Influence" (*VS*, 1962), where it is argued that Yeats's dramatic theory and practice were profoundly affected by his reading of "Shakespeare's English Kings," interpreted as a "thoughtful and authoritative rationale for the lyrical drama." It is unfortunate that no similar article has undertaken to examine James Joyce's response to Pater, though various writers, for example, Frank Kermode in *Romantic Image* (1954), have sensed an important influence. John J. Duffy looks to another great novelist for traces of Pater in what is essentially an elongated footnote, "Conrad and Pater: Suggestive Echoes" (*Conradiana*, 1968). Outside the British Isles, Pater's latter-day influence has been traced only sketchily. In the one article devoted to a major European writer's response to Pater, "Hugo von Hofmannsthal and Walter Pater" (*Comp. Lit. Stud.*, 1971), Penrith Goff presents a "preliminary sketch" of the deep impression made upon the Viennese poet, dramatist, and critic by Pater's theory and practice of criticism and by his sketch of the diaphanous personality in "Diaphaneitè."

Two well-executed essays have pointed out Pater's role, if not as a direct individual influence, at least as a precursor, of many elements of literary modernism. Ruth Z. Temple's "The Ivory Tower as Lighthouse," collected in *Edwardians and Late Victorians* (ed. R. Ellmann, 1960), defends Pater's critical method and notes how it and other aspects of his work anticipate later trends; while Wendell V. Harris, in "Pater as Prophet" (*Criticism*, 1964), usefully distinguishes Pater's particular prefiguration of modernism from that of the aesthetic movement generally. Throughout crisp and judicious, Harris' essay also offers a convincing defense of Pater's lasting importance as a man of letters.

COMPARATIVE STUDIES. Apart from considerations of context and influence, there is yet another kind of comparative study in which Pater has figured and may figure usefully still: that is the "affinity study" or treatment of two writers in which each serves to illuminate some salient aspects of the other. David A. Downes's *Victorian Portraits: Hopkins and Pater* (1965) is the most extensive affinity study (though it also estimates the probable influence on Hopkins of his early Oxford exposure to Pater's thought and interests). Unfortunately, Downes tends to remake Pater into a kind of crypto-Catholic, as he finds in "true holiness" the most compelling affinity between the two men. The book is seriously warped in this direction. Paul West regards André Malraux as a twentieth-century continuator of Pater's views on art in "Walter Pater and *The Voices of Silence*" (*Adelphi*, 1955), published again as "A Narrowed Humanism: Pater and Malraux" (*DR*, 1957). "What Pater and Malraux propose is a humanism founded on human creativity . . . a religion of art." Some striking general resemblances are observed, but the essay makes little effort to pursue them rigorously. Comparative essays of this sort are almost too easy to write, but where very marked parallels exist side by side with illuminating differences of attitude or approach, they can be of great value. These conditions are arrestingly met in the cases of Pater and Henry James, and Pater and Nietzsche, where useful work remains to be done.

REPUTATION. Although there is yet no study specifically devoted to the ebb and flow of Pater's reputation, useful documentation of its course can be garnered from d'Hangest, from the Introduction to the *Letters*, and from this essay. Robert Seiler is currently at work on a Pater volume for the Critical Heritage series, which should chronicle far more adequately than has yet been done the history of Pater's early reputation. But for the years between the first collected edition (1900–01) and World War II there is still no promise of a survey, and the territory seems open, at least insofar as Pater's fame in England and America is concerned. Light is shed on the history of his reputation in France between the wars by Angelo P. Bertocci's "French Criticism and the Pater Problem" (*BUSE*, 1955), and to a lesser degree by Charles G. Hill's "Walter Pater and the Gide-DuBos Dialogue" (*RLC*, 1967).

STYLE. Almost everyone says something about Pater's prose style, but virtually no one has done anything about it beyond quick impressionistic judgments dating back to Max Beerbohm, if not before. George Saintsbury discusses rhythmic aspects of Pater's prose style, worshipfully but not very helpfully, in *A History of English Prose Rhythm* (1912). Also concerned with rhythm, and somewhat more usefully, is Paull F. Baum's *The Other Harmony of Prose* (1952), though Baum's samples from Pater are not wholly representative and his focus is too narrowly restricted. In *An Analysis of the Stylistic Technique of Addison, Johnson, Hazlitt, and Pater* (1928), Zilpha E. Chandler chooses not the "Mona Lisa" but a more characteristic passage from the essay on Lamb as her sample for investigation. Though her attempt "to construct an apparatus for the objective study of literary expression" seems in many ways crude and naïve, she does succeed in describing certain representative features of Pater's diction and sentence structure. The two most recent discussions of Pater's style are both largely unhelpful. John J. Duffy (*Style*, 1967) tries to establish, on the basis of only two specimens, the provisional hypothesis that Pater's prose is best, most "melodic," when "he clearly retains the distinction between himself and the thing he is writing about" and least effective (*opsis* instead of *melos*) when this distinction is lost. G. S. Fraser's "Walter Pater: His Theory of Style, His Style in Practice, His Influence," printed in *The Art of Victorian Prose* (ed. George Levine and William A. Madden, 1968), returns to Saintsbury and advances no further.

The time is ripe for someone equipped with contemporary linguistic tools to bring a more sophisticated perspective to bear on the peculiarly Paterian qualities of Pater's prose. But even in the absence of such a study, there are still three discussions of his style that have value. Examining closely three consecutive paragraphs from Chapter iii of *Marius*, Vernon Lee's "The Handling of Words: A Page of Walter Pater" (*Life and Letters*, 1933) explores the qualities of sensibility revealed in Pater's narrative exposition. Edmund Chandler's study of textual revisions in *Marius* in *Pater on Style* (1958) leads to a valuable discussion of Pater's "special vocabulary," characterized by "the 'ideal' quality of the abstract nouns, and the great preponderance of 'precious' and 'intensive' adjectives." Finally, Germain d'Hangest makes valuable use of manuscript materials in his study of Pater's habits of composition in the last chapter of *Walter Pater: L'Homme et l'œuvre* (1961). D'Hangest also discusses with considerable intelligence qualities of vocabulary and rhythm, and wisely acknowledges the plurality of Pater's styles.

STUDIES OF INDIVIDUAL WORKS. The last large group of special studies consists of treatments of particular nonfictional works, or groups of works, not already discussed in Section IV. Pater's earliest known essay, "Diaphaneitè," is used by Derek Stanford in "Pater's Ideal Aesthetic Type" (*Cambridge J.*, 1954) to document his departure from the "prophetic collective voice" of the high Victorian sages. "Diaphaneitè" is also given pointed attention, with special notice taken of its original context—the Old Mortality essay society at Oxford—in Gerald Monsman's "Pater's Aesthetic Hero" (*UTQ*, 1971). Monsman interprets this somewhat cryptic document as "an attempt to define the moral temperament possible in a strongly rationalistic age." This is wholly plausible; but "Diaphaneitè" still remains opaque, and further work, perhaps drawing on manuscript evidences, is in order. The most controversial passage Pater ever wrote is the "Conclusion" to *The Renaissance*, and the most celebrated satire upon Pater was W. H. Mallock's acidulous portrayal of Mr. Rose in his *The New Republic* (1877). Two commentators have concerned themselves especially with the relation between the "Conclusion" and Mallock's work. In "Pater, Mr. Rose, and the 'Conclusion' of *The Renaissance*" (*E&S*, 1946; rpt. in *Criticism and the Nineteenth Century*, 1951), Geoffrey Tillotson demonstrates how Mallock adapted passages from the "Conclusion" into the speech of Mr. Rose. Jerome Hamilton Buckley argues in "Pater and the Suppressed 'Conclusion'" (*MLN*, 1950) that it was young antagonists like Mallock, and not impressionable Oxford aesthetes, to whom Pater referred in the 1888 footnote that accompanied the restoration of the (modified) "Conclusion." The preponderance of the evidence, however, suggests otherwise.

Among Pater's essays in the criticism of English literature, that on Wordsworth and the three on Shakespeare have drawn special notice. DeLaura's "The 'Wordsworth' of Pater and Arnold: The Supreme, Artistic View of Life" (*SEL*, 1967; partially incorporated in *Hebrew and Hellene*) not only explores the interaction of Pater and Arnold as critics of Wordsworth, but underscores the presence in Pater's 1874 essay of "one of the most crucial statements of his career." In the mid-seventies Pater seriously proposed to write a book on Shakespeare; and although only three essays were ever published, all are of some interest and one at least, that on *Measure for Measure* (1874), of real distinction indeed. In his *History of Shakesperian Criticism* (1932), Augustus Ralli gives Pater high marks for his perception of "the unity of Shakespeare—the core of poetry which everything else subserves." Since Ralli, however, the only commentator to deal closely with Pater's Shakespeare criticism is Germain d'Hangest. His "Walter Pater, critique shakespearien" (*EA*, 1964) argues that Pater was drawn by sure instinct toward those works of and elements in Shakespeare he was most capable of penetrating, and that he turned away from the major tragic masterpieces which might have overwhelmed him with "un choc insoutenable." Pater's well-known essay on "Style" is a much discussed text, and two works that deal with it (G. S. Fraser's essay and Edmund Chandler's monograph) have been mentioned earlier in this section during the general discussion of Pater's style.

Little attention has been paid to Pater's last complete volume, *Plato and Platonism* (1893); and, as Frean pointed out over a decade ago, a substantial study is in order, for this book significantly summarizes while it modifies some of the most central elements in Pater's thought. Bernard F. Huppé examines the last chapter, in odd isolation from the rest of the book, in "Walter Pater on Plato's Aesthetics" (*MLQ*, 1948), chiefly to instance it as a characteristic specimen of Pater's evasion of tough issues. But Huppé's own failure to recognize the general strategy of the book and his blurred use of key terms (especially the word "aesthetic") seriously cripple his argument. Knoepflmacher accords *Plato and Platonism* an important place in the Pater canon, reading it as a major document of nineteenth-century religious doubt. In *Religious Humanism and the Victorian Novel* (1965), substantially reworking his earlier "Pater's Religion of Sanity" (*VS*, 1962), he considers Pater's intention and strategies, which he compares strikingly to those of Arnold's theological writings. Whether Pater really recommends to young post-Darwinian intellectuals, as Knoepflmacher believes, that they "seek shelter in a compound of ritual and skepticism," the author makes a strong case for reading *Plato and Platonism* as a tract for the times. If such a tract, however, Pater's study is also an essay in the "aesthetic criticism" of philosophy, and should be looked at in the light of other Victorian interpretations of Plato, particularly Jowett's. The disquieting social and political vision of "Lacedaemon" calls for scrutiny too; and the complex relation between the Plato book and the unfinished *Gaston de Latour* may also prove a fertile subject for study—one among the many that Pater scholarship still awaits.

THE OXFORD MOVEMENT
1833-1845

·

Howard W. Fulweiler

Since the central figure of the Oxford Movement, Cardinal Newman, is treated elsewhere in the present collection, one is tempted to wonder what can be left to discuss. The Oxford Movement as a field for criticism and research is today somewhat undefined and uncertain, though not entirely neglected. The yearly Victorian bibliographies of 1932 and 1933, the centenary of the Movement, bring together a large body of scholarship under the heading, "Oxford Movement." As one continues down the years, however, in *Bibliographies of Studies in Victorian Literature* (ed. William D. Templeman, 1945), the "Oxford Movement" section grows smaller and smaller until in 1937 it disappears altogether except for an occasional cross-reference, the remaining crumbs being swallowed up under the headings of individual figures or in the general sections.

Although the Oxford Movement, as a Church of England phenomenon, remains a standard topic for introductions to the nineteenth century, its treatment—in the light of increased knowledge of the age itself and of modern theological developments—has grown increasingly perfunctory. The hortatory fervor of the *Tracts for the Times*, the innocent provincialism of Keble, the naïve severity of Pusey, even the sweet-tempered and literate dogmatism of Dean Church have seemed less compelling as students have come to know more about the theological depth of Maurice or the practical importance of figures like Blomfield or Samuel Wilberforce. Even more important, the theological revolution of the twentieth century, which has so transformed everyone's approach to religious matters—from Vatican II to the electronic prophets of contemporary rock groups—has made the theological controversies of the early nineteenth century seem dated in some respects.

The Oxford Movement was nevertheless a powerful and widely influential religious, social, and political phenomenon. It attracted the attention of the best minds of the nineteenth century, and it remains a rewarding field for scholarly investigation. Not only is the Oxford Movement important as an absorbing episode in Church history and as the occasion for the exercise of considerable literary talent, but it may be seen also as a significant channel for transmitting the Romanticism of the early decades of the century into the Victorian age, as part, in fact, of a now commonly recognized shift in the development of European consciousness.

The broader significance of the Oxford Movement for contemporary students of Western culture lies in its making explicit and conscious the English evolution from a "single society" to a pluralistic society. After the work of Locke, Hobbes, Bacon, Butler, and Hume had prepared the way, the Oxford Movement in the fourth decade of the nineteenth century signaled the end of the earlier participative system of social organization in which Church and State were at once mutually inclusive and coextensive. Ironically, the Movement's call for a revival of supernaturalism made it clear that belief in supernaturalism itself was a matter of human volition, of conscious choice—was not a given. Being a member of a divine society was henceforth to be quite separate from being a citizen of the State. The reaction of the Tractarians to Catholic Emancipation, the Irish Church Temporalities Bill, or even Lord Grey's mild warnings to the Church to set its house in order served to formulate the meaning of these significant events. In the prose of the Oxford Churchmen, marred as it sometimes is by provinciality or the odium theologicum, may be found some important means for interpreting not only the Victorian age but our own.

A vexing problem for the bibliographer of the Oxford Movement is how to define its chronological boundaries. Should it be limited to 1833-45, or should the aftermath of ritualism, the Roman Catholic revival, or later Catholic socialism be included? Since there are chapters on Newman and Victorian religion in this volume, this essay will focus on the years 1833-45 and writing that is essentially related to this period. The chapter will attempt first to define the primary materials of the Movement: relevant prose written either during the years 1833-45 or written by participants about those years. This section will be more a descriptive list than an evaluation. Unfortunately, this list must remain incomplete, touching only major works. The remaining parts will treat later scholarship and criticism in more traditional categories.

I. PRIMARY MATERIALS

Although it cannot be a part of this essay to make a definitive list of manuscript holdings, the major collections should be mentioned. Considerable material is held at Pusey House, Oxford. Printed pamphlets there have been described by Father Hugh, S.S.F, in *Nineteenth-Century Pamphlets at Pusey House* (1961). Other important repositories are the Newman archives at the Birmingham Oratory and the archives of Keble College, Oxford.

The *Tracts for the Times* are the basic documents of the Oxford Movement. Under the general editorship of Newman, the ninety tracts appeared between 9 September 1833 and 27 February 1841. There was a separate title and pagination for each tract. The first forty-six tracts were gathered together at the end of 1834 and published as Volume I of the series, which carried the general title, *Tracts for the Times*. The remaining tracts, which appeared in succeeding years, were collected in four more volumes, bringing the total to five. Tracts 89 and 90 were published separately although they are usually bound with the first five volumes.

There are several slightly varying lists of authorship of the tracts, which, except for Pusey's initialed numbers, were anonymous. The two most useful (and probably most reliable) are those found in Volume III of Henry Parry Liddon's *Life of Pusey* (1893) and in John William Burgon's *Lives of Twelve Good Men* (1891). Of the ninety tracts eighteen are reprints of earlier English divines: twelve (Nos. 37, 39, 42, 44, 46, 48, 50, 53, 55, 62, 65, 70) from Bishop Wilson; two from Bishop Cosin (Nos. 27 and 28); two from Bishop Beveridge (Nos. 25 and 26); one from Bishop Bull (No. 64); and one from Archbishop Ussher (No. 72). Four tracts were "Catenae" or "chains" of evidence from a number of English ecclesiastical or theological writers on specific issues (Nos. 74, 76, 78, 81).

Of the original tracts twenty-six were contributed by Newman according to Burgon (Nos. 1, 2, 3, 6, 7, 10, 11, 15, 19, 20, 21, 33, 34, 38, 41, 45, 47, 71, 73, 75, 79, 82, 83, 85, 88, 90). Liddon credits Newman with Numbers 8 and 31 as well. Charles Frederick Harrold in *John Henry Newman: An Expository and Critical Study of His Mind, Thought and Art* (1945) credits Newman with Numbers 40 and 8. Burgon attributes Number 8 to Froude; both Burgon and Liddon attribute Number 40 to John Keble.

Eight of the tracts were by Keble (Nos. 4, 13, 40, 52, 54, 57, 60, 89). Eight were by Pusey (Nos. 18, 66, 67, 68, 69, 70 which began as a tract by Bishop Wilson but later became the notes to Pusey's treatise on baptism, 77, and the introd. to 81). Five were by John William Bowden (Nos. 5, 29, 30, 56, 58). Four were by Thomas Keble (Nos. 12, 22, 43, 84). Four were by Archdeacon Benjamin Harrison (Nos. 16, 17, 24, 49), three by Hurrell Froude (Nos. 9, 59, 63), and three by Isaac Williams (Nos. 80, 86, 87). There was one tract by each of the following: Alfred Menzies (No. 14), Charles Page Eden (No. 32), R. F. Wilson (No. 51), Antony Buller (No. 61). Number 15 was prepared jointly by Newman and William Palmer.

Another source of Tractarian writing is found in the periodicals which served as outlets for the Movement. The *British Critic*, an old High Church monthly founded by W. Jones of Nayland in 1793, took articles from Newman and his friends. From 1838 to 1841 Newman was sole editor; from 1841 to its discontinuance in the autumn of 1843 Thomas Mozley edited the journal. The last two years of its life were notorious because of the extreme Anglo-Catholic radicalism of writers like William George Ward and Frederick Oakeley. The *British Magazine*, founded by Hugh James Rose in 1831, continued under his editorship until 1836, when Samuel Roffey Maitland edited it until 1849. In this journal appeared the *Lyra Apostolica*, poems by Newman, Keble, Isaac Williams, Hurrell Froude, J. W. Bowden, and Robert Wilberforce (published as a book in 1836). *The Christian Remembrancer* was founded and edited by William Scott and Francis Garden from 1841 to 1844; Scott and James Bowling Mozley continued it from 1844 to 1854; the editorship went on under Scott alone until 1868. *The Guardian* was founded in 1846 by Richard William Church, Frederick Rogers (Lord Blachford), and M. Bernard. Through this later periodical—especially in the contributions of Dean Church (up to 1871)—the Oxford Movement made its relationship to the main currents of Victorian thought.

Long-term scholarly projects of the Tractarians were *The Library of Anglo-Catholic Theology*, ed. William John Copeland, W. F. Audland, C. L. Cornish, and John Barrow (88 vols., 1841-63); *The Library of the Fathers of the Holy Catholic Church, Anterior to the Division of the East and West*, ed. John Keble, John Henry Newman, Edward Bouverie Pusey, and Charles Marriott (48 vols., 1838-85). The former "Library" was supposed to include the principal post-Reformation English divines (it was not completed); the latter contained translations of thirteen Fathers. A complete list with translators and editors appears in Liddon's *Life of Pusey*, 1 (1893). A third project was the ill-fated *Lives of the English Saints* (4 vols., 1844-45). Among the contributors were Newman, R. W. Church, Mark Pattison, F. W. Faber, and J. A. Froude.

Well-known early writing of Newman is treated elsewhere in this volume, but mention should be made of *The Arians of the Fourth Century* (1833); *Lectures on the Prophetical Office of the Church, Viewed Relatively to Romanism and Popular Protestantism* (1837; later included in *The Via Media of the Anglican Church*, 1877); *Parochial and Plain Sermons* (8 vols., 1834-43); *Sermons on Subjects of the Day* (1842); *University Sermons* (1843); *Lectures on Justification* (1838); *Essay on the Development of Christian Doctrine* (1845); and *Loss and Gain: The Story of a Convert* (1848). Newman's Anglican correspondence appears in *Letters and Correspondence during His Life in the English Church* (2 vols., ed. Anne Mozley, 1891) and *Correspondence of J. H. Newman with John Keble and Others, 1839-1849* (ed. Joseph Bacchus, 1917). Charles Stephen Dessain's monumental *Letters and Diaries of John Henry Newman* (1961-) will ultimately present Newman's Anglican period as it is now covering his Roman Catholic years.

An indispensable primary document is *Remains of the Late Reverend Richard Hurrell Froude, M.A.* (4 vols., 1838, 1839), which raised up a host of enemies to the Movement because of its supposed morbidity and its ultra-Catholicism. It was particularly offensive to Evangelicals and other Protestants because of its condemnation of the English Reformers. Important works of John Keble are his popular book of religious poetry, *The Christian Year* (1827); his *Praelectiones Academicae*, lectures on poetic theory delivered when Keble was Professor of Poetry at Oxford (trans. by E. K. Francis as *Lectures on Poetry, 1832-1841*, 2 vols., 1912); *Sermons, Academical and Occasional* (1848); *On Eucharistical Adoration* (1857); and *Occasional Papers and Reviews* (1877). A full bibliography of Keble's work is found in W. J. A. M. Beek's *John Keble's Literary and Religious Contribution to the Oxford Movement* (1959).

A work not usually thought of in connection with the Oxford Movement is William Gladstone's *The State in Its Relations with the Church* (1838). Gladstone's inscription to "The University of Oxford . . . and in the hope that the temper of these pages may be found not alien from her own" made the relationship clear enough for Victorian readers. Keble's reference to Gladstone as "Pusey in a blue coat" was appropriate.

A far more controversial—even notorious—literary product of the Movement was W. G. Ward's *Ideal of a Christian Church* (1844). This polemic was written as a defense of the later "Romanizing" articles in the *British Critic*, which had occasioned the orthodox High Churchman William Palmer to publish his conservative account of the progress of the Movement, *A Narrative of Events Connected with the Publication of the Tracts for the Times, with Reflections on Existing Tendencies to Romanism* . . . (1843). The *Ideal*, a book which drew admiring comment and analysis from John Stuart Mill and Auguste Comte, deserves to be more widely read than it has been. Ward, like Newman, based his theological and moral system on conscience. Not only did he insist upon an increased Catholic orthodoxy, but he promoted the social gospel as well, castigating the Church of England for its neglect of the poor. Ward concluded the book by asserting "that were we, as a Church, to pursue such a line of conduct as has been here sketched, in proportion as we did so, we should be taught from above to discern and appreciate the plain marks of Divine wisdom and authority in the Roman Church, to repent in sorrow and bitterness of heart our great sin in deserting her communion, and to sue humbly at her feet for pardon and restoration." Ward's bumptious and sometimes ecstatic Romanizing brought down a mixture of wrath and laughter upon his ultramontane head. The *Ideal* was condemned by Oxford and Ward was stripped of his degrees.

Although their publication dates do not fall within the twelve years under consideration, the theological works of Robert Wilberforce, which attempted to construct a systematic Anglo-Catholic theology, should be included in a canon of Tractarian prose: *The Doctrine of the Incarnation of Our Lord Jesus Christ* (1848); *The Doctrine of Holy Baptism* (1849); *The Doctrine of the Holy Eucharist* (1853); and *An Inquiry into the Principles of Church Authority, or Reasons for Recalling My Subscription to the Royal Supremacy* (1854), which signaled its author's conversion to Roman Catholicism.

Two classes of primary material which must be treated separately are the accounts of the Oxford Movement published long after 1845 but written by participants, and the considerable contemporaneous writing directed against the Tractarians.

Among general works on the Oxford Movement written by participants, the two best are Newman's *Apologia Pro Vita Sua* (1864) and R. W. Church's *The Oxford Movement* (1891). Church's study will be treated in more detail in a later section. *The Autobiography of Isaac Williams* (ed. George Prevost, 1892) is a useful and interesting source for many anecdotes about Keble, Froude, Pusey, and both John and Francis Newman. It is a valuable gloss on the events recounted in the *Apologia*. Thomas Mozley's *Reminiscences Chiefly of Oriel College and the Oxford Movement* (1882) has been generally criticized for its inaccuracy. As Mozley disarmingly says in his preface, "With all the care I can take, I find myself misspelling names." Although sometimes inaccurate, *Reminiscences* remains a chatty and entertaining source for Tractarian local color.

Unsympathetic accounts of the Movement by participants are found in James Anthony Froude's "The Oxford Counter-Reformation" in *Short Studies on Great Subjects*, Fourth Series (1881), and in Mark Pattison's *Memoirs* (1885). Froude's essay is an absorbing study, sympathetic to Newman personally, but deeply unsympathetic to the Movement itself and its outcome. It provides a history of Froude's involvement in the Movement and his lapse from it. Writing from a middle-class Protestant position, Froude regarded the infidelity of the latter part of the century as being caused in large part by the priestly intolerance of the Tractarians. Also valuable are Froude's two works of fiction, *Shadows of the Clouds* (1847) and *The Nemesis of Faith* (1849). Mark Pattison's waspish and anecdotal account of the Movement is sometimes informative, especially for Oxford politics and Newman's Littlemore period. Pattison ultimately became so alienated that he describes Newman's secession of 1845 as "a deliverance from the nightmare which had oppressed Oxford for fifteen years."

Although it is impossible to mention all the contemporaneous writing opposed to the Tractarians—especially in the voluminous literature of the periodicals and occasional pamphlets—some material should be noticed. Almost as influential as the Irish Church Temporalities Bill in starting the Oxford Movement was Thomas Arnold's *Principles of Church Reform* (1833), which attempted to solve the problems of the Church of England by recommending a broad national Church open to all who accepted the divinity of Christ. There is a good modern edition of Arnold's *Principles* with a sympathetic but judicious introduction by M. J. Jackson and J. Rogan (1962). The first serious attack on the Oxford Movement by an important figure was also made by Arnold: "The Oxford Malignants and Dr. Hampden" (*Edinburgh Rev.*, 1836). Another example of hostile journalistic treatment is John Wilson Croker's "Rubrics and Ritual of the Church of England" (*QR*, 1843). This reviewer (who "killed Keats" and condemned Tennyson's 1833 volume) was "sanguine enough to hope . . . that in a short period nothing will survive of this Tractarian agitation, but a renewed confirmation of the soundness of the Anglican doctrine as enshrined (we use the metaphor advisedly) in our articles." An amusing example of the pamphlet war waged during the thirties and forties is Charles Dickinson's *Pastoral Epistle from His Holiness the Pope to Some Members of the University of Oxford* (1836). Dickinson (domestic chaplain and secretary to Archbishop Whately), professing to be the Pope, expressed "the liveliest pleasure" in receiving "a collection of Tracts emanated from our ancient and well beloved University of Oxford." Another source of contemporaneous writing about the Oxford Movement which was generally hostile is to be found in the episcopal charges of the period. Most of them are collected by W. S. Bricknell in *The Judgment of the Bishops upon Tractarian Theology* (1845). Although this volume is useful and thorough, it is marred by the editor's Protestant partisanship and the confusing arrangement of its materials.

Aside from Newman, there has been little reprinting of Tractarian prose. There are two excellent critical anthologies: *The Mind of the Oxford Movement* (ed. Owen Chadwick, 1960) and *The Oxford Movement* (ed. Eugene R. Fairweather, 1964). Chadwick provides a good introduction to the Movement, followed by a number of brief excerpts from Tractarian writers, arranged under general topics, such as Faith, The Authority of the Church, Sanctification. The selections are taken from Newman, Pusey, Keble, Palmer, James Anthony Froude, and Isaac Williams. Fairweather's collection is on a considerably larger scale. Generally, he presents single works or larger portions of them, each selection having its own introduction. Especially valuable is the reprinting of some rarely seen texts like Keble's sermon on National Apostasy, Pusey's Tract 67, and Williams' Tract 87. There is also a good bibliography. *The Oxford Movement: Being a Selection from Tracts for the Times* (ed. W. G. Hutchinson, 1906) offers a selection of eighteen tracts.

II. GENERAL STUDIES

After the *Apologia*, the best-known general account of the Oxford Movement is R. W. Church's *The Oxford Movement, Twelve Years, 1833–1845* (1891). Church, later to become Dean of St. Paul's, was deeply committed to the Movement and was one of the Proctors who vetoed the attempt to condemn Tract 90 during the Convocation which deprived Ward of his degrees. Like the *Apologia*, Church's history has been influential in forming later opinion. Literate, charitable, and urbane, it is a classic. There is no doubt, however, that with all its benevolence and charm, the book is manifestly unfair to the opponents of the Tractarians. Newman and Church together may be said to have formed the myth of the Oxford Movement; modifications of the myth will in large part be modifications in our understanding of their books. Geoffrey Best has recently edited this work (1970) with an excellent introduction that succinctly describes Oxford in the 1830's, offers a sympathetic but judicious criticism of Church's book, and provides interesting commentary on other important scholarship concerning the Tractarians.

John Henry Overton's *The Anglican Revival* (1897) is a sensible and informative study of the Anglican revival of the nineteenth century as a whole, although it stresses the Oxford Movement and its aftermath. Overton sees the Tractarians as developing naturally out of the Evangelical Movement. He also modifies the generally low estimation of the pre-Tractarian Church by pointing out some of its positive assets in the first third of the century: for example, between government, private groups, and individuals, six million pounds were spent on the building and reparation of churches from 1818 to 1833—a sum far greater than the total expenditure in the hundred years previous to 1818.

A literary curiosity is Walter Walsh's *The Secret History of the Oxford Movement* (1897). This hysterical propaganda piece is concerned mainly with the evils of ritualism, describing the Church of England as "literally honeycombed with Secret Societies, all working in the interests of the scheme for the Corporate Reunion of the Church of England with the Church of Rome." The Oxford Movement itself is also characterized as a secret Romish plot. Walsh plays upon sexual fears— irregularities in convents, misuse of the confessional, and so on—in ways that range from the absurd to the comic.

An influential early twentieth-century study of the Movement has been S. L. Ollard's *A Short History of the Oxford Movement* (1915; a 3rd ed. appeared as late as 1963). This book, useful but partisan from an Anglo-Catholic point of view, is concerned not only with the Tractarians but devotes considerable space to the related issues of the later nineteenth century.

The centennial observances of the Oxford Movement elicited an avalanche of scholarship directed to the Tractarians. The three best general studies of this period, each written from a different bias, are Christopher Dawson's *The Spirit of the Oxford Movement* (1933), Geoffrey Faber's *Oxford Apostles: A Character Study of the Oxford Movement* (1933; 2nd ed. 1936), and Bishop E. A. Knox's *The Tractarian Movement 1833–1845: A Study of the Oxford Movement as a Phase of the Religious Revival in Western Europe in the Second Quarter of the Nineteenth Century* (1933). Dawson's study, written from the angle of a Roman Catholic intellectual, is a keenly intelligent treatment of the Anglican revival at Oxford in the context of European intellectual history. Dawson's focus on the significance of his subject is admirable: "The Tractarians were the contemporaries not only of Arnold, and Hampden and Stanley, but of Strauss and Feuerbach and of Comte and Renan. The real religious issue before the age was not whether High Church or Low Church views should prevail in the Church of England, but whether the Christian religion should preserve its spiritual identity, or whether it should be transformed by the spirit of the age and absorbed into the secularized culture of the modern world."

Dawson's emphasis on Froude's influence on Newman and on the social criticism of the Tractarians is especially informative, but his concluding chapter, which bewails the "liberal modernism" of twentieth-century Anglo-Catholicism and calls for a return to "Catholic intellectual principles," may seem dated to a contemporary reader. Faber's unsympathetic, though absorbing account is surely what graduate seminar professors used to call "an indispensable work." It is quite obviously part of the wave of Freudian literary biographies which washed over the decade preceding it; like Nicolson's *Tennyson* or Brooks's *Mark Twain*, much must be modified and added, but the book provides an important insight into the chief figures of the Oxford Movement. Although Newman is at the center of the book, as the object of its psychologizing, Faber is informative on early Victorian Oxford, Pusey, Froude, and the other "apostles." Following an excessive though always literate and intelligent Freudian bias, Faber suggests latent homosexuality as the force that drew Newman and Froude together, referring to "Newman with his escort of hermaphrodites." This book is very weak on both the theology and the spirituality of the Movement, subjects to which its author is generally indifferent. Bishop Knox's angry but perceptive study is written from an Evangelical position. Knox considers the relationship of the Tractarians to such subjects as the Reformation, eighteenth-century intellectual history, and to France, in the persons of Lamennais, Montalembert, Lacordaire, and others. In opposing the assertion that the Oxford Movement grew out of Evangelicalism, Knox states flatly his attitude to the two religious revivals: "One, the Evangelical, was progressive, associated with humanitarian reforms and world-wide missionary enterprise, the other, the Tractarian, was reactionary, guided by romanticism and desire to re-establish the rule of the clergy over the laity." Knox's own fierce partisanship brings him to detail forcefully what has been often overlooked by later scholars—the real intolerance of Newman, Froude, and Keble toward dissenters.

At once the most readable, the most thorough, and the most recent general account of the Oxford Movement is Marvin R. O'Connell's admirable *The Oxford Conspirators: A History of the Oxford Movement 1833–1845* (1969). Although this book does not attempt some of the larger critical goals of others and seems sometimes overly popular in tone, it is clearly the best history of the Oxford Movement to date. Unbiased, intelligent, and informed, it evokes the atmosphere of Oxford in the 1830's both powerfully and accurately. Particularly good are the fresh and detailed portraits of not only the leaders of the Movement, but the men around them at Oriel: not only Keble, Froude, and Pusey, but Copleston, Hawkins, Arnold, Whately, and Hampden. Similarly, there are useful critical summaries of little-read documents like Whately's *Letters from an Episcopalian*, Arnold's *Principles of Church Reform*, Hawkins' sermon on Tradition, and Keble's Assize Sermon. Again, there is a thorough treatment of the Hadleigh meeting and of Newman's subsequent tangled relationships with the more traditional High Churchmen (Palmer was never accepted as an equal by the Oriel men because of his Irishness). O'Connell's study will surely become a "standard work" on the Oxford Movement.

There are a number of briefer accounts of the Oxford Movement to be found as chapters in more comprehensive ecclesiastical histories. Paul Thureau-Dangin's *La Renaissance catholique en Angleterre* (2 vols., 1899; rev. and re-ed. from Wilfred Wilberforce's trans. in 1914 as *The English Catholic Revival in the Nineteenth Century*) is an early example. The solid and copiously detailed first volume treats the Movement and its background up to the conversion of Manning, but is considerably marred by its Roman Catholic partisanship. The second volume follows the progress of both the English and Roman Catholic revivals into the nineties. Another French contribution is H. Daniel-Rops, *L'Eglise des révolutions: En face des nouveaux destins* (1960; trans. John Warrington as *The Church in an Age of Revolution 1789–1870*, 1965, Vol. III of *The History of the Church of Christ*). Daniel-Rops's work is also heavily slanted in a Roman Catholic direction. His accuracy may be judged by his description of W. E. Gladstone and Matthew Arnold as members of the "small circle of impassioned men" who gathered around Newman to write the tracts.

Francis Warre Cornish's *The English Church in the Nineteenth Century* (1910) provides a judicious and straightforward account of the Movement, offering considerable information about the various publications of the Oxford men and about popular Tractarian literature. Notable in this book are fair and knowledgeable discussions of the Hampden controversy and the Jerusalem Bishopric. The author also gives a thoughtful analysis of Tract 90, not overlooking its occasional sophistries and unhistorical qualities.

A standard work is S. C. Carpenter's *Church and People, 1789–1889: A History of the Church of England from William Wilberforce to* Lux Mundi (1933). This well-written and intelligent study presents the Tractarians in the context of an entire century of Church history, with fine chapters on such related topics as the Evangelicals, Bishop Blomfield, and the Ecclesiastical Commission, and informed critical treatment of the Tracts and their relation to the existing reality of the English Church. Although Carpenter is sympathetic to the Tractarians, he does not fail to note the "remarkable and disappointing" fact "that with so many signs of Anti-Christ plain to be seen . . . vast areas of misery complacently regarded by the more comfortable as a thing inevitable, a penal system and a Poor Law full of cruelty, an almost complete lack of national education, Keble found National Apostasy in a point so purely ecclesiastical."

Two brief accounts are found in L. E. Elliott-Binns's *Religion in the Victorian Era* (1936), which offers two chapters on the Oxford Movement from a Protestant-oriented Anglican point of view, and in Kenneth Scott Latourette's *The Nineteenth Century in Europe: The Protestant and Eastern Churches* (1959, Vol. II of *Christianity in a Revolutionary Age*), which gives a generalized history within a very broad context.

Three valuable short studies are Basil Willey's "Newman and the Oxford Movement" in *Nineteenth-Century Studies: Coleridge to Matthew Arnold* (1948); C. F. Harrold's "The Oxford Movement: A Reconsideration" in *The Reinterpretation of Victorian Literature* (ed. Joseph E. Baker, 1950); and Part I of Owen Chadwick's *The Victorian Church* (1966). Although Willey's essay is more about Newman than the Oxford Movement, it does put the Movement in the general perspective of the history of ideas. There is also some serious treatment of Ward's *Ideal of a Christian Church*, emphasizing the philosophical aspects of its approach to ecclesiastical and social problems. Harrold's estimate of the Tractarians is expressed in social and political terms. He sees the Tractarians as recognizing the dangers of modern secular " 'state-ism'—what the twentieth century was to know as 'totalitarianism.' " The Oxford men were quick to see that in a secular society which believes that political and economic programs can establish the Kingdom of Heaven, one has no right to object to the claims of the State, even though it demands "the absolute submission of the individual will and conscience." Chadwick has written an excellent general study of the thirties and forties in *The Victorian Church*, with considerable new material and fresh, creative treatment of older material. Especially interesting is his detailed description of Irish civil disturbances preceding the Irish Church Bill of 1833 and his convincing demonstration of how many Anglican clergy became High Churchmen simply in political opposition to dissenters and Roman Catholics. The treatment of the Oxford Movement itself—the Oxford political scene, the Hampden affair, Ward's degradation—is required reading for students of the period.

David Newsome's "Newman and the Oxford Movement" in *The Victorian Crisis in Faith* (ed. Anthony Symondson, 1970) provides a succinct and perceptive description of the aims of the Movement focused primarily on the contrasting personalities of Keble and Newman. Two hostile and brief treatments are Owen E. Holloway's "The Tractarian Movement in Oxford" (*Bodleian Q. Record*, 1933) and Ronald Pearsall's "The Oxford Movement in Retrospect" (*QR*, 1966). An example of Pearsall's tone may be seen in his description of Newman, "whose logic is quite dotty but whose ideas have a certain wayward charm." Finally there is a somewhat unsympathetic treatment of the Tractarians in Desmond Bowen's *The Idea of the Victorian Church: A Study of the Church of England 1833–1889* (1968). Although Bowen's discussion does not treat the Tractarians in depth, it has the virtue of relating them to the other important issues of Victorian ecclesiastical history.

III. BIOGRAPHICAL STUDIES

There are many biographical studies of participants in the Oxford Movement. Although some of them are frankly hagiographic, a number are of scholarly and critical importance. The greater share are, of course, devoted to Newman. Since these are treated elsewhere in this volume, it will be necessary to mention only those with special relevance to Newman's Anglican career. Robert Dudley Middleton's *Newman and Bloxam: An Oxford Friendship* (1947) is a record of Newman's friendship with Bloxam, an antiquarian, scholar, and ecclesiologist, who was Newman's curate at Littlemore for a time and was especially interested in reunion with Rome. The book contains much interesting detail about Oxford and Littlemore. Middleton's *Newman at Oxford: His Religious Development* (1950) is a biographical study of Newman's Anglican career and treats the Oxford Movement generally. Maisie Ward's sprightly and intelligent *Young Mr. Newman* (1948) is also a study of the Anglican Newman, but especially concerned with the Oxford Movement and its historical background. Of particular relevance to the Oxford portion of Newman's life is Martin Svaglic's absorbing account of his initial examination failure at Trinity and the crucial importance of his election as Fellow of Oriel College (*PMLA*, 1955). Although not strictly biography and not about the Oxford Movement itself, A. Dwight Culler's excellent *The Imperial Intellect: A Study of Newman's Educational Ideal* (1955) should be mentioned here for its description of the Oxford educational system of the 1830's and 1840's.

There are two important biographies of John Keble: John Taylor Coleridge's *A Memoir of the Rev. John Keble, M.A., Late Vicar of Hursley* (2 vols., 1868; 2nd ed. with corrections and additions, 1869); and Georgina Battiscombe's *John*

Keble, A Study in Limitations (1963). Both books are more informative than critical. Coleridge provides large amounts of biographical material, letters and the like, but as in so many Victorian memoirs there is the inevitable pruning for the sake of delicacy so that one must read between the lines. Battiscombe's work is able and thorough, with considerable new information added; it is perhaps more readable than truly critical. Two brief studies devoted to Keble are M. A. McGreevy's "John Keble on the Anglican Church and the Church Catholic" (*Heythrop J.*, 1964) and Owen Chadwick's "The Limitations of Keble" (*Theol.*, 1964). The first essay discusses Keble's exposition of the branch theory, perhaps showing him to be more tolerant than he actually was. Chadwick also defends Keble against the traditional attacks of critics like J. A. Froude, Tom Mozley, and Francis Newman. Chadwick is nevertheless clear-eyed in estimating Keble's position as a leader. Despite Newman's generous description of him, "Keble was the author of no movement" and he "was no theologian."

It is difficult to know whether to consider H. P. Liddon's monumental *Life of Edward Bouverie Pusey, D.D.* (4 vols., 1893–97) as a part of the Oxford Movement or as a scholarly book about it. Liddon, a Victorian Anglo-Catholic partisan, was as indefatigable in his *Life* as Pusey himself was in belaboring the subject of baptismal regeneration. Just under 2,000 pages, Liddon's book is nearly indispensable for study of the Tractarians. Not only is there exhaustive treatment of Pusey himself, but the many lists, collections, and bibliographies found among the four volumes make them one of the best sources of information about the Oxford Movement. Leonard Prestige's *Pusey* (1933) is popular and sentimental hagiography, though it often shows wit and insight: for example, Pusey "wrote his love-letters like his lecture notes."

Froude biography begins, of course, with the *Remains*, after which there is Louise Imogen Guiney's *Hurrell Froude. Memoranda and Comments* (1904) and Gordon Huntington Harper's *The Froude Family in the Oxford Movement* (1933). Guiney's book is not a biography but consists of Froude's letters to Keble, Newman, and others, and Victorian writing about him, drawn from many sources. Harper's work treats the Froude family and their interesting connections throughout the intellectual establishment of Victorian England; the Oxford Movement and Hurrell's relation to it; and Newman's relationship with William Froude, Hurrell's scientist brother.

There are two semibiographical works on William George Ward by his son, Wilfrid Ward, *William George Ward and the Oxford Movement* (1889) and *William George Ward and the Catholic Revival* (1893). The latter, a study of Ward and the Roman Catholic revival in England after 1845, is less pertinent to the present essay. The former is an important source book, containing a detailed account of the later phase of the Oxford Movement and of the early life of Ward, with considerable quotation of contemporaneous response to the Oxford Movement and to Ward. Especially interesting is the publication of J. S. Mill's and Auguste Comte's correspondence concerning Ward's work and the coming struggle between positivism and Catholicism.

A. P. Stanley's *The Life and Correspondence of Thomas Arnold, D.D.* (2 vols., 1844) is a central document for Victorian studies as a whole as well as for the Oxford Movement. The liberal opposition to the Tractarians—also rooted in the Oriel common room—is perhaps best articulated in Arnold's life and letters. Letters like his to Whately (1836) calling for a series of "Church of England Tracts" to promote ecumenicity after "establishing again the supreme authority of Scripture and reason, against Tradition, Councils, and Fathers," or his letter to Bunsen (1838) suggesting that the root of the "Antichristian apostasy" is the "tenet of 'a priestly government transmitted by a mystical succession from the Apostles'" indicate an important portion of the ecclesiastical and theological opinions surrounding the Tractarians.

Interesting in detail, but anecdotal and uncritical, is J. W. Burgon's *Lives of Twelve Good Men* (2 vols., 1888). Among the lives treated are Martin Joseph Routh, Hugh James Rose, Charles Marriott, Edward Hawkins, Samuel Wilberforce, and Charles Page Eden. Another book of reminiscences written from a liberal point of view is W. Tuckwell's *Pre-Tractarian Oxford: A Reminiscence of the Oriel "Noetics"* (1909), with chapters on Eveleigh, Copleston, Whately, Arnold, Hampden, Hawkins, Baden Powell, and Blanco White. Tuckwell refers to Wilson, Keble, and Newman as "religious obscurantists of the higher sort."

Another more general biographical aid is Bertram C. A. Windle's *Who's Who of the Oxford Movement* (1926). Written from a Roman Catholic point of view, this book contains brief biographical notes on persons connected to the Oxford Movement, but is somewhat marred by inaccuracies and partisanship. A more scholarly effort, though from an Anglo-Catholic viewpoint, is R. D. Middleton's *Magdalen Studies* (1936), which contains studies of ten men associated with Magdalen College and the Oxford Movement. The biographical accounts, mainly based on letters, include Routh, Bloxam, Frederick Bulley, William Palmer, Roundell Palmer, J. B. Mozley, Henry Best, R. W. Sibthorp, Bernard Smith, and Henry Ramsden Bramley. Gertrude Donald's *Men Who Left the Movement* (1933) is a tendentious and sentimental treatment of the conversions of Newman, Manning, Thomas W. Allies, and Basil William Maturin.

A group of able and more recent biographical studies have considered figures closely related to the Oxford Movement. In addition to her *Keble* (1963), Battiscombe has a popular but detailed treatment of Tractarian rural life in *Charlotte Mary Yonge: The Story of an Uneventful Life* (1943). This book is not only a study of the best-known Tractarian novelist, but also describes the texture of human life in a pious Victorian family whose vicar was the Rev. John Keble. G. C. B. Davies' *Henry Phillpotts, Bishop of Exeter 1778–1869* (1954) is a capable biography of "Henry of Exeter," the cantankerous and litigious High Church bishop who was a principal in the Gorham trial. Full of detail, it sheds interesting sidelights on the Oxford Movement. Basil Alec Smith's *Dean Church: The Anglican Response to Newman* (1958) is a first-rate critical biography. Smith illuminates Church's function as the link between the Tractarians and the liberal Catholicism of Charles Gore. In Church's own writing, even dating from his articles in the *British Critic* of 1843, one finds the insistence that the Church speak out on social and economic questions. Smith stresses the importance of Church's continuing friendship with Frederick Rogers, the old friend of Newman and Hurrell Froude. Rogers (Lord Blachford), as a lawyer working at the Colonial Office, was a part of larger nineteenth-century English life. He founded the *Guardian*, a High Church weekly for which Church wrote intelligently and humanely up to 1871, helping to create the beginnings of a liberal Catholicism far different from the narrow orthodoxy first envisioned by Newman, Keble, and Pusey. David Newsome's *The Wilberforces and Henry Manning: The Parting of Friends* (1966), an absorbing biographical study which contains much new and unpublished material, presents the Oxford Movement from a novel point of view, that of the Wilberforces: the venerable William; his sons, Samuel, Robert, and Henry; and their brother-in-law, Henry Manning. In apologizing for his extended treatment of Robert Wilberforce's systematic theology, Newsome points in justification to the scholarly "neglect of the period which lies between the secession of Newman and the collapse of the Anglo-Catholic party after the Gorham judgment, with the result that insufficient attention has been paid to the movement, in which Manning played a leading rôle, to supply the Anglican Church with an effective ascetical theology." Newsome's excellent study as a whole serves to fill this notable gap in our knowledge.

IV. SPECIALIZED STUDIES

Literary Theory

Although Newman has received the greatest share of attention from students of literature, there has been considerable scholarly attention devoted to other literary topics connected with the Oxford Movement, the most widely discussed being Keble's poetic theories and Tractarian fiction.

John Campbell Shairp's *Studies in Poetry and Philosophy* (1868) contains, along with essays on Wordsworth and Coleridge, an essay on John Keble. Although Shairp's graceful discussion of the Oxford Movement itself is usually remembered best, his chapter attempts a critical estimate of Keble not only as clergyman, but as poet and literary theorist. Alba H. Warren, Jr. has chapters on both Newman and Keble in his *English Poetic Theory 1825–1865* (1950). Warren's intelligent essay on Keble is devoted to the Latin *Praelectiones Academicae* (1844). These "essays in Christian criticism" are chiefly influenced by Plato, Warren feels; they tend, however, to describe the basic function of poetry as catharsis in a proto-Freudian mode. Keble seems to treat the imagination both in a Coleridgean and in a psychotherapeutic sense. (Men become "their own physicians" through poetry.) Also stressing Keble's critical relationship to Freud is M. H. Abrams' excellent "Poetry as Catharsis: John Keble and Others" in *The Mirror and the Lamp: Romantic Theory and the Critical Tradition* (1953). The best recent study of Keble which joins his literary and religious interests is the Dutch scholar W. J. A. M. Beek's *John Keble's Literary and Religious Contribution to the Oxford Movement* (1959). Beek attempts to show how Keble's philosophical acceptance of Butler, his theories of poetry, and his sacramentalism all formed a coherent system. Beek's analysis of Keble's poetic theory is quite similar to those of Warren and Abrams, but he is especially perceptive in his discussion of Keble's emphasis on the analogy between symbolic apprehension and the Christian sacraments. "The symbolic view of nature, centering round the constant recollection of Christ's presence in the world, may justly be called Keble's seminal principle and the source of all his contributions to the Oxford Movement." Beek also stresses the influence of Wordsworth, to whom Keble's *Praelectiones* were dedicated. Keble apparently felt that the theories of Butler and Wordsworth might prepare for a return to the symbolic mode of thought of the Fathers. Beek's study is the most successful so far in illuminating the deep relationship among the Romantics, Keble, and the Oxford Movement—not a sentimental antiquarian Romanticism, but a more fundamental similarity in epistemological assumptions. "With the help of the new poetry, Keble hoped he might succeed in changing the mentality of many people and convince Anglican Churchmen that of all the doctrines on which their church, as a divine institution, depended for its existence and continuance, the doctrine of sacramental grace was the central one."

There are four able general surveys of imaginative literature associated with the Oxford Movement: Hoxie Neal Fairchild's chapter on "Catholic Christianity" in *Religious Trends in English Poetry: 1830–1880, Christianity and Romanticism in the Victorian Era*, IV (1957); Joseph E. Baker's *The Novel and the Oxford Movement* (1932); Margaret M. Maison's *The Victorian Vision: Studies in the Religious Novel* (1961); and Raymond Chapman's *Faith and Revolt: Studies in the Literary Influence of the Oxford Movement* (1970). Although somewhat disappointing in his more generalized approach, Fairchild is amusingly readable in his intelligent support of the general thesis that "the Catholic Revival and the Romantic Movement point in opposite directions." Among others, Fairchild treats Newman, Frederick Faber, Keble, R. C. Trench, and Isaac Williams. Baker's study of the novel is an important contribution to nineteenth-century scholarship, describing the relation of Victorian life to religious controversy as it is reflected in popular novels. There are general chapters on early Tractarian novels, Evangelical fictional attacks on the Oxford Movement, and Tractarian fictional attacks on that many-headed beast, Democracy. There are also chapters on individual novelists such as Newman, Disraeli, Kingsley, Charlotte Yonge, and Trollope, and a valuable essay on Joseph Henry Shorthouse and his sometimes neglected *John Inglesant* (1880), the exotic historical novel which revived the Anglican mysticism of the seventeenth century for Victorian Anglo-Catholics. Maison's *The Victorian Vision* is an amusing and informative survey of not only the literature treated by Baker but also later novelists of the nineteenth century such as Butler, Pater, Hardy, George Macdonald, and Marie Corelli. Although this book is entertaining and wide ranging, its scholarship is sloppy. Baker, for instance, in his review of it (*NCF*, 1962), demonstrates the author's extensive and unacknowledged use of his work in the earlier chapters (Baker's name is mentioned only twice and without bibliographical reference). Although it is popular in tone and presents little new information, Chapman's *Faith and Revolt* offers an excellent introduction to the Oxford Movement and its relation to nineteenth-century imaginative literature in general. Chapman treats fewer authors than Baker or Maison, but discusses them in a fuller context, including general chapters on both the background of the Movement and the Movement itself. He also considers not only the religious novelists of the period—Yonge, Newman, Kingsley, Froude, Wiseman, Shorthouse, and others—but also has good chapters on Christina Rossetti and the later Victorian mixture of Puseyism and medievalism to be found in Richard Watson Dixon, Digby Mackworth Dolben, William Morris, and Edward Burne-Jones.

Andrew L. Drummond provides what amounts to a brief summary of Baker's study in "Fiction and the Oxford Movement" (*CQR*, 1945). This essay contains little beyond plot summaries of material treated in Baker. John O. Waller's "A Composite Anglo-Catholic Concept of the Novel, 1841–1868" (*BNYPL*, 1966) traces changing Anglo-Catholic attitudes toward fiction in two periodicals, the *Christian Remembrancer* (1851–68) and the *Ecclesiastic* (1845–68), chronicling the Anglo-Catholic state of mind toward the novel from 1840 to 1860.

Interest in the fiction of Charlotte Yonge is continued in Margaret Mare and

Alicia C. Percivale's sentimental *Victorian Best Seller: The World of Charlotte M. Yonge* (1948). This work centers on the fiction of Yonge, but is damaged by its lack of documentation. A group of essays on Charlotte Yonge, some literary and some antiquarian, along with some reprints of rare short pieces of Yonge, is collected in *A Chaplet for Charlotte Yonge: The Proceedings of the Charlotte M. Yonge Society* (ed. Georgina Battiscombe and Marghanita Laski, 1965).

The relationship of the Oxford Movement to early Victorian periodicals is developed in Esther Rhoads Houghton's "The *British Critic* and the Oxford Movement" (*SB*, 1963) and Marion Lochhead's "Lockhart, the *Quarterly*, and the Tractarians" (*QR*, 1953). The former is a valuable research tool, based on MSS at the Birmingham Oratory and Pusey House, which details the history of the *British Critic* and its close relationship with the Tractarians; the latter is a popular but interesting description of the *Quarterly*'s inconsistent treatment of the Tractarians, that is, Lockhart's sympathy and Croker's hostility. As informative as this essay is, it is somewhat marred by carelessness, such as references to the "Oxford Movement of 1832" or Newman's Tract Number 80.

Shane Leslie's "Lewis Carroll and the Oxford Movement" (*London Mercury*, 1933) contends that Carroll reflected the religious controversies between the forties and the seventies in *Alice in Wonderland* (1865) and *Alice's Adventures through the Looking Glass* (1871). "It is not profane to suggest that *Alice in Wonderland* may contain a Secret History of the Oxford Movement. Lewis Carroll himself lived as a Don at Christchurch under the shadow of Pusey." Although Leslie's thesis is surely suggestive, the analogies he offers in its support are so forced and absurd that one suspects a marvelous hoax. A thoroughly admirable study of literary influence is David J. DeLaura's "Matthew Arnold and John Henry Newman: The 'Oxford Sentiment' and the Religion of the Future" (*TSLL*, 1965), now incorporated into *Hebrew and Hellene in Victorian England* (1969). Although DeLaura's aim in this monograph is to indicate Newman's literary influence on Matthew Arnold as it derives from the temper of mind at Oriel College in the thirties and forties, his thorough scholarship and critical insight shed a good deal of light on the Oxford Movement and the Victorian intellectual community in general.

Finally, Stephen Gaselee's "The Aesthetic Side of the Oxford Movement" in *Northern Catholicism: Centenary Studies in the Oxford and Parallel Movements* (1933) gives a brief account of the Cambridge Camden Society, the founding of *The Ecclesiologist* (1845–68), the literary labors of John Mason Neale in translating medieval Latin hymns, and the relation of the Oxford Movement to the Pre-Raphaelites, especially Christina Rossetti.

Social and Political History

Although the Oxford Movement is usually discussed in a theological or literary context, it took place within a social and political framework by which it was affected and upon which it had important effects. Consequently, there have been a number of studies particularly directed at political or social history connected with the Tractarians. An authoritative work in this regard is Olive J. Brose's *Church and Parliament: The Reshaping of the Church of England, 1828–1860* (1959). Although it does not deal with the Oxford Movement directly, it treats in detail the reform agitation (in the periodical press, in parliament, and elsewhere) surrounding the Church and the ecclesiastical reforms ultimately adopted. The focus is on "the

Church as an established institution in a time when all things established were called to account." The author emphasizes the work of the Ecclesiastical Commission and of Robert Peel and Bishop Blomfield. Although the Elizabethan concept of a single society had to be redefined in the nineteenth century, their work ensured that "the legal recognition of the church as the expression of the religion of the nation continued, despite the truth of Manning's remark to Gladstone that the Church had reverted to its pre-Constantine position." This book contains a good bibliography of works relating to the ecclesiastical history of the period. C. K. Francis Brown's *A History of the English Clergy, 1800–1900* (1953) provides detailed discussion of the status of the nineteenth-century clergy, including pluralism, the tithe system, disabilities of non-Anglican clergy, cathedral corporations, and so on. Brown also describes the large influence of the Tractarians on practical clerical reform. An earlier work that sheds some light on the Tractarians' relation to Church reform is W. L. Mathieson's *English Church Reform, 1815–1840* (1923). The Oxford leaders debated whether they should combine to agitate against the threatened inroads of liberalism (like the Ecclesiastical Commission) or whether they should simply restore Catholic theology. Mathieson brings out more clearly the part played by the "Associationists" who were more interested in the former course of action. The *British Magazine*, beginning its attack on Church reform in 1832, "became notorious for its defense or extenuation of almost every ecclesiastical abuse." There was, thus, more than met the eye at the Hadleigh meeting (Rose was editor of the *British Magazine*): a portion of the Oxford Movement's early popularity derived simply from its supposed defense of pluralism. Similarly, T. L. Harris in "The Conception of Authority in the Oxford Movement" (*Church Hist.*, 1934) stresses the Tractarian interest in current events: the counterrevolution in England crystalized around the Church "because the country clergy represented the landed interest." With the growth of Dissent, the parson needed theological reasons to keep his congregation.

Two able studies dealing with the social aspects of the Oxford Movement are William George Peck's *The Social Implications of the Oxford Movement* (1933) and Cyril K. Gloyn's *The Church in the Social Order: A Study of Anglican Social Theory from Coleridge to Maurice* (1942). The former, written from an Anglo-Catholic viewpoint, is concerned with the general background of the Oxford Movement—intellectual, political, and social. Peck assumes the failure of capitalism, which he associates with Protestantism and secularism, and sees the Catholic revival as a rebellion against both the totalitarian authority of the State and the injustices of the capitalist system. Although there are a few interesting references to the social criticism of Pusey, Newman, Froude, and Ward, the book lacks sustained consideration of the writing of the Tractarians themselves. Peck seems to assume that the Tractarians were very much like twentieth-century Catholic socialists, which—despite their defense of the poor—they were not. Gloyn's far more balanced study contains chapters on Coleridge, the Tractarians, Thomas Arnold, and Maurice. Emphasizing the Tractarian insistence both on authority and on "holiness" or works, Gloyn is particularly acute in perceiving the characteristic Tractarian schizophrenia toward the Church-State relationship. On the one hand, fearing the reformed parliament, they stressed the independence of the Church and discussed the possibilities of its separation from the State. On the other hand, they believed the Church was the agent of sanctification for the secular State, which ought to be made "*subservient* to the spiritual Church; for the good of the State, the

Church should not separate from it." Gloyn also analyzes the often-neglected social criticism of Ward and others in the *British Critic*. Although the Tractarians, unlike many Victorians, insisted that poverty was no sin, their assertion that it was actually an advantage may not have been received with intense enthusiasm by the poor. Although the Tractarians protested the employment of women and children, the exploitation of the agricultural poor, and the Poor Law, they upheld political and economic inequality, and their narrowness often kept them from cooperating with those outside the Church who sought social amelioration. Two shorter studies with an Anglo-Catholic orientation are Ruth Kenyon's "The Social Aspects of the Catholic Revival" (in *Northern Catholicism*, ed. N. P. Williams and Charles Harris, 1933) and her "Ideal Ward and a Catholic Sociology" (*Christendom*, 1932). The former treats Tractarian social criticism—especially Pusey's—but is also concerned with Anglo-Catholic social action of the late nineteenth and early twentieth centuries. The latter is a brief summary of Ward's trenchant attack on the social ills of his age—particularly the Church's neglect of the poor.

Richard A. Soloway's informative *Prelates and People: Ecclesiastical Social Thought in England 1783–1852* (1969) does not treat the Tractarians directly, but provides interesting insight into episcopal responses to the social background in which the Oxford Movement was formed and ran its course. Bishop Denison, for instance, in fighting the new Poor Law was "defining in social terms what the Tractarians were arguing in theological and historical terms." Soloway's "Episcopal Perspectives and Religious Revivalism in England 1784–1851" (*HMPEC*, 1971) is especially concerned with the attitudes of the bishops to Methodists and Evangelicals, but includes a brief treatment of their judgment of the Oxford Movement as well.

More directly political than social are John Neville Figgis' *Churches in the Modern State* (1913) and Harold J. Laski's monograph, "The Political Theory of the Oxford Movement," in *Studies in the Problem of Sovereignty* (1917). Although Figgis deals less directly with the Oxford Movement, his discussion of the history and development of the "established" Church of England in its legal relation to the secular State is suggestive in application to the anti-Erastianism of the Tractarians. Laski, fearing the "tremendous danger in modern times that people will believe the legal sovereignty of a State to be identical with its moral sovereignty," sees fruitful political significance both in the Oxford Movement and in the Disruption of 1843 in the Church of Scotland. Laski argues that both anti-Erastian movements offer a pluralistic theory of society to oppose the rise of the monistic secular State. Not inheriting the Presbyterian theory of Church and State, the Tractarians had to construct a new definition of the Church, "and they found almost immediately that to define its identity was to assert its exclusiveness." Laski's essay treats in some detail the late Victorian legal consequences of the Tractarian theory of the Church.

There have been, of course, a large number of brief or more limited historical studies of the Oxford Movement or subjects closely related to it. W. G. Roe, for instance, shows the political and theological influence of Lamennais on such figures as Newman, Froude, and William Palmer in his chapter "Lamennais and the Oxford Movement," in *Lamennais and England* (1966). He also discusses the specific relation of some of the Tracts to the French theorist. Howard W. Fulweiler's "Tractarians and Philistines: The *Tracts for the Times* vs. Middle-Class Values" (*HMPEC*, 1962) is a historical study based generally on the *Tracts* and contemporaneous pamphlet polemics, for example, *The Restoration of Churches Is the*

Restoration of Popery (1844) or *The Wooden Walls of England in Danger. A Defence of Church Pews* (1844). Fulweiler sees the *Tracts* as antagonistic both to middle-class Protestant religious opinion and to the secular ideals of the middle class as well. In "Mr. Gladstone and the Oxford Movement" (*NC*, 1933), the Archbishop of Canterbury, C. Gordon Lang, provides a general treatment of Gladstone's religion and his close relation both to Oxford and to the Tractarians. Kenneth M. Peck's "The Oxford Controversy in America: 1839" (*HMPEC*, 1964) chronicles the American periodical reception of the *Tracts* as they affected the already existing antagonism between the evangelistic, revivalistic school and the High Churchmen in the American Church.

The historical development from the Tractarians to the more liberal late Victorian Anglo-Catholicism is traced in "Oxford and the Origins of Liberal Catholicism in the Church of England" (*Studies in Church History: Papers Read at the First Winter and Summer Meetings of the Ecclesiastical History Society*, ed. C. W. Dugmore and Charles Duggan, 1964), where W. R. Ward argues convincingly that Oxford University politics helped in liberalizing the Tractarians and their successors, thus making possible the advent of a liberal Catholicism such as that found in *Lux Mundi* (1889). This argument is more fully developed in Ward's *Victorian Oxford* (1965). Gladstone was an important influence in this process, as were R. W. Church and J. B. Mozley. A less substantial essay by Hamilton Baynes, "From Newman to Gore" (*HJ*, 1933), is a very general attempt to trace the same evolution. Focusing on the development of liberalism in social theory, this study's thesis is that the new idea of the Church brought back the corporate theory of society. V. H. H. Green's *Religion at Oxford and Cambridge* (1965) has two pertinent historical chapters, "The Tractarians" and "Mark Pattison and the Oxford Movement," the latter being of interest in viewing the Movement through Pattison's hostile eyes. William J. Baker in his intelligent "Hurrell Froude and the Reformers" (*JEH*, 1970) suggests the interesting paradox that Froude's "essentially unhistorical" polemics against the sixteenth-century Reformers were on the one hand a useful corrective to the equally unhistorical glorification of them by the Evangelicals, but on the other hand stimulated the development of a sounder and more objective historical method in the second half of the nineteenth century.

Although this essay cannot concern itself with the Roman Catholic Revival of the nineteenth century, there has been some useful scholarship relating early Victorian Roman Catholicism to the Tractarians that should be mentioned. In *Lord Shrewsbury, Pugin, and the Catholic Revival* (1946), despite contrary opinions like Newman's remarks in his "Second Spring" sermon, Denis Gwynn shows that there was an extremely active Roman Catholic life in England both before and during the Oxford Movement. Another interesting and able contribution to this subject has been made by Charles T. Dougherty and Homer C. Welsh in "Wiseman on the Oxford Movement: An Early Report to the Vatican" (*VS*, 1958). This article gives a translation of a long letter of Wiseman to the Vatican written in 1839 and includes both Wiseman's opinions of the Oxford Movement and extracts from letters of Pugin, Ambrose Phillipps, George Spencer, and Bishop Walsh. A note by Louis Allen, "The Oxford Movement and the Vatican" (*VS*, 1960), also discusses ways in which the Vatican may have learned about the Oxford Movement.

The relation of the Tractarians to Victorian periodicals from a political point of view is considered by John L. Morrison in "The Oxford Movement and the British Periodicals" (*CHR*, 1959). The thesis of this essay is that periodicals like

Blackwood's, the *Quarterly Review,* the *Edinburgh Review,* and *Westminster Review* were essentially concerned with the secular implications of Tractarian thought.

A. O. J. Cockshut has produced two important books that, though not directly related to the Oxford Movement, have much tangential relevance. *Anglican Attitudes: A Study of Victorian Religious Controversies* (1959) contains judicious and informative accounts of three controversies: the Gorham Judgment, the publication of *Essays and Reviews,* and the Colenso affair—all of which may be said to have grown out of the earlier Tractarian controversy. *Religious Controversies in the Nineteenth Century: Selected Documents* (1966) provides selections from such writers as William Wilberforce, Coleridge, Newman, Thomas Arnold, Clough, Mansel, and others.

Theology

Although the Oxford Movement produced no great theologians, it was concerned above all things with restoring and defining a theological position. The amount of specifically theological investigation of the Tractarians has been surprisingly small, but there is, nonetheless, a body of scholarship which must be considered.

Despite its special concern with liturgical and devotional practice, J. Wickham Legg's *English Church Life from the Restoration to the Tractarian Movement* (1914) is a good place to start the study of the theological and ecclesiastical tradition the Tractarians inherited. This interesting work, filled with detailed information on such topics as Cathedral ceremonial usage, the number of services conducted regularly in London churches, the sacramental life of the Church of England, and the enormous number of devotional works published in the eighteenth century, provides an antidote to the usual generalizations about the moribund state of the Church before the Oxford Movement.

The end of the nineteenth century and the first third of the twentieth produced the first group of significant theological studies. An important, though often overlooked, general study is Andrew Martin Fairbairn's *Catholicism, Roman and Anglican* (1899). This humane and charitable, if not wholly sympathetic, work contains a number of related essays on the Church and Victorian religion and their relation to society. There is treatment not only of the Oxford Movement and the Roman and Anglo-Catholic revivals, but also of other theologians such as Lightfoot, Westcott, Hort, and even Jowett. Fairbairn's intuition of the tinge of deism brought on by a rigid Tractarian orthodoxy goes far to explain the spiritual agonies of mid-century agnostics or even converts like Gerard Manley Hopkins. It "made man an atheist by nature, and so confined divine influence to artificial and ordained channels as to make the common life which most needs to be illumined and ennobled by the divine, either vacant of God or alien from him." Fairbairn is again acute in seeing that "Newman, with all that he stands for, represents the struggle of English empiricism to remain empirical, and yet become imaginative and religious." Another able older study, basically unfriendly to Tractarian theology, is Vernon F. Storr's *The Development of English Theology in the Nineteenth Century 1800–1860* (1913). A general work, with three chapters devoted to the Oxford Movement and to Newman, it recognizes that "Tractarianism has left a permanent mark upon the English Church; though its power has been felt less in the sphere of thought than in that of practical Church life." The author emphasizes the Tractarians' interest in the past, but scores their uncritical and unhistorical use of the past. Only when their theology changed from static to dynamic within the context of later Anglo-Catholicism could the Oxford Movement become fruitful: in place of a theory of the Church as "the accredited organ for the transmission of divine truth, was set up a theory of the Church as an extension of the Incarnation, and the channel through which the living Christ works His age-long work of redemption."

The standard work on Tractarian theology is Yngve Brilioth's *The Anglican Revival: Studies in the Oxford Movement* (1925). This intelligent and informed study by a Swedish bishop treats the background (stressing Coleridgean influence) and the Movement itself thoroughly, but is particularly good on theological issues and on the devotional life engendered by the Movement. Although the "essential feature" of the remodeling of the nineteenth-century English Church is its revival of "Anglicanism in the narrower sense, which takes its conception of the Church from Laud and its piety from the Fathers of the Restoration," the Oxford Movement must be understood as a religious revival analogous to the Evangelical Movement. The deepening feeling in the life of the Church and the characteristic Tractarian sense of the *Mysterium Tremendum* were undoubtedly of greater significance than the political reaction against liberalism upon which Newman focuses in the *Apologia*, according to Brilioth. He is perceptive in analyzing an incipient Pelagianism in the strict and sometimes naïve moralism of the Tractarians, especially Froude. There are also theological chapters on "The Static View of the Church," "The Fundamental Forms of Tractarian Piety," "The Progressive Idea of the Church," "The Doctrine of Justification," and "Mysticism and Sacramentalism." Brilioth's briefer *Evangelicalism and the Oxford Movement* (1934) suggests that the Oxford Movement did not spring solely from the High Church tradition, but was based in the living religious tradition of the Evangelicals. Unfortunately, the Tractarian ignorance of the Continental Reformation "has been an important and perhaps a fatal factor in the history of the Oxford Movement." Thus the Movement was not itself theological, but could only stimulate later theological investigation. "It is part of the tragedy and crisis of the Oxford Movement that it sought to defend an historical view by methods that were essentially unhistorical."

Clement C. J. Webb's *A Century of Anglican Theology* (1923) and *Religious Thought in the Oxford Movement* (1928) are also concerned with theology. The former contains only one relevant essay, which attempts to relate Anglican theology to the "greater movement of European thought." The latter is a brief introductory study which makes the important point that the Oxford Movement was over before either the publication of *On the Origin of Species* or the advent of modern Biblical criticism. Thus its theological atmosphere is totally different from our own in ways that modern scholars sometimes overlook.

Evelyn Underhill in "The Spiritual Significance of the Oxford Movement" (*HJ*, 1933) sums up the spiritual results of the Movement as: "(1) the restoration of Catholic Tradition, the sense of the Church; (2) the revival of sacramental and liturgical worship; (3) the disciplined life; (4) sanctity." She stresses perceptively the importance of the "ritualist" phase which brought the Oxford Movement out of the intellectual circle of the University into the mainstream of Victorian life.

A useful collection of essays (a few of which have been mentioned above) published during the Oxford Movement centennial is *Northern Catholicism: Centenary Studies in the Oxford and Parallel Movements* (ed. N. P. Williams and Charles Harris, 1933). N. P. Williams' "The Theology of the Catholic Revival" is a competent survey which substantiates the general judgment that the Oxford Movement "made but a comparatively slight contribution to theology in the technical sense, whether systematic or historical." Eric Graham's "The Moral Ideals and Aims of the Movement" describes the Tractarian attack on Erastianism, while E. A. Down's "Pastoral Ideals and Methods of the Movement" is particularly concerned with the devoted Anglo-Catholic clergy who inherited the Movement, with their peculiar mixture of social concern and dogmatic ecclesiasticism. W. J. Sparrow Simpson, in "The Spiritual Independence of the Church," outlines the crisis in Church-State relations which confronted the Tractarians, detailing the developments from Hooker's *Ecclesiastical Polity* to modern times. A. S. Duncan Jones's "The Œcumenical Ideals of the Oxford Movement" is a homiletic Anglo-Catholic defense of the Lambeth "Quadrilateral."

Two short centenary studies by F. L. Cross summarize particular aspects of the Movement: *The Oxford Movement and the Seventeenth Century* (1933) and *The Tractarians and Roman Catholicism* (1933). The more useful of these is the first, which notes the coincidental publication of editions of many of the Caroline divines on the eve of the Oxford Movement and points to the Tractarian use of them in the "catenae" tracts and in the *Library of Anglo-Catholic Theology*. Cross argues that the Tractarian insistence on the Apostolic Succession would have found precedent in the seventeenth century, but with little of the rigidity of the nineteenth. It is undoubtedly true that the Tractarians were far more influenced by the devotional life of the Caroline Church than by its theology.

W. H. Mackean's *The Eucharistic Doctrine of the Oxford Movement: A Critical Survey* (1933) is a sensible, though not particularly sympathetic, study with concerns that are as much practical as scholarly. Mackean surveys the three characteristic seventeenth-century doctrines of the Eucharist—Virtualism, Memorialism, and Receptionism; the varying attitudes of the Tractarians toward them; and the modifications they made of them. He concludes that "A 'Catholic doctrine of the Eucharist' is meaningless, for it does not exist." P. E. Shaw's *The Early Tractarians and the Eastern Church* (1930), while providing some information on such topics as the Jerusalem Bishopric and William Palmer's (of Magdalen) abortive relations with the Russian Church, is an uncritical summary. It includes an appendix comparing Tractarian and Orthodox views on various theological issues.

Although interest in the Oxford Movement dwindled almost to the vanishing point after its apogee in 1933, there has been a renewal of first-class scholarly investigation in the last decade. A nearly indispensable work for Church history in general is Horton Davies' five-volume *Worship and Theology in England*. Of relevance to Newman scholarship is Volume IV: *From Newman to Martineau, 1850–1900* (1961). Volume III: *From Watts and Wesley to Maurice, 1690–1850* (1961) covers the Oxford Movement. Davies' approach is particularly useful since it is concerned with worship ("liturgical theology") and religious atmosphere rather than with formal doctrinal statement. This study, which is general and thematic rather than detailed and chronological, sees the Tractarians as being at the center of a widespread return to a more Catholic conception of Christianity. Even the Protestant tradition in English worship, in Davies' view, cannot be understood if the renewed liturgical expression of the nineteenth century is not considered along with the Evangelical revival of the eighteenth. The Oxford Movement is not an antithesis to Evangelicalism but a complement. It thus takes on practical importance even for Protestants who "begin to think and pray in terms of the *Ecclesia* instead of *ecclesiolae*" and therefore anticipate the advent of an Ecumenical Church.

The best theological study of the Tractarians since Brilioth is also by a Scandinavian: Alf Härdelin's *The Tractarian Understanding of the Eucharist* (1965). Although its title suggests a limited topic such as that of Mackean's earlier book, this work illuminates the entire theological stance of the Oxford Movement. Armed with solid scholarship, Härdelin analyzes freshly the relationship between Romantic epistemology and Tractarian sacramentalism suggested by Beek, especially as it appears in Newman's and Keble's admiration for Coleridge and Wordsworth. Keble's Tract 89 is not only influenced by the Alexandrian School but owes much to Coleridge's objective concept of the imagination. "The symbolic character of nature is then no mere invention of the imaginative mind, but an objective quality inherent in creation, impressed upon it in order to give us 'an index or token of the invisible.' " Thus Keble and Pusey, for instance, criticized Byron for his subjectivity. Härdelin brings to bear on the Tractarians a thorough knowledge of Continental theology, both Protestant and Roman Catholic, discussing, for example, the influence of the Tübingen theologian Johann Adam Möhler on figures such as Newman, Ward, and Oakeley. In addition, there are many detailed discussions of specific theological topics, for example, the generally ignored development of Keble and Newman from receptionist theories of the Eucharist to the more objective theories of their later years. Härdelin's book is excellent critical scholarship and necessary reading for students interested in the theology and philosophy of the Tractarian leaders.

Another important book, related to the recent British plan of ecumenical merger between the Methodist and Anglican Churches, is Trevor Dearing's *Wesleyan and Tractarian Worship* (1966). Dearing develops more thoroughly the recurrent theme of contemporary scholarship which sees the Oxford Movement as a part of the resurgent spirituality of the late eighteenth and early nineteenth centuries among both Protestants and Catholics. John Wesley's father, for instance, had strong sympathies for the Caroline Church and for the Non-Jurors. John himself admired William Law. These men were also strong influences on the old High Church "Hackney Phalanx." There was therefore a large and sympathetic audience for Keble, Newman, and the *Tracts*, even among Evangelicals and Methodists. Dearing follows the format of giving first Wesleyan, and then Tractarian, teaching and practice on various subjects, following the two by a comparison. This study is of a practical and topical nature, but shows once more the implicit continuity and organic unity of Church history.

Herbert Clegg's book-length monograph, "Evangelicals and Tractarians" (*HMPEC*, 1966, 1967), supports an argument similar to Dearing's, but is particularly concerned with the Evangelicals. In fact, this valuable study amounts to a fresh history of the Oxford Movement from a novel point of view. Like many other contemporary scholars, Clegg sees the Evangelical and Oxford Movements as being much closer in the earlier stages than has been generally realized. The divergence of the two came in the later 1830's, growing from differing opinions on the Eucharist, the general animosity aroused over the Hampden controversy, Froude's *Remains*, and Isaac Williams' tracts (No. 87 attacked the Evangelicals by name). Clegg analyzes what has sometimes been suspected: the large amount of Evangelical feeling in many of the Oxford leaders (esp. Pusey). Newman is treated in a reasonably objective, but unsympathetic, evaluation: for example, "it can be stated that Newman was the most unscrupulous of Tractarian writers."

The general question of theological development is examined in Owen Chadwick's perceptive *From Bossuet to Newman: The Idea of Doctrinal Development*

(1957). Chadwick explains the influence of Möhler on the Tractarians despite the fact that Newman could not read German. Ward read him in French and wrote about development in the *British Critic* in 1845. Chadwick also offers more analysis of Ward's *Ideal of a Christian Church* and its essentially unhistorical quality. Ward based his views upon the quasi-Kantian notion that intellect provides knowledge only of phenomena, conscience of realities. The truth of dogmas was therefore proved by the sanctity they elicited. Since intellect was unable to test truth, it followed for Ward that there was no need for historical investigation.

Alec R. Vidler's *The Church in an Age of Revolution: 1789 to the Present Day* (1965) has a very brief chapter, "The Anglican Revival, 1830–1845," which emphasizes the more limited academic and clerical appeal of the Oxford Movement in its early years and stresses the importance of the ecclesiastical reforms being conducted by Bishop Blomfield during those same years. An essay more tangentially related to the Oxford Movement is Kingsbury Badger's "Christianity and Victorian Religious Confessions" (*MLQ*, 1964). This generalized survey of liberal confessional literature, with specific reference to Francis Newman, William Rathbone Greg, and J. A. Froude, is an interesting contribution. Occasionally superficial, it nevertheless approaches the Oxford Movement and Victorian Christianity in a fresh way.

Two recent essays relate the *Tracts for the Times* to issues which have become relevant to the Christian Church in the twentieth century: liturgical reform and the Ecumenical Movement. Lawrence F. Barmann, S.J., in "The Liturgical Dimension of the Oxford Tracts, 1833–1841" (*JBS*, 1968), argues that a most important function of the *Tracts* was to establish and define a sound liturgical tradition for the Church of England on the basis of the past. This goal was to be reached especially by rejecting ill-conceived reform proposals. After quoting Palmer's fears in *A Narrative of Events* . . . (1843), Barmann remarks that "it was easy to imagine a desecration of the Church's liturgy, and a significant number of the *Tracts* were consequently written precisely to prevent such a development." In "The Vocation of Anglicanism" (*DubR*, 1968), John Pinnington suggests that after the *Tracts* "there was no longer any Anglican position as such, at least not in the sense in which there had been before." This well-informed and sprightly essay makes the additional point that the early fragmentation—even polarization—of Anglican theological opinion caused by the Tractarians may ultimately prove beneficial to the Ecumenical Movement.

It seems fitting, somehow, to close a discussion of the study of a Victorian ecclesiastical controversy with a controversial twentieth-century essay. John Kent's "The Victorian Resistance: Comments on Religious Life and Culture, 1840–1880" (*VS*, 1968) takes the general view that the leading theologians of the period, Coleridge, Maurice, and Newman, were all reactionaries; and that Matthew Arnold "was the most significant Anglican theologian of the nineteenth century." Arnold, according to Kent, was trying in works like *God and the Bible* to keep Christianity in touch with something called "the main direction of the historical process, whereas the dominant mood of institutionalized Christianity was still set in the mould of resistance." In a dazzling and bewildering reconciliation of disparities, Kent uses as examples of this "false spirituality" John Neville Figgis, the Stefan George circle in Germany, and the "passionately anti-intellectualist French Catholic novelists. The antimodernist ideology of Vichy France, which sought to reinstate the values of Hierarchy, Land, and Family, offered a rare political embodiment of this attitude." Although one could wish for a more objective and solidly researched effort, Kent's stimulating, though unguarded and sometimes inaccurate, essay (Tract 1 is dated 1834) points, oddly enough, in the direction future scholarship related to Victorian Christianity should go, not in the judgments expressed, but in the still incomplete general task of relating the theologians to the men of letters, the historians, and the philosophers—of seeing our past as Arnold's Sophocles saw life: steadily and whole.

THE VICTORIAN CHURCHES

·

Richard Helmstadter

I. GENERAL STUDIES

The most recent and certainly now the best general survey of religion in Victorian England is Owen Chadwick's *The Victorian Church* (2 vols., 1966, 1970). These graceful volumes by the Regius Professor of Modern History at Cambridge are part of *An Ecclesiastical History of England*, edited by John Compton Dickinson, which will supersede the multivolume *History of the English Church* edited by William R. W. Stephens and William Hunt at the beginning of the century. In *The Victorian Church* Chadwick deals with an impressive range of subjects. One finds here authoritative accounts of all the established topics in Victorian church history, beginning with Catholic emancipation, moving through the Oxford Movement, the mid-century controversies over doctrine and liturgy, the remodeling of the administration of the Church, the attempt to win the poor, and closing with the problem of secularization. It is one of the great merits of the work that Chadwick discusses as well, and in some detail, the non-Anglican denominations. His tidy summaries of nonconformist and Roman Catholic history are useful and convenient. Also very convenient is the competent survey of the statistics of religious success and failure which Chadwick, stressing success, includes in the second volume. The beautifully executed chapter on "The Village Church," also in the second volume, adds considerably to our knowledge of the Church in the countryside, a subject that has not received much serious attention. Perhaps the most impressive portion of this work is that which deals with doubt and the challenge to orthodoxy thrown up by history and science. Deemphasizing the disconcerting implications of the work of the geologists and biologists, Chadwick argues that most Churchmen found it easier to come to terms with the physical sciences than with historical criticism of the Bible. *The Victorian Church* is likely to remain for some time the necessary introduction to Victorian religion, but it must be noted that Chadwick, setting no new fashions, has written in the established tradition of ecclesiastical history. He has, especially in the first volume, concentrated his attention on a clerical elite and has not given as much attention to the social history of the Church. For failing to establish new avenues of approach to church history he has been rather sharply criticized, most thoughtfully, perhaps, by William R. Ward in "The Last Chronicle of Barset" (*JEH*, 1967).

Francis Warre Cornish's *The English Church in the Nineteenth Century* (2 vols., 1910), the standard history before Chadwick's work was published, is an excellent example of an even older style. It is essentially a political history of the Church of England, with reference to Catholics and dissenters only when they impinge upon the Establishment. Warre Cornish provides a carefully researched, straightforward, detailed account of the Church in its institutional dimension, dwelling on the leading "parties" among the clergy and the relations of Church and State. The short lists of authorities at the end of each chapter provide a good guide to the Victorian biographies and the sources for the major doctrinal controversies. Within the limits of its approach it is a valuable work, but on the whole it has been superseded by Chadwick.

No other general history of the Church in the nineteenth century is in the same class with those by Chadwick and Warre Cornish. All the others are less well balanced, but each of those discussed below, while weak as an authoritative general history, is worth serious consideration for its special strengths.

Religion in the Victorian Era (1936), by Leonard E. Elliott-Binns, is in most respects less solid and reliable than the work of Warre Cornish. Emphasis is on institutions, major figures, and theology. The attempt by Elliott-Binns to set his discussion of the Church in general secular history is misjudged, for his knowledge does not range widely enough. Even his most basic assertions about secular society cannot be trusted. Dealing with the institutional history of the Church, he is acceptably accurate, but his treatment is anecdotal and excessively unsystematic. In the discussion of theology, however, Elliott-Binns justifies this book. In this area he is very well informed, and his lucid description of theological trends, especially in the period after 1850, often displays considerable insight. His chapter on the Cambridge School of Westcott, Lightfoot, and Hort, combining sympathetic biography with a discussion of their work and ideas, is especially skillful. The excellent and difficult chapter on theological trends after 1870 can be thoroughly understood even by technically unequipped readers. The restrained, critical treatment of Bishop Gore and the *Lux Mundi* school is both provocative and convincing. Had the Elliott-Binns book limited its scope to theology, its reputation would be much higher.

Spencer C. Carpenter's *Church and People 1789–1889: A History of the Church of England from William Wilberforce to Lux Mundi* (1933) is a clearly conceived interpretive history which contains an admirably coherent, if somewhat too abstractly conceived and superficial, picture of the nineteenth-century Church. The book is loosely organized around a survey of the major Church parties—High Church, Broad Church, and Evangelical—and within parties the focus is on individuals rather than issues. There are, therefore, many brief biographies and character sketches, of which the best, charming and full of insight, is that of Bishop Wilberforce. Carpenter suggests that in the 1830's there were two streams of reform open to the Church: that offered by the Tractarians, and the practical, administrative reform movement associated with Charles James Blomfield, the Bishop of London. Associating Blomfield with F. D. Maurice and the Coleridgeans—more through sleight of hand than argument—Carpenter traces these two streams through the century to their union in Bishop Gore and the *Lux Mundi* group.

Alec Vidler's *The Church in an Age of Revolution* (1962) is largely devoted to the Church in England during the nineteenth century. The central theme is the development of liberal theology, and this theme is clearly and systematically presented. The chapters on German theology and historical criticism provide useful background to the central study of Frederick Denison Maurice and his Broad Church associates. Even more useful is the good discussion of liberal theology in Britain during Maurice's youth—Coleridge, McLeod Campbell, Erskine of Linlathen, and Julius Charles Hare are all well treated. While the *Lux Mundi* school of liberal Catholicism is discussed in some detail, the rest of Victorian Church history is given rather a short treatment.

Desmond Bowen, in *The Idea of the Victorian Church: A Study of the Church of England, 1835–1889* (1968), presents the interesting argument that the central "idea" of the Church of England was what he calls the ethic of service or Christian idealism. The ethic of service, according to Bowen, was gradually adopted by the Church as the century progressed. It saved England from Continental anticlericalism, and it softened the harshness of life in industrial society by materially aiding the poor and by restraining the selfishness of the rich. Round this central argument, which is itself rather doubtful, Bowen has written a general history of the Church, including all the standard topics, many of which neither benefit from nor add much to the thesis. Those matters closest to the central concern—Christian Socialism, the slum priests, *Lux Mundi*, and the theology of the Incarnation—are well described, but the contribution of the Evangelicals to social service is seriously undervalued. The conclusion that the 1890's constituted a "golden age" of pastoral concern is intriguing, but since it is here argued from the opinions of the great and powerful rather than from the activities of many pastors, it cannot yet be accepted as proved.

John R. H. Moorman's *A History of the Church in England* (1953) is the best single volume on the Church from Alban to the present. Necessarily, the treatment of the nineteenth century is slight.

All of the works mentioned above are essentially ecclesiastical histories; none of them makes a consistent effort to see church history as part of social history. Chadwick's second volume of *The Victorian Church* comes closer than the others, but even Chadwick treats the Church as an institution outside society, affected by rather than participating in social change. For an introduction to the history of the Church in society, one must turn to the social historians whose most relevant work is discussed in Section IV. None has yet written a general social history of religion, and until one appears it is well to keep in mind the work of Elie Halévy. In his *History of the English People in the Nineteenth Century* (esp. I, 1924; III, 1950; and IV, 1951) Halévy considers in some detail the relation of politics, society, and religion in the first half of the nineteenth century.

II. THEOLOGY

In this section only general histories of theology are considered, along with a note on the impact of science. Because so much of the history of Victorian religion has been conceived in terms of denomination or Church party, and because theology was so interwoven with ecclesiastical politics, studies of particular theologians are discussed under their appropriate party or denominational headings.

Unquestionably the best introduction to Victorian theology is to be found in Bernard M. G. Reardon's *From Coleridge to Gore: A Century of Religious Thought in Britain* (1971). This work is written as a textbook and does not aspire to orginality. It is enormously useful, for it surveys the entire range of British theology from the appearance of Coleridge's *Aids to Reflection* (1825) to the publication of Gore's *Lux Mundi* (1889). With no theological axe to grind, Reardon is a competent and judicious, not to say painstaking, guide to the major ideas of the more important theologians. Coverage is remarkably even; only F. D. Maurice, whose standing is high among current historians of nineteenth-century thought, receives more than summary consideration. So many men and so many ideas are dealt with that, inevitably, the book can be no more than an introduction. As an introduction its greatest failing is the absence of landmarks; there is no firm periodization, no clearly drawn pattern. Reardon has also put together a good collection of readings in *Religious Thought in the Nineteenth Century, Illustrated from Writers of the Period* (1966). His introductions to the readings, about half of which are from British writers—all liberals except Newman—are particularly perceptive. The short discussion of the British Hegelians John and Edward Caird, for example, makes clear in a few sentences the religious character of British idealism.

Vernon F. Storr in *The Development of English Theology in the Nineteenth Century* (1913) takes his subject up to 1860. Before the appearance of *From Coleridge to Gore*, Storr's work, in spite of its incomplete time span, was the most important basic account of Victorian theology. It remains a useful book, beautifully organized, clear, and written with a depth of understanding and sense of excitement which one misses in Reardon's much more efficiently inclusive text. Storr maintains that during the first sixty years of the nineteenth century there emerged all the forces that were to work a revolution in English theology in the latter half of the century. With considerable distinction he chronicles the disruptive forces and the extremely conservative, unintellectual, and provincial opposition to change within the English Church. He traces the impact of German historical, literary, and philological criticism from the 1820's through Coleridge to the mid-century liberals who wrote *Essays and Reviews*. He writes critically of the Oxford Movement, which he charges with introverted ecclesiasticism, and much more enthusiastically of F. D. Maurice, Erskine of Linlathen, and John McLeod Campbell whose *The Nature of the Atonement* (1856) he thinks "certainly the most important English contribution to dogmatic theology made in the first sixty years of the nineteenth century." It was, he argues, a turning point in the important and general shift in English theological thought away from the Atonement and toward the Incarnation, a progression that culminated in the Incarnationism of Gore and his circle. Storr insists on the central importance of Biblical criticism as the liberalizing force in English religious thought. The sciences were secondary; they helped to dramatize the necessity for the Church to abandon its rigid, provincial view of the literal inspiration of the

Bible and to force English theologians after 1860 "to hold commerce with the wider thought around them." Storr writes with a pronounced liberal bias which colors all of this tightly conceived book.

Storr's work was heavily influenced by John Tulloch's *Religious Thought in Britain during the XIXth Century* (1885). Tulloch covers almost exactly the same period, 1820–60; his general organization is essentially similar to that adopted by Storr; he deals with the same British thinkers, though not with the Germans; and his judgments are within the same liberal frame. Tulloch does not have Storr's strong sense of movements and tendencies. He deals more with individuals, his approach to history is more humane, and therefore his work is still valuable for its observations on the personalities of the British theologians.

Elliott-Binns, writing with a bias similar to Storr's, has attempted to carry on where Storr left off. His *English Thought, 1860–1900. The Theological Aspect* (1956) is a full-length development of his much shorter lectures on *The Development of English Theology in the Later Nineteenth Century* (1952). The shorter work is in some ways the better of the two. He narrates succinctly the continuing advance of liberal thinking and the collapse of narrow conservatism and concludes with an illuminating comment on the state of religion in 1900. In the longer work he attempts to relate progress in theology to progress in the social, intellectual, and economic realms. In this attempt he often fails, but he does produce some interesting associations. In the second half of the century, he suggests, the idea of progress became communal rather than individualistic, and he associates the increasing emphasis on the Incarnation with the tendency of history and science to combine in attacking individualism and the Evangelical stress on individual salvation. He tends to ramble, but he does present a great deal of useful information, well documented with helpful bibliographical footnotes. This is, apart from Reardon's work, the only comprehensive, detailed account of late Victorian theology.

Clement C. J. Webb's *A Study of Religious Thought in England from 1850* (1933) is a study of the development of English idealism in its theological manifestation. Webb successfully demonstrates the importance of theological idealism in the second half of the nineteenth century, and shows how it was associated with the sciences, historical criticism, and the drift away from individualism. His observations on the importance of the traditional English identification of ethics and theological orthodoxy are interesting and suggestive. British Hegelianism, the importance of Kant, and the influence of Ritschl and Lotze are thoroughly discussed. In "A Century of Anglican Theology in Relation to the General Movement of European Thought," published in his *A Century of Anglican Theology and Other Lectures* (1923), Webb insists strongly, perhaps too strongly, on the insularity of English thought in the early nineteenth century. He discusses the opening of English theology to a wider range of influences—historical, scientific, Continental, and philosophical—in the later part of the century.

For quite different reasons, two Victorian works on nineteenth-century theology remain valuable. John Hunt's *Religious Thought in England in the Nineteenth Century* (1896) is almost a biographical dictionary of Victorian religious thinkers, including dissenters and Roman Catholics as well as Anglicans. The special value of the book is in the extremely useful appendix on major Victorian lectures. Every published Bampton, Hulsean, Boyle, and Warburtonian lecture is listed, and the arguments of the most important are summarized. Andrew Martin Fairbairn's *The Place of Christ in Modern Theology* (1893) is itself a classic document of Victorian theology. One half of the book is a treatise in systematic theology, developing a Protestant alternative to the Catholic *Lux Mundi*. The other half is a history of theology, in which the discussion of nineteenth-century English theology is brilliantly organized around the idea of development and the progress of historical criticism.

Historians of theology have traditionally given much more attention to historical criticism than to the theological implications of the physical sciences. This is probably because the impact of science on theology was indirect and difficult to assess. Anxious to avoid a direct confrontation with science, those Victorian theologians who dealt with the problem tended to approach it through history and Biblical criticism. From the point of view of many theologians, accommodation rather than conflict characterized their relations with science in the later nineteenth century. John W. Draper, who wrote a *History of the Conflict between Religion and Science* (1875), and Andrew D. White, whose point of view in *A History of the Warfare of Science with Theology in Christendom* (2 vols., 1896) had been developed earlier in *The Warfare of Science* (1876), drastically oversimplified their subject. They considered hostility the natural relation of science and theology, and they looked upon theological accommodation of science as a victory for the latter.

While their view persists, for example, in David Lack's *Evolutionary Theory and Christian Belief: The Unresolved Conflict* (1957) and in William Irvine's popular joint biography of Darwin and Thomas Henry Huxley, *Apes, Angels and Victorians* (1956), it no longer dominates the scholarly approach to the problem. The modern approach is well illustrated in Robert M. Young's stimulating lecture on "The Impact of Darwin on Conventional Thought" (in *The Victorian Crisis of Faith*, ed. Anthony Symondson, 1970). Stressing the complexity of the tensions between science and religion in the twenty-five years before the publication of *On the Origin of Species* (1859), Young demonstrates that they constituted a web that included social theories, social prejudices, and ethical considerations. Charles C. Gillispie, in *Genesis and Geology: A Study in the Relations of Scientific Thought, Natural Theology and Social Opinion in Great Britain, 1790–1850* (1951), emphasizes the role of theological assumptions in the development of geological science. The emergence of the idea of evolution from the late seventeenth century is informatively surveyed by John C. Greene in *The Death of Adam: Evolution and Its Impact on Western Thought* (1959). Milton Millhauser's *Just before Darwin: Robert Chambers and* Vestiges (1959) contains an excellent discussion of the theological implications and public reception of Chambers' *Vestiges of the Natural History of Creation* (1844). Loren C. Eiseley's *Darwin's Century: Evolution and the Men Who Discovered It* (1959) is a good general history of the idea of evolution in the nineteenth century; it does not stress theological considerations.

Probably the most thoughtful study of the complex implications of Darwin's work is Gertrude Himmelfarb's *Darwin and the Darwinian Revolution* (1959). Himmelfarb's intelligent and penetrating discussion must, however, be treated with caution. Her hostility to Darwin and her exaggerated emphasis on the dogmatic element in Darwinian thought tend to mislead. Gavin de Beer's authoritative *Charles Darwin* (1963) supplies a useful corrective. Alvar Ellegård's brilliant *Darwin and the General Reader: The Reception of Darwin's Theory of Evolution in the British Periodical Press, 1859–1872* (1958) is an important, pioneering contribution to the study of religion, science, and public opinion.

III. THE CHURCHES

Church of England

General histories of the Church are discussed above in Section 1. The works considered here deal with the administrative structure of the Church and its reform, with politics, with the life of the clergy, and with the High Church, the Broad Church, and the Evangelical Movement.

CHURCH REFORM. From the late eighteenth century it had become increasingly clear that the Church, so obviously a corporation of the old regime, could not long continue without extensive reform. After the passing of the Reform Bill in 1832, many churchmen—Thomas Arnold, Richard Whately, Charles James Blomfield, and Robert Southey among them—believed that the Established Church was in fact doomed to such radical reformation that it would disappear. One response to this crisis was the Oxford Movement, another was practical institutional reform. There are four excellent studies of the surprisingly successful movement to modernize the institutional arrangements of the Church. William Law Mathieson's *English Church Reform, 1815–1840* (1923), a good general account of the movement and its eighteenth-century background, will remain a basic work and a useful source of information. Mathieson provides a particularly vivid illustration of the sense of crisis surrounding the Church when he describes the bishops' votes on the second and third reform bills and the public reaction to what seemed episcopal defense of aristocracy and privilege. Olive Brose's *Church and Parliament: The Reshaping of the Church of England, 1828–1860* (1959) is a stimulating study of the central role in reform played by Bishop Blomfield. Brose conceives Blomfield's work as an ecclesiastical parallel to the secular administrative reforms stimulated by the utilitarians. Her work gains considerably from the introductory chapter in which she discusses brilliantly the problems faced by the Church Establishment in a society newly recognized as religiously pluralistic. Geoffrey Best, one of the most talented English historians currently working, presents in *Temporal Pillars: Queen Anne's Bounty, the Ecclesiastical Commissioners and the Church of England* (1964) an authoritative and massive study of the financial arrangements of the Church in the eighteenth and nineteenth centuries. The book is especially strong for the period from 1820 to 1850, during which time the Ecclesiastical Commission was founded and Blomfield did his most important work. For this period Best broadens his scope and provides a fine general history of the Church in its relations with society and the state.

Very different in approach from the three books mentioned above is Kenneth A. Thompson's *Bureaucracy and Church Reform: The Organizational Response of the Church of England to Social Change, 1800–1965* (1970). Concentrating on the period between the foundation of the Ecclesiastical Commission in 1835 and the establishment of the Church Assembly in 1919, Thompson discusses the major changes in Church affairs in the light of sociological theory. The fruits of this pioneering effort are surprisingly various and fascinating. Thompson provides a new framework for understanding the three great Church parties, and he offers new insight into the changing relation of Church and State in the later nineteenth century. He discusses also, and freshly, the reactivation of Convocation, the proliferation of special agencies, and the need of the Church to find an active middle-class laity to replace the squirearchy in binding the Church to what was vital in the life of the nation. Unhappily Thompson's awkward style makes this book less attractive than it ought to be.

Turning to specifically financial issues within the area of administrative reform, Olive Brose provides in "The Irish Precedent for English Church Reform: The Church Temporalities Act of 1833" (*JEH*, 1956) a good example of the use of Ireland as a testing ground for reforms later carried out in England. She demonstrates that this Act, with its wide-ranging implications and enormous impact on England, arose out of opposition to the tithe in Ireland. The tithe in England aroused less opposition, but tithes, along with the even more important issue of Church rates, deserve more attention because they were a sensitive point of connection between Church and society. W. R. Ward's "The Tithe Question in England in the Early Nineteenth Century" (*JEH*, 1965) is a good introduction. While P. J. Welch's "Blomfield and Peel: A Study in Cooperation between Church and State, 1841–46" (*JEH*, 1961) has been superseded by Olive Brose's *Church and Parliament*, his article on "Bishop Blomfield and Church Extension in London" (*JEH*, 1953) is a solid account of Blomfield's church building activities and remains valuable. The best study of the strenuous effort and staggering sums of money that went into the campaign to provide Church accommodation for a population that was increasing rapidly, especially in the northern industrial towns, is Michael H. Port's *Six Hundred New Churches: A Study of the Church Building Commission, 1818–1856, and Its Church Building Activities* (1961). W. R. Ward's "The Cost of Establishment: Some Reflections on Church Building in Manchester" (in *Studies in Church History*, III, ed. Geoffrey J. Cuming, 1966) is an excellent discussion of a major struggle to strengthen Anglicanism at the parish level in the second half of the nineteenth century. In an interesting comparison of the investment decisions of the Church and nonconformity, Ward argues that the Church made serious mistakes, and did so for reasons inherent in its Establishment. The method of analysis developed in this important article might be applied usefully not only to other towns, but to other areas of religious life.

While Kenneth Thompson's *Bureaucracy and Church Reform* provides the best comprehensive discussion of Church government, P. J. Welch, in "The Revival of an Active Convocation of Canterbury, 1842–1855" (*JEH*, 1959), presents a useful account of the revival, sponsored by High Churchmen, of a governing body that had been merely formal since the early eighteenth century. This article, which emphasizes heavily the role of Samuel Wilberforce, the Bishop of Oxford, is interesting as an exploration of the intricate interplay of ecclesiastical and parliamentary politics. It would be interesting to know more about Henry Hoare, an important lay promoter of Convocation, whose significance is stressed by Kenneth Thompson. His only biography is James B. Sweet's *A Memoir of the Late Henry Hoare* (1869).

THE CLERGY. The clergy as a group rather than as individuals has received little attention from historians. Chadwick in the first volume of *The Victorian Church* acknowledges the importance of the subject and provides some interesting statistics on the education of ordinands which suggest a declining social status for the clergy in the nineteenth century. More systematic studies are needed, however, before it will be possible to comment with authority on the social position of the clergy, their backgrounds, or their role in society. Charles K. Francis Brown's *A History of the English Clergy, 1800–1900* (1953) deals largely with legal and institutional questions, such as pluralism, tithe, and Cathedral chapters. More systematic and more basic is Diana McClatchey's careful study of *Oxfordshire Clergy 1777–1869* (1960), a model of the sort of investigation that is needed. This well-documented work contains a detailed analysis of the ecclesiastical patronage of the county and of the financial and legal status of the clergy which McClatchey uses as an index of social status. The most interesting, and largest, portion of the book is devoted to a description of the social role of the clergy as landowners, educators, guardians of health, custodians of local charities, Justices of the Peace, and political propagandists. While in its way a magnificent work, Henry I. Longden's *Northamptonshire and Rutland Clergy from 1500* (6 vols., 1938–52) is not a history but a biographical dictionary akin to *Crockford's Clerical Directory* which was issued first in 1858. There are no good local histories apart from that by McClatchey.

The works of Arthur Tindal Hart, *The Nineteenth Century Parson* (1954), *The Country Priest in English History* (1959) and *The Curate's Lot: The Story of the Unbeneficed English Clergy* (1970), are amusing, anecdotal compilations drawing on fictional clergymen as well as the real thing. Roy P. Flindall's "The Parish Priest in Victorian England" (*CQR*, 1967) is a mistitled summary of eight meetings of the Flegg Deanery Clerical Society in the later 1850's.

Owen Chadwick's *Victorian Miniature* (1960) is a beautifully written story of the relations of an obscure East Anglian parson and his squire in the middle decades of the century. No great issues of ecclesiastical or national politics intrude into this charming tale of parochial life.

There are as yet no good surveys of the education of the clergy, but there are several histories of the educational institutions designed for prospective clergymen. The best is by Chadwick, *The Founding of Cuddesdon* (1954). Frederick William Bagshawe Bullock's rather mechanical works, *The History of Ridley Hall* (2 vols., 1941, 1953) and *A History of Training for the Ministry of the Church of England in England and Wales from 1800 to 1874* (1955), are informative.

Alan Savidge has written the best book on *The Parsonage in England: Its History and Architecture* (1964). This work, by a former assistant secretary to the Church Commissioners, is splendidly well informed, beautifully illustrated, and a serious contribution to the social history of the clergy. Margaret Hewitt Watt has written the only book on *The History of the Parson's Wife* (1943).

POLITICS. During the nineteenth century the Church was deeply involved in politics at both the Parliamentary and local levels. The political and social roles of the churches in local communities are considered below in Section IV, as are the campaigns for disestablishment and the involvement of the churches in social reform.

Among politicians of the first rank on the national level, none was more consistently concerned with religious questions than Mr. Gladstone, and any general study of religion and politics in the nineteenth century must consider Gladstone of central importance. His standard biographies are John Morley's *The Life of William Ewart Gladstone* (3 vols., 1903) and Philip Magnus' *Gladstone, A Biography* (1954). The most detailed history of Gladstone as a churchman is Daniel C. Lathbury's excellent *Mr. Gladstone* (1907), which was conceived as a religious supplement to Morley's *Life*. Lathbury also edited *Correspondence on Church and Religion of William Ewart Gladstone* (2 vols., 1910). Gladstone's Church patronage is discussed by Dudley Bahlman in "The Queen, Mr. Gladstone, and Church Patronage" (*VS*, 1960) and by M. D. Stephen in "Gladstone's Ecclesiastical Patronage, 1868–74" (*Hist. Stud., Australia and New Zealand*, 1964). Stephen also considers "Gladstone's Relations with Manning and Acton, 1832–70" (*JRH*, 1961) and "Gladstone and the Composition of the Final Court in Ecclesiastical Cases, 1850–1873" (*Hist J*, 1966).

In *The Orb and the Cross* (1945), Alec Vidler has written an interesting essay on Gladstone's *The Church in Its Relations with the State* (1838). He demonstrates that F. D. Maurice shared many of Gladstone's ideas. The most interesting and stimulating work on Gladstone as churchman and politician is that of W. R. Ward. In "Oxford and the Origins of Liberal Catholicism in the Church of England" (in *Studies in Church History*, 1, ed. G. J. Cuming, 1964), Ward develops an explanation of the relation of the *Lux Mundi* group to post-Tractarian Oxford. He argues that Gladstone during the election of 1847 forged an alliance of Tractarians and Liberals at Oxford, and that he held that alliance together until he was deserted by many churchmen in 1865. From this alliance developed the socially aware, liberal Catholicism of Gore and Scott Holland. Ward provides a detailed setting for this essentially political explanation of theological change in *Victorian Oxford* (1965).

Among the very few good special studies of the reactions of the churches to major political events is Olive Anderson's perceptive and well-organized discussion of "The Reaction of Church and Dissent towards the Crimean War" (*JEH*, 1965). Anderson deals with the general problem of religious opinion and war, comments on the strikingly widespread assumption of an active and direct Providence, and traces the development of the *Maud* theme, that the war would redeem the nation from Mammon worship.

Perhaps the most persistent political issue involving the Church was the education question, which has attracted a vast literature that cannot be surveyed here in detail. The basic books are John William Adamson's *English Education, 1782–1902* (1930) and Mary Sturt's *The Education of the People* (1967). Because it is a brilliant analysis and evocation of religiosity in the Victorian public schools, David Newsome's *Godliness and Good Learning* (1961) cannot escape mention. The nature of the political problem, a problem of primary education, is well explained in Geoffrey Best's "The Religious Difficulties of National Education in England, 1800–1870" (*Cambridge Hist. J.*, 1956). This important article is the best introduction to the subject. Marjorie Cruickshank's *Church and State in English Education: 1870 to the Present Day* (1963) provides a good general account of the issue after the passing of Forster's Education Act. John T. Ward and J. H. Treble in "Religion and Education in 1843: Reaction to the 'Factory Education Bill' " (*JEH*, 1969) discuss the crisis that more than any other illuminates the antagonism and distrust dissenters felt for churchmen and both felt for the State. A. J. Marcham's "The Church and the 'Conscience Clause,' 1860–70" (*JEH*, 1971) is an important study of the diminution of that antagonism and the emergence of a spirit of compromise as it became clear that Church and State were drifting apart.

Much of the work on politics and the Church has appeared in the biographies of leading churchmen and politicians.

THREE LIVES. Church historians have been methodologically very conservative. Following the pattern established by the secular political historians, they have written much Church history in the form of biographies, and they have assumed, perhaps too readily, the basic significance of the three parties in the Church. *Leaders of the Church of England, 1828–1944* (1971), twenty fresh sketches well drawn by David L. Edwards, is an admirable epitome of this tradition. Ecclesiastical biographies are so numerous that it is possible to acknowledge only a few of the most important in this survey, and most of those appear below under their appropriate party banners. Studies of three men only—an archbishop, a bishop, and a parish priest—are noticed here. Their biographies are in themselves important and they serve as illustrations of a large body of significant work. Peter T. Marsh's *The Victorian Church in Decline* (1969) is a study of Archibald Campbell Tait as Archbishop of Canterbury from 1868 to 1882. Marsh considers Tait the strongest Archbishop since the seventeenth century and concentrates on Tait's role as the most effective representative of the Church in Parliament at a time when the Church faced more political crises than it had since the decade following the constitutional changes of 1828–32. Tait was a central figure in the ritualist controversy and the passing of the Public Worship Regulation Act of 1874, in the disestablishment of the Irish Church in 1868, in the abolition of Church rates in 1868, and in the foundation of a national system of education in 1870. Marsh's discussion of Tait's role in these affairs is definitive. His argument that the declining importance of Church matters in Parliament during the time when Tait was Archbishop can be seen as an index of the general decline of the Church as an important part of the life of the nation is not altogether convincing. For a fuller and less politically oriented biography that deals with his entire career—Tait was Dean of Carlisle and an important Bishop of London before he became Archbishop—one may turn to *The Life of A. C. Tait* (2 vols., 1891), by Randall Thomas Davidson and William Benham.

Standish Meacham's *Lord Bishop: The Life of Samuel Wilberforce, 1805–1873* (1970) is an excellent life of the bishop who did more than any other to modernize the episcopate, to shift the focus of episcopal energies from parliamentary politics to diocesan administration and pastoral concern. Wilberforce was a great pastoral bishop, and Meacham's study of this aspect of his career is penetrating, authoritative, and of general significance. One need only contrast Wilberforce's strenuous episcopal life with that of the last aristocratic Archbishop of York, well sketched by Alan M. G. Stephenson in "Archbishop Vernon Harcourt, 1807–1847" (*Studies in Church History,* iv, ed. G. J. Cuming, 1967), to see what a great change had come over the temper of the Church by the middle decades of the century. Meacham also deals well, and sympathetically, with Wilberforce's early Evangelical life, with his political activities, and with his attempt to defend orthodoxy against the liberalism of *Essays and Reviews* and the heretical implications of *On the Origin of Species*. In most respects—it does not of course reprint letters and diary extracts —this study supersedes *The Life of Samuel Wilberforce* (3 vols., 1880–83), by Arthur Rawson Ashwell and Reginald Garton Wilberforce.

Walter Farquhar Hook, Vicar of Leeds from 1837 to 1859, did for the parish what Wilberforce did for the diocese. Perhaps the greatest Victorian parish priest, Hook has no full-scale modern biography. Charles James Stranks's *Dean Hook* (1954) is a worthy short study based on Hook's unpublished papers, while the most important work on Hook remains that of his son-in-law, William Richard Wood Stephens, in *Life and Letters of Dean Hook* (2 vols., 1878).

High Churchmen

Ironically, William John Conybeare, who deplored the division of the Church into factions, helped confirm the fashion that encourages Church historians to consider ecclesiastical parties fundamentally important categories in the history of the Victorian Church. Calling for unity so that the struggle with atheism might not end in disaster, Conybeare surveyed the division of the Church among High, Low, and Broad Churchmen in "Parties in the Church" (*Edinburgh Rev.*, 1853). His mischievous, vividly written caricatures of the foibles of each party are amusing. While his guess as to the number of clergy belonging to each party cannot be accepted uncritically, his description of the most important institutions round which the parties were organized is unquestionably useful, and so is his analysis of the divisions within each camp. It would be useful to have a detached modern study of the general role of parties in the Victorian Church, and very interesting indeed to have a reliable guide to the numerical strength of the parties among both the clergy and the laity. Church historians, with more loyalty than imagination, have tended to concentrate on the histories of their own parties.

The Oxford Movement has received so much attention and so much emphasis has been placed on the Movement's impact on the life of the Church that the High Church party in the second half of the century seems oddly neglected. There is no good general account. While it is slight, Marcus Donovan's *After the Tractarians* (1933) is probably the best general survey. William J. Sparrow Simpson's *The History of the Anglo-Catholic Revival from 1845* (1932) is a set of highly partisan, discursive essays on Anglo-Catholic themes, and not, strictly speaking, a history. Herbert L. Stewart's *A Century of Anglo-Catholicism* (1929) is a poorly informed, wordy comment on Anglo-Catholicism as a Good Thing. *Northern Catholicism* (1933, ed. Norman Powell Williams and Charles Harris) is an uneven collection of essays. The best among them are Williams' "The Theology of the Catholic Revival" and especially Ruth Kenyon's "The Social Aspect of the Catholic Revival." Kenyon is strongest when she deals with the Oxford Movement and its opposition to materialism and commercial values. Her treatment of the second half of the century is slight and mistakenly assumes that Anglo-Catholics led the other Church parties in philanthropy and social work among the poor. This fundamental error, surprisingly widespread among High Church historians, illustrates the distorting power of the party view. Paul Thureau-Dangin's *The English Catholic Revival in the Nineteenth Century* (rev. and re-ed. from a translation by Wilfred Wilberforce, 2 vols., 1914) is dominated by the Oxford Movement, Newman, and Manning. George H. Tavard's *The Quest for Catholicity, A Study in Anglicanism* (1963) is a perceptive short study of Anglo-Catholic theology from the Reformation, written by a bilingual French priest. The chapter on the post-Tractarian period concentrates on Charles Gore, Henry Scott Holland, and Darwell Stone, dwelling on the tension between their Catholicism and their Anglican nationalism.

For the substantial history of the High Church party one must turn to the rich array of biographies. Among non-Tractarian High Churchmen in the early and mid-Victorian period, the most striking was the fearsomely irascible Bishop of Exeter. George C. B. Davies' *Henry Phillpotts, Bishop of Exeter, 1778–1869* (1954) is a good scholarly biography with a most inappropriately mild tone. Phillpotts was the leading figure in the Gorham controversy, of which *Gorham and the Bishop of Exeter* (1951) by John C. S. Nias is the best account. Alan B. Webster's *Joshua Watson, The Story of a Layman, 1771–1855* (1954) is a good study of the most important figure in the Hackney Phalanx, a group of non-Tractarian High Church laymen. Watson's activities in the Church Building Commission and in other Church societies are well described and so is the character of his religious life.

The history of the movement after 1845 is best presented in the biographies of Edward Bouverie Pusey and Richard William Church. Henry Parry Liddon's *Life of E. B. Pusey* (4 vols., 1893–97) is a massive work by Pusey's chief disciple. It is a rich storehouse of information and its importance cannot be overestimated. Liddon, one of the greatest Victorian preachers, was a person of considerable importance in his own right, and John O. Johnston's *Life and Letters of Henry Parry Liddon* (1904) is a solid biography. Basil A. Smith's *Dean Church: The Anglican Response to Newman* (1958) is a fine study of the dominant figure in High Church circles between the death of Pusey and the emergence of Gore. This literate, sympathetic biography is the most important modern contribution to the history of the High Church party after 1845. With an excellent command of late Victorian Church history, Smith describes convincingly Dean Church's influence and intellectual standing. His influence was particularly great in the 1880's when he was Gladstone's principal adviser on ecclesiastical affairs. One might doubt that he had "a shrewder grasp than his patron had of the politics of the age," but on the whole Smith's is a work of well-balanced judgment.

George L. Prestige's *The Life of Charles Gore, A Great Englishman* (1935) is a good comprehensive life of the editor of *Lux Mundi*, the leading Anglo-Catholic of the turn of the century. Although it is without scholarly apparatus this is a serious, thoroughly well-informed biography and the best introduction to a study of Gore's career. James Carpenter's *Gore: A Study in Liberal Catholic Thought* (1960) is an intelligent introduction to *Lux Mundi* and Gore's Incarnation-centered theology. Unfortunately, Gore's thought is considered in isolation. Calling for a wider examination of Anglo-Catholic thought, David Newsome discusses the relation of Anglo-Catholic theology and social reform in "The Assault on Mammon: Charles Gore and John Neville Figgis" (*JEH*, 1966).

A useful guide to lesser figures among High Churchmen is provided by the two dozen essays in Benjamin Consitt Boulter's *The Anglican Reformers* (1933). These charming sketches have little scholarly significance but they constitute almost a dictionary of High Church biography. For the domestic atmosphere of High Church life and the flavor of High Church piety there is a splendid source in Charlotte Anne Elizabeth Moberly's *Dulce Domum* (1911), a collection of reminiscences, diaries, and letters relating to George Moberly, Headmaster of Winchester, 1835–66, and Bishop of Salisbury, 1869–85, put together by one of his fifteen children. Moberly's book is a rich source of comment on Charlotte Mary Yonge and John Keble who lived near Winchester and played a large role in the life of the Moberlys.

The impact of the Tractarian movement on parochial life is well illustrated in Brian Heeney's "Tractarian Parson: Edward Monro of Harrow Weald" (*Canadian J. of Theol.*, 1967, 1968). Edward Monro, influenced especially by Keble, developed a systematic program of parochial activity which he used in his obscure parish and described in *Parochial Work* (1850). Heeney describes in detail the system, its inspiration, and its application. One might note that it is a little difficult to discover the distinctively Catholic elements in Monro's ideas which seem, on the whole, surprisingly similar to those of socially concerned Broad Churchmen and Evangelicals. This is not the case with Nathaniel Woodard, who founded schools to attract the middle classes to Anglo-Catholicism and conservatism. Brian Heeney has written the authoritative account of Woodard's work in *Mission to the Middle Classes: The Woodard Schools, 1848–1891* (1969).

Several studies of the revival of Anglican religious communities have recently appeared, including *The Park Village Sisterhood* (1965), by Thomas Jay Williams, and Allan Walter Campbell and Thomas Jay Williams' *Priscilla Lydia Sellon: The Restorer after Three Centuries of the Religious Life in the English Church* (1965). These books provide a detailed, intimate study of the sisterhood. A good general survey is found in Arthur Allchin's *The Silent Rebellion, Anglican Religious Communities 1845–1900* (1958). The authoritative work on religious communities is Peter F. Anson's *The Call of the Cloister: Religious Communities and Kindred Bodies in the Anglican Communion* (1955; rev. and ed. Allan Walter Campbell, 1964). Massive, surprisingly readable, utterly reliable, and pleasingly larded with odd bits of curious information, this history is the indispensable introduction to the subject.

The best general survey of the dramatic changes, one might fairly say improvements, in Victorian liturgical fashions and styles of worship is Horton Davies' *Worship and Theology in England* (III and IV, 1961 and 1962). Davies includes nonconformity as well as the Established Church. James F. White's *The Cambridge Movement: The Eccelesiologists and the Gothic Revival* (1962) is a full history of the Cambridge Camden Society of the 1840's and its subsequent influence on liturgy and the architecture and furnishings of churches. Elliot Rose, in "The Stone Table in the Round Church" (*VS*, 1966), provides a careful and amusing account of the crisis that resulted in the breakup of the Cambridge Camden Society and a brief assessment of the importance of the Society for ritualists.

While G. J. Cuming's *A History of the Anglican Liturgy* (1969) and Ronald Claud Dudley Jasper's *Prayer Book Revision in England 1800–1900* (1954) contain short summaries of the ritualist controversies; there is no comprehensive history of "ritualism." Perhaps one is not needed. *The Victorian Church in Decline* (1969) by Peter Marsh contains a good account of the controversy from the perspective of established authority, and the case for the other side is put in Michael Reynolds' *Martyr of Ritualism: Father Mackonochie of St. Alban's, Holborn* (1965), which chronicles in wearisome detail the travails of the most distinguished ritualist slum priest. While Reynolds' book is dominated, as was Mackonochie's life, by the ritualist trials, it contains as well a fine description of High Church parochial work from Butler of Wantage through Charles Lowder and Mackonochie to Arthur Stanton. Stanton, Mackonochie's protégé at St. Albans, has received a sympathetic biography from George W. E. Russell, *Arthur Stanton* (1917).

Broad Churchmen

W. J. Conybeare thought the Broad Church party the smallest of the three. Broad Churchmen, with their emphasis on national unity and their opposition to rigid dogmatism, did not acknowledge that they belonged to any party at all. Their party, if we may call it such, was certainly not like the others and is perhaps better considered a network of liberal friends and relations. Walter F. Cannon analyzes the nature of the group in his brilliant article, "Scientists and Broad Churchmen: An Early Victorian Intellectual Network" (*JBS*, 1964). Cannon traces the relationships among the central group of Broad Churchmen, which he calls a "self-reviewing circle," and emphasizes the importance of Julius Charles Hare and German scholarship for the clerical members of the network. He also comments on the character of their liberalism, which recognized no conflict between religion and science. The fullest survey of Broad Churchmen remains Charles R. Sanders' *Coleridge and the Broad Church Movement* (1942), which contains worthy studies of Coleridge, Thomas Arnold, Carlyle, F. D. Maurice, and J. C. Hare. No biography of Hare has yet been written and therefore the chapter on him is the most valuable in the book. Still valuable for their evocation of liberal Christian thought and for their perceptive re-creations of personality are the many short essays on Broad Churchmen in Julia Wedgwood's *Nineteenth Century Teachers* (1909). Another collection of essays on Broad Churchmen, stressing the importance of F. D. Maurice, is Alec Vidler's *F. D. Maurice and Company* (1966), which contains a good summary of the recent revival of interest in Maurice. The essays on Coleridge, Thomas Arnold, and Carlyle in Basil Willey's *Nineteenth Century Studies* (1949) should be noted, as should Asa Briggs's essay on "Thomas Hughes and the Public Schools" in his *Victorian People* (1954).

Perhaps the most penetrating thematic study of Broad Church thought is Duncan Forbes's *The Liberal Anglican Idea of History* (1952). This impressive analysis of the historical approach and ideas of Thomas Arnold, Richard Whately, J. C. Hare, Connop Thirlwall, and Henry Hart Milman deserves to be much better known. Forbes shows how these men, with Thomas Arnold in the lead, pessimistically rejected the simple theory of material progress and developed a theory of history in which the moral and spiritual aspects of civilization were central.

The basic biography of Thomas Arnold, now a minor classic, is Arthur Penrhyn Stanley's *The Life and Correspondence of Dr. Arnold* (2 vols., 1844). The best modern life is by Arnold's great-grandson, Arnold Whitridge, *Dr. Arnold of Rugby* (1928). This book contains, as an introduction, a magnificent character sketch of Arnold by Michael E. Sadler. Whitridge's intelligent, sympathetic biography provides no more than a slight discussion of Arnold's religious ideas and churchmanship. It is stronger on Arnold's social radicalism and on Rugby. The most recent biography is Thomas W. Bamford's *Thomas Arnold* (1960), a slightly awkward study that concentrates on Arnold as a schoolmaster. Norman Wymer's *Dr. Arnold of Rugby* (1953) is a popular biography, badly out of balance, which concentrates on Arnold's personal life. The most comprehensive account of Arnold as a churchman is in Reginald John Campbell's *Thomas Arnold* (1927). Eugene L. Williamson's *The Liberalism of Thomas Arnold: A Study of His Religious and Political Writings* (1964) is a reliable guide to Arnold's works that gives too little attention to social and intellectual context. Michael J. Jackson and John Rogan have written a long introduction, not original but useful, to a new edition of Thomas Arnold's *Principles of Church Reform* (1962).

Frederick Denison Maurice is currently the center of much interest; two important books on him have recently appeared. Frank M. McClain's *Maurice, Man and Moralist* (1972), based on a close study of the manuscript sources, is now the best and most systematically conceived introduction to the enigmatic Maurice. *Frederick Denison Maurice: Rebellious Conformist* (1971), by Olive Brose, is a searching inquiry into the emotional and intellectual core of Maurice's theology. Emphasis is placed on Maurice's young manhood, on *Eustace Conway*, and on his conversion experience. The best biography of Maurice remains, surprisingly, Frederick Maurice's *The Life of Frederick Denison Maurice* (2 vols., 1884), which consists largely of Maurice's letters, many no longer available in manuscript. Florence Higham's *Frederick Denison Maurice* (1947) is slight, unreliable, and hagiographic.

After the works of Brose and McClain, the two best studies of Maurice as a theologian are Herbert G. Wood's *Frederick Denison Maurice* (1950) and Arthur Michael Ramsey's *F. D. Maurice and the Conflicts of Modern Theology* (1951). Both are short, solid, comprehensive introductions to Mauricean thought; neither tries to do much more than explain what Maurice said. Wood's book is particularly interesting for its discussion of Maurice's enormous influence among Congregationalists in the later nineteenth century and for the clear descriptions of the controversies in which Maurice, professing peace, was frequently embroiled. Walter M. Davies' *An Introduction to the Theology of F. D. Maurice* (1964) is not comprehensive and tends toward paraphrase. The most prolific Mauricean scholar, Alec Vidler, has published a number of his excellent lectures and essays on Maurice in *The Theology of F. D. Maurice* (1948) and *F. D. Maurice and Company* (1966). One regrets that he has not attempted a sustained book on Maurice. Torben Christensen's "F. D. Maurice and the Contemporary Religious World" (in *Studies in Church History*, III, ed. G. J. Cuming, 1966) is a curious and interesting criticism of Maurice's life of his father. Christensen argues that the religious press received Maurice generously up until the publication of the *Theological Essays* (1853) and that Maurice's influence declined thereafter. While this argument should not be received uncritically, it is to be hoped that Christensen's attempt to see Maurice in a broader context will be emulated. The works of Christensen and others on Maurice as a Christian Socialist are discussed below in Section IV.

There is no modern life of Arthur Penrhyn Stanley, an interesting figure and the most important Broad Churchman of the Arnoldian school. *A Victorian Dean: A Memoir of Arthur Penrhyn Stanley, Dean of Westminster* (1930) by Hector Bolitho and the Dean of Windsor is not a scholarly performance; it provides a popular sketch of Stanley's life and incorporates the newly discovered letters which were the occasion for the book. A good, accessible sketch of Stanley's career appears as a chapter in Frances J. Woodward's *The Doctor's Disciples* (1954), a popular account of four men influenced by Arnold. Rowland E. Prothero's *Life and Letters of Dean Stanley* (2 vols., 1893) is a peculiarly excellent example of its type. Prothero, an able and prolific historian, writes with sympathetic appreciation of Stanley's ebullient personality. Prothero also edited *Letters and Verses of Arthur Penrhyn Stanley* (1895), which includes many letters not published in the *Life*.

Charles Kingsley deserves a better study than he has so far received from his modern biographers. Margaret Ferrand Thorp's *Charles Kingsley, 1819–1875* (1937) and Robert B. Martin's *The Dust of Combat, A Life of Charles Kingsley* (1959) are both scholarly treatments of Kingsley, but they are slight, uncritical, and not rooted in knowledge of historical context. While it is marred by untrustworthy judgments, Una Pope-Hennesy's popular life, *Canon Charles Kingsley, A Biography* (1948), is a slightly better book. The basic work on Kingsley is still Mary Kingsley's *Charles Kingsley, His Letters and Memoirs of His Life* (2 vols., 1876). G. Egner's misleadingly titled *Apologia pro Charles Kingsley* (1969) is a book about Newman.

Thomas Hughes: The Life of the Author of Tom Brown's School Days (1952) by Edward C. Mack and Walter H. G. Armytage is a good modern study and so are Charles Smyth's *Dean Milman* (1949) and John Connop Thirlwall's *Connop Thirlwall, Historian and Theologian* (1936). Ralph A. D. Owen's *Charles Bunsen and Liberal English Theology* (1924) calls attention to an influential figure who warrants further investigation. Frederick W. Robertson of Brighton, a great preacher of the elder Arnold's generation and a liberal Churchman who stood outside the central circle of Broad Church friends, has received no modern consideration beyond A. C. Curnow's brief "Robertson of Brighton: A Centenary Tribute" (*London Q. and Holborn Rev.*, 1953). In the decade following *Essays and Reviews* when the liberal threat to orthodoxy seemed most dangerous, a mild sensation greeted Stopford Brooke's *Life and Letters of F. W. Robertson* (2 vols., 1865).

Geoffrey Faber's *Jowett: A Portrait with a Background* (1958) is an important study of the great Master of Balliol who became the chief figure among intellectual Broad Churchmen in the second half of the century. More than merely a life of Jowett, this excellent biography is also a serious study of liberal Anglicanism. It supersedes Evelyn Abbott and Lewis Campbell's *The Life and Letters of Benjamin Jowett* (2 vols., 1897). Another important and suggestive foray into Broad Church history of the later nineteenth century is Richard T. Shannon's "J. R. Seeley and the Idea of a National Church" (in *Ideas and Institutions of Victorian Britain*, ed. Robert Robson, 1967). Shannon argues that Seeley, by developing the idea of providential dispensation for English imperialism, advanced the Broad Church tradition that was faltering with Matthew Arnold.

Margaret Anne Crowther's *Church Embattled: Religious Controversy in Mid-Victorian England* (1970) contains an intelligent general consideration of the Broad Church group up to the publication of *Essays and Reviews* (1860), an interesting attempt to determine the "generations" in the group, and a severely critical discussion of Broad Church scholarship. The general chapter on the education of the Victorian clergy, a trifle out of place in this book, is nevertheless welcome for it is well done. Less attractive is the major portion of the book which Crowther devotes to the orthodox attack on liberal Churchmen. Arguing that liberalism, with its criticism of the Bible, seemed to the orthodox the most dangerous threat to faith, Crowther proceeds to recount in a shrill tone the "persecuting" of liberals. Her focus is on the controversy surrounding *Essays and Reviews*. Another view of that controversy is reported by Stephen Paul Booth in "*Essays and Reviews*: The Controversy as Seen in the Correspondence and Papers of Dr. E. B. Pusey and Archbishop Archibald Tait" (*HMPEC*, 1969). Anthony O. J. Cockshut's *Anglican Attitudes: A Study of Victorian Religious Controversies* (1959) is a helpfully organized though slight survey of the major battles, including *Essays and Reviews* and the Colenso affair. Peter Hinchliff in "John William Colenso: A Fresh Appraisal" (*JEH*, 1962) and *J. W. Colenso, Bishop of Natal* (1964) presents a sympathetic discussion of Colenso and his difficulties, with much information on the African situation.

Evangelicals

While the High Church and Broad Church movements were intellectually disciplined, elitist, and important for their impact on ecclesiastical and literary culture, the Evangelical movement was rooted in a complicated tangle of emotionally conditioned attitudes. It was popular and enormously important for its impact on English culture generally. Diffuse and difficult to define, Evangelicalism was much more than an ecclesiastical party, and it was not confined to the Church. Indeed, Evangelicalism probably involved more Methodists, Congregationalists, Baptists, and Quakers than Churchmen. Nor can there be any doubt, when the laity are included, that Evangelical Churchmen overwhelmingly outnumbered their High

Church and Broad Church brethren. Unfortunately, most historians of Evangelicalism treat the movement narrowly as a Church party. In spite of the recognized importance of the Evangelical movement in the nineteenth century, studies on the subject are less abundant and, on the whole, less good than those on Anglo-Catholicism and the Broad Church.

The best introduction to Evangelicalism in the eighteenth century is John Dixon Walsh's "Origins of the Evangelical Revival" (in *Essays in Modern Church History*, ed. Gareth V. Bennett and John Dixon Walsh, 1966), an important new interpretation of the matrix from which the movement developed. Ronald Knox's *Enthusiasm* (1950) is a lively and perceptive inquiry into the psychology of revivalism. The quality of religious and social life at Clapham in the late eighteenth and early nineteenth centuries is sensitively portrayed by Standish Meacham in *Henry Thornton of Clapham* (1964) and by E. M. Forster in *Marianne Thornton: A Domestic Biography* (1956). Ford K. Brown's *Fathers of the Victorians: The Age of Wilberforce* (1961) is a massive account of pre-Victorian Evangelicalism, with emphasis on popular education and philanthropy. While this work is valuable for its detailed description of Evangelical societies, the book is seriously marred by Brown's tendentious attack on Evangelical motives which he dogmatically identifies with social and political conservatism.

George R. Balleine's *A History of the Evangelical Party in the Church of England* (1908) is essentially an ecclesiastical history. The eighteenth century receives the greatest emphasis, but this is nevertheless the best easily accessible account of Victorian Evangelicalism as a Church party. The leading clergymen, the major controversies with other Church parties, and the most important changes in styles of worship and revival are reliably discussed. While it is difficult to get at, the most detailed and perceptive history of the Evangelical movement in the Victorian Church is scattered through the four monumental volumes of Eugene Stock's *The History of the Church Missionary Society* (1899 and 1916). This magisterial work by the secretary of the Society discusses the sources for Evangelical history and presents a well-documented, carefully conceived narrative. Stock, like most historians of Evangelicalism, exhibits parti pris, although the judgments in his large work are much more soundly balanced than in his short, acerbic history of *The English Church in the Nineteenth Century* (1910). Handley C. G. Moule's *The Evangelical School in the Church of England, Its Men and Its Works in the Nineteenth Century* (1901) is a collection of brief essays which originally appeared in the *Record*, the most militant of Evangelical periodicals. Moule's essays contain an interesting suggestion for the periodization of Evangelical history, and there is a useful, brief discussion of the societies around which the party was organized.

There are no good modern histories of Victorian Evangelicalism. *Anglican Evangelicalism* (ed. Alexander C. Zabriski, 1943) contains only a slight sketch of the movement in the nineteenth century and is seriously misleading on the important question of Evangelical social action. L. E. Elliott-Binns, in *The Evangelical Movement in the English Church* (1928), raises some interesting questions about the geography of Evangelicalism, but this slight work adds little to Balleine. Geoffrey Best's fine lecture on "Evangelicalism and the Victorians," printed in *The Victorian Crisis of Faith* (ed. Anthony Symondson, 1970), is an excellent brief characterization of the movement which suggests some of the directions future research might take.

Herbert Clegg's three-part article, "Evangelicals and Tractarians" (*HMPEC*,

1966, 1967), contains a very good close analysis of early nineteenth-century Evangelical theological emphases, and a convincingly well-written account of the relations between Evangelicals and Tractarians up to the condemnation of the Tracts at the Islington Clerical Meeting in 1837. Standish Meacham's "The Evangelical Inheritance" (*JBS*, 1963) is a fascinating comment on how some of the descendants of the Clapham Sect moved away from orthodoxy; his focus is on the Stephen family.

Charles Smyth's *Simeon and Church Order* (1940) is the most important biography of an Evangelical clergyman. Very well written and lively, this intelligent study of Charles Simeon argues that the fundamental divergence between Evangelicals and Methodists was over church order, and that Simeon did more than any other man to maintain an Evangelical stream within the Church of England. Marcus Loane's *Makers of Our Heritage* (1967) contains biographies of J. C. Ryle, H. C. G. Moule, E. A. Knox, and H. W. K. Mowll. Although written from a highly partisan Evangelical point of view, these are informative, well-documented studies. Particularly perceptive is the essay on Ryle, a brilliant scholar and cricket player at Eton and Oxford in the thirties, a great tract writer, the leader of the militant Evangelicals from the mid-seventies, and Bishop of Liverpool from 1880. John S. Reynolds' *Canon Christopher of St. Aldgate's, Oxford* (1967) is a leisurely, well-illustrated life of the leading Evangelical clergyman in late-nineteenth-century Oxford. It is useful for the sympathetic discussion of Christopher's religious temper and for the description of his wide circle of Evangelical friends. Harold Kirk-Smith's *William Thomson, Archbishop of York* (1958) is a short study of a draper's son who rose to prominence in the Church through success at Oxford. Shocked into orthodoxy by *Essays and Reviews*, Thomson became famous in the seventies for his vow to "put down ritualists." Kirk-Smith, perhaps, is too critical of Thomson and not sufficiently critical of his sources. John Battersby Harford and Frederick Charles Macdonald, in *Handley Carr Glyn Moule, Bishop of Durham* (1922), provide a good account of the life of the man who dominated Cambridge Evangelicalism in the later part of the century. Moule, more sensitive and articulate than most prominent Evangelicals, was a theologian of some merit and a devotee of the Keswick Convention. The discussion of his spiritual life in this biography is especially interesting. David E. H. Mole's "John Cale Miller, A Victorian Rector of Birmingham" (*JEH*, 1966) is a first-rate description of an Evangelical peculiarly successful at the parish level in the middle decades of the century. As well as Miller's impact on his parish, Mole discusses the religious and social structure of Birmingham and Miller's political role in the city. For a charming memoir of a philanthropic lady author who moved at the top of Evangelical clerical society and seemed to know everyone who counted, one may read L. E. O'Rorke's *The Life and Friendships of Catherine Marsh* (1917).

The most powerful Victorian Evangelical in both ecclesiastical and political circles was the seventh Earl of Shaftesbury. From the later 1840's until his death in 1885 he was the undisputed leader of the Evangelical party, and his influence was enormous. His life is authoritatively chronicled by Edwin Hodder in *The Life and Work of the Seventh Earl of Shaftesbury* (3 vols., 1886), a sympathetic, well-balanced biography which probably will never be superseded. Shaftesbury, in company with many Evangelicals, religiously kept a diary in which he reported the state of his soul as well as his daily activites. Hodder used the diaries with Victorian discretion, never drawing on the personal religious portions. Geoffrey Best has also consulted the diaries and his less restrained short life, *Shaftesbury* (1964), should be read as a supplement to Hodder.

Since the time of Simeon, Evangelicalism has been more closely associated with Cambridge than Oxford. J. S. Reynolds, in *The Evangelicals at Oxford 1735–1871: A Record of an Unchronicled Movement* (1953), demonstrates that at Oxford Evangelicalism was very strong indeed until Newman's defection in 1845 frightened Evangelical parents. Reynolds also challenges the widely held assumption that Evangelicals did not achieve academic distinction, and he produces an impressive list of Evangelical firsts and double firsts. One suspects that Reynolds is right and that the Ritualists were probably, among Churchmen, academically the weakest group. A closely related and more important problem which Reynolds does not take up is the nature of Evangelical vulgarity. There is a good comparison of the religious atmosphere of mid-century Oxford and Cambridge by John Roach in "'The Rudiments of Faith and Religion': Religious Controversy at Oxford, 1860–1865" (*JEH*, 1971). Vivian H. H. Green, in *Religion at Oxford and Cambridge* (1964), covers 800 years but still manages a densely packed forty pages on the second half of the nineteenth century. During that period Cambridge was a peculiarly enthusiastic center of Evangelical activity, much of which is described in the works of John C. Pollock. The most basic of Pollock's books, *A Cambridge Movement* (1953), is a sound, descriptive history of the Cambridge Intercollegiate Christian Union. Pollock, alas, does not attempt to explain why in the second half of the century Evangelicalism became attractive to so many young men of good family. Neither does Tissington Tatlow in *The Story of the Student Christian Movement of Great Britain and Ireland* (1933).

Before the middle of the century enthusiasm and revivalism were associated with Methodism and disapproved by the hierarchy. This disapproval is well documented by Richard Allen Soloway in "Episcopal Perspective and Religious Revivalism in England, 1784–1851" (*HMPEC*, 1971). By the 1850's Evangelicalism had become eminently respectable and fear of the nonreligious poor made revivalism seem desirable to many. The Evangelical revival that spread from North America to Britain in 1859 is described in great detail but mechanically by J. Edwin Orr in *The Second Evangelical Awakening in Britain* (1949). Dealing with the period 1859–65, Orr traces the expansion of the revival throughout Britain and argues that it was fundamentally important for the great outpouring of Evangelical philanthropy that followed. R. C. Morgan, an Evangelical publisher of no fixed denomination, was a key figure in organizing the revival. George E. Morgan's *R. C. Morgan, His Life and Times* (1909) is a useful biography that contains a good history of Morgan's firm. While his major concern is with America, there is much material on England in William G. McLoughlin's *Modern Revivalism: Charles Grandison Finney to Billy Graham* (1959); the greatest strength of McLoughlin's work is the treatment of Victorian revivals as phenomena of the North Atlantic triangle. The greatest of the evangelists was D. L. Moody. His career in England is given heavy emphasis by J. C. Pollock in *Moody without Sankey* (1963), the first competent survey of Moody's life. While there is less on the English revivals in James Findlay's *Dwight L. Moody, American Evangelist* (1969), the stimulating discussion of the relation of revivalism and social change is of general significance. Findlay's important suggestion that English revivals should be seen in the context of democratization deserves attention. J. C. Pollock's *The Keswick Story* (1964) is the official history of a curious, institutionalized form of middle-class revivalism. An excellent book on a minor theme, Dieter Voll's *Catholic Evangelicalism* (1963) presents an interesting and scholarly discussion of the revivals which were led by Anglo-Catholics.

There has been little investigation of Evangelical literature in the Victorian period, and no sympathetic study of the ways in which Evangelical attitudes were propagated. J. D. Walsh in "Joseph Milner's Evangelical Church History" (*JEH*, 1959) describes the contents and career of *The History of the Church of Christ* (1794), which Julius Hare in 1847 called "the main, if not the sole, source from which a large portion of our church derive their notions of ecclesiastical history." Religious journalism flourished in the nineteenth century. While historians have used the journals as sources, they have rarely treated religious journalism as a subject, and never systematically. A welcome expedition into this world of which we have so little conception is undertaken by Patrick Scott in " 'Zion's Trumpet': Evangelical Enterprise and Rivalry, 1833–1835" (*VS*, 1969).

Having noted the prevalence of cricket players among prominent Evangelicals, Patrick Scott undertakes another exploratory mission into the little-worked field of sport in "Cricket and the Religious World in the Victorian Period" (*Church Q.*, 1970). His interesting argument that Evangelicals were attracted to cricket as a badge of social prestige is not altogether convincing, but it does suggest another area in which Evangelicalism and democratization might be linked.

Evangelicals were readier than other Churchmen to cooperate with like-minded dissenters and foreigners. A brief look at the problems involved in ecumenical activity is provided in John E. Pinnington's "Denominational Loyalty and Loyalty to Christ" (*Canadian J. of Theol.*, 1968), a study of the early years of the Evangelical Alliance.

FOREIGN MISSIONS. Foreign missions were the glory of the Evangelicals, and in their search for missionaries Evangelicals within the Church were eager to cooperate with their brethren outside. The history of British missions is a vast subject and cannot be fully surveyed here. Our attention is focused on the organization of missions at the home base, a subject that has received surprisingly little modern treatment. The best introduction to the general history of missions is Stephen Neill's *A History of Christian Missions* (1964), Volume VI in the *Pelican History of the Church*. This is a very good book indeed, straightforward history, well organized and with a fine bibliography. The only rival to Neill's book is Robert Hall Glover and J. Herbert Kane's *The Progress of World Wide Missions* (rev. ed., 1960). Not very readable, almost a handbook, this work is a full and reliable guide, packed with information about the areas in which missionaries worked. Max Warren surveys Victorian missions briefly in "The Church Militant Abroad: Victorian Missionaries" (in *The Victorian Crisis of Faith*, ed. Anthony Symondson, 1970), and he has published two books of essays, *Social History and Christian Missions* (1967) and *The Missionary Movement from Britain in Modern History* (1965). In *The Missionary Movement*, "Missionary Motives 1784–1859" is an imaginative comment on a difficult theme. The essay on "The Social and Economic Background of the Nineteenth Century Missionary," in *Social History*, suggests what might be done if this subject were studied closely; "The Public Image of the Missionary in the Nineteenth Century" is delightful; "Church and State in the British Colonial Empire from Palmerston to Macmillan" organizes a difficult problem clearly and calls for more use of the vast archives of the missionary societies. Hans Cnattingius discusses the relation of the early missionary societies to the traditional structure of

Church authority in *Bishops and Societies: A Study of Anglican Colonial and Missionary Expansion, 1698–1850* (1952) and shows how the quarrels of the Church parties were exported into the mission field.

The domestic history of the missionary movement is not thoroughly recorded. It is best studied in the histories of the missionary societies. The only good modern history covering a society in the nineteenth century is Henry Paget Thompson's *Into All Lands. The History of the Society for the Propagation of the Gospel in Foreign Parts 1701–1950* (1951). This long book is virtually a history of the Anglican Church abroad; there is not much space for domestic concerns. Charles Frederick Pascoe's *Two Hundred Years of the S. P. G.* (1901) contains a useful list of S. P. G. missionaries and their dates. The best of all the society histories is Eugene Stock's impressive *History of the Church Missionary Society* (4 vols., 1899 and 1916), which puts considerable emphasis on the history of the Society in England. Max Warren has edited *To Apply the Gospel, Selections from the Writings of Henry Venn* (1971), with a good general introduction. Venn, a powerful Evangelical, was secretary of the C. M. S., 1841–72, and did much to establish the pattern of Victorian Missionary enterprise. Norman Goodall's *A History of the London Missionary Society 1895–1945* (1954) contains an excellent discussion of interdenominationalism, the "Fundamental Principle of the Society." Goodall's work continues the history of the L. M. S. begun by Richard Lovett in *The History of the London Missionary Society* (2 vols., 1899). William Canton's *The History of the British and Foreign Bible Society* (5 vols., 1904–10) and George Browne's *The History of the British and Foreign Bible Society* (2 vols., 1859) are fascinating, detailed histories, loaded with extracts from the archives of the Society that sent George Borrow to Russia and Spain, battled Popery everywhere, and pacified the Canadian Indians with the Word. William Thomas Gidney's *The History of the London Society for Promoting Christianity among the Jews, from 1809 to 1908* (1908) contains the story of another major Evangelical society. The pioneering work of the Baptists has an excellent modern history in E. Daniel Potts's *British Baptist Missionaries in India, 1793–1837* (1967), a useful addition to Fred Townley Lord's popular *Achievement: A Short History of the Baptist Missionary Society* (1941). The work of the Methodists is recorded by George Gilanders Findlay and William West Holdsworth in *The History of the Wesleyan Methodist Missionary Society* (5 vols., 1921–24).

The impact of the mid-century Evangelical revival in the universities, especially in Cambridge, is reflected in the recruitment of missionaries among the undergraduates. George Herbert Wilson has written *The History of the Universities' Mission to Central Africa* (1936). This was the Mission that sent out Mackenzie, whose tragically brief career is movingly reconstructed by Owen Chadwick in *Mackenzie's Grave* (1959). J. C. Pollock's *The Cambridge Seven* (1955) is a popular study of the prominent undergraduate sportsmen who caused a national sensation by joining the China Inland Mission in 1885.

Nonconformists

No satisfactory major general history of Victorian nonconformity has yet been written. The most thoughtful and perceptive discussion is contained in those brief chapters in G. Kitson Clark's stimulating essay, *The English Inheritance* (1950), which place dissent in its social and political setting. A short, more ecclesiastically oriented survey by a distinguished Baptist historian, Ernest A. Payne's *The Free*

Church Tradition in the Life of England (1944), deals largely with the pre-Victorian period; unfortunately, so does Horton Davies' *The English Free Churches* (1952). Eric Routley's *English Religious Dissent* (1960) is an excellent brief survey by a historian with a good sense of the mixture of social and ecclesiastical factors that shaped Victorian nonconformity. David M. Thompson's collection of excellently chosen documents, *Nonconformity in the Nineteenth Century* (1972), contains a sensible introduction to Victorian dissent.

On the whole, the books written to commemorate the tercentenary of the "great ejection" of 1662 have been disappointing. Francis G. Healey's *Rooted in Faith: Three Centuries of Nonconformity, 1662–1962* (1962) barely mentions the nineteenth century. John Thomas Wilkinson's *1662 and After: Three Centuries of English Nonconformity* (1962) contains only a brief sketch of the Victorian period, with a bias toward organizational history and nothing on the character of nonconformist life. E. A. Payne's useful short chapter in *From Uniformity to Unity, 1662–1962* (ed. Geoffrey F. Nuttall and Owen Chadwick, 1962) sets out in clear schematic form the changing legal status of nonconformity after 1689. To the same book, Edward Carpenter contributes a discursive essay on some of the central themes in the relations of Church, State, and dissent. Recognizing the general importance of nonconformity, Charles F. Mullett calls for more research in "Religious Nonconformity: A Central Theme in Modern English History" (*HMPEC*, 1968).

The older histories also concentrate on the seventeenth century and tend to slight the nineteenth. In Volumes VII and VIII of *The History of Religion in England* (1884), however, John Stoughton deals with the first fifty years of the nineteenth century in detail. Stoughton was an eminent Congregationalist, and his *History* contains a good account of dissent. Herbert S. Skeats and Charles S. Miall, also Congregationalists, devote considerable space to a politically oriented history of both early and late nineteenth-century dissent in their *History of the Free Churches of England, 1688–1891* (1894). Henry W. Clark's *History of English Nonconformity* (2 vols., 1913) contains only a brief sketch of the nineteenth century. The same is true of C. Silvester Horne's *A Popular History of the Free Churches* (1903). Horne's *Nonconformity in the XIXth Century* (1905) is more polemical than historical. Bernard Lord Manning, in *The Protestant Dissenting Deputies* (1952), provides an invaluable record of the opinions on public affairs of a group of politically concerned dissenters. His work covers the whole of the nineteenth century and is tightly tied to the Deputies' minutes.

The role of dissent in parliamentary politics has recently received promising attention. Richard W. Davis, in *Dissent in Politics, 1780–1830: The Political Life of William Smith, M.P.* (1971), has written the best history so far of the successful campaign to repeal the Test and Corporation Acts, the most pressing of dissenters' civil grievances. Geoffrey Best's article, "The Whigs and the Church Establishment in the Age of Grey and Holland" (*History*, 1960), provides a clear summary of the political positions of the Church and dissent on the morrow of the Reform Act. Norman Gash, in two long chapters of his important work on *Reaction and Reconstruction in English Politics, 1832–1852* (1965), surveys and analyzes brilliantly a critical period in the Parliamentary battle between Church and dissent. Raymond G. Cowherd's *The Politics of English Dissent* (1956) covers the first half of the century. While it contains some useful information, Cowherd's work is so ill organized and ill conceived that it is both misleading and difficult to read. William G. Addison's knowledgeable essay, *Religious Equality in Modern England* (1944), outlines well the major grievances and political campaigns of Victorian dissenters.

A brief and rewarding general introduction to the politics of dissent in the second half of the century is contained in Frank Salter's informative lecture, *Dissenters and Public Affairs in Mid-Victorian England* (1967). Salter surveys the variety of issues that interested dissenters, among which their central hope was disestablishment. The best history of the emergence and early years of the disestablishment movement is still buried in Arthur Miall's *The Life of Edward Miall* (1884). Miall, the redoubtable editor of the *Nonconformist*, was the principal organizer of the mid-century parliamentary politics of militant dissent. The strongest leader among moderate dissenters of the same period, Edward Baines, editor of the *Leeds Mercury*, has no biography. The later history of the disestablishment movement is competently chronicled by S. M. Ingham in "The Disestablishment Movement in England, 1868–74" (*JRH*, 1964) and by Noel J. Richards in "Disestablishment of the Anglican Church in England in the Late Nineteenth Century: Reasons for Failure" (*J. of Church and State*, 1970). Philip Michael Hitt Bell's *Disestablishment in Ireland and Wales* (1969) is an excellent, full study of the successful attacks on the Celtic outworks of the Establishment.

Some aspects of the part played by nonconformity in the Liberal politics of Gladstone's era are brilliantly discussed by John Vincent in *The Formation of the Liberal Party 1857–1868* (1966). Vincent's first two chapters include an original and imaginative approach to the role of nonconformity at the constituency level. Many suggestions for further research emerge, and some of them are amplified in John Vincent's *Pollbooks: How Victorians Voted* (1967). In *Elections and Party Management: Politics in the Time of Disraeli and Gladstone* (1959), Harold J. Hanham also considers dissent at the constituency level and emphasizes the financial importance of dissenting political organizations. John F. Glaser traces the relations of Liberalism and dissent through the crises of the 1880's in "English Nonconformity and the Decline of Liberalism" (*AHR*, 1958). Harry F. Lovell Cocks, in *The Nonconformist Conscience* (1943), discusses briefly and in general terms that curious ethicism which colored late Victorian dissenting opinion on public affairs.

For most of the nineteenth century, nonconformity was a peculiarly provincial phenomenon, very much more important in local politics than in national. The history of the place of dissent in local politics, especially town politics which were often dominated by religious tensions, is found scattered among the multitude of local histories. The more recent volumes of the *Victoria County History* are often good sources, as are some of the recent urban histories, especially A. Temple Patterson's *Radical Leicester* (1954), Conrad Gill and Asa Briggs's *History of Birmingham* (2 vols., 1952), Asa Briggs's *Victorian Cities* (1963), and Robert Newton's *Victorian Exeter* (1968). Frank Tillyard discusses some of the factors influencing "The Distribution of the Free Churches in England" (*Sociological Rev.*, 1935). The only comprehensive study of dissent in a provincial town is Alan Brockett's mechanically descriptive work on *Nonconformity in Exeter, 1650–1875* (1962).

Congregationalists

Among nonconformist denominations the Congregationalists have attracted the richest written history for the Victorian period. Their history, in quality and amount, is rivaled only by that of the Methodists. Only a mere portion is surveyed here. R. Tudur Jones's *Congregationalism in England 1662–1962* (1962) is a major contribution to Victorian religious history; the emphasis of the book is on the period 1815–1914. It is the most comprehensive, useful introduction to the history of the denomination, and the good bibliography and many footnotes provide an excellent guide to the literature on Congregationalism. Jones is at his best when he deals with theology—an unusual strength among nonconformist historians—and he is only slightly less secure with politics. The leading clergy and chapels are well noticed, with an emphasis on London that is perhaps misleading. The social composition of the denomination is discussed superficially. Erik Routley's *The Story of Congregationalism* (1961) is merely a short sketch, but Routley understands so well the interaction of religious and social factors that his book is a valuable complement to the work of Tudur Jones. Albert Peel's *These Hundred Years, A History of the Congregational Union of England and Wales, 1831–1931* (1931) is a reliable and intelligently conceived study of the central organization that debated all questions of serious denominational concern. After Tudur Jones's history, this is the most important work on Victorian Congregationalists. Still valuable for their wealth of detail and numerous small biographies are the last two volumes of John W. Waddington's *Congregational History* (1869–80). Robert William Dale's literate *History of English Congregationalism* (2nd ed., ed. Alfred W. W. Dale, 1907) is so strongly colored by Dale's liberal antipathy to early Victorian Evangelicalism that it must be read with considerable caution. *The Congregational Two Hundred* (1948), compiled by Albert Pell, is a useful collection of biographies of eminent Congregationalists. John W. Grant's *Free Churchmanship in England, 1870–1940, with Special Reference to Congregationalism* (1955) is a detailed survey of Congregational opinion on ecclesiastical polity, the area in which Congregationalists located their distinctive identity.

Thomas Binney was the leading mid-Victorian Congregational minister. Clyde Binfield's "Thomas Binney and Congregationalism's 'Special Mission'" (*Trans. of the Congregational Hist. Soc.*, 1971) is an interesting, short comment on Binney's famous remark that the special mission of his denomination was to the middle classes. Binfield contrasts the attitude of the denomination in Binney's day to that in the 1890's when Alexander Mackennal, influenced by F. D. Maurice, repudiated Binney's social orientation. There has been no major study of Binney since E. Paxton Hood's *Thomas Binney* (1874), but Elaine Kaye has written a good history of his chapel, *The History of the King's Weigh House Church* (1968). John H. Taylor's "London Congregational Churches since 1850" (*Trans. of the Congregational Hist. Soc.*, 1965) is a well-documented, precise investigation of the relations between social and ecclesiastical geography and the financing of chapels. Taylor, making good use of maps, shows clearly that Congregational chapels were established in areas where the middle classes lived and were shut down in those areas the middle classes abandoned. Ian Sellars' "Congregationalists and Presbyterians in Nineteenth Century Liverpool" (*Trans. of the Congregational Hist. Soc.*, 1965) contains a guide to the literature on Lancashire nonconformity and a most interesting brief comment on the sociology and politics of dissent in Liverpool.

Reflecting rather belatedly the rising importance of provincial dissent, R. W. Dale of Birmingham succeeded Binney as the most influential Congregationalist. It is surprising that Dale, liberal in politics, social thought, and theology, has not been more studied. The attractive biography by his son, A. W. W. Dale, *The Life of R. W. Dale* (1898), is a beautifully written, moving book, but it is neither comprehensive nor critical. Especially useful for Dale's view of the social sciences and their implications for Christian social action is Stephen Mayor's "R. W. Dale and Nineteenth Century Thought" (*Trans. of the Congregational Hist. Soc.*, 1965). The best treatments of Dale's theological liberalism and his reception of Biblical criticism are found in Tudur Jones's *Congregationalism* and in W. B. Glover's *Evangelical Nonconformists and Higher Criticism in the Nineteenth Century* (1954). There is no sustained modern work on A. M. Fairbairn, the most significant Congregationalist theologian of the late nineteenth century. John H. Rodgers has written a study of the last important dissenting theologian, *The Theology of P. T. Forsyth* (1965). Although this is a misty, sometimes awkward work, it does provide a good description of the German and Mauricean influences at work among late Victorian Congregationalists.

The most influential layman among the Congregationalists of the mid-century was Samuel Morley, an enormously wealthy hosier and one of the great Victorian philanthropists. He cooperated frequently with Shaftesbury, with whom he shared his biographer, Edwin Hodder, who wrote the only *Life of Samuel Morley* (1887). David Newton has recently studied another Congregationalist businessman and philanthropist, *Sir Halley Stewart* (1968). Newton's work is a welcome addition to the scattered and sparse literature on religiously committed businessmen.

Baptists

The best introduction to Victorian Baptists is provided by Ernest A. Payne in *The Baptist Union: A Short History* (1958). This richly informed book by the best contemporary Baptist historian is organized around an account of the central denominational organization. Payne discusses the Baptists in the broader context of Protestant nonconformity and attempts to assess their place in the general life of the nation. Alfred Clair Underwood's *A History of the English Baptists* (1947) is the best modern history of the denomination from the seventeenth century, but the nineteenth-century chapters are slight and consist largely of short notes on important men. The Victorian portions of William T. Whitley's *A History of British Baptists* (1923) and John C. Carlile's *The Story of the English Baptists* (1905) are valuable only for their material on foreign missions.

The two great men among Victorian Baptists were Charles Haddon Spurgeon and John Clifford. Spurgeon, a talented evangelist, a great preacher, and a complex, fascinating man, lacks a good biography. *C. H. Spurgeon's Autobiography Compiled from His Diary, Letters and Records, by His Wife and His Private Secretary* (4 vols., 1897–1900) is poorly constructed and surprisingly slight. William Young Fullerton's *Charles Haddon Spurgeon: A Biography* (1920; rpt. 1966) is informal, anecdotal, but much more informative. John C. Carlile's *C. H. Spurgeon: An Interpretive Biography* (1933) is based on little research and badly marred by interpretive digressions. Ernest Wallace Bacon's *Spurgeon: Heir of the Puritans* (1967) is too short and simple for its substantial subject, but it is a useful introduction to Spurgeon and the activities of his Metropolitan Tabernacle. Sir James Marchant's *Dr. John Clifford, C. H.* (1924) is a well-constructed compilation from Clifford's reminiscences, diaries, letters, and sermons. There is a considerable store of material on the Downgrade Movement, the important Baptist doctrinal controversy in which the conservative Spurgeon and the liberal Clifford were deeply involved. Clifford was at the forefront of nonconformist politics at the end of the century, and this biography emphasizes his outward-looking, nonsectarian view which contrasted sharply with Spurgeon's denominational orientation.

Methodists

The first fully comprehensive history of Methodism, and still the best, is *A New History of Methodism* edited by William J. Townsend, Herbert B. Workman, and George Eayrs (2 vols., 1909). This work, like others written in that decade peculiarly productive of standard church histories, is strongest as a narrative of the constitutional and ecclesiastical history of the denomination. There is virtually nothing on the social life of Methodism, and little on the place of the denomination in the community. The *New History* is currently being replaced by a newer, edited by Ernest Gordon Rupp and Rupert Eric Davies. The first of three projected volumes of *A History of the Methodist Church in Great Britain* appeared in 1965. It ends with Wesley's death. Davies' *Methodism* (1963) contains only one slim chapter on the nineteenth century.

Robert Currie's *Methodism Divided: A Study in the Sociology of Ecumenicalism* (1968) is the most stimulating and important recent work on the denomination. Currie analyzes brilliantly the major theme of nineteenth-century Methodism —schism and reunion—and demonstrates clearly the intimate relation between ecclesiastical conflict and Methodist social history. Constitutional conflict and the problem of authority dominate John Kent's excellent and learned essays collected in his *The Age of Disunity* (1966). Included here is Kent's fine lecture on Jabez Bunting. Keen on refining ideas and demolishing myths, Kent argues that "evangelicalism, like the Feudal system, never existed." He criticizes in detail Halévy's discussion of Methodism in the 1830's and 1840's, and he provides a useful survey of Methodist historiography. His major investment, and his greatest contribution, is in his discussion of the theological background of the authoritarianism of Jabez Bunting. Bunting was overwhelmingly the most powerful Wesleyan in the first half of the century, and Methodist history of that period is dominated by reactions to his authority. Kent argues that his personal authoritarianism was secondary, and that Bunting's impersonal, theological conception of the ministerial office is the key to understanding his career. Kent is too critical of Ernest R. Taylor's *Methodism in Politics, 1791–1851* (1935) in which Bunting's personal love of power is clearly demonstrated if somewhat overemphasized. Taylor's discussion of the tension between the Tory Bunting and the increasingly liberal Wesleyan laity is still valuable. Especially important is Taylor's suggestion that the source of Methodist liberalism should be sought outside the denomination in the secular community, a reminder that Currie's tendency to see Methodism as a closed system with almost exclusively internal dynamics is not without danger.

The drift from conservatism to liberalism during the years between the death of Wesley and the death of Bunting is chronicled by Maldwyn Edwards in *After Wesley, A Study of the Social and Political Influence of Methodism in the Middle Period, 1791–1849* (1935), a slight and unsystematic study. Edwards' succeeding volume, *Methodism and England, A Study of Methodism in Its Social and Political Aspects during the Period 1850–1932* (1943), is a much stronger and richer book, packed with solid information. Edwards' discussion of Hugh Price Hughes, the leading Methodist of the later nineteenth century, is especially well done. Dorothea Price Hughes's *The Life of Hugh Price Hughes* (1904), leisurely, immense, and well constructed, is written very much from within the family and does not do justice to Hughes as a public figure. Edwards helps redress the balance; to his work one must add the searching analysis of Hughes's version of Social Christianity in John Kent's "Hugh Price Hughes and the Nonconformist Conscience" (in *Essays in Modern English Church History*, ed. G. V. Bennett and J. D. Walsh, 1966). No serious contribution is made by J. Wesley Bready in *England before and after Wesley* (1938); it is little more than an unsystematic list of social reforms undertaken by men and women more or less influenced by Evangelicalism. The books on Methodism and the working classes by Robert Wearmouth are discussed below in Section IV, as is the well-known Halévy thesis.

Regional histories of Methodism are beginning to appear and they are most welcome. Frank Tice, in *The History of Methodism in Cambridge* (1966), shows how the tension between liberalism and authority operated at the local level. Thomas Shaw's *A History of Cornish Methodism* (1967) is a richly informative book that deals well with styles of worship, the social status of the laity and the ministers, and trends in membership. Shaw's intriguing bibliography includes J. J. Beckerlegge's *Two Hundred Years of Methodism in Mousehole* (1954).

Thomas Shaw has also written a very good history of *The Bible Christians* (1965), one of the early nineteenth-century schisms from the Wesleyans which was particularly strong in the West Country. Curiously, the Bible Christians, like the Salvation Army later, exhibited the same pattern of conflict that continued to split the Wesleyans. Holliday B. Kendall's *The History of the Primitive Methodist Church* (2 vols., ca. 1907) is a surprisingly good official history, illustrated with photographs. Kendall writes with sensitivity and insight. His massive history is far superior to Joseph Ritson's popular account, improbably called *The Romance of Primitive Methodism* (1909).

Quakers

Elizabeth Isichei's *Victorian Quakers* (1970) is a fine illustration of what good denominational history can and ought to be. This excellent work, with its elaborate, full bibliography, is the necessary starting place for any further investigation of nineteenth-century Quakers. Influenced by the school of religious sociology developed by Bryan Wilson at Oxford, Isichei concentrates her attention on the relation between theological change and organizational change. She also describes with finesse the style of life favored in wealthy Quaker families and includes an interesting analytical study of the types of Quaker philanthropy. The major weakness of Isichei's approach is her tendency to consider too exclusively the denomination as the framework of Quaker action. Consequently there is little here about the place of Quakers in the secular community.

Victorian Quakers in both England and the United States are dealt with in the second volume of Rufus M. Jones's *The Later Periods of Quakerism* (2 vols., 1921). In this magisterial but uncritical work Jones emphasizes Quaker work in the world. His accounts of theology and the inner life are weak compared to those of Isichei, whose work is superior in every way except grace of style. Warren Sylvester Smith's "London Quakers at the Turn of the Century" (*Quaker Hist.*, 1964) is a useful description of the drift of Quakers from Evangelicalism through social action to secularism. Auguste Jorns's *The Quakers as Pioneers in Social Work* (trans. T. K. Brown, 1931) and Isabel Mackenzie's *Social Activities of the English Friends in the First Half of the Nineteenth Century* (1935) are conceptually weak and useful only for their catalogs of Quaker philanthropies. A much more stimulating inquiry into this area is Asa Briggs's *Social Thought and Social Action: A Study of the Work of Seebohm Rowntree 1871–1954* (1961).

George Macaulay Trevelyan's *Life of John Bright* (1913) is the classic biography of the great Quaker politician. David E. Swift's *Joseph John Gurney: Banker, Reformer and Quaker* (1962) is a solid, scholarly study of a leading representative of a great Quaker family, the brother of Elizabeth Fry and the brother-in-law of T. F. Buxton of antislavery fame. Anne Vernon's *A Quaker Businessman: The Life of Joseph Rowntree, 1836–1925* (1958) is disappointing, popular, and anecdotal. Alfred G. Gardiner's worthy *Life of George Cadbury* (1923) is a good biography of the founder of the firm who moved his factory out of smoky Birmingham in 1878 and established the first "garden city" at Bournville in 1898.

Unitarians

Unitarians, who attracted the rich and powerful in many provincial towns and maintained the most genuinely intellectual ministry among all the Victorian denominations, deserve better treatment from their historians. There is no satisfactory history of Victorian Unitarianism. *The English Presbyterians from Elizabethan Puritanism to Modern Unitarianism* (1968) by Charles Gordon Bolam, Jeremy Goring, Harry Lismer Short, and Roger Thomas must serve until a full general history is written. Short's chapter on the late eighteenth and nineteenth centuries includes a useful survey of theological trends—with emphasis on the dominance of James Martineau in the fifty years before 1900—and a good summary of organizational development and the major issues faced by the denomination. There is no space in Short's brief outline for the role of Unitarianism in provincial life. Earl Morse Wilbur's *A History of Unitarianism in Transylvania, England and America* (1952) contains very little about Victorian Unitarianism beyond an abbreviated outline of the legal crises of the early nineteenth century and a short discussion of James Martineau. Herbert McLachlan's *The Unitarian Movement in the Religious Life of England* (1934) deals with Unitarian scholarship, education, theology, and journalism; it is not a general history. McLachlan's study of journalism especially is very well done. It provides a good overview of the intellectual life of the denomination in the nineteenth century.

Raymond V. Holt's *The Unitarian Contribution to Social Progress in England* (1938) includes a valuable record of Unitarian activities in progressive causes. The tone is tendentious, the approach uncritical, and the organization unhistorical, but the information is useful. Arthur Peacock, in "Social Factors in British Unitarian History" (*Faith and Freedom*, 1969), calls attention to the growing conservatism of late Victorian Unitarians and suggests how it might be explained.

In *The Dissidence of Dissent: The Monthly Repository 1806–1838* (1944), Francis Mineka has written a first-rate intellectual history of the denomination in the early nineteenth century. His treatment of W. J. Fox, editor of the *Monthly Repository* for ten years after 1827, is a particularly useful introduction to the quality of Unitarian radicalism in its most fruitful period. The best work on James Martineau is J. Estlin Carpenter's *James Martineau, Theologian and Teacher* (1905). Massive and well documented, this careful biography might be considered a history of the denomination as well as a life of its leading minister. *The Life and Letters of James Martineau* (2 vols., 1902), by James Drummond and Charles B. Upton, is not as good a book as Carpenter's, but it is useful for its concentration on

Martineau's philosophy. Edgar Wright includes a good discussion of the quality of Mrs. Gaskell's Unitarianism in *Mrs. Gaskell: The Basis for Reassessment* (1965), and Herbert McLachlan describes William Gaskell's ministry in "Cross Street Chapel in the Life of Manchester" (*Memoirs and Proc. of the Manchester Lit. and Phil. Soc.*, 1939–41). In *The Story of the Old Meeting House, Mansfield* (1959), J. Harrop White describes the drift from Presbyterianism to Unitarianism in a midlands town, and discusses the changing style of worship and the social composition of the congregation. Unitarianism in early nineteenth-century Norwich is described very well indeed by Robert K. Webb in his important life of *Harriet Martineau: A Radical Victorian* (1960). Unitarian theology is discussed from an interesting point of view in Dennis G. Wigmore-Beddoes' *Yesterday's Radicals: A Study of the Affinity between Unitarianism and Broad Church Anglicanism in the Nineteenth Century* (1971).

Minor Sects

The study of Victorian sects has recently been greatly encouraged by the work of Bryan Wilson, the liveliest and most original sociologist of religion working in England. In *Sects and Society* (1961) Wilson developed his goals and methods in the course of studying three sects, one of which, the Christadelphians, has a considerable nineteenth-century history. The fully developed method is well described in his essay, "An Analysis of Sect Development," in his *Patterns of Sectarianism* (1967). He establishes a typology of sects, and, transcending the approach used by H. Richard Niebuhr in *The Social Sources of Denominationalism* (1929), locates the principal dynamic of sectarian history in the structure of the sects themselves. Three works inspired by the Wilson approach are noticed above: Thompson's *Bureaucracy and Church Reform*, Currie's *Methodism Divided*, and Isichei's *Victorian Quakers*. Some others are noticed below. Bryan Wilson's *Religious Sects: A Sociological Study* (1970) is a popular short survey of all the world's sects, not a serious contribution.

Among the smaller English sects the Plymouth Brethren have received the most attention. W. Blair Neatby's *A History of the Plymouth Brethren* (1901) is the standard account, but it must now be supplemented with Harold H. Rowdon's *The Origins of the Brethren, 1825–1850* (1967) and F. Roy Coad's *A History of the Brethren Movement* (1968). The history of the sect is dominated by the doctrinal split between the Open and the Closed Brethren. Neatby, Rowdon, and Coad all make clear how complicated and fundamental is this fissure. The major Wilsonian contribution to Brethren history, P. L. Embley's "The Early Development of the Plymouth Brethren" (in *Patterns of Sectarianism*, ed. Bryan Wilson, 1967), provides a neat framework within which the complicated quarrels of the Brethren take on general significance. Wilson himself contributes two stimulating pieces on the Brethren to the same book.

The Brethren figure prominently in Ernest R. Sandeen's *The Roots of Fundamentalism: British and American Millenarianism 1800–1930* (1970), an important scholarly work which surveys the entire millenarian movement with comprehensive care. Principally interested in the intellectual history of the movement, Sandeen traces with authority the origin and interrelationships of the major themes in the millenarian view of this life and the world to come. Not much attention is paid to the social context of the movement.

The best history of a working-class Pentecostal sect is G. R. Balleine's *Past*

Finding Out: The Tragic Story of Joanna Southcott and Her Successors (1956), a good straightforward narrative. Balleine devotes considerable space to Southcott's Victorian successors: John Ward, whose orthodoxy was shattered by Richard Carlile's reports of German scholarship; John Wroe, the founder of the British Israelites; and the fascinating "James Jershom Jezreel" of the New and Latter House of Israel, builder of the Jezreel tower. In *Patterns of Sectarianism* the essay by J. Wilson on "British Israelism: The Ideological Restraints on Sect Organization" argues that British Israelism, in its many variations a major theme in the Victorian sectarian world, was a form of nationalism. Louis Billington's "The Millerite Adventists in Great Britain, 1810–50" (*J. of American Stud.*, 1967) and P. A. M. Taylor's *Expectations Westward: The Mormons and the Emigration of Their British Converts in the Nineteenth Century* (1966) both deal with minor aspects of the problem of transatlantic influence which constitutes a major theme for Sandeen. Sandeen's work includes the only serious critical study of Edward Irving, socially and intellectually the most prominent figure among the British millenarians. Andrew L. Drummond's *Edward Irving and His Circle* (ca. 1936) is an unsystematic but informative description of Irving and his literary and clerical friends up to the foundation of the Catholic Apostolic Church in 1836. In the 1820's Irving attracted an influential circle of London intellectuals, including Carlyle, Maurice, Hazlitt, and Crabb Robinson, and held some of them as he slipped into millenarianism and speaking with tongues during the turbulent two years before the Reform Bill was passed.

At the end of the Victorian period spiritualism had a fascination for intellectuals much stronger than that excited by Irving's Pentecostalism at the beginning of the reign. The careers of the most famous Victorian mediums are reported by Trevor H. Hall in *The Spiritualists: The Story of Florence Cook and William Crookes* (1962). Alan Gould's *The Founders of Psychical Research* (1968), a scholarly study of the late Victorian interest in spiritualism by a professional psychologist who is a believer, is a serious contribution to intellectual history as well as to the history of the sects. Geoffrey K. Nelson's *Spiritualism and Society* (1969) treats spiritualism as a sect and discusses the organization, doctrinal basis, and social views of the movement.

Roman Catholics

The best introduction to the modern history of English Roman Catholics is David Mathew's *Catholicism in England, 1535–1935* (1936), a brief survey by a distinguished historian. The last volumes of Bernard Ward's seven-volume history of Catholicism from 1781, published as *The Sequel to Catholic Emancipation, 1830–1850* (2 vols., 1915), is the authoritative work on this period. Ward considers a variety of subjects including music, architecture, and the work of the laity, but his major concern is the leading ecclesiastical figures. In "The English Catholics in 1850" (in *The English Catholics, 1850–1950*, ed. George A. Beck, 1950), Philip Hughes provides a richly detailed picture of the Catholic community which is a valuable complement to Ward's history. The other essays in this collection are also of high quality; the book is a major contribution to the history of Victorian Catholics. Unfortunately not of the same caliber, most of the short essays in *Catholic Emancipation, 1829–1929* (introd. Cardinal Bourne, 1929) are disappointing. The most useful is Viscount Fitzalan's clear description of the civil disabilities imposed before 1829 and during the following century. Denis Gwynn's *The

Second Spring, 1818–1852 (1944) adds nothing to Ward's scholarly account. Because there is no history equivalent to Ward's for the period after 1850, Denis Gwynn's *A Hundred Years of Catholic Emancipation, 1829–1929* (1929) is valuable as an introduction. Gwynn's view of Catholic history after 1850 is dominated by the four great Cardinals, Wiseman, Newman, Manning, and Vaughan. Their biographies, along with the lives of a few less elevated men, are the most important histories of the period.

The standard life of Wiseman is Wilfrid Ward's literate and thoroughly informed *Life and Times of Cardinal Wiseman* (2 vols., 1912). In *Nicholas Wiseman* (1963), a semipopular, attractively presented biography, Brian Fothergill corrects Ward on some points of detail. Ernest E. Reynolds' *Three Cardinals, Newman— Wiseman—Manning* (1958) is an interesting literary exercise in interleaved biography. Written from secondary sources and popular in tone, it adds nothing to the conventional lives.

Edmund S. Purcell's hasty and venomous *Life of Cardinal Manning* (2 vols., 1896) does not merit respect, even bearing in mind Lord Acton's comment that "a wrong opinion is never conquered until it has reached its most perfect expression." The only reliable life of Manning is Shane Leslie's *Henry Edward Manning: His Life and Labours* (1921). It is substantial but certainly not definitive. The ten pleasant essays in *Manning: Anglican and Catholic*, edited by John Fitzsimmons (1951), are slight and do not contribute significantly to Manning scholarship. Vincent Alan McClelland's *Cardinal Manning, His Public Life and Influence, 1865–1892* (1962) contains a solid study of Manning's role in the politics of education, a good discussion of Manning's relation with Gladstone, and a thorough, sympathetic account of his social work and philanthropy.

Arthur McCormack's *Cardinal Vaughan, The Life of the Third Archbishop of Westminster* (1966) is a popular life designed to enhance Vaughan's reputation. It draws heavily on John G. Snead-Cox's *Cardinal Vaughan* (2 vols., 1911) which remains the only serious biography.

Probably the second most distinguished Catholic intellectual of the nineteenth century was Lord Acton, the historian. David Mathew's definitive *Lord Acton and His Times* (1968) is a magnificent, widely ranging biography which must be considered a major contribution to the history of Victorian Catholicism. Wilfrid Ward's *W. G. Ward and the Catholic Revival* (new ed., 1912) is a work that retains its significance. Well written, well documented, and impressively well informed, this is an excellent study of Catholic intellectual life in the period 1845–82. Maisie Ward's *The Wilfrid Wards and the Transition, I: The Nineteenth Century* (1934) describes life among the late Victorian intelligentsia. Ronald Chapman's perceptive *Father Faber* (1961) takes as its main theme the dominant influence of Newman. Heavy with letters and other papers, *The Life and Times of Bishop Ullathorne, 1806– 1889* (2 vols., 1926) by Dom Cuthbert Butler is a worthy old-fashioned life of a distinguished ecclesiastic. Gertrude Donald produces journalistic sketches of Newman, Manning, T. W. Allies, and B. W. Maturin in *Men Who Left the Movement* (1933). More interesting and vastly more useful is W. Gordon Gorman's *Converts to Rome, A Biographical List of the More Notable Converts to the Catholic Church in the United Kingdom during the Last Sixty Years* (1910). A fascinating occupational analysis precedes the several thousand entries.

Written from archival material, Claude Leetham's *Luigi Gentili, A Sower of the Second Spring* (1965) is a thorough account of the most famous among the

Continental missionaries to England in the 1840's. There is much of interest here. The missions to England are comprehensively surveyed in Conrad Charles's "The Origins of the Parish Mission in England and the Early Passionist Apostolate" (*JEH*, 1964). Josef L. Altholz has written an excellent essay on mid-century Catholic thought in *The Liberal Catholic Movement in England: The* Rambler *and Its Contributors 1848–1864* (1962) and a solid account of "The Political Behaviour of the English Catholics 1850–1867" (*JBS*, 1964). Damian McElrath's thorough and painstaking survey of the principal crisis in the Victorian Catholic Church, *The Syllabus of Pius IX, Some Reactions in England* (1964), can be supplemented with *The Roman Question: Extracts from the Dispatches of Odo Russell from Rome, 1858–1870* (ed. Noel Blakiston, 1962). John Jay Hughes's *Absolutely Null and Void: The Papal Condemnation of Anglican Orders, 1896* (1968) is an intriguing and convincing description of a complex episode in ecclesiastical politics. George Tyrell, the most important English Catholic in the Modernist movement, is gracefully discussed by John Ratté in *Three Modernists* (1968), while the movement as a whole is described in Michele Ranchetti's *The Catholic Modernists: A Study of the Religious Reform Movement 1864–1907* (trans. Isabel Quigly, 1969).

The life of the Catholic poor in England has not been thoroughly investigated. The only comprehensive work, John A. Jackson's *The Irish in Britain* (1963), is a useful introduction. John Hickey's *Urban Catholics* (1967) is an informed but unsystematic history of the Irish community in Cardiff. The best study is Lynn Lees's "Patterns of Lower Class Life: Irish Slum Communities in Nineteenth-Century London" (in *Nineteenth-Century Cities: Essays in the New Urban History*, ed. Stephen Thernstrom and Richard Sennett, 1969).

Walter Arnstein's "Victorian Prejudice Reexamined" (*VS*, 1969) is a helpful introduction to the recent literature on Victorian anti-Catholicism. Geoffrey Best has written a brilliant essay on this theme, "Popular Protestantism in Victorian Britain" (in *Ideas and Institutions of Victorian Britain*, ed. Robert Robson, 1967). In *Anti-Catholicism in Victorian England* (1968), Edward R. Norman discusses five episodes in which anti-Catholic prejudice clearly emerged. *Anglo-Saxons and Celts* (1968), by Lewis P. Curtis, Jr., is a study of anti-Irish prejudice in Victorian England. Although his suspicions of Peel and the higher echelons of the Tory party are not convincing, Gilbert Cahill's articles on "Irish Catholicism and English Toryism" (*Rev. of Pol.*, 1957) and "The Protestant Association and the Anti-Maynooth Agitation of 1845" (*CHR*, 1957) demonstrate the political significance of Protestant prejudice. An illustration of prejudice made effective through organization is discussed in Vincent McClelland, "The Protestant Alliance and Roman Catholic Schools, 1872–74" (*VS*, 1964).

IV. RELIGION AND SOCIETY

Social History

There is as yet no authoritative general assessment of the role of religion in Victorian society. Nor is there an established method for considering the social history of religion. There is no language of systematic analysis, and there is no recognized set of major questions. This absence of guides and guidelines is underlined by Geoffrey Best in *Mid-Victorian Britain, 1851–75* (1971). In the case of religion, writes Best, "the social historian is driven to rely more completely than usual on his own judgement." Deeply influenced by their particular interests in secular history, historians of both the right and the left have tended to conceive the social history of Victorian religion in terms of the relations of the churches and the working classes. By suggesting other areas of concern, Best shows how narrowing this tendency has been. The place of religion among the middle classes, for example, has received little attention, the religious life of the aristocracy is unexplored, and the important role of the churches in organizing the society of industrial towns deserves much more consideration. The sociologists are beginning to offer suggestions as to how areas such as these might be systematically explored.

While focusing on the twentieth century in *Religion and Secular Society* (1966), Bryan Wilson includes a rich variety of potentially creative comments on Victorian religion. In his important analysis of the nature of secularization and its Victorian roots, Wilson characteristically argues that the pattern of development within religious institutions was itself one of the sources of secularization because it encouraged utilitarian goals. Wilson also goes beyond his usual institutional perspective to remark, sometimes with brilliant insight, on the general place of religion in Victorian society; he stresses the role of nonconformity. The relation of religion and social class and the impact of social change on the organization of churches are themes taken up also by David A. Martin. In his article on "The Denomination" (*Brit. J. of Sociology*, 1962), he takes issue with Ernst Troeltsch, Max Weber, and Wilson, arguing that the "denomination" is the type of organization most appropriate to industrial society, that it is therefore a post-church type of institution. The first chapter of Martin's *A Sociology of English Religion* (1967) contains a brief but convenient survey of the relation of churches and social classes during the nineteenth century.

The role of the denominations in nineteenth-century English society has yet to be considered in detail, but there are two excellent studies concerned with the Celtic fringe that deserve to be taken as models. In *Religion in the Industrial Revolution in South Wales* (1965), Ebenezer T. Davies describes brilliantly the fascinatingly close relation between social and denominational change in Monmouthshire over the course of the nineteenth century. Davies explains in convincing detail why the shift from the English-managed iron and steel industry to the Welsh-managed coal industry profoundly affected the alignments of social classes and denominations. A. Allen MacLaren's "Presbyterianism and the Working Class in a Mid-Nineteenth Century City" (*Scottish Hist. Rev.*, 1967) is an imaginatively researched study of the quite different ways Kirk discipline affected the middle classes and the working classes in Aberdeen. MacLaren concludes that the Kirk was attractive to the middle classes because its harsh treatment of bankruptcy—the characteristic middle-class sin— made membership in good standing an advertisement of financial respectability. Harsh treatment of sexual immorality and drunkenness, on the other hand, carried no counterbalancing benefits for the working classes.

Harold Perkin's *The Origins of Modern English Society, 1780–1880* (1969) contains the most ambitious and sustained discussion of the social role of religion in nineteenth-century England. Perkin contends, almost certainly correctly, that denominational rivalries and tensions both reflected and affected the relations of social classes. But Perkin has tried to describe and explain too much on the basis of too little detailed research and too simple an idea of class. His analysis, therefore, tends to degenerate into abstract patternmaking. As a guide to what is known of the social history of Victorian religion, however, Perkin's work is useful. It does contain a great deal of reliably reported information. As a guide to further research the work is useful because of the questions Perkin asks, and answers prematurely.

George Kitson Clark, in his informative chapter on "The Religion of the People," in *The Making of Victorian England* (1962), addresses himself to an older set of questions and describes, with considerable literary grace, many of the official responses of the Church and nonconformists to social changes in the early and mid-Victorian period. A. W. Smith calls attention to folklore as a source through which the religious concerns of the poor might be investigated in "Popular Religion" (*P&P*, 1968).

Standish Meacham in "The Church in the Victorian City" (*VS*, 1968) surveys briefly and competently the major problems of the Established Church in the larger towns. He discusses the established central question, why the Church did not attract the working classes in larger numbers, and the leading explanations which revolve around the financial dominance of the middle classes. He includes also a discussion of the breakdown of the parish system and reports some interesting Victorian hopes that the parish might serve as a manageable social unit capable of withstanding the depersonalizing pressures of large cities. The same themes pervade Edward R. Wickham's *Church and People in an Industrial City* (1957), a study of Sheffield in the nineteenth and twentieth centuries. Wickham, at one time the head of the Sheffield Industrial Mission, is principally concerned with the failure of the Church to attract the working classes. So overriding is this concern that it narrows Wickham's conception of his subject to an unfortunate extent. Within its limits, however, this fully detailed record of the efforts of the Church and the dissenters to make Christians of the workingmen of Sheffield is a valuable mine of information. R. B. Walker's informative articles, "Religious Change in Cheshire, 1750–1850" and "Religious Change in Liverpool in the Nineteenth Century" (*JEH*, 1966, 1968), are also dominated by the nonattendance problem.

The institutionalized religious habits of the various social classes in London are the subject of the remarkably little-used survey by Charles Booth, *Life and Labour of the People in London. Third Series: Religious Influences* (7 vols., 1902). The religious life of London is described from neighborhood to neighborhood, with impressive sociological maps in which streets are color coded for social type, and the social complexion and social work of the individual congregations are discussed.

The most complete survey of church attendance in the nineteenth century was sponsored by the State and taken in connection with the census of 1851. The results are published in *Parliamentary Papers*, 1852–53, Vol. LXXXIX. While the accuracy of this survey is doubted, its value is nonetheless considerable, especially as a guide to the social and economic geography of religious worship. The uses and limitations of the census are well discussed by Kenneth S. Inglis in "Patterns of Religious Worship in 1851" (*JEH*, 1960), by W. S. F. Pickering in "The 1851 Religious Census—A Useless Experiment?" (*Brit. J. of Sociology*, 1967), and by David M. Thompson in "The 1851 Religious Census: Problems and Possibilities" (*VS*, 1967). The *Daily News* sponsored an elaborate survey of attendance at London churches over a twelve-month period in 1902–03. The results are published by Richard Mudie-Smith in *The Religious Life of London* (1904), a work that also reprints the results of a count of attendance at 1,500 places of worship undertaken for the *British Weekly* in 1886.

Social Thought

The literature on Christian social thought in the nineteenth century is not large, perhaps because there were few distinctively Christian social thinkers. Most Churchmen and dissenters, more interested in politics and philanthropy than in social theory, were more at ease with points of view than with ideas. Their tendency to attitudinize rather than analyze is noted by John Kent in "The Victorain Resistance, Comments on Religious Life and Culture, 1840–1880" (*VS*, 1968). Less convincing and more provocative is Kent's argument that the characteristic religious attitude was opposition to modernization. He is certainly correct to suggest that the view of Christian Socialists as "advanced" thinkers in tune with the more progressive streams of social consideration is a view that should be revised, and his comments on Coleridge, Newman, Maurice, and Matthew Arnold are in themselves perceptive. While Kent's framework is more clever than solid, he has nonetheless suggested a potentially productive approach to a discouragingly shapeless subject.

Unsystematic and weakly organized, Richard Soloway's *Prelates and People, Ecclesiastical Social Thought in England 1783–1852* (1969) is a meticulously researched record of the bishops' views on social questions, rather mechanically written, with very little attempt to place prelatical attitudes in historical context. It is nevertheless useful, for it provides more basic information about nineteenth-century ecclesiastical social thought than does any other work. The discussion of J. B. Sumner, the bishop most interested in social analysis, is particularly full and interesting, far richer than the account of Sumner in Robert S. Dell's "Social and Economic Theories and Pastoral Concerns of a Victorian Archbishop" (*JEH*, 1965). Soloway suggests that the bishops' views during the first half of the nineteenth century were generally considered important, particularly by politicians. And he demonstrates that the bishops moved rapidly away from their earlier laissez-faire position to become, by mid-century, generally anxious not to associate the Church with positions that might appear antagonistic to the working classes. Unfortunately, Soloway does not distinguish pastoral concern and ecclesiastical strategy from what might more properly be called social thought; he is therefore unable to discuss the relationship between them.

Cyril K. Gloyn's *The Church in the Social Order* (1942) contains essays on the "social theology" of Coleridge, Arnold, the Tractarians, and Maurice. In these informative essays Gloyn dwells on the importance of the corporate view of society which, he maintains, was shared by the Broad Churchmen and the Tractarians. He argues that the Evangelicals evolved no significant theory of Church and society because, stressing the ultimate importance of individual salvation, they undervalued the corporate character of society. This argument, which harmonizes with a favorable view of the Catholic revival, is of doubtful validity. Individualistic economists developed serious social theory, and individualistic Evangelicals were effectively active in philanthropy and social reform. Maurice B. Reckitt's Scott Holland Memorial Lectures, *Maurice to Temple: A Century of the Social Movement in the Church of England* (1947), provide a pleasant, brief survey of social thinking in the Church, more interesting for the period after 1884 when Reckitt's Christian Socialist passions are engaged. Among the ten slight essays in *Christian Social Reformers of the Nineteenth Century*, ed. Hugh Martin (1927), Fenner Brockway's piece on Keir Hardie is the most interesting.

For the later nineteenth century, Melvin Richter's brilliant major study, *The Politics of Conscience: T. H. Green and His Age* (1964), is required reading. Through lucidly written, substantial, and definitive accounts of Green's theology, metaphysics, and politics, Richter constructs a satisfyingly coherent assessment of Green's thought and its historical significance. Green, Richter suggests, is more significantly understood as a sensitive reflector of the main intellectual currents of his time than as a cause for renewed interest in social action. Retaining the Evangelical piety which Richter thinks was fundamental to his view of life, Green moved to a Hegelian position in which corporate-oriented philosophy superseded individualistic theology. Similarly, he retained much from Manchester liberalism as he moved away from individualism to preach the duty of political obligation in the name of community. Along with Richter's work, one must read Reba N. Soffer's "The Revolution in English Social Thought, 1880–1914" (*AHR*, 1970), an incisive and forcefully analytical description of the intellectual movement in which Green participated.

Religion and the Working Classes

The dominant theme for the first half of the nineteenth century was established by Elie Halévy in *England in 1815* (trans. E. I. Watkin and D. A. Barker, 1924). Halévy argues that Methodism saved England from revolution during the period of the French Revolution; and in subsequent volumes of his *History of the English People in the Nineteenth Century*, he maintains that Methodism and Evangelicalism remain a significant stabilizing force throughout the century. Methodism, according to Halévy, attracted the potential leaders of working-class rebellion into a highly disciplined association which stressed otherworldly values and submission to authority. In his excellent introduction to Halévy's *The Birth of Methodism in England* (1971), Bernard Semmel discusses Halévy's thesis sympathetically and traces the surprisingly long history of the idea that Methodism was an obstacle to revolution. Eric Hobsbawm in *Primitive Rebels* (1965), and especially in "Methodism and the Threat of Revolution in Britain" (*Labouring Men*, 1964), attacks Halévy's thesis. The sects, Hobsbawm claims, provided the working class with a mode of radical activity, not an alternative to radicalism. He argues that the overlapping geographies of Methodism and radicalism support his claim that only the official Wesleyan leadership was conservative. Edward P. Thompson's sparkling, hostile treatment of Methodism in *The Making of the English Working Class* (1963) is more persuasively complex. Recognizing the importance of Methodism as a central institution for the developing working-class community, Thompson agrees with Hobsbawm that sectarian commitment was not always incompatible with secular radicalism. He also argues that Methodism tended to direct the psychic energies of its members toward otherworldly goals, and he suggests that this tendency itself made Methodism attractive to radicals whose secular mission had ended in failure and repression.

Among the books of Robert F. Wearmouth, the best is *Methodism and the Working-Class Movements of England, 1800–1850* (1937). This uncomplicated but well-informed work directs attention to much material that has not yet been profitably studied. Wearmouth describes, convincingly, the conservatism of the Wesleyan leadership early in the century. He reports substantially the very interesting activities of class meetings during three periods between 1817 and 1848, drawing on a pool of evidence that deserves more investigation. Finally, distinguishing between the conservatism of the Wesleyan Conference and the underlying liberalism of the laity, he provides many examples of the association of Methodist religious passion with zeal for political and social reform. Wearmouth's *Some Working Class Movements of the Nineteenth Century* (1948) concentrates on the Chartist period and draws attention to the relation of Chartist activities to class meetings and camp meetings. His *Methodism and the Struggle of the Working Classes, 1850–1900* (1954) is much less thoroughly researched than his work on the first half of the century, but it contains a useful description of the drift of Methodist leadership toward liberalism. *Methodism and the Trade Unions* (1959) is a derivative work in which Wearmouth adds little to George Nicoll Barnes's *Religion in the Labour Movement* (1919).

Harold Underwood Faulkner's *Chartism and the Churches* (1916) explores some of the links between Methodism and radicalism. Faulkner argues that Chartist antipathy to the existing churches had a theological basis and that the rhetoric linking the Charter with the New Testament should be taken seriously. Trygve R. Tholfsen provides a case study of an unusual Chartist Church in "The Chartist Crisis in Birmingham" (*IRSH*, 1958). Examples of Methodist and Evangelical support for social reform during the Chartist period are described in Cecil Driver's *Tory Radical: The Life of Richard Oastler* (1946), John C. Gill's *The Ten Hours Parson* (1959) and *Parson Bull of Byerley* (1963), and in J. T. Ward's *The Factory Movement 1830–1855* (1962). The extent and significance of this support has not yet been systematically assessed.

The leading theme for the second half of the century, the alienation of the working classes from the churches, is treated competently by K. S. Inglis in *Churches and the Working Classes in Victorian England* (1963). A slightly super-ficial survey of the situation of each denomination is followed by substantial, well-researched chapters on the Settlement Movement, the Salvation Army, and the Labour Church. Inglis, especially in the more general first portion of his work, asks interesting questions but tends to accept Victorian opinions too uncritically as "explanations" rather than as raw historical data. *The Churches and the Labour Movement* (1967) by Stephen Mayor is an unprofessional survey, chiefly useful for the discussion of the half-dozen newspapers upon which it is based.

The Labour Church movement of the 1890's is described by K. S. Inglis in "The Labour Church Movement" (*IRSH*, 1958), in Stanley Pierson's "John Trevor and the Labour Church Movement" (*Church Hist.*, 1960), and in F. Reid's "Social-ist Sunday Schools in Britain" (*IRSH*, 1966), which reprints the "Socialist Ten Commandments." The Labour Church movement is a fascinating example of the adaptation of ecclesiastical forms and ceremonies to secular political purposes.

Until recently, secularism and free thought were considered almost exclusively in the context of the history of ideas. Alfred W. Benn's monumental and still valuable *History of English Rationalism in the Nineteenth Century* (2 vols., 1906) concentrates on major thinkers, including the Utilitarians, Comte, Carlyle, Mill, and the Bible critics. Considering rationalism a condition of progress in philosophy, Benn argues that the association of political radicalism and rationalism was pecu-liarly French and not significant in England. John M. Robertson's *History of Free Thought in the Nineteenth Century* (2 vols., 1929) is also written as a record of progress from superstition to objectivity. Robertson indiscriminately includes in this well-informed survey the work of many different sorts of men and women who criticized orthodox Christianity in the language of rationalism. Tom Paine, George

Combe, Bishop Colenso, Darwin, and George Eliot are all treated as similarly engaged in the battle of truth against error.

More recent work on the rejection of orthodoxy among the literary elite is much less sectarian. The essays in Basil Willey's *More Nineteenth Century Studies* (1956) sensitively explore doubt and the quality of unbelief among a number of major figures. A. O. J. Cockshut's *The Unbelievers: English Agnostic Thought, 1840–1890* (1964) is a useful if poorly ordered survey of the major texts of the leading literary humanists. U. C. Knoepflmacher's *Religious Humanism and the Victorian Novel* (1965) and J. Hillis Miller's *Disappearance of God* (1963) are both sophisticated studies of the nature of unbelief among major authors. Howard R. Murphy, in "The Ethical Revolt against Christian Orthodoxy in Early Victorian England" (*AHR*, 1955), distinguishes between the intellectual and moral causes for loss of faith among the intelligentsia. The influence of positivism is ably considered by Walter M. Simon in "Auguste Comte's English Disciples" (*VS*, 1964), and brilliantly by Sydney Eisen in "Huxley and the Positivists" (*VS*, 1964), "Frederick Harrison and the Religion of Humanity" (*SAQ*, 1967), and "Herbert Spencer and the Spectre of Comte" (*JBS*, 1967).

Secularism, considered as a religiously oriented form of social and political radicalism, is currently receiving attention. Edward Royle's *Radical Politics 1790–1900: Religion and Unbelief* (1971) is a regrettably short but very useful survey of the varieties of unbelief that were rooted in radical opposition to established social and political authority. The only comprehensive history of organized secularism—another is needed—is John E. McGee's *A History of the British Secular Movement* (1948). David Tribe's *100 Years of Free Thought* (1967), written for the centenary of the National Secular Society, is journalistic, confused, and irresponsibly inaccurate. The association of rationalism and working-class radicalism in the decade after 1815 is described well in William H. Wickwar's excellent account of Richard Carlile's trials for blasphemy, *The Struggle for the Freedom of the Press* (1928). The interesting relationship of unbelief and millennialism in Owenite socialism is studied for the first time by J. F. C. Harrison in *Robert Owen and the Owenites in Britain and America* (1969).

In "The Atheist Mission, 1840–1900" (in *Ideas and Institutions of Victorian Britain*, ed. Robert Robson, 1967), Francis B. Smith discusses the rhetoric and ideological roots of working-class secularism. The political radicalism of the secularists, he maintains, flowed from their rejection of Christian orthodoxy. This view, familiar to Victorian magistrates, is effectively challenged in Susan Budd's important "The Loss of Faith: Reasons for Unbelief among Members of the Secular Movement in England, 1850–1950" (*P&P*, 1967). Budd analyzes more than 150 secularist biographies and discovers that the revolutions in scientific and theological thinking were not significant causes in most conversions to atheism. She concludes that most conversions were preceded by moral rejection of the established social order. In what he calls a contribution to the sociology of irreligion, John Eros, in "The Rise of Organized Free Thought in Mid-Victorian England" (*Sociological Rev.*, 1954), stresses the role of social dissatisfaction in creating G. J. Holyoake's secularist movement. Joseph McCabe's *Life and Letters of George Jacob Holyoake* (2 vols., 1908) is the only biography of this attractive figure. David Tribe's biography of the leading secularist of the late nineteenth century, *President Charles Bradlaugh M.P.* (1971), does not replace Hypatia Bradlaugh Bonner's *Charles Bradlaugh: A Record of His Life and Work, with an Account of His Parliamentary*

Struggle, Politics and Teaching, by *J. M. Robertson* (2 vols., 1895). The best study of Bradlaugh, albeit not a full biography, is Walter Arnstein's *The Bradlaugh Case: A Study in Late Victorian Opinion and Politics* (1965). Warren Sylvester Smith's *The London Heretics, 1870–1914* (1967) is a misguided attempt to survey every variety of heterodoxy in London. After suggesting that poverty and oppression were the basic causes of heresy, Smith describes the activities of the secularists, the spiritualists, the theosophists, the ethicists, the positivists, the Unitarians, the Quakers, the Christian Scientists, the Forward Movement, the Catholic Modernists, and others. Smith's work is less detailed and lacks the immediacy of Charles Maurice Davies' *Heterodox London: or Phases of Free Thought in the Metropolis* (2 vols., 1874; rpt. 1969).

Missions to England

The churches in the Victorian period were deeply involved in philanthropy, and the religious roots for many charities and social reform movements are often apparent. It is difficult to establish with precision the complex links between theology and social action, but there can be no doubt that connections existed. Surprisingly, no one has approached this problem through comparing the very different styles of social action favored by High Churchmen, Broad Churchmen, Evangelicals, and dissenters. Slum priests, Anglo-Catholic and Broad Church Christian Socialists, and Evangelical activists have thus far been studied in isolation. Among these groups, High and Broad Church reformers have generally received more sympathetic attention than Evangelicals in spite of the fact that Evangelical social reformers appear to have been more numerous and more active.

Ford K. Brown's hostile treatment of early nineteenth-century Evangelical social action and the works of Edwin Hodder and Geoffrey Best on Shaftesbury are noticed above. Kathleen Heasman provides an overview of *Evangelicals in Action: An Appraisal of Their Social Work in the Victorian Era* (1962). Her work is unsophisticated and uncritical, but it suggests the comprehensive range of Evangelical social work, especially in the second half of the century. By investigating the directorates of the charities listed in Sampson Low's *Charities of London in 1861* (1861), Heasman concludes that seventy-five percent were dominated by Evangelicals. Only a small portion of the activity surveyed by Heasman has received attention from historians.

Among Evangelically dominated reform movements, the temperance movement probably touched the largest number of people most profoundly. Brian Harrison's brilliant account of this movement, *Drink and the Victorians: The Temperance Question in England 1815–1872* (1917), is a major contribution to Victorian social history and the most important work so far on popular culture in the nineteenth century. This impressively well-researched, irrepressibly analytical study demonstrates clearly the close association of Evangelicalism, especially Evangelical nonconformity, with political liberalism, temperance, and respectability. Among Harrison's several vigorous articles on temperance which preceded the book, " 'A World of Which We Had No Conception.' Liberalism and the Temperance Press: 1830–1872" (*VS*, 1969) explores the links between temperance and a broad range of other reforming causes, and "Drink and Sobriety in England, 1815–1872. A Critical Bibliography" (*IRSH*, 1967) suggests subjects that might repay further research. Harrison's "Religion and Recreation in Nineteenth Century England"

(*P&P*, 1967) includes perceptive discussions of the Royal Society for the Prevention of Cruelty to Animals, patronized by Evangelical ladies, and the Lord's Day Observance Society, a paternalistic Anglican society supported by Evangelical clergy, which did battle with the free-trading, free-thinking National Sunday League. That battle is closely analyzed in Harrison's "The Sunday Trading Riots of 1855" (*HistJ*, 1965). The official centennial history of the RSPCA, *A Century of Work for Animals* (1934), has been written by E. G. Fairholme and W. Pain.

The typical pattern of Evangelical social work was set before the middle of the century by the London City Mission, the best known of the city missions which eventually spread throughout the kingdom. From its foundation in 1835, the L. C. M. was operated jointly by Evangelical nonconformists and Churchmen. Its initial purpose was to save souls through conversion, but it soon became involved in temperance and housing reform and helped to found the Ragged Schools in the 1840's. There is no modern history of the L. C. M., but John Matthias Weylland's *These Fifty Years, Being the Jubilee Volume of the London City Mission* (1884) is a mine of information. The early history of the YMCA, well reported in J. E. Hodder Williams' *The Life of Sir George Williams* (1906), displays a similar pattern. Founded as a nondenominational prayer meeting for introspective, Evangelical young businessmen, the YMCA gradually became a philanthropic, social-working agency. The shift from emphasis on spiritual salvation to social work occurred much more rapidly in the case of Dr. Barnado's homes. J. Wesley Bready, in *Doctor Barnado: Physician, Pioneer, Prophet* (1930), describes how Barnado was converted to the cause of homeless children in the East End of London while he was training to join the China Inland Mission.

The Salvation Army was the greatest of the Evangelical social-working organizations. It, too, began with exclusively spiritual concerns. William Booth was a very successful lay preacher who, feeling uncomfortably fettered by Methodist discipline, established an independent mission in London's East End in the 1860's. Out of this mission the Salvation Army emerged in the next decade as an Evangelical sect, much as the other sects spun off from Wesleyan Methodism. The history of the Army as a conversionist sect is well discussed in Roland Robertson's "The Salvation Army: The Persistence of Sectarianism" (in *Patterns of Sectarianism*, ed. Bryan Wilson, 1967). Robertson develops an interesting explanation for why the Salvation Army did not feel the pressures for reunion that affected other schismatic Methodist groups. Not until the end of the 1880's did the Salvation Army turn purposefully to philanthropy and social reform. The shift of emphasis is described without sufficient attention to the Army's previous history by Herman Ausubel in "General Booth's Scheme of Social Salvation" (*AHR*, 1951). Much sounder and more thoughtful is the chapter on the Army in K. S. Inglis' *Churches and the Working Classes in Victorian England* (1963). The general history of the Salvation Army in the nineteenth century is fully but officially and uncritically recorded at a leisurely pace in Robert Sandall and Arch R. Wiggins' *The History of the Salvation Army* (5 vols., 1947–68). Bernard Watson's *A Hundred Years War* (1965) is inaccurate popular journalism. The best biography of William Booth is St. John Ervine's *God's Soldier: General William Booth* (2 vols., 1934), a sympathetic and beautifully written character study. Harold Begbie's *Life of William Booth* (2 vols., 1920), full of letters and information, is uncritical and anecdotal. Richard Collier's *The General Next to God: The Story of William Booth and the Salvation Army* (1965) is useful only for its photographic illustrations. Frederick St. George de

Latour Booth-Tucker's *The Life of Catherine Booth* (2 vols., 1912) contains much of interest for the early history of the Army.

The Church Army was founded a little later than Booth's Army and made the transition to social concern a little earlier. Its history is found in Edgar Rowan's *Wilson Carlile and the Church Army* (1905). Kathleen Heasman's *Army of the Church* (1968) is inspirational propaganda.

Founded by Samuel Barnett, an Evangelical clergyman, Toynbee Hall was the first and most prestigious institution in the settlement movement of the 1880's. Its activities are described by Werner Picht in *Toynbee Hall and the English Settlement Movement* (1914) and by John A. R. Pimlott in *Toynbee Hall: Fifty Years of Social Progress, 1884–1934* (1935). The only biography of Barnett, who considered a sense of sin the starting point of social progress, is by his wife, Henrietta Octavia Barnett, *Canon Barnett, His Life, Work and Friends* (2 vols., 1918).

Christian Socialism

While the slippery ideas of F. D. Maurice remain elusive, the history of mid-century Christian Socialism has been exhaustively investigated. The central work is Charles E. Raven's *Christian Socialism, 1848–1854* (1920). His unfortunately violent dislike of the Tractarians leads Raven to some curious and unfair judgments —he suggests that Tractarian neglect of social problems blackened the reputation of the Church and ensured that "social reform followed Marx and not Maurice." His unmeasured admiration for Maurice, moreover, dulls his view of the ambiguities in the ideas and attitudes of the man he considers "incomparably the greatest Churchman of the nineteenth century." He also considers Maurice and his colleagues more unreservedly progressive than they probably were. Raven's basic account of the movement is nevertheless sound and remains essentially unchallenged. His treatment of J. M. Ludlow's important role is surprisingly good even though the Ludlow papers were not available to him, and his description of the sect-like quality of the Christian Socialist brotherhood is especially perceptive. Torben Christensen's *Origin and History of Christian Socialism* (1962) corrects a number of minor errors in Raven's work and emphasizes with a slightly tendentious tone the conservatism of Maurice and the radicalism of Ludlow. Using the Ludlow papers, Christensen discusses well the French influence on the movement. More interested in ideas, Christensen does not describe as fully as Raven the practical activities of the movement in the 1850's. Neville C. Masterman's *John Malcolm Ludlow, The Builder of Christian Socialism* (1963) dwells on the significance of Ludlow's practical executive ability and examines with insight Ludlow's emotional dependence on Maurice and his "hunger for the comradeship and loyalty of membership of a party or sect." Unhappily this generally sensible, well-grounded work is marred by minor inaccuracies and a suspiciously harsh attitude toward Maurice. Also hard on Maurice is Philip Backstrom, Jr., in "The Practical Side of Christian Socialism in Victorian England" (*VS*, 1963). Backstrom surveys E. V. Neale's great contributions to the Cooperative movement after 1854, and the work of Ludlow and Thomas Hughes with the Trade Union movement in the 1850's and 1860's. In his polemical effort to reestablish on practical grounds the progressive character of the Christian Socialists, Backstrom, in the face of massive contrary evidence, discounts the importance of Maurice. Both the centrality of Maurice and the conservatism of the movement are stressed by John Saville's "The Christian Socialists of 1848," in his *Democracy and the Labour Movement* (1954). Much less argumentative and very much more interesting is Peter Allen's stimulating "F. D. Maurice and J. M. Ludlow: A Reassessment of the Leaders of Christian Socialism" (*VS*, 1968). Avoiding the widespread recent tendency to distinguish sharply the theoretical and conservative Maurice from the practical and progressive Ludlow, Allen argues that each put religious concern and moral reform ahead of social reform. Allen's sophisticated attempt to trace their different styles of social reform to their different theological emphases is provocative and, at least in the case of Maurice, convincing. The difference between the position of Maurice and Ludlow, he concludes, was the difference between the Coleridgean and Arnoldian streams in the Broad Church movement. Lord Altrincham's essay on "F. D. Maurice and Christian Socialism," in his *Two Anglican Essays* (1958), stresses Maurice's ethical ideals and his essential conservatism in theology as well as politics. The influence of Maurice on the Christian Socialist revival in the last two decades of the century has often been remarked but never systematically studied. In an interesting and original discussion, Altrincham dismisses that influence as more apparent than real.

Donald O. Wagner's informative and intelligently constructed study, *The Church of England and Social Reform since 1854* (1930), contains the best account of the old Christian Socialists after 1854, a good investigation of the changing views of the Bishops, and the only comprehensive discussion of ecclesiastical opinion on social questions reflected in Convocation, the Lambeth Conferences, and Church Congresses. Nowhere else is the involvement of the country clergy in the movement for agrarian unionism examined in detail. There is also a careful study of the burst of philanthropic activity in the last two decades of the century which is sometimes called the Christian Socialist revival. In Wagner's judgment, the Church made no serious contributions to practical social reform or to social theory during this period, but he considers profoundly important the general reorientation of official ecclesiastical opinion toward greater concern for the poor and the working classes. At the end of the century, Wagner concludes, the Bishops tended to take a more liberal view of social questions than did the generality of the clergy, while the laity were much more conservative than either. Gilbert Clive Binyon's socialist critique of Christian social action, *The Christian Socialist Movement in England* (1931), is neither solid nor informative, but it does contain a useful review of the period before 1848.

Painstakingly researched, Peter d'A. Jones's enormous and erudite work on *The Christian Socialist Revival, 1877–1914* (1968) provides an excellent introduction to a most interesting period in the relations of religion, conscience, and social action. Jones calls attention to the remarkably widespread flowering of small Christian Socialist groups in the 1880's; almost every city and every denomination had a Christian Socialist society by the end of the century. It is unfortunate that he does not place Christian Socialism more firmly in the context of the general reorientation in middle-class social attitudes. And perhaps he misses the point when he stresses the curiosity of the fact that the Christian Socialists, whom he considers genuinely progressive, were weak in their understanding of social and economic theory. However, his long, detailed studies of the Guild of St. Matthew, the Christian Social Union, and the Church Socialist League are splendidly informative and probably definitive. His excellent discussion of the nonconformists among the Christian Socialists helps correct the established impression that Anglo-Catholics dominated the movement and underlines the merging of styles of social action and the blurring of denominational distinctions toward the end of the century. Jones does not deal with the Roman Catholics, who were led into social action by Cardinal Manning during this period, but Georgiana P. McEntee has written a good history of *The Social Catholic Movement in Great Britain* (1927).

Inglis examines the leading social reformers among the Congregationalists and Wesleyans in "English Nonconformity and Social Reform, 1880–1900" (*P&P*, 1958) and discovers that they were progressive in theology as well as politics, having abandoned both Evangelicalism and Gladstonean liberalism. His conclusion that Evangelicalism was inherently opposed to social reform is not convincing. Anthony S. Wohl's "The Bitter Cry of Outcast London" (*IRSH*, 1968) demonstrates that the old Evangelical interest in social reform as a part of the strategy of conversion was still very much alive in the 1880's.

The quality of Anglo-Catholic socialism, well discussed by Jones, is shrewdly assessed in Frederick G. Bettany's thoughtful biography of the founder of the Guild of St. Matthew, *Stewart Headlam* (1926). Headlam, Bettany suggests, was more interested in the social implications of Christianity than in practical solutions to real problems. This was certainly true of the Christian Social Union, dominated by Bishop Gore and Henry Scott Holland, whose paternalistic conservatism pervades his *Bundle of Memories* (1915), a collection of brilliantly written, self-revealing sketches of contemporaries. That the socialism of the Christian Social Union amounted in action to little more than a kindly attitude toward the poor is illustrated in Geoffrey Best's penetrating lecture on the first president of the C. S. U., *Bishop Westcott and the Miners* (1967).

THE CRITICS

•

Wendell V. Harris

Much basic research into nineteenth-century critical thought has yet to be undertaken; at present one cannot be entirely sure who were the most important of the lesser critics. Included in this survey are Walter Bagehot, Eneas Sweetland Dallas, Edmund Gosse, Richard Holt Hutton, "Vernon Lee" [Violet Paget], George Henry Lewes, George Moore, George Saintsbury, Algernon Swinburne, John Addington Symonds, Arthur Symons, and Oscar Wilde. These dozen figures have been chosen as representative, on the one hand, of various types of aesthetic orientation of importance in the Victorian period, and, on the other, of the state of existing scholarship. The omissions are obvious, including most notably William Rossetti, Leslie Stephen, David Masson, Augustine Birrell, Andrew Lang, Walter Raleigh, John Morley, Frederic Harrison, and R. L. Stevenson; the life-spans of some of those who are included intrude deeply enough into the twentieth century to have provided considerable justification for including Yeats as well. Lewes is also treated in the chapter on the Unbelievers, as are three of the omitted—Stephen, Morley, and Harrison.

The importance of the literary criticism of an age extends well beyond whatever intrinsic value it may have as commentary on specific works. Criticism written in an earlier age is, with certain classic exceptions, less likely to be read for its intrinsic value than for the purposes of charting literary reputations, tracing the history of criticism, or providing important indications of the cultural, aesthetic, and ultimately philosophical presuppositions of the age. The lesser critics of the Victorian period have most often been approached for the first of these ancillary purposes, less often for the second, and, as yet, very rarely for the third. That the value of this criticism as a cultural and philosophical index has been relatively neglected is somewhat surprising, since Victorian scholarship has been for at least a decade consciously—at times perhaps too self-consciously—attempting to become more interdisciplinary. At least two causes can, however, be assigned. First, the reputations of few of the lesser critics were made wholly on their literary criticism. This is true not only of Swinburne, Moore, and Wilde. Symons was of course a poet as well as a critic, Lewes a philosopher, Hutton a wide-ranging journalist, Bagehot an editor and economic and political theorist. Second, there has been a tendency to look to the critical writings of some of these only in relation to certain special questions. Wilde and Symons are most often considered simply as examples of decadence, or, what amounts to the same thing, the aesthetic movement gone to seed. Lewes is best known as the companion and adviser of George Eliot. Wilde's and Symonds' homosexuality, Swinburne's algolagnia and attitudes toward Whitman, the possibility that Gosse was implicated in Thomas J. Wise's forgeries, and Vernon Lee's ruffling of Henry James have usurped more than their share of interest. All in all, while a rich store of anecdote and legend has accumulated around these figures, their critical pronouncements and aesthetic principles have more often been given cursory summation than careful analysis.

Few studies have dealt with enough of the minor critics to make possible a meaningful comparison of the major points of difference. The most sweeping survey is René Wellek's *A History of Modern Criticism, 1750–1950*, the fourth volume of which (1965) gives substantial treatment to seven of the figures here considered, Bagehot, Dallas, Lewes, Saintsbury, Swinburne, Symonds, and Wilde. Wellek's discussions of these men are much more helpful than those of any of the earlier surveys; what he provides is essentially a cogent summation of contemporary judgment of their importance. The most original of his comments are on Saintsbury, who is seen as having different standards for poetry and the novel (the first are formalistic, the second much broader), and on Symonds, the importance of whose evolutionary theories is emphasized. However, the soundness and incisiveness of the sections on each of the critics considered make them perhaps the best starting points for the student. Older broad surveys, including Saintsbury's *A History of Criticism and Literary Taste in Europe* (1900–04), may be dismissed as too superficial in their brief mention of the lesser critics.

The most important among more specialized studies of criticism in the nineteenth century are Geoffrey Tillotson's *Criticism and the Nineteenth Century* (1951), Alba H. Warren's *English Poetic Theory, 1825–1865* (1950), Richard Stang's *The Theory of the Novel in England, 1850–1870* (1959), and Kenneth Graham's *English Criticism of the Novel, 1865–1900* (1965). Tillotson's volume is a collection of essays, most of which consider problems of critical method or individual critics. Warren's study devotes a chapter to introducing the major topics of English poetic theory during the period studied, a chapter each to studies of nine important statements of poetic theory, and a chapter to summary. Stang and Graham search out statements by both novelists and critics that indicate the major attitudes toward the novel and the general direction in which these shifted in the years 1850–70. Tillotson's book is valuable for various helpful but disparate insights; Warren's, Stang's, and Graham's for their summation of the amount and direction of the critical thought on poetry and the novel in the Victorian period. Tillotson ignores the lesser figures, however, as does Warren to some extent (the nine statements Warren examines are by Newman, Keble, Mill, Carlyle, Hunt, Browning, Dallas, Arnold, and Ruskin). Stang's and Graham's studies of criticism of the novel are more wide-ranging—the views of Bagehot, Hutton, and Lewes, for instance, are given significant consideration by Stang, and Lee, Moore, and Saintsbury by Graham.

An important but controversial study of one grouping of critics is Ruth Z. Temple's *The Critic's Alchemy: A Study of the Introduction of French Symbolism. into England* (1953). Temple explores the soundness of the grasp of French Symbolist poetry shown by Arnold, Gosse, Swinburne, Symons, and Moore. The book gathers together a mass of information to support the clearly announced thesis that the three last critics, who belong to the aesthetic or impressionist school, understood what was important in nineteenth-century French poetry much better than the more conventional Arnold and Gosse. Whether or not one comes to agree with this thesis, it is argued too forcibly to be ignored. The bibliography is valuable for any investigation of Anglo-French relationships in the second half of the century. Bruce A. Morrisette's "Early English and American Critics of French Symbolism" (*Studies in Honor of Frederick W. Shipley*, 1942; rpt. 1968), which finds Moore, Symons, Gosse, and others unable fully to grasp French Symbolist intent, should be consulted in connection with Temple's book. Morrisette is perhaps a bit too eager to praise American critics of Symbolism at the expense of English, but he has gathered the relevant material and cited it in helpful bibliographic footnotes. James K. Robinson's "A Neglected Phase of the Aesthetic Movement: English Parnassianism" (*PMLA*, 1953) is important for the light it throws on both the development of one stream of English aestheticism and the French influence thereon.

Albert J. Farmer's *Le Mouvement esthétique et "décadent" en Angleterre (1873–1900)* (1931) presents what has come to be the most orthodox account of the rise of a decadent aesthetic, tracing the origins from Keats, the Pre-Raphaelite Brotherhood, and Pater (the first of the inclusive dates is that of *Studies in the History of the Renaissance*) that combine with new French moral and aesthetic doctrines announced in Moore's *Confessions of a Young Man* to produce the "decadence," the doctrine of the pursuit in life and art of emotions both subtle and ecstatic. This doctrine, exemplified in Wilde's life and in his works, presented as a manifesto by Symons, and translated into the *Yellow Book* and the *Savoy*, is seen as gathering its strength from the need to reject Victorian values. Thus all the forces which went to the making of the decadence "convergent vers cet idéal d'affranchissement qui séduit tous les cœurs, et elles s'unissent dans la commune reaction contre les dogmes périmés du victorianisme." Louise Rosenblatt's *L'Idée de l'art pour l'art dans la littérature anglaise*, published the same year, gives greater emphasis to Swinburne's role, and indicates the breadth of the movement by pointing to the aestheticism of Stevenson and James. Rosenblatt strives to emphasize the importance of both the French influences and the native forces that created the revolt against the identification of art and morality. The studies of Farmer and Rosenblatt are accurate enough in pointing to the obvious sources of the literary attitudes that came to be called "decadent" in England in the 1890's, though there is considerable room for variation in emphasis. Both books, with their interest in the more spectacular manifestations of a developing "decadence," and that of Temple with its emphasis on the importance of three critics, should be compared with the admittedly less striking but quite balanced summary of Anglo-French relations that makes up the first part of Enid Starkie's *From Gautier to Eliot: The Influence of France on English Literature, 1851–1939* (1960).

Another group of relevant studies are those that trace the attitudes toward and critical contributions to the study of major writers or schools: James G. Nelson's *The Sublime Puritan: Milton and the Victorians* (1963), George Ford's *Keats and the Victorians* (1944; rpt. 1962), Deborah Dorfman's *Blake in the Nineteenth Century* (1969), Joseph E. Duncan's *The Revival of Metaphysical Poetry: The History of a Style, 1800 to the Present* (1959; rpt. 1969), and Kathleen Tillotson's "Donne's Poetry in the Nineteenth Century" (*Mid-Victorian Studies,* 1965). Such studies and their more sweeping counterparts—Augustus Ralli's *A History of Shakespearean Criticism* (1932), Arthur M. Eastman's *A Short History of Shakespearean Criticism* (1968), Samuel Chew's *Byron in England* (1924), and Mary Katherine Peek's *Wordsworth in England* (1943)—are valuable for the analysis of the critical tendencies of an age, but are only indirectly helpful in understanding the systems and values of individual critics. Finally, one should know Stephen Potter's *The Muse in Chains* (1937), which concentrates on the place of literary study in the universities and traces the struggle to make English literature a formal part of the curriculum.

Most prominently lacking are substantial studies of the development of significant critical principles and particular attitudes toward literary criticism in the nineteenth century as exhibited in critics less well known than Arnold, Ruskin, and Pater. Examples of this sort of approach on a limited scale are the first two essays in *The Art of Victorian Prose* (1968), edited by George Levine and William Madden. Travis R. Merritt's "Taste, Opinion, and Theory in the Rise of Victorian Prose Stylism" analyzes a selection of nineteenth-century discussions of prose style, tracing the development of various views of style and the conflicts among those views. Included is consideration of Saintsbury's championship of the cult of style and Lewes' attempt to liberalize Spencer's positivist philosophy of style. G. Robert Stange's "Art Criticism as a Prose Genre" traces the growth of expressionism with special attention to Ruskin and Pater. Sui generis is John Gross's *The Rise and Fall of the Man of Letters* (1969). Vivacious in style and wide-ranging in scope, it briefly treats most of the important nineteenth-century English critics. Well-marshaled biographical facts are salted with occasional penetrating critical insights, though it is mainly the personality rather than the thought of Gross's subjects that emerges. The volume provides a useful overall view of the variety of levels and functions of nineteenth-century criticism. The general survey of reviewing which Gross offers is supplemented by the chapter on "Literature and Dogmas" in Edwin Everett's *The Party of Humanity*: The Fortnightly Review *and Its Contributors, 1865–1874* (1939), the chapter "Literary Insignificancies" in George L. Nesbitt's *Benthamite Reviewing* (1934), and R. G. Cox's "Victorian Criticism of Poetry: The Minority Tradition" (*Scrutiny,* 1951). Cox establishes that there was a considerable amount of critical protest against intellectual feebleness and disassociation from contemporary life in nineteenth-century poetry. Nesbitt's survey is useful, but it exhibits the common defect of studies of this sort in failing to pursue fully the extent to which literary judgments reflect extraliterary principles. Everett does somewhat better in this respect.

It should be noted that while Volume III of the *New Cambridge Bibliography of English Literature* (1969) deserves to be welcomed for its general usefulness, it must be used with caution; at least in the listings of minor authors it is frequently inaccurate and incomplete.

I. GEORGE HENRY LEWES (1817–78)

George Henry Lewes divided his interests between three major areas: literary criticism, science (esp. physiology), and philosophy. Beside his *Life of Goethe* (1855, with many later editions) must be set his *Biographical History of Philosophy* (1845–46) and his *Problems of Life and Mind* (1874–79).

Lewes' first literary articles were on the drama, but from the beginning his range as a free-lance contributor to periodicals was broad. A great part of his essays, articles, reviews, and dramatic criticisms (many of the latter over the pseudonym "Vivian" in the *Leader*) remain scattered through periodicals. The important, separately published volumes of his literary criticism are *The Spanish Drama* (1846), *The Life of Goethe* (1855), *On Actors and Acting* (1875), *The Principles of Success in Literature* (1896), and *Dramatic Essays* (selected from the *Examiner*, 1896). Alice R. Kaminsky's volume in the Regents Critics series, *Literary Criticism of George Henry Lewes* (1964), is a good selection; the introduction and bibliography are helpful. The most detailed accounts of Lewes' life are found in Anna Theresa Kitchel's *George Henry Lewes and George Eliot: A Review of Records* (1933), which also includes a bibliography of secondary sources, a list of the books published by Lewes, and a list of his early essays (to 1850); and Gordon Haight's *George Eliot: A Biography* (1968). *The George Eliot Letters* (1954–56), edited by Haight, contains 528 items by Lewes as well as his record of literary receipts. The most complete bibliography of Lewes' books, articles, and reviews, an admirable compilation, is found in Alice R. Kaminsky's *George Henry Lewes as Literary Critic* (1968).

The position Lewes had achieved by the time of his death is summed up in James Sully's "George Henry Lewes" in the *New Quarterly* (1879). Also of interest as an informed contemporary evaluation is Anthony Trollope's "George Henry Lewes" (*FortR*, 1879).

Alice Kaminsky's *George Henry Lewes as Literary Critic*, the one full-scale study of Lewes' criticism, provides a comprehensive survey of his commentary on critical theory, poetry, the novel, and the drama. The book offers more summary than analysis and is finally somewhat disappointing in relating Lewes' criticism to his philosophical principles. It is, nevertheless, the indispensable introduction to Lewes' criticism. (Kaminsky's "George Eliot, George Henry Lewes, and the Novel," *PMLA*, 1955, is incorporated into the volume.) Edgar W. Hirshberg's *George Henry Lewes* (1970) offers substantial chapters on Lewes as literary critic and dramatic critic. Lewes' doctrines of "sincerity" and "realism" are accepted rather too uncritically as adequate basic principles for his criticism, but Hirshberg's summary of Lewes' critical positions is clear and convenient. The bibliography includes many of Lewes' contributions to periodicals.

As might be expected from his relationship with George Eliot, Lewes' criticism of fiction has received considerable attention. Morris Greenhut (*SP*, 1948) offers the thesis that Lewes "developed a coherent aesthetic of the novel" and summarizes his views of contemporary and earlier novelists. Gordon Haight (*PMLA*, 1956) argues that Lewes' review of Forster's *Life*, with its attack on the weaknesses in Dickens' novels, shows a better understanding of Dickens than Forster possessed. Franklin Gary's "Charlotte Brontë and George Henry Lewes" (*PMLA*, 1936) is an interesting study of the effect of Lewes' advice and criticism. In the fourth chapter of *The Theory of the Novel in England, 1850–1870* (1959), Richard Stang explores the way Lewes comes to identify true realism and true idealism. Allan R Brick gives Lewes credit for being the first important critic to appreciate the greatness of *Wuthering Heights* (*NCF*, 1960).

Lewes' dramatic criticism has been surveyed by Morris Greenhut (*PMLA*, 1949), who points to the soundness of Lewes' judgments on the drama and the way in which he applied a theory of the historical process of development and decay of the drama in a given culture. M. Glen Wilson, Jr., on the other hand, finds that Lewes' judgment of Charles Kean's acting was unfairly harsh (*ETJ*, 1964). Edgar W. Hirshberg's "George Henry Lewes and Victor Hugo's Reputation in England" (*LangQ*, 1963) examines Lewes' pronouncements on Hugo to show that the reversal of his first favorable judgments and adoption of the lower estimate which has become standard corresponds to Lewes' reaction against the Romantic drama. Hirshberg's "G. H. Lewes and A. W. Schlegel" (*LangQ*, 1967) examines the parallels and contrasts between Lewes' theories on the drama and those Schlegel set forth in *Über dramatische Kunst und Litteratur*, upon which Lewes commented in an article in 1843; the comparison is of value in sharpening our understanding of Lewes' theories.

The most extensive treatments of Lewes' total critical theory are those of R. L. Brett, "George Henry Lewes: Dramatist, Novelist and Critic" (*E&S*, 1958), and Morris Greenhut's "George Henry Lewes and the Classical Tradition in English Criticism" (*RES*, 1948). Brett's position is that Lewes' "claim to rank as the most important critic between Coleridge and Arnold is a considerable one." Lewes takes the responsibilities of literature seriously and combines the insights of Hegel and Mill in his criticism (no inconsiderable feat). Greenhut sees Lewes as fighting against the excesses of both Romantic and neoclassic criticism, viewing the importance of culture in giving perspective much as Arnold was to do.

It seems a likely assumption that a writer so strongly influenced by Mill, Comte, and the German Idealists would try to keep his mental house in order by developing a consistent aesthetic. No one has yet fully investigated the relation between Lewes' aesthetic beliefs and his changing philosophical beliefs; the most relevant works would seem to be his book on Goethe, his *Principles of Success in Literature* (in itself rather pedestrian but interesting in its denial of anything mystical or extraterrestrial in the imagination of the artist), and his *Problems of Life and Mind*. Anyone undertaking such an investigation will find Jack Kaminsky's "The Empirical Metaphysics of George Henry Lewes" (*JHI*, 1952) an excellent starting point.

II. WALTER BAGEHOT (1827–77)
AND RICHARD HOLT HUTTON (1826–97)

Walter Bagehot and Richard Holt Hutton, close friends from their University of London days in the early 1840's, not only represent the lively yet solid intellectual life of the time, but, through their roles as leaders in the "higher journalism," they successfully spread their attitudes and opinions. At University College, London, they were exposed to both a stimulating intellectual life and the prevailing bias toward science and political economy. They edited the *National Review* jointly; first

Hutton and then Bagehot served as editor of the *Economist*; Hutton achieved his greatest prominence as editor of the *Spectator*. Both were men with wide interests, a belief in informed common sense, and a distrust of the wayward, eccentric, or overly imaginative. Their writing is both analytical and judgmental; at times it appears digressive because neither thought that one could write about any topic in isolation. They represent what those of the generation educated in the 1840's—at least those not rigidly tied to the positions of a particular philosophical or political party—believed the function of the thoughtful writer to be, and as their influence grew, their method of approach to a subject became a model for others. Those who wish to know what the typical contributor to the literary criticism of the Victorian journals was trying to achieve should begin with Bagehot and Hutton.

Walter Bagehot's literary studies have been kept before the public in a succession of editions since he first published the bulk of them in *Estimates of Some Englishmen and Scotchmen* in 1858. These essays were not limited to strictly literary figures, and, as has several times been remarked, there seems little reason to follow Hutton in separating Bagehot's essays into "literary" and "biographical" since his interest was the same in both cases: he wished to analyze personality and mental constitution. Hutton was the first editor of Bagehot's work; his two-volume edition of the *Literary Studies* appeared in 1879, the volume of *Biographical Studies* in 1881. Forrest Morgan's five-volume edition of 1889 and Emily Barrington's nine-volume collected edition of 1915 followed. These and lesser editions based on them are being superseded by *The Collected Works of Walter Bagehot* now in progress under the editorship of Norman St. John-Stevas, who has long labored in Bagehot's cause. The first two volumes (1965) contain all the literary essays known to be Bagehot's, several of which are there republished for the first time. (See Robert H. Tener's "Bagehot's Literary Essays," *UTQ*, 1967, for an indictment of the inaccuracy of the editing.) A useful bibliography of works on Bagehot appears in St. John-Stevas' *Walter Bagehot* (1959). The major biography is *The Spare Chancellor* (1959) by Alastair Buchan. Barrington's *Life*, printed as Volume x of her edition of his *Works* (1918), is an account by a member of the family who had known him. Hutton's memoir in the *Fortnightly Review* (1877) and the brief biography Hutton contributed to the *DNB* are important as representing the judgments of a close friend and associate; the first was reprinted in Hutton's edition of Bagehot's *Literary Studies* (1879), the *DNB* article joining it in later printings. A useful brief biographical account is that by St. John-Stevas, which, together with a general survey of Bagehot's work, occupies the first portion of *Walter Bagehot: A Study of His Life and Thought together with a Selection from His Political Writings* (1959) and appears in an expanded version in the first volume of the new *Collected Works*.

Much of the writing on Bagehot touches his literary criticism only tangentially or summarily. The most extended survey appears as Chapters v through x of William Irvine's *Walter Bagehot* (1939). Irvine's treatment is rambling and discursive, but perceptive in its emphasis on Bagehot's preference for the typical, for the delineation of what seemed to him the permanent and significant qualities of man, and for the point of view of the "broad, many-sided, moderate man of the world." These standards Irvine finds, not altogether helpfully, to be Classical, and, especially, Aristotelian. The brief chapter on Bagehot in Gertrude Himmelfarb's *Victorian Minds* (1968), entitled "A Common Man with Uncommon Ideas," provides what is probably a needed counterbalance to such emphasis on Bagehot as the literary representative of the practical world; she finds a fascinating interplay between the visionary and practical valuations of life which produces his sense of irony, complexity, and incongruity.

A stimulating, brief commentary on Bagehot's criticism appeared as the leading article of the *TLS* of 28 January 1926. It cites Bagehot's belief that "the materials for the creative faculty must be provided by the receptive faculty" as the basis of all his literary criticism, thus explaining why Bagehot put so much emphasis on the necessity of "an experiencing nature." A competent survey of the literary pieces by William Haley appears in the first volume of the new *Collected Works*. Other such studies which deserve notice are those by Leslie Stephen (in the third volume of *Studies of a Biographer*, 1902), Augustine Birrell (collected in *Essays and Addresses*, 1907), Herbert Read (in *The Sense of Glory*, 1929, where Bagehot is pronounced to be, except for Arnold, the best critic of his time), and John Wain (*REL*, 1960). None of these four, however, can be regarded as a major contribution to an understanding of Bagehot. Somewhat tangential to Bagehot's literary criticism but important for understanding the whole cast of Bagehot's mind is Jacques Barzun's brilliant "Bagehot, or the Human Comedy," in his *Energies of Art* (1956; this essay is a much revised version of "The Critic as Statesman," *AM*, 1946). Charles Hubert Sisson's *The Case of Walter Bagehot* (1972) is wholly devoted to depreciation; its unceasing contempt for Bagehot's banker-like mind is finally, and tediously, self-defeating.

George Malcolm Young advanced the proposition that Bagehot was the greatest Victorian of his time—"greatest" in the sense of being the most typical of vital Victorian thought in the breadth and vigor of his mind—in two articles in the *Spectator* (1937; rpt. in his *Today and Yesterday*, 1948), and Woodrow Wilson paid high compliments to the sanity of his mind in articles in the *Atlantic Monthly* (1895, 1898). Bagehot's importance as representative of the emphasis on balance—with all the virtues and defects of such an emphasis—in much of the best Victorian thought calls for more attention to the consistency of his literary judgments with the basic principles of his total thought. For instance, the objections to Dickens are hardly surprising in the man who wrote *The English Constitution* and *Physics and Politics*, and to realize this is not only to understand the educated English mind of the mid-century better but to understand the barriers Dickens was breaking through. And to examine Bagehot's distinction between the "creative taste" which Dickens had and the "passive taste" which he had not is to understand the implications of a not untypical distrust of the creative imagination undisciplined by taste and fidelity to experience.

Richard Holt Hutton was as much devoted to theological questions as Bagehot to economic and political ones. It is therefore perhaps appropriate that the first collection of his literary studies makes up one of the two volumes entitled *Essays, Theological and Literary* (1871). His other major literary essays are to be found in *Modern Guides to English Thought in Matters of Faith* (1887), which treats Carlyle, Newman, Arnold, George Eliot, and F. D. Maurice, and in the two volumes of *Criticism on Contemporary Thought and Thinkers* (1894). His *Sir Walter Scott* (1878) is of smaller importance. Lesser essays have been collected in *Brief Literary Criticisms*, selected from the *Spectator* by Elizabeth M. Roscoe (1906). There is no collected edition of Hutton's work, and many of his essays remain to be retrieved from periodicals. The devoted efforts of Robert Tener have resulted in an excellent checklist of Hutton's writings which makes up the seventeenth number of *Victorian Periodicals Newsletter* (1972); two notes by Tener (*N&Q*, 1967, 1971) give the evidence for attributing another thirty-six *Spectator* articles to Hutton.

The only book-length study of Hutton is John Hogben's *Richard Holt Hutton of* The Spectator (1899). This provides useful information but is not a penetrating study of Hutton's thought or writing. As Sir William Watson noted in his chapter on Hutton in *Excursions in Criticism* (1893), "Mr. Hutton is the *Spectator*," and the two most important later studies, those of Gaylord LeRoy (*PMLA*, 1941) and Robert A. Colby (*NCF*, 1956), emphasize the degree to which Hutton impressed his personality and views on the *Spectator* and the resulting weight of his influence. The information gathered in LeRoy's notes and bibliographical appendix would be of considerable value by themselves; the text they support is admirable in outlining Hutton's attack on materialist philosophy with his own mixture of weapons drawn from Coleridge, Maurice, and Martineau, his attack on Carlyle, Arnold, and the positivists who remained illogically suspended between faith and doubt, and his attempt, by means of consciously formulated principles and techniques, to understand and appraise the important English and American writers of the nineteenth century. Colby makes clear that Hutton saw literature primarily "in its relationship to the culture of the mind and to moral consciousness" and stresses the degree to which Hutton's literary criticism "was a phase of his theology." Between them these two articles examine the way Hutton's attitudes are imbedded in his total thought with much more success than has been achieved in any examination of Bagehot. For instance, in pointing out the degree to which Hutton ascribed the faults he found in particular novels to the result of an "aberration" in the author's way of seeing, Colby is touching on an aesthetic theory, which, like Bagehot's, is tied to suspicion of any personal idiosyncrasy. The high regard in which Hutton was held in his own time, a regard that justifies close study of his literary judgments and their philosophical and religious base, is made clear in Robert H. Tener's "The Importance of Being Hutton" (*DR*, 1964) in which one finds, for instance, Gladstone's statement that Hutton was the "finest critic of the nineteenth century" and Morley's opinion that Hutton was a better critic than Arnold.

One sees more clearly the more one reads them that Bagehot and Hutton combined judicial criticism, in which a work or author is judged by standards the critic assumes or hopes the reader will share, and what finally can only be called impressionistic criticism. The open re-creation in fine writing of a more or less personal reaction to a work of art begins, of course, later in the century, but a covert rendering of a personal impression by such critics as Bagehot and Hutton is common. In a passage the importance of which was recognized by William Irvine, Bagehot comments that "The only way to criticize a work of the imagination, is to describe its effect upon the mind of the reader—at any rate, of the critic; and this can only be adequately delineated by strong illustration, apt similes, and perhaps a little exaggeration." Bagehot's description of Shelley's mind, for instance, though prefaced with some theorizing about possible types of minds, is essentially impressionistic, as are such sentences scattered through Hutton's essay on Carlyle as: "He was always trying to paint the light shining in darkness and the darkness comprehending it not, and therefore it was that he strove so hard to invent a new sort of style which should express not simply the amount of human knowledge, but also, as far as possible, the much vaster amount of human ignorance against which that knowledge sparkled in mere radiant points breaking the gloom."

III. ENEAS SWEETLAND DALLAS (1828–79)
AND VERNON LEE (1856–1935)

In contrast to this tendency toward impressionism, there were, of course, attempts to establish an aesthetic doctrine grounded in psychology or physiology. The two most interesting are by Eneas Sweetland Dallas and "Vernon Lee" (Violet Paget's pseudonym appears to be established quite as firmly as that of Mary Ann Evans).

Dallas, the corpus of whose identifiable critical work is constituted by his reviews in the *Times*, articles on "Currer Bell" (*Blackwood's*, 1857) and Blake (*Macmillan's*, 1864), the *Poetics* (1852), *The Gay Science* (1866), and, according to William E. Buckler (*N&Q*, 1950), the introduction to the 1868 edition of Shenstone's prose, set himself the goal of putting criticism on a scientific basis. The attempt aroused no enthusiasm in his own time, and commentary has continued to be meager despite the appreciative essay by John Drinkwater in *The Eighteen-Sixties* (1932), which tries to awaken interest by abundant quotation of striking passages. Derek Hudson has recently made a new attempt to call Dallas to notice, this time by giving interesting details of his life (*REL*, 1967).

In brief, the psychological theory on which Dallas based his structure was that the Imagination, which is responsible for both the creation and enjoyment of poetry, is not a faculty but a special function of the unconscious mind. The shifting of the description of the Imagination from a "faculty" to a "function" suggests solutions for many a problem with which Coleridge battled (he was never quite sure what other faculties the Imagination mediated between) while freeing from weighty metaphysical explanations Kant's recognition that the mind is least aware of its most creative acts. In rejecting Aristotelian "imitation" he was opening up possibilities for seeing art as truly creative without having to make claims for it as a form of knowledge superior to ordinary experience.

The earliest analytical essay of value on Dallas, Michael Roberts' "The Dream and the Poem: A Victorian Psychoanalyst" (*TLS*, 18 Jan. 1936), is clear, intelligently appreciative, and incisive. Roberts cites some of the more important of Dallas' reviews for the *Times* (others can be gleaned from Ch. xxii of the 2nd vol. of *The History of the* Times, 1939, and from the notes in articles listed below).

A summary and critique of Dallas' theory that the end of art is pleasure and that the Imagination is the unconscious functioning of the mind makes up Francis X. Roellinger's "E. S. Dallas on Imagination" (*SP*, 1941). Roellinger's "E. S. Dallas: A Mid-Victorian Critic of Individualism" (*PQ*, 1941) surveys some of Dallas' more perceptive opinions as expressed in his reviews, emphasizing his critique of the growing sentimental individualism he found in the literature of the time. Alba H. Warren, Jr. provides a thoughtful chapter on Dallas' *Poetics* in *English Poetic Theory, 1825–1865* (1950). Warren's analysis is especially valuable in placing Dallas within the traditional and contemporary debates on aesthetics, but unfortunately the *Poetics* is merely a tentative exploration of a point of view much more fully worked out in *The Gay Science*. The weakness of Dallas' penchant for schematizing emerges clearly, but so also does his originality. R. A. Forsyth's "'The Onward March of Thought' and the Poetic Theory of E. S. Dallas" (*BJA*, 1963) sets Dallas' efforts against the cultural temper of the time, pointing out that Dallas was not only trying to put literary criticism on a more scientific basis, but trying to preserve the value of imaginative literature against scientific materialism. This he saw as of particular importance because of the cultural changes making the written word more and more powerful for the guidance of the total population.

The critical and aesthetic writing of Vernon Lee is wide in range, controlled in approach, and of special interest as a record of the struggle between purely aesthetic and unmistakably moral attitudes toward art. She published almost fifty volumes of fiction, travel essays, historical studies, and books on aesthetic theory. The important historical studies, all of which cast light on her aesthetic theories, are *Studies of the Eighteenth Century in Italy* (1880), *Euphorion: Being Studies of the Antique and the Medieval in the Renaissance* (1884), and *Renaissance Fancies and Studies* (1895). The volumes specifically devoted to aesthetics are *Belcaro: Being Essays on Sundry Aesthetical Questions* (1881), *Juvenilia: Being a Second Series of Essays on Sundry Aesthetical Questions* (1887), *Beauty and Ugliness* (1912), *The Beautiful: An Introduction to Psychological Aesthetics* (1913), and *The Handling of Words* (1923; rpt. 1968). The most accurate bibliography of her works appears in Peter Gunn's *Vernon Lee* (1964); there is no extensive list of her periodical publications. Arthur Lane is preparing an annotated bibliography of writings about Lee for *ELT*. An important collection of letters and other manuscript material is located in the Colby College Library; descriptions of the collection, together with other biographical and bibliographical information, comprise the November 1952 and June 1960 issues of the *Colby Library Quarterly*; Vernon Lee letters and other ana appear in that journal from time to time. A collection, *Vernon Lee's Letters*, was edited by Irene Cooper Willis in 1937.

Peter Gunn's very readable biography, the only full-scale study of Lee, gives helpful summaries of the points of view adopted in her various books on aesthetic matters. As becomes clear there, she was from the time of her early studies in *Belcaro* an advocate of the moral neutrality of art and beauty; in her later writings on aesthetics, undertaken in collaboration with Kit Anstruther-Thomas, she carried her insistence on the preeminence of form in art into a physio-psychological aesthetic theory that traced the pleasure created by beauty to subtle physiological reactions to pure form. Her belief that subject matter did not determine the beauty of a work—a point on which she differed strongly from Ruskin—was thus given a theoretical base. Yet from her early writings on, one finds her expressing strongly moral views, even to the censuring of the subjects of certain works of art. A sort of compromise appears in an ultimately teleological expression of her poetics (one immediately reminiscent of Kant) which identifies the response to beauty with an increase in the well-being of the beholder, but one senses a continuing struggle between the two norms in her work. Her aesthetic theory will repay closer study than it has received; in view of the relevance of her writing on aesthetics for study of late Victorian cultural and historical attitudes, the paucity of published work on Vernon Lee is surprising.

She has not lacked admirers. Harriett Preston Waters gave three of her early volumes an appreciative review in the *Atlantic Monthly* in 1885, which in its praise of her intelligence and sensitivity set the dominant tone for later reviewers. Desmond MacCarthy has been an untiring advocate: "Vernon Lee" (*Bookman*, 1931), "Out of the Limelight" (rpt. in MacCarthy's *Humanities*, 1953), and three notices in the *New Statesman* (3 July 1920, 10 Feb. 1923, and 28 Mar. 1925) are all attempts to call attention to the value of her work. Van Wyck Brooks's "Notes on

Vernon Lee" (*Forum*, 1911) compares her aesthetic thought with that of J. A. Symonds and Walter Pater, comments on various other genres of her writing, and concludes that the structure of her ideas is so little known because "Her gift has been so gracious that she seems not to have asked for austere consideration." A brief but intelligent discussion of her mixture of scientific theory and a bias toward art for art's sake is offered in Madeleine L. Cazamian's *Le Roman et les idées en Angleterre, II: L'Anti-intellectualisme et l'esthétisme* (1935). Kenneth Graham praised Lee for her originality and comprehensiveness (*English Criticism of the Novel, 1865–1900*, 1965) and Royal Gettmann has edited and provided an appreciative introduction for the 1968 reprint of her *Handling of Words*; a version of the introduction appeared in *Prairie Schooner* in 1968.

Nevertheless, a detailed examination of her critical writing has yet to be undertaken. The only other works of any significance that I have been able to discover are short articles by Burdett Gardner, Carl J. Weber, and Leon Edel in *PMLA* (1953, 1954) treating episodes in her relationship with Henry James, and three 1970 articles in the *Colby Library Quarterly*: Richard Cary's "Vernon Lee's Vignettes of Literary Acquaintances," Richard Ormond's "John Singer Sargent and Vernon Lee," and Leonee Ormond's "Vernon Lee as a Critic of Aestheticism in *Miss Brown*."

IV. ALGERNON CHARLES SWINBURNE (1837–1909)

Swinburne's critical writings occupy six of the twenty volumes of the standard (though not entirely reliable) Bonchurch edition (*The Complete Works of Algernon Charles Swinburne*, 1925–27) edited by Edmund Gosse and Thomas J. Wise; the opinions expressed there are supplemented by passages in *The Swinburne Letters* (6 vols., 1959), edited by Cecil Y. Lang, which supersedes many previous partial collections of Swinburne's correspondence. Two previously unpublished pieces of literary criticism were printed by Clyde Kenneth Hyder in *PMLA* in 1943; the first of these and other pieces not to be found in the Bonchurch edition appear in *New Writings by Swinburne*, edited by Cecil Y. Lang (1964). Hyder also published more accurate texts of "Notes on Poems and Reviews" and "Under the Microscope" than those in the Bonchurch edition, together with the "Dedicatory Epistle" of 1904 (omitted from the Bonchurch ed.) as *Swinburne Replies* (1966). Swinburne's notes in an edition of Middleton appear as "Swinburne on Middleton" by T. Larsen (*TLS*, 17 June 1939).

The standard bibliography (in need of revision) is that by Wise, published as Volume xx of the Bonchurch edition. Wise's *A Swinburne Library* (1925) is a catalog of books and manuscripts in the Ashley Library held by the British Museum. William B. Todd (*TQ*, 1959) gives the history and a checklist of the manuscripts in the John H. Wrenn collection and the Stark and Hanley libraries acquired by the University of Texas. Despite its date, the list of bibliographical, biographical, and critical works on Swinburne, including reviews, to be found in *Bibliographies of Twelve Victorian Authors* (1936), edited by Theodore George Ehrsam et al., is still useful. (Eleven additional items are added in Joseph G. Fucilla's supplement, *MP*, 1939.) Despite numerous later studies that treat all or portions of Swinburne's life, one must know Gosse's biography (1917; rpt. with a few revisions in the Bonchurch ed.); the necessary additions to and corrections of Gosse's account are for the most part to be found in Georges Lafourcade's *La Jeunesse de Swinburne* (1928) and *Swinburne: A Literary Biography* (1932).

No one has ever questioned the vigor of Swinburne's response to literature or ever doubted that the central evaluative question concerning his critical prose is whether his pronouncements were based on sufficiently coherent principles, or sufficiently profound insights, to offset their frequent lack of organization and extravagance of statement. A full review of opinions on Swinburne's criticism to the date of publication (1933) and a good secondary bibliography is found in Hyder's *Swinburne's Literary Career and Fame*. The 1895 review of Swinburne's *Studies in Prose and Poetry* in the *Dublin Review* by Charles Coupe, S.J., is unfair, its author driven to almost Swinburnian prejudice by his subject's impiousness, but it serves well to sum up all the major faults urged against both the style and the content of Swinburne's critical prose. A severe judgment is Henry James's in a review of *Essays and Studies* in the *Nation* (1875; rpt. in *Views and Reviews*, 1908): "To note, however, the points at which Mr. Swinburne's judgment hits the mark, or the points at which it misses it, is comparatively superfluous, inasmuch as both of these cases seem to us essentially accidental. His book is not at all a book of judgment; it is a book of pure imagination. His genius is for style simply, and not in the least for thought nor for real analysis; he goes through the motions of criticism, and makes a considerable show of logic and philosophy, but with deep appreciation his writing seems to us to have very little to do." T. S. Eliot's "Swinburne as Critic" (*The Sacred Wood*, 1920) praises Swinburne for the depth of his knowledge of and interest in literature, but places him among the "appreciators" rather than the critics of literature. Coulson Kernahan summed up (*London Q. and Holborn Rev.*, 1936) the frequently expressed view that Swinburne's insurmountable defect was his inability to qualify his praise and blame in remarking that "the road which Swinburne travelled, led, almost invariably, to one of two destinations—the City of Detestation or the City of Delight."

One answer is that of Thomas Earle Welby in "The Poet as Critic" (*A Study of Swinburne*, 1926); he argues that despite "the dust-devils that spring up almost causelessly and obscure the view of the subject which he is really capable of giving us," worthy compensation is to be found in scattered insights and great passages. Newton S. Arvin (*SR*, 1924) finds Swinburne's criticism valuable because "His capacity for *feeling himself into* a piece of literature that enlists his devotion is almost incredible." He is able to give the flavor of a work beautifully and one can allow for his exaggeration, which at times leads him astray, since his fundamental taste is sound. The chapter on Swinburne's prose in Harold Nicolson's *Swinburne* (1926) sympathetically explains the way in which personal associations led into diatribes, and defends the value of his criticism in spite of that tendency. In "Swinburne's 'Internal Centre'" (*QQ*, 1933; rpt. in *Science and Literary Criticism*, 1949), Herbert Dingle finds Swinburne's oscillations of opinion, as well as the extremity of many of those opinions, the result of a passion for infinity which he tried to satisfy by looking at things so closely that the finite approximates the infinite. The result is myopic concentration on isolated aspects of a writer's work. To answer directly Meredith's doubt that Swinburne had an "internal centre" by establishing at least that he had a core of aesthetic theory or procedures has been the aim of those who have most strongly defended his critical writings. An attempt to find greater consistency in Swinburne's critical writings by distinguishing between his early pronouncements while under the influence of the art-for-art's-sake movement (esp. in "Notes on Poems and Reviews" and his *William Blake*) and his more responsible positions after 1867 is made by Ruth C. Child in "Swinburne's Mature Standards of Criticism" (*PMLA*, 1937). Her article points out the ethical overtones of Swinburne's use of such words as "noble," "profound," and "lofty" and his increasing use of the word "moral" itself as a standard of judgment after 1867.

Thomas E. Connolly's *Swinburne's Theory of Poetry* (1964) bases itself on "the assumption that behind every piece of Swinburne's criticism and behind every effusion of appreciation lies a solid core of poetic theory that can be recovered by careful analysis." Connolly argues that Swinburne's criticism was grounded in a view of the object of poetry like that of Victor Hugo, and that his espousal of art for art's sake was merely a temporary wandering from the path of his basic and lifelong poetic theory. In this he is close to Child's essay in emphasizing Swinburne's identification of the noblest art with that having humanitarian ends. Robert L. Peters' *The Crowns of Apollo* (1965)—a more substantial book—attempts to work out certain basic principles: the placing of beauty first, followed by truth, the demand that detail be "integral," the idea of a creative tension between "passion" and "tact." Connolly and Peters are able with some success to find consistency and meaning in Swinburne's sets of terms such as "Gods" and "Giants," "singers" and "poet-prophets," "inner" and "outer" music, but ultimately a certain amount of misty impressionism seems to cling to these terms and the distinctions they imply. That the value of such terminology is in its suggestive power rather than its accuracy, as Samuel C. Chew says in his general chapter on the criticism in his *Swinburne* (1929), seems the truest estimate. (Chew also reminds us of a point of history that should not be overlooked—the admitted influence of Swinburne's "Notes on Designs of the Old Masters at Florence" on Pater's critical approach.)

The other studies touching significantly on Swinburne as a critic focus on narrower points. John A. Cassidy's "Robert Buchanan and the Fleshly Controversy" (*PMLA*, 1952) pulls together the strands of the situation out of which grew one of Swinburne's most famous quarrels and several of his best-known critical statements. Oscar Maurer's "Swinburne vs. Furnivall" (*SEng*, 1952) traces the famous battle over the editing of Shakespeare, the intuitive judgment versus the analytical. Swinburne's reversal of his estimate of Whitman—high praise followed by violent denunciation—has been taken, for instance by Nicolson, as the result of the influence of Watts-Dunton. Georges Lafourcade (*MLR*, 1927), William B. Cairns (*AL*, 1931), and William J. Goede (*VN*, 1968) challenge this explanation, finding Swinburne's change gradual and not wholly inconsistent. See also Will S. Monroe's "Swinburne's Recantation of Walt Whitman" (*RAA*, 1931). Cecil Y. Lang lists the Whitman volumes in Swinburne's library (*MLN*, 1949); James Coutts Maxwell explains the allusion to Whitman's Calamus poems in Swinburne's sneer at Symonds and "the cult of the calamus" (*N&Q*, 1959). (The contemporary struggle for greater freedom of expression, the interest in sexual perversity which lies just below the surface of certain later Victorian aesthetic pronouncements, and a wide nexus of personal aversion and preference lie behind the published criticism of Whitman by men like Gosse, Symonds, and Swinburne.)

The relationship between the *Spectator* and Swinburne and the significance of some of his early reviews published there are analyzed by K. S. Leaf (*Spectator* Literary Supp., 4 April 1925); attributions of some *Spectator* articles which may have been by Swinburne are discussed by Samuel Chew (*MLN*, 1920), Robert H.

Tener (*TLS*, 25 Dec. 1959), Eileen Souffrin (*RLC*, 1960), and William D. Paden (*Six Studies in Nineteenth-Century English Literature and Thought*, ed. Harold Orel and George Worth, 1962).

As a final note, I am not aware that anyone has linked the fury of Swinburne's denunciations when he violates his own definition of criticism as "the noble art of praising" to the difficulties a predominantly impressionistic critic encounters when he chooses to condemn. The flavor that gives value to a work in the eyes of the critic can perhaps be approximated by a kind of re-creation, but attack, other than parody, must almost of necessity proceed by some sort of judicial standards or degenerate into vituperation.

V. JOHN ADDINGTON SYMONDS (1840–1893)

John Addington Symonds, like Swinburne and Moore, is usually associated with the "aestheticism" rather than the "decadence" of the latter half of the nineteenth century. His books wholly or partially devoted to literary criticism are too many to be listed here, but for the core of his critical thought *Essays Speculative and Suggestive* (2 vols., 1890), *In the Key of Blue* (1893), *The Renaissance in Italy* (7 vols., 1875–86), and *Studies of the Greek Poets* (2 series: 1873, 1876) are essential. Fortunately, a full-scale descriptive bibliography which includes helpful annotations exists: Percy L. Babington's *Bibliography of the Writings of John Addington Symonds* (1925). An annotated bibliography of writings about Symonds by Carl J. Markgraf is scheduled for publication in *ELT*.

Phyllis Grosskurth's *John Addington Symonds: A Biography* (1964; Amer. ed., *The Woeful Victorian*, 1965) is one of the most generally acclaimed literary biographies of recent years. Her account of Symonds' life is more accurate and complete than the two earlier biographies: Horatio Brown's *John Addington Symonds: A Biography Compiled from His Papers and Correspondence* (1895) and Van Wyck Brooks's *John Addington Symonds* (1914), but the real advance in Grosskurth's biography is that it is the first to announce and explore the effect of Symonds' homosexuality. This adds more than candor; it rescues the unwary from being misled by Brown's account of Symonds' personal conflicts as "spiritual" and "religious" and the crisis he went through around 1870 as a struggle between abstract thought and a sensuous temperament; it rescues them also from random interpretations of Van Wyck Brooks's speculations about the conflict in Symonds between "impenetrable reserve" and "rhetorical candour." (Those who read much in the period never could have believed for long that Brown's biography fully explained Symonds' psychological difficulties; Arthur Symons' review of the book, which appeared in *Studies in Prose and Verse*, 1904, broadly suggests the degree of Brown's reticence.) Grosskurth also makes clearer the extent of homosexual interests and practice within a circle of well-known literary men (including Gosse) at the end of the century.

Still to be adequately evaluated, however, is the precise effect of homosexuality on Symonds' thought as found in his published works. Louis J. Bragman's "The Case of John Addington Symonds: A Study in Aesthetic Homosexuality" (*Amer. J. of Psychiatry*, 1936; rpt. in *Homosexuality and Creative Genius*, ed. Hendric Ruitenbeek, 1967) does not, despite its promising title, make any real contribution to the problem. The conclusions in Brooks's summary chapter, in which he tries to sum up the value and place of Symonds as a thinker, historian, and critic, must be reexamined in light of the fuller knowledge now available, but that knowledge does not wholly invalidate them. Brooks's insight into the importance of Symonds' use of evolution in his literary theory and his search for a new religion need to be reinterpreted, not rejected. The massive (2700+ pages) three-volume edition of *The Letters of John Addington Symonds, 1844–1868* (1967–69), edited by Herbert M. Schueller and Robert L. Peters, supersedes Horatio Robert Forbes Brown's 1923 edition of the *Letters and Papers* (except for a few diary entries); James Coutts Maxwell's "The Letters of John Addington Symonds, 1" (*N&Q*, 1970) should be consulted for an extensive list of errors. However, any significant attempt at reinterpretation will be premature for a few years yet: Symonds' autobiographical memoirs now in the London Library—quoted in part by Brown and frequently referred to by Grosskurth—cannot be published until 1976. Symonds contributed a number of case histories to Havelock Ellis' studies of homosexuality; Leslie B. Mittleman identifies case history 20 in the Modern Library edition of *Studies in the Psychology of Sex* (1, Part 4, pp. 139–44) as Symonds' own (*N&Q*, 1968).

Study of Symonds' published work has been meager. Frederic Harrison's review article, prompted by the publication of Brown's biography and collected in *Tennyson, Ruskin, Mill and Other Literary Estimates* (1900), is an interesting analysis of an aesthete by a sympathetic Comtist; Harrison's major criticisms are of the lusciousness of Symonds' style, his lack of selectivity, and his neglect of science in the *Renaissance*. The most significant general study is Robert L. Peters' "Athens and Troy: Notes on John Addington Symonds' Aestheticism" (*ELT*, 1962). Peters provides a good summary of Symonds' kind of aestheticism with its blending of Paterian "intensity," idealism, classicism, homosexuality, and interest in psychology and evolutionary theory. Justice is done both to Symonds' speculative bent and to his wide knowledge of the arts, the latter at times dangerous in tempting him to explain a work in one medium in terms of a second work in a quite different medium. Peters also makes a beginning in the evaluation of the relationship between Symonds' homosexuality and his other predilections and beliefs. Phillip Appleman's "Evolution and Two Great Critics of Art and Literature" (*Proc. of the Third Int. Congress on Aesthetics*, 1957) examines Symonds' exploitation of the idea of evolution "throughout his working life as a critic." Symonds was looking for an objective principle, but, says Appleman, he was too rigid in his attempts to apply a three-stage law of development. Of interest for the understanding of Symonds' early responses to literature is Phyllis Grosskurth's examination of Symonds' annotations in a copy of Lamb's *Specimens of English Dramatic Poets* (*MLR*, 1964).

The remaining significant studies have concentrated on Symonds' treatment of the Renaissance. The most important of these is Gian Napolene Giordano Orsini's "Symonds and De Sanctis: A Study in the Historiography of the Renaissance" (*Stud. in the Ren.*, 1964). Orsini's article includes useful information about Symonds' reputation as a historian of the Renaissance, the influences on and attitudes of Symonds, and his critical theory. Wallace Klippert Ferguson's pages on Symonds in *The Renaissance in Historical Thought: Five Centuries of Interpretation* (1948) give tribute to Symonds for achieving "the thorough naturalization of Renaissancism in the English-speaking world," filling out "the careful economy of Burckhardt's outline." The influence of Burckhardt on Symonds and the parallel emphases on culture rather than politics, on individualism, and on the revival of learning are reviewed. Ferguson also points to Symonds' dramatizing tendencies in dealing with his material. The eighth chapter of John Rigby Hale's *England and the Italian Renaissance: The Growth of Interest in Its History and Art* (1954) is devoted to Symonds. Hale does not try to penetrate the basis of Symonds' thought, but he points out the excessive subjectivity and other weaknesses in his handling of the Italian Renaissance. Hale makes a point others have also made, that Symonds was drawn to the Renaissance as a time of "highly perfected individuality"; he perhaps saw in a culture favoring individual development the best solution of his own conflicts. That for all his praise for the Renaissance Symonds recognizes and explicitly indicts the tyranny and immorality which accompanied the new culture is argued in Alan P. Johnson's "The Italian Renaissance and Some Late Victorians" (*VN*, 1969).

VI. GEORGE MOORE (1852–1933)

Max Beerbohm began an essay on George Moore by remarking the "luminous vagueness" of his appearance—"there was something blurred about him." Moore the critic is as difficult to see in focus as was Moore the subject of the portrait-painter. Like Wilde, Moore has been the subject of a vast number of appreciations, reminiscences, literary portraits, and repetitious general articles. The comments that suggest themselves to anyone attempting an overview are obvious, trite, and somehow unavoidable: "Moore never wrote anything (or, anything of value) which was not about himself"; "Moore was no more than the literary chameleon he admitted himself to be"; "Moore's style is enduring, his subjects dated, and his opinions trivial"; and so forth. One obvious approach to the side of himself that Moore called "Critico Moorini" is through his role as, in Stuart Pratt Sherman's words, "The Boswell of a literary generation" (see Ch. v of Sherman's *On Contemporary Literature*, 1917). But we do not ordinarily think of Boswell as a critic of Johnson; and in Moore, autobiographic confession, the chronicling of literary movements, direct criticism, and not a little fiction flow together in a unique blend.

The fact is that the form taken by Moore's comments on literature and art changed from volume to volume quite as strikingly as did his approaches to the novel. The pamphlet *Literature at Nurse* (1885) follows the style of infighting developed early in the century in the Reviews and continued more shrilly in such conflicts as that between Swinburne and Buchanan. *Confessions of a Young Man* (1888) takes the form of the autobiographical report of foreign discoveries, much of it being essentially "adventures among the masters" as well as "adventures among masterpieces," a method that Gosse and others began to employ at about the same time. *Impressions and Opinions* (1891) is, on the whole, made up of the sort of literary essays—attempts at capturing the importance of a work or writer—that one associates with the mid-century; the pieces gathered from the *Speaker* and reprinted in *Modern Painting* (1893) are only a little less conventional. The form of these two volumes of essays is not so different from that which Bagehot or Hutton would have given them. The "confessional" form is resumed in *Reminiscences of the Impressionist Painters* (1906). *Hail and Farewell* (1911–14), behind which one feels Borrow as well as Boswell, is essentially "adventures in a movement." *Avowals* (1919) is a mixed volume—the dialogues with Gosse and Balderstone are modifications of Landor, the rest a development of the approach of *Confessions. Conversations in Ebury Street* (1936) mixes personal portraits, dialogue, and reminiscences. Even the introduction to *An Anthology of Pure Poetry* (1924) includes a dialogue and divagations into impressionist painting.

Though its variety makes Moore's criticism difficult to discuss, at least one important common element runs through all of it (though to a lesser extent in *Impressions and Opinions* and *Modern Painting*): Moore creates structures that do not demand logical development of thought, or a step-by-step exposition, or even conclusions to particular trains of thought. He can start idea after idea, dropping each at the point where it no longer interests him, or when the burden of carrying it forward becomes too great. It does not matter, in this kind of presentation, whether the reader agrees with each particular point—the structure of the essay does not depend on the granting of sequential steps. What Moore created was thus a new form of impressionist criticism—he tries not so much to re-create a particular impression made on him by an individual work or author as to record a continuing series of impressions of works, events, men, and ideas. So much of his life was devoted to responses to literature and art that his biography becomes a record of critical insights. Moreover, he tacitly rejects the assumption that each critic is a kind of invariable norm—William Archer said that Moore was the reverse of an impressionist because "he always sees things in the light of a preconceived idea." It is probably more accurate to say that Moore's impressions always took the cast of his mood at a particular time and that he felt no anxiety about justifying the resulting inconsistencies. Desmond MacCarthy points out (*Portraits*, 1954) that Moore's literary sincerity is of the sort "which consists in the writer allowing each experience to impinge with all its force upon him, as though it were the only impression he had ever received. This is sincerity of mood, and it is Mr. Moore's great merit as a literary artist." Moore says in *Ave* that the artist must keep himself free from "all creed, from all dogma, from all opinion . . . all his feelings and his ideas must be his own, for Art is a personal re-thinking of life from end to end." Such rethinking, apparently, was never intended to arrive at a final conclusion. Finally, Moore is able to vary his appeals to the reader's interest by mixing his genres. Wilde was right in saying to Beerbohm that Moore continually conducted his education in public—what he omitted was that Moore had found a way to make the process interesting.

The standard biography has long been Joseph Hone's *The Life of George Moore* (1936); the most important interpretive and biographical study published since is Malcolm Brown's *George Moore: A Reconsideration* (1955). Helmut Gerber's *George Moore in Transition: Letters to T. Fisher Unwin and Lena Milman (1894–1910)* (1968) offers a commentary sufficiently complete and informed to make it a study of the middle portion of Moore's literary life. (A second volume, *George Moore on Olympus: Letters to His Publisher, 1910–1933*, is in preparation.) Since it is almost impossible to write on any aspect of Moore without touching on his autobiographical/critical works, a bibliography of all works on Moore that might contribute insight into his critical strategies would come close to coinciding with a bibliography of all comment on Moore. The latter has, in fact, been provided by Helmut Gerber's "George Moore: An Annotated Bibliography of Writings about Him" (*ELT*, 1959, with supplements in 1960 and 1961 and brief additions in many subsequent issues—it is the admirable practice of *ELT* to continue to add to the bibliographies it publishes). Good select bibliographies of secondary sources are to be found in Alexander Norman Jeffares' pamphlet on George Moore in the Writers and Their Work series (1965), and in Georges-Paul Collet's *George Moore et la France*. Both works also provide annotated lists of Moore's separately published works; Collet's includes thirty-five articles and prefaces. A bibliography of first editions of Moore from 1878 to 1921 by Henry Danielson appears in John Freeman's *A Portrait of George Moore* (1922). The definitive bibliography of Moore's works is Edwin Gilcher's *A Bibliography of George Moore* (1970); the number of revisions made between editions by Moore make this volume indispensable.

An exhaustive study of Moore's critical opinion would have to include his letters, though significant critical statements are sparse in his correspondence. The more important published collections are: *Letters from George Moore to Edouard Dujardin, 1886–1922*, edited by "John Eglinton" [William Magee] (1929), *Letters of George Moore*, addressed to and edited by Eglinton (1942), George Moore's *Letters to Lady Cunard*, edited by Rupert Hart-Davis (1957), and those edited by Gerber mentioned above.

Faced with the peculiarities of Moore's critical writing, most critics have preferred to cite only Moore's most striking comments or survey whatever portions of his views commend themselves to their particular interests. The exceptions are not numerous. Humbert Wolfe's chapter on Moore's criticism in *George Moore* (1933) collects his views with a wide sweep; Malcolm Brown's chapter on "The Craftsman as Critic" in *George Moore: A Reconsideration* (1955) emphasizes Moore's more consistent positions: his dislike of ideas as opposed to "things," his devotion to form, his advocacy of "pure" literature. Ruth Temple's chapter in *The Critic's Alchemy* (1953) finds Moore's criticism of poetry reasonably consistent. "Here then are the crucial Parnassian precepts: art is not the handmaid of morality; the subject matter of poetry is irrelevant to its excellence; the poem should be objective and in rhymed verse. By and large Moore's criticism, though impressionistic, is faithful to these principles." Herbert Howarth's chapter on Moore in *The Irish Writers, 1880–1940* (1958) emphasizes Moore's impressionism and the relation between his interest in painting and his writing. The two best overall treatments of Moore as critic seem to me to be the chapter entitled "Critique impressioniste et strategic" in Jean C. Noel's *George Moore: L'Homme et l'œuvre* (1966) and Helmut Gerber's "George Moore: From Pure Poetry to Pure Criticism" (*JAAC*, 1967). Moore's alogical mode of progression, his easy changes of position, his impressionistic judgments, and the various forms taken by his criticism are discussed by Noel as parts of an aesthetic strategy. Noel also collects several of the more interesting earlier, brief judgments passed on Moore. Gerber's article, though not focused wholly on Moore as critic, cogently urges that Moore's emphasis on the autonomy of art and perfection of form was unchanging, that his views were not simply borrowed from France, and that his views on poetry lead directly into twentieth-century positions. Gerber also surveys and evaluates the comments made on Moore's doctrine of pure poetry by Ruth Temple in *The Critic's Alchemy*, John Crowe Ransom in *The World's Body* (1938), Suzanne K. Langer in *Feeling and Form* (1953), and Herbert Read in *Reason and Romanticism* (1926).

There are a few helpful studies on matters tangential to Moore's criticism. Wayne Shumaker's *English Autobiography: Its Emergence, Materials, and Form* (1954) discusses the art with which Moore constructed *Hail and Farewell* so as to blend his materials to pursue the mission he sees for the volume: "Nothing less than to destroy the Roman Catholic Church and bring back Art to Ireland." William C. Frierson argues that Moore's criticism and autobiography were much more effective than his novels because in the latter he consciously compromised with the Victorian reader's demands (*Trollopian*, 1947). Rappalla M. Ustenghi's "Una prospettiva du unita nell'arte di George Moore" (*EM*, 1964) traces Moore's view of the novel in his own practice. Graham Hough discusses Moore as a figure who brings into relief the influences operating on the writers of the 1890's (*Edwardians and Late Victorians*, English Institute Essays, 1959); see also "George Moore and the Novel" (*REL*, 1960); both are reprinted in Hough's *Image and Experience* (1960). Moore "was more completely involved in French literature than any other writer of the 1890's—more so even than Symons; and we can see in him a complete microcosm of the French influences that were then reshaping English literature." Georges-Paul Collet's *George Moore et la France* (1957) brings together Moore's comments on French subjects from all his critical and biographical works. A strong negative evaluation of Moore is to be found in Seán O'Faoláin's "Pater and Moore" (*London Mercury*, 1936). O'Faoláin argues that Pater was much more serious than Moore and much more balanced, not having been led astray by too great an emphasis on form. (Those who wish to pursue the influence of Pater on Moore's critical thought will perhaps appreciate knowing that Robert Sechler's *George Moore: A Disciple of Walter Pater*, 1931, touches significantly on the thought of neither man; it does cite all Moore's references to Pater.) Beside O'Faoláin's essay should be put that by Gilbert Keith Chesterton in *Heretics* (1909). Moore's rejection of Roman Catholicism could have been expected to arouse Chesterton, as it does, but Chesterton also presents the interesting paradox that Moore's pride prevented him from being able to project himself clearly in his confessions.

VII. GEORGE SAINTSBURY (1845–1933) AND EDMUND GOSSE (1849–1928)

Two men stand out as the true professionals of literary criticism in the later part of the Victorian period: George Saintsbury and Edmund Gosse. Both produced works that are still standard references, both influenced the general view of literature, both fought their way to positions of importance and influence, and both are of interest as representatives of literary trends viewed with suspicion when manifested in other quarters. In his evaluation of literature, Saintsbury not only substituted a frank hedonism for the aesthetically based Cyrenaicism of Pater, but, without being charged with immorality, opened his career as a journalist-critic with an essay on Baudelaire (*FortR*, 1877), following this in the next decade with a number of studies of French writers regarded as immoral by British philistinism. Edmund Gosse, who also avoided any attempt to ground his criticism on first principles or consider literature as a criticism of life, labored for a right appreciation of French literature, and introduced the English to many of the Scandinavian writers of the time, including the "scandalous" Ibsen, laying the foundation of his reputation with *Studies of the Literature of Northern Europe* (1879).

A most readable yet detailed brief biography of Saintsbury is that by Adam Blyth Webster, reprinted from the *University of Edinburgh Journal* (1933) in 1934 as a thin volume entitled *George Saintsbury, 1845–1933*, and reprinted again in *George Saintsbury: The Memorial Volume* (1945; Amer. ed., *A Saintsbury Miscel-*

lany, 1947). It is a fine example of the old-fashioned biographical memoir at its best—the intelligent and illuminating tribute of one man of letters to another. Oliver Elton's brief survey of Saintsbury's life (*PBA*, 1933) may also be recommended.

The immediate difficulty in treating Saintsbury is apparent from the length of the Saintsbury bibliography compiled by W. M. Parker for inclusion in *A Last Vintage* (ed. John W. Oliver et al., 1950), the most complete listing available, though it does not include still uncollected contributions to periodicals. The "Selected Bibliography" in Walter Leuba's *George Saintsbury* (1967) lists fifty-one separately published items and refers to "four hundred and fifty or more other volumes in which he had a hand as editor, anthologist, introducer, or contributor." Of this mass of work, the early essays on French writers, *A History of Elizabethan Literature* (1887), *A History of Nineteenth Century Literature* (1896), *A Short History of English Literature* (1898), *A History of Criticism and Taste in Europe* (3 vols., 1900–04), *A History of English Prosody* (3 vols., 1906–10), *The Peace of the Augustans* (1916), *A History of the French Novel* (2 vols., 1917–19), and the many contributions to the *Cambridge History of English Literature* are the most important.

A second difficulty is that, since Saintsbury avoided, at times explicitly, the setting up of first principles, aesthetic systems, or metaphysical justifications for literature, it is difficult to find a way of getting a grip on his mind, of finding any underlying unity in his criticism. Moreover, Saintsbury rejects any form of identification of art with morality or with "a criticism of life." The relationship of literature to other forms of thought and cultural expression is thus severed.

Leuba's *George Saintsbury*, the most extensive and, with the exception of essays frankly intended as "tributes" rather than criticism, the most laudatory, shirks Saintsbury's antitheoretical stance not at all. Leuba defends at every turn the view represented particularly clearly perhaps by the sentence he quotes from *The Peace of the Augustans*: "Art has its own morality—a pretty severe and complicated one. It is sometimes called 'Taste.'" It would not misrepresent Saintsbury's thought, I believe, to phrase his view of the value of literature in the same form: "Art has its own purpose—a high and important one. It is called pleasure." Such a position Leuba also defends in his partisan but readable and essentially sound study. His bibliography of secondary works, though it is not complete and requires to be supplemented by attention to the notes to the text of the volume, contains by far the most complete listing of studies of and substantive references to Saintsbury's thought. (The annotations, like the books as a whole, are at times unduly defensive of Saintsbury.)

Others have defended Saintsbury's approach to literature. Oliver Elton's "George Saintsbury" (*Life and Letters*, 1933) gives his emphasis on form and style credit for making it possible for Saintsbury to ignore content which in itself he could not approve so long as the sound, style, and form were such as to give pleasure. John Boynton Priestley's well-developed tribute (*London Mercury*, 1922; rpt. in *Figures in Modern Literature*, 1924) finds his literary enthusiasm and cultivated taste sufficient to give his criticism both charm and value. It is not surprising, however, that a man who gives no apology for habitually offering his readers what is essentially description of the particular pleasure a work gives his literary palate would seem lacking in fundamental soundness as a guide. A brief but sharp attack that views Saintsbury's lack of a hierarchy of critical values as an example of "Victorian evasion" and his "gusto" in writing of literature as the result of a lack of discrimination is found in Sir Herbert Read's *A Coat of Many Colours* (1945). These few pages are worth pondering as a succinct statement of the direction the twentieth-century interpretation of the critic's role has taken. Irving Babbitt's review of *A History of English Criticism* (*Nation*, 1912; rpt. in *The Spanish Character and Other Essays*, 1940) debates the value of English criticism and concludes that the fact that Saintsbury's "reputation should be as great as it is, is perhaps in itself a proof that the English are not critical." Dorothy Richardson's "Saintsbury and Art for Art's Sake in England" (*PMLA*, 1944, with which should be compared the comments on Saintsbury in James K. Robinson's "A Neglected Phase of the Aesthetic Movement: English Parnassianism," *PMLA*, 1953) attacks Saintsbury's impressionism, cites inconsistencies in his thought, and points to the dangers of too great an emphasis on form and style. Her quotation of an earlier reference to Saintsbury as "a great connoisseur . . . but not a great critic" reminds us of the inevitable parallels that the hostile have been able to draw upon in treating a man who boasted his palate both for literature and vintages. One recalls Wordsworth's gibe at those "who talk of Poetry as of a matter of amusement and idle pleasure; who will converse with us as gravely about a *taste* for Poetry, as they express it, as if it were a thing as indifferent as a taste for rope-dancing, or Frontiniac or Sherry."

It is perhaps surprising that Saintsbury avoided for so long and to so great an extent being more heavily tarred with the "art-for-art's-sake" brush. Perhaps the secret is the avoidance of preciousness in his writing—he boasts his palate rather than his sensibilities, combining the tone of the fully armed scholar with that of the country squire praising a good joint of beef. Saintsbury was thus able to adopt what are very close to Pater's views of criticism (see, e.g., Theodore Stenberg's "The Pater-Saintsbury Definition of Criticism," *MLN*, 1947) without being regarded as one of those attempting to subvert moral foundations.

Three other objections have been consistently lodged against Saintsbury: his style has been held to be atrocious, his high Tory politics to have influenced his critical judgment, and his scholarship to be factually unreliable. The harshest statement of the first two objections is that of Robert Duncanson in "The Tory Professor" (*Univ. Mag. and Free Rev.*, 1897); both points are also strongly made by Richard Jennings in the 25 August 1945 issue of the *New Statesman and Nation*. The most famous attack on Saintsbury's inaccuracy is made in John Churton Collins' review of *A Short History of English Literature* (*SatR*, 1898; rpt. in *Ephemera Critica*, 1901).

I have touched on only a small number of the many essays on Saintsbury, but the selection reflects the fact that almost all consist of tributes from admirers or attacks from those who cannot stomach his approach or his style. The one important exception of which I am aware is the brief but sensible and judicious commentary in Volume IV of René Wellek's *A History of Criticism, 1750–1950* (1965).

The differences between the personalities of Saintsbury and Gosse are striking. (For Saintsbury's view of Gosse, see "Some Memoirs of Sir Edmund Gosse," an obituary notice in the *London Mercury* in 1928; for Gosse's view of Saintsbury, see his essay in *Silhouettes*, 1925.) Equally obvious are the differences between the compendious approach that Saintsbury's omnivorous reading made possible and the "portraits of the author" in which Gosse specialized, though Gosse is like Saintsbury in being generally valued for, in the words of Gosse's biographer Charteris, "the high spirits and general vision with which he approached his task," rather than profundity of insight or daringness of vision. Gosse's apologia appears as the preface to the first series of his *Selected Essays*. "But my object has never been to teach. I have not the peculiar gift which the teacher needs. Let me say quite clearly that I have always been an artist and never a tutor. . . . [These essays] represent my irresistible desire to share with others the infinite pleasures which literature has afforded me."

The standard life remains Sir Evan Charteris' *The Life and Letters of Sir Edmund Gosse* (1931), on the whole a reliable study though neither critical nor detailed. The list of "more important writings" in the appendix is quite useful, since no full bibliography of Gosse has yet appeared. Charteris is often unexpectedly perceptive as the compiler of a "life and letters" study. He sees clearly that although important literary and cultural essays by Hutton, Brooks, Stephen, and Arnold were appearing in the 1870's, Gosse's interests were focused on a lighter, more gossipy kind of criticism. "The band of writers to which he belonged sought to please and charm by their style, to 'gossip in a library,' or give the reader 'Silhouettes,' 'Kit-Kats,' and 'Profiles.'" (The inconsequentiality into which this can degenerate is nicely parodied in Max Beerbohm's *A Christmas Garland*, 1912.)

Gosse's *Collected Essays* were published in twelve volumes (1912–27). The most important of his volume-length studies are *Studies in the Literature of Northern Europe* (1879), *Northern Studies* (1890), and the biographies of Gray (1882, rev. 1889), Raleigh (1886), Congreve (1888), Donne (1899), Taylor (1904), Browne (1905), Patmore (1905), and Swinburne (1917). James D. Woolf's generously annotated "Sir Edmund Gosse: An Annotated Bibliography of Writings about Him" (*ELT*, 1968) provides a remarkably complete list of the commentary on Gosse; additions appear in *ELT* from time to time. (Woolf's bibliography offers a ready means of tracing the various evaluations that have been made of Gosse's role in establishing the reputations of Donne, Stevenson, and Swinburne, questions which there is insufficient room to examine here.) An important collection of letters and other manuscript material, located at the Brotherton Library, Leeds, is listed in *A Catalogue of the Gosse Correspondence in the Brotherton Collection* (1950). Leslie Marchand's "The Symington Collection" (*JRUL*, 1948) cites the Gosse material at Rutgers. Of interest also is Euan Cox's catalog of the greater part of Gosse's Library (*The Library of Edmund Gosse*, 1924). Probably the best brief account of Gosse's steady rise to success as a man of letters and his subsequent career as a highly respected critic is Lord David Cecil's essay in the *Sunday Times* (London) series titled "Great Writers Rediscovered" (12 May 1957), though it is well to balance this against the less sympathetic appraisal in Chapter vi of Malcolm Elwin's *Old Gods Falling* (1939). Two other interpretive essays deserve mention. John Freeman's essay on Gosse in *English Portraits and Essays* (1924) emphasizes Gosse's interest in the personality behind the work and his avoidance of all speculation as to the meaning of art and beauty. A more recent article by Paul F. Mattheisen, "Gosse's Candid Snapshots" (*VS*, 1965), discusses Gosse's theory of the interrelationship of a writer's personality and his works, preliminary to printing some of Gosse's "portraits." As Charteris, Freeman, and Mattheisen all make clear, Gosse's highest talent was that of the prose-portrait painter.

The introduction to *Sir Edmund Gosse's Correspondence with Scandinavian Writers* (1960), edited by Elia Bredsdorff, competently and interestingly traces the development of Gosse's interest in Scandinavian literature (pursued partly because of the advantage its novelty offered in helping to make his name), his importance in bringing Scandinavian writers to English notice, and his errors of fact and judgment. Bredsdorff's account of Gosse's failure to keep current in Scandinavian literature is paralleled by an earlier and otherwise favorable commentary on Gosse in Eskil Sundström's "The Strange Case of Swedish Literature" (*London Mercury*, 1935). Bredsdorff publishes all that is available from either side of Gosse's correspondence with over fifty writers. The appendices list and briefly annotate Gosse's writings on Scandinavia and books that refer to "Gosse and Scandinavia." (To this list should be added Einar Østvedt's "Henrik Ibsens pioner i England—Sir Edmund Gosse," published in *Samitiden*, 1962.) Paul Vincent traces some of Gosse's judgments about Dutch writing in his introduction to Couperus' *Footsteps of Fate* (1891) to his correspondence with Frederik Van Eeden (*MLR*, 1971). Vincent also reviews Gosse's interest in and knowledge of Dutch literature. Gosse's correspondence with Hans Christian Andersen is published in Bredsdorff's *H. C. Andersen og England* (1954), with Georg Brandes in *Correspondence de Georg Brandes* (1956), edited by Paul Kruger. *The Correspondence of André Gide and Edmund Gosse* (1959), edited by Linette F. Brugmans, contains helpful introductory matter on Gosse's position as interpreter of French literature and on "Gosse as Critic of Gide." Gosse's importance in interpreting French literature to England is examined in the larger context of the influence of French aesthetic theory in James K. Robinson's "A Neglected Phase of the Aesthetic Movement: English Parnassianism" (*PMLA*, 1953). Ruth Temple's *The Critic's Alchemy* (1953) devotes a detailed but hostile chapter to Gosse: "Neither by temperament nor by critical method was he equipped to serve the cause of French poetry in England as did the aesthetic critics Swinburne, Moore, and Symons." *Transatlantic Dialogue: Selected American Correspondence of Edmund Gosse*, edited by Paul F. Mattheisen and Michael Millgate (1965), is a carefully edited and selected collection that includes correspondence with Howells, James, Stedman, and Wharton; the introduction summarizes Gosse's relationships with American writers.

Gosse has not been spared derogation. Virginia Woolf's "Edmund Gosse" (*FortR*, 1931; rpt. in *The Moment and Other Essays*, 1947) says clearly what others have implied: Gosse's great defect was his concern for correctness and respectability. "How much better Gosse would have been as a writer, how much more important he would have been as a man, if only his fragrant sensual joy had not been deadened by perpetual caution." Thus does a later generation tend to view the quality Gosse's contemporaries praised as discretion and good taste.

Stronger charges have been made. The two MS letters from Gosse to Whitman quoted by William White (*VS*, 1957) and the entry from a Gosse diary now in the Huntington Library quoted by Robert L. Peters (*WWR*, 1965) indicate that Gosse was more interested in his own respectability and reputation than in accurately recording the details of his visit with Whitman in *Critical Kit-Kats*. John Churton Collins, the earliest to attack Gosse for factual inaccuracies, was able to show serious errors in Gosse's *From Shakespeare to Pope* ("English Literature at the Universities," *QR*, 1886). Collins returned to the attack in 1898 with a review of Gosse's *A Short History of Modern English Literature* (*SatR*, 1898; rpt. in *Ephemera Critica*, 1901). (Collins gashed and rent a number of reputations; for a sympathetic view of Collins and a summary of his attacks on Symonds, Swinburne, Tennyson, and Gosse—that on Saintsbury is omitted—see Phyllis Grosskurth's "Churton Collins: Scourge of the Late Victorians," *UTQ*, 1965.)

A charge more severe than inaccuracy has been urged against Gosse; since the exposure of the forgeries of Thomas J. Wise, it has occurred to a number of scholars that his friend and bibliographic collaborator may not have been unaware of Wise's dishonesty. The major attempt to implicate Gosse was made by Fannie E. Ratchford in *Letters of Thomas J. Wise to John Henry Wrenn: A Further Inquiry into the Guilt of Certain Nineteenth-Century Forgers* (1944), though her charges have generally been judged unproven. A reasoned defense of Gosse by William O. Raymond, "The Forgeries of Thomas J. Wise and Their Aftermath," was published in *JEGP* in 1945 and reprinted in *The Infinite Moment and Other Essays* (1950; 2nd ed., 1965). One of the discoverers of Wise's forgeries, John Carter, reviews the evidence in his *Books and Book-Collectors* (1956) and concludes that Gosse was gulled, but not an accomplice. Such a view is supported by E. E. Bissell's argument (*BC*, 1959) that Gosse was careless and inept as a scholar. Donald K. Adams' "A Certain 4to 'Elegy' " (*PBSA*, 1961) also argues that Gosse was taken in by Wise. Arguments on the other side include Ralph Hagedorn's "Edmund Gosse and the *Sonnets from the Portuguese*" (*PBSA*, 1952), which cites most of the other essays that have been written on the question. Nicholas Barker tries to show, with what seems to me a highly untrustworthy interpretation of certain events, that Gosse had some sort of hold over Wise and that this must have resulted from his knowledge of the forgeries ("So Gosse Was in It after All," *BC*, 1964).

Gosse's approach to literature now being out of fashion, it is difficult to remember the awe he was capable of inspiring during the latter part of his career. Osbert Sitwell's sympathetic and anecdotal chapter in *Noble Essences* (1950) helps one to see Gosse as he appeared to all but the wholly iconoclastic members of the next literary generation.

VIII. OSCAR WILDE (1854–1900) AND ARTHUR SYMONS (1865–1945)

Two things have made it difficult to get a true picture of the late 1880's and the 1890's: the audacity of its prophets and the artistry of its autobiographical chroniclers; these difficulties continue to obscure evaluation of the key critical writings of the time. Though Wilde's addiction to exaggeration and paradox and Symons' desire to advertise the importance of the literary scene are recognized by all, these are seldom adequately compensated for. And, though I think no one takes George Moore's account of the Irish revival in *Hail and Farewell* as absolutely accurate, relatively few allow for the amount of artistic focusing that occurs in Yeats's autobiographies. Beerbohm's drawings and essays provide the standard humorous appraisal, Arthur Symons' "The Decadent Movement in Literature" the accepted statement of theory, and Yeats's chapter "The Tragic Generation" the standard serious explanation. "Three or four years ago," writes Yeats, "I re-read *Marius the Epicurean* expecting to find I cared for it no longer, but it still seemed to me, as I think it seemed to us all, the only great prose in modern English, and yet I began to wonder if it, or the attitude of mind of which it was the noblest expression, had not caused the disaster of my friends." But the fact is that however sad or messy the personal fates of many of the members of Yeats's "tragic generation," more is obscured than explained by the conventional view that Symons and Wilde were either misled by Pater or misled themselves by misinterpreting his doctrine.

A well-written recent restatement of the orthodox view of the "decadent" strain in the later nineteenth century is Barbara Charlesworth's *Dark Passages* (1965). Her description of the decadents as those "whose ideal was the attainment of as many moments as possible of heightened sensory experience, enjoyed within the mind outside society" leads her to give considerable emphasis to the psychological confusions of the writers she treats, but the chapters on Wilde and Symons, while conventional in their emphasis on both men's "decadence," reflect the recent serious scholarly study of their aesthetic theories.

Wilde's critical prose bulks larger than one is apt to remember. The standard edition remains the fourteen-volume *Works* edited by Robert Ross and issued by Methuen (*Dorian Gray* appearing under the imprint of Charles Carrington, Paris) in 1908. The critical pieces, with the volumes of the 1908 edition in which they appear, are: "The Rise of Historical Criticism" (split between vols. VII and XIV), the four essays Wilde published as *Intentions* ("The Decay of Lying," "Pen, Pencil, and Poison," "The Critic as Artist," and "The Truth of Masks" in VIII), his reviews (mostly from the *Pall Mall Gaz.*, the *Woman's World*, and the *Dramatic Rev.*, XIII), and the essays, lectures, and criticism published as *Miscellanies* (XIV). Wilde's aesthetics are so closely tied to the rest of his thought that any study should extend to *The Soul of Man under Socialism* (VIII) and *De Profundis* (XI, though the complete and accurate text first became available only in Rupert Hart-Davis' ed. of *The Letters of Oscar Wilde*, 1962). One of the better bargains available is the one-volume *Works of Oscar Wilde* with an introduction by Wilde's son, Vyvyan Holland (1948; rev. and improved ed., 1966), which is slightly more complete and accurate in printing the plays and poems than the 1908 edition, though it omits Wilde's reviews and miscellaneous essays. Good selections of these are available in two editions of Wilde's critical writings, *The Artist as Critic* edited by Richard Ellmann (1969) and *Literary Criticism of Oscar Wilde* edited for the Regents Critics series by Stanley Weintraub (1968).

Wilde was generally well served by the 1908 edition, which not only collected his reviews but printed previously unpublished manuscripts and other material; he was equally fortunate in his bibliographer, "Stuart Mason" (Christopher Sclater Millard), whose *Bibliography of Oscar Wilde* (1914; rpt. 1967) is most comprehensive (more than justifying Robert Ross's description of it as "astonishing and ingenious") to the date of publication by which time all the important editions except Hart-Davis' beautifully annotated collection of the letters had appeared. (Owen Dudley Edwards' review of the reissue of the bibliography, *BC*, 1967, finds Millard's work "ill-organized, insufficiently indexed, deficient in some important matters." These charges all have foundation, but the virtues of the work remain great. What Edwards really makes clear is the danger inherent in succumbing to the temptation to photoreproduce older volumes which would profit from correction and improvement.) The most complete collection of Oscar Wilde material is that held by the W. A. Clark Memorial Library; see the well-indexed *Oscar Wilde and His Literary Circle: A Catalogue of Manuscripts and Letters in the William Andrews Clark Library* (1957) compiled by John Charles Finzi.

No single biography of Wilde can be recommended as adequate, though one may hope that the collection of Wilde's letters by Hart-Davis will provide the foundation needed for a definitive life. At present one must read Robert Harborough Sherard's *The Life of Oscar Wilde* (1905), Lord Alfred Douglas' *Oscar Wilde: A Summing Up* (1940), "Frances Winwar's" [Frances Grebanier's] *Oscar Wilde and the Yellow Nineties* (1940), Hesketh Pearson's *The Life of Oscar Wilde*

(1946), Patrick Byrne's *The Wildes of Merrion Square* (1953), and Philippe Julli-an's *Oscar Wilde* (1968; English trans. by Violet Wyndham, 1969), and hope, by making due allowance all around, to arrive at a reasonably accurate composite portrait. If one is capable of making especially large allowances, Frank Harris' *Oscar Wilde: His Life and Confessions* (1918) should also be looked into.

Philippe Jullian's *Oscar Wilde* illustrates the difficulty that faces Wilde's would-be biographer. Though writing with the advantage of the Hart-Davis edition of Wilde's letters and able to evoke scene and atmosphere, Jullian produced a biog-raphy that strikes the reader with tedious familiarity. The bon mots, the striking incidents have all been told many times before, and told in so many variants that one can neither rekindle one's interest in them nor lean on them for support of any thesis about Wilde. One almost imagines that only a "Variorum Wildeana" in which versions of incidents and epigrams would be collated and evaluated, each page consisting of one third text and two thirds notes, would be necessary to (perhaps) clear the air.

The relationship between Wilde's homosexuality, creative writing, and aesthetic theorizing has been wearisomely but largely profitlessly discussed. An example of how unilluminating an analysis of the significance of Wilde's homosexuality can be is Clifton Allen's "Homosexuality and Oscar Wilde: A Psychological Study" in *Homosexuality and Creative Genius*, edited by Hendric Ruitenbeek (1967).

Note has frequently been taken of the strength and persistence of interest in Wilde on the Continent. As one looks back over the seventy years of criticism since Wilde's death, it becomes apparent that in general the Continental critics began to see what was important in Wilde's thought sooner than the English and American critics, who assumed for so long that Wilde's aesthetics were simply a bubble to be pricked. Those who have carefully tried to examine Wilde's thought and resisted the temptation merely to summarize his more outrageous statements have generally tended toward the judgment expressed in the perceptive chapter on Wilde in Made-leine L. Cazamian's *Le Roman et les idées en Angleterre*, II (1935) that there is in Wilde a "cohérence intérieure d'une pensée exceptionnellement riche, le timbre forte-ment défini et cependant complexe d'une sensibilité personnelle."

It was obvious from early in Wilde's career that his thought in some sense derived from Walter Pater, though too often the relationship was summed up by simply calling Wilde an erring disciple. Eduard J. Bock's *Walter Paters Einfluss auf Oscar Wilde* (1913) was the first important attempt to examine the exact nature of Pater's influence. Bock finds that Wilde emphasized different portions of Pater's thought from time to time, coming closest to Pater's total view in *De Profundis*. Alice Wood's "Oscar Wilde as a Critic" (*North Amer. Rev.*, 1915; rpt. in Karl Beckson's *Oscar Wilde: The Critical Heritage*, 1970) raises the important question of the relationship between the "active principle" which Pater thought a writer's work should express and Wilde's emphasis on the impression of a work on the individual critic, but reaches no resolution.

Less attention has been given to Wilde's adoption of Arnoldian views, though in his essay on "Criticism" in the seventh series of *Shelburne Essays* (1910), Paul Elmer More argued that Wilde (and Pater) fell into aesthetic and moral error through grasping only a part of Arnold's system. On the other hand, Merritt Y. Hughes's "The Immortal Wilde" (*Univ. of Calif. Chron.*, 1928) emphasizes the interesting continuity. Beginning deceptively as a review of a recent edition of *Salome*, Hughes's excellent essay points out that despite Wilde's rejection of the goal of the critic as seeing the object as it really is, "the whole practical, political gospel of *Culture and Anarchy* is implied in Gilbert's interpretation of 'self-culture as the true ideal of man.'" "Four Arnold Letters," edited by David DeLaura (*TSLL*, 1962), includes a letter from Arnold to Wilde and a résumé of Wilde's expressions of admiration for Arnold.

The two-step progression of thought from Arnold to Pater to Wilde has been variously evaluated. T. S. Eliot of course implied the progression in his well-known attack on the reduction of religion to aesthetics that he finds in Arnold and Pater ("The Place of Pater," *The Eighteen-Eighties*, ed. Walter de la Mare, 1930; rpt. as "Arnold and Pater" in *Selected Essays*, 1932 et seq.). Eliot states the purpose of the essay as the indication of "a direction from Arnold, through Pater, to the 'nineties, with, of course, the solitary figure of Newman in the background," but Newman is much less in evidence than the sinister figure of Wilde waiting in the wings. Richard Ellmann's "The Critic as Artist as Wilde," printed in slightly differing versions in *Wilde and the Nineties: An Essay and an Exhibition* (1966), *The Poet as Critic* (1967), and the introduction to *The Artist as Critic* (1968), develops the view that there were "three critical phases in the late nineteenth century, with Pater transitional between Arnold and Wilde." Wendell Harris argues (*SEL*, 1971) that the definitions of criticism upon which Arnold and Pater built were finally untenable, and that Wilde's theory, paradoxical as it seems, recognizes this. A considerable portion of Ellmann's essay is devoted to tracing the Wildean paradoxes and jugglings of the relationship of ethics, and thus of life, to art. The degree of Wilde's consistency at this point is, of course, of first importance in the interpretation of his aesthetic position; it has been discussed from a variety of directions. Léon Lemonnier, in his chapter on *Intentions* in *Oscar Wilde* (1938), points out that what Wilde is centrally fighting against is the identification of the good and the beautiful but that he contradicts this point in his handling of the argument that life imitates art. Some of the same points emerge from Eduard Roditi's chapter on Wilde's prose in his *Oscar Wilde* (1947). In Chapters vii, ix, and x he strives to show the relations between Wilde's ethics, politics, and aesthetics, and examines the irreducible confusion between his ethics and aesthetics. The argument of the book as a whole is excellent, though the influence of Chuang Tzu's *Taoism* is probably exaggerated. (A very careful assessment of Wilde's use of ideas found in Chuang Tzu—and an unusually thoughtful example of a source study—has been provided by Isobel Murray, *DUJ*, 1971.)

The chapter on Wilde in Gaylord C. LeRoy's *Perplexed Prophets* (1953) makes the interesting observation that Wilde's ethics are influenced by his belief that nature constantly changes. The full ramifications of this premise on the interpretation of Wilde's aesthetics and the relations of ethics to aesthetics are not worked out by LeRoy but are in the direction pursued by Graham Hough in "The Artist as a Man of Action" (*Listener*, 1954). Hough, who rates Wilde low as a writer, nevertheless argues that he truly wanted aesthetic doctrines to change personal life, and that those doctrines made life flexible, an affair of improvisation. That can lead us, though it is not necessarily intended to, to the point A. E. Dyson made seven years later on the Third Programme (*Listener*, 1961), that although life continually changes (and therefore must be an affair of improvisation), life must be less beautiful than art—which is the reason life can only follow behind art. Dyson also effectively makes the point that Wilde's "cynicism" is largely a myth—the conventional beliefs he mocks are usually clichés behind which lie hypocrisy and cant. In a beautifully organized essay, "L'Intellectualisme d'Oscar Wilde" (*RAA*, 1935), J. Charbonnier argues for Wilde's belief in the importance of constant improvisation from different premises. Wilde was, says Charbonnier, very much an intellectual and "La confiance de Wilde en l'intellect est sans limite." But what the intellect must grasp is not static; it must be grasped by personal experiment and it often may be expressed only in the form of art. It is precisely because art can grasp change that art is higher than ethics. Moreover, literature is the highest form of art because language is the instrument of the intelligence. But the intellect, and artistic expression, must never become static by yielding to a rigid view or unchanging passion. Charbonnier closes with a discussion of the ways in which *Dorian Gray* supports his interpretation. That novel and Wilde's plays are used by A. G. Woodward (*ESA*, 1959) to argue that Wilde's works of art fail because his own aesthetic theories were faulty and Wilde could not give his doctrine with "any essential seriousness." The argument is one with which I cannot agree, but it is clearly and cogently argued. An engaging counter to Woodward's doubts about Wilde's seriousness is J. D. Thomas' (*ELT*, 1969). The appropriateness of the dialogue form for the presentation of a view of art that is many-sided and constantly extending is here illustrated by a close look at Wilde's strategies in "The Decay of Lying" and "The Critic as Artist."

A stimulating treatment is Hilda Schiff's "Nature and Art in Oscar Wilde's 'The Decay of Lying'" (*E&S*, 1965), which argues that Wilde anticipated the modern view of literature as an organization of images or symbols intended to create "significant images for our contemplation." The importance of Wilde's anti-Romanticism in placing man above nature, the antididacticism which results from his emphasis on the symbolic, and his insistence on the imagination as an independent faculty emerge clearly.

There are a number of other very good essays on Wilde's criticism and aesthetics that touch on the above and other problems. Robert Merle's sixth chapter in *Oscar Wilde* (1948) contains good analyses of the problems in the usual interpretations of Wilde's thought and of the claims for various influences on Wilde. E. B. Partridge's "The Importance of Not Being Earnest" (*BuR*, 1960) argues that Wilde wished not merely to astound or shock the public but to rescue poetry from it. Chapters iv and v of Part i of Aatos Ojala's *Aestheticism and Oscar Wilde* (1954, as Series B, xc, 2 of *Suomalainen Tiedakatemian Toimituksia*) stress the influence of Ruskin's thought (as developed by Morris) which exists alongside the Paterian goal of contemplation in Wilde, and the importance of the difference in the conceptions of art held by Wilde and Whistler. Ojala traces well the changes in Wilde's views, pointing out, for instance, that the criticism in his early reviews "may be said to possess all those qualities which he later disclaimed in *The Critic as Artist*: it was fair, sound, and reliable." Leonard A. Willoughby's "Oscar Wilde and the Life of Art" (*PEGS*, 1964–65) argues that "no other Englishman of his century, with the possible exception of Coleridge, betrays such awareness of the complex process of mirroring and inter-mirroring that is constantly going on between art and life." Nevertheless, for all his attempt to integrate Art and Life as he understood Goethe to have done, Wilde failed, says Willoughby, because he tried to deny the claims of Life, just as he failed fully to integrate the different forms of aestheticism offered by Ruskin and Morris, on the one hand, and Pater, on the other. Philip Rieff (*Encounter*, 1970) interestingly examines Wilde's view of the artist as the guide for mankind in the "next culture" in the light of the state of our society today. Lewis J. Poteet

(*Stud. in Short Fiction*, 1970) reads "The Portrait of Mr. W. H." as a statement about literary theory which emphasizes the necessarily subjective and creative na ture of criticism.

The chapter on Wilde's aesthetics and literary criticism in *The Art of Oscar Wilde* (1967) by Epifanio San Juan provides a summary of Wilde's major pronouncements on art which, more comprehensive than coherently integrated, calls attention to Wilde's reviews and lesser-known criticism. Chapters vii, viii, and xi of George Woodcock's *The Paradox of Oscar Wilde* (1949) are also of interest: Woodcock's line of argument, which is at times tedious and at times perceptive, resolves paradoxes in the common ground of Wilde's intense individualism. J. D. Thomas (*RUS*, 1965) analyzes the individualism that runs through *The Soul of Man under Socialism* and indicates why Wilde would have felt it necessary to assert the importance of the individual at a time when neither socialists nor their opponents were inclined to grant it. Though not directly on literary criticism, the essay so beautifully fulfills the task of putting Wilde's essay in context and so helpfully makes clear the difference between the role of the artist for Morris, whom Wilde otherwise largely follows in *The Soul of Man*, and the role Wilde envisions that it cannot be overlooked. A final interesting analysis of Wilde's individualist solution to the conflict between Pater's aestheticism and an interpretation of art which, like Morris', led to socialism is Masolino D'Amico's "Oscar Wilde between 'Socialism' and Aestheticism" (*EM*, 1967). D'Amico argues that Wilde's individualist bent actually made him an anarchist rather than a socialist.

Of at least tangential interest are essays citing the possible influence of Renan on Wilde's thought by Joan Harding (*ConR*, 1953) and Brian Nicholas (*MLR*, 1964). Two other studies in parallels and influences are Norbert Loeser's "Friedrich Nietzsche en Oscar Wilde" in *Nietzsche en Wilde en andere Essays* (1960) and Guido Glur's *Kunstlehre and Kunstanschauung des Georgekreises und die Aesthetik Oscar Wildes* (1957). Richard Ellmann concentrates on a review of the themes of "The Decay of Lying" and traces the influence of that essay on Yeats in the chapter "Oscar and Oisin" in *Eminent Domain* (1967).

Arthur Symons suffered a serious mental breakdown in 1908; all his work written after that period is generally thought to contain much less insight and intellectual power. Roger Lhombreaud (*Arthur Symons: A Critical Study*, 1963) argues that the work produced between 1919 and 1931 cannot so easily be dismissed, but does not adequately support this view. *An Introduction to the Study of Browning* (1886, enlarged 1906), *The Symbolist Movement in Literature* (1899), *William Blake* (1907), and the earlier essays, some of which are collected in *Studies in Two Literatures* (1897), *Studies in Prose and Verse* (1904), and *Studies in Seven Arts* (1906, rev. 1925), are his important critical works. There is as yet no even reasonably complete bibliography of Symons' works though Roger Lhombreaud has announced that he has one in preparation. The bibliography in John Munro's *Arthur Symons* (1969) is very useful, but it should be supplemented by reference to the bibliographies in Lhombreaud's biography and T. Earle Welby's *Arthur Symons: A Critical Study* (1925). Only nine of the projected sixteen volumes of *The Collected Works of Arthur Symons*, an edition begun by Martin Secker in 1924, appeared (Munro points out that it is safer in all cases to consult the original editions). The acquisition of a number of Symons' papers, including notebooks, was announced in the *Princeton Library Chronicle* in 1952.

T. Earle Welby's *Arthur Symons: A Critical Study* was the first and long the only volume-length study of Symons. Welby had the advantage of having read widely in the literature of the latter part of the nineteenth century, but his volume, which avoids biography, is too discursive and loose to be of great value. It is an impressionist study of an impressionist—an unfortunate combination, found rather too often in early twentieth-century studies of the immediately previous generation.

Roger Lhombreaud, who has painstakingly collected material, gives us in *Arthur Symons: A Critical Study* (1963) a comprehensive survey of Symons' life for which students of the period must be grateful. It is not, however, truly a "critical" biography—the task of evaluating Symons' work and integrating the main lines of his thought (if that can be done) remains. Lhombreaud entitles the third section of his book "A Theory of All the Arts" and quotes Symons' statements that he was attempting to formulate such a comprehensive theory. However, he fails to outline it adequately. Most writers on Symons have been equally unsuccessful in this matter. Welby's review, "The Work of Arthur Symons" (*SatR*, 1924), and his critical study also assert the unity of Symons' personal system of aesthetics without describing that system. Certainly we cannot accept as a comprehensive theory Symons' statements that criticism is the evaluation of forces or his Paterian pronouncement that "The aim of criticism is to distinguish what is essential in the work of a writer; and in order to do this, its first business must be to find out where he is different from all other writers." Osbert Burdett's strongly appreciative assessment of Symons in *The Beardsley Period* (1925) denies that Symons ever worked out his set of first principles; Burdett thinks Symons offers simply "an exposition of the quality of beauty peculiar to the work of each author or artist whom he treats."

John M. Munro's *Arthur Symons* is the first study to attempt to assess carefully the development and establish the unity of Symons' aesthetic theories. Munro, who finds Symons' poetry of comparatively little importance, devotes the bulk of his volume to outlining the influence of the younger generation of French poets on Symons at the beginning of the 1890's, Symons' search for a kind of transcendence through literature, the relationship with Yeats which led to *The Symbolist Movement in Literature*, the shift from the subsumption of symbolism under decadence to the reverse of this position, the progress of Symons' "spiritual enlightenment" as traced through "his criticism of the dance," and finally his attempt from about 1900 to 1908 to apply Symbolist doctrine to all the arts. The doctrine that Symons saw as explaining all the arts, according to Munro, is simply that the perfect work of art is "a harmony of forces which defies cerebral analysis yet induces an emotion analogous to spiritual ecstasy." That is, the total work is a symbol whose meaning may be intuited but not analyzed. The conclusions arrived at in many of the briefer studies listed below have been incorporated into Munro's volume.

Two of the major starting points for the discussion of Symons have been his relationships to Pater and to Yeats. There is no doubt that Symons was greatly influenced by Pater; in 1885 he writes to Churchill Osborne that the style of the essay he has been working on is modeled on Pater, and allusions from and appreciative references to Pater recur in his writings throughout his life. John Pick's "Divergent Disciples of Walter Pater" (*Thought*, 1948) urges that Symons never got beyond the Cyrenaicism of the Conclusion to *The Renaissance*. Richard Jennings' depreciatory obituary notice (*New Statesman and Nation*, 1945)—which begins by remarking that Symons had really died in 1908—complains of the bad influence exerted by Pater. Arnold B. Sklare (*JAAC*, 1951) emphasizes Symons' discipleship to Pater, making the additional points that Symons tried to be the sort of creative critic Wilde called for and that Symons' *The Symbolist Movement* represents a necessary development in his thought.

Derek Stanford, in "Arthur Symons as Literary Critic (1865–1945)" (*QQ*, 1965), points to the ways in which Symons diverged from Pater after a period of Pateresque subjective impressionism. (This essay makes up the first portion of a two-part article under the same title in *ConR*, 1965, the second portion of which—a discussion of comments on Symons by Hough and Kermode—appears in the *SoR*, 1965, as "Arthur Symons and Modern Poetics.") Stanford finds that Symons applied to contemporary literature the approach Pater had applied to that of the past. More important, where aestheticism had come to be the proper response to life for Pater, mysticism became the answer for Symons. However defiantly Symons had urged (in reply partly to Le Gallienne's sneers at "decadence") the importance of decadence as represented in its essence by Pater's "morbid subtlety of analysis" and "morbid curiosity of form," it is not surprising that in cooler moments he began to look away from the sunset toward a hoped-for new literary dawn.

It used to be assumed that Symons had introduced Yeats to Symbolism; recently the importance of Yeats in giving Symons an understanding of the mysticism which provided the key to the Symbolists has been asserted. Richard Ellmann suggested this evaluation of the relation between the two men in his 1958 introduction to a reprinting of *The Symbolist Movement* ("It seems reasonably clear that Yeats's mind was the dominant one in the friendship"); it is summarized in the chapter "Oscar and Oisin" in his *Eminent Domain* (1967). Ian Fletcher makes a similar point in "Explorations and Recoveries—II: Symons, Yeats and the Demonic Dance" (*London Mag.*, 1960), which also sets forth the claim to be made for Symons as a link to the Imagist movement. Frank Kermode touches on Symons' debt to Yeats in his chapter on Symons in *Romantic Image* (1957), but he insists that Symons would have known much about mysticism and magical correspondences directly from the French writers. John M. Munro has argued, partly on the evidence of jottings made by Symons before he knew Yeats well, that it is not true that "before Symons met Yeats he was a 'decadent'; and only afterwards did he turn 'symbolist'" (*ELT*, 1964; see also Edward Baugh's note on Munro's article and Munro's reply in the next issue). In "Arthur Symons and W. B. Yeats: The Quest for Compromise" (*DR*, 1965), Munro discusses the mutual influence of the two men, indicating why Symons moved toward mysticism; he concludes, however, that Symons' search for transcendence was unsuccessful; Symons was never able to find a proper compromise between body and soul, meditation and energy. A very interesting essay by Francis Gribble, "The Pose of Mr. Arthur Symons," published in the *Fortnightly Review* in 1908, considers this desire for transcendence and concludes that what Symons really desired was an escape from the Methodism which clung to him from childhood. T. S. Eliot's review of Symons' translation of Baudelaire gives major attention to Symons as a representative, especially in his Preface to the translation, of "the childish attitude of the nineties toward religion, the belief . . . that there is a religion of Evil, or Vice, or Sin" (*Dial*, 1927; rpt. *For Lancelot Andrewes*, 1929). Ruth Temple's chapter on Symons in *The Critic's Alchemy* (1953) is highly appreciative, strongly defending the value of *The Symbolist Movement*. Symons' influence on others besides Yeats has been more often assumed than explored; Max Wildi (*OL*, 1964) traces the ways Symons influenced and aided the young Joyce (principally by opening up French aesthetic thought to him); Karl

Beckson and John Munro published a number of Arthur Symons' letters to Joyce (*James Joyce Q.*, 1967) during the time Symons was attempting to find publishers for Joyce's early poems and stories.

Broader than any of the foregoing are Max Wildi's *Arthur Symons als Kritiker der Literature* (1929) and Frank Kermode's chapter on Symons in *Romantic Image*. Wildi surveys Symons' criticism on each figure or topic, keeping in mind Symons' definition of criticism as the evaluation of forces. He concludes that Symons sees the connections within a work of art but is unable to go outside it or deal with either detail or the truly abstract. Kermode, whose interest in Symons is the special one dictated by his topic, stimulatingly explores Symons' view of image and symbol as expressing the power of the imagination through mystic or magic correspondences. William S. Peterson (*RES*, 1968) surveys Symons' predecadent literary apprenticeship in the early 1880's, when his enthusiasm for Browning led him into the Browning Society and secured his introduction to F. J. Furnivall and James Dykes Campbell. An interesting earlier essay on Symons by William M. Urban (*AM*, 1914) analyzes the results in Symons' prose and verse of his impressionism, finding that in suppressing all relationships in order to regard an object, scene, or event wholly aesthetically, Symons produces a curious kind of abstraction from reality.

THE UNBELIEVERS

•

John W. Bicknell

* Among the many scholars who have helped me prepare this chapter, I should like to thank
particularly Lord Annan, Albert Ashforth, Cyril Bibby, Charles S. Blinderman, Sydney Eisen,
Walter E. Houghton, Stephen Koss, Peter Stansky, A. F. Thompson, Samson Ullmann, Martha
S. Vogeler, and Robert M. Young.

I. GENERAL MATERIALS

While students of the Victorian period soon learn about the Death of God and become facile in quoting the appropriate passages from Tennyson, Clough, and Arnold, few of them have read or can comment on the classic texts written by the deicides themselves. Students know all about the prose and verse of those who agonized, but not the works of those who vigorously attacked the citadel of orthodoxy and were anything but infants crying in the night over the dissolution of Urizen. This ignorance produces a gap in their panorama of cultural history which tends to be filled with a gallery of caricatures. One thinks, for example, of Arnold's image of Leslie Stephen at a social science conference, of Frederic Harrison as a young man with a guillotine, of Charles Bradlaugh as a nasty, crude atheist, and Bishop Colenso as a "mere arithmetician." Students will be at the mercy of such images until they read the texts, understand their import, and grasp their historical significance. The situation is not made better by the fact that whereas Jerome H. Buckley in his Goldentree Bibliography *Victorian Poets and Prose Writers* (1966) includes Darwin and Huxley among his individual bibliographies, he omits Frederic Harrison, John Morley, and Leslie Stephen. Likewise, in his provocative essay, "Method in the Study of Victorian Prose" (*VN*, 1956), A. Dwight Culler speaks of "three great ways of life contending with each other" in nineteenth-century England: the Romantic, the Utilitarian, and the Christian-humanist. The classification is suggestive, but surely omits a fourth "way"—that of the non-Christian humanist, the adherents of which often drew on elements from the other three, though in varying degrees, and attracted a significant audience in the second half of the nineteenth century.

One direct way of getting acquainted with the literature of and about Victorian unbelief is simply to read the works that sapped the faith of a number of major figures and that illustrate the particular forms unbelief took. Taking first the pre-Darwinian period, one might begin with two of the books we know helped to produce or confirm George Eliot's loss of faith: Charles C. Hennell's *An Inquiry concerning the Origins of Christianity* (1838) and David Strauss's *Das Leben Jesu* (1835). Reading Strauss in George Eliot's own translation (1846) will give the proper flavor, as will reading her translation of Ludwig Feuerbach's *Essence of Christianity* (1853). Nor should the work of Auguste Comte be neglected; the abridged version of the *Cours de philosophie positive* (1830–42), published by Harriet Martineau in 1853, gives the temper of the lady and the period. Another influential but sometimes neglected text is George Combe's *The Constitution of Man in Relation to External Objects* (1828); "Phrenology," Sir William Hamilton exclaimed, "is implicit atheism."

Bearing in mind the model and influence of Carlyle's *Sartor Resartus*, one might then turn to three stories of deconversion: James Anthony Froude's *Nemesis of Faith* (1849; rpt. 1969), Francis W. Newman's *Phases of Faith, or Passages from the History of My Creed* (1850; rpt. 1969), and Carlyle's own *Life of John Sterling* (1851). To these one might add William Rathbone Greg's *The Creed of Christendom* (1850), a book Fitzjames Stephen later described as one that might have been written by a disciple "who had heard the Sermon on the Mount, whose attention had been called to the miracles, and who had died before the Resurrection." Then there are the scientific works: Charles Lyell's *The Principles of Geology* (3 vols., 1830–33; rpt. 1970); Robert Chambers' *The Vestiges of the Natural History of Creation* (1844), which went through twelve editions by 1884, the first of which is newly edited (1969) from The Centre for Victorian Studies, Leicester, and the extensively revised tenth (1853) newly edited by David Bakan (1970); and finally, of course, *On the Origin of Species* (1859) available in a variety of editions, including a variorum text edited by Morse Peckham (1959). Few even philosophically inclined readers will be anxious to work through J. S. Mill's *System of Logic* (2 vols., 1843), but all should be aware that, as John Morley tells us in his *Recollections* (2 vols., 1917), it became a standard text at Oxford and along with Mill's other works, including *On Liberty* (1859), gave traditional theology little support. Nor did Henry L. Mansel's Bampton Lectures, *The Limits of Religious Thought* (1858), which were intended to defend the faith, but convinced Huxley, among others, that the rational ground for Christian faith had been blown up. This reading period might be concluded with a perusal, first, of a few sample issues of the *Leader* and the *Westminster Review* during the 1850's, keeping an eye out in the former for Herbert Spencer's "The Development Hypothesis" (1852; rpt. in *Essays: Scientific, Political, and Speculative*, 3 vols., 1901), and in the latter for George Eliot's "Evangelical Teaching: Dr. Cummings" (1855); and second, a few issues of the *Oracle of Reason*, edited by Charles Southwell, and its successor, the *Freethinker's Magazine and Review*. A look at George Jacob Holyoake's *Rationalism* (1845) and *The Trial of Theism* (1857) will help to give one the flavor of the militant Secularists.

Post-Darwinian texts are plentiful indeed as the atmosphere of controversy begins to dominate. *Essays and Reviews* (1860; rpt. 1970) together with Frederic Harrison's "Neo-Christianity" (*Westminster Rev.*, 1860; rpt. in *The Creed of a Layman*, 1907) and Bishop Wilberforce's "Essays and Reviews" (*QR*, 1861; rpt. in

Replies to Essays and Reviews, 1862) will bring the student vividly in touch with one of the first violent public controversies. Thomas Henry Huxley's *Man's Place in Nature* (1863) made everything implicit in Darwin explicit, while J. S. Mill's *Examination of Sir William Hamilton's Philosophy* (1865) turned out to be the nemesis of Mansel. For the next fifteen years the pages of the *Fortnightly Review* are crowded with classical texts of unbelief. Here one may find the first printed versions of Huxley's "The Physical Basis of Life" (1869), John Tyndall's assault on J. B. Mozley (1867) and his famous "Belfast Address" (1874), William Kingdon Clifford's "The Unseen Universe" (1875) and "The Ethics of Belief" (1877), some of the corrosive essays by Leslie Stephen collected in *Essays on Freethinking and Plainspeaking* (1873) and in *An Agnostic's Apology* (1893), the separate essays that became John Morley's *On Compromise* (1874), and Frederic Harrison's attack on what he called Fitzjames Stephen's "Religion of Inhumanity" (1873). In 1872, Gladstone selected two English works as special examples of the current "noxious crop" of infidel literature: Herbert Spencer's *First Principles* (1862) and Winwoode Reade's *Martyrdom of Man* (1872), a text still in print and still read. Gladstone might also have mentioned the *Ecce Homo* (1865) by John Seeley, Darwin's *The Descent of Man* (1871), and Edward Tylor's *Primitive Culture* (1871). The Duke of Somerset's *Christian Theology and Modern Scepticism* (1872) and Walter Cassel's *Supernatural Religion* (1874) are works worth setting beside Matthew Arnold's excursions into reformed religion, and a session with several issues of Charles Bradlaugh's *National Reformer* (begun in 1860) will illuminate one of Arnold's bêtes noires.

When the student has completed this course of reading, he will be ready for some comic relief, which he will find in abundance in *The New Republic* (1877) by William Hurrell Mallock, who delighted himself and all his readers with this satirical houseparty novel in which he made fun of several earnest Victorians; it should be read in J. Max Patrick's annotated edition (1950). Having refreshed himself at this fountain of delight, the student can take a deep breath and plunge into the problems of cultural and intellectual history.

Studies in the History of Unbelief

How the Unbelievers made their conquests and attracted their audience is a historical question involving a number of subsidiary questions not susceptible of easy answers even for the expert in historical sociology, the historian of ideas, or the Erik Erikson of Victorian patterns of alienation and revolt. For the earliest historians, the battle was between science and religion in which science is hero and religion villain. Two such histories are Andrew Dickson White's *The Warfare of Science* (1876), later expanded into *A History of the Warfare of Science with Theology in Christendom* (2 vols., 1897; rpt. 1955), and John W. Draper's *The History of the Conflict between Religion and Science* (1875; rpt. 1970); neither of these resembled the dispatches of a detached war correspondent; they were both salvos fired on the battlefield. In his *Genesis and Geology* (1951), Charles C. Gillispie called attention to the German scholar, D. O. Zöckler, who, in his *Geschichte der Beziehung zwischen Theologie und Naturwissenschaft, mit besonder Rücksicht auf Schopfungsgeschichte* (2 vols., 1877–79), took a wider view and attacked the White-Draper thesis explicitly.

Though clearly sympathetic to the cause of rationalism, two twentieth-century historians—Alfred William Benn and John Mackinnon Robertson—also take a wider perspective.

Benn (*The History of Rationalism in the Nineteenth Century*, 2 vols., 1906; rpt. 1966) claimed that his subject had never been "treated before as a whole" and proceeded to cast his net as widely as his definition of Rationalism would permit, so widely in fact that he was able to include Browning. His definition of Rationalism ("the mental habit of using reason for the destruction of religious belief") is not entirely satisfactory and is not always systematically employed. His book is a blend of intellectual history and the exposition of the ideas of individuals, with comments on the effect of political events thrown in from time to time. Somewhat defective in its lack of a modern perspective, in its slighting of the role of the Secularists, and in an inadequate rationale for the sequence of chapters, especially in the second volume, Benn's history is nonetheless a compendious, informative, and entertaining account of persons, controversies, and tendencies, sprinkled with enough suggestive and dubious generalizations to set off a dozen doctoral dissertations, and equipped with a bibliography long enough to keep a reader busy for years. Though Robertson (*A History of Free Thought in the Nineteenth Century*, 2 vols., 1929) covers much the same ground, he includes sections on developments in Continental thought and pays far more attention than Benn to the work of Holyoake, Bradlaugh, and other Secularists. In fact, while respectful of Benn, he inveighs against what he considers to be the latter's tendency to overpraise the respectable middle-class freethinkers; in Robertson's view, Bradlaugh put the case against orthodoxy more effectively than the Huxleys and the Stephens and at greater personal cost. Though narrow and often dogmatic in his judgments, Robertson peoples his volumes with a host of now-forgotten names of men and women who talked out their lives on street corners and lists a whole range of publications, most of them short-lived, that form a body of primary materials for any historian of nineteenth-century unbelief. While omitting a formal bibliography, he provides extensive documentation, some of it based on his personal involvement in the movement and friendship with its leaders.

From these two works emerges a judgment on the causes, the course, and the nature of the movement as a whole. As for the causes, both emphasize science and the higher criticism of the Bible, Benn the relativism induced by the historical method, and Robertson the increasing dissatisfaction with the Christian ethic as expounded by the church. Both chart the course of the movement through ebbs and flows of controversy up through the sixties, asserting the seventies as the decade when the tide turned against the orthodox faith, philosophically, politically, and socially. Robertson in particular makes us aware of the fight conducted by the Secularists throughout the century, a movement that preceded and then paralleled the action led by men who were of the establishment.

This parallel movement is the central theme of Noël Annan's "The Strands of Unbelief" (*Ideas and Beliefs of the Victorians*, ed. Harman Grisewood, 1949). Students of the strand of radical Secularism will find themselves in a complicated study of the interactions among Secularists, Owenites, trade unionists, birth-controllers, and the rank-and-file members. The Secularist periodicals such as the *Oracle of Reason*, the *Freethinker's Magazine and Review*, and the *National Reformer* become required reading in conjunction with such works as Richard D. Altick's *The English Common Reader: A Social History of the Mass Reading Public, 1800–1900* (1957) and, even more pertinent, Robert K. Webb's *English Working Class Reader, 1790–1848* (1955), not to mention the work of such labor historians as the Webbs and E. P. Thompson. The student will also find that until very recently little has been done to bring up to date our understanding of the work of the principal agitators; there is no published full-length study of G. J. Holyoake subsequent to Joseph McCabe's *Life and Letters* (2 vols., 1908). Charles Bradlaugh, whose life was written by his daughter in collaboration with J. M. Robertson (1895) and by Robertson in 1921, has been restudied by David Tribe, President of the National Secular Society, in *President Charles Bradlaugh, MP* (1971). One of the most colorful of the Secularists, Annie Besant, has been given full and lively treatment in Arthur H. Nethercot's *The First Five Lives of Annie Besant* (1960), which deals with her career as Bradlaugh's colleague, as a socialist, and her eventual movement into the arms of Madame Blavatsky.

There are three surveys of the Secular movement: *A Chronology of British Secularism* by G. H. Taylor (1957) is a handy pamphlet obtainable from the National Secular Society; John Edwin McGee's *History of the British Secularist Movement* (1948), though difficult to locate, is competent and thorough, with only minor errors; David Tribe's *A Hundred Years of Free Thought* (1967) is an intelligent account of the movement since 1866, based on primary materials and equipped with a useful but selective bibliography. These three texts will give the student the fundamental historical data.

For short, challenging, and interpretive studies, one may turn to two articles, one by a sociologist, the other by a historian. "The Rise of Organized Free Thought in Mid-Victorian England" (*Sociological Rev.*, 1954) by John Eros is an interesting attempt to apply the categories of Max Weber in judging the "social role of irreligion" and "its close association with mid-Victorian social and political conflicts." Tracing the rise of the movement intellectually to the tradition of Thomas Paine and socially to the political and economic dissatisfaction of the underprivileged, Eros credits Holyoake and Bradlaugh with "reassembling the scattered hosts of Owenites and Chartists and of leading them under the flag of free thought . . . towards cooperation with middle-class radicals" in order to democratize English politics and achieve a republic; he notes the moderation of the leaders and concludes that since they could not create the image of a new community or evoke the messianic power of socialism, the historic function of the Secularists was transitory; "unable to satisfy the moral and the material needs of the fourth estate," they helped "prepare the soil for the socialist creed." Eros concludes further that comparative studies of organized infidelity in various countries will help us to understand its social role. The historian F. B. Smith, in "The Atheist Mission, 1840–1900" (*Ideas and Institutions of Victorian Britain*, ed. Robert Robson, 1967), is more concerned to give us data, graph the historical curve, estimate the Secularists' influence, and determine the reasons for its ultimate diminution. Two notable emphases emerge: one, on the way in which persecution and prosecution drove them into militant atheism and political action, especially in agitation against church control of education and in the creation of rival schools, libraries, and magazines; the other, on the way in which the high moral tone of Holyoake and other earnest atheists estranged them from many working people, who enjoyed the exposure of salacious stories in the Bible and tales of orgies in convents, but had little ear for the gospel of duty and self-help, or for concerts of Handel and Haydn at which they were forbidden to smoke. Smith also points to the factiousness that constantly led to quarrels among the leaders and disunity in their program—some were socialist minded, others not; some favored birth control, others not; some temperance, some not. Finally, Smith believes, the movement lost power as the church made concessions; the intellectual agnostics breached the forts of orthodoxy and moved into controlling positions with the formation of the Rationalist Press Association in 1899 (see A. Gowans White, *The Story of the R. P. A., 1899–1949*, 1949).

That the organized Secularists were not the only dissenters from orthodoxy is made clear in *The London Heretics, 1870–1914* (1967) by Warren Sylvester Smith, who while not invalidating Annan's two-strand approach to the forces of unbelief certainly complicates it by relating Secularism to a number of other threads of heresy. Though marred by a number of minor errors of fact, Smith's book is entertainingly written, informative, and illuminated by significant generalizations. Beginning by reminding us of the climate of doubt and poverty in the 1870's and thus supporting the claim of those who see economic distress and unbelief as closely connected, he sets forth three major groups of heretics: Non-Christians, New Christians, and Independent Seekers. Paying almost no attention to such notables as Huxley, he treats, among the first group, the Secularists, the Positivists, the Free Thought Congregations, and the lunatic fringe of spiritualists and theosophists; among the second, such figures as the rebel Anglican Stewart Headlam, Joseph Parker, the Quakers, and the Unitarians; and among the third, men like William Thomas Stead, Bernard Shaw, and Wilfrid S. Blunt, whose *My Diaries* (2 vols., 1919–20), along with Beatrice Webb's *My Apprenticeship* (1926), Edward Clodd's *Memories* (1926), and Moncure Conway's *Autobiography* (2 vols., 1904), comprise a group of volumes of reminiscence throwing light on what it was like to be involved in late Victorian upheavals of thought and faith. Such works and a number of others listed in Smith's bibliography, including *Heterodox London* (2 vols., 1874; rpt. 1971) by C. M. Davies, an excellent reporter of what he saw and heard, provide a strong basis in primary sources for the liveliness of Smith's book.

Voluminous accounts of primary and other sources for the study of English Secularism may be found in the bibliographies of four recent doctoral dissertations: "British Rational Secularism: Unbelief from Bradlaugh to the Mid-Twentieth Century" (Washington 1963) by Walter David Nelson; "G. J. Holyoake and the Secularist Movement in Britain, 1841–1861" (Cambridge 1968) by Edward Royle; "The British Secularist Movement: 1860–1966" (Oxford 1968) by Susan Budd; and "G. J. Holyoake: A Study in the Progress of Labor and the British Reform Tradition" (Chicago 1970) by Lee F. Grugel. Royle's work takes a fresh look at the period of Holyoake's leadership, based on, among other materials, the Holyoake collections at the Cooperative Union Library, Manchester, and at the Bishopsgate Institute (now in a microfilm version together with an index prepared by Royle in 1969). Though Royle is primarily concerned with the political significance of Holyoake and his movement, he is also sensitive to the intellectual elements that produced its ideology and is fully aware of the variety of causes that led to unbelief. Apart from the familiar causes, such as historical criticism and science, he notes that the Bible itself—its inconsistencies, its indecencies, and its objectionable ethos—as well as the work in comparative religion led many true believers out of the ecclesiastical household into rationalism, non-Christian theism, or free thought. In his handling of the political history of the movement, he fills in countless details of the story Smith can only summarize and brings to our attention the relationships that Holyoake established with Mill, Francis Newman, George Henry Lewes, as well as with dissenters, in his campaign for reforms in the secular sphere. Royle's study concludes with five useful appendices, some designed to establish data concerning the extent and occupational makeup of the Secularists, one a useful collection of thumbnail sketches of the principal participants, and a dictionary of pseudonyms. Grugel's work is primarily biographical in emphasis.

The dissertations by Nelson and Budd cover the same ground, the history of the Secularist movement from the 1860's, but in radically different ways. Nelson's work is a prodigious affair, crammed with data and sprinkled with challenging remarks, but lacking focus and a consistent methodology. That the study of such a movement as Secularism has its methodological problems is starkly revealed in Budd's introductory chapter as she points out that "the humanist movement cannot successfully be fitted into the sociological analysis of religious movements. Rather it can be seen as an eddy between the two main streams of religious and sociopolitical bodies." Her central concern is to examine the organizational forms that grew out of the ideological commitment of the National Secular Society, the Ethical Union, and the Rationalist Press Association as well as the characteristic membership and activity of each. She notes that when the N.S.S. could mount a campaign of social and political reform in addition to its atheistic propaganda, it achieved relative success; mere "Bible-bashing" was not enough and became a bore, especially after the churches made their accommodations to science and higher criticism. Like John Eros, Budd sees the movement as a halfway house for dissidents on their way into radical politics and economics; as Bradlaugh became openly antisocialistic, as the socialist movement itself gathered strength, and as the churches became less identified with the status quo, the dissidents either left the N.S.S. to join the socialistic groups or, if they were Christian already, could join the socialists without going through the stage of unbelief. One of Budd's more interesting chapters has already been published under the title "The Loss of Faith: Reasons for Unbelief among Members of the Secular Movement, 1850–1950" (P&P, 1967). After reading 150 "deconversion ̉xperiences" and 200 briefer biographical sketches, she found that the two books most influential in producing unbelief were Paine's *Age of Reason* and the Bible; only two of her subjects had read Darwin or Huxley before losing their faith and only one had read Strauss; the chief experience productive of doubt was resentment of the resistance of the Church and its ministers to social improvement. This important article suggests the generally high quality of her dissertation now being revised for publication. Shortly, therefore, Victorian scholars will have before them genuine contributions to an understanding of the Secularist movement, works that will need to be taken together with the important studies of insurgent movements such as Eric Hobsbawm's *Primitive Rebels* (1958) and John F. C. Harrison's *Robert Owen and the Owenites* (1969). What has not been done with the Secularists is to consider to what extent, if any, their writings have literary value. Sectarian, polemical prose is admittedly ephemeral; too often it stings and dies. Too often also we may assume that the "wicked" write badly; perhaps someone should have a look at the prose of George W. Foote, Edward Aveling, Annie Besant, Bradlaugh, and W. S. Ross ("Saladin") at their best and bring in a report.

Of the other strand of unbelief, that of the educated middle class, there is no comprehensive treatment, possibly for the good reason that it was not organized. There have been a few group studies of the individuals involved. One thinks of Janet Courtney's *Freethinkers of the Nineteenth Century* (1920) which presents portraits of Arnold, Bradlaugh, Huxley, Stephen, Harriet Martineau, and includes, curiously enough, John Frederick Denison Maurice and Charles Kingsley, while omitting John Morley and Frederic Harrison because they were still alive. One also thinks of Basil Willey's two volumes, *Nineteenth Century Studies* (1949) and *More Nineteenth Century Studies: A Group of Honest Doubters* (1956), with which most students of Victorian literature are familiar, and the more recent book by A. O. J. Cockshut, *The Unbelievers: English Agnostic Thought, 1840–1890* (1964), which, like Willey's, is not a history but a study of single figures. Though neither is concerned to unearth new materials, Willey is the more thorough expositor while Cockshut, though occasionally perceptive, tends to be impressionistic and sometimes superficial.

More scholarly fare will be found in Alan Willard Brown's *The Metaphysical Society: Victorian Minds in Crisis, 1869–1880* (1947). To Brown were available the papers and minutes of this remarkable society, organized by James Knowles, in which freethinker and churchman debated the philosophical and theological problems that lay before the age. Since many of the papers read before the Society were published in *Contemporary Review* and in *Nineteenth Century* and since Brown has presented us with sketches of each member and with detailed accounts of meetings, we have here indeed a most intimate account of a remarkable chapter in intellectual history. Among his many insights, Brown laid to rest forever any notion that the rationalists and the scientists (the classification is his) formed a solid front: "the personal disagreements among the opponents of theism were even greater than among the Churchmen." This fact did not diminish the influence of the infidels, however, for one of the results of the meetings of the Society was to convince the theists "that the days of theological and ecclesiastical influence over the minds of 'free spirits' had already drawn to a close." What Brown shows is that the Society and its journalistic counterpart, *Nineteenth Century*, provided a forum in which the new thought of the seventies and eighties, both in its philosophical and political form, gained a wide and, if anything, a too respectable audience. In Brown's study we see the strands of unbelief entwined and their colors blurred.

The most recent and the most systematic attempt to deal with the characteristic thought of the principal agnostics is to be found in an article by D. W. Dockrill on "The Origin and Development of Nineteenth Century English Agnosticism" (*Hist. J.*, Univ. of Newcastle, New South Wales, 1971). Beginning by showing why the term Agnosticism became necessary to distinguish the thought of Huxley, Spencer, Stephen, and others from Comtean Positivism and Mill's empiricism, Dockrill goes on to display in cogent detail the positions developed by the major agnostics vis-à-vis theology, epistemology, science, and ethics. He also sets forth the positions of their opponents. His command of the literature is thorough, his notes are sprinkled with references others will wish to follow up, and his sensitivity to the philosophic problems encountered by the agnostics is acute. His article is the most succinct presentation we have of agnostic thought treated from a purely philosophic point of view.

The agnostics, however, were not only philosophers. Their objectives were also political and social, and they made no bones about it, as anyone can see who glances through the pages of the *Fortnightly Review*, the most militant of middle-class rationalist periodicals of the post-Darwinian period. Students are fortunate indeed to have at hand a thorough and intelligent treatment of its contributors, policies, and contents in Edwin Mallard Everett's *The Party of Humanity: The Fortnightly Review and Its Contributors, 1865–1874* (1939). Everett's book impresses one with the fact that respectable publishers were willing to sponsor a periodical so outspoken in its rationalism, in its attack on the Church, and in its support of the labor movement and Radical politics, both at home and abroad. The evidence also led Everett to the important conclusion, one that needs further examination, that the rationalist assaults were based "not always so much upon new scientific concepts as upon the almost unanimous liberal dissatisfaction with the part played by the nineteenth-century Church." Since, as Everett remarks, the *Fortnightly Review* reached "its highest pitch of radicalism" between 1874 and 1880, an opportunity is open for someone to produce a sequel. The *Fortnightly Review* in its sphere was quite as important as the *Nineteenth Century* in its, and a careful study of its most radical period is certainly in order, as is one of Bradlaugh's *National Reformer*.

The work of Everett makes it difficult to accept Noël Annan's assertion in his *Leslie Stephen* (1951) that English "middle class rationalists were . . . political quietists." Otherwise, however, Annan's two chapters, "Evangelicalism" and "Cambridge Rationalism," brilliantly expound the nature of these two forces and present them, not as strands of unbelief, but as strands of influence that determined the character of unbelief, not only in Stephen but in other Unbelievers of similar background, tending to make them, in Annan's words, "a new nonconformist sect." It was important to be moral, to show that unbelief did not produce ethical anarchy, but being moral also demanded that one believe only what was demonstrable and that one act virtuously in order to be virtuous, not to avoid a hell or buy a heaven. This emphasis on the moral objections to the Christian faith as a motive in producing unbelief among the intelligentsia is also brought to the fore in Howard R. Murphy's "The Ethical Revolt against Christian Orthodoxy in Early Victorian England" (*AHR*, 1955). Complaining that "the factors usually cited in explanation of the decline of nineteenth-century orthodoxy are the rise of the concept of evolution . . . and of the 'higher criticism' in Biblical scholarship," he advances the thesis that the revolt against orthodoxy before Darwin "was generated by a sensed incongruity between a vigorous and hopeful meliorism and the doctrinal legacy of the Christian tradition." By examining the personal histories of George Eliot, J. A. Froude, and F. W. Newman, he shows that the basis of their alienation was not so much their feeling that Christianity was untrue, but that it was wicked. The higher criticism and the idea of evolution only reinforced the argument for the abolition of Christianity. Though Murphy's thesis was not as new as he implied (see Robertson), his article was a forceful reminder of what had become neglected, and was therefore greeted with some critical acclaim. While confirmed by Susan Budd's article (*P&P*, 1967) for the Secularists, his thesis has not produced the studies it should have stimulated, however, for it is significant enough to be tested further and developed in a related direction. His term "meliorism" carries with it not only ethical but political implications which suggest, and which varied sources of evidence tend to support, that the revulsion against orthodoxy among the middle class as well as among workers needs to be seen as an aspect of political and social insurgency. Charles Kingsley's abuse of the Church for using the "Bible as if it were a mere special constable's handbook—an opium-dose for keeping beasts of burden patient" and John Morley's angry charge that the Church was not one "of the nation but the Church of a class. . . . She is as inveterate a foe to new social hope as we know her to be to a new scientific truth" echo each other across the Darwinian divide. Justin McCarthy's *Reminiscences* (2 vols., 1899) and A. W. Benn's *Modern England* (1908) give vivid personal testimony, confirmed by such later scholars as Royden

Harrison (*Before the Socialists*, 1965), Budd, and Royle, that the history of unbelief cannot be separated from an analysis of social and economic discontents.

Meanwhile, the historians of science have been busy, especially so in the years encompassing the centenary of the publication of *On the Origin of Species*; thus 1959 brought forth a spate of volumes, conferences, commemorations, and Darwinian convocations. (I have made no attempt to give an account of the vast Darwinian bibliography. Students might well begin with Jerome H. Buckley's section on Darwin in his Goldentree Bibliography, *Victorian Poets and Prose Writers*, 1966, and consult the bibliographies of such works as Gertrude Himmelfarb's *Darwin and the Darwinian Revolution*, 1959 and annual bibliographies in *VS* in recent years.) The aim here is to sort out those works that either revise our notions of the warfare between science and religion or throw light on the history of unbelief. One such work has already been mentioned, C. C. Gillispie's *Genesis and Geology: A Study in the Relations of Scientific Thought, Natural Theology, and Social Opinion in Great Britain, 1790–1850* (1951; paperback, 1958). Gillispie has produced a searching and original work, equipped with a voluminous bibliography, which successfully defends the thesis that the development of the evolutionary hypothesis was obstructed less by theology from without the scientific community than by the religious conceptions imbedded within it. Of equal importance is the evidence he finds to assert that the scientists themselves feared the social consequences of evolutionary conceptions; their social and ethical predilections made them feel that "the stability of society not only depended upon, but was justified by, the direct and immediate attention of a Providence whose arrangements could be empirically demonstrated in the physical universe." The book is a landmark in its precision and its sense of the interaction between scientist, theologian, and society.

At the end of the last century Josiah Royce remarked that "with the exception of Newton's 'Principia' no single book of empirical science has ever been of more importance to philosophy than this work of Darwin" (*The Spirit of Modern Philosophy*, 1892). What that importance was to philosophy and theology has been dealt with in general terms by George G. Simpson in *The Meaning of Evolution* (1951), by Rudolf Metz in *A Hundred Years of British Philosophy* (1938), and by John Passmore in his *A Hundred Years of Philosophy* (1957), and more specifically in a number of the works on Darwin published on or near the centenary year, several of which, together with other useful Darwinian materials, may be found in the admirable Norton Critical Edition, *Darwin*, edited by Philip Appleman (1970). Of particular interest because of its point of view is "Darwin's Impact on Philosophy" by James Collins, in the volume *Darwin's Vision and Christian Perspectives* (ed. Walter J. Ong, 1960), a collection that could be fruitfully juxtaposed to David Lack's able *Evolutionary Theory and Christian Belief* (1957). Collins makes the point that whereas it is usually said that Darwin destroyed the argument from design, in fact Darwin destroyed only one form of that argument, the argument from final causes. More concerned with Darwin's impact "upon such diverse tendencies as agnosticism, naturalism, and idealism" is Passmore's "Darwin and Metaphysics" (*VS*, 1959), a cautious and scholarly survey, especially useful for its observations of "Darwin's influence . . . in those who fought against his teachings as in those who fully accepted them" and for its awareness of Continental perspectives. For a study of Darwin's reception by the public and the press Alvar Ellegård's *Darwin and the General Reader* (1958) should be consulted as well as his "Public Opinion and the Press: Reactions to Darwinism" (*JHI*, 1958), both of which will give some precision to generalizations about Darwin's impact. Of equal importance is Robert M. Young's "Non-Scientific Factors in the Darwinian Debate" in *Actes du XIII Congrès International d'Histoire des Sciences* (1968). Of particular significance is Young's "The Impact of Darwin on Conventional Thought," in *The Victorian Crisis of Faith* (ed. Anthony Symondson, 1970).

Darwin's impact on the field of ethics has been a more controversial issue. During the conflicts of the 1870's, Goldwin Smith remarked that "the dogmas [were] remaining with the orthodox, the ethics often going to the infidel," and all are now familiar with George Eliot's encounter with F. W. H. Myers in which she announced that God was inconceivable, Immortality unbelievable, and Duty peremptory and absolute. To Unbelievers of like temper the idea that "if God did not exist everything was permissible" would have seemed to be arrant nonsense. While comment on work dealing with the ethical theories of the principal Unbelievers will appear below, it should be noted that there has been a continuing debate over what the Unbelievers actually said about the grounds for ethical choice and over the viability of an evolutionary ethic. William F. Quillian's *The Moral Theory of Evolutionary Naturalism* (1945) has its uses as does Sir Arthur Keith's *Evolution and Ethics* (1946); both are challenged, in part on grounds of inaccuracy, by Julian Huxley in *Touchstones of Ethics* (1949) and by George G. Simpson in Part III of his *The Meaning of Evolution* (1951). David Lack's *Evolutionary Theory and Christian Belief* (1957), especially Chapters ix and x, offers a knowledgeable and reasoned presentation of the issues, in both historical and contemporary terms. Both Simpson and Lack provide documentation and references useful to the student who wishes to read further. A briefer but perhaps more incisive analysis of the issues raised by Darwin and Huxley can be found in "Darwinism and Ethics" by D. Daiches Raphael in *A Century of Darwinism* (ed. Samuel A. Barnett, 1958). The Dockrill article cited above is also pertinent.

It has been argued by A. W. Benn in the last chapter of his *History of Rationalism*, John Morley in his *Recollections*, Vol. I, G. M. Young in his *Victorian England* (1936), and by others that one of the strongest dissolvents of orthodoxy was the development of evolutionary theories of social change. While the defenders of the forerunners of Darwin have been refuted in one sense, they have performed the service of showing the extent to which the notion of historical development was in the air before Darwin and thus strengthened one link in the argument that theories of change were implicitly hostile to Christian theories of history. The idea of the mutability of ideas and institutions preceded the idea of the mutability of species. The importance of this dissolvent of belief is highlighted in Annan's essay, "Science, Religion, and the Critical Mind" (*1859: Entering an Age of Crisis*, ed. Philip Appleman, William A. Madden, and Michael Wolff, 1959). In drawing attention to the growth of historical theory and technique and in particular to the impetus Darwin gave to the study of origins, Annan suggests that such studies led Victorians to find the origin of religion in less than edifying modes of thought—primitive delusions—and to explore cultures that seemed more attractive than their own and that produced ethical ideals superior to those of Christianity. Annan thus distills the inferences to be made from an examination of nineteenth-century historiography. Whether history was written by a member of the rationalist-utilitarian school as exemplified by Mill, Grote, and Buckle, or by a disciple of Comte, or by the liberal Anglicans (see Duncan Forbes, *The Liberal Anglican Idea of History*, 1952), the results were not hospitable to orthodoxy. If the first saw history as a struggle for the liberation of reason from superstition, the second saw it as the inevitable working out of stages, and the third saw it as a gradual unfolding of God's purpose, all assumed a process of mutability, an assumption that the rationalist used against Christianity and the liberal Anglican as a justification for modernizing his theology. Whether Darwin made a significant contribution to this historical perspective has been debated: Leslie Stephen in his assessment of Buckle (*FortR*, 1880) and later in *The English Utilitarians* (1900) argued that Darwin provided the ecological approach (as it has been lately called) for lack of which both Comte and Buckle were unable to develop adequate theories of history. John W. Burrow, however, in his *Evolution and Society: A Study in Victorian Social Theory* (1966), makes a strong case, also presented in Irving Goldman's "Evolution and Anthropology" (*VS*, 1959), that pre-Darwinian social theory was already heavily "evolutionary" and that Darwin's work was not a watershed in the development of social theory. Burrow's work is important not only for the challenge of its initial proposition, but for its able exposition of the "tension between positivism and the romantic reading of history," for its chapters on Herbert Spencer, Tylor, McLennan, and others, as well as for its bibliography. While neither Goldman's article nor Burrow's longer study is designed to uncover sources of unbelief, both can be used to illuminate the sociological and anthropological dimensions of a historical method which made Providential theories of history difficult to sustain. Moreover, as Morse Peckham reminds us (*Victorian Revolutionaries*, 1970), the work of Tylor in examining primitive religion could be extrapolated to undermine contemporary Christianity.

Further study of the theories of history espoused by the post-Millite Unbelievers is thus indicated; theories of history are theories of change and the Unbelievers wanted change. If one believed with Mill or Comte that social change was produced by ideas, one might then emphasize the idea of an elite educating the mass toward innovation—and not too fast; if one believed with the Marxists that ideas were the by-products of social change, one might then emphasize the primacy of mass social action. Just where did the Unbelievers stand on these issues and what is the relation of their social action to their theories and to their positions in society? The questions need attention, though they are partially addressed by Granville Hicks in *Figures in Transition* (1939). Finally, it is important to emphasize that, as Robert Young put it in the essay mentioned above, "the impact usually associated with Darwin, Spencer, Wallace, Huxley, *Essays and Reviews*, and John Tyndall, was part of a larger movement embracing a number of naturalistic approaches to the earth, life, and man in utilitarianism, in population theory, in geology, phrenology, psychology, and in theology itself."

Rows: Gentlemanly and Otherwise

The history of the struggle between Believers and Unbelievers is dotted with its share of dramatic incidents which have often been treated as historical and biographical narrative and sometimes as foci for the analysis of forces and issues. The biographical sections of Gertrude Himmelfarb's *Darwin and the Darwinian Revolution* (1959) and almost all of William Irvine's *Apes, Angels and Victorians* (1955) illustrate this approach by covering the major controversies in which Darwin and Huxley found themselves, including the famous meeting of the British Association in which Huxley found himself pitted against Bishop Wilberforce. Shortly after this celebrated event came the uproar over *Essays and Reviews* (1860). Told by such older writers as Benn and Robertson (*The Dynamics of Religion*, 2nd ed., 1926), the tale has been repeated, with additions of fact and insight, by Basil Willey (*More Nineteenth Century Studies*, 1956), by Geoffrey Faber in his *Jowett* (1957), by Anthony O. J. Cockshut in *Anglican Attitudes: A Study in Victorian Religious Controversies* (1959), and most recently by Stephen Paul Booth in "*Essays and Reviews*: The Controversy as Seen in the Correspondence of Dr. E. B. Pusey and Archbishop Archibald Tait" (*HMPEC*, 1969), an article that reveals the deep personal bitterness engendered by the whole affair. These writers approach the event and its significance from their separate interests and thus stress different elements in the case. There are, however, sources of information still untapped—unpublished letters, for example—so that we do not yet have the whole story. Both Benn and Robertson also recount *l'affaire* Colenso stirred up by his *Critical Examination of the Pentateuch* (1862), another ecclesiastical debacle that roused the emotions of the conservative and religious clergy alike and disgusted the Unbelievers. Cockshut treats the episode as a crisis in authority—still unresolved. A more detailed study, both of the event and of Bishop Colenso himself, is available in Peter Hinchliff's *John W. Colenso: Bishop of Natal* (1964). An interesting and provocative survey of all these episodes will be found in the first three chapters of Owen Chadwick's *The Victorian Church: An Ecclesiastical History of England*, II (1970). Chadwick is not convinced that the real quarrel was between science and religion; his point of view provides a tonic contrast to such rationalist historians as Benn and Robertson.

"The Jamaica massacre made a political agitator of Herbert Spencer"—so wrote Justin McCarthy, and it was Spencer himself who observed in his *Autobiography* (2 vols., 1908) that on the committee to prosecute Governor Eyre "the evolutionists, considering their small number, contributed a far larger proportion . . . than any other class." Only Tyndall, in fact, of the leading evolutionary propagandists, joined Carlyle, Tennyson, and Froude in defense of Eyre, an action that strained his friendship with Huxley almost to the breaking point. The connections between ideology and politics come to the fore in this affair, as can be seen in George H. Ford's article, "The Governor Eyre Case in England" (*UTQ*, 1948) and in Bernard Semmel's *Jamaica Blood and Victorian Conscience* (1963; published in England, 1962, under the less gaudy title, *The Governor Eyre Controversy*). Though W. L. Burn complains (*VS*, 1964) that Semmel failed to consult Colonial Office records and the papers of Fitzjames Stephen at Cambridge, the student interested primarily in the reactions and activities of the leaders of both committees will find them presented in detail and, further, will find no reason to dissent from Benn's earlier judgment (*Modern England*, 1908) that "on the whole the division of opinion corresponded to the division on the American [Civil] War, and, like that, indicated a conflict between two ideals of society—more than that, between two different theories of the world."

Fifteen years later, in 1880, Charles Bradlaugh, elected to Parliament by Northampton, made life complicated for everyone by attempting to affirm his allegiance instead of taking the oath requiring him to evoke the deity. Speaker Brand made the mistake of throwing the question to the Commons, who proceeded to kick the issue back and forth until Speaker Peel finally settled the question in 1886. As Walter J. Arnstein has shown in his detailed examination of the behavior of bigoted and hypocritical Whigs and Tories and of fearful Liberals, the case for Mill's *On Liberty* had hardly weakened in thirty years (*The Bradlaugh Case: A Study in Late*

Victorian Opinion and Politics, 1965). On this occasion, the Unbelievers presented no solid phalanx of vocal support: both Huxley and Frederic Harrison remained silent, and Morley took the oath when he entered the House in 1883; those who gave forthright, public support included Leslie Stephen, Moncure Conway, the *Westminster Review*, the Unitarians, Jews, Dissenters, and liberal Anglicans like Stewart Headlam. Another test of the Unbelievers' principles arose when they were called upon to petition the Home Office to reduce the sentence of G. W. Foote, the editor of the *Freethinker* imprisoned for blasphemy in 1883 (see *Verbatim Report of the Two Trials of Foote . . . 1883, 86*; rpt. 1971). At his trials, Foote read aloud passages from Arnold, Huxley, Mill, Spencer, Leslie Stephen, Morley, Swinburne, and James Thomson, implying that if he were being tried for blasphemy, why not they? It was Gladstone's view that the exclusion of Bradlaugh and the harassment of Bradlaugh and Foote discredited Christians and served the cause of atheism. Accounts of these episodes and others like them illuminate the attitudes and behavior of the Unbelievers in times of stress; they also suggest that we might learn more about the Unbelievers if we examined their positions, comparatively, on such touchstone issues as Irish Home Rule, the Boer War, woman suffrage, the Franco-Prussian War, the Paris Commune, and the major episodes in England's advancing imperialism.

There are also the controversies among the Unbelievers themselves to be considered. That these differences of opinion on philosophical issues can be fruitfully studied has been clearly demonstrated by Sydney Eisen. In a series of articles (which will be taken up in their appropriate positions below) he has followed up the hint from Alan Brown that there was more agreement among the Unbelievers about what they did not believe than about what they did. They also quarreled. Eisen is now preparing a book, based in part upon his articles, on the varieties of Unbelief in late Victorian England, which will deal with such men as Spencer, Clifford, Tyndall, Harrison, Leslie Stephen, and Huxley, a book which will be the first major effort in many years to cover these figures as a complete group.

Topics for Further Study

The books and articles discussed so far have shed light on the causes, course, and nature of unbelief in the nineteenth century. While scholars have reinforced the notion that unbelief arose from developments in science, especially from the work of Darwin, and from the development of Biblical criticism, the notion has been given substance that moral and political motivations form a powerful ingredient of the mixture that gave Victorians theological indigestion; moreover, the theory that the rise of the historic way of looking at things, both before and after Darwin, tended to make Christianity seem to be a transient set of doctrines has been developed and explored in greater depth than before. That there are social and psychological forces at work below, in, and among these four causes may be taken for granted, but just what these forces are and how they worked has not really been set forth; the difficulties involved are ably stated by Morse Peckham in "Darwin and Darwinisticism" (*VS*, 1959), an essay that is also suggestive of other problems for study. The fact that new biographies are being written and that manuscript sources hitherto unavailable are now open to inspection or being prepared for publication enlarges the opportunity for research and scholarship in these areas.

Such resources also make possible further study of the actual course of unbelief and the forces that facilitated or hindered its development. We need, for example, to know more about the relationships, covert or open, among Secularists, Positivists, and middle-class agnostics; we need to know the extent of private unbelief and the specific reasons why it remained private rather than public. We also need to determine the extent to which the militant rationalists of the seventies collaborated in planning the strategy and tactics of their crusade against the faith; there is some evidence that they did. Were there also strategy sessions among the faithful? We do know that Huxley was skillful at securing strategic posts for key people; to what extent was the deliberate positioning of persons part of the whole campaign? The possibility of exploring these questions has recently been enhanced by the discovery of the Minute Books of the famous "X Club," now accessible on microfilm at the Royal Institution of Great Britain. Basing his conclusions on this new material, J. Vernon Jensen has published two articles, "The X Club: Fraternity of Victorian Scientists" (*Brit. J. for the Hist. of Sci.*, 1970) and "Interrelationships within the Victorian X-Club" (*DR*, 1971). Among other conclusions, he shows the extent to which the X Club was an organized caucus to defend science against hostile theologians and even to attack Gladstone's Irish policy.

Thanks to Noël Annan, we have a vivid image of the nature and quality of Stephen's unbelief, and to the extent that Annan uses the comparative method we see into the faith of other Unbelievers, but new comparative studies will give us more insight into the lives and ideas of the principal actors in the drama and provide a basis for judging their effectiveness and relevance for their own and our times. Much might be learned by examining the Unbelievers' responses to key figures from the past and in their own times. As John Lucas has demonstrated ("Tilting at the Moderns," *Ren. and Mod. Stud.*, 1966), Voltaire is one such figure; other candidates might be Burke, Goethe, Hume, and Rousseau, to name a few. In their own time, Matthew Arnold was a figure none of the Unbelievers could avoid, or Carlyle, or Mill, or Ruskin, not to mention Arthur J. Balfour with whom Huxley, Stephen, and Harrison crossed swords. At least two major comparative studies in a larger dimension also suggest themselves. Has anyone really attempted to compare the infidels of the Romantic period with those of the post-Darwinian period? Has anyone attempted to consider the differences and similarities between the Victorian non-Christian humanists with those of our own day, both in and outside the Christian faith, with, for example, Milan Machovec, the Czechoslovakian leader from the side of atheism in the current Christian-Marxist dialogue, Ernst Bloch, or Roger Garaudy?

Perhaps the most revealing studies, however, would be examinations of the prose style of the Unbelievers. This chapter began with a reference to A. Dwight Culler's "Method in the Study of Victorian Prose" (*VN*, 1956), an essay that argues that each of "the three great ways of life" contending for mastery in the nineteenth century produced "a characteristic mode of expression." "The Utilitarian, the way of science," Culler wrote, "does not create an inner world of meaning but analyzes and describes an external world which is given, and thus its characteristic mode of expression is scientific prose." Ultimately, he went on to say, the utilitarians "speak not through symbols at all but through the practical activities whereby they changed the face of England in the 19th century." Thus for Culler the utilitarian-scientists became for the nineteenth century what the Romans became for Shelley—the poets of institutions. Objection has already been raised that the classification is incomplete, but there are two others to be made. First, modern analysts of language have reminded us that even the most referential prose may embody emotive and subjective elements and, moreover, that it is not only by words and images that emotive elements are carried, but also by sentence pattern, rhythm, and other structural elements. Second, Ways of Life do not write books; individuals do—however much they may be influenced by a Way of Life. What is required is not deductive constructs, but estimates of the extent to which the non-Christian humanists, or Unbelievers, wrote memorable prose, estimates based on empirical examinations of their texts by those techniques, both traditional and novel, which we have come to find most rewarding in literary criticism. We may then discover that it was not only the Christian humanists who "created a form of discourse which bears in all its lineaments both the pressure of reality and the pressure of an individual soul" (Culler).

Some of the problems involved in analyzing scientific-philosophical prose may be illustrated by recent critical studies of *On the Origin of Species*. In his introductory essay to *1859: Entering an Age of Crisis* (1959), Howard Mumford Jones remarked that it was time to admire Darwin as a writer of prose, and called attention to his fine ear, his rhetorical devices, and the excellence of his "ordonnance." Jones probably did not anticipate that the *Origin* would soon emerge as a pattern of tragic action in Stanley E. Hyman's *The Tangled Bank: Darwin, Marx, Frazer and Freud as Imaginative Writers* (1962) or as conducive to a pattern of comedy in A. Dwight Culler's "The Darwinian Revolution and Literary Form" (*The Art of Victorian Prose*, ed. George Levine and W. A. Madden, 1968). Hyman brought to bear on Darwin the weighty construct of archetypal criticism, but made the great mistake, as Walter Cannon has shown, of distorting Darwin to fit his own thesis. Cannon's essay, "Darwin's Vision in *On the Origin of Species*" (in the Levine and Madden vol.), is far more important, however, than as a refutation of pretentious nonsense. It is a model of common sense, critical tact, and sound method.

There is no question that the most notable Unbelievers are tractable subjects for the kind of study the editors of *The Art of Victorian Prose* are attempting to encourage. John Holloway's *The Victorian Sage* (1953) provides one kind of model, though as Dwight Culler suggested in his 1956 essay, the rhetorician needs to be wary of arguing in a circle. Another model is provided by Alan Donaghan's "Victorian Philosophical Prose: J. S. Mill and F. H. Bradley" (also in the Levine and Madden vol.). Donaghan's distinction between polemical prose and the kind that, he believes, Mill approached and Bradley at his best achieved is particularly useful in evaluating the style of the principal Unbelievers, for much of what they wrote was, perforce, polemical. They also had their moments when they were attempting to evoke their own sense of the mystery of man and the universe, or of "an intelligibility in things that is not directly intelligible to every mind," or of "the pressure of reality and the pressure of the individual soul." Another of Donaghan's points is worth considering before we accept too easily the position that scientific or philosophical prose always directs us outward to an external world of things or principles and seldom, if ever, inward, to a world of feeling. Donaghan makes his point by quoting R. G. Collingwood to the effect that "the progressive intellectualization of language . . . represents not a progressive drying-up of emotion, but its progressive articulation and specialization. We are not getting away from an emotional atmosphere into a dry, rational atmosphere. We are acquiring new emotions and new means of expressing them."

At all events, it should be clear that any of the approaches illustrated by

Levine and Madden are capable of being used to advantage and tested in studies of the Unbelievers, provided they be used with the sophistication and sense of proportion demanded of all good literary criticism. It should also be clear that fruitful studies will come from those who, like Walter Cannon, have a sure sense of cultural history, a sense that will suggest what in the writer before them is carried over from an older rhetoric expressive of a more traditional vision and what is expressive of a new vision of human destiny in new terms, for the Unbelievers were trying to live into a new faith, a faith in veracity, in living without opium, and in the power of human beings to live significantly without knowing whether the universe was, or was not, ontologically absurd.

II. FREDERIC HARRISON (1831–1923)

Harrison stands out among the Unbelievers as one who lost his Anglican faith, but insisted on the necessity for religious belief and became an energetic defender of secular religion, the Religion of Humanity, as propounded by Auguste Comte. He was also a consistent critic of the agnostics, whose creed he deplored as "negative." Unlike Morley, he was untroubled by political ambitions; unlike Leslie Stephen, he enjoyed political activism; and, like Huxley, he throve on controversy. Moreover, Harrison had no fear of being regarded as peculiar in adopting the formalized doctrine of Positivism, which Huxley christened "Catholicism *minus* Christianity." After some doubts about his vocation, Harrison became a missionary in politics and religion (as he saw it), and a versatile man of letters. He is, in a curious sort of way, the William Morris of Positivism, the "happy humanist," as his son called him, who embraced a foreign ideology and comprehensive views of history and man just as Morris became an apparently cheerful and energetic apostle of Marxist socialism. Like Morris, Harrison worked with and for the labor movement, but, in contrast to Morris, drifted away for various reasons and at about the same time that Morris became active politically; their careers are analogous in their separate movements.

However, Morris has retained his interest, in part because socialism has survived, while Harrison lost his public when Positivism faded into a historical curiosity. Yet a fresh reading of his life and works impresses one not with his originality, but with the simplicity of his humanism, his integrity (no civil list honors for him), and with the astonishing variety of his activities and of his contacts with the life and persons of his time. His opponents in controversy range from Huxley, Arnold, Fitzjames Stephen, and Herbert Spencer to the Essayists and Reviewers, Mark Pattison, Ruskin, and Arthur Balfour, while his friends include some of those figures as well as George Eliot, John Morley, Leslie Stephen, and George Gissing. His essays suggest that had he chosen to specialize, he might have been a more notable figure than he was in any of several fields, not excluding jurisprudence. He had, for example, the talents of a major satirist: both his "Culture: A Dialogue," directed at Arnold, and "The Religion of Inhumanity," directed at Fitzjames Stephen, are devastating.

His special quality may be suggested by noting that while the rationalist has in the twentieth century been the subject of destructive if sympathetic analysis by novelists (Virginia Woolf's *To the Lighthouse* and Roger Martin du Gard's *Jean Barois* are cases in point), no one has really portrayed a rationalist like Harrison—

happy in his marriage, happy in his work, and so disarmingly downright. As his son remarked, "My father's life was Humanism. It explains his work, his enthusiasms, his concessions, and his negations."

Works and Bibliography

Harrison's own *Autobiographic Memoirs* (2 vols., 1911) contains a full but not complete list of his voluminous writings through 1910. For his books written after that date, the usual sources are available; for his articles and more fugitive items, the bibliographies of recent dissertations should be consulted, notably those by Sydney Eisen, "Frederic Harrison: The Life and Thought of an English Positivist" (Johns Hopkins 1957); Martha Salmon, "Frederic Harrison: The Evolution of an English Positivist, 1831–1881" (Columbia 1959); Herbert W. McCready, "Frederic Harrison and the Working Class Movement, 1860–1875" (Harvard 1952); and Paul Adelman, "The Social and Political Ideas of Frederic Harrison in Relation to English Thought and Politics, 1855–1886" (London 1967). A more complete bibliography of Harrison's works will be published in the full-scale study of Harrison now being written by Martha Salmon Vogeler.

Until very recently, almost all of Harrison's works were out of print. Exceptions were the 1907 edition of *The Philosophy of Common Sense* (1968) and an essay "Imprisonment for Breach of Contract" in *1868: Year of the Unions*, edited by E. Frow and M. Katanka (1968). At the moment, however, thanks to the reprint houses, the list of exceptions can be extended. Three of his books of literary criticism are now available: the 1895 edition of *Studies in Early Victorian Literature* (1969), the 1900 edition of *Tennyson, Ruskin, Mill, and Other Literary Estimates* (1970), and the 1912 edition of *Among My Books* (1970). In addition, his lectures given in America, *George Washington and Other American Addresses*, as published in 1901 (1969), his biographical study *William the Silent*, as published in 1896 (1970), *Memories and Thoughts* (1971), and *On Society* (1971) are now available. This still leaves several of his important works, such as *The Creed of a Layman, The Choice of Books*, and *Realities and Ideals*, difficult to locate as only the larger libraries seem to have adequate holdings of Harrison's books. The critical edition of *Order and Progress*, to be published by Harvester Press in 1973 and edited by Martha Salmon Vogeler, will thus fulfill a real need. It would be convenient if someone would publish a selection of his best essays representing his various interests, especially as *Selected Essays* edited by Amarantha Jha (1925) is long out of print.

For work about Harrison, the student should examine the bibliographies of the dissertations mentioned above, for there is no other adequate source.

Biography, Letters, Etc.

Apart from the *DNB* article and Austin Harrison's delightful impressions of his father in *Frederic Harrison: Thoughts and Memories* (1927), there is no published biography of Harrison. In fact, Austin's book is not, strictly speaking, a biography. Nor are Harrison's own *Autobiographic Memoirs* a substitute. Though presenting the facts of his life and quoting extensively from his letters and journals, Harrison is no Rousseau, baring the secrets of his inner life. Here are biographical materials, loosely ordered it is true, but from which we may learn the astonishing range of Harrison's remarkable life.

Thus the need for a definitive, critical biography is obvious. Harrison lived so long and touched so many other Victorian lives, was active in so many causes and explored so many fields of intellectual inquiry that industry, patience, and a reasonable competence in several fields are required. Moreover, the life is so wrapped up in his ideas that a mere biography will not do. This task, now nearing completion, has been undertaken by Martha S. Vogeler, who has spent fifteen years accumulating materials, published and unpublished.

Sources for the study of Harrison's careers, friendships, ideas, and activities are plentiful enough to challenge the courageous and the enterprising. The most extensive manuscript collection, consisting of approximately 2,000 letters and clippings, is lodged in the British Library of Political and Economic Science at the London School of Economics. Here readers will find, for example, the letters to Morley quoted by Francis W. Hirst in his *Early Life and Letters of John Morley* (2 vols., 1927), by Royden Harrison in *Before the Socialists* (1965), and by David A. Hamer in *John Morley* (1968), and many more which they do not quote. Other materials will be found in the Positivist Archives in the British Museum; the Congreve and the Eugene Oswald papers in the Bodleian Library; the George Howell correspondence at the Bishopsgate Institute (see Simon Maccoby, *English Radicalism, 1853–1886*, 1935, pp. 409–10); and the extensive collection at the Musée d'Auguste Comte in Paris. The Huxley Papers at the Imperial College also include letters from Harrison. Other letters are scattered throughout libraries and private collections in the United States and Great Britain: Colby College, for example, possesses a MS of Harrison's essay on Tennyson, and the British Museum, many letters from Harrison to Macmillan; there are Harrison letters at Cornell, Harvard, Yale, and Texas Universities; at the Huntington Library, the Library of Congress, the National Library of Scotland, the Brotherton Collection at Leeds, and elsewhere.

The extent of this material may well explain why scholars have focused on special aspects of his career, though two recent general articles may be mentioned. The first of these has some special interest because it reflects continued French interest in Harrison. Without saying anything really new or using sources other than the obvious, S. Marandon gives the reader a sound sketch of Harrison's career and ideas in *Etudes Anglaises* (1960). Marandon will not go so far as Morton Luce, who proposed that Harrison should be given the title "Prose Laureate" (*NC*, 1923), but sums up by saying "il est juste de dire qu'Harrison fut une homme intelligent, jouissant dans le maniement des idées et de la langue d'une rare dextérité, et une conscience toujours prête à répondre, dans le sens de la générosité, aux problèmes de son temps." More recently, Sydney Eisen distilled his sympathetic studies of Harrison in "Frederic Harrison and the Religion of Humanity" (*SAQ*, 1967); and John Gross has written a few sprightly pages in his *Rise and Fall of the Man of Letters* (1969). Both serve as useful twentieth-century sketches of his life and work.

Eisen's essay reminds the student that no real comprehension of Harrison's life and ideas is possible without an acquaintance with the work of Auguste Comte and his English disciples. Apart from reading the essential primary sources, study should begin with John Edwin McGee's *A Crusade for Humanity: The History of Organized Positivism in England* (1931). Though McGee did not have available to him the Congreve, Beesly, or Harrison papers, his account is generally accurate and straightforward, his bibliography excellent, and his research done when interviews with surviving Positivists were still possible. More recently, the English Positivists have been treated, though not exhaustively, by the late Walter M. Simon in his *European Positivism in the Nineteenth Century* (1963) and in "Auguste Comte's English Disciples" (*VS*, 1964). Both scholars tend to gloss over the acerbity of the sectarian conflicts within the movement. Harrison's gradual conversion to the faith has been treated in the dissertations of Salmon and Eisen, the latter devoting a good deal of detail to the inner conflicts and intrigues that resulted in the split between those who remained with Congreve and those who followed Harrison, E. S. Beesly, and J. H. Bridges to Newton Hall.

Harrison and Labor

Such studies will prepare the reader for the published works on Harrison's life from 1860 to 1875, the period in which Harrison and his fellow Positivists were most active in the cause of organized labor. These works serve to impress the reader that, as in the case of John Morley and Leslie Stephen, unbelief in Christianity was virtually indistinguishable from Radical politics. For a Positivist like Harrison, the new faith was inextricable from the new politics. As Royden Harrison reminds us, Comte had urged the intellectuals to unite themselves with the proletariat (*Before the Socialists*, 1965, Ch. vi). It is thus not surprising that Comte's English converts should have turned their attention to the plight of labor. R. Harrison's chapter gives us a trenchant and detailed analysis of their relation to the labor movement, with considerable attention to F. Harrison. What R. Harrison spells out in one chapter, Herbert McCready has treated in even greater detail in four important articles which, though not always focused directly on Harrison, nevertheless deal with events in which Harrison was a prominent actor. Among other reasons, these articles are of prime significance because McCready was the first scholar to consult the collection of papers then in the hands of Frederic Harrison's grandson and now partly at the London School of Economics.

Though Harrison himself had described his experience in Northern England during the Cotton Famine of 1863 (when the workers were supporting the Union in the Civil War), McCready was able to add considerably to the picture of Harrison's break from his middle-class background as he came into personal contact with members of the working class ("The Cotton Famine in Lancashire, 1863," *Trans. of the Hist. Soc. of Lancashire and Cheshire*, 1954). McCready's second article, "British Labour and the Royal Commission of Trade Unions, 1867–9" (*UTQ*, 1955), is a searching analysis of Harrison's "skill and energy" as "the official representative of organized labour." McCready concludes that Harrison was not only "the most energetic examiner and cross examiner" on the Commission, but also that he must be credited with (though to a lesser extent than Harrison claimed) revision of the Majority Report as well as being the chief author of the Minority Report, which was finally embodied in legislation in 1875, and was considered to be "a classic defense of . . . mid-Victorian unionism." In contrast to the Webbs (*History of Trade Unionism*) both R. Harrison and McCready play up the extent to which Harrison consulted Beesly and the labor leadership, but neither denies the central importance of Harrison's work in the Commission.

While McCready in his third article, "British Labour's Lobby, 1867–75" (*CJEPS*, 1956), expands his focus to include a number of persons and organizations, he singles out Harrison and Beesly as middle-class radicals who were most active in demanding repeal of the egregious clauses of the labor legislation of 1871.

His article concludes with a summary of the problems of the labor lobby as it confronted the election of 1874 and with the story of the success of the lobby, assisted by Harrison, in gaining complete legislative victory under a Tory ministry in 1875.

Finally, though written earlier, McCready's study of Harrison's difficulties in attempting to formulate his position in the 1874 election rounds out the chronological sequence (*CJEPS*, 1954). Harrison and Morley and Chamberlain are seen in a three-cornered correspondence about Chamberlain's quadrilateral program, with Morley stressing the need of a single issue—National Education; and Harrison insisting on the need for the liberals to right the wrongs of labor and finally appearing to support Gladstone, but hardly with any enthusiasm.

Part of the value of the studies by McCready and R. Harrison lies in their use of such contemporary sources as the minutes of trade union organizations, newspapers, the files of the *Fortnightly Review* and the *Beehive*, and the archives of the Home Office. From these materials, they draw somewhat different conclusions about the role of F. Harrison and the Positivists. Whereas R. Harrison insists on the importance of the Comtist influence (though in fact Eisen's dissertation provides more background material) and sees the Positivists as "labor's intellectuals," McCready is unwilling to see them as significantly different from other academic, middle-class radicals. McCready's position is supported by Christopher A. Kent in his dissertation "Aspects of Academic Radicalism in Mid-Victorian England: A Study in the Politics of Thought and Action with Particular Reference to Frederic Harrison and John Morley" (Sussex 1968), now being revised for publication under the proposed title, *Academic Radicalism: Politics and the Clerisy in Mid-Victorian England*.

R. Harrison also claims for the Positivists a more significant role in later history than that played by the early Christian Socialists. Frederic Harrison's impatience with the latter, comparable to his impatience with the Broad Church movement, is recorded in "Early Documents Relating to the Formation and Activities of the College, 1854–1880" now located at the Working Men's College, and in less detail in the work of still another Harrison, John F. C., in his *A History of the Working Men's College, 1854–1954* (1954).

Apart from these publications, there is nothing further to record of significant studies of Harrison's career in the labor movement. The field is wide open for further investigation and further debate, especially on the point at issue between McCready and R. Harrison.

Critical Studies

Politics

Certainly, Harrison's political position and its development is an integral aspect of his whole life and work. Anti-imperialist from the middle fifties, he supported the Indian Mutiny, deplored the Crimean War and the bombardment of Kagosima in 1863, publicly sympathized with the Commune and invited Communard refugees to dinner, interrupted his career as a barrister by joining the Royal Commission on Trade Unions, vigorously supported Home Rule for Ireland—the tale is long. He broke with his class (or did he?), joined an exotic sect which the *Pall Mall Gazette* labeled Reds, knew but distrusted Marx, supported Ruskin against the classical political economists but opposed land nationalization, socialism, national education, and woman suffrage, all in the name of Positivism, which proposed alternative solutions to economic and educational problems of the age. Harrison was also, as Kingsley Martin has suggested, a leading theoretician of the republican movement against the monarchy (*The Magic of Monarchy*, 1937).

Much of Harrison's earlier political writing, though partially represented in *Order and Progress* (1875), is to be found in the *Fortnightly Review* under the editorship of his lifelong friend, John Morley. His contributions have been discussed enthusiastically by Frances N. Knickerbocker (*Free Minds: John Morley and His Friends*, 1943; rpt. 1970) and wittily by Edwin M. Everett (*The Party of Humanity*, 1939). What is clear from both of these sources is that Harrison differed from his colleagues on a number of points: during the Franco-Prussian War he was pro-French when they were pro-German, he was not convinced that the United States possessed the model polity, he had no use for traditional political economy, and he quarreled with his editor sharply by opposing Bismarck's Falk Laws, which Morley vehemently supported. In fact, one way of uncovering Harrison's political views is to juxtapose him to Morley; both wrote books on Oliver Cromwell, for example. Their differences, especially as they appeared before 1886, have been indicated by Everett, Knickerbocker, and Eisen (in his dissertation). Though not particularly concerned with their politics, Muriel Harris drew an interesting comparison of the two men in "Two Victorian Portraits" (*North Amer. Rev.*, 1920) and Austin Harrison makes a few comparative observations in *Frederic Harrison* (1927), but both authors deal with their subjects as they were late in life. Christopher Kent sees Morley and Harrison as paradigms of two forms of "the intellectual in politics" in Part IV of his "Aspects of Academic Radicalism," dealing at length with Morley's *On Compromise* and Harrison's *Order and Progress* as "elitist manifestos which offer differing formal statements of the creed of academic radicalism." Harrison, Morley, and the *Fortnightly Review* also loom large in Kent's "Higher Journalism and the Mid-Victorian Clerisy" (*VS*, 1969), in which they are shown to be debating the proper role of the intellectual as journalist, an article that both supplements and corrects the sections dealing with Morley and Harrison in Gross's *Rise and Fall of the Man of Letters*. A complete story of this friendship would throw light on the personalities and the political ideas and tactics of both.

On at least one matter they agreed wholeheartedly. Enraged by Fitzjames Stephen's attack on Mill in *Liberty, Equality, Fraternity* (1873), Morley goaded Harrison to thwack the ribs of Goliath. Harrison responded with "The Religion of Inhumanity" and promptly labeled Stephen's position as "Calvinism minus Christianity." The importance of this donnybrook in defining Harrison's position is touched on by Knickerbocker, Everett, and Eisen, who base their accounts in part on Leslie Stephen's life of his brother and on Hirst's early life of Morley. Benjamin Lippincott's *Victorian Critics of Democracy* (1938) gives a good account of Fitzjames Stephen's position.

Religion

When we turn to published work on Harrison's religious ideas, we discover that, like studies of his political views, most of it has concentrated on his controversies with rival schools of thought. The focus on the controversies is easily explained. First, Harrison has so clearly and simply expounded his own faith (in

The Creed of a Layman, and *Apologia pro Fide Mea*, and his *Autobiographic Memoirs*) that it hardly needs exegesis; second, controversy brought out, as it did in Huxley, Harrison's liveliest powers; and third, controversy is interesting.

The first of these gentlemanly rows was provoked by Harrison's article, "Neo-Christianity," in the *Westminster Review* (Oct. 1860; rpt. with additions as "Septem contra Fidem," in *The Creed of a Layman*, 1907), an attack on the authors of *Essays and Reviews* (1860). The tale has been told frequently, but most succinctly by Basil Willey in *More Nineteenth Century Studies* (1956) and by Geoffrey Faber in two chapters of his *Jowett* (1957); the significance of the debacle for the Church has been indicated by A. O. J. Cockshut in his chapter "The Doctrinal Crisis" in *Anglican Attitudes* (1959). Willey's urbane and graceful chapter tends to minimize the grasp that Harrison had of the real issue by juxtaposing his words to those of Bishop Wilberforce, who agreed with Harrison, that the "seven against Christ" had no business still calling themselves Christians. Willey disagrees with both. Yet were not Harrison and Soapy Sam right? If one did not believe in the Incarnation as "a divine eschatological event in history" (Richard V. Sampson, *VS*, 1957), or if one interpreted the life of Jesus in some way not imagined by the usual holder of the creed, how was one a Christian? Harrison laid his rough finger on a nerve that still quivers among theologians. It may be possible to argue, as Willey does, that Harrison feared that if the Church of England became completely modernized it would provide a bear's embrace for the Religion of Humanity, but there is also a good deal to be said for Harrison as the kind of man who tried to call things by their right names. Like Leslie Stephen in his handling of the Broad Church, Harrison insisted that there was something hypocritical about losing one's faith but retaining one's clerical collar. In another connection, he remarked that while Arnold and others could parade their heresies without fear, men like Bradlaugh, who lacked sweetness and light and high positions, were being persecuted and prosecuted. The episode needs telling from Harrison's point of view.

Two other notable controversies in which Harrison was a duelist involved Thomas Henry Huxley and Herbert Spencer. These have been admirably treated in two detailed articles by Sydney Eisen. The first of these, "Huxley and the Positivists" (*VS*, 1964), lays stress on Huxley and the harm he did to the Positivist cause by damning it as "Catholicism *minus* Christianity," but Eisen's secondary theme is that the Positivists, and particularly Harrison, demanded that Huxley define his ethical position, a demand, in Eisen's judgment, that Huxley found some difficulty in meeting. Eisen traces this controversy through its three stages, showing Harrison as a prime catalytic agent in pushing Huxley toward the position he took in the famous Romanes Lecture. Eisen's second essay, "Frederic Harrison and Herbert Spencer: Embattled Unbelievers" (*VS*, 1968), recounts the sometimes comic, sometimes bitter, sometimes unseemly, war of words in the 1880's between Harrison and Spencer, which finally ended amicably, each convinced that their religious views were more alike than later judges might discern. Harrison enjoyed discomfiting his opponents by calling them crypto-Positivists. Eisen notes that Harrison's tactics, at least in the earlier stages of the quarrel, repeated those used in "Neo-Christianity," but claims that Harrison distorted Spencer's position "so that he could more easily turn his wit on the Unknowable and expose it as a mere bubble." More than in his earlier essay Eisen attempts to explore the roots of this clash below the level of the argument, and finds reasons deep in the personality structure and early environments of the two contestants. Eisen's essays are models for others to emulate.

Harrison's other debates with his contemporaries on the subject of religion have engaged the attention of Eisen and Salmon in their dissertations and Walter Maneikis in "Frederic Harrison: Postivist Critic of Society and Literature" (Diss. Northwestern 1943), but no one has yet made full studies of Harrison's engagements with Ruskin or Mark Pattison. Nor has anyone made a study of Harrison's individual brand of the Religion of Humanity that would illuminate its relation to other secular religions either of his own time or of ours. The developments in our century of what might be called Christianity minus God and the blending of religion and social action in assorted figures from Gandhi to Norman Thomas and Martin Luther King might well draw attention to a man who had been there before and from whom something might be learned.

Culture

Harrison's entanglement with Matthew Arnold inevitably takes us into the realm of culture. Here Harrison's posture has been admirably defined by Martha Salmon Vogeler in "Matthew Arnold and Frederic Harrison: The Prophet of Culture and the Prophet of Positivism" (*SEL*, 1962). This essay not only traces the role Harrison played in the development of *Culture and Anarchy* (once again we see him as catalyst), but also rescues Harrison from being forever left in our minds by Arnold as the young man sharpening up a guillotine in his dress clothes. (One suspects that more might be done to rehabilitate others in what Vogeler calls "Arnold's rogues' gallery.") She then goes on to trace Arnold's modifications of his position and his textual revisions in the light of his interchange with Harrison, and more important, to support Harrison's charge (which Arnold never answered) to the effect that Arnold's "Culture" was far closer to Positivism than he would admit. Though concluding with more charity to Arnold than he perhaps deserves, she sums up thoroughly the parallels and the sharp distinctions between the prophet of culture and the prophet of Positivism as they faced the political, social, and religious issues of their times. For Positivism itself and Harrison in particular had rather distinct notions of how culture should be spread; Harrison among his other activities was a teacher, not only at the Working Men's College in his younger days but in the Positivist center at Newton Hall; moreover, he contributed to the "Choice of Books" discussion popularized by Sir John Lubbock and continued in the pages of the *Pall Mall Gazette* in the 1880's (see Vogeler, "The Victorians and the Hundred Best," *TQ*, 1968). It would be useful indeed to explore Harrison's concept of education and his career as a popular educator, not only for the sake of Harrison himself, but also to see his ideas and work in the context of the wider movement for mass education in the years after the second Reform Bill.

Topics for Further Study

Since Martha Salmon Vogeler's critical biography of Harrison may be expected to light up much of Harrison's life and thought left in shadow up to now, it is difficult to predict what topics will need further study. Of Harrison the man of letters much more needs to be said. Harrison's position as a literary critic needs establishing, especially the merit of his judgments on his contemporaries; his style— so much admired by his contemporaries—might well be a rewarding study. His skill as a satirist is well worth investigating, especially in connection with his classicism and his interest in Gibbon and the eighteenth century. Other topics might lie in Harrison's friendships with such authors as George Eliot, to whom he was an adviser, and in his patronage of others like George Gissing and Maurice Hewlett. No one has yet commented adequately on Harrison's importance as a reporter of and commentator on French politics, or evaluated his work in jurisprudence (he studied under Henry Maine). Eisen, in his dissertation, touched briefly on Harrison the historian, whose work on Chatham, Gibbon, and Cromwell, and on Byzantine history merits analysis. Eisen also suggested that a study of Harrison's extensive club memberships might deepen our understanding of the social matrix in which Victorian intellectuals and politicians spun their threads of power and influence. These are only some of the projects that will come readily to mind as one becomes acquainted with his work. Like Annie Besant, Harrison lived a number of lives, but in each there is a curious consistency and a characteristic energy. The interesting question to ask about each of these lives is: how much of its quality is due to Harrison's Positivism, how much to his being a Victorian, and how much to his individual talents and circumstances?

III. THOMAS HENRY HUXLEY (1825–95)

Darwin's bulldog, the nemesis of Bishop Wilberforce and the baiter of Gladstone, needs no justification to stand among the Unbelievers. In fact, because of his polemical enthusiasm, his trenchant intellect, his political cunning, and his tragic moments, he might well be considered (to shift the image) as being simultaneously the Prince Hal and the Hotspur of the hosts of rationalism. Ready to thrust himself into any breach, to challenge innumerable Glendowers to fetch spirits, to be pestered by popinjays and slaughter them out of hand, to woo his wife and children with wit and gallantry, he died at seventy, worn out, wondering if time were not life's fool and thought the slave of life. No one has expressed one view of the paradox of Huxley more sharply, if debatably, than Loren Eiseley in his introduction to *On a Piece of Chalk* (1967): Huxley "embodies man unbeaten, but rendered intellectually impotent before space, time, and the unknowable. . . . He is of the generation that Charles Darwin at once enlightened and spiritually destroyed."

Of the four Unbelievers here treated, Huxley achieved the greatest fame, nationally and internationally; he has been the most anthologized, and the most vigorously defended and excoriated. As the prophet of Science Militant, he seemed to be a simple man and a simple thinker; his apparent clarity thus tended to prevent earlier writers from giving us the man in his full complexity. For the paradoxes remain: the man ready to prosecute Governor Eyre defended repression in Ireland and opposed Home Rule; the crusader for the right of the poor and of women to have education took a Hobbesian view of human nature and was attracted to the determinism of a Jonathan Edwards. The loving student of nature who adapted Goethe's youthful *Aphorisms on Nature* into rhapsodical English later damned Nature as embodying a demonic power and repudiated her as a model for human conduct. As a stylist he claimed to be a plain blunt man who would not "plaster the fair face of truth with that pestilent cosmetic, rhetoric," which, as Gilbert K. Chesterton later remarked, was "about as well-plastered a piece of rhetoric as Ruskin himself could have managed" (*The Victorian Age in Literature*, 1913).

Chesterton preceded his comment by announcing that "Huxley was much more a literary than a scientific man" and three years later Henry L. Mencken went even further by saying that Huxley was "a master writer even more than a master biologist, one of the few truly great stylists that England has produced since the time of Anne." Others have claimed that his true place in fame is as an educator, as a statesman for science, and the impresario for *On the Origin of Species*; still others praise him as the forceful presenter of the materialism of Democritus; and still others as an artist, a creator of orderly forms and patterns of thought. Ronald Clark, the author of *The Huxleys* (1968), credits Huxley, in addition to eminence in science and education, with being the man who conducted the defense of the *Origin*, who forced upon his generation a confrontation with the implications of evolution for their understanding of man and morality, and with being the man who "mellowed passionate arguments with sweet reasonableness" and thus made acceptance of the new ideas less traumatic than it might have been.

Despite such remarks, Huxley has suffered the fate of the accepted culture hero by being oversimplified and therefore ignored, except by a few scholars who refuse to allow his life and work to die of the indifference of later generations. (While it is not the purpose of this essay to assess Huxley's scientific achievements, those who wish to look into the matter should consult the *Scientific Memoirs* and the special supplement of *Nature*, 1925, pp. 697–732, as the first step and then turn to *Scientist Extraordinary: The Life and Scientific Work of Thomas Henry Huxley*, 1972, by Cyril Bibby.)

Works and Bibliography

In his handsome edition of *On a Piece of Chalk* (1967), Loren Eiseley listed only two books by Huxley still in print, the Crofts Classics *Selections from the Essays of T. H. Huxley* (1948) and *Man's Place in Nature* (1959), with an introduction by Ashley Montague. Since Eiseley wrote, however, the nine-volume *Collected Works* (1893–94) has been reprinted (1968) as well as the Brander Matthews edition of the *Autobiography and Essays* (1919), the *Darwiniana* (1896), the EML *David Hume* (1879), *Evolution and Ethics, and Other Essays* (1896), and Huxley's *On the Origin of Species* (1859), also with an introduction by Montague. Particular essays, of course, have been reprinted or anthologized in too many volumes to list here. A selection from his writings, *The Essence of T. H. Huxley*, has been edited by Cyril Bibby (1967). Since Huxley's death, the major publications of previously unpublished material have been Julian Huxley's edition of T. H. Huxley's *Diary of the Voyage of* HMS Rattlesnake (1936; rpt. 1970), the *Scientific Memoirs*, edited by Michael Foster and E. Ray Lankaster (1898–1903), and the text of the unfinished essay on Arthur J. Balfour in an appendix to Houston Peterson's *Thomas H. Huxley: Prophet of Science* (1932).

The *Collected Essays* were, of course, edited by Huxley before his death and therefore represent the authoritative texts, but by no means of his complete works, some of which have not even yet been officially listed. Studies of the text are certainly in order, not only to examine the revisions Huxley made in his final versions, but also to discover his methods of composition by looking at manuscript versions. Also in order is a complete checklist of Huxley's works. The most complete listings in print are those to be found in J. R. Ainsworth Davis, *Thomas H. Huxley* (1907; rpt. 1970) and in Leonard Huxley's *Life and Letters of Thomas H.*

Huxley (2 vols., 1901; rpt. 1968). Shorter listings may be found in Cyril Bibby's *T. H. Huxley: Scientist, Humanist and Educator* (1960). The materials to accomplish these tasks can hardly be claimed as unavailable. The manuscript material, not only letters but texts of essays and lectures, account books, and memoranda, is enormous. The largest and most important collection is that held by the Imperial College of Science and Technology, London, which includes some 4,500 letters to more than 800 correspondents. This collection has been cataloged by Warren R. Dawson and published under the title, *The Huxley Papers, a Descriptive Catalogue of the Correspondence, Manuscripts and Miscellaneous Papers of the Rt. Honorable Thomas Henry Huxley, Preserved in the Imperial College of Science and Technology* (1946). Jeanne Pingree of the Imperial College has also prepared *T. H. Huxley: A List of His Scientific Papers* (1968) and Huxley's correspondence with his wife before their marriage (*Correspondence with Henrietta Heathorn, 1847–1854*, 1969). Other collections of letters and papers are located in universities and special libraries in England and America, as mentioned in Bibby's Preface. Letters to and from Huxley can also be found in the published lives and letters of his scientific colleagues and friends: Darwin, Hooker, Lyell, Spencer, Kingsley, et al. There are also the papers of the Royal Commissions (Huxley served on ten), the London School Board, the minutes of Eton College and of the universities of Edinburgh, Aberdeen, and London, as well as the records of all the other institutions with which Huxley was connected. An account of Huxley's addresses and lectures given on his American tour will be found in Extra No. 56 of the New York *Tribune*, 1876, as well as in "Thomas H. Huxley's American Lectures on Evolution" (*SSJ*, 1952), by Wayne C. Minnick, and "Huxley in America" (*PAPS*, 1970), by William P. Randel.

Just as there is no complete checklist of Huxley's works so there is no up-to-date bibliography of work on Huxley. The anthologies of Victorian prose edited by Charles F. Harrold and William D. Templeman (1938) and F. W. Roe (1947) both contain useful listings up to the date of publication; another, more recent but shorter, bibliography will be found in Jerome Hamilton Buckley's Goldentree Bibliography, *Victorian Poets and Prose Writers* (1966), which lists three editions and fourteen items of biography and criticism. William Irvine also includes a selective listing in his *Thomas Henry Huxley* (Writers and Their Works, 1960). In addition, the sources listed by Bibby, both in his footnotes and in his list of sources for each chapter, should be examined carefully, as well as the selected bibliography in Albert Ashforth's *Thomas Henry Huxley* (1970).

Biography

Of the earlier biographies, Leonard Huxley's *Life and Letters* has the old-fashioned virtues and deficiencies, and, until the letters are published, will be the readiest source of Huxley's private correspondence; Edward Clodd's *Thomas Henry Huxley* (1902) has its value for being written by one of Huxley's students and colleagues; and J. R. Ainsworth Davis' study in the English Men of Science series (1907; rpt. 1970) draws part of its importance from its bibliographical information; but perhaps the most penetrating of the early short lives is *Huxley: A Sketch of His Life and Work* (1901) by P. Chalmers Mitchell. In 1932, two workmanlike biographies appeared, *Huxley* by Clarence Edwin Ayres and Peterson's *Huxley: Prophet of Science*; both go over familiar ground effectively. Much the same may be said of

F. W. McBride's *Huxley* in the Great Lives series (1934). Peterson's book, however, should be noted for its psychological interpretation of Huxley's aggressiveness as rooted in a neurotic fear produced by his traumatic experience at a postmortem examination when he was a boy. Two more recent short biographical essays should be mentioned, one by Charles S. Blinderman in the *Scientific Monthly* (1957), based on a substantial amount of material from the Huxley Papers, and the other by William Irvine mentioned above. Two earlier studies, throwing light primarily on Huxley's character, should be looked into—Leonard Huxley's *Thomas Henry Huxley: A Character Sketch* (1920) and George Gissing's pages on Huxley in his *Autobiographical Notes* (1930). Huxley's diary of his voyage on *HMS Rattlesnake*, his letters to Henrietta (1969), and the commentary on his whole Australian experience given by the late A. J. Marshall in *Darwin and Huxley in Australia* (1971) provide us with rich materials for understanding the young Huxley; *The Diary*, as its editor Julian Huxley emphasized, reveals that his grandfather did not escape the typical Victorian soul crisis. The role Carlyle's works played in Huxley's recuperation and shaping his temperament is spelled out clearly by William Irvine in his "Carlyle and T. H. Huxley" (*Booker Memorial Studies: Eight Essays in Victorian Literature*, 1950; rpt. in *Victorian Literature: Modern Essays in Criticism*, 1961).

Irvine enlarged his scope by painting a full-length portrait of Huxley in his by now well-known *Apes, Angels and Victorians: Darwin, Huxley and Evolution* (1955; rpt. 1959), a joint biography, notable, in Loren Eiseley's words, "for demonstrating that a reliable and dignified treatment of Darwin and Huxley demands neither muck-raking nor breathless rhetoric" (*YR*, 1955). Part i interweaves and compares the two lives in the context of the scientific and ideological struggles of the era, while Part ii is concerned exclusively with Huxley's later career as "a figure upon every intellectual battlefield in Europe and the living embodiment of science militant," thus contributing to the legendary view of Huxley long held. Irvine, however, by no means neglects Huxley the father, the husband, and the friend; nor does he exempt the legendary Huxley from ironic criticism. Each major episode in Huxley's career is treated vividly, highlighted with significant detail drawn from both published and unpublished materials, though as Anthony West pointed out ("Darwin and Huxley," in *Principles and Persuasions*, 1958), some of Irvine's psychologizing is far from convincing. One question that Irvine does not answer (nor does anyone else) is why Huxley attacked Chambers' *Vestiges of Creation* so harshly only a few years before he accepted Darwin and why he shifted his position so suddenly. While Irvine wrestles with the question, he admits that the causes for Huxley's failure to draw conclusions from Chambers and Lyell "go deep." How deep we need to know.

Another biographical episode, one that has been recited so many times as to have achieved the fixed form of legend, is the Oxford Debate. Irvine follows the legend, extracting high drama from its simplicity. Students will wish to compare his account with that of Gertrude Himmelfarb in her *Darwin and the Darwinian Revolution* (1959); she reminds us that there is no single verbatim account of the encounter with Bishop Wilberforce, indicates the different versions recorded in the *Life and Letters*, and is less disposed than many to make Huxley the hero of the occasion, putting forth the claims of Hooker to be the real victor over Wilberforce. The precise status of J. W. Draper in the affair has been indicated by Eiseley (*YR*, 1955) and further details and matters of interest have been brought to our attention by Blinderman in "The Oxford Debate and After" (*N&Q*, 1957), a source apparently not tapped by Himmelfarb, and by A. MacC Armstrong, "Samuel Wilberforce vs. T. H. Huxley" (*QR*, 1958). Cyril Bibby adds a document to the story in his *T. H. Huxley* (1960) by citing Huxley's own version written in a letter to his friend Dyster. The most recent version is by Ronald Clark in his *The Huxleys* (1968), who also quotes the letter to Dyster and speculates that it implies an interchange between the Bishop and the Bishop-eater *before* the meeting took place; like Himmelfarb, he is inclined to give Hooker full honors as playing "Blucher to Huxley's Wellington." It should be noted that if legend has tended to make Huxley the sole hero in the affair, this was not his doing, for in his letter to Dyster he gives credit not only to Hooker, but to Lubbock: "Among us," he wrote, "we shut up the bishop and his party."

Huxley's famous correspondence with Charles Kingsley is another legendlike episode in Victorian cultural history. Almost every biographer has treated it as in one way or another demonstrating a close kinship between the two men, despite their opposed religious views—Glaucus and Diomedes, Irvine calls them. Blinderman is not prepared to accept the legendary image. In his article, "Huxley and Kingsley" (*VN*, 1961), he reviews the correspondence and other materials, concluding that "the view that [they] were close in temperament and attitude needs qualification, that while their friendship is undeniable, their ideological differences, however obscured by social amenities, prevail as barriers to the reconciliation of irreconcilable world views." Kingsley also enters Blinderman's account of the disputes and enmity between Richard Owen and Huxley in "The Great Bone Case" (*Perspectives in Biology and Medicine*, 1971), an entertaining account of the way in which this dispute found its way into the popular press and the world of caricature, making a strong case for crediting Huxley with being the first to assemble the evidence that man was descended from an anthropoid ape.

Huxley's *passages d'armes* with the Positivists, Gladstone, Herbert Spencer, the Duke of Argyll, and the Reverend Wace, and the final, incomplete debate with Arthur J. Balfour have all been discussed by his biographers. Some of these controversies, too, took on the character of myth, but recent years have brought disenchantment. Irvine treats them with detached irony, believing that too often the logomachies "stagnated among the muddy technicalities of allegation and counter allegation." Sydney Eisen deflates the hero somewhat in his "Huxley and the Positivists" (*VS*, 1964) by showing that Huxley displayed a certain defensiveness when challenged by Frederic Harrison to state an affirmative position. What emerges from these studies is that Huxley is far more complex and human than we have sometimes believed—without being any the less heroic.

The most impressive recent scholarship on Huxley's life has been performed, however, by Cyril Bibby, whose book is focused on Huxley's career as a promoter of educational reform. Bibby has consulted an extraordinary number of hitherto untapped sources to give us a vivid portrait of Huxley's skill as committee chairman, as member of assorted commissions, boards, and other official posts from which vantage points he deployed all his polemical and parliamentary skill in promoting his ideas and programs and all his influence in getting key persons placed in strategic educational posts. If students of Huxley have had reason to wonder at Huxley's incredible energy and alert vitality, their wonder will now turn to awe. If Huxley became a myth in his own lifetime, Bibby demonstrates how. Looked at from the mid-twentieth century, he writes, "the most striking thing about Thomas

Henry Huxley is his sheer effectiveness. . . . Compounding a clear view of objectives with immense determination and enormous energy, an unyielding devotion to principle with great flexibility of application, and a capacity for occasional ruthlessness with an habitual captivating charm, he was indeed a formidable figure." In short his mythic status was genuine, not a fabrication of public relations experts. Bibby also elucidates a number of other events and situations in which Huxley played a significant part. In fact, his book teems with lively anecdote illuminating Huxley's life and the Victorian scene.

What perhaps is missing from Bibby's study is a stronger sense of the melancholia, of the tormented elements in Huxley's personality, for Huxley dreamed strange dreams and was haunted, not only by illness, but by dark images from which the Alps, or hard work, or a new adversary provided the only relief.

Critical Studies

While the biographies already mentioned are all (except for the *L & L*) critical in the sense that they to some degree expound and comment on Huxley's ideas, the fact remains that we need a thorough reexamination of his whole philosophical position, first in order to assess traditional views and second to make use of what Bibby calls the "hundreds of folios of notes [that] bear witness to the seriousness with which he studied theology and philosophy." In the view of Albert Ashforth (*Thomas Henry Huxley*, 1970), Huxley was the most farsighted of his contemporaries in understanding "the impact the new findings were having upon the traditional values and assumptions which underlie Western culture—more specifically upon education, theology, philosophy, politics, morality, and art." Though Ashforth's little book is not exhaustive, it lucidly sets forth Huxley's positions in these areas and is based upon unpublished as well as published material.

Historically, studies in Huxley's ideas have moved in opposing directions. Conservatives like James McCosh (*The Agnosticism of Hume and Huxley*, 1884), or Paul Elmer More ("T. H. Huxley," *The Drift of Romanticism, Shelburne Essays*, VIII, 1913), or More's disciple Robert Shafer (*Christianity and Naturalism*, 1926) tend to insist that Huxley's agnosticism was a kind of cover for an almost fanatical dogmatism: "he used [his skepticism] as a tool, as a fighting weapon, as a retreat when difficulties threatened, as a means of escape from vigorous thought—he used it, in short, when it suited him and carefully shielded from it his sacred verities." Lenin's famous remark that Huxley's agnosticism served "as a fig-leaf for materialism" (*Materialism and Empirio-Criticism*, 1908) provides an echo to the Right from the Left. The implication is that Huxley's agnosticism was a tactical term that concealed a genuine atheism and a thoroughgoing materialism.

More recent students of Huxley, especially those who have also consulted unpublished materials, tend to look at the same question in a different light. They note the dogmatism, but they observe that beneath Huxley's dogmatism stirs a genuine uncertainty on ultimate questions and serious doubts about the future of humanity. Such an emphasis will be found in Irvine, in Bibby, and in Eiseley's introduction to *On a Piece of Chalk* (1967). Irvine and Bibby both find this bewilderment registered early in life, in the *Rattlesnake* diary; Bibby also mentions the lecture Huxley gave to the Royal Institution in 1856. Curiously enough, in an impressionistic but unsystematic essay on Huxley in *The Unbelievers* (1964), A. O. J. Cockshut suggests, as others have, that Huxley's "ferocity masked interior misgivings," but in other passages maintains that Huxley "was all of a piece . . . undisturbed by any hint of mysterious reserves and unplumbed spiritual depths." Few would now agree.

Blinderman's "T. H. Huxley: A Re-Evaluation of His Philosophy" (*Rationalist Annual*, 1966) indicates the direction that a new examination of his thought should take. More systematic and searching than Bibby, Blinderman begins by reviewing the traditional critiques of Huxley's materialism and then examines the evidence, both published and unpublished. He draws the inference that Huxley in his earlier work does indeed give credence to the popular opinion of Huxley as a materialist. "Yet," Blinderman goes on to say, "in the very heart of his apparently robust materialism there is always a tremor of idealism." Pulling together the relevant passages, Blinderman shows that on the issues of the ultimate nature of reality, the limits of human knowledge, and determinism versus free will, Huxley can sound like an idealist, or better, a nominalist. He finds, however, that late in life in the replies to Balfour and in his private attacks on Plato, Huxley seems to move back to his earlier materialism. "Huxley then is inconsistent." But Blinderman does not stop there. He explains the inconsistency by suggesting strongly that Huxley was attempting to find a philosophical position which, foreshadowing logical Positivism, admitted that scientific propositions were only symbols, but which would in no way give comfort to those who would denigrate the power of science or deny the physiological basis of mind and the respectability of matter. To Blinderman, Huxley's failure to solve his problem is less significant than his "refusal to be bound by mind-forged abstractions."

Another apparent contradiction (or ambiguity) in Huxley's thought lies in his differing definitions of Agnosticism—did he think the term applied to the limits of human knowledge, or was it a description of scientific method? The question is faced by D. W. Dockrill in "T. H. Huxley and the Meaning of 'Agnosticism'" (*Theol.*, 1971), who attempts, without reference to unpublished work, to resolve the issue by examining the relevant texts and their contexts. Disposing of Victorian critics of Huxley, Dockrill concludes that the contradiction is more apparent than real, a conclusion that would not surprise such Huxley scholars as Bibby or Blinderman, whose work Dockrill seems not to have read.

The articles by Dockrill and Blinderman are thus useful preludes to the longer study that is now required. That there is some gap between Huxley's usual clarity and the uncertainty of his philosophical exposition is now generally accepted. Blinderman has suggested that the gap is not caused by a deliberate or unconscious masking of his real views, but by genuine inner conflicts. He also points out that much of Huxley's thought is expounded when he is "talking for victory"; what he wrote in his study and said to the public, and the historical context of both, need to be studied carefully to do justice to his position and to assess the judgment that his Agnosticism was merely polemical or merely muddled.

Such study is also necessary for an examination of Huxley's ethics. The literature on the subject of evolutionary ethics is vast and has been selectively referred to in the first section of this chapter. To students of Huxley, Quillian's *The Moral Theory of Evolutionary Naturalism* (1945) and Julian Huxley's reply (*Touchstones of Ethics*, 1947) are of some special interest. In any case, it is clear to all that Huxley's position differs sharply from that of Spencer and other social Darwinians. It has also been said that despite Huxley's attempt to extricate himself from the position that man must combat nature while yet being a part of nature, he fails to do so. In his *Leslie Stephen* (1951), Annan opined that Huxley had not really answered the question: "is there a moral law in human society which will make men do good even when the sanctions of religion vanish?" Richard W. Noland, however, notes that in his "Prolegomena" to *Evolution and Ethics* (1894) Huxley found the sources of morality and moral sanction in society itself, in the primary family affections, in man's desire to imitate others for pleasure, which (Noland points to the link with Freud) produces an "artificial personality . . . built up beside the natural personality," and further by the development in society of the idea of justice ("T. H. Huxley on Culture," *Personalist*, 1964). Though based only on published texts, Noland's essay is an able statement of Huxley's view, emphasizing that for Huxley the development of morality is a completely "naturalistic process." What that morality was, most scholars agree, resembled a number of Victorian pieties, not excluding Carlylean "veracity." Whether Noland convinces us that Huxley was a sound ethical theorist is less important, here, than his clear presentation of the basis on which that judgment may be made.

What is not in question is that Huxley changed his view of Nature; that he changed it after a reading of John Stuart Mill's "Nature" (1873) is made a strong possibility by Oma Stanley's pedestrian but competent examination of the published evidence ("T. H. Huxley's Treatment of 'Nature,'" *JHI*, 1957). Stanley has collected all of Huxley's published remarks on the subject and found significant verbal parallels between Mill's essay and Huxley's *Hume*, "The Struggle for Existence in Human Society," and other writings after 1874. Those who have noticed the parallel will find the argument persuasive. What is more to the point is to ask why Huxley would be receptive to Mill's stern image of Nature's indifference to human morality. To comprehend Huxley's notion of how morality developed one needs to study his view of human history. Here, too, the facile idea that he embraced a typically Victorian belief in progress has long since been abandoned. Basic study is needed, however, to relate his views of the history of nature and the history of man to those of his contemporaries. Huxley was neither a historian nor an anthropologist, but he studied history and was a member of the Anthropological Society. His introductions to *Science and the Hebrew Tradition* and *Science and the Christian Tradition* as well as "The Evolution of Theology: An Anthropological Approach" are excursions into the field and, though commented on briefly by J. W. Burrow in *Evolution and Society* (1966), need further analysis.

What is important is to see the *vision* that is embodied here and elsewhere in Huxley's work. Most recent critics have seen the dark Calvinistic streak in this vision and the fierce anti-Utopianism of the prophet's gaze into the future, as well as the image of man insistently staving off the chaos of the cosmos and in himself, building a garden on the darkling plain, relighting the candle again and again. It is this vision that has suggested to Cockshut that "Huxley, more than any of his contemporaries, foreshadows the pessimistic humanism of Faulkner and Camus" and to Noland, Huxley's kinship with Hardy and Conrad. Such insights should stimulate further study of Huxley's vision of history, especially its haunting images, and the close connection of his views to those of men whom it is now fashionable to admire for their alienation from man and nature.

Educator

Pessimism, of course, never reduced Huxley to inaction. It would be a nice exercise to decide whether he was more active on behalf of Rationalism or on behalf of education. For Cyril Bibby, in fact, "it is as an educator that T. H. Huxley has the greatest significance," now that his scientific work is superseded and his "controversial writings become pieces to be admired for their craftsmanship but no longer put to daily use" (*T. H. Huxley: Scientist, Humanist, and Educator*), a view that echoes Irvine's remark that "the bishop eater has tended to be more famous, though less read, than Huxley the teacher and the statesman of science" (*Apes, Angels and Victorians*). Thanks to Bibby, moreover, we now know more than ever before, not only of Huxley the agitator for educational reform, but of his ideas on the subject. Henry Fairfield Osborn, one of Huxley's students, wrote a general study (*Huxley and Education*) in 1910, but until Bibby began publishing his articles in the 1950's, the only essay is by Louis Foley, "The Huxley Tradition of Language Study" (*MLJ*, 1942). In his notes Bibby lists his earlier articles, several of them in specialized English journals, the essence of which has been incorporated in his book. Two of these deserve mention here: "T. H. Huxley's Idea of a University" (*Universities Q.*, 1956), based partly on unpublished materials, is an important and interesting comparison of Huxley's "idea" to those of Arnold and Newman; "Thomas Henry Huxley and University Development" (*VS*, 1958) details Huxley's enormous role in the shaping and reshaping of university education in England, culminating in his being in old age towed into line to fight for a great federated University of London. Bibby admits that Huxley left no great texts on university education, but is convinced by the evidence that "he had more influence on the actual development of the universities in the nineteenth century" than Newman, Pattison, or Jowett.

All this and more is encompassed in Bibby's book, which is so well documented that it will really be impossible for anyone now to see Arnold and Huxley in simple terms of opposition, or to say, as Irvine did, that Huxley's idea of education was the creation of a mind like a well-oiled machine. Though published before the C. P. Snow-F. R. Leavis "Two Cultures" debacle, Bibby's account of Huxley impresses one with the fact that the issue has been with us for a long time indeed and suggests the possibility of a fruitful comparison between the terms and persons of the argument in the two centuries. Moreover, one must be impressed by Bibby's interpretation of Huxley's ideas in the context of the educational and larger politics of the times. Consistently, Huxley thought of the whole child, of the background of poverty from which the child might come, and thus found himself a spokesman, not only for the scientific community, or for ambitious middle-class students, or for those who saw Germany outflanking England in national education, but of the working class and the poor, with whom he had a singular rapport.

Prose Stylist

Loren Eiseley has remarked that "there are really two faces that comprise the face of Thomas Henry Huxley. The one in youth—sensitive, mobile, somewhat sad—is that of a poet. The other . . . could be the face of a great barrister . . . of a fighter who expects no mercy and gives none" (Introd. to *On a Piece of Chalk*, 1967). Eiseley's image of the barrister's face is not quite, as Walter Houghton earlier remarked, what the older critics of Huxley's rhetoric said it was—the face of an honest controversialist scorning rhetoric to whom, as his grandson Aldous said, "truth was more important than personal triumph" ("T. H. Huxley as a Man of Letters," *The Olive Tree*, 1937). Houghton's essay, "The Rhetoric of T. H. Huxley" (*UTQ*, 1949), marks the recognition that "when Huxley turned from straight exposition to generalization about the values of science or religion . . . and to cognate passages on scientists and clergymen, he was by no means reluctant to bolster a shaky or a biased argument . . . with the extra emotional influence . . . of exaggeration and insinuation." Houghton proceeds to document his thesis by an examination of selected passages, devoting to them the close textual analysis they deserve, noting en passant that Huxley's rhetoric is sometimes "suddenly swept by a gust of personal emotion which he cannot check or master." Houghton's anatomy of Huxley's use of rhetorical devices, however, does not lead him to condemn Huxley's tactics as either "vicious or unscrupulous" or those of "a slick politician with a party platform to defend." Rather they are the outcome, as Wilfrid Ward asserted, "of deep conviction" on the part of an "able and lucid exponent of one side" (*Problems and Persuasions*, 1903, cited by Houghton).

Two later discussions of Huxley's controversial rhetoric tend to pass summary judgments without close analysis. Irvine (*Apes, Angels and Victorians*) gives high marks to "The Physical Basis of Life," "Mr. Darwin's Critics," and "Science and Culture," but lower marks to "Agnosticism" and the Gladstonian essays; Bibby, in "The Prince of Controversialists" (*TC*, 1957), recites triumphs rather than literary judgments. In 1962, however, Blinderman published an essay supplementing Houghton's approach, dealing with "the effectiveness of [Huxley's] communication of Darwinism" ("Semantic Aspects of T. H. Huxley's Literary Style," *J. of Communication*). Drawing on a variety of sources including the Huxley Papers, Blinderman shows us what Huxley thought about the problem of being a popular lecturer and writer, how the tensions between the need to be accurate and the need to persuade worked themselves out "in prose which has outlasted not only his scientific memoirs but also the literary remains of most of his contemporaries." While Blinderman analyzes a few characteristic passages (and in so doing substantially agrees with Houghton), he lifts up only one passage that would illustrate his conclusion quoted above. He has made a large claim that drastically challenges William E. Buckler's view that Huxley (along with Mill) as a stylist was only a journeyman, though of a high order (Introd. to *Prose of the Victorian Era*, 1959). The essays by Houghton and Blinderman are not only competent in themselves, but, taken together with "The Rhetorical Strategy of Thomas H. Huxley and Robert G. Ingersoll: Agnostics and Roadblock Removers" (*Speech Monographs*, 1965), by J. Vernon Jensen, are suggestive of further studies along the same line. Houghton's essay particularly stimulates attention to those "gusts of personal emotion," or as Eiseley has called them, those "passages that erupt as belligerently as the murky fires of the first blast furnaces." Blinderman, who calls attention to Huxley's interest in grace, force, exactness, and beauty, leads us to consider the face of Huxley as poet.

Students who have read the beautiful essays on chalk and on the lobster might do well to begin with Aldous Huxley's attempt to display how his grandfather's prose both in "scientific and emotive statements arouses aesthetic feelings." The analytic section of his essay ("T. H. Huxley as a Man of Letters") begins with brief quotations of Huxley's notions of style and a classification of his writings under three headings—the descriptive, the philosophical and sociological, and the "controversial and the emotional." He continues by illustrating each and commenting in particular on Huxley's techniques of rhythm and iteration, especially what he calls the "caesura-sentences." He also notes Huxley's spare use of imagery and the effectiveness of his Biblical allusions. "The analysis," as Aldous remarked, "might be carried further," for if indeed his grandfather had something of the poet in him, this needs to be demonstrated more than it has been up to now. That the demonstration is possible is made clear by Joseph H. Gardner's striking article, "A Huxley Essay as 'Poem'" (*VS*, 1970), which applies clear criteria and perceptive textual analysis to argue that "The Physical Basis of Life" is better read as a poem than as rhetoric. Gardner's argument should provoke discussion and stimulate others to produce comparable studies.

Those who venture into this territory, however, should be aware of the extent to which Huxley's artistry is an expression of his considered views, not only on sentence rhetoric, but on the function of the artist and the close relationship between artist and scientist, the latter view anticipating those of our own day and not usually attributed to Huxley. That he held such views is now put beyond dispute by another article by Blinderman, "T. H. Huxley's Theory of Aesthetics: Unity in Diversity" (*JAAC*, 1962). "Huxley's unpublished papers," writes Blinderman, indicate that "a sense of structure pervaded his thinking" and writing and that Huxley moved "towards a synthesis which demonstrates that the bridging of the gap between the 'two cultures' can be achieved through an engagement with form as well as through . . . commitment to man's welfare." That Huxley was "a born lover of form" and that his method of exposition "was simply the method of anatomy" is not, as Blinderman is well aware, a new idea in Huxley scholarship; what Blinderman presents as new, however, is a series of tantalizing quotations from unpublished texts which "comprise the closest statement one can get of Huxley's theory of art." What these quotations show is that Huxley regarded both scientists and artists as those who "arrest the flux of phenomena" and who are, to use Coleridge's phrase, "the tamers of chaos." Readers of this essay will wish to juxtapose it to Noland's (discussed above) and note, though it is not Noland's purpose, how the famous image of the garden as an emblem of order and civilization pervades Huxley's "Prolegomena" and how Noland's exposition, though based only on published sources, seems to be confirmed by Blinderman's view that in Huxley "the structuring of chaos . . . can almost be said to have been an element in his personality."

Topics for Further Study

Recent scholarship on Huxley has been generally sound, but the few scholars working on him would welcome a swelling of their ranks. Obviously there is still much to be done. One fact, for example, emerges from a reading of Bibby and Irvine: the need for a thorough study of Huxley's political activities and ideas. Irvine (*Apes, Angels and Victorians*) asserts that Huxley's "political excursions began in 1888." But surely this ignores his participation in the Governor Eyre protests and, more important, his whole educational campaign, which is nothing if not political. Moreover, though Huxley astutely refused to enter Parliament, he was a citizen-statesman-politician bent on removing or immobilizing the forces in English life and thought that obstructed what he considered to be necessary change. To look at his political life demands not only a consideration of the essays he wrote after 1888, but also examination of his day-to-day reactions to political events as well as his more theoretical formulations. Irvine's assertion that "Huxley was as cautious in politics as he was extreme in religion" also needs testing. Why was Huxley opposed to Home Rule? Why did he give Henry George such a blast? Are there real inconsistencies in his political life and thought? Some clear light needs to be shed on these matters.

Another topic for study is the question of Huxley's reading and the influences that played upon his thought and life, especially his knowledge of Continental writers and thinkers. To turn the coin over, we also need studies of the nature of his contribution to Western thought. How much of that influence took the form of receiving his words clearly and accurately and how much the form of distortion and oversimplification, as in the case of other prophets? Bibby has also suggested that there may be some kinship between Huxley's philosophy and dialectical materialism; the suggestion needs testing.

IV. JOHN MORLEY (1838–1923)

Though his parents thought John Morley safe for the clergy when they left him in John Wesley's rooms at Lincoln College, the heady atmosphere of Oxford in the fifties proved too strong for the Wesleyan emanations. Losing his religious faith and, as a result, the parental allowance, in 1860 he went to London where he became a journalist, wrote for the *Saturday Review* and other periodicals, and made friends with Leslie Stephen and other members of the Victorian radical intelligentsia —Frederic Harrison, George Henry Lewes, and George Meredith, and eventually with their Gamaliel, John Stuart Mill.

Chosen in 1867 to succeed Lewes as editor of the *Fortnightly Review*, Morley began a remarkable career as editor, historian, literary critic, biographer, Member of Parliament, Secretary of State for Ireland, and Secretary of State for India. In 1908, he took his seat in the Lords and was Lord President of the Council from 1910 to 1914, when he resigned from the cabinet to spend the last quiet nine years in recollections.

As an Unbeliever, Morley carried the war to the enemy in the *Fortnightly Review* until 1882, opening its pages to Huxley, Tyndall, Stephen, Harrison, Arnold, Swinburne, and Pater, all of whom attacked received views on a number of fronts: the Church, the Crown, an outmoded educational system, and Philistinism of whatever variety. Though he wrote no text of unbelief—that is, no "Creed of a Layman" or "Agnostic's Apology"—he carried out the work of destructive criticism of theology in his studies of the leaders of the French Enlightenment. His most famous book, *On Compromise* (1874), is a major polemic, a continuation of Mill's *On Liberty*, a severe critique of the art of muddling through and intellectual double-bookkeeping, and a search for the proper stance for the liberal intellectual bent on changing the world. It is a book to set beside Leslie Stephen's *Freethinking and Plainspeaking* (1873).

Editing the *Fortnightly Review* and later the *Pall Mall Gazette*, the English Men of Letters, and the Twelve English Statesmen series was not enough for this ambitious man, who could not resist the desire to translate liberal ideas into politics while he rose in place and power. From the early 1880's until his famous resignation he continued to combine his political and literary careers, writing on Cobden, Walpole, Cromwell, and finally composing the monumental *Life of William Ewart Gladstone*, while rising to the loftier circles of the Liberal Party and achieving high place, though never the Foreign Office, which he craved.

A baffling figure, Morley is for some the paradigm of the liberal intellectual in politics and for others the image of an intellectual used by politicians to give a liberal and respectable aura for otherwise unsuitable policies and programs. Another problem is raised by those who felt that Morley's adventure into politics spoiled a great man of letters; Hardy's view that Morley could have been the Gibbon of his age is a case in point. Still other sources of interest are his inner conflicts. "Cut him open," said George Meredith of the man who spelled God with a small "g," "and you will find a clergyman inside"; Frederic Harrison summed him up as "Diderot *plus* John Wesley." Morley described himself in 1885 as being "a cautious Whig by temperament, a sound Liberal by training, and a thorough Radical by observation and experience." The resultant mixture varied from time to time, depending on the relative amounts of each ingredient Morley chose to pour in, and, if sometimes unpalatable, was seldom bland.

Works and Bibliography

The most complete, single listing of Morley's works is to be found in the British Museum Catalogue, though briefer lists are in the bibliographies of Stanley Wolpert's *Morley and India* (1967), D. A. Hamer's *John Morley: Liberal Intellectual in Politics* (1968), and Stephen E. Koss's *John Morley at the India Office, 1905–1910* (1969). The *edition de luxe, The Works of John Morley* (1921), runs to fifteen volumes, but consisted of only 750 copies; for ordinary purposes, students will find it easier to use the twelve-volume 1923 edition or the earlier editions of the separate works, but if collation of texts is to be attempted the *de luxe* or the 1923 edition is essential. Neither of these editions, however, includes Morley's lives of Cobden (1881) or of Gladstone (1903), *The Struggle for National Education* (1873), *Indian Speeches* (1909), nor the posthumously published *Memorandum on Resignation* (1928), and other miscellaneous items. Two of these, *Modern Characteristics* (1865) and *Studies in Conduct* (1867), were published anonymously and are difficult to locate outside the British Museum (a copy of the latter is in the Boston Athenaeum); they are described in "Two Anonymous Books by Lord Morley," by F. B. Harvey (*ConR*, 1927). In 1895, several of his essays were translated into French and published under the title *Essais critiques* with an introduction by Augustin Filon. In 1923 H. G. Rawlinson edited a volume of *Selected Essays*. Morley has hardly been anthologized since his death, nor, with the exception of *On Compromise*, have his works been reprinted until recently. Peter Stansky has edited a selection of his historical and critical studies, entitled *Nineteenth Century Essays* (1970), an indication of possibly renewed interest, which is strengthened by the reprinting of the 1872 edition of *Voltaire* (1970), the 1887 *Burke* (1968), the 1889 *Walpole* (1970), the 1897 *Machiavelli* (1970), the 1897 *Diderot* (1968), the 1903 *Life of William Ewart Gladstone* (1969), and the 1923 *Oracles on Man and Government* (1968). Finally, Asa Briggs has edited Morley's *The Struggle for National Education* (1970), in the Harvester Press series, Society and the Victorians.

Still incompletely listed and uncollected are a large number of essays contributed by Morley to the *Fortnightly Review* and other monthlies, quarterlies, and newspapers, not to mention his Parliamentary speeches quoted in Hansard. The first volume of the *Wellesley Index* may be consulted for his essays in *Macmillan's*; many others can be located by signature. Also identifiable, but not without effort, are assorted letters and items printed in newspapers such as the *Newcastle Daily Chronicle*, the *Times*, and the *Pall Mall Gazette*. Morley's essays in the *Saturday Review* are clearly identified in Merle Mowbray Bevington's *The Saturday Review*,

1855–1868 (1941) but not beyond the terminal date. Finally, there are political speeches, lectures, and other fugitive items to be listed. Hamer has apparently tracked down many of these, for he quotes Morley from the *Pall Mall Gazette* frequently and the *Times* copiously, but he gives us no checklist.

Hamer also reports two interesting finds in the Morley Library at the University of Manchester: a proof copy of a book on Ireland which Morley never published and a commonplace book. Hamer does not date the period in Morley's life that the latter covers.

A virtually complete bibliography of work on Morley may be compiled from the bibliographies of Wolpert, Hamer, and Koss, and from the dissertation by Valentine John Healy, "John Morley, Interpreter of the French Enlightenment" (St. Louis 1961).

Biography and Letters

The manuscript sources for the study of Morley's biography are voluminous, as is to be expected for a man who led such an active public life. The largest single collection reposes in the India Office Library and has been cataloged by Molly Poulter and published in two volumes (1965). A second major collection is in the custody of A. F. Thompson of Wadham College, Oxford. This material is not yet accessible, but it is expected that in due course it will be made available to scholars. Wolpert and Koss give differing accounts of the disposition of Morley's papers since his death; conversation with Thompson convinces me that the Koss account is the more accurate. Morley's correspondence with Frederic Harrison and T. H. Huxley will be found in the London School of Economics and the Imperial College, respectively. American scholars may be particularly interested in the more than 400 letters Lord Haldane, among others. Hamer, Koss, and Wolpert are the best guides to to Andrew Carnegie held by the Library of Congress. Of relevance to historians are the papers of statesmen who were Morley's colleagues, such as those of Joseph Chamberlain, William Ewart Gladstone, William Harcourt, Lord Rosebery, and these materials, of which I have listed samples.

At the moment, no single, definitive biography of Morley exists. His life up to the election of 1885 may be studied in *The Early Life and Letters of John Morley* (2 vols., 1927) by F. W. Hirst, also author of the *DNB* life. Hirst planned to treat the later life, but never did so, though his *In the Golden Days* (1947) includes several reminiscences of Morley's later years. Hirst had access to the Morley family papers and produced a detailed, but by no means complete, picture of the early years, which Morley himself scanted in his *Recollections* (2 vols., 1917). Through Morley's correspondence with his friends we get a vivid and dramatic picture of his life as editor of the *Fortnightly Review* and an intimate account of his movement into the political arena in the 1880's. While maddeningly reticent about Morley's life from 1860 to 1867 and full of admiration for his subject, Hirst is by no means uncritical; his judgments on Morley's thought and action are independently formed, and his analyses of the works shrewd. Thus, there are a number of matters in Morley's private life that need clarifying before we can see the whole man (see, for example, "Who Was Mrs. Morley?" by John W. Bicknell and Clarence L. Cline, *VN*, 1973).

Supplementary to Hirst's *Early Life* and valuable for conveying the excitement of Morley's years as a radical journalist are a series of articles by Frances Knickerbocker in the *Sewanee Review* (1924, 1927, 1933, 1939) that formed the basis of her book *Free Minds: John Morley and His Friends* (1943; rpt. 1970). Though Janet Courtney's *The Making of an Editor: W. L. Courtney, 1850–1928* (1930) contains a chapter on Morley as editor of the *Fortnightly Review*, the most detailed and scholarly treatment of Morley and the *Fortnightly Review* is Edwin M. Everett's *The Party of Humanity* (1939), an excellent piece of scholarship which, unfortunately, tells the story to 1874 only, leaving the final years of Morley's editorship still to be examined. Studies of other phases of his journalistic career, by men who knew him, include T. H. S. Escott's *Masters of English Journalism* (1911) and "John Morley" (*FortR*, 1923); dealing with his editorship of the *Pall Mall Gazette* is W. T. Stead's "The Right Honorable John Morley" (*Rev. of Reviews*, 1890), and J. Robertson Scott's somewhat undependable *The Life and Death of a Newspaper: An Account of the Temperaments, Perturbations, and Achievements of J. Morley, W. T. Stead, etc.* (1952). Morley's related career as a reader for Macmillan's and as editor of the English Men of Letters and Twelve English Statesmen series is described, but not thoroughly, in *The House of Macmillan* (1944) by Charles Morgan. Most recently Morley the journalist has been discussed by John Gross in his *The Rise and Fall of the Man of Letters* (1969) and by Christopher Kent in "Higher Journalism and the Mid-Victorian Clerisy" (*VS*, 1969).

Students of Morley must be warned that they are dealing with a public man of many contacts in the great world; to grasp his life, especially his political career, one must consult a large number of biographical and autobiographical works about and by his friends and colleagues. Frederic Harrison's *Autobiographic Memoirs* (1911), A. G. Gardiner's *Life of William Harcourt* (1923), and Garvin and Amery's four-volume life of *Joseph Chamberlain* (1932, 1933, 1934, 1951) are only samples of such works listed in greater detail by Wolpert and Hamer. The enormity of the biographical task may well explain why, until very recently, the only studies of Morley's later life and career have been brief, many of them composed by acquaintances shortly after his death. Of these (which are listed in Wolpert) the more interesting are the early chapters of *John, Viscount Morley* (1924) by John H. Morgan, an old friend and admirer, and a penetrating essay by Augustine Birrell reprinted in *Things Past Redress* (1937). Recently, however, one gap left by Hirst is being filled. Using not only the India House collection but other papers recently made available, M. N. Das, Stanley Wolpert, and Stephen Koss have much to relate that is new on Morley's behavior as Secretary of State for India. Das, in *India under Morley and Minto: Politics behind Revolution, Repression and Reforms* (1964), gives us the Indian point of view; Wolpert, sophisticated and thorough, provides in his final chapter an admirable summing up of the dual movements of reform and "its darker face," repression, that characterized Morley's administration of India in a difficult and "turbulent era"; Stephen Koss makes his contribution to our understanding of Morley's role by emphasizing the way in which Morley carried Gladstonian presuppositions into an era and a situation in which they did not fit and by bringing us close to the almost day-by-day battles that Morley conducted with the Army, the Indian bureaucracy, and the criticism of English Radicals. The three studies supplement each other. Other gaps left by Hirst will be filled when A. F. Thompson completes his work, in part biographical and in part political, of Morley's role in English politics.

Of equal interest to historians, but covering a shorter time span, are two works which deal with Morley's role in Liberal Party rivalries at the end of the century. Peter Stansky's *Ambitions and Strategies: The Struggle for the Leadership of the Liberal Party in the 1890's* (1964), Stephen Koss's "Morley in the Middle" (*EHR*, 1967), and Kenneth O. Morgan's "John Morley and the Crisis of Liberalism, 1894" (*Nat. Lib. of Wales J.*, 1968), with their references to the papers of Sir William Harcourt, Viscount Esher, Lord Haldane, and to recent biographies of Randolph Churchill and Lord Rosebery, only illustrate the complexity of the task of unraveling Morley's political role in this or that governmental predicament. Those who undertake it must be stung by the "fascination of what's difficult."

The most recent and by far the most searching examination of Morley's whole career in the light of his character is D. A. Hamer's *John Morley: Liberal Intellectual in Politics* (1968). Hamer attempts to come to grips with "the interplay between the political ideas and the principles of John Morley and the various situations and problems in which he was involved as a practical politician." He has written an extremely challenging book, rich in hitherto untapped sources, which he uses to argue a cogent and provocative thesis. From the point of view of students of Victorian unbelief, his thesis is significant, for it starts with the proposition that Morley is to be seen, first, as "an intellectual preoccupied with the consequences of loss of religious faith," searching desperately to work out a system to guide his life, thought, and politics, but not quite able to commit himself to any, and therefore resorting to the expedient of concentrating on "one question at a time" in politics and of attaching himself to a series of heroes, both in the past and in his own time. Hamer's treatment of Morley's career and his role in the Liberal Party is thus controlled by his thesis, which presides over his presentation of all the details of election issues, party programs, and cabinet intrigue.

Hamer's brief early chapters deal with Morley's combined search for a father and a creed. Thus Hamer sees Morley's attraction to Mill as an example of the former and his study of Comte of the latter. Skillfully, Hamer shows us how many of Morley's French studies deal with conflicts between father and son and between order and anarchy in the lives of his subjects, as well as with conflicts between intellect and power. In effect, Morley's early biographies "appear as extremely personal works, used to explore his own situations and resolve dilemmas." This approach to Morley's French studies is fascinating and differs from (without contradicting) the usual interpretation of them as overly didactic tracts for the times. While illuminating, Hamer's approach may suggest to the untutored reader that Morley's works and career are solely expressive of his personal psychic problems. Since Hamer does not evaluate Morley's works and ideas as intellectual creations but as personal instruments, we do not see so much of the *intellectual* in politics, but a great deal of John Morley in politics. For a study of Morley's ideas, qua ideas, consult Kenneth Zimmerman, "The Political Thought of John Morley" (Diss. Minnesota 1967).

As a matter of fact, Hamer could have pressed his psychological approach more vigorously by examining the personality in even greater depth, as Peter Stansky suggests (*VS*, 1969). There is nothing here of Morley's early Bohemianism, of his marriage, of his inordinate sensitivity about rank and status, or of his personal ambition, just as there is little if any real analysis of the validity and importance of Morley's ideas for his own time or ours. The Morley that emerges appears to be a kind of failure, wrong on too many occasions. These caveats, however, should not diminish the importance of Hamer's book: its thesis is significant even if overridden, its use of sources voluminous, and its incidental insights too numerous to mention. Hamer has taken a giant step into the thickets of Morley's contradictions and paradoxes: the tensions between the reformer and the ambitious politician, between the radical democrat and the seeker after men of power, between his caution and his audacity, and between all those other contending impulses that made J. H. Morgan describe Morley as being "in a ministry . . . like Hamlet fallen among a conventicle of all the sons of Polonius, and like Hamlet . . . brooding, solitary, scrupulous and passionate, flashing out the most tragic of truths."

Setting Morley in the wider context of a generation of like-minded university men is the dissertation by Christopher Kent, "Aspects of Academic Radicalism in Mid-Victorian England: A Study in the Politics of Thought and Action, with Particular Reference to Frederic Harrison and John Morley" (Sussex 1968), now being prepared for publication under the title *Academic Radicalism: Politics and the Clerisy in Mid-Victorian England*. Kent widens the lens used by Melvin Richter to study T. H. Green in *The Politics of Conscience* (1964) and surveys, first, a number of figures comprising the intellectual elite, then contracts his lens to examine the Radicals, the Comtists, and finally Harrison and Morley as two exemplars of the intellectual in politics.

Critical Studies

Among the earlier critical studies of Morley's works, the student will find some amusement in reading Robert Buchanan (who shared with Morley the dubious honor of attacking fleshly poetry) in the *Contemporary Review* (1871) and two good samples of hostile criticism at the hands of W. S. Lilley in the *Dublin Review* (1887) and of W. H. Mallock in the *Quarterly Review* (1889), both reviews of the nine-volume collected works (1886). Mallock is particularly searching and hostile; since Morley is "the Fénelon or Cardinal Newman of the Radical movement," he must be subjected to a solid blast: Morley believes in an immoral philosophical system that makes men who embrace it immoral; he is inconsistent in simultaneously embracing democratic principles and undermining "every main proposition on which his formulated radicalism depends." It is a trenchant attack that every Morleyite must confront.

Two other conservative estimates are also worth consideration: Algernon Cecil's in *Six Oxford Thinkers* (1909) and Paul Elmer More's in *A New England Group and Others, Shelburne Essays*, xi (1921). More's essay is the less significant. Cecil's study sets Morley off against Newman and presents Morley as the last of the liberal breed, who connected the Edwardians with the mid-Victorians as he had formerly linked Victorian radicals with the French Enlightenment. Like More and Mallock, Cecil detects a contradiction between Morley's radical credo and his actions. He finds him more moderate and sympathetic "than his creed from start to finish." He sees, moreover, Morley's interest in Burke as a sign of conservative instincts somewhat at war with the radical creed, and the radical creed at war with the moralistic historian who must approve of Cromwell, but is silent on the moral issues of the massacres at Drogheda and Wexford. Though thus critical, Cecil nevertheless looks back on Morley's career with admiration and offers the judgment that he made the House of Commons less common and that his passionate love of truth drew him closer to Newman than he ever knew. Perhaps, as Healy has suggested, a study of Morley's relation to the Oxford Movement is in order.

Cecil has thus set down the issues all students of Morley must face, the central paradoxes of his thought. Until 1940, general studies had done little more than elaborate and explore them in detail. Lytton Strachey's review of *Recollections*, "A Statesman: Lord Morley," reprinted in *Characters and Commentaries* (1937), is another of his acid dissolvents of Victorian Eminence, and J. A. Spender in *Fortnightly Review* (1938) celebrates the centenary of Morley's birth with the ambivalent judgment that while honest John would work "indefatigably at any literary task" that would gain him "a footing in . . . the real world of the great," his early works "hold a high place in the literature of political edification."

More sympathetic than any so far mentioned are books by Warren Staebler (*The Liberal Mind of John Morley*, 1943) and by Frances Knickerbocker. Staebler's fourth chapter is a sixty-page critical summary of Morley's major works and essays, though curiously he omits *On Compromise*. His major effort is to exhibit Morley as "applying the historical method to criticism" and traces Morley's theory primarily to Darwinism; though he discusses Comte, Staebler underestimates his influence on Morley's whole historical perspective, an influence Morley admits more than once in letters to Harrison, though denying emphatically any sectarian connections. In such a survey Staebler is unable to analyze any one of Morley's works in detail, but his summaries are succinct and the criticisms apt. His chapter serves as an excellent introduction for the uninstructed student. It concludes, moreover, with a cogent and eloquent defense of Morley's relevance for the twentieth century: "it is exactly this body of thought which exhibits such startling pertinency to our own day and relates him more closely, perhaps, than any of the other Victorians to the twentieth century." Staebler might have quoted Morley's journal entry of 1 September 1910 as evidence of his prescience: "Talk of India and other 'insoluble problems' of great States, I declare the American Negro often strikes me as the hardest of them all."

The most passionate defense of Morley's importance is to be found in the series of articles by Knickerbocker mentioned above and later reworked into the texture of her book, *Free Minds* (1943). While uncritical in its praise and overemotional in tone, her book has the virtue of its defect—enthusiasm. It is also well documented. It is clear that for Knickerbocker the image of an embattled liberal was an important one to hold up before an audience agitated by the struggles of the 1930's and by the rise of fascism when liberalism seemed to be stumbling its compromising way to Munich. Morley is for her, as he is for her opposite, W. H. Mallock, the Fénelon of the Radical movement, but she approves.

The most recent brief study is the chapter on Morley in Basil Willey's *More Nineteenth Century Studies: A Group of Honest Doubters* (1956). Unconcerned with Morley's political career and writings, Willey focuses on his historical studies, *On Compromise*, and the literary criticism. It is a deft, urbane, and sometimes witty performance, emphasizing those elements in Morley's thought that bear on the theme of his whole book, "agnosticism and religious liberalism." Even more recent and more thorough is *John Morley* (1972) by Edward Alexander, an excellent study, which "undertakes a critical survey of his work as a man of letters with the emphasis placed upon the methods and principles of his historical studies and literary criticism as well as on his ethical and political ideas."

On Compromise

Though not widely read and studied today, Morley's *On Compromise* (1874) continues to be recognized as a central document both in the history of his mind and of late Victorian liberalism. In his *John Morley and Other Essays* (1920),

George Harper called it "the moral portrait of the author," and more recently Milton Konvitz linked it with Mill's *On Liberty* as representing "the most cogent statement of Victorian liberalism" ("John Morley on Liberty and Compromise," *Essays in Political Theory Presented to George H. Sabine*, 1948). In the same year, however, Byron Dexter ("Morley and Compromise," *Foreign Affairs*, 1948) challenged the assertion of H. H. Massingham ("Morley the Humanist," *FortR*, 1923) that Morley's life was guided by the principles of his great polemic. Beginning with a masterly exegesis of the text and reminding the reader that Morley, far from denouncing all forms of compromise, was concerned only to set limits, Dexter turns to the political career and finds that, from the point of view of political tactics, Morley did not always follow his own principles; he did not compromise enough! Dexter has an interesting thesis, but he does not really work out its implications; the essay is too brief, and, at the end, more busy making points about American foreign policy than shaping a final assessment of Morley. The task he began should be taken up again.

Hamer suggestively treats *On Compromise* as a principal source of Morley's key political principles, seeing the book as "a kind of manual of conduct for the élite . . . of mid-Victorian England . . . a *Prince* or *Courtier* of Victorian liberalism," and showing us how it was thus read, in fact, by Haldane, Asquith, and Grey in the late 1880's. Hamer also sees it as a treatise on the "higher expediency," an updating of Burke. Another treatment of *On Compromise* as an "elitist manifesto" will be found in Part IV of Christopher Kent's dissertation, "Aspects of Academic Radicalism in Mid-Victorian England," mentioned above. While it is interesting that recent scholars are finding strains of conservatism in the early Morley and thus blunting the charge that the later Morley was a kind of turncoat, one must, as Alexander reminds us, still recall that Morley's readers in the seventies were most impressed by his insistence on the primacy of truth, his attacks on the Church and on the so-called Utility of Error. *On Compromise* needs careful rhetorical analysis of the sort employed by Kenneth Burke or John Holloway before we can see what it reveals to us of Morley and what it communicated to its public in that time and place.

French Studies

The recognition that Morley's French Studies (as they are often called) are polemical as well as academic, though emphasized by such modern critics as Knickerbocker, Staebler, Willey, and Alexander, came early. Not only the sympathetic Buchanan and the fellow unbeliever Leslie Stephen ("Voltaire," *Fraser's*, 1872), but also Mallock and W. S. Lilley knew very well what Morley was about. That the French Studies are, as Basil Willey remarks, "tracts for the times" is incontestable; that they also constitute critiques of the great figures of the Enlightenment and include sympathetic studies of conservative figures, such as his *De Maistre* (1868) provides evidence of the way in which Morley and other sons of Mill had taken to heart the master's interest in syncretizing Coleridge and Bentham. The road into the French Studies begins with Morley's first *Burke* (1867) and especially (as Staebler reminds us) with its last eighty-five pages, continues by way of his shorter essays, and stretches out into his major volumes on Voltaire, Rousseau, and his beloved Diderot.

The most extensive and judicious account of these French Studies will be found in Alexander; nonetheless their full significance is yet to be explored. Three major areas suggest themselves: one, a study of Morley's methodology in what he called the history of opinion; two, a study of the extent to which his work stands up against modern historical scholarship; three, a close examination of the way in which his nineteenth-century concerns affected his interpretation of his eighteenth-century analogues. A correlative study would be the attempt to extract the evidence so pervasive, but unsystematized, of Morley's philosophical position and the bearing of this evidence on his other work. On Morley's historical method, the critics already mentioned have had something to say and agree that Morley, like Stephen, thought that ideas and men were motivated by the social forces around them, but no one has really determined what, if any, theory he really espoused.

Older historians credit Morley with a leading role in reversing Carlyle's judgment on the bankrupt eighteenth century (G. P. Gooch, *History and Historians in the Nineteenth Century*, 1913); and biographers of Voltaire, Rousseau, and Diderot have in the past cited Morley with approval, as, for example, Ferdinand Brunetière, *Etudes critiques sur l'histoire de la littérature française*, III, VII (1899) and his "La Bilan de Voltaire" (*RDM*, 1890). More recently, if the views of Peter Gay be typical, Morley's value as a guide to the philosophes is being discredited. Although in his *Voltaire's Politics* (1959) Gay cited Morley's *Voltaire* as a good starting point for the modern reader, in his *The Party of Humanity: Essays on the French Enlightenment* (1964), he blamed Morley for being the perpetrator of the view of Rousseau as a confused thinker who neglected history and experience, and damned Morley's *Rousseau* as "thoroughly dated in all respects." He passed then to a wider judgment of Morley's biographies of the philosophes: "sympathetic and intelligent as they are, [they] perpetuated the misconceptions and gave weight to the kind of criticism they were designed to eradicate. . . . if a sympathizer could call the Enlightenment impractical and immoral, why should an opponent not feel the same?" Gay raises a real question, but he has perhaps forgotten the impact Morley's French Studies had on his contemporaries and the extent to which they answered Arnold's cry for a fresh current of ideas to deprovincialize English intellectual life. Nevertheless, it is worth considering Gay's point, if only to determine how much of Morley's disapproval of certain Enlightenment tendencies (e.g., loose morals) was motivated by genuine conviction and how much by a deliberate attempt to throw sops to Philistine opinion in order to carry his main points. Such consideration might lead into a third area of investigation: it may well be that Morley, like Leslie Stephen with the Deists, was concerned to expose the failures of the philosophes as well as their liberating doctrines in order to determine how failure could be avoided in his own time. A sector of this area has been plotted by Healy and by Hamer in his early chapters, though the latter's focus is on the way in which these books satisfy Morley's private needs rather than on his needs as a Radical crusader. Hamer's view comes from a different angle of vision from that of Knickerbocker, Staebler, Willey, or Healy. He cites passage after passage from the French Studies revealing Morley's concern—virtually obsessive according to Hamer—with the problem of order and disorder, in both public and private life, and with the problem of being intellectually radical and politically cautious. To the extent that Hamer extrapolates from the French Studies texts for understanding Morley's later career he has illuminated an important aspect of the *Voltaire*, the *Rousseau*, and to a lesser extent, the *Diderot*, but his emphasis needs to be balanced by Kent's sense of historical context and by Alexander's critical acumen.

Literary Criticism

The full extent of Morley's literary criticism is not to be found either in his *Critical Miscellanies* (3 vols., 1886; 4 vols., 1908) or his *Studies in Literature* (1891), but must be pursued in the pages of the *Saturday Review*, the *Fortnightly Review*, and elsewhere. Students should also be aware of Morley's literary estimates in *Recollections* and of his deep and abiding study of Dante, Shakespeare, and Lucretius. Like his contemporaries Arnold and Stephen, he believed in art for man's sake, as befitted an unbelieving crusader in the cause of humanity. Known too often only by his famous (or infamous) review of Swinburne's *Poems and Ballads* (*SatR*, 1866; rpt. in Houghton and Stange, *Victorian Poetry and Poetics*, 1968), and by Osbert Sitwell's denunciation (Preface to *Victoriana*, 1931), Morley's criticism has a wider range and a good deal more sympathy with the avant-garde than that single review might suggest.

No substantial study of Morley's literary essays appeared between James Dow McCallum's dissertation, "Lord Morley's Criticism of English Poetry and Prose" (Princeton 1921) and 1943, the year in which Staebler and Knickerbocker published their works. Staebler's book, written first, provides us with brief commentaries on a series of essays and concludes with a conscientious assessment. He gives Morley high marks for his ability to recognize literary merit in the new writer, citing as examples Morley's praise of Meredith, George Eliot, Pater, Morris, and Hardy; for his breadth of mind in distinguishing between the character of the writer and the merit of his work; for his use of psychological analysis; for his vigorous efforts to create, under Arnold's influence, "a literary atmosphere" in which creative artists could work; and finally, for his historical approach and "synthetic method" in which mode Staebler places him second only to Leslie Stephen. Staebler's admission, however, that Morley lacked the sympathetic intuitions of a Pater is one that both Knickerbocker and Willey are forced to make, even while they urge his merits upon us. The former develops her chapter ("Art and the Rationalist: Morley as Critic") chronologically, noting the growth of Morley's artistic taste as his premises interact with his intuitions and experience. She sets the Swinburne review in perspective and sees Morley (contra Strachey and Osbert Sitwell) as the repudiator of Victorian prudery and Tennyson's "ethics of the rectory parlour set to sweet music"; as the bold interpreter of *The Ring and the Book* and even bolder judge of the aging Carlyle; and as the encourager of Pater, both by publishing the essays collected later in *The Renaissance* and by reviewing the book favorably in the *Fortnightly Review*. Finally (and here Willey and Staebler concur), she proclaims the essay on Macaulay to be Morley's most brilliant effort. "If it is hard for us to realize," she remarks, "how new and daring the essays on Carlyle and Browning first seemed, this is because their findings have entered into our ways of thought." Both Alexander and Willey take the essay on Byron as their exemplum of Morley's historical method and appropriately warn us not to expect from Morley (or from any major Victorian critic) the kind of detailed analysis of texture the twentieth century looks for. "The fact is," writes Willey, "that Morley was more interested in tendencies than in poets; or putting it another way, he was chiefly interested in poets when they were clearly representative" of tendencies. Morley was interested in poetry that served humanity, placing the life of action above the life of letters. The great exception, Willey claims, is the essay on Macaulay where, for once, Morley quotes his writer and subjects his sentences and rhythms to devastating technical analysis.

Was Morley merely an eclectic critic or did he, as Edward Alexander asserts, try to "suggest ways in which literature might minister to morality, to scientific truth, and to social well-being without ceasing to be literature"? Did the fact that he was a rationalist make a difference? This is the crucial question to ask of the Unbeliever as Critic.

Of Morley's political biographies of English statesmen (Walpole, Cobden, Gladstone, and Cromwell) little has been written in recent years. Perhaps, indeed, little more need be said. The *Walpole* (1889) is a competent labor of duty not love; the *Oliver Cromwell* (1900) won the praise of Gardiner, but is now quite dated; the Cobden and the Gladstone lives are monumental and impressive. Morley's methods of composition in the *Gladstone* are criticized by M. R. D. Foot in his introduction to the first volume of his edition of *The Gladstone Diaries* (1968) and in a more extensive evaluation, "Morley's Gladstone: A Reappraisal" (*BJRL*, 1969). There is also a pedestrian study of Morley as a historian of England by W. Menzies Whitelaw in *Some Modern Historians of Britain*, edited by Herman Ausubel (1951). Hamer treats the Cobden and the Gladstone as illustrations of crucial stages in Morley's search for order and effectiveness.

At least two other areas of investigation suggest themselves. How does Morley stand as an interpreter of Mill as compared with Leslie Stephen and Frederic Harrison? Second, more work needs to be done with Morley's style, not only in itself, but also in relation to the whole study of Victorian prose now in its early stages. While Knickerbocker, Willey, and Staebler in particular have all touched on the question, we know from Morley's correspondence with Harrison (as recorded in Hirst) that the problem of style concerned him all his life. What is its range, what does his style reveal about the man, what of his style remains vital for later centuries despite its unfashionable grandiloquence? Or must we, as Staebler says, weigh Morley not by his syntax and his tone but "by his body of thought"?

V. LESLIE STEPHEN (1832–1904)

In his Leslie Stephen Lecture of 1937, Desmond MacCarthy remarked that among "go-between thinkers of that century who disseminated ideas without originating them, he must be reckoned among the first. I cannot think of a fourth to set beside Huxley, Matthew Arnold, and Leslie Stephen." Yet, while Huxley and Arnold have been reprinted, anthologized, and taught in universities, Stephen, though an eloquent agnostic, a leading critic, the editor of the *Cornhill* and the *DNB*, and the historian of eighteenth-century and utilitarian thought, has been neither anthologized, nor taught, nor much written about, and not even reprinted until the mid-twentieth century. Since then he has received more attention, but it is clear that scholars do not agree about what he should be remembered for. Two writers of recent, short critical estimates disagree sharply. For Phyllis Grosskurth (*Leslie Stephen*, Writers and Their Work, 1968), the *DNB* "was his supreme achievement" and his histories of ideas are near masterpieces, but his literary criticism seems of little use. For Samson O. A. Ullmann, however, "it is as a critic that Stephen will be remembered longest. Except for Matthew Arnold, no other Victorian produced so large a body of distinguished criticism" (*Men, Books, and Mountains*, 1956). To Basil Willey, Stephen is notable for being "perhaps the most honest, and the most doubting, of all the agnostic group," the "perfect exemplar and fine flower of the type" (*Christianity Past and Present*, 1952). While F. W. Bateson admires Stephen's *English Thought in the Eighteenth Century*, he is more concerned to bracket Stephen with Blake as a slayer of Old Nobodaddy and proclaim him "a major prophet" of agnosticism (*New Statesman*, 21 June 1963). Most recently John Gross has denied Stephen the status of prophet, but ranks him, along with Walter Bagehot and G. H. Lewes, as one of the three best examples of the Victorian Man of Letters as "higher journalist" (*The Rise and Fall of the Man of Letters*, 1969). Thus, there would seem to be sufficient cause to remember and to stimulate examination of the achievement of this often neglected man of letters.

His life and character, lived through and shaped by the major agonies of the Victorian age, have also produced radical differences of opinion. Apparently his personality was sufficiently interesting to provoke two novelists to use him as a basis for fictional characters and one poet to take him as a subject. Was Stephen more like Vernon Whitford, or more like Mr. Ramsay, or more like Hardy's "Schreckhorn"? And what were the central emotional experiences in his life?—being bullied at Eton, losing his faith, watching the sunset on Mont Blanc, or standing at the graves of his two wives? Perhaps the character has as many facets as the career.

Stephen predicted that he would live only in footnotes. He has certainly done that, but anyone who has read his major works knows that footnotes will not do justice to his passionate intellect.

Works and Bibliography

While there is no complete edition of Stephen's works, *Collected Essays* (1907) contains *Hours in a Library, Studies of a Biographer*, and *Essays on Freethinking and Plainspeaking, The Science of Ethics*, and *English Literature and Society in the Eighteenth Century*. In 1950 only four of his works were in print; today the situation is somewhat different. *English Literature and Society in the Eighteenth Century* (1904) is available from three publishers; *The History of English Thought in the Eighteenth Century* (1902 ed.) can be had both in paper and hard cover; and there have been two reprints of *The English Utilitarians* (1900) and one of *Hobbes* (1904). Of his literary studies, we now have two reprints of the 1907 edition of *Hours in a Library* and one of the 1892 edition, one reprint of the 1898 two-volume *Studies of a Biographer* and another of the 1898–1902 four-volume edition; and, for the first time, a reprint of his EML *Samuel Johnson* (1878), *Alexander Pope* (1880), and *Swift* (1882). The reissue of the twenty-four-volume 1879 edition of Thackeray makes Stephen's essay, "The Writings of W. M. Thackeray" (Vol. xxiv) more accessible. Finally, *Essays on Freethinking and Plainspeaking* (1873), *The Science of Ethics* (1882), *An Agnostic's Apology* (1893), *The Life of Sir James Fitzjames Stephen* (1895), *Social Rights and Duties* (1896), and *Some Early Impressions* (1924), long out of print, are now to hand.

Since Stephen's death there have been only two publications of previously uncollected essays. In 1924, Leonard and Virginia Woolf collected his reminiscences from the *National Review* (1903) under the title, *Some Early Impressions*; in 1956, S. O. A. Ullmann edited *Men, Books, and Mountains*, a selection of eleven essays prefaced by an introduction. *Selected Essays in Intellectual History* is now being prepared by Noël Annan for the Classics of British Historical Literature series.

Readers of Stephen should be warned that, with the exception of those mentioned in the preceding paragraph, reprints of his books have been made without strict editorial supervision. His notorious misprints remain in all their glory. Readers should also be aware that, apart from about forty manuscripts of essays he wrote for the *Cornhill*, the texts of these essays are from the periodicals in which they first appeared. So far very little has been done to compare the texts as originally published with those in republished collections. To the best of my knowledge, no one is planning to do for Stephen what is being done for Arnold. "Still uncollected," writes Ullmann, "are hundreds of articles that appeared in over two dozen periodicals in the course of more than forty years." The task of collecting, even if advisable, will stretch the scholar's patience and ingenuity. Nevertheless, as Ullmann's collection shows, far more should be done to exhibit the full range of Stephen's intellectual interests and abilities.

One of the problems of collection will be to identify those essays by Stephen not now assigned to him. Real progress has been made, however. The most complete, single listing of Stephen's works is to be found in "A Check-List of Works" composed by Ullmann for the volume already mentioned. Apart from books, Ullmann includes essays contributed by Stephen to monthlies and refers the reader for a complete list of Stephen's articles in the *Nation* to Daniel C. Haskell's *The* Nation (2 vols., 1951) and for a partial listing of Stephen's pieces for the *Saturday Review* to Merle Bevington's *The* Saturday Review *1858–68* (1941), as well as to Frederic W. Maitland's *Life and Letters of Leslie Stephen* (1906; rpt. 1970). The attribution of articles in the *Saturday Review* made by Edwin Sheen in "Leslie Stephen: Man of Letters and Critic of Literature" (Diss. Illinois 1957) should not be accepted without careful scrutiny. Ullmann's assignment of authorship of Stephen's essays in the *Cornhill* was based on the publisher's file and is confirmed in the *Wellesley Index*, Volume I. There still remain many unidentified articles written for the *Pall Mall Gazette* and other weeklies.

Likewise, there is no single bibliography of work about Stephen. Students will find suggestive listings, however, in Phyllis Grosskurth's "Select Bibliography," attached to her *Leslie Stephen* (Writers and Their Work, 1968); in the bibliographies of five dissertations: John J. Timmerman, "Sir Leslie Stephen as a Biographer" (Northwestern 1948), John W. Bicknell, "Leslie Stephen as an Intellectual Historian" (Cornell 1950), S. O. A. Ullman, "The Philistine Pose: A Study in the Literary Criticism of Leslie Stephen" (Harvard 1954), Floyd Tolleson, "The Relation between Leslie Stephen's Agnosticism and Voltaire's Deism" (Washington 1955), and Edwin Sheen, noted above. In addition to these, the "Notes and References" to Annan's *Leslie Stephen* (1951) should be consulted.

Letters and Biography

The only significant group of Stephen letters in print are those to be found in Maitland's *Life and Letters*, though a small selection may be found in *Thackeray's Daughter: Some Recollections of Anne Thackeray Ritchie*, compiled by Harriet T. Fuller and Violet Hammersley (1951). The material from which this selection was taken is now in the possession of Belinda Norman Butler, the daughter of Mrs.

Fuller. The largest group of letters is in the Houghton Library at Harvard; there, in the Norton, Holmes, and Lowell papers will be found all the originals of the letters printed by Maitland and addressed to O. W. Holmes, Jr., C. E. Norton, J. R. Lowell, and E. L. Godkin; the published letters of Lowell (1894, 1932), Holmes (1953), and Norton (1913) should also be consulted. There are also a number of letters to William Knight in the Morgan Library. A collection of Stephen papers in the Duke University Library is described by C. R. Sanders as containing "298 items, nearly all letters except for about forty holograph manuscripts of articles . . . contributed in his early days to the *Cornhill Magazine*." A group of letters from Stephen to Gosse is to be found in the Brotherton Collection at the University of Leeds, and a brief exchange between Stephen and Mark Pattison is in the Pattison papers at the Bodleian; also at the Bodleian are about 100 letters to Sidney Lee dealing with *DNB* matters; a few to the Huxleys are among the Huxley papers at the Imperial College. In 1935, C. E. Engel published "Leslie Stephen's Letters to Some French Friends," in the *Alpine Journal*; in 1954 Richard L. Purdy reproduced six letters to Hardy in *Thomas Hardy: A Bibliographical Study*.

Stephen's long "letter" to his children written after his second wife's death is in the custody of the family and is admirably described by Quentin Bell in "The Mausoleum Book" (*RES*, 1965). Two of Stephen's notebooks, containing notes on his reading and the draft of a projected (but never finished) study in philosophy, are now in the possession of the Drew University Library.

Two works only come strictly within the category of biography. F. W. Maitland's *Life and Letters* is a full-scale Victorian commemorative volume, written with love, but not a piece of mere hagiography. It is dense in detail useful to the interpreter and critic: the books that shaped Stephen's mind are listed with dates, his letters are copiously quoted, and the range of his friendships with other Victorian sages indicated. A passionate biographer can find here a network of trails fascinating to follow: Stephen's friendships with Hardy, Meredith, Morley, Holmes, Lowell, and Norton; his connections with the contributors to the *Cornhill* (Henry James, R. L. Stevenson, and W. E. Henley, for example); and other contacts with the Victorian great and near-great.

It is his contribution to our knowledge of some of these contacts that makes the biographical sections of Annan's *Leslie Stephen: His Thought and Character in Relation to His Times* (1951) the most interesting study of Stephen's life and character. Not a biography in the strict sense, it is an attempt to fulfill Maitland's demand that for Stephen be done what "he to our admiration did for many others: illustrate in a small compass his life by his books, his books by his life, and both by their environment." To Maitland's account Annan adds little for the years after 1868; what he does add is a most penetrating and informative section on Stephen's early years, defining the environment of Clapham and the rising cluster of families that supplied so many lively minds to the later Victorian intelligentsia—the Venns, Diceys, Macaulays, Trevelyans, Darwins—and their interconnections (see also Annan's "The Intellectual Aristocracy," *Studies in Social History: A Tribute to G. M. Trevelyan*, 1955, ed. J. H. Plumb). As the reader travels from Clapham to Bloomsbury, he is aware that his guide knows the road and enjoys the journey. Annan is also enlightening on the inner workings of mid-Victorian Cambridge and the interplay between Cambridge rationalism and Evangelical morality.

If Annan does not provide us with a new life, he does explore Stephen's character critically, bringing to bear on the problem more details of the early life

and more material from "The Mausoleum Book" than Maitland chose to draw on
Readers of Maitland and of Virginia Woolf are aware that the portrait of Stephen
drawn by his friends and that drawn of Mr. Ramsay (*To the Lighthouse*) hardly
match. The self-pity and the emotional blackmail revealed in Mr. Ramsay and "The
MB" tempt the student to use them as exposés of the honorable, equable public
man, beloved of his friends. To this temptation Gertrude Himmelfarb succumbs in
her "Leslie Stephen: The Victorian as an Intellectual" (*Victorian Minds*, 1968)
and scores a glib victory over her subject. Annan is aware, however, as Himmelfarb
is not, that Mr. Hilbery in *Night and Day* reveals Virginia Woolf's different view of
her father as does her *Times* essay (1932) reprinted in *The Captain's Deathbed*
(1950). Further information about the complexity of her feelings for her father are
detailed in Quentin Bell's *Virginia Woolf* (1972).

Though perhaps not solving the problem of Stephen's character, Annan avoids
oversimplification; he does insist that we look "upon this picture and upon that"
and considers the issue with compassionate realism—a posture Stephen would have
approved. Annan's compassion emerges especially in the development of his thesis
that Stephen's crisis came not so much over religious questions, but earlier when he
attempted to save himself from his extreme sensitivity by forcing himself into the
contemporary masculine and muscular mode. Since Annan's appraisal of Stephen's
mind will be considered below, suffice it to say here that despite its errors, Annan's
is the most significant study of Stephen's character we have, and all scholars will be
happy to know that Annan is working on a new edition in which he hopes "to
eliminate errors, bring into the text the results of recent research by others, and
insert any new material which comes to hand."

Whether a definitive biography is desirable or necessary is debatable. Stephen
claimed his life was not interesting; certainly it was not glamorous. Perhaps Maitland was right in his demand, but the life of a man who touched so many other
Victorians and their movements of mind could, if hitherto unused materials were
brought to bear, be made interesting to those who wish to feel the interaction of
people, ideas, and movements, not just the history of propositions. Of some particular interest would be a more detailed study of his relation to America and Americans. There is also some dispute whether Stephen's loss of faith was painful or
painless and over just what books or influences eroded that faith. There are, therefore, still some unresolved issues to which attention should be paid, including
Stephen's tantalizing statement to his children in "The MB" that no full life could
be written because he is taking certain facts about his personal life with him into
the grave.

Critical Studies

Since Annan did not deal with Stephen as an intellectual historian and only
briefly with his editorship of the *Cornhill* and the *DNB*, Stephen's total achievement
has not really been estimated by recent scholars, not even by David D. Zink's *Leslie
Stephen* (1972), a short book largely dependent on earlier studies and which breaks
no new ground.

Mountaineering

Like several of his fellow intellectuals, Stephen was a passionate mountaineer.
Though Ruskin growled at his pipe-smoking in the Alps, Stephen's companions and

many others who never knew him in any other connection have been delighted by his essays in the *Alpine Journal* and by *The Playground of Europe* (1871), which enjoyed some popular success and has been reprinted, though not since 1946. Those interested in mountain-climbing or in the cultural and psychological significance of this mid-Victorian sport should turn to Annan's pages and his sources, notably an essay by W. R. Irwin ("Because It Is There," *QQ*, 1946); C. E. Engel, *A History of Mountaineering in the Alps* and C. W. F. Noyce, *Scholar Mountaineers*, both published in 1950; and a more recent work, *The Victorian Mountaineers* (1953) by Ronald Clark.

Agnosticism and Ethics

It is an extraordinary fact that until 1951 no one could read a substantial treatment of Stephen's agnosticism—this despite the fact that in 1906 A. W. Benn had pronounced him, rather than Huxley, to be the man who gave "world-wide celebrity" to the word "agnostic," and J. M. Robertson had called attention to Stephen's work in 1929. True, Charles R. Sanders collected all of Stephen's animadversions on F. D. Maurice in "Sir Leslie Stephen, Coleridge, and Two Coleridgeans" (*PMLA*, 1940), and H. G. Wood defended Maurice from Stephen's attacks in his *F. D. Maurice* (1950); true also, Stephen's views and role are briefly sketched in Allan Brown's *The Metaphysical Society* (1947) and by Frances Knickerbocker in 1943. But the student will find nothing of real depth in earlier studies unless he returns to the Victorian period itself, to such critiques as may be found in Richard Holt Hutton's defense of Newman against Stephen in his *Cardinal Newman* (1891) and in his *Contemporary Thought and Thinkers* (1894), or to reviews of Stephen's major works by such writers as Henry Sidgwick and G. Croom Robertson, or to Arthur Balfour's *The Foundations of Belief* (1895) which, while not treating Stephen specifically, assails the whole rationalist position. Joined by Harrison and Huxley, Stephen replied to Balfour with his usual mordant irony. Still another late nineteenth-century debate is the exchange between Gladstone (*NC*, 1895) and Stephen (*NC*, 1896) concerning Stephen's earlier estimate of Bishop Butler. Such interchanges took place at a level far above the fulminations of frightened and vindictive clerics—the kind that wrote Mrs. Huxley proclaiming their delight at her husband's demise—and give the reader some guidance as to the issues raised and the modes by which they were handled in Stephen's lifetime. Robert Flint's chapter on Stephen in *Agnosticism* (1903) and Janet Courtney's in *Free Thinkers of the Nineteenth Century* (1920) are also useful in presenting the Edwardian point of view.

Acquaintance with these materials will prepare one for the encounter with Annan's chapters on Stephen's philosophical position. These chapters present Stephen's agnosticism and his ethical theories cogently, critically, and in more depth than any previous study. Annan judges Stephen to be a better expounder of agnosticism than Huxley ("Stephen's writings appear by comparison more distinguished, acute and oecumenical"). While Huxley concerned himself with Biblical criticism and got bogged down with Gladstone among the Gadarene swine, Stephen did not concentrate on the truth or falsity of points in theology or history: "theology and metaphysics were not so much untrue as unreal . . . [he] presented agnosticism as a composite intellectual structure." So far, Annan follows close on the heels of A. W. Benn.

Annan then proceeds to expound what he considers to be Stephen's three main assertions, dramatizing them by juxtaposing Stephen to Arnold, Newman, Maurice, and various twentieth-century figures, but not (except for Huxley or in often intriguing footnotes) to his contemporary rationalists. By implication Stephen emerges as a better expositor of the faith than Clifford, Spencer, and Morley, but the explicit judgment is not worked out. Readers of Stephen's *Essays on Freethinking and Plainspeaking* (1873) and his *English Thought* (1876) will be surprised to read that not until old age did Stephen see that "religion, whether true or false, has its roots in society and is not superimposed." Stephen's militant agnosticism needs to be seen in the context of the radical movement of the seventies, and also in the context of the interaction between the Coleridgean and Benthamite strains as influenced by Comte. Seen thus, it may well appear that Stephen deals with religion in two ways: contemporary theological positions are to be treated as propositional in order to be attacked and refuted; at the same time they are to be seen in a historical perspective, as emerging at a particular stage of development. The future of organized religion or of the new faith depends less on their propositional viability than on their ability to satisfy human needs, material and spiritual. It is difficult to quarrel, however, with Annan's central verdict that Stephen "armed unbelief with a short sword to slash theology and vitalized it as a noble conception of life."

Like most of his fellow agnostics, Stephen felt the need to assert that morality would not collapse with the disintegration of traditional theology, or, as Annan wittily puts it, "he who loses his faith will find it." But where will he find it when the supernatural sanctions and the fear of hell are removed? The huge book that Stephen wrote (*The Science of Ethics*, 1882) to examine this question he hoped would be a masterpiece, but neither his contemporaries, such as R. H. Hutton and Henry Sidgwick (both of whom reviewed it), nor posterity has agreed. Sidgwick's review (*Mind*, 1882) is of particular interest because he, like Stephen and like Spencer, Huxley, and others, had explored and continued to explore the same terra incognita of naturalistic ethics. Although Stephen, following Comte, argues that men's ethical postures are derived from their environment, thus denying their divine origin, he also borrows Darwinian conceptions in order to explain the process by which men have selected good from bad, and so far takes a few, halting steps in the direction of Durkheim and Weber. Although Rudolf Metz (*A Hundred Years of British Philosophy*, 1938) judged *The Science of Ethics* to be "the maturest and best thought out contribution to establishing morals upon the foundation of an evolutionist philosophy," later critics of this work have centered their attack on Stephen's failure to deal with the problem of moral choice and his assertion that what is good is that which is good for the social organism and its progress. Both J. A. Irving ("Evolution and Ethics," *QQ*, 1948) and Annan, at greater length and with apt comparison to Victorian and later exponents, make hay of *The Science of Ethics*. Annan finds little to choose between Huxley and Stephen, citing George E. Moore as the modern dynamiter of all evolutionary ethics. It is certain that if one judged Stephen by this book alone one would be judging him at the point where his character and morality were most closely tethered to the preconceptions of his own age.

An excellent basis for the understanding of Stephen's philosophical position has thus been laid. Future study might well concentrate on the development of his ideas as he grew older, taking note of his later tendency to regard philosophical propositions as being close kin to poetry and myth, as being instrumental rather than definitive, and as being rationalizations rather than reasons.

The Biographer

No study of nineteenth-century biography can afford to sidestep Stephen, not merely because of his formidable accomplishment in creating the *DNB*, but also in writing his EML studies of George Eliot, Johnson, Swift, Pope, and Hobbes, not to mention the essays collected in *Studies of a Biographer* (1907), others not collected, and his lives of Henry Fawcett and J. F. Stephen. Francis Thompson's essay, "Leslie Stephen as a Biographer" (1915), reprinted in *Literary Criticisms*, collected by Terence L. Connolly (1948), has been superseded by John J. Timmerman's unpublished dissertation, "Sir Leslie Stephen as a Biographer" (Northwestern 1948), a superb blend of scholarship and criticism which deserves to be better known. Timmerman extracts Stephen's theory of biography from comments strewn about his essays, examines his interest in the technique and the different kinds of biography, and analyzes his practice in the major texts mentioned above. Timmerman's final chapters deal ably and in detail with Stephen's work on the *DNB*, and commend his skill in distilling essences and in "the purposive articulation of fact." Considering the thoroughness of his reading, Timmerman's statement that he had not found "a dull article in the whole range of Stephen's publications" is remarkable indeed. Students of Stephen's theory of history will find here an elucidation of his view of the role of great men and will note how it dovetails into his theories of literary and intellectual history and is of a piece with his humanistic materialism. Timmerman's bibliography points clearly to his sources and to the criticism of the *DNB* which preceded his own careful, scholarly work.

Journalist

In his career as a journalist, Stephen played two roles: the prolific writer of articles and the harried editor. He began writing for *Macmillan's* and as one of John Douglas Cook's bright young men on the *Saturday Review*. It is worth reading John Morley's comments on this period of British journalism in *Recollections,* i (1917) and Stephen's own descriptions in his *Life of Fitzjames Stephen* (1895) and *Some Early Impressions* (1924) before tackling Bevington's important and meticulous study of the *Saturday Review* (1941).

By and large, studies of Stephen's relation to periodicals have been made in books, or in articles dealing with a periodical as a whole, as in Edwin Everett's *The Party of Humanity* or in Oscar Maurer, Jr.'s "Froude and *Fraser's Magazine*, 1860–74" (*SEng*, 1949). Other studies have used his periodical essays to define and expand Stephen's position as philosopher, critic, or commentator on things in general. What has not been done is to study them thoroughly from the point of view of the history of nineteenth-century journalism. To what extent, for example, must we weigh the effect of the audience (and the corresponding editorial policy) for which Stephen was writing when we evaluate both the ideas and the style embodied in his periodical essays? To what extent would it be worthwhile to compare the texts of his essays as they appeared in periodicals and as they later appeared in book form? In a letter to Edwin Lawrence Godkin, as Maurer tells us, Stephen reports submitting "Are We Christians?" in a mutilated form to *Fraser's*, where it was rejected; then to the *Fortnightly Review*, which printed the mutilated version; the original text finally appeared in *Freethinking and Plainspeaking*. The possibilities for re-search suggested by this episode are self-evident.

Another useful project would be an analysis of Stephen's contributions to the *Nation*. As the task of identification is complete, the camera can now be focused on these pieces from different points of view. What did Stephen think would interest Americans? What books does he mention, what political and social events, and what does all this contribute—both to our knowledge of his political and other attitudes as well as to our picture of him as a working journalist?

Stephen edited three periodicals: in 1864, as a worker in the campaign to elect Henry Fawcett to Parliament, he put together the short-lived political journal, the *Brighton Election Reporter*; from 1868 to 1872 he edited the *Alpine Journal* to which he contributed articles both before and after his editorship; and from 1871 to 1882 he edited the *Cornhill*, a significant phase of his career commented on by his many friends and contributors and thoroughly discussed by Oscar Maurer in his "Leslie Stephen and the *Cornhill Magazine*, 1871–82" (*SEng*, 1953) and in a dissertation by Samuel J. Tindall, "Leslie Stephen as Editor of the *Cornhill Magazine*" (South Carolina 1969). Maurer challenges Annan's declaration that editing the *Cornhill* was "a sideline" by showing how carefully and conscientiously Stephen worked with his contributors and succeeded in making his magazine the best of its kind—so good, in fact, that it began to lose money because the public wanted something more sensational. One of the moot points in evaluating Stephen's editor-ship has been to determine the extent to which his censorship involved a conflict between the man and the editor. Annan's view that many "excisions which he excused on editorial grounds were agreeable to him for personal reasons" is re-garded by Maurer as an oversimplification. Reinforced by his later study, " 'My Squeamish Public': Some Problems of Victorian Magazine Publishers and Editors" (*SB*, 1959), Maurer's argument seems to be the more balanced presentation of this issue, though one does not expect the debate to end there.

Critic and Literary Historian

Since his death, Stephen's value as a literary critic has been disputed, some-times sharply. Unlike that of his great contemporaries, his criticism has not been anthologized; as a result twentieth-century students are not exposed to Stephen as they are to Arnold, Ruskin, Pater, and even Mill. The reasons may be found in Desmond MacCarthy's Leslie Stephen Lecture (1937) and in René Wellek's chapter on Stephen in *A History of Modern Criticism*, IV (1965). Neither MacCarthy nor Wellek finds Stephen's theory or practice of much use today: Stephen's aesthetic is too corrupted by Positivism, by the intentional fallacy, by an interest in the author and in the moral element in literature. MacCarthy's position was sharply attacked by Q. D. Leavis in "Leslie Stephen: Cambridge Critic" (*Scrutiny*, 1939; rpt. in *A Selection from* Scrutiny, 1968), who laid the lash on Bloomsbury and traced the basis for the study of literature at Cambridge from a Stephen tradition. This dispute, however, produced no immediate attempt to survey the corpus of Stephen's criticism, analyze his theory and practice, and compare his work with that of his contemporaries. Not until Annan's chapter in his *Leslie Stephen* was that task approximated. In a delightful jeu d'esprit, Annan imagines a debate among literary critics assembled in a Chamber of Deputies presided over by a weary Apollo, with Stephen sitting next to Arnold, wondering as he listens whether or not he should cross the chamber. The chapter then proceeds to analyze and evaluate Stephen's critical position. Annan's judgment is reasonably balanced and appreciative, especially of Stephen's penetrating analyses, his trenchant irony, his self-criticism, and his vivacity. He gives more credit to Stephen's appreciation of Coleridge, for example, than does C. R. Sanders (*PMLA*, 1940); he also notes that Stephen "did for English fiction what Arnold had tried to do for poetry" but still finds Arnold the greater critic. Annan observes that Stephen is not given to close analyses of poetry, but is there any such in Arnold, that is, to a degree that would satisfy the recent passion for explication de texte? What Annan finds most objectionable in Stephen is his moralism, his diffidence, and his distrust of literature and criticism.

That another view of Stephen's apparent diffidence can be taken is revealed in S. O. A. Ullmann's "The Philistine Pose" (Diss. Harvard 1954). Ullmann argues, in effect, that both Wellek and Annan take too seriously Stephen's deprecatory remarks about his own criticism, and sees his self-confessed Philistinism as something of a pose which "enabled him to undermine the position of extremes on both sides. He could join forces with his fellow Philistines in attacking estheticism and artiness, at the same time that he could help to destroy Philistinism by exaggerating the worst faults of the Philistines." Ullmann also attempts to qualify Annan's position on Stephen's moralism by pointing out that Stephen changed his mind and that in practice he was less prudish than charged, a view also stated in his introduction to *Men, Books, and Mountains*. Stephen's modification of his earlier views on art and morality is also noted by Richard Stang in *The Theory of the Novel in England, 1850–1870* (1959), as well as by David Zink. Ullmann further reminds any reader who takes his judgment of Stephen's view of the relation between philosophy and poetry from the early essay on Wordsworth that here, too, Stephen changed his mind, not only about Wordsworth, but on the main issue. Thus Ullmann both supports and supersedes J. Dover Wilson's *Leslie Stephen and Matthew Arnold as Critics of Wordsworth* (1939) and would find an ally in Judson S. Lyon, who maintained in *The Excursion: A Study* (1950) that the twentieth century has repudiated the Arnoldian view of Wordsworth. Ullmann is also more effective in his argument contra Annan than Edwin Sheen, who in "Stephen and Modern Criticism" (*CLAJ*, 1958) weakens his thesis by utilizing quotations from articles in the *Saturday Review* that cannot be attributed with certainty to Stephen. What is really needed in future comparisons of Stephen and Arnold as critics is hardheaded judgment based on a systematic juxtaposition of their principles and practice of criticism. We have had too much automatic genuflection toward Arnold and not enough setting Arnold on Gray and Shelley next to Stephen on Gray and Shelley, or Arnold on Tolstoi and Flaubert next to Stephen on Balzac.

While scholars disagree about Stephen's critical principles, their opinion is generally united in judging him as more at home with fiction than with poetry. Both Richard Stang and Kenneth Graham (*English Criticism of the Novel, 1865–1900*, 1965) devote several pages to Stephen's criticism of the novel, Stang choosing the essay on Charlotte Brontë to illustrate Stephen's critical method and giving Stephen high marks for his flexibility in handling the problems of realism and his use of the term "organic unity." Graham is likewise respectful.

The debate about Stephen's position as critic and literary historian remains, however, between Ullmann's position that it is as a critic that he "will be remembered longest" and Grosskurth's that "Stephen's contemporary reputation as one of the foremost critics of his time has not been sustained."

Stephen's posture as judicial critic was gradually modified by his theory of literary history, a theory that emphasized the social basis of literature and received its fullest exposition in *English Literature and Society in the Eighteenth Century* (1904), a book frequently reprinted and regarded by Annan as "a prolegomena to a new branch of learning." As Ullmann points out, Stephen's earliest literary criticism shows "an awareness of literature in its historical background and his continuing concern with method led him to examine the historical theories of his age with his usual hard-headed scepticism." While many scholars tend to assume that the sociological approach to literature is primarily the product of German, usually Marxist, historical theory, or of Continental theories of *Wissensociologie*, the British empirical tradition, as modified by French thought, has too often been neglected; while Stephen dismissed Taine's simplistic formula, like Mill he learned from Comte, whose theories he modified, producing independently what is close to a Marxist position. A critical analysis of *Literature and Society in the Eighteenth Century*, placing it historically, may be found in the final chapter of Bicknell's dissertation and in Ullmann. The Darwinian influence on Stephen's approach to literature and literary history is developed by Philip D. Appleman in his dissertation "Darwin and the Literary Critics" (Northwestern 1955).

Stephen is also recognized as a leading but unsentimentalizing Queen Anne revivalist by Oscar Maurer in his "Pope and the Victorians" (*SEng*, 1944) and in an able dissertation by Gene B. Montague, "The Queen Anne Revival" (Texas 1957).

Intellectual Historian

Though Stephen's work on Swift, Pope, and other Augustan literary figures is considered rather out of date, his work as a historian of eighteenth-century and utilitarian thought continues to be read, admired, and reprinted. To this achievement may be added his *Hobbes* and essays on such figures as Spinoza, Jonathan Edwards, and Pascal. Published general accounts of his work as a historian of ideas may be found in "Sir Leslie Stephen" by Sidney A. Burrell (*Some Modern Historians of Britain*, ed. Herman Ausubel, 1951) and in a chapter by Zink (*Leslie Stephen*).

Some of the latter's observations are based on an article by John W. Bicknell ("Leslie Stephen's *English Thought in the Eighteenth Century*: A Tract for the Times," *VS*, 1962) in which Bicknell argues that Stephen's book is a document not only in Victorian but also in Stephen's own intellectual history, a view shared by F. W. Bateson (*New Statesman*, 1963). Bicknell's approach explains Stephen's impatience with some of the Deists, his respect for Butler (surprising in an agnostic), and his praise for Hume in terms of Stephen's position in the nineteenth-century drama for which the earlier ideological conflicts were a rehearsal. Bicknell sees Stephen's approach to intellectual history as an aspect of the way in which he as a rationalist (joined by Harrison and Morley) was building an alternative theory of historical development to those of the theologians, the idealists, and the pre-Darwinian rationalist historians. That Stephen was an originator in England of a quasi-Marxist theory of intellectual history is expounded in Bicknell's dissertation, which challenges MacCarthy's view that Stephen was only a go-between thinker and supports Annan's view that Stephen's philosophical position was not so much a foray into antitheological warfare, but was developed as a total view of human life.

There remains, then, the task of determining why *English Thought* has remained a classic even after objections to Stephen's specific judgments on particular figures or issues have been raised by both his contemporaries and more recent critics. Even these critics, however, remain respectful, even worshipful (Peter Gay calls the book "majestic" in *The Enlightenment: An Interpretation*, 1966), but no one, including the book's unqualified admirers, has told us what makes it a masterpiece.

Topics for Further Study

Other areas of investigation and analysis suggest themselves. Sheldon Rothblatt's *The Revolution of the Dons: Cambridge and Society in Victorian England* (1968) and the earlier monumental studies of Victorian Cambridge by D. A. Winstanley give us an excellent context in which to pull together Stephen's views on university reform and compare them with those of his contemporaries, not only vis-à-vis Cambridge but in relation to other "ideas of a university." Annan has indeed considered the major sources for such a synthesis and judges Stephen to have been ahead of his times in some ways and retrograde in others, but Annan is primarily concerned with these ideas in relation to Stephen's character and development; he is not writing a discourse on Stephen's idea of a university.

Likewise, Stephen's political position needs more thorough analysis than it has yet received. While he removed himself from the political scene after the Gladstone defeat of 1874, before that disaster, in his own way, he shared actively in the Radical movement. A good deal of this is treated by Annan, Maitland, and Bicknell, though in general terms, and we do not therefore have the whole story. More use needs to be made of his *Nation* pieces, where, as Maitland says, he felt freest, and his work for the *Pall Mall Gazette*, for which he for a time acted as parliamentary reporter. Moreover, about his attitudes after 1874 there are differences of opinion. Annan thinks that Stephen became disgusted with Gladstone for being too liberal. The evidence is not so clear; there are some grounds for thinking that he felt, as some of his fellow Radicals did, that Gladstone had failed because he had not been liberal enough, for example, with the Education Act of 1870. Some of his letters suggest that Stephen was not opposed to "Home Rule" as James Bryce and Herbert Paul believe. And is not John Morley misleading in his *Recollections* where he wrote that Stephen supported the government during the Boer War? The answers to these questions need to be put together with the facts of Stephen's defense of Bradlaugh (*FortR*, 1880) and of G. W. Foote (*Pall Mall Gaz.*, 8 March 1883), the atheist tried for blasphemy.

His specific political acts and attitudes need also to be related to his theoretical writings on social questions. Annan views the essays in *Social Rights and Duties* as second-rate stuff, revealing Stephen's inability to rethink the catchwords of liberalism as time and circumstance changed, but in another area of political and social theory, he at least rethought the arguments of Mill's *On Liberty*. His two-part essay, "Toleration," in *An Agnostic's Apology* (1893), is a hardheaded reorientation and critique of Mill, a significant document in the development of utilitarian thought, worthy of comparison with Bagehot's "The Metaphysical Basis of Toleration."

Another useful project would be to consider the underlying quality of Stephen's thought as found by an analysis of his style, its rhythms, its characteristic turns and images, and above all its shades of irony and humor. Some writers on Stephen take him more seriously than he took himself.

INDEX

•

Waters, Harriett Preston, 445
Watkin, E. I., 425
Watkins, Charlotte Crawford, 62
Watson, Bernard, 429
Watson, Edward A., 152
Watson, George, 4, 191, 294, 298, 300, 312,
  320, 324
Watson, John Gillard, 306
Watson, Joshua, 400
Watson, William, Sir, 308, 443
Watt, Frank W., 74, 195
Watt, H., 50
Watt, Margaret Hewitt, 397
Watt, W. Montgomery, 94
Watts, Isaac, 383
Watts-Dunton, Walter Theodore, 448
Wead, Mary Eunice, 38
Wearmouth, Robert F., 416, 425, 426
Weatherby, H. L., 164
Webb, Beatrice, 476
Webb, Clement C. J., 119, 318, 382, 393
Webb, Robert K., 418, 474
Weber, Carl J., 446
Weber, Max, 311, 422, 475, 522
Weber, Ronald, 25
Webster, Adam Blyth, 454
Webster, Alan B., 400
Wedderburn, Alexander D. O., 221, 222,
  225, 226, 227, 229, 230, 237
Wedgwood, Julia, 91, 403
Weidemann, Carla, 83
Weinberg, Adelaide, 200, 211
Weintraub, Stanley, 460
Weintraub, Wiktor, 68
Welby, Thomas Earle, 447, 464, 465
Welch, P. J., 396
Wellek, René, 9, 11, 25, 66, 82, 87, 88, 294,
  302, 339, 340, 436, 456, 524, 525
Wells, H. G., 307
Wells, John T., 96
Welsh, Alexander, 67
Welsh, Homer C., 380
Welty, Gordon A., 206
Wenger, C. N., 215
Wentworth, Harold, 83
Wernekke, H., 66
Wesley, John, 383, 384, 415
Wesling, Donald, 243, 244
West, Alick, 337, 338
West, Anthony, 498
West, Julius, 212
West, Paul, 84, 337, 341, 356
Westcott, Brooke Foss, 381, 390, 432
Westlake, Neda, 253
Wethered, Herbert N., 215
Weylland, John Matthias, 429
Wharton, Edith, 458
Wharton, Thomas, 25
Whately, Richard, Archbishop, 116, 138, 173,
  208, 317, 368, 370, 373, 374, 395, 403
Wheeler, Charles Stearns, 71

Wheeler, T. S., 140
Whewell, William, 191, 209, 210
Whistler, James Abbot McNeill, 229, 463
Whitcomb, S. L., 90
White, A. Gowans, 476
White, Andrew Dickson, 394, 473
White, Blanco, 151, 156, 374
White, Helen C., 272
White, J. Harrop, 418
White, James F., 402
White, W. D., 182
White, William, 458
Whitehouse, John Howard, 223, 224, 225,
  227, 240
Whitelaw, W. Menzies, 516
Whitford, Vernon, 517
Whitley, William T., 414
Whitman, Walt, 59, 71, 436, 448, 458
Whitmore, Charles, 209
Whitridge, Arnold, Mr. and Mrs., 237, 255,
  271, 403
Whittaker, Thomas, 198
Whittier, John Greenleaf, 71, 103
Whittingham, Selby, 245
Whyte, Alexander, 160
Whyte, J. H., 139
Wickelgren, Florence L., 271
Wicker, Brian, 174
Wickham, Edward R., 423
Wickwar, William H., 427
Widger, Howard D., 103
Wiecki, Ernst von, 64, 94
Wiggins, Arch R., 429
Wightman, Francis Luci, 257
Wigmore-Beddoes, Dennis G., 418
Wilberforce, Henry, 131, 375
Wilberforce, Reginald Garton, 399
Wilberforce, Robert, 163, 365, 367, 375
Wilberforce, Samuel, Bishop, 119, 126, 363,
  374, 375, 396, 399, 472, 482, 493, 495,
  498, 499
Wilberforce, Wilfred, 370, 400
Wilberforce, William, 371, 375, 381, 390
Wilbur, Earl Morse, 417
Wilbur, William C., 76
Wilde, Oscar, 51, 143, 164, 247, 267, 302,
  303, 307, 308, 330, 337, 355, 436, 437,
  452, 459–64, 466
Wildi, Max, 338, 466, 467
Wilenski, Reginald H., 3, 222, 223, 225, 229,
  231, 232, 233, 240, 241, 247
Wilhelmi, J. H., 68
Wilkenfeld, Roger B., 284
Wilkens, Charles T., 259
Wilkinson, D. R. M., 61
Wilkinson, John Thomas, 411
Willam, Franz M., 173
Willebrands, Jan G. M., 173
Willey, Basil, 8, 16, 74, 124, 163, 171, 314,
  315, 320, 371, 403, 427, 478, 483, 493,
  512, 513, 514, 515, 516, 517